RELIGIOUS OFFENCES IN COMMON LAW ASIA

This book provides in-depth comparative analysis of how religious penal clauses have been developed and employed within Asian common law states, and the impact of such developments on constitutional rights. By examining the theoretical and conceptual underpinnings of religious offences as well as interrogating the nature and impact of religious penal clauses within the region, it contributes to the broader dialogue in relation to religious penal clauses globally, whether in countries which practise forms of secular or religious constitutionalism. Asian practice is significant in this respect, given the centrality of religion to social life and indeed, in some jurisdictions, to constitutional or national identity.

Providing rigorous studies of common law jurisdictions that have adopted similar provisions in their penal code, the contributors provide an original examination and analysis of the use and development of these religious penal clauses in their respective jurisdictions. They draw upon their insights into the background sociopolitical and constitutional contexts to consider how the inter-relationship of religion and state may determine the rationale and scope of religious offences. These country-by-country chapters inform the conceptual examination of religious views and sentiments as a basis for criminality and the forms of 'harm' that attract legal safeguards. Several chapters examine these questions from a historical and comparative perspective, considering the underlying bases and scope, as well as evolving objectives of these provisions. Through these examinations, the book critically interrogates the legacy of colonialism on the criminal law and constitutional practice of various Asian states.

Constitutionalism in Asia series

NUS National University of Singapore | Centre for Asian Legal Studies Faculty of Law

Religious Offences in Common Law Asia

Colonial Legacies, Constitutional Rights and Contemporary Practice

Edited by
Li-ann Thio
and
Jaclyn L Neo

•HART•
OXFORD • LONDON • NEW YORK • NEW DELHI • SYDNEY

HART PUBLISHING
Bloomsbury Publishing Plc
Kemp House, Chawley Park, Cumnor Hill, Oxford, OX2 9PH, UK
1385 Broadway, New York, NY 10018, USA
29 Earlsfort Terrace, Dublin 2, Ireland

First published in Great Britain 2021

A catalogue record for this book is available from the British Library.

Library of Congress Cataloging-in-Publication data

Names: Thio, Li-ann, editor, author. | Neo, Jaclyn L, editor, author.

Title: Religious offences in common law Asia : colonial legacies, constitutional rights and contemporary practice / edited by Li-ann Thio and Jaclyn L Neo.

Description: Oxford, UK ; New York, NY : Hart Publishing, an imprint of Bloomsbury Publishing, 2021. | Series: Constitutionalism in Asia series | Includes bibliographical references and index.

Identifiers: LCCN 2020052049 (print) | LCCN 2020052050 (ebook) | ISBN 9781509937295 (hardback) | ISBN 9781509946037 (paperback) | ISBN 9781509937318 (pdf) | ISBN 9781509937301 (Epub)

Subjects: LCSH: Offenses against religion—Law and legislation—Asia. | Common law—Asia. | Freedom of religion—Asia. | Religious law and legislation—Asia.

Classification: LCC KM982.O34 R45 2021 (print) | LCC KM982.O34 (ebook) | DDC 345.5/0288—dc23

LC record available at https://lccn.loc.gov/2020052049

LC ebook record available at https://lccn.loc.gov/2020052050

ISBN: HB: 978-1-50993-729-5
ePDF: 978-1-50993-731-8
ePub: 978-1-50993-730-1

Typeset by Compuscript Ltd, Shannon

Acknowledgements

A BOOK IS the product of many hands, and we would like to express our appreciation for the help we received in bringing this project to glad fruition.

This book is made possible with funding from a Ministry of Education Academic Research Fund Tier 1 Grant No R-241-000-162-115, and with the support of the Centre for Asian Legal Studies at the National University of Singapore.

The genesis of this book is sited in a conference on *Religious Penal Clauses: Colonial Legacies and Colonial Practice* held at the Faculty of Law, National University of Singapore, on 5–6 December 2018. Earlier versions of the chapters in this book were presented then, and we would like to thank Kevin Tan, Mario Gomez, Ann Black, Dian Shah, Masum Billah, Mrinal Satish, Syed Ali Raza and Arif Jamal for their hard work in finalising their papers into the polished chapters in this book. We are grateful to our moderators and commentators, Nyi Nyi Khaw, Jeremiah Lau, Ronojoy Sen and Tan Hsien Li, for their support and contributions to the conference. In particular, we would like to express our especial gratitude to Professor Thi Thi Lwin from the East Yangon University Faculty of Law, for sharing with us her paper and insights on Myanmar.

Our burdens were made lighter by our superb research and editorial assistants at the National University of Singapore Faculty of Law – we are thankful to Jiang Zhi Feng, Louis Lai, Philip Teh, Muhammad Nurshazny Bin Ramlan and Ashleigh Gan for their hard work, dedication and fast turnover. Special thanks to Yvonne Lim and Wendy Wee from the NUS Law Office of Research for their excellent assistance on the workshop organisation and research grant administration. Last, but not least, we would like to convey our appreciation to the Series Editors for the Hart Constitutionalism in Asia Series, the anonymous referee for the helpful and enriching comments, and to Kate Whetter, Rosemarie Mearns and the editorial staff at Hart Publishing for their kind patience and energetic enthusiasm. It has been a pleasure to work with you all.

Li-ann Thio and Jaclyn L Neo
Singapore, 15 July 2020

List of Contributors

SM Masum BILLAH is an Associate Professor at the Department of Law at Jagannath University Dhaka. A graduate of Rajshahi University Bangladesh, he started his teaching career at Stamford University Bangladesh and later Northern University Bangladesh. He was a recipient of Victoria University Doctoral Scholarship and completed his doctoral studies at the School of Law, Victoria University Wellington, New Zealand, in 2017. He has published in reputed journals, and his research interests include land law and poverty in South Asia, constitutional law, interpretation of statutes, law and literature, and legal history.

Ann BLACK is an Associate Professor and Reader at the TC Beirne School of Law, The University of Queensland, Australia. She is also the Deputy Director of the Centre for Public International and Comparative Law. Although admitted as a barrister-at-law, she has spent several decades as a legal academic, teaching and researching in the field of comparative law, in particular Islamic law, the law and legal systems of Asia, and comparative criminal law, having particular research interest in the Sultanate of Brunei Darussalam.

Mario GOMEZ is the Executive Director at the International Centre for Ethnic Studies, an independent think-tank in Sri Lanka. He was previously a Lecturer at the University of Colombo. Recent and forthcoming publications include 'The Courts Respond to Executive Tyranny in Sri Lanka', 'The Politics of Dealing with the Past in Deeply-Divided Sri Lanka', 'Reform and Reconciliation in Post-War Sri Lanka', 'The Right to Information and Transformative Development Outcomes', 'The Death Penalty in Sri Lanka', 'Constitutional Change and Institutional-Resilience in Sri Lanka', 'Advancing Economic and Social Rights through National Human Rights Institutions', and 'Institutional-Resilience and Political-Transitions in Sri Lanka and Beyond'.

Arif A JAMAL is an Associate Professor of Law at the National University of Singapore and the Deputy Director of the Centre for Asian Legal Studies there. Arif is also the co-Editor-in-Chief of the *Asian Journal of Comparative Law*. His research and teaching interests include legal and political theory, law and religion, comparative law, and law in Muslim contexts. He has authored *Islam, Law and the Modern State: (Re)imagining Liberal Theory in Muslim Contexts* (Routledge, 2018). Arif has held visiting appointments with the law schools of the University of Trento, Tel Aviv University, the City University of Hong Kong, and at the Centre for Transnational Legal Studies in London.

Jaclyn L NEO is an Associate Professor of Law at the National University of Singapore and the Director of its Centre for Asian Legal Studies. She is a Professorial Fellow with the Attorney-General's Chambers Academy and an elected Council Member of the International Society for Public Law (ICON-S). Jaclyn has published in leading journals in her field and is editor/co-editor of more than five books. She has won the *Asian Yearbook of International Law*'s DILA International Law Prize and, in 2017, was awarded the inaugural SHAPE-SEA Research Award for her scholarly work on religious freedom in Southeast Asia.

Syed Ali RAZA is a founding partner at Common Law Chambers and also a Visiting Faculty Member at Pakistan College of Law. Ali has served as a Member & Legal Advisor at the Public Affairs Unit of the Chief Minister's Office of Punjab, where he provided strategic legal and policy support to top political leadership, ministers and rank government officials. At present, he is serving as a Director on the Board of one of the oldest listed companies of Pakistan. Ali was a Draper Hills Fellow with Stanford University and holds an LLM from the National University of Singapore.

Mrinal SATISH is a Professor of Law at the National Law School of India University, Bengaluru. He was formerly the Chairperson of the Delhi Judicial Academy. He specialises in criminal law. Mrinal's teaching and research interests include laws on sexual violence, sentencing, gender and the law, medical jurisprudence, empirical analysis of law, and reproductive justice. Mrinal holds degrees from National Law School, Bengaluru and Yale Law School. He is the author of *Discretion, Discrimination and the Rule of Law: Reforming Rape Sentencing in India* (Cambridge University Press, 2016).

Dian AH SHAH is an Assistant Professor of Law at the National University of Singapore. Her research spans the fields of law and religion, comparative constitutional law and human rights. Dian is the author of *Constitutions, Religion and Politics in Asia: Indonesia, Malaysia and Sri Lanka* (Cambridge University Press, 2017), the co-editor of *Law and Society in Malaysia: Pluralism, Religion and Ethnicity* (Routledge, 2018) and the editor of the *Asian Journal of Comparative Law*'s Special Issue on 'Religion and Constitutional Practices in Asia' (December 2018). She has also published in the *International Journal of Constitutional Law* and the *Oxford Journal of Law and Religion*.

Kevin YL TAN is one of Singapore's leading constitutional law scholars and legal historians. He is the author and editor of over 50 books on the law, history and politics of Singapore, including *Constitutionalism in Asia* (Hart Publishing, 2014), *The Singapore Constitution: A Contextual Analysis* (Hart Publishing, 2015) and *Constitutional Foundings in Southeast Asia* (Hart Publishing, 2019). He is currently Adjunct Professor at the Faculty of Law, National University of Singapore, and Visiting Professor at the S Rajaratnam School of International

Studies, Nanyang Technological University. He is also Editor-in-Chief of the *Asian Journal of Comparative Law*.

Li-ann THIO is Provost Chair Professor at the Faculty of Law, National University of Singapore. A graduate of Cambridge University (PhD), Harvard Law School (LLM), and Oxford University (BA Hons), she is a barrister with Gray's Inn and was a Nominated Member of the Singapore Parliament (2007–09). She teaches and researches in the field of constitutional and administrative law (Singapore and comparative), human rights in Asia and public international law. She is currently Chief Editor, *Singapore Journal of Legal Studies*, an Advisory Board Member of the *Max Planck Encyclopaedia of Comparative Constitutional Law* and, with Kevin YL Tan, Co-Editor of the Hart Series on Constitutionalism in Asia.

Historically, anti-blasphemy laws have operated as the primary way by which common adherence and loyalty to a majority religion were upheld through law. Defining blasphemy is not always easy but, generally speaking, blasphemy can be understood as the 'disrespectful or offensive treatment' of sacred material.[6] Blasphemy was closely associated with heresy, which in Western Christendom includes a denial of Jesus or attribution of his miracles to Satanic forces.[7] Where the legitimacy of the state is closely tied to a particular religion, either because there is a state religion or when the state strongly identifies itself with a particular religion, religious offences may be viewed as attacks on the state itself and are accordingly threatened with severe penalties that may extend to the death penalty.[8] Indeed, blasphemous speech may be seen as attacking the dominant values and norms of society, threatening social cohesion as well as state integrity. In the context of English laws, for example, William Blackstone has argued that blasphemy was justified because 'Christianity is part of the laws of England.'[9] In a major case on the criminal offence of blasphemy in England in 1676, *R v Taylor*, the King's Bench articulated this connection between offence to religion with protection of the state. It held that the accused's utterance was 'not only an offence to God and to religion, but a crime against the laws, state and Government'.[10]

Anti-blasphemy laws are clearly contrary to robust protection of individual freedom of religion and beliefs; they strike a discordant tone in religiously pluralistic societies. Today, there are laws that focus on prohibiting blasphemy as an offence against God or religion, as well as laws that focus on prohibiting offence to religious believers. It is more common now to talk about laws of religious offence (wounding of religious feelings) and laws of religious hatred (hate speech targeting religious groups), rather than laws criminalising blasphemy. We discuss the conceptual distinctions between these in section III, and further situate it within a broader discussion about the idea of defamation of religion. What bears emphasising here is that religious offence can also be connected to the protection of the state, but in a more indirect fashion. State legitimacy may not be directly attacked; rather, religious offence could be seen as a direct attack on the sensibilities of religious groups, which could provoke violent responses, precipitating social disorder. This is because insults to one's religion can be

[6] Neville Cox, 'Pourquoi Suis-Je Charlie? Blasphemy, Freedom of Religion, and the Nature of "Offensive" Cartoons' (2015) 4 *Oxford Journal of Law and Religion* 343, 351.

[7] John C Knechtle, 'Blasphemy, Defamation of Religion and Religious Hate Speech: Is There a Difference that Makes a Difference?' in András Koltay and Jeroen Temperman (eds), *Blasphemy and Freedom of Expression: Comparative, Theoretical, and Historical Reflections after the Charlie Hebdo Massacre* (Cambridge University Press, 2017) 199, 200.

[8] Henning Radtke, 'Religious Offenses' in Hans Dieter Betz, Don S Browning, Bernd Janowski and Eberhard Jungel (eds), *Religion Past and Present* at http://dx.doi.org/10.1163/1877-5888_rpp_SIM_124602 accessed 16 July 2020.

[9] William Blackstone, *Commentaries on the Laws of England*, book IV, ch 4 (University of Chicago Press, 1979).

[10] *R v Taylor* (1676) 1 Vent 293.

perceived as an attack on a cherished facet of one's self-identify and worldview, as well as an attempt to undermine a corporate way of life grounded in deeply and personally felt religious relationships. Religious hatred could also be apprehended as an intrinsic harm to the person and group, rather than having a necessary connection to public order or disorder. Waldron, for instance, justifies hate speech regulation as necessary to protect the *dignity* of persons who are identified as part of a community.[11]

Criminal laws regulating speech relating to religion therefore can have multiple focal points and multiple justifications, and serve multiple purposes. In this book, we use the term 'religious penal clause' to signify this range of criminal provisions, though we also seek to identify key conceptual distinctions between the different types of provisions: blasphemy, religious offences, hate speech and defamation of religion. Religious penal clauses are distinctive because they are criminal provisions implicating religion, religious ideologies, or a person or group identified specifically by their religion. A broad range of conduct can be prohibited as religious offences, including behaviour that 'discredit[s] the religious convictions of the population or a segment thereof',[12] disrupts religious practices or causes damage to a place of worship.

This book employs the specific lenses of the religious penal clauses written into the laws of former English colonies in Asia in order to broadly examine the impact of such laws in contemporary settings and the intersection of such criminal regulation with constitutional rights, and to investigate the enduring effects of colonial legacies. Our concern is with those specific laws written into the criminal codes of these countries in common law Asia. These laws originated from the 1860 Indian Penal Code (IPC), authored by English drafters who drew from English common law while modifying the rules as they deemed appropriate for the colonies. Chapter XV of the IPC was entitled 'Of Offences Relating to Religion', and broadly dealt with three categories of offences relating to defiling places of worship or objects, wounding of religious feelings and disturbing of religious assemblies. Macaulay, the author of the IPC, appreciated that India's religious composition was distinct from that of England, and as such did not seek to codify the English criminal law on blasphemy law for the colony. This reflected the English colonial rulers' realist disposition in taking religion seriously as a key social feature in India, and in appreciating the need to have laws dealing with inflamed religious passions that could precipitate social fragmentation along religious lines.

However, far from protecting religious feelings for the sake of religious feelings, the English laws were aimed at the maintenance of inter-religious, inter-group harmony, which was key to public order. These public-order considerations motivating the religious penal clauses in the IPC are distinguishable

[11] Jeremy Waldron, *The Harm in Hate Speech* (Harvard University Press, 2012).
[12] Radtke, 'Religious Offenses' (n 8).

from contemporary approaches to protect religious sensitivities in the form of what may be termed hate speech laws, designed to protect the *security and dignity of religious minorities* (or what may be viewed as other vulnerable sectors of society) and their members, to promote their integration and participation as citizens in a democratic society. The authors of the religious penal clauses intended that they be founded on 'true principles of toleration',[13] and sought to provide for 'fair latitude to religious discussion' while preventing 'intentional insults' to what others considered sacred.[14] This showed solicitude for freedom of conscience and civil debate, without foregrounding the language of rights. Furthermore, the religious offence clauses extended the criminal law's 'protection' to all religious traditions in India.

The IPC was later exported to other English colonies around Asia. After decolonisation and the attainment of independence, these criminal codes were retained. Some were subsequently modified and augmented, as they appeared to be effective and expedient legislative tools in managing religious sensitivities and keeping civil peace. For example, Pakistan not only preserved its penal code and the religious penal clauses, it also expanded the chapter to include new offences addressing specific holy names. The religious penal clauses were also often employed in conjunction with other related criminal offences, such as obscenity and sedition. In Singapore, the clauses operated alongside the 1990 Maintenance of Religious Harmony Act, an overarching law directed at regulating religious harmony.

There are several factors influencing how religious penal clauses have been deployed and modified in various common law jurisdictions in Asia. These include the constitutional state-religion relationship, whether the state maintains a posture of neutrality or preferentialism towards a religion, religious demography, the presence of 'strong religion' of a dominant group and its stance towards religious freedoms, as 'our concept of religious freedom cannot be divorced from our concept of religion'.[15] Additionally, the degree to which a polity is authoritarian or democratic affects the valuation of expressive freedoms. It is worth noting that in some cases, the religious penal clauses have had the effect of solidifying the hierarchical position of a particular religion, such as Buddhism in Sri Lanka and Islam in Pakistan and Brunei, which imperils the religious freedom of religious minorities or minorities within a religious majority. Furthermore, related to the problem of offences criminalising hurt to religious sensitivities is the broader task of how religious diversity is constitutionally accommodated. Models may range from pluralist constitutions[16] to constitutions based on an

[13] The Indian Law Commissioners, *A Penal Code Prepared by The Indian Law Commissioners* (GH Huttman at the Bengal Military Orphan Press, 1837).

[14] ibid 50.

[15] Arvind Sharma, *Problematizing Religious Freedom* (Springer, 2012) 86. For example, a religion like Islam, which views itself as the perfected final religion, may allow other faiths to coexist with Islam but would not include the freedom to leave the faith.

[16] See generally Jaclyn L Neo and Bui Ngoc Son (eds), *Pluralist Constitutions in Southeast Asia* (Hart Publishing, 2019).

absolute truth, the keeper of which is 'above the constitution', which prevents the constitution from being 'a comprehensive regulation of public power.'[17] The latter model imperils the robustness of religious liberty guarantees, in the face of the politicised use of 'religion-as-ideology', which seeks homogeneity and to uphold the privileged religion, as distinct from 'religion-as-faith', which supports plurality.[18]

In examining these factors, this book seeks to provide a critical perspective on religious penal clauses and examine the theoretical and conceptual underpinnings of religious penal clauses, as well as interrogate the nature and impact of these religious penal clauses within Asian common law jurisdictions. It seeks to contribute to the academic literature by building a constitutional and comparative perspective to the study of how these religious penal clauses have been developed and employed within the common law world. Thus far, only one other book in recent times has examined the sharp rise in the number of blasphemy accusations in the twenty-first century in four former English colonies. The approach there has been socio-political, whereas our book takes a legal-political approach, which is nonetheless informed by the social context.[19] Further, an additional contribution of this book is that by situating itself within a conversation about legal transplantations and transformations, it sheds light on the afterlife of colonial legacies where these are retained, rejected or revised according to autochthonous particularities. It further engages with the global dialogue on religious penal offences, and aims to modulate and enrich that dialogue with a close, contextual analysis of Asian practice. Asian practice is significant in this respect, given the centrality of religion to social life and even to constitutional or national identity in some jurisdictions. The discussions in this book demonstrate that laws restricting religious speech take on a different complexion in different social, political and constitutional contexts, whether the polities in question practise secular or religious forms of constitutionalism.

We have arranged this book into two parts. Part I consists of four chapters that provide historical and conceptual perspectives of the religious penal clauses. Chapter 1, by Kevin Tan, serves as a historical primer to the IPC and the religious penal clauses. It provides a skilful overview in exploring the initial drafting and promulgation of the IPC and how it, including the legal tools it contained

[17] Dieter Grimm, 'Types of Constitutions' in Michel Rosenfeld and Andras Sajo (eds), *The Oxford Handbook on Comparative Constitutional Law* (Oxford University Press, 2012) 98, 114.

[18] Ashis Nandy, 'The Politics of Secularism and the Recovery of Religious Tolerance' (1988) 13 *Alternatives* 177, 178.

[19] Paul Rollier, Kathinka Froystad and Arlid Engelsen Ruud (eds), *Outrage: The Rise of Religious Offence in Contemporary South Asia* (UCL Press, 2019). The editors and authors have identified four conditions that have sustained religious offence controversies and have formed the contextual canvass to appreciate their case studies drawn from India, Pakistan, Bangladesh and Myanmar: (i) the advent of social media and smartphones; (ii) how deepening or declining democracy influences the articulation of political and religious rivalry; (iii) how a 'split public' deepens the suspicion between religious and secular reasoning; and (iv) the growing demands for recognition, whether from religious majorities or minorities.

to manage inter-religious group relations, was exported to other common law countries. Tan discusses, in three distinct phases, the historical evolution of the criminal code, its normative origins, debates and eventual enactment as the IPC, as well as the later transplantation into other English colonies in Asia. Chapter 2, by Li-ann Thio, examines the rationale and assumptions of laws that regulate religious feelings, whether through targeting the manner of delivery or through the material content of 'offensive' speech and action. It considers the extent to which law or cognate 'soft law' methods can promote liberty, nurture tolerant self-restraint and resilience, and secure effective pluralism and social cohesion. Chapter 3, by Arif Jamal, points to the internal plurality within religious traditions and the tendency in the operation of the religious penal clauses to over-simplify religious doctrines; or, as he puts it, 'Penal codes were structured and organised but also stylised and de-pluralised.' Jamal examines *hudud* in Islamic law, a cognate of religious penal offences, to show considerable internal plurality in understandings of how *hudud* should be understood and applied. Chapter 4 by Jaclyn Neo, the last chapter in this part, provides an analysis of the divergent paths that common law countries in Asia have taken in how they understand, conceptualise and apply the same religious penal clauses. Neo points to three factors underlying these divergent paths as countries pursue public order premised upon religious coexistence versus religious hierarchy: the degree of constitutional identification between state and religion; religious demography; and the extent to which the government relies on religion to legitimise its power. In examining the development of these laws, Neo reflects on legal transplants and legal transformation, showing that colonies are not merely passive receptors of legal ideas but exercise their social and political agency in transforming colonial laws to respond to local conditions. Her chapter contextualises developments in Singapore, Pakistan and Myanmar, and analyses points of divergence and convergence.

Neo's chapter segues into Part II, which comprises in-depth analysis of religious penal clauses in various common law countries in Asia, providing context to further the conceptual understanding of religious views and sentiments as a basis for criminality and the forms of 'harm' that attract legal safeguards. The chapters in Part II critically examine the use of religious penal clauses within each country, and situate the developments in their particular social, political and constitutional contexts. In chapter 5, Mrinal Seekay Satish goes to the first criminal code – the IPC – and examines the interpretation of Sections 295 to 298 of the Indian Penal Code, which deal with offences against religion, as well as Section 153A, which deals with promoting enmity between different groups, including religion. Within a context of Hindu majoritarianism and a troubled secularism, he argues that these provisions have been used more to quell dissent and alternative voices, rather than to maintain religious harmony. This is followed by Syed Ali Raza's chapter (chapter 6) on Pakistan, where Islam is the state religion, which he notes has the strongest blasphemy law in the world and led the push to promote the concept of 'defamation of religion' on the international stage.

He points to the expansion of the chapter on 'Offences Relating to Religion' in the Pakistani Penal Code in seeking to define Islamic orthodoxy on heresy, and using the law to stipulate that Ahmadis are not Muslim. He further situates the expansion and the employment of the religious penal clauses within an environment of heightened religiosity that fuelled the constitutional Islamisation of Pakistan. A sharp contrast can be drawn with SM Masum Billah's chapter on Bangladesh (chapter 7), where political debates have centred on whether the principle of secularity should be constitutionally entrenched, as it initially was after secession from Pakistan. In this Muslim majority country, the religious penal clauses have become embroiled in the country's religion-centric politics, but have not taken the same harsh turn as in Pakistan. To round up the discussion on the impact of the religious penal clauses in South Asia, Mario Gomez examines the situation in Sri Lanka in chapter 8, showing that there has been a lack of attention to the religious penal clauses there. He sees these clauses as possible legislative tools among other laws to quell ethno-religious violence primarily, but not exclusively, between the Sinhala Buddhists and Hindu Tamils, and views the neglect of these laws as symptomatic of broader political ambivalence towards the protection of ethnic-religious minorities.

With respect to Southeast Asia, Dian Shah in chapter 9 shows how these religious penal clauses have also not been invoked much in Malaysia, whose Constitution 'confesses' Islam as the religion of the Federation, although other religions may be practised in peace and harmony. However, this does not mean that religious speech is greatly protected in the country. To the contrary, she points to how the use or lack of use of these clauses are an outcome of the federal–State (and, by extension, the civil–syariah) division of powers in matters implicating religion. Religious orthodoxy thus tends to be regulated under Syariah laws rather than by the criminal code, which falls within the province of the Federal Government. Formerly part of Malaysia, Singapore does not associate the objectives of the religious penal clauses with the enforcement of religious orthodoxy, given its commitment to an anti-theocratic model of accommodative secularism. Li-ann Thio argues in chapter 10 that these provisions are viewed as part of a broader legal framework within which race and religion issues are addressed through formal and informal modes of regulation. The impact of historical race-religious riots has scarred the national psyche, and accounts for the acute government solicitude towards racial and religious sensitivities in contemporary law and practice. The chapter examines the rationale for retaining and renovating the religious penal clauses within a secular state, given that ... h tradition of treating offences against religion as criminal acts dates ... her ... asphemy laws were linked to sedition, and the church was ... e.

... n Black's chapter on Brunei (chapter 11) shows the ... he religious penal clauses as the country moves from ... self a product of colonial rule – towards a consoli- ... y Islamic law. Malay Islamic Monarchy (MIB) is the proclaimed national philosophy, and in this context the reach of Islamic law, which affects Muslims as well as non-Muslims in some respects, has grown apace. The author sees the bureaucratisation of Islamic law as part of a trend started by the English and now employed by the Sultan of Brunei as a way to consolidate religion-political power, which has weakened the protection of religious freedom. It should here be noted that Myanmar, another common law country in Asia that has adopted the IPC, is discussed in Jaclyn Neo's chapter in Part I.

Our introduction here sets the stage for these conceptual and empirical chapters in the book. We first examine in section II the phenomenon of religious penal clauses in common law Asia and globally. In section III, we provide a conceptual framework to distinguish among different types of religious penal clauses, their focal points, justifications and purposes. In section IV, we examine the clash between constitutional rights and religious penal clauses. In section V, we consider the lasting impact these colonial era laws have had on the former colonies, and reflect on how this legal transplant has engendered legal transformation.

II. RELIGIOUS PENAL CLAUSES IN COMMON LAW ASIA AND WORLDWIDE

A. The Indian Penal Code, the Religious Penal Clauses and Their Progenies

The spread of English style criminal law in codified form is among the lasting legacies of English colonialism. As mentioned in section I, the 1860 IPC was drafted by Thomas Babington Macaulay and legally extended/transplanted to other English colonies in Asia.[20] However, the intent was never to introduce the 'arcane common law of blasphemy'.[21] Instead, Macaulay drafted provisions that 'recognised cultural plurality and anticipated modern measures against cultural denigration'.[22] The religious penal clauses were therefore not meant to function as blasphemy laws, to uphold a national religion and to protect *religious orthodoxy*. Blasphemy laws would surely have been considered inappropriate in

[20] Legal historian Andrew Huxley, in discussing the national independence of Burma/Myanmar in 1948, points out that the principal question then was not how much of the transplanted law to jettison but how much to keep: Andrew Huxley, 'The Last Fifty Years of Burmese Law: E Maung and Maung Maung' (1998) *Lawasia: Journal of the Law Association of East Asia and the West Pacific* 14athttp://burmalibrary.org/docs/The_last_50_years_of_%20Burmese_%201aw.htmaccessedon 16 July 2020.

[21] Barry Wright, 'Macaulay's Indian Penal Code: Historical Context and Originating Prin[illegible] in Chan Wing-Cheong, Barry Wright and Stanley Yeo (eds), *Codification, Macaulay and t[illegible] Penal Code: The Legacies and Modern Challenges of Criminal Law Reform* (Ashgate, [illegible]

[22] ibid.

a religiously heterogeneous setting like India. The religious penal clauses were therefore designed as instruments of *public order*, aimed at the management of religious tensions and to prevent communal riots. Given India's religiously diverse society comprising 'millions of Mohamedans of differing sects', 'tens of millions of Hindoos' and a Christian minority that disproportionately occupied the highest government posts, there was 'much to apprehend from religious excitement among the people'.[23] The religious penal clauses were clearly based on an assumption (some may say prejudice) that Indians were easily excitable and readily offended by any slight, perceived or real, against their religion, necessitating legal regulation to contain their 'uncivilized religious passions'.[24]

The religious penal clauses were instruments of control for the English. They create a legal infrastructure for managing religion-related tensions within ethnically and religiously plural societies, with the goal of fostering *le vivre ensemble* (or pacific coexistence) within a religiously plural setting. In other words, to safeguard social harmony and public order. Guarding against social dissolution was important to maintaining English colonial rule. The English thought that as long as they, as neutral and rational arbiters, were implementing the law, discussion over controversial religious matters would be permitted and managed.[25] In time, it was hoped that legal regulation would facilitate temperate self-restraint in their colonial charges and moderate the tone of their language.[26]

As Kevin Tan's chapter goes into intricate detail on the history of the IPC and the religious penal clauses, we will not traverse the same ground. Readers should refer directly to his chapter (chapter 1), which provides a crucial background to understanding the original impetus and thought behind the religious penal clauses. Furthermore, the country-specific chapters in Part II of this book will consider more closely how the religious penal clauses are (or are not) deployed in the contemporary setting, as well as the interests of those who champion and deprecate these clauses.

It is clear that the problem of managing religious sensitivities remains an acute, contemporary one, given the increase in the number of religious-offence-related controversies, whether in liberal European societies[27] or liberal and non-liberal societies in Asia.[28] In 2011, Punjab Governor Salman Taseer was assassinated by his own bodyguard for criticising harsh blasphemy laws that

[23] Indian Law Commissioners, *A Penal Code*, note J (n 13).

[24] Cassie S Adcock, 'Violence, Passion and the Law: A Brief History of Section 295A and its Antecedents' (2016) 84(2) *Journal of the American Academy of Religion* 337–51, 342.

[25] Asad Ali Ahmed, 'Specters of Macaulay: Blasphemy, the Indian Penal Code, and Pakistan's Postcolonial Predicament' in Raminder Kaur and William Mazzarella (eds), *Censorship in South Asia: Cultural Regulation from Sedition to Seduction* (Indiana University Press, 2009) 181.

[26] Adcock, 'Violence, Passion and the Law' (n 24).

[27] Jeroen Temperman and Andras Koltay, *Blasphemy and Freedom of Expression: Comparative, Theoretical and Historical Reflections after the Charlie Hebdo Massacre* (Cambridge University Press, 2017); Jytte Klausen, *The Cartoons that Shook the World* (Yale University Press, 2009).

[28] Rollier, Froystad and Ruud (eds), 'Outrage' (n 19).

provide for capital punishment; Taseer had also sought the pardon of Asia Bibi, a Christian woman sentenced to death for allegedly insulting Prophet Muhammad.[29] A Christian couple in Pakistan were lynched and thrown into a brick kiln after being falsely accused of blasphemy, as they allegedly threw away pages of the Quran, desecrating the Muslim holy book.[30] Atheist bloggers have been targeted and murdered for hurting religious sentiments in Bangladesh,[31] while feminist self-exiled author Taslima Nasreen has been sentenced to imprisonment for books that apparently hurt religious feelings by casting aspersions on Islam.[32] Complaints about the hurting of religious sentiments in India are legion. In 2014, Penguin India responded to a suit by a Hindu Right activist by announcing that it would cease production of historian Wendy Doniger's *The Hindus: An Alternative History*, as the book's fixation on the erotic elements in Hindu literature apparently hurt the religious feelings of millions of Hindus.[33] The ease and virality of communications through social media and smartphones have also introduced more platforms for religiously offensive transgressions, exacerbated by a culture of easily taking offence.

In 2016, it was reported that the Gujarat High Court was asked to ban Pokemon Go, as its images of eggs in front of places of worship were blasphemous to Hindus and Jains and hurt the religious sentiments of vegetarians. Musicians, celebrities, Amazon India and Netflix films have also been charged or investigated for hurting religious sentiments.[34] In Myanmar, the owner of a bar sparked controversy on social media and was charged and found guilty under Article 295A of the Myanmar Penal Code for insulting religion, by posting on Facebook a promotional poster featuring an image of Buddha wearing

[29] M Ilyas Khan, 'Punjab Governor Salman Taseer assassinated in Islamabad', *BBC News* (South Asia, 4 January 2011); Ed Husain, 'Explaining the Salman Taseer Murder' (Council on Foreign Relations, 7 January 2011).

[30] 'Pak sentences 5 to death for burning of Christian couple for "blasphemy"', *Hindustantimes* (23 November 2016).

[31] Ali Riaz, *Bangladesh: A Political History Since Independence* (IB Taurus, 2016) 106–07.

[32] See generally Ali Riaz, 'Constructing Outraged Communities and State Responses: The Taslima Nasreen Saga in 1994 and 2007' (2008) 2 *South Asia Multidisciplinary Academic Journal* 1 at https://doi.org/10.4000/samaj.1262; Alain Salles, 'Bangladeshi author's book banned for attack on Islam' *The Guardian* (UK, 26 September 2002); Md Mahmudul Hasan, 'Free speech, ban and "fatwa": A study of the Taslima Nasrin affair' (2010) 46 *Journal of Postcolonial Writing* 540.

[33] Brian K Pennington, 'The Unseen Hand of an Underappreciated Law: The Doniger Affair and its Aftermath' (2016) 84(2) *Journal of the American Academy of Religion* 323.

[34] 'Bombay HC stays probe against band accused of hurting religious sentiments' *The Indian Express* (Panaji, 12 November 2020); 'Complaint filed against Amazon for hurting religious sentiments in India' *Fashion Network* (13 January 2020) (for selling toilet mats with the image of the Golden Temple, which Sikhs revere); Vineeta Kumar, 'Netflix Film Krishna and His Leela's Sexual Content hurts religious sentiments, Rana Daggubati Speaks' *India.com* (2 July 2020); Apurva Vishawanath, 'SC quashes criminal case against M.S. Dhoni' *livemint* (5 September 2016) (a cricketer charged under Section 295 for allegedly hurting religious sentiments by portraying himself as Lord Vishnu on a magazine cover); 'Comedy Nights actor Kiku Sharda arrested for mimicking Dera Chief Gurmeet Ram Rahim' *The Indian Express* (New Delhi/kaithal, 15 January 2016) (a television comedian was arrested and booked for mimicking a leader of the Dera Sacha Sauda cult, following the complaint of a cult member).

headphones. Observers consider this case as indicative of growing religious intolerance fuelled by the pro-Buddhist groups seeking to protect majoritarian Buddhist sentiments, and widening restraints on expressive freedoms.[35]

B. Religious Penal Clauses: A Global Phenomenon

Lest we think that religious penal clauses are a distinctly common law Asian phenomenon, it bears noting that the English common law of blasphemy, their historical precursor, dated back to medieval times and was only abolished in 2008.[36] It had by then been replaced by the 2006 Racial and Religious Hatred Act, which criminalises threatening speech and conduct that stirs up religious hatred.[37] Many European countries abolished blasphemy laws only in the last decade: this includes the Netherlands (2012);[38] Iceland (2015);[39] Norway (2015);[40] France (2016);[41] Denmark (2017);[42] and Ireland (2020).[43] Even the United States, whose First Amendment boasts some of the broadest free-speech protections, only properly abolished blasphemy legislation in 1952.[44] That many

[35] Joe Freeman, 'Myanmar's "Buddha bar" case highlights rise of religious conservatism' (2015) *Nikkei Asian Review*. See also Iselin Frydenlund, 'The rise of religious offence in transitional Myanmar' in Paul Rollier et al (eds), *Outrage: The Rise of Religious Offence in Contemporary South Asia* (UCL Press, 2019) 77.

[36] The Criminal Justice and Immigration Act 2008, s 79(1) provides 'The offences of blasphemy and blasphemous libel under the common law of England Wales are abolished.' See Russell Sandberg and Norman Doe, 'The Strange Death of Blasphemy' (2008) 71(6) *Modern Law Review* 971.

[37] The Racial and Religious Hatred Act 2006, s 29B(1) provides 'A person who uses threatening words or behaviour, or displays any written material which is threatening, is guilty of an offence if he intends thereby to stir up religious hatred.' See at www.legislation.gov.uk/ukpga/2006/1/schedule accessed 16 July 2020.

[38] Esther Janssen, 'The Rise and Fall of the Offence of Blasphemy in the Netherlands' in Jeroen Temperman and Andras Koltay (eds), *Blasphemy and Freedom of Expression: Comparative, Theoretical, and Historical Reflections after the Charlie Hebdo Massacre* (Cambridge University Press, 2017) 619.

[39] 'Iceland makes blasphemy legal', *BBC News* (3 July 2015) at www.bbc.com/news/world-europe-33378778 accessed 16 July 2020.

[40] 'Norway ends blasphemy law after Charlie Hebdo attack' *The Local.no* (Norway, 7 May 2015) at www.thelocal.no/20150507/norway-scraps-blasphemy-law-after-hebdo-attacks accessed 16 July 2020.

[41] 'Le Sénat supprime le délit de blasphème qui s'applique en Alsace-Moselle' ['The Senate repeals the offence of blasphemy in Alcace-Moselle'] *Loractu.fr* (France, 14 October 2016) at http://loractu.fr/france/14345-le-senat-supprime-le-delit-de-blaspheme-qui-s-applique-en-alsace-moselle.html accessed 16 July 2020.

[42] 'Denmark scraps 334-year-old blasphemy law' *The Guardian* (France, 2 June 2017) at www.theguardian.com/world/2017/jun/02/denmark-scraps-334-year-old-blasphemy-law accessed 16 July 2020.

[43] 'Blasphemy officially abolished as a criminal offence' *Irish Legal News* (20 January 2020) at www.irishlegal.com/article/blasphemy-officially-abolished-as-a-criminal-offence accessed 16 July 2020. Notably, a referendum was held asking voters to decide whether to strike out the legal ban on blasphemy, which had a constitutional imprimatur dating back to the time when a conservative Catholic Church dominated the Republic's affairs.

[44] In *Joseph Burstyn Inc v Wilson* 343 US 495 (1952), the Supreme Court held that allowing a censor to prohibit a movie on grounds that it was 'sacrilegious' was a restraint on free speech that violated the First Amendment.

Anglo-European countries today no longer retain anti-blasphemy laws, strictly defined, can be explained as a result of a shift to secularisation in society in the post-Enlightenment era. Radtke elaborates:

> The Enlightenment led either to the removal of religious offenses from the statutes of criminal law or to the transformation of religious offenses from penal provisions for the protection of God to provisions that were intended to guarantee the free practice of religion and thus the respective liberties of human beings with the most varied religious and ideological convictions.[45]

Even if the strong secularisation claim that religion would decline has not been fully realised in Europe,[46] there has been secularisation in the sense of clearer differentiation between the secular and the religious[47] in many European states. Religiously driven politics is not as influential as it currently is in other parts of the world, including in parts of South and Southeast Asia. In this post-secular society, as Habermas calls it,[48] there is a realisation that religion remains a significant social force, and this demands renewed engagement in the intersection of religion and politics.[49] In this post-secular society, blasphemy laws appear to be less relevant.

Even so, religious penal clauses have not been entirely abolished in Europe. Indeed, they have retained their salience, for two primary reasons. First, anti-blasphemy laws remain on the statute books of several European countries. According to a 2016 Pew Research Centre Report, as of 2014, seven out of 45 European states (16 per cent) still criminalise blasphemy,[50] and some still periodically invoke these laws. For instance, as recently as 2011, Austria invoked Section 188 of the Austrian Criminal Code of 1974[51] against a member of the

[45] Radtke, 'Religious Offenses' (n 8).

[46] Peter Berger, 'The Desecularization of the World: A Global Overview' in Peter Berger (ed), *The Desecularization of the World: Resurgent Religion and World Politics* (Eerdmans Publishing, 1999) 1. See also Rodney Stark, 'Secularization, R.I.P. – Rest in Peace' (1999) 60(3) *Sociology of Religion* 249.

[47] 'Secularisation' can refer to at least three analytically distinctive propositions: the decline of belief; the differentiation of public and private spheres (with religion's being assigned to the latter); and the marginalisation of religion. See also José Casanova, *Public Religions in the Modern World* (University of Chicago Press, 1994) 7; Charles Taylor, 'The Meaning of Secularism' (2010) 12(3) *Hedgehog Review* 23, 25.

[48] Jurgen Habermas, 'Notes on post-secular society' (2008) 25(4) *New Perspectives Quarterly* 17; Clayton Fordahl, 'The post-secular: Paradigm shift or provocation?' (2016) 20(4) *European Journal of Social Theory* 550.

[49] Weiler, 'The Idea of the Holy' (n 4). See also Gila Stopler, 'The Challenge of Strong Religion in the Liberal State' (2014) 32 *Boston University International Law Journal* 101.

[50] Angelina E Theodorou, 'Which countries still outlaw apostasy and blasphemy', *Pew Research Centre*, 29 July 2016 at www.pewresearch.org/fact-tank/2016/07/29/which-countries-still-outlaw-apostasy-and-blasphemy/ accessed 16 July 2020.

[51] 'Whoever, in circumstances where his behaviour is apt to arouse justified offence, publicly disparages or ridicules a person who, or an object which, is the subject of veneration of a domestically established church or religious community, or a dogma, a lawful custom or a lawful institution of such a church or religious community, shall be liable to a prison sentence of up to six months or a fine of up to 360 daily units.' See Greg Taylor, 'Austria's Law Against Defamation of Religion: A Case Study' (2015) 30(1) *Journal of Law and Religion* 80.

Freedom Party of Austria who 'denigrated' Prophet Muhammad and criticised his marriage to six-year-old Aisha.[52] The European Court of Human Rights later upheld her conviction.[53] Indeed, one might note that an administrative code on insulting religious feelings was revitalised and criminalised in a 2013 amendment to the Russian criminal code carrying enhanced penalties, after the Pussy Riot incident in 2012.[54]

Second, even in countries that no longer have blasphemy laws, some form of legal restriction on speech relating to religion is retained, couched as religious offence or religious hatred laws. At the global level, such religious offence or religious hatred laws, restricting 'insult to' or 'vilification of' or 'offence against' religion, can be found in many countries. Reports from the Pew Research Centre indicate that religious defamation or religious hatred laws were found in 44 per cent of the countries surveyed,[55] while only about a quarter of the world's countries and territories had anti-blasphemy laws and policies.[56] Article 525 of the Spanish Penal Code, which punishes the 'vilification' of religious feelings, dogmas, beliefs or rituals as a crime, is one such example.

Third, there is a possibility that we may see a resurgence of anti-blasphemy laws to manage inter-religious group relations, which have become increasingly fraught as a result of radical changes in the religious demography in many European countries, driven by rapid migration (including by asylum seekers) and changing birth patterns. Drawing on the Austrian example again, it is noteworthy that Section 188 of the Austrian Criminal Code was used to criminalise denigrating speech against Islam even though Austria has a long history as part of Christian Europe. This may be contrasted with the English response in a case arising from the Salman Rushdie affair, where the High Court in *R v Chief Stipendiary Magistrate, ex parte Choudhury* held that the common

[52] 'Blasphemy bans are struck out in Ireland and reinforced in Austria' *The Economist* (29 October 2018) at www.economist.com/erasmus/2018/10/29/blasphemy-bans-are-struck-out-in-ireland-and-reinforc ed-in-austria accessed 16 July 2020. Conor Gallagher, 'Calling Muhammad paedophile "not protected by free speech"' *The Irish Times* (29 October 2018) at www.irishtimes.com/news/world/calling-muhammad-paedophile-not-protected-by-free-speech-1.3678825 accessed 16 July 2020.

[53] *Case of ES v Austria* App no 38450/12 (ECtHR, 25 October 2018). See also *Otto-Preminger-Institut v Austria* [1994] ECHR 26 (upholding Austrian ban of film on grounds that it insulted the Christian religion); *Wingrove v the United Kingdom* App no 19/1995/525/611 (ECtHR, 25 November 1996) (upholding an English decision to reject for classification a film that involved erotic scenes between Jesus and St Theresa d'Avila on grounds that it violated national obscene publications law and national blasphemy law).

[54] Yulia Ponomareva, 'New law protecting religious feelings divides Russians' *Russia Beyond* (14 June 2013) at www.rbth.com/society/2013/06/14/new_law_protecting_religious_feelings_divides_russians_27089.html accessed 16 July 2020.

[55] Brian J Grim, 'Laws Penalizing Blasphemy, Apostasy and Defamation of Religion are Widespread', *Pew Forum on Religion and Public Life* (21 November 2012) at www.pewforum.org/2012/11/21/laws-penalizing-blasphemy-apostasy-and-defamation-of-religion-are-widespread/ accessed 16 July 2020.

[56] Theodorou, 'Which countries still outlaw apostasy and blasphemy' (n 50).

law of blasphemy did not apply to Islam.[57] However, Muslims argued that it was discriminatory, as blasphemy law privileges Christianity, where the Church of England is the established Church.

It is important to recognise that while religious penal clauses involve religion, they are deeply political. Even the use of terminology can be politicised. The term 'blasphemy' is today often used to pejoratively invoke passion, emotionalism and arcaneness, to refer to something that resides in a backward past. This is contrasted with the more 'rational' and 'modern' West, which has been associated with a 'history of increasing emotional restraint', with modernity bringing in 'self-discipline, control and suppression', and a view of law as an emanation of reason that is engaged in the project of controlling passion.[58] There is also a contemporary tendency to associate blasphemy almost exclusively with Islam. This is inaccurate, driven by sensationalistic, selective accounts of religiously-related conflicts. The image of the intolerant Islamic state is fuelled by the highly controversial ways in which many Muslim-majority countries restrict freedom of speech and religion, not only through blasphemy laws but also through heresy and apostasy laws that attract draconian penalties. Pakistan is one such country, where cases involving blasphemy have periodically been prosecuted and the death penalty pronounced at the lower court levels. These decisions are heavily influenced by local politics; but as Syed Ali Raza points out in his chapter (chapter 6), no person has ever been put to death for a blasphemy charge in Pakistan. Nonetheless, occasional sensational publicity surrounding such cases contributes to this (mis)conception that blasphemy is distinctly Eastern or Islamic, and particularly barbaric and backward. The choice of language can therefore be both illuminating and de-legitimating.

III. CONCEPTUAL DISTINCTIONS: OFFENCE AGAINST GOD VERSUS OFFENCE AGAINST RELIGIOUS BELIEVERS?

As mentioned in section II, religious penal clauses are criminal provisions implicating religion, religious ideologies, or a person or group identified specifically by their religion, and can involve a broad range of conduct. Conceptual clarity is necessary for analytical precision and comparative study of the developments surrounding religious penal clauses in common law Asia. A distinction could be made on the basis of the subject of protection. While blasphemy, strictly speaking, is conceptualised as an offence against God or religion, religious offence and religious hatred is better understood as an offence against religious believers. A further distinction could be drawn between religious offence, which is often tied to public order considerations, and religious hatred. The former could

[57] *R v Chief Stipendiary Magistrate, ex parte Choudhury* [1991] 1 QB 429.

[58] Barbara H Rosenwein, 'Worrying about Emotions in History' (2002) 107(3) *American Historical Review* 821.

be said to protect religious believers instrumentally, while the latter could be said to protect religious believers intrinsically.

A. Blasphemy: Offence against God

Famous historical personages have been accused of blasphemy. Jesus was accused by the Jewish High Priest at the trial before the Sanhedrin of blasphemy for claiming to be 'the Christ, the Son of God'.[59] The ancient Greek philosopher Socrates stood trial for blasphemy and impiety for not believing in the gods of the state and for corrupting its youth.[60] While Western Christianity has had a strong influence in institutionalising blasphemy laws, the concept of blasphemy pre-dated the three major Abrahamic religions under which it correlated to a betrayal of covenant or connoted the opposite of a declaration of faith or statements that revile God (as per Exodus 22:28), an intangible harm against a people and their God(s).

The etymology of the word 'blasphemy' is Greek, being a combination of *blapto* ('to harm') and *pheme* ('speech'). It means 'malicious remark', and refers to 'defamatory mockery, insult, slander and cursing of a deity in word, writings or actions',[61] and constitutes a value judgement on someone's communication. Blasphemy is *inherently religious*, in that it is proscribed because it accords 'disrespectful or offensive treatment'[62] and attacks sacredly-held persons, objects or doctrines within religion.[63] It is thus closely associated with heresy. Protestant reformers during the Reformation revived the claims of blasphemy as a way to condemn dissidents among their ranks.[64] A chapter entitled 'Of Offences against God and Religion' in Blackstone's eighteenth-century monumental *Commentaries on the Laws of England*, included blasphemy as well as the crimes of apostasy and heresy, and the offence of reviling the ordinances of the established Church.[65] He defined blasphemy as an offence 'against the Almighty', entailing 'all profane scoffing at Holy Scripture, or exposing it to contempt and ridicule', a denial of the Almighty's 'being or providence' or 'contumelious reproaches of our Saviour Christ'.[66] In comparison, apostasy

[59] Matthew 26:63. See Darrell Bock, 'Blasphemy and the Jewish Examination of Jesus' (2007) 17(1) *Bulletin for Biblical Research* 53.

[60] Leonard Williams Levy, *Blasphemy: Verbal Offense against the Sacred, from Moses to Salman Rushdie* (University of North Carolina Press, 1995) 6–7.

[61] Herman L Beck, 'Blasphemy' in Hans Dieter Betz et al (eds), *Religion Past and Present Online* (Brill, 2011) at www.referenceworks.brillonline.com/entries/religion-past-and-present/blasphemy-SIM_08937 accessed 16 July 2020.

[62] Cox, 'Pourquoi Suis-Je Charlie?' (n 6) 351.

[63] Knechtle, 'Blasphemy, Defamation of Religion and Religious Hate Speech' (n 7).

[64] ibid 200.

[65] Also included in this chapter are crimes of 'open and notorious lewdness' and 'having bastard children'.

[66] Blackstone, *Commentaries on the Laws of England* (n 9).

is defined as 'a total renunciation of Christianity, by embracing either a false religion, or no religion at all'; while heresy is defined as 'not a total denial of Christianity, but of some of its essential doctrines'.[67] Blasphemy expanded the scope of ecclesiastical law since, unlike apostasy and heresy, it could be applied to both religious and non-religious persons.[68]

Within Islam, a major religious tradition in Asia, blasphemy is also strongly associated with heresy. Notably, there is in fact an absence of a specific definition for blasphemy in the works of *fiqh* in Islam, and Kamali argues that this is because blasphemy had generally been subsumed under apostasy (*riddah*), and treated as part of it.[69] In addition, blasphemy has also been regarded as heresy (*zandaqah*) and denial of Islam (*kufr*).[70] In Islam, the key distinction between blasphemy and apostasy seems to be that of coverage, given that blasphemy applies to non-Muslims. A Muslim who utters a statement considered blasphemous may also be accused of apostasy on the basis that a person who 'blasphemes the essentials of the faith cannot fail, at the same time, to renounce it'.[71] In contrast, a non-Muslim who makes the same statement can only be accused of blasphemy.

Blasphemy law, in policing the boundaries of religious orthodoxy, is deeply *political*. Blasphemy requires an authoritative interpreter of religious doctrine, which may bring about an unholy alliance between Caesar and God, as when the Roman Emperor Constantine convened the Nicene Council, which produced orthodoxy in the form of the Nicene Creed.[72] There are often complex interlocking reasons for prohibiting blasphemous speech. For instance, in ancient Greece and Rome, the fear was that blasphemous speech would attract the displeasure of the gods because proper respect was not shown to them, and that retribution would be wrought on the polity.[73] During and after the Reformation, when secular (political) authority was unified with religious authority in the King, this meant that 'any verbal disagreement on religion was also a verbal disagreement with the king, neither of which was tolerated'.[74] Heresy and blasphemy were no longer crimes under church or ecclesiastical law, enforced by ecclesiastical authorities, but incorporated as part of state law.[75] Thus, religious orthodoxy became intertwined with political authority, such that 'blasphemy is an orthodoxy's way of demonising difference in order to perpetuate violence against it'.[76]

[67] ibid 43–45.
[68] Knechtle, 'Blasphemy, Defamation of Religion and Religious Hate Speech' (n 7) 200.
[69] Mohammad Hashim Kamali, *Freedom of Expression in Islam* (Berita Publishing, 1994) 206.
[70] ibid 207.
[71] ibid.
[72] Although the Nicene Council, in seeking universal doctrine, was concerned more with heresy than blasphemy; see David A Lawton, *Blasphemy* (University of Pennsylvania Press, 1993) 51–53.
[73] Taylor, 'Austria's Law Against Defamation of Religion' (n 51) 80.
[74] Knechtle, 'Blasphemy, Defamation of Religion and Religious Hate Speech' (n 7).
[75] Radtke, 'Religious Offenses' (n 8).
[76] Lawton, 'Blasphemy' (n 72) 202.

Furthermore, practice shows that blasphemy laws could and have been used to control a religious population, since religion is a useful means of ensuring obedience to the laws – as even Napoleon cynically appreciated[77] – offensive speech could thus undermine the foundation of the law.[78] Where state legitimacy is closely aligned with a religious identity, religious offences may be viewed as attacks on the state itself and attract severe penalties, including capital punishment.[79] In this regard, blasphemy has been regarded as akin to treason.[80] In Blackstone's view, blasphemy was justified in England because 'Christianity is part of the laws of England'.[81] This view was echoed by the King's Bench in *R v Taylor*, holding that the accused's blasphemous utterance was 'not only an offence to God and to religion, but a crime against the laws, state and Government'.[82]

B. From 'Offences against God and Religion' to 'Offences against Religious Believers'?

The secularisation of the state and the religious pluralisation of society meant that blasphemy laws served a less obvious purpose in ensuring state preservation and maintaining social cohesion. Indeed, the Treaty of Westphalia's recognition of the rights of members of religious minorities within a polity to profess and practise their religion sparked off an international recognition of the right to the protection of religious freedom, which further undermined the need for blasphemy laws. The decoupling of the state from the majority religion in Anglo-European countries thus led to a shift from protecting the state and religion through laws against offending God and religion, to protecting religious believers. The primary function of religious penal clauses was to 'safeguard public and religious peace, mainly through the prosecution of external interferences in the free practice of religion'.[83] This was reflected in Britain, with shifting opinions that the social fabric did not depend on sound religious opinions.[84] For instance, it was stated in the 1917 case of *Bowman v Secular Society Ltd* that

[77] Hippolyte A Taine, 'Napoleon's views on Religion' (1891) 152(414) *The North American Review* 567.

[78] Taylor, 'Austria's Law Against Defamation of Religion' (n 51).

[79] Radtke, 'Religious Offenses' (n 8).

[80] Knechtle, 'Blasphemy, Defamation of Religion and Religious Hate Speech' (n 7) 203.

[81] Blackstone, *Commentaries on the Laws of England* (n 9).

[82] Hale CJ, in *R v Taylor* [1676] 1 Vent 293 (KB), stated that 'For to say, religion is a cheat, is to dissolve all those obligations whereby the civil societies are preserved, and that Christianity is parcel of the laws of England, and therefore to reproach the Christian religion is to speak in subversion of the law.' See Elliot Visconsi, 'The Invention of Criminal Blasphemy: R v Taylor (1676)' (2008) 103(1) *Representations* 30.

[83] ibid.

[84] Knechtle, 'Blasphemy, Defamation of Religion and Religious Hate Speech' (n 7).

'reasonable men do not apprehend the dissolution or the downfall of society because religion is publicly assailed by methods not scandalous'.[85]

This change from offences against God or religion, to offences against religious believers is crucial. The latter focuses not on religion but on deviant or anti-social acts involving religion. The objects of protection are individual members of religious groups. In relation to offences against religious believers, one can further distinguish between those that protect individuals for instrumental reasons, because of the potential impact on public order, and those that protect individuals as an intrinsic value. The latter tend to be conceptualised as hate speech, which serves to protect members of vulnerable groups from harm arising from denigratory speech and vilification. The harm is here conceptualised broadly to also include the psychological and emotional health of persons belonging to the group.[86] The offence of hate speech has also been justified as necessary to protect the dignity of persons who are identified as part of a community.[87] Waldron distinguishes the protection of dignity from protection from offence.[88] Dignity refers to a person's equal status in the community, their entitlement to basic justice and the fundamentals of their reputation. Group-directed attacks in the form of hate speech undermine a person's dignity, as they proclaim that members of the group are, 'by virtue of their race or some other ascriptive characteristic, not worthy of being treated as members of society in good standing'.[89] Interestingly, Waldron understands dignity not as an individual right but as 'a status sustained by law in society in the form of a *public good*'.[90]

C. Denigration or Defamation of Religion: Between Blasphemy and Religious Hate Speech?

A discussion of religious penal clauses, particularly blasphemy, necessarily implicates another discussion at the international level concerning the defamation of religion. This was a concept promoted by Muslim-majority states to counter 'hatred, discrimination, intolerance, and acts of violence, intimidation, and coercion'. It was initially proposed in 1999 by Pakistan, on behalf of the Organisation of Islamic Conference (OIC, now known as the Organisation of Islamic Cooperation), before the UN Commission on Human Rights, but with a focus on Islam. The draft resolution entitled 'Defamation of Islam' was fuelled by a longstanding grievance of Muslim-majority states against the negative

[85] *Bowman v Secular Society Ltd* [1917] AC 406.

[86] Katharine Gelber, 'The False Analogy between Vilification and Sedition' (2009) 33 *Melbourne University Law Review* 270, 285.

[87] Waldron, 'The Harm in Hate Speech' (n 11).

[88] ibid 105.

[89] ibid 106.

[90] ibid 106 (emphasis added).

depiction of Islam as an obstruction to human rights within the UN context.[91] Its proposers argued forcefully against the 'negative stereotyping of Islam and the tendency to associate human rights violations and terrorism with Islam'.[92] The initial draft called upon the Special Rapporteur on religious tolerance to report on 'attacks against Islam and attempts to defame it'.[93] After objections primarily from EU states, the final resolution retained the concept of defamation but made it more inclusive by referring to all religions, even though Islam was still given particular prominence.[94] The resolution adopted urged:

> [A]ll States, within their national legal framework, in conformity with international human rights instruments to take all appropriate measures to combat hatred, discrimination, intolerance, and acts of violence, intimidation, and coercion motivated by religious intolerance, including attacks on religious places, and to encourage understanding, tolerance, and respect in matters relating to freedom of religion or belief.[95]

Following this, resolutions on defamation of religion were passed at the Commission on Human Rights annually until it was disbanded in 2006, and thereafter at the Human Rights Council until it was abandoned in 2010.[96]

In the meantime, there was a lack of conceptual clarity as to what defamation of religion means. Proponents referred to existing concepts, such as racism, discrimination and freedom of religion, but without clearly setting out how defamation relates to these.[97] In this context 'defamation' is confusing, since it is commonly understood to relate to the reputation of a person, rather than criticism of religious tenets and practices. Opponents argue that defamation of religion is an euphemism for blasphemy and the resolutions represent a backdoor attempt to create 'international blasphemy laws'.[98] For instance, in discussing defamation of religion, Knechtle considers it 'closely related to

[91] For a historical sweep of this concept on the international forum, see Brett G Scharffs, 'International Law and the Defamation of Religion Conundrum' (2013) 11(1) *The Review of Faith & International Affairs* 66; Lorenz Langer, *Religious Offence and Human Rights: The Implications of Defamation of Religions* (Cambridge University Press, 2014).

[92] Langer, *Religious Offence and Human Rights* (n 91) 169.

[93] ibid.

[94] United Nations Commission on Human Rights, *Racism, Racial Discrimination, Xenophobia and All Forms of Discrimination* (E/CN.4/1999/L.40/Rev.1, 30 April 1999); see also discussion in Langer, *Religious Offence and Human Rights* (n 91) 165–70. In tandem with this are efforts to avoid paying undue attention to one religion, as in the context of religious discrimination and violence, [illegible] 'arly refers to cases motivated by 'Islamophobia, anti-Semitism and [illegible] s ag[illegible] inst persons of other religions or beliefs': General Assembly [illegible] *Religion or Belief* (A/RES/72/177, 29 January 2018). The use [illegible] dimension: Lauren Moustakas, 'The Label Christianophobia [illegible] *re for Law and Justice* (24 June 2020) at https://eclj.org/ [illegible] phobia-in-human-rights-law accessed 16 July 2020.

[95] [illegible] 0 (n 91) para 5. Draft resolution E/CN.4/1999/L.40/Rev 1, [illegible] without a vote: CHR Summary Record 55th Session, E/ [illegible]

[96] [illegible] of religion movement at the United Nations, see Scharffs [illegible] of Religion Conundrum' (n 91).

[97] [illegible] an Rights (n 91) 170.

[98] [illegible] 5) 353.

blasphemy'[99] because it involves 'criticism or ridicule of religious practice or belief whether reasoned, satirical or contemptuous'.[100] The focus is on the relationship with the sacred.

Cox, however, argues that a 'fair reading' of the defamation of religion resolutions show that they do not envisage blasphemy law, strictly speaking, but rather are aimed at 'protecting religious groups (and in particular, Islam) from quasi-xenophobic vilification through statements which falsely and negatively stereotype the entire group by references to unrepresentative actions from a minority of members of the group'.[101] Cox points out that there is a conceptual difference between speech that 'offends against some sacred aspect of the ideological vision of a religion' (properly, blasphemy) and speech that 'demonizes the religion itself (and, by inherent extension, its members)', which also 'may and probably will transgress on the sacred' (properly, denigration or defamation of religion).[102] He says that the conceptual differences between blasphemy and defamation of religion can be determined from the terms of the resolutions, which contain 'three key interlocking purposes':

> First, they seek to target speech which is xenophobic in relation to a religion, through a process of negative stereotyping which links that entire religion with terrorism or human rights violations. Second (and even more prominently) they seek to uphold the rights of those individuals that might be under threat as a result of such xenophobic vilification. Third, they seek to encourage states and other actors to promote values of tolerance and diversity which are conducive to global and social harmony.[103]

Accordingly, Cox argues that defamation of religion 'inescapably implies that what is targeted is factual, false and demonizing rather than merely disrespectful' speech.[104] In this regard, one may see defamation of religion as closer to hate speech, which serves to protect the individual from vulnerable groups, unlike blasphemy, which serves to protect the religious majority.

IV. CONSTITUTIONAL RIGHTS

Drafted in the second half of the nineteenth century, the IPC was adopted in India and elsewhere way before there were independence constitutions or constitutional bills of rights. The religious penal clauses have remained in Penal Codes in Asian common law jurisdictions in the twenty-first century, where they are not moribund but sites of sometimes feverish activity. Their operation has a bearing on fundamental liberties, particularly freedom of speech and freedom

[99] Knechtle, 'Blasphemy, Defamation of Religion and Religious Hate Speech' (n 7) 198.
[100] ibid.
[101] ibid 350.
[102] Cox, 'Pourquoi Suis-Je Charlie?' (n 6) 345.
[103] ibid 355.
[104] ibid 355.

of religion. Even though Macaulay did allude to the need to have 'fair latitude' for religious discussion when drafting the IPC, this was not conceptualised as a basic constitutional right. At best, having fair latitude to discuss religious matters is an individual and public interest to be taken into consideration in a negotiated balance. For instance, in the 1862 'Maharaj libel case', public opinion about religious matters was seen as susceptible to reasonable argument, such that a religious reformer had the right to publicly criticise a religious community in Bombay.[105] However, in a subsequent 1915 case, Arya Samaj preacher Dharm Bir was found guilty under Section 298 for delivering a public lecture that was critical of Islam, with the deliberate intent of wounding the religious feelings of Muslims in the audience, after which some Muslims beat up several Arya Samaj lecturers. The court rejected the defence that this constituted reasonable, fair debate that warranted protection as free speech. Marking a shift in understanding, religion was no longer seen as susceptible to rational deliberation; instead, the judge opined that 'religion is rooted in the emotions and sentiments' and that 'logic has never saved a soul'.[106]

The question today is whether, in relation to religious offences, the fundamental status now accorded to freedom of speech and religion affects or should affect how religious penal clauses are to be interpreted and applied in jurisdictions with supreme written constitutions. This further raises the issue of whether these religious penal clauses should be re-examined in light of these constitutional rights. For example, Lorenz Langer argues that 'defamation of religions' or religious offence, as championed by Islamic states, is irreconcilable with human rights and would undermine the universal aspirations of human rights law.[107]

Religious penal clauses clearly impinge upon freedom of speech. Under the common law, free speech was a residual liberty, left over after statutory regulation. In the 'age of rights', the response in some common law courts has been to 'read up' fundamental rights and increase the weight accorded to free-speech guarantees.[108] It is instructive to note that when the House of Lords Select Committee on Religious Offences in England and Wales declared the offence of blasphemy to be a dead letter in 2003, it observed that 'any prosecution for blasphemy today … is likely to fail on grounds either of discrimination or denial of the right to freedom of expression'.[109] In recent years, blasphemy, and by association religious penal clauses, has emerged as a major flashpoint in

[105] Adcock, 'Violence, Passion and the Law' (n 24) 345.

[106] Uttar Pradesh Government (India), General Administration Department, 51, 49, cited in Adcock, ibid 346.

[107] Langer, 'Religious Offence and Human Rights' (n 91).

[108] See eg *Reynolds v Times Newspaper* [2001] 2 AC 127; *Review Publishing Co Ltd v Lee Hsien Loong* [2010] 1 SLR 53 [261]–[264].

[109] See House of Lords Select Committee on Religious Offences in England and Wales (2003, vol I, app (3), para 9). Since the freedom of expression was included in the Human Rights Act, a 'constitutional' statute that came into force in 2000, it has been accorded greater weight, as the right is

free-speech and religious-freedom debate. The incidents involving the *Jyllands-Posten* (Danish) cartoons and *Charlie Hebdo* caricatures were cast as a clash between free speech and religious bigotry.[110] Both provoked and roiled religious sensitivities, and resulted in violence.[111] Nonetheless, it bears emphasising that free speech is not an absolute right.[112] If legitimate criticism, which may contain truth and which may be hurtful, is too easily characterised as religiously offensive or wounding speech, this could undermine the value of expressive freedom in the marketplace of ideas as well as democratic development. However, if speech is used to denigrate religious persons and provoke religious offence, it fractures relationships and social solidarity. Ultimately, this requires a balancing of rights and goods.

Where speech or conduct proscribed under the religious penal clauses arises from religious motivations, or where it is considered to constitute a religious obligation, such criminalisation also adversely affects the right to religious freedom. For instance, where the 'offensive' speech or conduct is undertaken in the course of religious proselytisation, proscribing such conduct could be seen as constraining both free speech and religious freedom. While the Indian and Singapore Constitutions define religious freedom as including a right to religious propagation,[113] this has been viewed as a contentious liberty, capable of provoking inter-religious group tension. While evangelism is viewed as integral to missionary faiths like Islam and Christianity and key to religious liberty for example, to others, proselytism as a form of religious criticism is viewed as 'intolerant and intolerable'.[114] In Malaysia, its constitutional provision guaranteeing the right to propagate one's religion is subject to laws controlling or restricting the 'propagation of any religious doctrine or belief among persons professing the religion of Islam.'[115]

'based on a constitutional or higher legal order foundation', such that 'freedom of expression is the rule and regulation of speech is the exception requiring justification': Lord Steyn, *Reynolds v Times Newspaper* [2001] 2 AC 127, 207–08.

[110] See eg Jytte Klausen, *The Cartoons That Shook the World* (Yale University Press, 2009); Caroline Warman, et al (eds & trs), *Tolerance: The Beacon of the Enlightenment* (Open Book Classics, 2016).

[111] Josh Levs, '10 killed, churches torched in protests over Charlie Hebdo' *CNN World* (21 January 2015) at https://edition.cnn.com/2015/01/20/world/charlie-hebdo-violence/index.html accessed 16 July 2020; NPR, 'Muhammad Cartoon Protests Turn Deadly Again' *NPR* (18 February 2006) at www.npr.org/templates/story/story.php?storyId=5223591 accessed 16 July 2020.

[112] This is evident in the legal constraints regulating speech in the law of defamation, sedition, contempt of court or incitement to discrimination, hostility or violence on the basis of racial or religious hatred. See Sydney Kentridge, 'Freedom of Speech: Is it the Primary Rights?' (1996) 45(2) *International & Comparative Law Quarterly* 253.

[113] Li-ann Thio, 'Caesar, Conscience and Conversion: Constitutional Secularism and the Regulation of Religious Profession and Propagation in Asian States' [2011] *Fides et Libertas: The Journal of the International Religious Liberty Association* 127; Sarah Claerhout and Jakob de Roover, 'Religious Freedom and the Limits of Propagation: Conversion in the Constituent Assembly of India' (2019) 10(3) *Religions* 157.

[114] Adcock, 'Violence, Passion, and the Law' (n 24) 339.

[115] See Art 11(4), Federal Constitution.

If religion, drenched in sentiment, is beyond reason, then religious debate is pointless, being 'nothing but a provocation, an act calculated to arouse hatred',[116] as claims to absolutist truth are accompanied by criticism of another religion, which is frequently considered denigratory. Propagation as religious criticism was considered intolerant and not to be tolerated as it was prone to incite violence. This critical view against religious propagation diminishes the role of religious critique as an impetus to religious reform and privileges religious feeling by punishing upsetting views, since it was assumed the offended would be unable to act with self-restraint. Some consider propagation to be incompatible with secularism, insofar as the secular ideal is not to engage in religious criticism. It has been argued within more plural societies like India, that the state should exercise more censorship, or individuals should be required to exercise more self-censorship, in the interests of peace. Muslim philosopher Shabbir Akhtar considered this to be 'a meaningful demand in a world of varied and passionately held convictions' around the time of the Salman Rusdhie affair.[117] The view that civil peace is contingent on preserving restraint when it comes to religious discussions is embodied in laws like Section 295A of the Indian Penal Code, under which religious sentiment and violence are tethered. For the sake of social harmony, religious propagation should be avoided, it is argued, bearing in mind that Section 295A was meant to provide 'a legal tool to restrain the religious criticism associated with proselytizing by the Arya Samaj'.[118] The robustness of religious freedom guarantees is then affected by whether religious propagation is viewed as part of a valued constitutional right or an unvalued threat to social harmony.

In interpreting constitutional chapters on rights, courts are engaged in identifying and balancing the competing rights of individuals and groups, duties and public goods, which speaks to the organisation of social relations. In the context of religious penal clauses, this could include the right to the expression of religious views and propagation, pitted against competing interests. These competing interests vary and could entail wide-ranging public order and public morality considerations, as well as the protection of the religious feelings of others in the interest of religious peace.[119] A Singapore court has even referred to a competing right not to be offended,[120] without clearly articulating the legal basis of such a putative right.[121] The scope of rights could be qualified by duties, such as the duty to respect religious others and so not to denigrate any other religion in propagating one's faith.[122] The European Court of Human Rights

[116] Adcock, 'Violence, Passion, and the Law' (n 24) 346.
[117] Quoted in Kenan Malik, 'Changing Landscape of Freedom' *The Hindu* (India, 12 February 2014).
[118] Adcock, 'Violence, Passion, and the Law' (n 24) 346.
[119] *ES v Austria* App no 38450/12 (ECtHR, 18 March 2019) paras 52–57.
[120] *PP v Koh Song Huat Benjamin and Anor* [2005] SGDC 272.
[121] Jaclyn Neo, 'Seditious in Singapore! Free Speech and the Offence of Promoting Ill-Will and Hostility between Different Racial Groups' [2011] *Singapore Journal of Legal Studies* 351.
[122] *Evangelical Fellowship of India v State of Himachal Pradesh* (30 August 2012) CWP No 438 of 2011A (High Court, Himachal Pradesh) para 16: 'The right to propagate one's religion may

has recognised that with expressive freedom comes 'a duty to avoid expressions that are gratuitously offensive to others and profane'.[123] There may be a duty to be resilient, 'tolerate and accept the denial by others of their religious beliefs and even the propagation by others of doctrines hostile to their faith'.[124] Rights may be qualified by public goods, which may justifiably restrict free expression, such as guarding against religious intolerance or sacraphobia, ensuring religious peace[125] and protecting the religious feelings of citizens.[126]

Another constitutional rights issue arising from religious penal clauses concerns the subject of protection. Classic international human rights law tends to valorise the individual as the object of protection, consonant with the tenets of liberal individualism. However, religious practice entails a communal dimension, which is recognised under religious freedom clauses.[127] There needs to be a recognition that the individual is embedded within the religious community from which they derive their identity and meaning. Indeed, the protection of religious minority groups was a core purpose of the inter-war international minority protection system underwritten by the League of Nations, which was the historical precursor to the human rights system implemented by the United Nations.[128] The communitarian nature of religious worship would mean that the denigration of any one person's religion would be seen or felt keenly as an attack on all fellow religious believers. This is reflected in Kamali's exposition in identifying two aspects of blasphemy: first, a 'contemptuous and hostile attack on the fundamentals of religion'; second, that it 'offends the religious sensibilities of the community of believers'.[129] As such, while religious hate speech laws in some jurisdictions may be orientated towards protecting believers as individuals, in other jurisdictions, such religious denigration or hate speech laws seek to protect individuals as members of religious groups. In this regard, religious

entitle a person to extol the virtues of the religion which he propounds. He, however, has no right to denigrate any other religion, thought or belief. One may promise heaven to the followers of one's religion, but one cannot say that damnation will follow if that path is not followed. The essence of secularism is tolerance and acceptance of all religions. The right to propagate can never include the right to denigrate any other thought, religion or belief …'

[123] *İA v Turkey* App no 42571/98 (ECtHR, 13 September 2005) para 24.

[124] ibid, para 28: 'Those who choose to exercise the freedom to manifest their religion, irrespective of whether they do so as members of a religious majority or a minority, cannot reasonably expect to be exempt from all criticism. They must tolerate and accept the denial by others of their religious beliefs and even the propagation by others of doctrines hostile to their faith.'

[125] *Otto-Preminger-Institut* (n 53). The ECtHR held that the seizing of a satirical religious film, *Council of Heaven*, did not breach Art 10 as there was a pressing social need to ensure religious peace; the method was proportionate and did not overstep the margin of appreciation.

[126] *Gay News Ltd v United Kingdom* (1983) 5 EHRR 123. The European Commission held that the restriction imposed by the common law offence of blasphemous libel, which sought to protect the right of citizens not to be offended in their religious feelings by publications, was a legitimate purpose recognised by the Convention, ie to protect the rights of others.

[127] See eg Art 18 of the Universal Declaration of Human Rights, which appreciates that religious practices are to be enjoyed 'either alone or in community'.

[128] Linde Lindkvist, 'The Politics of Article 18: Religious Liberty in the Universal Declaration of Human Rights' (2014) *Humanity Journal* at http://humanityjournal.org/issue4-3/the-politics-of-article-18-religious-liberty-in-the-universal-declaration-of-human-rights/ accessed 16 July 2020.

[129] Kamali, 'Freedom of Expression in Islam' (n 69) 206, 210.

penal clauses in common law Asia must be seen as operating within a conception of religious profession that is more communitarian than individualistic, reflecting the close link between protecting religion, religious groups and their individual constituent members.

The interpretive approach towards religious penal clauses is shaped by the extant rights jurisprudence, whether viewed as atomistic, individualistic rights that are prioritised over collective interests, or as structured rights, which focuses the judicial enquiry on whether the reasons for justifying regulation over a sphere of human activity are legitimate.[130] This is shaped by the values espoused within the constitutional context, whether liberal, communitarian or statist (or a mix of these) in orientation, which influence issues such as whether restrictions on liberties should satisfy a test of reasonableness, proportionality or expediency. Interpretive approaches are also affected by whether religious or secular constitutionalism is practised (official religion, protectionism), whether an official religion informs the national character, how the good of public order and religious harmony is understood, the official state view towards religion and whether citizens are expected to act with the disciplined self-restraint of a 'rational person', as opposed to being given over to the excesses of religious passion as an 'emotional person'.[131]

Additionally, the status given to rights within the constitutional order also influences the extent to which religious penal clauses may be read restrictively or expansively. Where rights are given a fundamental status, having priority or even serving as trumps over other interests, it is likely that religious penal clauses would be read more restrictively unless they are conceptualised narrowly as protecting other individual rights. Hate speech laws, for instance, could be justified on the basis of protecting the individual right to dignity. In contrast, where rights are conceptualised as coequal or subordinate to competing interests, religious penal clauses are more likely to be employed more extensively given the weaker constitutional constraints. Accordingly, the intervention of the written constitution and constitutional bill of rights does not necessarily translate to a constriction of religious penal clauses. Much depends on the way rights are conceptualised, and the constitutional context and philosophy that determine the normative weight attributed to rights in the adjudicatory process.

V. RECEPTION, RETENTION, RENOVATION, AND REIMAGINATION: LEGAL TRANSPLANTS AND COLONIAL LEGACIES

The legacy of the IPC continues to resound across the common law world. Religious penal clauses, as we shall see in the rest of this book, remain legally relevant in all the common law jurisdictions studied, except perhaps Sri Lanka,

[130] Richard H Pildes, 'Why Rights are not Trumps: Social Meanings, Expressive Harms and Constitutionalism' (1998) 27(52) *Journal of Legal Studies* 725, 730.

[131] See Li-ann Thio's chapter on Apollonian Restraint and Dionysian Impulse (ch 10) in this volume.

where decades of civil war have inhibited development of its legal system. As Alan Watson once said, a 'successful legal transplant ... will grow in its new body, and become part of that body just as the rule or institution would have continued to develop in its parent system'.[132] After all, legal transplants bring 'legal transformation'.[133] As Jaclyn Neo points out in her chapter (chapter 4), religious penal clauses have adapted to local contexts and transformed these legal and political systems. The impact of these laws continues to reverberate. Here, we identify four ways in which the religious penal clauses have transformed state-society relations as well as inter-group relations in common law Asia.

A. Consolidating State Power

As mentioned, the colonial powers saw the religious penal clauses as expedient though probably effective tools to manage inter-group relations. The terms of some of the religious penal clauses are vague, and it is difficult both to quantify and qualify the harm or damage done by religiously 'offensive' or 'wounding' speech and conduct. For example, what degree of wounding is required, and what degree of tolerance is expected? The response towards religiously offensive conduct may vary, both in terms of how easily one is offended by religious insults and speech, and how one reacts, which may range from sober disquiet and simmering resentment to rage and riot. The religious penal clauses allowed the colonial government to appropriate the role of making normative judgement calls about what is religiously offensive. It cast itself as the benevolent, neutral arbiter, charged with maintaining public peace among a colonial population prone to religious excitation, so that pacific coexistence between different religious communities would be possible.[134] In so doing, the colonial government controlled religious discourse in determining prohibited and permitted degrees of religious offensiveness. The implementation of the religious penal clauses therefore constituted an assertion and legitimation of colonial authority in regulating religion, in disciplining and sanctioning religious passion.

[132] Alan Watson, *Legal Transplants: An Approach to Comparative Law*, 2nd edn (University of Georgia Press, 1993) 27.

[133] ibid 116.

[134] It is argued that the English, through their conduct of censuses, where questions about religious affiliation were prominent, manufactured a particular set of political identities in India by dividing communities along religious lines, discounting their overlapping identities. If religion is the basis of division, this conveys to the census subject that this is the most important aspect of their identities, which were essentialised. This divide-and-rule strategy created competitive group identities, for religious 'us' and 'others', and set the stage for communal tension, particularly between the Hindus and Muslims, driving a wedge between religious groups, especially Hindus and Muslims. Such communal tensions persist today: Aziz Rahman, Mohsin Ali and Saad Kahn, 'The British Art of Colonialism in India: Subjugation and Division' (2018) 25(1) *Peace and Conflict Studies*, Article 5, at https://nsuworks.nova.edu/pcs/vol25/iss1/5 accessed 16 July 2020; Maria Misra, 'Lessons of Empire: Britain and India' (2003) 23(2) *SAIS Review* 133, 144–45.

When the English left, the colonial structures and laws they implemented were reproduced by retention, with different players taking up the reins of control and authority. Retaining the religious penal clauses in turn kept the colonial view of religion as something rooted in sentiment and passion, something that often defies rational deliberation,[135] as well as the operating English stereotype that 'religious violence was a feature of Indian society',[136] requiring legal control. Hence, the criticised or offended party would not be able to restrain himself from having a violent reaction. It has been argued that this colonial construct enhanced the legitimacy of imperial rule.[137] This legal regime and its underlying assumptions about the need to subdue or civilise unruly native religious passions were later transplanted into other English colonies and augmented, indicating the vital importance attributed to the religious penal clauses. In Singapore, new provisions were added in 2007 to the relevant chapter in the Penal Code to criminalise acts promoting enmity between different groups on grounds of religion or race and doing acts prejudicial to maintenance of harmony. Provisions in the chapter were also recently invoked to address speech considered offensive to religious groups, resulting in the legal prosecution of an Indian national who is an Imam and a teenage blogger, discussed in Li-ann Thio's chapter (chapter 10), demonstrating their continuing utility.

B. New Elite, Back to the Past in Entrenching Religious Hierarchy

As several of the country chapters show – India, Pakistan, and Myanmar stand out among them – these religious penal clauses could be used by a dominant majority driven by majoritarian religious nationalism to appropriate state power to 'discipline' and subordinate religious minorities, thereby entrenching a religious hierarchy. For example, in Pakistan, several provisions were added to the Chapter that appear to be specifically directed at controlling unorthodox minorities like the Ahmaddiyas, in the context of a Muslim-majority state. With the end of English colonial rule, new local elites entered into power and sat in determination of what constituted a religious offence and threat to public order. The religious penal clauses have become useful tools for these new elites to advance a religious vision of the state, alongside other legal or constitutional tools that

[135] In *Veerabadran Chettiar v EV Ramaswami Naicker & Others* AIR 1958 SC 1032, the Supreme Court of India, in interpreting Section 295 of the Penal Code, stated that courts had to be 'very circumspect' where religious susceptibilities were concerned, and were to pay 'due regard to the feelings and religious emotions of different classes of persons with different beliefs, irrespective of the consideration whether or not they share those beliefs, or whether they are rational or otherwise, in the opinion of the court'.

[136] Adcock, 'Violence, Passion, and the Law' (n 24) 341.

[137] Gyanendra Pandey, 'The Colonial Construction of "Communalism": British Writings on Bañaras in the Nineteenth Century' in Veena Das (ed), *Mirrors of Violence: Communities, Riots and Survivors in South Asia* (Oxford University Press, 1990) 94.

serve to erect a religious hierarchy through constitutional proclamation. This is the case in Malaysia and Brunei, where state resources are brought to bear not only to support one version of Islam, such as Sunni Islam in Malaysia, but also to promote Islamic *dakwah* (religious propogation) activities.

The trajectory for religious dominance was in some cases laid by the English colonial rulers. In Brunei, the robust system of Islamic criminal law today is actually a colonial legacy given the English support for a dual system of penal law, residing in the common law and Islamic law. The concentration of religious and political power in the Sultan, the only absolute monarch in Asia, has been brought to bear in efforts to realise a *zikir* nation that upholds the laws of Allah.[138] Islam is a matter of the government, and Section 2 of the 1959 Constitution identifies Islam with that of the Shafeite sect. This diminishes the inherent interpretative plurality within Islam through the centralised control of religious debates and of religious orthodoxy. The neutral tenor of the colonial era religious penal clauses was reversed in the form of protectionist treatment of Islam, on the backs of new syariah laws: the 2013 Syariah Penal Code Order, which criminalises blasphemy and apostasy, and the 2018 Syariah Penal Code Procedure Order. The civilisational superiority-inferiority debate re-emerged in the form of a new law introduced in 2013 that created an offence against black magic, targeted at the animistic practices of non-Muslim indigenous tribes that are considered primitive and civilisationally inferior to the values of the Malay Islam Monarchy. Ironically too, the enactment of Syariah penal laws means that the religious penal clauses are likely to be less relevant, though the types and range of religion-related conduct and speech subject to legal sanction will continue to expand. Ann Black's chapter (chapter 11) demonstrates that within the dual legal system, the pendulum has swung to favour robust implementation of religious law, to the detriment of other liberties.

Where there are political forces motivated to entrench religious preferentialism through political dominance, this bodes ill for religious minorities as well as minority sects within a dominant religious group, like the Ahmadis in Pakistan and Shia Muslims in Sunni-majority Malaysia. In India, the religious penal clauses have been used as a tool for the Indian Hindu right-wing nationalists, for example, to advance their nationalist agenda by harassing religious minorities through violent performative displays of religious emotions that serve as proof of wounded religious feelings. If a law encourages or makes space for people to feel offended without requiring them to restrain their emotions and outrage, more people will seize the opportunity to feel offended, fuelling tribalist conflict and interest group politics. It diminishes the willingness of the offended to accept the pain of being offended as the price for the 'pleasures of pluralism'.[139]

[138] Hajah Sainah Haji Saim, 'Brunei Darussalam in 2012: Towards a "Zikir" Nation' [2013] *Southeast Asian Affairs* 63.

[139] Malik, 'Changing Landscape of Free Speech' (n 117).

C. Legal Protection for Religious Minorities

While some post-colonial states have instrumentalised the religious penal clauses to preserve religious majoritarian dominance, in other post-colonial states, the religious penal clauses are seen as a way for minorities to protect themselves against other religious groups, including the majority group. While the English Raj imposed these religious penal clauses in a top-down fashion to secure public order, these laws were subsequently extended, in some cases in response to demands for such a law emanating from minorities. This is evident in the origins of Section 295A of the IPC,[140] which augmented the existing laws in 1927 and made it easier to secure convictions of those in breach of religious offence.

It was passed in the aftermath of the controversial 1924 *Rangila Rasul* ('The Colourful Prophet') case,[141] which led to violent protests after the publisher was acquitted. The case involved a satirical pamphlet authored by a Hindu group and published by a Hindu publisher in Urdu, containing poems about the Prophet and his multiple marriages.[142] While condemning the publication as malicious, the Lahore High Court reluctantly ruled that satire concerning the personal life of a deceased religious teacher fell outside Section 153A because otherwise, a serious historical work adversely discussing the life and character of the Prophet might fall within Section 153A. The judge suggested instead that the work should be sanctioned for 'wounding the religious feelings of any person or of insulting the religion of any person', which unfortunately was not an offence under the Penal Code.[143]

Protests in response to the acquittal aggravated Hindu–Muslim communal tensions. Article 295A was drafted for a legal solution to address the agitation of Indian Muslim minorities to protect them from future similar instances; this was justified in terms of the need for great restraint in discussing religion in service of the pacific coexistence of distinct religious groups in plural societies. Punjab Governor Hailey met with Muslims to hear their grievances after the trial, and publicly commented that the situation posed 'a very serious danger of disorder, for an attack on the Prophet was a concrete offence against Islam that stung them to the quick and they could not bear the thought that Hindus could repeat

[140] Section 295A reads 'Whoever, with deliberate and malicious intention of outraging the religious feelings of any class of citizens of India, by words, either spoken or written, or by signs or by visible representations or otherwise, insults or attempts to insult the religion or the religious beliefs of that class, shall be punished with imprisonment of either description for a term which may extend to three years, or with fine, or with both.'

[141] *Raj Paul v Emperor* AIR 1927 Lahore 590. The case is discussed in greater detail in Mrinal Satish's chapter on India (ch 5), Masum Billah's chapter on Bangladesh (ch 7) and Syed Ali Reza's chapter on Pakistan (ch 6).

[142] Richa Raj, 'A Pamphlet and its (Dis)contents: A Case Study of Rangila Rasul and the Controversy Surrounding it in Colonial Punjab, 1923–29' (2015) 9(2) *History and Sociology of South Asia* 150; Ranbir Vohra, *The Making of India: A Historical Survey*, 2nd edn (ME Sharpe, 2001) 101–02.

[143] *Raj Paul v Emperor* (n 141) 592.

it with impunity'.[144] Section 295A[145] was added to the Indian Penal Code to placate the minorities. It was 'not instituted by Hindu society, but against it',[146] being a English imposition on Hindus to shield Islam, a minority religion, from criticism. This equipped the Indian subcontinent with 'one of the strictest regulations of religious offence that the world had ever seen',[147] which later became part of the Penal Code of independent India and other common law Asian jurisdictions like Pakistan, Bangladesh and Myanmar.

D. Non-State Actors and Political Theatre, Manufactured Indignation

In more contemporary settings, the religious penal clauses arguably have caused rather than curtailed violence, by providing a site for political theatre. The clauses have become a basis for non-state actors to demand legal sanctions for their hurt emotion and outrage through protest statements and violent conduct, as a performance act, to obtain political attention and legal redress. The clauses have the potential to become weaponised; they have been strategically used by pressure groups to mount and mobilise political campaigns against other religious persons or groups, through staging collective demonstrations of wounded religious feeling, or to initiate legal action. Complaints are framed in a way that closely follows the legal language used in formulating a religious offence,[148] thus using law to articulate emotional offence and to narrate 'religious affect … in terms that were politically legible'.[149] The goal of this tactic is to induce the government to take action against religious opponents who voice 'criminalised' speech, demonstrating a hurt or harm that needs government protection. Accordingly, the worry is that the religious penal clauses and attendant laws have inculcated a culture of being readily offended, fuelling 'the politics of religious sentiment'.[150] This undermines a unifying sense of solidarity through encouraging religious tribalism. This translates into enforced self-restraint and self-censorship on the part of the offending speaker, if there is no expectation that the offended hearer should be responsible and demonstrate resilience and

[144] Gene Thursby, *Hindu-Muslim relation in British India: a study of controversy, conflict and communal movements in Northern India 1923-1928* (Brill, 1975) 41. See also Julia Stephens, 'The Politics of Muslim Rage: Secular Law and Religious Sentiment in Late Colonial India' (2014) 77(1) *History Workshop Journal* 45.

[145] See also n 140.

[146] Koenraad Elst, 'In Favour of Freedom of Expression: Section 295A as Cornerstone of Censorship' (2016) 18(1) *Dialogue* at www.researchgate.net/publication/308725181_In_Favour_of_Freedom_of_Expression_Section_295A_as_Cornerstone_of_Censorship accessed 16 July 2020.

[147] Rollier, Froystad and Ruud (eds), 'Outrage' (n 19).

[148] Adcock, 'Violence, Passion, and the Law' (n 24) 343–44.

[149] J Barton Scott, 'Aryas Unbound: Print Hinduism and the Cultural Regulation of Religious Offense' (2015) 35(2) *Comparative Studies of South Asia, Africa and the Middle East* 301.

[150] Adcock, 'Violence, Passion, and the Law' (n 24) 345.

restraint, or refrain from vigilantism and aggressive demonstrations as performance acts. This effectively democratises demands for censorship issued not just by the state but by non-state actors. This may mark the end of rational deliberation in the public sphere, displaced by 'affect' engineering,[151] involving the display of upset or outraged religious sentiments to galvanise government action. For example, if something is considered blasphemous, the playbook is to threaten violence as evidence of offence.

Such displays of outrage are presented as spontaneous responses, rather than as calculated, manufactured indignation – as part of what Brass terms 'institutionalised riot systems' in which emotions are systematically incited, which triggers collective violence against another religious group like the Muslims in India, and then controls the narrative to present it as a natural, spontaneous reaction of the religiously offended.[152] The law on religious penal clauses, designed to curtail violent expressions of religious passions, could be said to have an effect opposite to its intent, insofar as it 'incites' or specifically encourages collective violent displays of wounded feelings,[153] justified as a response to hurt feelings, sustaining a 'political culture of violence'.[154] In an environment where violence elicits political gain, where he who shouts loudest and acts most violently is most rewarded, self-restraint is a virtue prudent only for the intimidated. In this way, the religious penal clauses can be said to have provoked rather than prevented inter-group violence.

One sees the instrumentalisation of these religious penal clauses in Malaysia, in the wake of serious political upheavals after the last 2018 General Election, when the incumbent coalition, which has been in power since 1957, lost its majority in Parliament for the first time.[155] As Dian Shah discusses in her chapter (chapter 9), the religious elite that had largely been in support of the incumbent coalition had encouraged the reporting of cases against persons they considered to have 'insulted' Islam, and threatened to rally the masses if the new government did not act against such cases. They used the prosecution of the religious penal offences as a way to signal the new government's support or otherwise of Islam.[156] Indeed, the study on Malaysia highlights how religious penal clauses

[151] William Mazzararella, 'Affect: what is it good for?' in Saurabh Dube (ed), *Enchantments of Modernity: Empire, Nation, Globalization* (Routledge India, 2010) 291–309.

[152] Paul E Brass, *Forms of Collective Violence: Riots, Pogroms, and Genocide in Modern India* (Three Essays Collective, 2006).

[153] Ahmed, 'Specters of Macaulay' (n 25) 174.

[154] Adcock, 'Violence, Passion, and the Law' (n 24) 347.

[155] It has since regained power through a series of political backroom tactics: Dian AH Shah and Andrew Harding, *Constitutional Quantum Mechanics and a Change of Government in Malaysia* at www.iconnectblog.com/2020/04/constitutional-quantum-mechanics-and-a-change-of-government-in-malaysia/ accessed 16 July 2020.

[156] 'PAS says govt too lenient with those who insult Islam' *The Straits Times* (Kuala Lumpur, 26 February 2019) at www.straitstimes.com/world/pas-says-govt-too-lenient-with-those-who-insult-islam accessed 16 July 2020.

may not only be employed to discipline religious minorities and the non-religious, but also used against reformers within the religious majority. For instance, Dian Shah discusses how members of one religious group – the Sisters in Islam – have periodically had police reports and criminal charges filed against them under the religious penal clauses for their reformist stance on gender issues in Islam, as a form of intimidation. The instrumentalisation of the religious penal clauses as a form of political and social intimidation can also be seen in Pakistan and India, as discussed further in Syed Ali Raza's and Mrinal Satish's chapters (chapters 6 and 5 respectively).

Most recently, the religious penal clauses became embroiled in impassioned election campaigning for Singapore's General Elections in July 2020. A 'netizen' uncovered earlier social media posts by a young opposition candidate, Raeesah Khan, a Muslim, and proceeded to file a police report alleging that the posts were written with deliberate intent to wound religious or racial feelings and promoted enmity between different groups on grounds of religion or race.[157] The police confirmed that Khan was under investigation for a Section 298A offence. The ruling political party, the People's Action Party (PAP), issued a statement questioning whether the opposition political party should field Khan.[158] In response, a private citizen filed a police report against the PAP statement that had apparently wrongly claimed that the opposition candidate had 'admitted to making highly derogatory statements about Chinese and Christians'.[159] The intent in filing this police report was to hold the incumbent party accountable under a Section 298A offence for 'promoting false narratives which seek to divide rather than unite Singaporeans'.[160] Another police report was also filed against a 2019 remark made by the Deputy Prime Minister (from PAP), that 'the older generation of Singaporeans was not ready for a minority Prime Minister': the allegation was that the remarks were 'socially divisive' and caused the accuser to feel 'unsafe'.[161] The police later stated that no offence was disclosed in the

[157] Khan had alleged that rich Chinese and white people were treated differently under the law, and that mosque and church leaders received different treatment: Tham YC and R Kurohi, 'Singapore GE2020: WP Candidate Raeesah Khan apologises for "insensitive" remarks in posts' *Straits Times* (Singapore, 6 July 2020) at www.straitstimes.com/politics/wp-candidate-raeesah-khan-apologises-for-insensitive-remarks-in-posts accessed 12 October 2020; Anna Maria Romero, 'Despite police report, support for WP's Raeesah Khan is growing' *The Independent* (Singapore, 7 July 2020) at http://theindependent.sg/despite-police-report-support-for-wps-raeesah-khan-is-growing/ accessed 16 July 2020.

[158] People's Action Party, 'The Worker's Party's position on Sengkang Candidate Ms Raeesah Khan' (6 July 2020) at www.pap.org.sg/news/the-workers-partys-position-on-sengkang-candidate-ms-raeesah-khan/ accessed 16 July 2020.

[159] The report was allegedly made by one Alfred Goh Jing Heng: 'Man files police report against PAP over statement on Raeesah Khan' *Coconuts Singapore* (Singapore, 7 July 2020) at https://coconuts.co/singapore/news/man-files-police-report-against-pap-over-statement-on-raeesah-khan/ accessed 16 July 2020.

[160] ibid.

[161] Basia Chow, 'GE 2020: How 298A of S'pore's Penal Code Failed Raeesah Khan' *Vulcan Post* (Singapore, 7 July 2020) at https://vulcanpost.com/703901/raeesah-khan-penal-code-singapore/ accessed 17 July 2020.

PAP statement[162] or in the Deputy Prime Minister's remarks.[163] Investigations against Khan continue, however. She nevertheless made a public apology, and her team later won their constituency in a surprise victory over the incumbent.[164] These competing police reports have led to criticism that these religious penal clauses are bad law that are easily 'weaponized'.[165] They are examples of how religious penal clauses have become a site of political theatre, as it seems that anyone who discusses race or religious issues may potentially be swept into the dragnet of a religious offence, given its breadth. It becomes embroiled in a 'You accuse? I accuse you' show of political thrust and parry by governor and citizen alike, showing how this offence can capture both trivial and potentially serious incidents.[166]

VI. CONCLUSION

Religious penal clauses have not fallen into desuetude and suffered the fate of being relegated to the obscurity of dusty colonial statute books; instead, they have continued to produce case law and shape legal-political governance approaches in post-colonial states in common law Asia. In some cases, this has constricted rights and diminished a commitment to pluralism. From their almost indiscriminate use in India to control religio-political discussion, to expansion in Pakistan against religious minorities, to their reinforcement as a tool for managing inter-group harmony in Singapore and finally to their seemingly inevitable decline (in form but not in substance) in Brunei, these religious penal clauses continue to hold immense power in law and in our imaginations. They shape how we think about inter-group relations, constituting rather than simply being constituted by them. This book, in providing a conceptual and country-based discussion of the use and development of religious penal clauses in common law Asia, therefore serves to expand our understanding of the intersection of

[162] Asyraf Kamil, 'Police say no offence committed by PAP, after reports lodged against party for statement on Raeesah Khan' *Today* (16 July 2020); see also Amir Hussain, 'GE2020: PAP's statement on WP candidate Raeesah Khan not unlawful, says police' *Yahoonews Singapore* (Singapore, 8 July 2020) at https://sg.news.yahoo.com/ge-2020-pa-ps-statement-on-wp-candidate-raeesah-khan-not-unlawful-says-police-152155032.html accessed 16 July 2020.

[163] 'Police confirm reports made against DPM Heng over comments at NTU forum, but no offence found' *Channel News Asia* (Singapore, 7 July 2020) at https://www.channelnewsasia.com/news/singapore/heng-swee-keat-police-reports-ntu-forum-12910236 accessed 17 July 2020.

[164] There was evidence that younger voters and minorities were unhappy with the incumbent party's statement and treatment of the opposition candidate, with the hashtag #IStandWithRaeesah trending on social media over the campaign period. Audrey Tan, 'Singapore GE2020: How Workers' Party won over Sengkang' *Straits Times* (Singapore, 12 July 2020) at www.straitstimes.com/politics/how-wp-won-over-sengkang accessed 16 July 2020.

[165] Chow, 'GE2020' (n 161).

[166] On this point, for a discussion of how religious harmony has been internalised as a social norm and used by groups to make claims against one another, see Jaclyn Neo, 'Dimensions of Religious Harmony as Constitutional Practice: Beyond State Control' (2019) 20 *German Law Journal* 966.

law and religion, the relationship between law and politics, and the confluence of constitutional rights and criminal law, as well as the enduring transformative impact of legal transplants.

BIBLIOGRAPHY

—— *Bowman v Secular Society Ltd* [1917] AC 406
—— *Case of ES v Austria* App no 38450/12 (ECtHR, 25 October 2018)
—— *Evangelical Fellowship of India v State of Himachal Pradesh* (30 August 2012) CWP No 438 of 2011A (High Court, Himachal Pradesh)
—— *Gay News Ltd v United Kingdom* (1983) 5 EHRR 123
—— *İA v Turkey* App no 42571/98 (ECtHR, 13 September 2005)
—— *Joseph Burstyn Inc v Wilson* 343 US 495 (1952)
—— *Otto-Preminger-Institut v Austria* [1994] ECHR 26
—— *PP v Koh Song Huat Benjamin and Anor* [2005] SGDC 272
—— *R v Taylor* (1676) 1 Vent 293
—— *Raj Paul v Emperor* AIR 1927 Lahore 590
—— *Review Publishing Co Ltd v Lee Hsien Loong* [2010] 1 SLR 53
—— *Reynolds v Times Newspaper* [2001] 2 AC 127
—— *Veerabadran Chettiar v EV Ramaswami Naicker & Others* AIR 1958 SC 1032
—— *Wingrove v the United Kingdom* App no 19/1995/525/611 (ECtHR, 25 November 1996)
Ahmed, AA, 'Specters of Macaulay: Blasphemy, the Indian Penal Code, and Pakistan's Postcolonial Predicament' in Raminder Kaur and William Mazzarella (eds), *Censorship in South Asia: Cultural Regulation from Sedition to Seduction* (Indiana University Press, 2009) 181
Adcock, CS, 'Violence, Passion and the Law: A Brief History of Section 295A and its Antecedents' (2016) 84(2) *Journal of the American Academy of Religion* 337
Amir Hussain, 'GE2020: PAP's statement on WP candidate Raeesah Khan not unlawful, says police' *Yahoonews Singapore* (Singapore, 8 July 2020) at https://sg.news.yahoo.com/ge-2020-pa-ps-statement-on-wp-candidate-raeesah-khan-not-unlawful-says-police-152155032.html accessed 16 July 2020
Asyraf Kamil, 'Police say no offence committed by PAP, after reports lodged against party for statement on Raeesah Khan' *Today* (16 July 2020)
Beck, HL, 'Blasphemy' in Hans Dieter Betz et al (eds), *Religion Past and Present Online* (Brill, 2011) at www.referenceworks.brillonline.com/entries/religion-past-and-present/blasphemy-SIM_08937 accessed 16 July 2020
Berger, P, 'Further Thoughts on Religion and Modernity' (2012) 49 *Society* 313
—— 'The Desecularization of the World: A Global Overview' in Peter Berger (ed), *The Desecularization of the World: Resurgent Religion and World Politics* (Eerdmans Publishing, 1999) 1
Bhuiyan, JH, 'Secularism in the Constitution of Bangladesh' (2017) 49(2) *Journal of Legal Pluralism and Unofficial Law* 204
Blackstone, W, *Commentaries on the Laws of England*, book IV (University of Chicago Press, 1979)
Bock, D, 'Blasphemy and the Jewish Examination of Jesus' (2007) 17(1) *Bulletin for Biblical Research* 53

Brass, PE, *Forms of Collective Violence: Riots, Pogroms, and Genocide in Modern India* (Three Essays Collective, 2006).
Casanova, J, *Public Religions in the Modern World* (University of Chicago Press, 1994)
Chow, B, 'GE 2020: How 298A of S'pore's Penal Code Failed Raeesah Khan' *Vulcan Post* (Singapore, 7 July 2020), at https://vulcanpost.com/703901/raeesah-khan-penal-code-singapore/ accessed 17 July 2020.
Coconuts Singapore, 'Man files police report against PAP over statement on Raeesah Khan' (Singapore, 7 July 2020) at https://coconuts.co/singapore/news/man-files-police-report-against-pap-over-statement-on-raeesah-khan/ accessed 16 July 2020.
Cox, N, 'Pourquoi Suis-Je Charlie? Blasphemy, Freedom of Religion, and the Nature of "Offensive" Cartoons' (2015) 4 *Oxford Journal of Law and Religion* 343
Channel News Asia, 'Police confirm reports made against DPM Heng over comments at NTU forum, but no offence found' (Singapore, 7 July 2020) at https://www.channelnewsasia.com/news/singapore/heng-swee-keat-police-reports-ntu-forum-12910236 accessed 17 July 2020.
Claerhout, S, and Roover, JD, 'Religious Freedom and the Limits of Propagation: Conversion in the Constituent Assembly of India' (2019) 10(3) *Religions* 157
Elst, K, 'In Favour of Freedom of Expression: Section 295A as Cornerstone of Censorship' (2016) 18(1) *Dialogue* at www.researchgate.net/publication/308725181_In_Favour_of_Freedom_of_Expression_Section_295A_as_Cornerstone_of_Censorship accessed 16 July 2020.
Express News Service, 'Bombay HC stays probe against band accused of hurting religious sentiments' *The Indian Express* (Panaji, 12 November 2020)
Express Web Desk, 'Comedy Nights actor Kiku Sharda arrested for mimicking Dera Chief Gurmeet Ram Rahim' *The Indian Express* (New Delhi/Kaithal, 15 January 2016)
Fordahl, J, 'The post-secular: Paradigm shift or provocation?' (2016) 20(4) *European Journal of Social Theory* 550
Gallagher, C, 'Calling Muhammad paedophile "not protected by free speech"' *The Irish Times* (29 October 2018) at www.irishtimes.com/news/world/calling-muhammad-paedophile-not-protected-by-free-speech-1.3678825 accessed 16 July 2020
Gelber, K, 'The False Analogy between Vilification and Sedition' (2009) 33 *Melbourne University Law Review* 270
Grim, BJ, 'Laws Penalizing Blasphemy, Apostasy and Defamation of Religion are Widespread' *Pew Forum on Religion and Public Life* (21 November 2012) at www.pewforum.org/2012/11/21/laws-penalizing-blasphemy-apostasy-and-defamation-of-religion-are-widespread/ accessed 16 July 2020
Grimm, D, 'Types of Constitutions' in Michel Rosenfeld and Andras Sajo (eds), *The Oxford Handbook on Comparative Constitutional Law* (Oxford University Press, 2012) 98
Habermas, J, 'Notes on post-secular society' (2008) 25(4) *New Perspectives Quarterly* 17
Harper, *Online Etymology Dictionary* at www.etymonline.com/word/religion accessed 16 July 2020
Hasan, MM, 'Free speech, ban and "fatwa": A study of the Taslima Nasrin affair' (2010) 46 *Journal of Postcolonial Writing* 540
Hindustantimes, 'Pak sentences 5 to death for burning of Christian couple for "blasphemy"' (23 November 2016)
Hoyt, SF, 'The Etymology of Religion' (1912) 32(2) *Journal of the American Oriental Society* 126

Husain, E, 'Explaining the Salman Taseer Murder' (Council on Foreign Relations, 7 January 2011)

Huxley, A, 'The Last Fifty Years of Burmese Law: E Maung and Maung Maung' (1998) *Lawasia: Journal of the Law Association of East Asia and the West Pacific* 14 at http://burmalibrary.org/docs/The_last_50_years_of_%20Burmese_%20law.htm accessed on 16 July 2020

Indian Law Commissioners, The, *A Penal Code Prepared by The Indian Law Commissioners* (GH Huttman at the Bengal Military Orphan Press, 1837)

Kamali, MH, *Freedom of Expression in Islam* (Berita Publishing, 1994) 206

Kentridge, S, 'Freedom of Speech: Is it the Primary Rights?' (1996) 45(2) *International & Comparative Law Quarterly* 253

Khan, MI, 'Punjab Governor Salman Taseer assassinated in Islamabad' *BBC News* (South Asia, 4 January 2011)

Klausen, J, *The Cartoons that Shook the World* (Yale University Press, 2009)

Knechtle, JC, 'Blasphemy, Defamation of Religion and Religious Hate Speech: Is There a Difference that Makes a Difference?' in András Koltay and Jeroen Temperman (eds), *Blasphemy and Freedom of Expression: Comparative, Theoretical, and Historical Reflections after the Charlie Hebdo Massacre* (Cambridge University Press 2017) 199

Kumar, V, 'Netflix Film Krishna and His Leela's Sexual Content hurts religious sentiments, Rana Daggubati Speaks' *India.com* (2 July 2020)

Langer, L, *Religious Offence and Human Rights: The Implications of Defamation of Religions* (Cambridge University Press, 2014)

Lawton, DA, *Blasphemy* (University of Pennsylvania Press, 1993) 51

Levs, J, '10 killed, churches torched in protests over Charlie Hebdo' *CNN World* (21 January 2015) at https://edition.cnn.com/2015/01/20/world/charlie-hebdo-violence/index.html accessed 16 July 2020

Levy, LW, *Blasphemy: Verbal Offense against the Sacred, from Moses to Salman Rushdie* (University of North Carolina Press, 1995) 6

Lindkvist, L, 'The Politics of Article 18: Religious Liberty in the Universal Declaration of Human Rights' (2014) *Humanity Journal* at http://humanityjournal.org/issue4-3/the-politics-of-article-18-religious-liberty-in-the-universal-declaration-of-human-rights/ accessed 16 July 2020

Malik, K, 'Changing Landscape of Freedom' *The Hindu* (India, 12 February 2014)

Mazzararella, W, 'Affect: what is it good for?' in Saurabh Dube (ed), *Enchantments of Modernity: Empire, Nation, Globalization* (Routledge India, 2010) 291

Misra, M, 'Lessons of Empire: Britain and India' (2003) 23(2) *SAIS Review* 133

Moustakas, L, 'The Label Christianophobia in Human Rights Law' European Centre for Law and Justice (24 June 2020) at https://eclj.org/religious-freedom/un/the-label-christianophobia-in-human-rights-law accessed 16 July 2020

Nandy, A, 'The Politics of Secularism and the Recovery of Religious Tolerance' (1988) 13 *Alternatives* 177

Neo, J, 'Dimensions of Religious Harmony as Constitutional Practice: Beyond State Control' (2019) 20 *German Law Journal* 966

——, 'Seditious in Singapore! Free Speech and the Offence of Promoting Ill-Will and Hostility between Different Racial Groups' [2011] *Singapore Journal of Legal Studies* 351

—— and Bui Ngoc Son (eds), *Pluralist Constitutions in Southeast Asia* (Hart Publishing, 2019)

NPR, 'Muhammad Cartoon Protests Turn Deadly Again' (18 February 2006) at www.npr.org/templates/story/story.php?storyId=5223591 accessed 16 July 2020
Pandey, G, 'The Colonial Construction of "Communalism": British Writings on Bañaras in the Nineteenth Century' in Veena Das (ed), *Mirrors of Violence: Communities, Riots and Survivors in South Asia* (Oxford University Press, 1990) 94
Pennington, BK, 'The Unseen Hand of an Underappreciated Law: The Doniger Affair and its Aftermath' (2016) 84(2) *Journal of the American Academy of Religion* 323
People's Action Party, 'The Worker's Party's position on Sengkang Candidate Ms Raeesah Khan' (6 July 2020) at www.pap.org.sg/news/the-workers-partys-position-on-sengkang-candidate-ms-raeesah-khan/ accessed 16 July 2020
Pildes, RH, 'Why Rights are not Trumps: Social Meanings, Expressive Harms and Constitutionalism' (1998) 27(52) *Journal of Legal Studies* 725
Ponomareva, Y, 'New law protecting religious feelings divides Russians' *Russia Beyond* (Russia, 14 June 2013) at www.rbth.com/society/2013/06/14/new_law_protecting_religious_feelings_divides_russians_27089.html accessed 16 July 2020
Radtke, W, 'Religious Offenses' in Hans Dieter Betz, Don S Browning, Bernd Janowski and Eberhard Jungel (eds), *Religion Past and Present* at http://dx.doi.org.libproxy1.nus.edu.sg/10.1163/1877-5888_rpp_SIM_124602 accessed 16 July 2020
Rahman, A, Mohsin, A, and Kahn, S, 'The British Art of Colonialism in India: Subjugation and Division' (2018) 25(1) *Peace and Conflict Studies*, Article 5, at https://nsuworks.nova.edu/pcs/vol25/iss1/5 accessed 16 July 2020
Riaz, A, *Bangladesh: A Political History Since Independence* (IB Taurus, 2016)
—— 'Constructing Outraged Communities and State Responses: The Taslima Nasreen Saga in 1994 and 2007' (2008) 2 *South Asia Multidisciplinary Academic Journal* at https://doi.org/10.4000/samaj.1262
Rollier, P, Froystad, K, and Ruud, AE (eds), *Outrage: The Rise of Religious Offence in Contemporary South Asia* (UCL Press, 2019)
Romero, AM, 'Despite police report, support for WP's Raeesah Khan is growing' *The Independent* (Singapore, 7 July 2020) at http://theindependent.sg/despite-police-report-support-for-wps-raeesah-khan-is-growing/ accessed 16 July 2020
Rosenwein, BH, 'Worrying about Emotions in History' (2002) 107(3) *American Historical Review* 821
Saim, HSH, 'Brunei Darussalam in 2012: Towards a "Zikir" Nation' [2013] *Southeast Asian Affairs* 63
Salles, A, 'Bangladeshi author's book banned for attack on Islam' *The Guardian* (UK, 26 September 2002)
Scharffs, BG, 'International Law And The Defamation Of Religion Conundrum' (2013) 11(1) *The Review of Faith & International Affairs* 66
Scott, JB, 'Aryas Unbound: Print Hinduism and the Cultural Regulation of Religious Offense' (2015) 35(2) *Comparative Studies of South Asia, Africa and the Middle East* 301
Shah, DAH, and Harding, A, *Constitutional Quantum Mechanics and a Change of Government in Malaysia* at www.iconnectblog.com/2020/04/constitutional-quantum-mechanics-and-a-change-of-government-in-malaysia/ accessed 16 July 2020
Sharma, A, *Problematizing Religious Freedom* (Springer, 2012) 86
Stark, R, 'Secularization, R.I.P. – Rest in Peace' (1999) 60(3) *Sociology of Religion* 249
Stopler, G, 'The Challenge of Strong Religion in the Liberal State' (2014) 32 *Boston University International Law Journal* 101

Stephens, J, 'The Politics of Muslim Rage: Secular Law and Religious Sentiment in Late Colonial India' (2014) 77(1) *History Workshop Journal* 45
Taine, HA, 'Napoleon's views on Religion' (1891) 152(414) *The North American Review* 567
Tan, A, 'Singapore GE2020: How Workers' Party won over Sengkang' *Straits Times* (Singapore, 12 July 2020) at https://www.straitstimes.com/politics/how-wp-won-over-sengkang accessed 16 July 2020
Taylor, C, 'The Meaning of Secularism' (2010) 12(3) *Hedgehog Review* 23
Taylor, G, 'Austria's Law Against Defamation of Religion: A Case Study' (2015) 30(1) *Journal of Law and Religion* 80
Temperman, J, and Koltay, A, *Blasphemy and Freedom of Expression: Comparative, Theoretical and Historical Reflections after the Charlie Hebdo Massacre* (Cambridge University Press, 2017)
Tham, YC, and Kurohi, R, 'Singapore GE2020: WP Candidate Raeesah Khan apologises for "insensitive" remarks in posts' *Straits Times* (Singapore, 6 July 2020) at https://www.straitstimes.com/politics/wp-candidate-raeesah-khan-apologises-for-insensitive-remarks-in-posts
Theodorou, AE, 'Which countries still outlaw apostasy and blasphemy' *Pew Research Centre* (29 July 2016) at www.pewresearch.org/fact-tank/2016/07/29/which-countries-still-outlaw-apostasy-and-blasphemy/ accessed 16 July 2020
The Economist, 'Blasphemy bans are struck out in Ireland and reinforced in Austria' (29 October 2018) at https://www.economist.com/erasmus/2018/10/29/blasphemy-bans-are-struck-out-in-ireland-and-reinforced-in-austria accessed 16 July 2020
The Straits Times, 'PAS says govt too lenient with those who insult Islam' (Kuala Lumpur, 26 February 2019) at www.straitstimes.com/world/pas-says-govt-too-lenient-with-those-who-insult-islam accessed 16 July 2020
Thio, LA, 'Caesar, Conscience and Conversion: Constitutional Secularism and the Regulation of Religious Profession and Propagation in Asian States' [2011] *Fides et Libertas: The Journal of the International Religious Liberty Association* 127
Thursby, G, *Hindu-Muslim Relation in British India: a study of controversy, conflict and communal movements in Northern India 1923–1928* (Brill, 1975) 41
Visconsi, E, 'The Invention of Criminal Blasphemy: R v Taylor (1676)' (2008) 103(1) *Representations* 30
Vishawanath, A, 'SC quashes criminal case against MS Dhoni' *livemint* (5 September 2016)
Waldron, J, *The Harm in Hate Speech* (Harvard University Press, 2012)
Warman, C, et al (eds and trs), *Tolerance: The Beacon of the Enlightenment* (Open Book Classics, 2016)
Watson, A, *Legal Transplants: An Approach to Comparative Law*, 2nd edn (University of Georgia Press, 1993) 27
Weiler, JHH, 'The Idea of the Holy: Nomos as Holiness' in Hoger Hestermeyer (ed), *Coexistence, Cooperation and Solidarity: Liber Amicorum Rudiger Wolfrum* (Brill, 2011) 2165
Wright, B, 'Macaulay's Indian Penal Code: Historical Context and Originating Principles' in Chan Wing-Cheong, Barry Wright and Stanley Yeo (eds), *Codification, Macaulay and the Indian Penal Code: The Legacies and Modern Challenges of Criminal Law Reform* (Ashgate 2011) 47

Part I

Religious Penal Clauses: Historical and Conceptual Perspectives

1

Religious Penal Clauses in Commonwealth Asia: A Brief History

KEVIN YL TAN*

I. INTRODUCTION

THIS CHAPTER OFFERS a brief survey of religious penal clauses in the countries making up what might loosely be called Commonwealth Asia. These are states that were formerly part of the British Empire and that are now part of the Commonwealth. Two former British colonies – Hong Kong and Myanmar – are also common law countries but are not dealt with in this chapter. Legislation in the following Commonwealth states in Asia will be considered: Brunei, Malaysia, Singapore, India, Pakistan, Bangladesh, Sri Lanka and the Maldives. This chapter will consider the historical antecedents of these clauses, how they came to be included in the Indian Penal Code 1860, and how the Code was subsequently exported to and adopted by other British territories in Asia. I will further examine how the offence of sedition – originally a common law offence to protect the Crown – has been adapted and used as a religious criminal statute. While many of these penal provisions applied with some degree of uniformity when these territories were still part of the British Empire, post-independence developments show how many of the provisions have been further strengthened and augmented, especially in countries that proclaim an official or state religion.

II. BLASPHEMY AND THE INDIAN PENAL CODE

A. Blasphemy in England

Blasphemy is committed when one speaks profanely of sacred matters. Societies have long punished individuals for blasphemous speech.[1] In England, the offence

*I would like to thank my former student Bryont Chin, who assisted with the research into various facets of this chapter. All opinions and errors are mine alone.

[1] Leonard W Levy, *Blasphemy: Verbal Offense against the Sacred from Moses to Salman Rushdie* (University of North Carolina Press Books, 1995) 3–14.

of blasphemy had its origins in ecclesiastical law dating back to the fourteenth century.[2] From the mid-sixteenth century, the English Parliament also sought to control blasphemous acts through legislation. The first of these was the 1547 Sacrament Act, which made it an offence to revile the sacrament of the Lord's Supper.[3] In 1648, the Rump Parliament passed the draconian Ordinance for the Punishing of Blasphemies and Heresies, which made the denial of God or anything stated in the Bible punishable by death.[4] This legislation also made it an offence to preach or repeat certain heretical 'errors'. What follows in the statute is a litany of 'errors', including that:

> [A]ll men shall be saved, or that man by Nature hath free will to turn to God, or that God may be worshipped in or by Pictures of Images, or that the soul of any man after death goeth neither to Heaven or hell, but to Purgatory, or that the soul of man dieth or sleepeth when the body is dead, or that Revelations or the workings of the Spirit are a rule of Faith …

Anyone convicted of heresy would be ordered by the court to renounce his or her errors at a public congregation in the same parish where the complaint arose. Failure to do so would render the heretic liable to imprisonment. This extreme law was the work of Presbyterians who controlled Parliament at the time, and was targeted at other Christian sects, such as the Baptists.[5]

Two years later, in 1650, Parliament, in fulfilling its 'duty, by all good ways and means to propagate the Gospel in this Commonwealth, to advance Religion in all Sincerity, Godliness and Honesty', passed yet another Blasphemy Act targeted at the Ranters, a 'movement among lower-class people numbering several thousands' who rejected the Puritan Establishment, 'its ethics, its values and its goals'.[6] The long title of the Act read 'An Act against several Atheistical, Blasphemous and Execrable Opinions, derogatory to the honour of God, and destructive to humane Society'.[7] The Act makes puzzling reading on its own; it can only be understood against the backdrop of the Ranters' philosophical mindset. Ellens explains:

> Ranters were said to regard themselves as God, and to be free of all the ordinary restraints of decent human society. Smoking and drunkenness were common to all of them, and they were reputed to practice adultery and fornication freely and in public, and buggery too, and to curse and swear in the most fulsome and blasphemous way

[2] See *Rex v Taylor* (1676) 1 Vent 293; (1676) 86 ER 189.

[3] The long title of the statute reads 'An Acte against suche as shall unreverentlie speake against the Sacrament of the Bodie and blude of Christe commonlie called the Sacrament of the Altar, and for the receiving thereof in bothe kyndes'.

[4] The statute is found in Charles Harding Firth and Robert Sangster Rait, *Acts and Ordinances of the Interregnum, 1642–1660*, vol 1 (HM Stationery Office, 1911) 1133–36.

[5] See Chung Youngkwon, 'Parliament, the Heresy Ordinance of 1648, and the Religious Toleration in Civil War England' (2015) 57 *Journal of Church and State* 119.

[6] GFS Ellens, 'The Ranters Ranting: Reflections on a Ranting Counter Culture' (1971) 40(1) *Church History* 91.

[7] Firth and Rait, *Acts and Ordinances* (n 4) 409–12.

> without restraint … [as] there was a Ranter doctrine that a man could not be free from sin until he had committed it in the belief that it was not sinful, and that, in order to be perfect, it was necessary to have committed every sin.[8]

Before the end of the seventeenth century, Parliament passed yet another Blasphemy Act that made it an offence for any person, being educated in or having made the profession of Christianity, to deny the Holy Trinity or to claim that there was more than one god, to deny the truth of Christianity or to deny the Bible as divine authority.[9] Those found guilty might be imprisoned for up to three years.

Despite Parliament's attempts at criminalising blasphemy, these various statutes were hardly used and prosecutions were uncommon, even in the seventeenth century.[10] One key reason could have been the very draconian nature of these statutes, passed during a time of great religious intolerance in Puritan England. While at least one of these statutes remained on the law books right up till the twentieth century, they largely fell into disuse, especially after the common law courts stepped in and made blasphemy a common law offence.[11] This occurred in the landmark case of *Rex v Taylor*, decided by Chief Justice Sir Matthew Hale.[12] Taylor was charged for blaspheming Christianity when, among other things, he declared himself the younger brother of Christ and called Christ 'a bastard' and 'a whore's master'. Hale CJ found him guilty of blaspheming Christianity, which 'is part of the law itself', and as such made 'injuries to God … as punishable as to the King'. Taylor was fined 1,000 marks (about £660) and pilloried for one hour each in Westminster and Guildford, with the words '[f]or blasphemous words, tending the subversion of all government'.[13] Significantly, Hale CJ held that

> such kind of wicked blasphemous words were not only an offence to God and religion, but a crime against the laws, State, and Government, and therefore punishable in this Court. For, to say religion is a cheat, is to dissolve all those obligations whereby the civil societies are preserved, and that Christianity is parcel of the laws of England; and therefore to reproach the Christian religion is to speak in subversion of the law.[14]

Kenny, in one of the earliest articles outlining the law of blasphemy in England, considered Hale's pronouncement a 'cognate innovation'.[15] Visconsi noted that Hale CJ's judgment – flawed as it was on the basis that Christianity was indeed

[8] Ellens, 'The Ranters Ranting' (n 6).

[9] Blasphemy Act 1697 (9 Will III 3, c 35).

[10] John Hamilton Baker, *An Introduction to English Legal History*, 5th edn (Oxford University Press, 2009) 512.

[11] There have been no criminal prosecutions under the Blasphemy Act of 1697. See Courtney Kenny, 'The Evolution of the Law of Blasphemy' (1922) 1(2) *Cambridge Law Journal* 127, 132.

[12] *Rex v Taylor* (1676) 1 Vent 293; (1676) 3 Keb 607.

[13] On *R v Taylor*, see Elliott Visconsi, 'The Invention of Criminal Blasphemy: *Rex v Taylor* (1676)' (2008) 103(1) *Representations* 30.

[14] ibid 31.

[15] Kenny, 'The Evolution' (n 11) 129.

part and parcel of the common law – was an attempt to 'protect the common law from the potential reappearance of scripturalist hardliners'.[16] Regardless of Hale CJ's motivations, the crime of blasphemy had been established as a common law offence and remained intact until it was abolished in 2008 by the 2008 Criminal Justice and Immigration Act.[17]

B. The Indian Penal Code

The offence of blasphemy travelled wherever the common law landed in Britain's many colonies. Its application was largely unproblematic in colonies that were settled and populated by Christians (nominal or otherwise), such as those in America, Canada, Australia and New Zealand. However, this proved problematic in colonies where large native populations either professed religions of their own or did not profess any religion. The British first settled in India in the 1600s, and began asserting sovereignty over the Indian territories after the Battle of Plassey in Bengal in 1757. Because of the manner in which the British East India Company exerted its influence over different parts of India, the law that applied to its inhabitants varied from place to place.

In terms of criminal law, the applicable law was a mix of Hindu law, local customary law and Muslim criminal law as interpreted by British judges. While the common law is commonly accepted as having been introduced into India from about 1780, the common law offence of blasphemy was never applied in India. As Jain noted, 'the system of law prevailing in India near about the beginning of the 19th century ... is one confusion and chaos'.[18] The law applicable in the Presidency Towns of Calcutta, Madras and Bombay was antiquated, and the law in the mofussil (regions beyond the Presidency Towns) varied from region to region, with great uncertainty as to whether any particular legal principle was applicable or not.[19] An opportunity to clear this mess up came in June 1831 when the British Parliament, in considering the renewal of the East India Company's Charter, appointed a Select Committee to 'inquire into the present state of the affairs of the East-India Company', especially 'how far the administration of justice, and the government of the country generally, were suited to the wants and wishes of the inhabitants of that great continent'.[20] The Committee's subsequent reports revealed a 'broad consensus' that 'the state and practice of the law in India required reform'.[21]

[16] Visconsi, 'The Invention' (n 13) 41.

[17] See Russell Sandberg and Norman Doe, 'The Strange Death of Blasphemy' (2008) 71(6) *Modern Law Review* 971.

[18] MP Jain, *Outlines of Indian Legal and Constitutional History*, 6th edn (LexisNexis, 2012) 417.

[19] ibid.

[20] HC Deb, 28 June 1831, vol 4, cols 436–440, 436.

[21] Elizabeth Kolsky, 'Codification and the Rule of Colonial Difference: Criminal Procedure in British India' (2005) 23 *Law and History Review* 631, 638.

Reform was effected through the passage of the 1833 Charter Act, which made three specific provisions for the uniformisation of law in India.[22] First, it established an omni-competent all-India legislature with powers to make law for all of India; second, it created the office of the Law Member in the Government of India; and, third, it provided for the appointment of a Law Commission in India[23] to rectify perceived deficiencies in British India's legal system and to report on the practicability of establishing a uniform system of law and judicature throughout British India.[24] The Act further provided for the drafting of 'such laws as may be applicable in common to all classes of the inhabitants of the said territories, due regard being had to the rights, feelings and peculiar usages of the people'.[25] In the debates leading up to the passing of the Charter Act, Thomas Babington Macaulay (1800–1859), then Member of Parliament for Calne and Secretary of the Board of Control (which oversaw the East India Company), pushed assiduously for the codification of law for India,[26] arguing that 'no country ever stood so much in need of a code of laws as India'.[27] When the Act was passed, and at his own instigation, Macaulay was appointed Chairman of the Commission, and he set sail for India in 1834.

When members of the first Indian Law Commission – Macaulay as Chairman, Frederick Millet as Secretary and the other members, being Charles Hay Cameron, John Macpherson Macleod and George William Anderson – arrived in India, they found British courts simultaneously administering a diverse plurality of laws, including 'regional regulations, Acts of Parliament, Hindu and Muslim personal law, Islamic criminal law, and the widely interpreted Roman principle of "justice, equity and good conscience"'.[28] The criminal law that was administered in British India – at the time, the Presidency Towns – was either Muslim law (Bengal and Madras) or Regulations of the East India Company (Bombay).[29] The Law Commission was constituted in May 1835, and work on a penal code for India began immediately.

By 14 October 1837, the Commission had finished its draft Code. In their report to the Governor-General, Lord Auckland, the members explained how they evaluated the existing laws operating in British India: Mahomedan law

[22] Charter Act 1833 (3 & 4 Will 4, c 85). This Act is also known as the Saint Helena Act or the Government of India Act.

[23] Jain, *Outlines* (n 18) 423.

[24] In response to corruption in the East India Company, the British Government assumed partial control over the governance of India with the passage of the Regulating Act of 1773, appointing a Governor-General and Council to rule over the Presidency of Bengal. These were replaced by the Governor-General and Council of India by the Charter Act of 1833.

[25] Charter Act 1833 (n 22), s 5.

[26] Jain, *Outlines* (n 18) 422–23; MC Setalvad, *The Common Law in India* (London, Stevens & Sons, 1960) 122–23.

[27] HC Deb, 10 July 1833, vol 19, col 531.

[28] Kolsky, 'Codification' (n 21) 632.

[29] Setalvad (n 26) 119.

was 'defective and inconvenient', full of 'peculiarities to perplex and encumber the administration of justice',[30] in contrast to the British Regulations, which, despite their shortcomings, gave a 'great advantage' to the British administrators by 'placing the whole law in a written form before those who are to administer, and those who are to obey it'.[31] The Commission thus preferred codifying all the criminal laws into a single Code. In doing so, it did not consider it 'desirable' to base this new Code on any of the legal systems that were then in force in India,[32] as the existing legal system was 'so flawed that it had to be discarded and a new system created to take its place'.[33] Neither was it desirable to base it on English criminal law, a 'very artificial and complicated system' that 'even in the country for which it was framed is generally considered as requiring extensive reform'.[34] Instead, the Commission looked to 'the most celebrated systems of Western jurisprudence', especially the French Code and the French courts' interpretation of the same, as well as the Code of Louisiana.[35] With these considerations in mind, the Commission drafted its Code, mindful of two main principles: (i) that laws 'should be as far as possible precise [and] easily understood'; and (ii) that 'a loosely worded law is no law' – to the extent a legislature 'uses vague expressions [it] abdicates its functions'.[36] In October that year, a complete version was presented to the Governor-General's Council.[37]

Chapter XV of the Report is entitled 'Of Offences Relating to Religion', and the Commission proposed the creation of four related offences, all of which were aimed at preventing the inflaming of religious passions by the disruption or disturbance of religious ceremonies, or the intentional wounding the religious feelings of individuals by insulting their religion by words or deeds. Note J of the Report laid down the underlying philosophical bases of these offences. The Commission understood that in India – which had large numbers of Hindus and Muslims – religion was a subject that would easily excite the passions of their respective adherents to the extent that it could lead to an outbreak of violence or even to the collapse of the society:

> There is perhaps no country in which the Government has so much to apprehend from religious excitement among the people. The Christians are numerically a very

[30] *A Penal Code Prepared by The Indian Law Commissioners* (Calcutta, Bengal Military Orphan Press, 1837) 3 (hereinafter '*A Penal Code*').

[31] ibid.

[32] ibid 6.

[33] David Skuy, 'Macaulay and the Indian Penal Code of 1862: The Myth of the Inherent Superiority and Modernity of the English Legal System Compared to India's Legal System in the Nineteenth Century' (1998) 32(3) *Modern Asian Studies* 513, 524.

[34] *A Penal Code* (n 30) 6.

[35] ibid.

[36] ibid 7.

[37] Barry Wright, 'Macaulay's Indian Penal Code: Historical Context and Originating Principles' in Wing-Cheong Chan, Barry Wright and Stanley Yeo (eds), *Codification, Macaulay and the Indian Penal Code: The Legacies and Modern Challenges of Criminal Law Reform* (Farnham, Ashgate, 2011) 19, 34.

> small minority of the population, and in possession of all the highest posts in the Government, in the tribunals, and in the army. Under their rule are placed millions of Mohamedans, of differing sects, but all strongly attached to the fundamental articles of the Mohamedan creed, and tens of millions of Hindoos, strongly attached to doctrine and rites which Christians and Mohamedans join in reprobating. Such a state of things is pregnant with dangers which can only be averted by affirm adherence to the true principles of toleration. On those principles the British Government has hitherto acted with eminent judgment, and with no less eminent success: and on those principles we propose to frame this part of the penal Code.[38]

Macaulay and the Indian Commissioners were patently conscious that the demographic and religious make-up of India was vastly different from that of England, and knew that it was necessary to accommodate this difference. For a start, the English common law of blasphemy could not possibly be imported into India even if it had taken root in the North American colonies or in Australia, for example. The Christians were a very small minority. Hence, offences that merely punished those who insulted Protestant Christianity made no sense, and would have been rejected and reviled by the majority of Indian inhabitants who felt that their religions needed protection too. For instance, some scholars consider that laws protecting Islam against blasphemy have existed from the mid-sixteenth century.[39] The Commissioners' Report proposed the religious penal clauses set out in Table 1.1.[40] The clause numbers do not appear to run sequentially because clauses 277, 279, and 281 sought to emphasise the gravity of these offences by making punishment for infractions of these provisions cumulative when committed alongside any other offence in the Code. clause 283 deals with the offence of *dhurna* (a method of extortion invoking divine displeasure), while clause 284 makes it an offence to cause someone to lose his or her caste.

Table 1.1 Proposed Religious Offences under the Indian Law Commissioners' Report 1837

Clause	Offence
275	Whoever destroys, damages, or defiles any place of worship, or any object held sacred by any class of persons, with the intention of thereby insulting the religion of any class of persons, or with the knowledge that any class of persons are likely to consider such destruction, damage, or defilement as an insult to their religion, shall be punished with imprisonment of either description for a term which may extend to seven years and must not be less than one year, and shall also be liable to fine.

(continued)

[38] *A Penal Code* (n 30) note 26.

[39] Akhtar Rasool Bodia, 'Genesis of Blasphemy Laws in Colonial India' (2017) 38(2) *Pakistan Journal of History and Culture* 139,140.

[40] *A Penal Code* (n 30) 71–73.

Table 1.1 *(Continued)*

Clause	Offence
276	Whoever voluntarily causes disturbance to any assembly lawfully engaged in the performance of religious worship, or religious ceremonies, if in causing such disturbance he assaults any person, or makes shew of assaulting any person, or threatens to assault any person engaged in such worship or ceremonies, shall be punished with imprisonment of either description for a term which may extend to three years and must not be less than six months, and shall also be liable to fine.
278	Whoever, in any place of worship, does anything whereby he voluntarily causes disturbance to any assembly lawfully met therein for the performance of religious worship or religious ceremonies, shall be punished with imprisonment of either description for a term which may extend to one year, or fine, or both.
280	Whoever, with the intention of wounding the feelings or insulting the religion of any person, commits any trespass on any place of sepulture, offers any indignity to any human corpse, or causes disturbance to any assembly assembled for the performance of funeral ceremonies, shall be punished with imprisonment of either description for a term which may extend to one year, or fine, or both.
282	Whoever, with the deliberate intention of wounding the religious feelings of any person, utters any word or makes any sound in the hearing of that person, or makes any gesture in the sight of that person, or places any object in the sight of that person, shall be punished with imprisonment of either description for a term which may extend to one year, or fine or both.
285	Whoever intentionally causes any food belonging to any person to be in a state in which that person, according to the rules of his religion or caste, cannot use it as food, shall be punished with a fine which may extend to fifty rupees.

Under Macaulay's scheme, the most severe punishment was reserved for persons who intentionally defiled or destroyed places of worship under clause 275. Offenders might face up to seven years' imprisonment for such an offence. The Commissioners explained why:

> We have provided a punishment of great severity for the intentional destroying or defiling of places of worship, or of objects held sacred by any class of persons. No offence in the whole Code is so likely to lead to tumult, to sanguinary outrage, and even to armed insurrection. The slaughter of a cow in a sacred place of Benares in 1809 caused violent tumult, attended with considerable loss of life. The pollution of a mosque at Bangalore was attended with consequences still more lamentable and alarming. We have therefore empowered the Courts in cases of this description, to pass a very severe sentence on the offender.[41]

[41] ibid note 26.

The maximum punishment for the other offences was imprisonment for a term of one year. In addition, the offender might also be subjected to a fine.

Even though the first Indian Law Commission completed its work on the Indian Penal Code in 1837, it was not until 1860 that it was finally enacted into law.[42] The enforcement of the Code was deferred until 1 January 1862, when it came into force.[43] This delay was due to

> [g]overnmental and legislative inertia, resistance by European residents to having the same legal status as indigenous populations and the loss of reforming momentum in the metropole, as professional resistance to ambitious legislative projects that threatened the common law solidified and positivist legal scholars distanced themselves from Bentham's legacy.[44]

In the interim, Macaulay's draft underwent several refinements and amendments. When it was finally enacted in 1860, the sequence of offences was reorganised and the section numbers changed. The severity of punishment for defiling places of worship was also reduced from seven years' to two years' imprisonment. The offence of deliberately and maliciously 'outraging the religious feelings' of a particular class of Indian citizens was inserted in 1927 as the new section 295A. This offence also carries the maximum punishment of two years' imprisonment.

Table 1.2 Table of Religious Penal Offences enacted under the Indian Penal Code 1860 and its corresponding provisions under the Indian Law Commissioners' Report 1837

1837 Draft Clause No	IPC 1860 Section No	Offence
275	295	Whoever destroys, damages or defiles any place of worship, or any object held sacred by any class of persons with the intention of thereby insulting the religion of any class of persons or with the knowledge that any class of persons is likely to consider such destruction, damage or defilement as an insult to their religion, shall be punished with imprisonment of either description for a term which may extend to two years, or with fine, or with both.
282	295A[45]	Whoever, with deliberate and malicious intention of outraging the religious feelings of any class of [citizens of India], by words, either spoken or written, or by signs or by visible representations or otherwise insults or attempts to insult the religion or the religious beliefs of that class, shall be punished with imprisonment of either description for a term which may extend to two years, or with fine, or with both.

(continued)

[42] KN Chandrasekharan Pillai (ed), *Essays on the Indian Penal Code* (Indian Law Institute, 2005) 41.

[43] ibid.

[44] Wright, 'Macaulay's Indian Penal Code' (n 37) 38.

[45] Inserted vide Criminal Law (Amendment) Act 1927, s 2, Act 25 of 1927.

Table 1.2 *(Continued)*

1837 Draft Clause No	IPC 1860 Section No	Offence
278	296	Whoever voluntarily causes disturbance to any assembly lawfully engaged in the performance of religious worship, or religious ceremonies, shall be punished with imprisonment of either description for a term which may extend to one year, or with fine, or with both.
280	297	Whoever, with the intention of wounding the feelings of any person, or of insulting the religion of any person, or with the knowledge that the feelings of any person are likely to be wounded, or that the religion of any person is likely to be insulted thereby, commits any trespass in any place of worship or on any place of sepulture, or any place set apart for the performance of funeral rites or as a depository for the remains of the dead, or offers any indignity to any human corpse, or causes disturbance to any persons assembled for the performance of funeral ceremonies, shall be punished with imprisonment of either description for a term which may extend to one year, or with fine, or with both.
282	298	Whoever, with the deliberate intention of wounding the religious feelings of any person, utters any word or makes any sound in the hearing of that person or makes any gesture in the sight of that person or places any object in the sight of that person, shall be punished with imprisonment of either description for a term which may extend to one year, or with fine, or with both.

The Indian Penal Code retained the same *mens rea* for all religious offences, by requiring that the accused act with deliberate intention or malice. The Commission had explained why this *mens rea* was necessary. In drafting clause 282, the Commission stated that it had a two-fold objective to 'allow all fair latitude to religious discussion, and at the same time to prevent the professors of any religion from offering, under the pretext of such discussion, intentional insults to what is held sacred by others'.[46] This is because no one could conceivably be justified in wounding 'with deliberate intention' the religious feelings of his neighbours by his 'words, gestures, or exhibitions'.[47] The Commission stressed that deliberate intention to wound religious feelings was required, nothing less:

> [A] warm expression dropped in the heat of controversy, or an argument urged by a person not for the purpose of insulting and annoying the professors of a different creed, but in good faith for the purpose of vindicating his own [would not suffice].[48]

[46] *A Penal Code* (n 30) 50.
[47] ibid.
[48] ibid.

This approach was clearly Macaulay's, as evinced in his famous speech before the Committee of the Whole House in the House of Commons on the abolition of civil disabilities of the Jews:

> In my opinion it is monstrous to see any judge try a man for blasphemy under the present law ... Every man, I think, ought to be at liberty to discuss the evidences of religion; but no man ought to be at liberty to force on the unwilling ears and eyes of others sounds and sights which must cause annoyance and irritation. The distinction is clear ... [But a man] must use all his rights so as not to infringe the rights of others. These, Sir, are the principles on which I would frame the law of blasphemy.[49]

Macaulay's liberal approach was significant in that unlike the old common law which privileged Christianity, he recognised the importance of the cultural context in which the provision was intended to operate and the practical ramifications should any religion be similarly privileged. This approach was condemned by the Evangelists and even by Macaulay's admirer Sir James Fitzjames Stephen.[50] That said, there was no doubt that Macaulay's approach represented 'a huge advance on the existing common law' and 'reflected toleration while addressing intangible harms in a manner that minimised contested moral and ethical criteria'.[51]

C. The Penal Code Beyond India

From India, the British exported the Indian Penal Code to many of its other colonies: the Straits Settlements, Ceylon (Sri Lanka),[52] Brunei, Burma (Myanmar),[53] the Sudan, Kenya, Uganda,[54] Malawi, Tangayika and Zanzibar (now Tanzania).[55] When some of these territories decolonised, they splintered into smaller states, with the result that the Indian Penal Code became the primary

[49] HC Deb, 17 April 1833, vol 17, cols 205–44.

[50] Wright, 'Macaulay's Indian Penal Code' (n 37) 48. Stephen thought that Macaulay had carried 'the principle of tolerating and protecting all religions whatever to a length which cannot be justified, and which might lead to horrible cruelty and persecution if the government of the country ever got into Hindoo or Mohammedan hands'. See also James Fitzjames Stephen, *History of the Criminal Law of England*, vol 3 (Macmillan, 1883) 312.

[51] Stephen, ibid 48.

[52] It will be noted that as Ceylon's Legislative Council had undertaken its own review of the Indian Penal Code for the purposes of adapting it to their circumstances, the section numbers of the same provisions in the Ceylon Code are not identical to those of the Indian Penal Code. For example, section 290 of the Ceylon Penal Code corresponds with section 295 of the Indian Penal Code, section 295A with section 290A; section 296 with section 291; section 297 with section 292; and section 298 with section 291B.

[53] Stanley Yeo, 'Giving Precedence to the Indian Penal Code' in Mahendra Pal Singh and Niraj Kumar (eds), *The Indian Yearbook of Comparative Law 2018* (Springer, 2019) 341.

[54] James S Read, 'Criminal Law in the Africa of Today and Tomorrow' (1963) 7(1) *Journal of African Law* 5.

[55] Law Library of Congress Global Legal Research Directorate, 'Blasphemy and Related Laws' (*The Library of Congress*, 3 March 2017) at www.loc.gov/law/help/blasphemy/index.php.

criminal law for Singapore and Malaysia (formerly Straits Settlements), as well as India, Pakistan and Bangladesh (formerly British India). In British Asia, the Code was adopted by the Straits Settlements in 1871, by Ceylon and Burma in 1886, and Brunei in 1951. The Maldives adopted the Penal Code of Ceylon on 11 July 1962 but without all criminal offences prescribed by the Shariah.[56]

III. SEDITION

A. The Offence of Sedition in the Penal Code

Beyond the religious offences under the Penal Code, the offence of sedition[57] has also been used to criminalise religious insult and incendiary speech that fomented discord between religious groups. Like the offence of blasphemy, sedition began as a common law offence that was created to protect the Crown from actions designed to 'excite disaffection' against it and subjecting it to contempt or hatred. Sir James Fitzjames Stephen, in Article 93 of his *Digest of the Criminal Law*,[58] described the offence as follows:

> A seditious intention is an intention to bring into hatred or contempt, or to excite disaffection against the person of, Her Majesty, her heirs or successors, or the government and constitution of the United Kingdom, as by law established, or either House of Parliament, or the administration of justice, or to excite Her Majesty's subjects to attempt, otherwise than by lawful means, the alteration of any matter in Church or State by law established, or to excite any person to commit any crime in disturbance of the peace, or to raise discontent or disaffection against Her Majesty's subjects, or to promote feelings of ill-will and hostility between different classes of such subjects.[59]

It is, however, not 'a seditious intention' if all the maker of the statement only wishes to

> shew that Her Majesty has been misled or mistaken in her measures, or to point out errors or defects in the government or constitution as by law established, with a view to their reformation, or to excite Her Majesty's subjects to attempt by lawful means the alteration of any matter in Church or state by law established, or to point out, in order to their removal, matters which are producing, or have a tendency to produce, feelings of hatred or ill-will between classes of Her Majesty's subjects ...[60]

The offence of sedition also makes it a crime to promote feelings of ill-will or hostility between different classes or groups of persons within the state.

[56] Husnu Al Suood, *The Maldivian Legal System* (Maldives Law Institute, 2014) 86.
[57] On the history of sedition, see Roger B Manning, 'The Origins of the Doctrine of Sedition' (1980) 12(2) *Albion: A Quarterly Journal Concerned with British Studies* 99.
[58] James Fitzjames Stephen, *A Digest of the Criminal Law (Crimes and Punishments)*, 4th edn (Macmillan, 1877).
[59] ibid, 56.
[60] ibid.

The common law was put on legislative footing in 1819 with the enactment of 'An Act for the More Effectual Prevention and Punishment of Blasphemous and Seditious Libels'.[61] The offence of sedition appeared in the first draft of Lord Macaulay's Indian Penal Code (1837–1839) as clause 113 which provides that:

> 113.—Whoever, by words, either spoken or intended to be read, or by signs, or by visible representations, attempts to excite feelings of disaffection to the Government established by law in the territories of the East India Company, among any class of people who live under that Government, shall be punished with banishment for life or for any term from the territories of the East India Company, to which time may be added, or with simple imprisonment for a term which may extend to three years, to which fine may be added, or with fine.
>
> *Explanation.* Such a disapprobation of the measures of the Government as is compatible with a disposition to render obedience to the lawful authority of the Government, and to support the lawful authority of the Government against unlawful attempts to subvert or resist that authority, is not disaffection. Therefore the making of comments on the measures of the Government, with the intention of exciting only this species of disapprobation, is not an offence within this Clause.[62]

The essence of the offence, as Macaulay makes clear, is the exciting of disaffection – to 'inflame the people against the Government'.[63] However, when the Penal Code was finally passed into law in 1860, it was omitted. Later, in 1870, it was added with a verbal amendment by Sir James Stephen in 1870 as section 124A of the Penal Code, which provides that:

> 124A.—Whoever, by words, either spoken or written, or by signs, or by visible representation, or otherwise, brings or attempts to bring into hatred or contempt, or excites or attempts to excite disaffection towards, the Government established by law in India, shall be punished with imprisonment for life, to which fine may be added, or with imprisonment which may extend to three years, to which fine may be added, or with fine.
>
> *Explanation 1.* — The expression 'disaffection' includes disloyalty and all feelings of enmity.
>
> *Explanation 2.* — Comments expressing disapprobation of the measures of the Government with a view to obtain their alteration by lawful means, without exciting or attempting to excite hatred, contempt or disaffection, do not constitute an offence under this section.
>
> *Explanation 3.* — Comments expressing disapprobation of the administrative or other action of the Government without exciting or attempting to excite hatred, contempt or disaffection, do not constitute an offence under this section.

The 1870 addition did not go as far as Macaulay's initial draft, as it restricted itself to acts against the Government only and not against other 'classes' or

[61] An Act for the More Effectual Prevention and Punishment of Blasphemous and Seditious Libels 1819 (60 Geo III and 1 Geo IV, c 8).
[62] *A Penal Code* (n 30) 30.
[63] ibid 104.

groups of persons. The law was broadened to deal with the stirring of enmity or hatred against particular groups or classes in 1898 when the Government of India amended the Indian Penal Code by inserting a new section 153A. The original version of this provision read:

> 153A.—Whoever by words, either spoken or written, or by signs, or by visible representations, or otherwise, promotes or attempts to promote feelings of enmity or hatred between different classes of Her Majesty's subjects shall be punished with imprisonment which may extend to two years, or with fine, or with both.
>
> *Explanation* — It does not amount to an offence within the meaning of this section to point out, without malicious intention and with an honest view to their removal, matters which are producing, or have a tendency to produce, feelings of enmity or hatred between different classes of Her Majesty's subjects.

At first glance, this appears very similar to section 124A of the Penal Code, but the words or actions of the offender are in this case directed at 'different classes of Her Majesty's subjects' rather than at the state directly. As Professor KD Gaur noted, section 153A

> punishes stirring up of class hatred, which is an offence against public tranquillity, whereas section 124A IPC punishes the offence of sedition, which is essentially an offence against the State … The offence under section 153A affects the State indirectly by disturbing the public peace, whereas the offence under section 124A affects the State directly.[64]

As with the other Indian Penal Code provisions, sections 124A and 153A were exported verbatim to all parts of British Asia that adopted the Penal Code as its primary criminal legislation – Brunei, Burma, Ceylon, Malaya and the Straits Settlements. Today, section 124A remains on the statute books of Bangladesh, Brunei, India, Myanmar, Pakistan, and Sri Lanka. However, Malaysia, Singapore and Brunei have gone beyond section 124A and enacted separate sweeping legislation to deal with sedition.

B. The Sedition Acts in the Straits Settlements, Malaya and Brunei

The first of these territories to have its own standalone sedition legislation was the Straits Settlements in 1938. Steps towards having separate legislation to deal with sedition and seditious publications had already been set in motion in 1915, following the Sepoy Mutiny in Singapore, when the Straits Settlements Legislative Council passed the 1915 Seditious Publications (Prohibition) Ordinance.[65] The object of this law was to 'suppress the circulation in the Colony of seditious publications'.[66]

[64] KD Gaur, *Textbook on the Indian Penal Code*, 4th edn (Universal Law Publishing, 2009) 262–63.

[65] Ordinance 11 of 1915 (Straits Settlements).

[66] 'Speech of Attorney-General GA Goodman, First Reading of the Seditious Publications (Prohibition) Bill, 25 June 1915' in *Proceedings of the Legislative Council of the Straits Settlements for the Year 1915* (Singapore, Government Printing Office, 1916) B40.

In 1938, the Straits Government proposed amending the Penal Code to abolish minimum sentences that were 'objectionable in principle', but took the opportunity to include a provision that would complement section 124A of the Penal Code to make it a 'punishable offence to promote hatred between different classes of the community'.[67] As Attorney-General Howell informed the Legislative Council, this new provision was drawn 'from the corresponding provision in the Indian Penal Code'[68] and it read as follows:

> 153A. – Whoever by words, either spoken or written, or by signs or by visible representations, or otherwise, promotes or attempts to promote feelings of enmity or hatred between different classes of the public shall be punished with imprisonment of either description which may extend to two years, or with fine, or with both.[69]

The introduction of this Bill proved controversial and objections to its enactment came from several quarters, including the Straits Settlements (Penang) Association, which considered the new law 'wholly unnecessary in a country where class hatred and feelings of enmity between different classes of the public have hitherto been so conspicuously absent'.[70] Questions were even raised in the House of Commons about the impending amendment. On 22 June 1938, John Parker (Member of Parliament for Romford) asked Malcolm MacDonald, the Secretary of State for the Colonies, whether he was aware that the proposed amendment was 'likely to lead to further restrictions on the right of free speech', and whether he had approved these changes. MacDonald replied that

> the proposed amendment ... is designed to prevent the fomentation of enmity between the various races and classes of the community and is based upon the corresponding section of the Indian Penal Code. The right of non-malicious criticism is preserved, and no Court will be empowered to take cognizance of any offence under this section unless upon complaint by the Attorney-General or on his authority ...[71]

Parker followed this up with another query to MacDonald on 4 July 1938, when he asked the Secretary for the Colonies if he was 'aware that public opinion in the Straits Settlement, both European and Asiatic' was 'strongly opposed' to the proposed amendment and whether it could be reconsidered. This time, MacDonald informed Parker that the proposed section 153A had 'now been deleted from the Bill' and that the matter was 'being dealt with in the new Sedition Bill, which is based upon the law' of the United Kingdom.[72]

[67] 'Speech of Attorney-General CG Howell, First Reading of the Penal Code (Amendment) Bill, 25 April 1938' in *Proceedings of the Legislative Council of the Straits Settlements for the Year 1938* (Singapore, Government Printing Office, 1939) B25.

[68] ibid.

[69] Penal Code (Amendment) Bill 1938 (Straits Settlements).

[70] 'Penal Code Amendment Protest' *Singapore Free Press* (Singapore, 30 May 1938) 9; see also 'Freedom of Speech' *Sunday Tribune* (Singapore, 15 May 1938) 12.

[71] HC Deb, 22 June 1938, vol 337, cols 1117–1232.

[72] HC Deb, 4 July 1938, vol 338, cols 59–104.

It may well be for these reasons that this amendment bill never went through to a Second Reading. Instead, a separate Sedition Ordinance,[73] with a complementary Undesirable Publications Ordinance,[74] was enacted in 1938. Speaking at the First Reading of the Sedition Bill on 13 June 1938, Attorney-General CG Howell explained:

> The present law of the Colony with regard to sedition is briefly dealt with in section 124A of the Penal Code, but it is desirable that this subject should be dealt with in rather more detail than it is possible to do in that way, and the present Bill reproduces substantially the provisions of the common law of England with regard to sedition.[75]

Curiously, Howell went on to state that the clause in the proposed section 124A of the Penal Code that makes it a seditious intention if a person promotes 'feelings of enmity or hatred between different classes of the public', was now being removed. This was a sleight of hand, as the same objectionable and problematic clause found its way into the new Sedition Ordinance, a fact that did not go unnoticed by a critical press.[76] What had hitherto been cast as an ordinary public order criminal offence was 'elevated' to the much more serious crime of sedition.

The Sedition Act absorbed the crime of sedition under section 124A of the Penal Code (offence against the state) and enlarged it to include the incitement of feelings of enmity and hatred to other groups or classes of individuals in the community. The definition of the offence is to be found in section 3 of the Ordinance, which defines the meaning of 'seditious intention' as follows:

> 3.—(1) A 'seditious intention' is an intention:
>
> (a) to bring into hatred or contempt or to excite disaffection against the person of His Majesty or the Government established by law in the Colony or in the United Kingdom of Great Britain and Northern Ireland or in British India or in any other British Possession or the Ruler of any Malay State under His Majesty's protection or the Government or Governments established by law therein; or
>
> (b) to excite His Majesty's subjects or inhabitants of the Colony to attempt to procure the alteration, otherwise than by lawful means, of any other matter in the Colony as by law established; or
>
> (c) to bring into hatred or contempt or to excite disaffection against the administration of justice in the Colony; or
>
> (d) to raise discontent or disaffection amongst His Majesty's subjects of inhabitants of the Colony; or

[73] Ordinance 18 of 1938 (Straits Settlements).

[74] Ordinance 19 of 1938 (Straits Settlements).

[75] 'Speech of Attorney-General CG Howell on the Sedition Bill, 13 June 1938' in *Proceedings of the Legislative Council of the Straits Settlements for the Year 1938* (Singapore, Government Printing Office, 1939) B46.

[76] Editorial, 'The Sedition Bill' *Singapore Free Press* (Singapore, 11 June 1938) 8; 'The "Sedition" Bill' *Malaya Tribune* (Singapore, 18 June 1938) 10; '"Savours of Fascism" Comments Opposition' *Singapore Free Press* (Singapore, 20 June 1938) 9.

(e) to promote feelings of ill-will and hostility between different races or classes of the population of the Colony.

However, section 3(1) provides that an act, speech or publication is not considered 'seditious' by reason only that it intends:

(a) to show that His Majesty has been misled or mistaken in any of his measures; or
(b) to point out errors or defects in the government or constitution as by law established of any British possession or of any Malay State or in legislation or in the administration of justice with a view to the remedying of such errors or defects; or
(c) to persuade His Majesty's subjects or inhabitants of the Colony to attempt to procure by lawful means the alteration of any matter in the Colony as by law established; or
(d) to point out, with a view to their removal, any matters which are producing or have a tendency to produce feelings of ill-will and enmity between different races or classes of the population of the Colony.

The caveats were designed to maintain a balance between speech or acts that are seditious because the perpetrator has the intent to foment discontent, disaffection or promote feelings of ill-will and hostility. If the intention had been simply to highlight a situation or persuade the government or people to effect a lawful change in law or policy, no seditious intent could be imputed.

As a result of the broadening of the offence of sedition, section 124A of the Penal Code was accordingly repealed. Likewise, the new 1938 Sedition and Undesirable Publications Ordinances[77] rendered the 1915 Seditious Publications (Prohibition) Ordinance otiose, and it was accordingly repealed as well.[78] The offence of sedition under the Sedition Ordinance is punishable by imprisonment for to two years or a fine of up to $1,000 in the case of a first-time offender, while a subsequent offender is subject to a term of imprisonment of up to three years.[79] The punishment is no different whether one is charged under the old sedition provisions of the Penal Code or the new Sedition Ordinance. The following year, the British-controlled Federated Malay States of Selangor, Perak, Pahang and Negri Sembilan adopted similar legislation and enacted the Sedition Enactment[80] and the Undesirable Publications Enactment.

Just three years after the passage of the Sedition Ordinance and Sedition Enactment, British Malaya and Singapore were overrun by the Japanese, who occupied these territories from 1942 to 1945. When the British returned at the end of World War II to reclaim their territories, they had determined to constitutionally reorganise them. The Straits Settlements – comprising Penang, Malacca and Singapore – were disbanded in 1946, and Penang and Malacca joined the rest of the Federated Malay States and Unfederated Malay States,

[77] Ordinance 19 (n 74).
[78] Sedition Ordinance 1938 (Straits Settlements), s 10.
[79] ibid s 4(1).
[80] Enactment No 13 of 1939 (Federated Malay States).

forming a new entity, the Malayan Union. Singapore would be administered as a separate Crown Colony. Due to Malay opposition, the Malayan Union was disbanded in 1948 and replaced by the Federation of Malaya. In the meantime, the Communist Party of Malaya (CPM) began an armed insurrection in 1948 to displace the British. This led to the proclamation of a state of emergency – a euphemism for what was effectively an undeclared civil war.

To combat the spread of anti-British propaganda, the Government proposed a number of legislative measures, including strengthening legislation on restricted residence, seditious publications, printing presses and emergency.[81] It was in these circumstances that the British Government decided to reinvigorate and strengthen the old Sedition Enactment by passing a new Sedition Act. Speaking at the Second Reading of the Sedition Bill on 6 July 1948, the Acting Attorney-General for the Federation of Malaya, EPS Bell, stated that previous enactments on sedition within the Federation were identical, as they followed 'very much the same pattern … based on a model Ordinance … sent to this country some years ago by the Colonial Office'.[82] Bell explained that the new Bill was 'very substantially – indeed, a re-enactment – the same as the existing Sedition Enactments in force throughout the Federation'.[83] At the same time, the Government was taking the opportunity to 'increase the maximum penalties in respect of seditious offences … and incorporate two new sections which did not exist' previously – giving the court the power to suspend the publication of a newspaper convicted of publishing matters having a seditious tendency as well as a procedure to govern this process.[84]

What Bell did not inform the Legislative Council was that the new version of the Sedition Act changed the structure and elements of the offence of sedition altogether. The new section 4(1)(a) provided:

> 4.—(1) Any person who—
>
> (a) does or attempts to do, or makes any preparation to do, or conspires with any person to do, any act which has or which would, if done, have a *seditious tendency* … [emphasis added]
>
> shall be guilty of an offence …

The words of section 4(1)(a) of the 1938 Ordinance remained the same, except that the words 'seditious tendency' replaced the phrase 'seditious intention' under the earlier legislation. The meaning of 'seditious tendency' is found in section 3, as follows:

> 3.—(1) A 'seditious tendency' is a tendency:
>
> (a) to bring into hatred or contempt or to excite disaffection against any Ruler or against any Government;

[81] See 'Decisive Action Being Prepared' *Straits Times* (Singapore, 17 June 1948) 1.

[82] 'Speech of the Acting Attorney-General EPS Bell, Second Reading of the Sedition Bill, 1948, 6 July 1948' in Proceedings of the Legislative Council of the Federation of Malaya for the Period (First Session) February 1948 to February 1949 (Kuala Lumpur, Government Press, 1951) B351.

[83] ibid B352.

[84] ibid.

(b) to excite the subjects or inhabitants any Ruler or the inhabitants of any territory governed by any Government to attempt to procure in the territory of the Ruler or governed by the Government the alteration, otherwise than by lawful means, of any other matter as by law established;
(c) to bring into hatred or contempt or to excite disaffection against the administration of justice in the Colony; or
(d) to raise discontent or disaffection amongst the subjects of the Yang di-Pertuan Agong or of the Ruler of any State or amongst the inhabitants of Malaya or of any State; or
(e) to promote feelings of ill-will and hostility between different races or classes of the population of Malaya.

The new provision now made it easier to charge someone for sedition, since the *mens rea* for the new offence made 'intention' to actually incite or excite disaffection irrelevant. All that was required was for the prosecution to show that the accused intended to either speak the words spoken or execute the deed in question. It did not matter why the accused was motivated to act. The intention of acting was sufficient to satisfy the *mens rea* element of the crime.

Malaya's 1948 Sedition Act was extended to Singapore in May 1964 when Singapore became part of the new Federation of Malaysia, along with the Borneo states of Sabah and Sarawak.[85] This legislation was retained in Singapore even after it seceded from the Federation of Malaysia in 1965, and is currently found in Chapter 290 of the Singapore Statutes. The British Protectorate of Brunei also adopted its own Sedition Enactment in June 1948, just a month before the Federation of Malaya enacted its new Sedition Act. However, unlike the Federation of Malaya, Brunei did not have its own law-making legislature till independence in 1984. The British Resident had, in the meantime, arrogated to himself all of the executive and legislative powers of Brunei, and was able to enact laws without objection. It was only from about 1950 onwards that the Sultan's State Council began asserting itself to block legislation it did not like.[86] Thus, when the British Resident introduced the Sedition Enactment in 1948,[87] it adopted what was effectively the 1938 Sedition Ordinance of the Straits Settlements, which was concerned with punishing words spoken or acts done with 'seditious intent' rather than that having a 'seditious tendency'.

IV. POST-INDEPENDENCE DEVELOPMENTS

There were many changes in religious penal law in the former British Asian territories after they became independent. This was largely because many of these states adopted official or state religions and amended their laws to make

[85] 'Sedition Act extended' *Straits Times* (Singapore, 30 May 1964) 1.
[86] See Bachamiya Abdul Hussainmiya, '"Manufacturing Consensus": The Role of the State Council in Brunei Darussalam' (2000) 31(2) *Journal of Southeast Asian Studies* 321.
[87] Enactment 3 of 1948 (Brunei).

blasphemous speech or acts against the state religion much more serious offences. Among them are Pakistan, Bangladesh, Malaysia, Brunei and the Maldives (all Islamic countries), and Sri Lanka (which privileges Buddhism). Only India's laws remained largely unchanged from the colonial era. Even Singapore amended its laws by passing the 1990 Maintenance of Religious Harmony Act, which was amended in 2019 to incorporate the old Penal Code offences therein. We now consider how the laws have changed in each of these territories.

A. Pakistan and Bangladesh

The break-up of British India in 1947 led to the partitioning of the sub-continent into Hindu-dominated India and Muslim-dominated Pakistan (which then consisted of two geographically separate territories – East and West Pakistan). Following partition from India, Pakistan became a British Dominion and remained so till 1956, when it adopted a new constitution and proclaimed itself the Islamic Republic of Pakistan. The 1956 Constitution was rejected by the Hindu minority parties and the Awami League – the largest Muslim political party in East Pakistan – and this led to a period of political instability throughout the state. In 1958, General Ayub Khan seized control of the government and ruled under martial law. He promulgated the 1962 Constitution through an executive order, but this was replaced in 1973 by a third Constitution drawn up by a constituent assembly. Article 1(1) of the Constitution proclaims the state as 'the Islamic Republic of Pakistan', while Article 2 stipulates that 'Islam shall be the State religion'. Article 20 nonetheless guarantees every citizen the 'right to profess, practise and propagate his religion', and guarantees every religious denomination or sect 'the right to establish, maintain and manage its religious institutions'.

Article 106 of the Constitution deals with the seats in the Provincial Assemblies and the Provinces of Baluchistan and the North-West Frontier. In September 1974, it was amended to classify Ahmadis as non-Muslims. Article 260, which deals with the interpretation of the Constitution, was also amended to define 'non-Muslims' to include 'a person of the Quadiani Group or the Lahori Group who call themselves "Ahmadis"'. A decade later, the religious offences provisions of the Pakistan Penal Code – which was in essence the old Indian Penal Code – were expanded to include two new offences, which both specifically protect Islam from insult:[88]

> *Defiling, etc, of Holy Qur'an*
>
> 295B.—Whoever wilfully defiles, damages or desecrates a copy of the Holy Qur'an or of an extract therefrom or uses it in any derogatory manner or for any unlawful purpose shall be punishable with imprisonment for life.

[88] Pakistan Penal Code (Amendment) Ordinance 1 of 1982. See also Raza Rumi, 'Unpacking the Blasphemy Laws of Pakistan' (2018) 49(2) *Asian Affairs* 319.

Use of derogatory remarks, etc, in respect of the Holy Prophet

295C.—Whoever by words, either spoken or written, or by visible representation or by any imputation, innuendo, or insinuation, directly or indirectly, defiles the sacred name of the Holy Prophet Muhammad (peace be upon him) shall be punished with death, or imprisonment for life, and shall also be liable to fine.

In 1971, East Pakistan broke away from West Pakistan to become the Republic of Bangladesh. While Bangladesh is a predominantly Muslim country, it resisted making Islam its state religion till 2014, when Article 2A was inserted into the Constitution to provide that the 'state religion of the Republic is Islam'. Article 2A further provides that the State will 'ensure equal status and equal right in the practice of Hindu, Buddhist, Christian and other religions'.[89] Successive Bangladeshi governments have resisted Islamists demands that Bangladesh emulate Pakistan in enacting more blasphemy laws to protect Islam.[90]

B. Malaysia

The Federation of Malaya became independent from the United Kingdom in 1957. Although it has a multi-racial and multi-religious society,[91] a concession was made to the Malay-Muslim majority through Article 3(1) of the Federal Constitution, which proclaims Islam as 'the religion of the Federation' but provides that 'other religions may be practised in peace and harmony'. This provision is largely hortatory, as matters of religion are strictly within the purview of the states and not the federal Government. Furthermore, Article 11(1) of the Constitution guarantees every person the right 'to profess and practise his religion' and to 'propagate it'. However, Article 11(4) provides that the states – and the Federal Government (in the case of the Federal Territories of Kuala Lumpur, Labuan and Putrajaya over which it has legislative jurisdiction) – may 'control or restrict the propagation of any religious doctrine or belief among persons professing the religion of Islam'. This caveat has led to the promulgation of state laws[92] in all but three of the Federation's 13 states to restrict the propagation of non-Islamic religions to Muslims.[93] For examples, the Federal Government

[89] Art 2A was inserted by section 4 of the Constitution (Fifteenth Amendment) Act 2011, Act 14 of 2011.

[90] See, eg, Anbarasan Ethirajan, 'Bangladesh PM Sheikh Hasina Rejects Blasphemy Law' (*BBC News*, 8 April 2013) at www.bbc.com/news/world-asia-22058462.

[91] See generally, Andrew J Harding, 'Malaysia: Religious Pluralism and the Constitution in a Contested Polity' (2012) 4 *Middle East Law and Governance* 356.

[92] See Zuliza Mohd Musrun, Zaini Nasohahm, Mohd Al-Adib Samuri and Mat Noor Mat Zain, 'Legal Provisions and Restrictions on the Propagation of Non-Islamic Religions Among Muslims in Malaysia' (2013) 31(2) *Kajian Malaysia* 3.

[93] Between 1980 and 2002, 10 state laws, most of which are entitled 'Control and Restriction of the Propagation of Non-Islamic Religion Enactments', were passed by the states: Terengganu (1980); Kelantan (1981); Kedah, Malacca, Perak, Selangor (all 1988); Pahang (1989); Negri Sembilan and Johor (1991). The latest of these restrictive laws is the Control and Restriction of the Propagation of Religious Doctrine which is Contrary to the Religion of Islam (Perlis Enactment No 6 of 2002).

passed the Syariah Criminal Offences (Federal Territories) Act in 1997, which applies to all Muslims living in the Federal Territories.[94] Section 5 of the Act reads:

> 5.—Any person who propagates religious doctrines or beliefs other than the religious doctrines or beliefs of the religion of Islam among persons professing the Islamic faith shall be guilty of an offence and shall on conviction be liable to a fine not exceeding three thousand ringgit[95] or to imprisonment for a term not exceeding two years or to both.

In 1983, the Malaysian Parliament took steps to strengthen the religious offences provisions in the Penal Code by introducing a new section 298A.[96] This is a lengthy and complex provision with eight sub-clauses, the significant parts of which are set out below:

> 298A.(1)Whoever by words, either spoken or written, or by signs, or by visible representations, or by any act, activity or conduct, or by organising, promoting or arranging, or assisting in organising, promoting or arranging, any activity, or otherwise in any other manner—
>
> (a) causes, or attempts to cause, or is likely to cause disharmony, disunity, or feelings of enmity, hatred or ill will; or
>
> (b) prejudices, or attempts to prejudice, or is likely to prejudice, the maintenance of harmony or unity, on grounds of religion, between persons or groups of persons professing the same or different religions, shall be punished with imprisonment for a term of not less than two years and not more than five years.
>
> ...
>
> (3) Where any person alleges or imputes in any manner specified in subsection (1) —
>
> (a) that any other person, or any class, group or description of persons, professing any particular religion —
>
> (i) has ceased to profess that religion;
>
> (ii) should not be accepted, or cannot be accepted, as professing that religion; or
>
> (iii) does not believe, follow, profess, or belong to, that religion; or
>
> (b) that anything lawfully done by any religious official appointed, or by any religious authority established, constituted or appointed, by or under any written law, in the exercise of any power, or in the discharge of any duty, or in the performance of any function, of a religious character, by virtue of being so appointed, established or constituted, is not acceptable to such person, or should not be accepted by any other person or persons, or does not accord with or fulfil the requirements of that religion, or is otherwise wrong or improper,
>
> he shall be presumed to have contravened the provisions of subsection (1) by having acted in a manner likely to cause disharmony, disunity or feelings of enmity, hatred

[94] Syariah Criminal Offences (Federal Territories) Act 1997 (Act 559).

[95] A ringgit is a Malaysian dollar, the value of which is approximately US$0.25 at the time of writing.

[96] Penal Code and Criminal Procedure Code (Amendment) Act 1983 (Act A549).

or ill will, or likely to prejudice the maintenance of harmony or unity, between persons or groups of persons professing the religion referred to in the allegation or imputation.

(4)(a) Where, on any ground of a religious character, any person professing any particular religion uses for burial or cremation of any human corpse a place other than one which is lawfully used for such purpose by persons professing that religion, he shall be presumed to have contravened the provisions of subsection (1) by having acted in a manner likely to cause disharmony, disunity or feelings of enmity, hatred or ill will, or likely to prejudice the maintenance of harmony or unity, between persons or groups of persons professing that religion.

(b) Where any person, on any ground of a religious character, counsels, advises, instigates, urges, pleads with, or appeals or propagates to, or in any manner or by any means call upon, whether directly or indirectly, any other person or persons professing any particular religion—

(i) to use for burial or cremation of any human corpse a place other than one which is lawfully used for such purpose by persons professing that religion;
(ii) not to use for burial or cremation of any human corpse any place which is lawfully used for such purpose by persons professing that religion; or
(iii) not to use for worship any place which is lawfully used for such purpose by persons professing that religion,

he shall be presumed to have contravened the provisions of subsection (1) by having acted in a manner likely to cause disharmony, disunity or feelings of enmity, hatred or ill will, or likely to prejudice the maintenance of harmony or unity, between persons or groups of persons professing that religion or different religions.

(5) Where any person who is not a religious official appointed, or a religious authority established, constituted or appointed, by or under any written law purports to exercise any power, or to discharge any duty, or to perform any function, of a religious character, being a power, duty or function which can be lawfully exercised, discharged or performed only by a religious official appointed, or a religious authority established, constituted or appointed, by or under any written law, he shall be presumed to have contravened the provisions of subsection (1) by having acted in a manner likely to cause disharmony, disunity or feelings of enmity, hatred or ill will, or likely to prejudice the maintenance of harmony or unity, between persons or groups of persons professing the same or different religions.

(6) The foregoing provisions of this section shall not apply to —

(a) anything done by any religious authority established, constituted or appointed by or under any written law and conferred by written law with power to give or issue any ruling or decision on any matter pertaining to the religion in respect of which the authority is established, constituted or appointed; or

(b) anything done by any person which is in pursuance of, or which accords with, any ruling or decision given or issued by such religious authority, whether or not such ruling or decision is in writing, and if in writing, whether or not it is published in the Gazette.

(7) It shall not be a defence to any charge under this section to assert that what the offender is charged with doing was done in any honest belief in, or in any honest interpretation of, any precept, tenet or teaching of any religion.

> (8) If in any proceedings under this section any question arises with regard to the interpretation of any aspect of, or any matter in relation to, any religion, the Court shall accept the interpretation given by any religious authority referred to in subsection (6), being a religious authority in respect of that religion.

It is beyond the scope of this chapter to offer a detailed analysis of section 298A of the Malaysian Penal Code, but the following observations may be noted. First, this section makes it an offence to say anything or do any act that 'prejudices, or attempts to prejudice, or is likely to prejudice' the maintenance of religious harmony. This is extremely wide, since what constitutes 'likely to prejudice religious harmony' is highly arguable. Furthermore, the punishment for this offence is severe – between two and five years' imprisonment. Second, anyone who 'alleges or imputes' that someone or a group of persons of a particular faith has ceased to profess that religion or 'should not be accepted' or 'cannot be accepted' as professing that religion, or 'does not believe, follow, profess, or belong to' that religion is *presumed to* violate section 298(1) 'by having acted in a manner likely to cause disharmony, disunity or feelings of enmity, hatred or ill will, or likely to prejudice the maintenance of harmony or unity, between persons or groups of persons professing the religion referred to in the allegation or imputation'. This is almost a strict liability offence, as the presumption appears irrebuttable; it also applies to clauses (4) and (5) of the same section. To make these provisions even stricter, section 298(7) states that it is no defence for an accused to assert that he or she had acted 'in any honest belief in, or in any honest interpretation of, any precept, tenet or teaching of any religion'. Finally, section 298(8) requires the Court to accept the interpretation 'given by any religious authority' in the event where a question arises as to the interpretation of any aspect of or matter relating to any religion.

C. Brunei

Brunei is an absolute monarchy that gained her independence from Britain in 1984. The Brunei Constitution, which dates to 1959, contains no guarantees of fundamental rights or liberties, including no guarantee of religious freedom. Article 3(1) of its Constitution – similar to that of the Federation of Malaysia – proclaims Islam to be the 'official religion' of the state but guarantees that 'all other religions may be practised in peace and harmony'. It further proclaims the Sultan as the 'Head of the official religion' of Brunei[97] and that a Religious Council will be responsible for advising the Sultan 'on all matters relating to the Islamic Religion'.[98] At his Declaration of Independence Speech on 1 January 1984, Sultan Hassanal Bolkiah proclaimed the state's national

[97] Constitution of Brunei Darussalam 1959, Art 3(2).
[98] ibid Art 3(3).

ideology – *Melayu Islam Beraja* (literally, Malay Islamic monarchy) or MIB – and soon began promoting ideology with systematic fervour.[99] In 1990, the Sultan announced that all laws would 'be brought in line with Islam', and established a committee of Islamic scholars to advise him on how this could be achieved.[100] The Penal Code of Brunei, which was adopted from the Indian Penal Code in 1951, carried the same offences against religion as the original version enacted in 1860–70, though section 124A (sedition) was deleted in light of the operation of similar provisions in Brunei's own Sedition Act. However, in 2014, the Penal Code was supplemented by a new Syariah Penal Code Order 2013, which would be administered by the Syariah Court.[101] The passage of the latter legislation immediately raised questions as to whether the civil courts or the Syariah Court would have jurisdiction in matters covered by both statutes.

The remarkable thing about the Syariah Penal Code is that some of its provisions apply to non-Muslims as well. Most of these offences are to be found in Part IV of the Syariah Penal Code, which covers 'General Offences'. It is impossible within the framework of this chapter to cover every new offence created by the new Code, but the most significant offences that apply to all persons regardless of their faith merit highlighting. Section 195 makes it an offence for any person to sell or consume 'in public, any food, drink or tobacco during the fasting hours in the month of *Ramadhan*'. Those found guilty are liable to a fine not exceeding $4,000 or imprisonment for up to one year or both. Section 197 criminalises acts of 'indecent behaviour in any public place [by] any person', and defines such indecent acts as those that tend 'to tarnish the image of Islam, deprave a person, bring bad influence or cause anger to the person who is likely to have seen the act'. The punishment for infractions under section 197 is a fine of up to $2,000 or imprisonment for up to six months or both. It is likewise a crime for any man to dress or pose as a woman, or for any woman to dress and pose as a man 'in any public place without reasonable excuse'. Those found guilty may face a fine of up to $1,000 or imprisonment for up to three months or both. However, if it is found that the purpose of cross-dressing or impersonation is 'for immoral purposes', the punishment is a fine of up to $4,000 or imprisonment for up to one year or both.

Section 209 forbids any person from propagating any religion other than Islam – either to a Muslim or to 'a person having no religion' – on pain of a maximum fine of $20,000 or imprisonment for up to five years or both. Any person who 'persuades, tells, causes, offers payment to, influences, incites, encourages or lets a Muslim' change his religion or 'leave or dislike the religion of Islam' may

[99] See Dominik M Müller, 'Sharia Law and the Politics of "Faith Control" in Brunei Darussalam: Dynamics of Socio-Legal Change in a Southeast Asian Sultanate' (2015) 46 *Internationales Asienforum* 313, 316–17.

[100] ibid 321.

[101] Syariah Penal Code Order 2013 (Brunei), s 69. For a detailed discussion of this Code and its provisions, see Tim Lindsey and Kerstin Steiner, 'Islam, the Monarchy and Criminal Law in Brunei: The Syariah Penal Code Order, 2013' (2016) 25(4) *Griffith Law Review* 552.

similarly be punished with a fine of up to $20,000 or with imprisonment for up to five years or both.[102] It is immaterial whether the accused succeeded in causing the subject of his efforts to change religion or abandon Islam.[103] Any person who 'persuades, tells, causes, offers payment to, influences, incites, encourages or lets a Muslim child, or a child whose parents have no religion, who is under the age of 18' either to 'accept the teachings of religions other than the religion of Islam' or to 'attend any ceremony, act of worship or religious activities of any religion other than' that of Islam, or 'participate in any activities held for the benefit of any religion other than the religion of Islam', may be liable to a fine of up to $20,000 or a term of imprisonment of up to five years.[104] Any person who uses certain words listed in the Fifth Schedule,[105] either in speech or publication, for the purpose of stating or expressing 'any fact, belief, idea, concept, act, activity, matter or instances of or relating to religion other than the religion of Islam' is guilty of an offence and is liable to a fine of up to $12,000 or imprisonment for up to three years or both.[106] Any person who 'accuses, alleges or imputes' that any Muslim is *kafir* (an infidel or unbeliever) or is no longer professing the faith of Islam is also guilty of an offence, with punishment of a maximum fine of $8,000 or imprisonment for up to two years or both.[107] Any person who 'brings into contempt, insults, makes fun of, mocks, mimics or ridicules' Islamic teachings, ceremonies, holy words, law, tenets or *fatwa* (Islamic scholars' ruling on a religious point of law) may be fined up to $12,000 or imprisoned for up to three years or both.[108] Finally, it is an offence to hold in contempt, neglect, contravene, oppose or insult any *titah* (command) of the Sultan 'with respect to religion in his capacity as the Head of the official religion of Brunei'. Committing such an offence may result in imprisonment for up to five years.[109] A person who is guilty of contempt of the *Majlis* (Islamic Religious Council) or its members, the Syariah Court or the administration of Syariah justice may be fined up to $8,000 or imprisoned for up to two years or both.[110]

D. The Maldives

Although the British occupied the Maldives as a Dominion and then as a Protectorate from 1796 till 1965, it was not until 1932 that the territory had any

[102] Syariah Penal Code Order 2013 (Brunei), s 210(1).
[103] ibid s 210(2).
[104] ibid s 212.
[105] Under the Fifth Schedule, the following words may not be used in respect of any religion except for Islam: *Allah*, *Al-Qu'ran*, *Azan*, *Baitullah*, *Fatwa*, *Firman Allah*, *Hadith*, *Haji*, *Hukum Syara*, *Ilahi*, *Imam*, *Ka'bah*, *Kalimah al-syahadah*, *Kiblat*, *Masjid*, *Mufti*, *Mu'min*, *Solat* and *Wali*.
[106] Syariah Penal Code Order 2013 (Brunei), s 217.
[107] ibid s 219.
[108] ibid s 220.
[109] ibid s 230.
[110] ibid.

written laws of its own. This was facilitated by its first written Constitution, which empowered the People's *Majlis* (People's Council) to make law for the territory. It would appear that no over-arching penal statute was adopted until 1961 when the Maldivian Parliament enacted the Maldives Penal Code[111] – an enactment that drew on selected portions of the Ceylon Penal Code except 'all criminal offences from which Islamic Shari'ah prescribes punishment'.[112] While the Maldives Penal Code of 1961 provides for seditious offences, there are no offences against any religion. However, section 88 of the Code does make it an offence to 'disobey an order issued lawfully within the Shari'ah or Law', and those found guilty are liable to a fine not exceeding Mrf 150.00 (about US$10.00).

Islam is the predominant religion of the people of the Maldives; an estimated 99 per cent of the population are Muslims. As a result, Islam and Islamic law have always been given constitutional prominence. Except for the short-lived Third Constitution (1953–54), all Maldivian Constitutions have proclaimed Islam the official state religion. The current Constitution, which dates from 2008, does likewise, and forbids any 'law contrary to the tenets of Islam' to be enacted.[113] The Constitution further prohibits non-Muslims from becoming citizens of the country. All rights in Chapter II (Fundamental Rights and Freedoms) are guaranteed 'to all persons, in a manner that is not contrary to any tenet of Islam'.[114]

In 2004, the Maldives Government commissioned Professor Paul H Robinson of the University of Pennsylvania to draft a new Penal Code and a Criminal Procedure Code. The draft Penal Code was completed in January 2006 and was enacted into law in 2014. Robinson stated that in his Code, 'a high priority' was 'given to ensuring that it reflects Maldivian values (not European, American, or any other values)' and that three sources of law were relied upon: (i) current Maldivian statutes; (ii) principles of Shari'ah; and (iii) shared community values.[115]

The new Penal Code contains four specific religious offences. Section 410 makes it an offence for any woman to marry a non-Muslim man or for any man to marry a non-Muslim woman 'not belonging to adherent faiths which have revealed scripture'. Offenders may be imprisoned for up to a year. Section 616 makes it an offence if a Maldivian citizen does not fast, or gives up fasting 'during the month of Ramadan without an acceptable medical or health-related reason', or who 'consumes pork or pork products' or alcohol. Offenders

[111] Maldives Penal Code 1961 (Act No 1/81).

[112] Al Suood, *The Maldivian Legal System* (n 56) 86.

[113] Constitution of the Maldives 2008, Art 10.

[114] ibid Art 16. The phrase 'tenet of Islam' is defined in Art 274 to mean 'the Holy Qur'an those principles of Shari'ah whose provenance is not in dispute from among those found in the Sunna of the Noble Prophet, and those principles derived from these two foundations'.

[115] Paul H Robinson et al, *Final Report of the Maldivian Penal Law & Sentencing Codification Project*, vol 2 (University of Pennsylvania Carey Law School, 2006) 3.

under this section may be imprisoned for up to three months and given up to 40 lashes.[116] Under section 617, any person may be punished for criticising 'Islam in public or in a public medium with the intention to cause disregard for Islam', or producing, selling, distributing or offering material for the same purpose. A person may run afoul of the same section for attempting 'to disrupt the religious unity of the citizens of Maldives' or 'conversing and acting in a manner likely to cause religious segregation amongst people'. Offenders may be imprisoned for up to one year.

E. Singapore

Like Malaysia, Singapore retained its Penal Code religious offences as well as the Sedition Act after independence from the Federation of Malaysia in 1965. The punishments for the religious offences under the Penal Code were enhanced under the 2007 Penal Code (Amendment) Act.[117] In 1990, Parliament passed the Maintenance of Religious Harmony Act,[118] to establish a Presidential Council for Religious Harmony as well as to give the Government power to issue restraining orders against 'any priest, monk, pastor, imam, elder, office-bearer or any other person who is in a position of authority in any religious group or institution' if the Minister is satisfied that that person has committed or is attempting to commit one of the following acts:

> (a) causing feelings of enmity, hatred, ill-will or hostility between different religious groups;
> (b) carrying out activities to promote a political cause, or a cause of any political party while, or under the guise of, propagating or practising any religious belief;
> (c) carrying out subversive activities under the guise of propagating or practising any religious belief; or
> (d) exciting disaffection against the President or the Government while, or under the guise of, propagating or practising any religious belief.[119]

The restraining order may be issued for the following purposes:

> (a) restraining him from addressing orally or in writing any congregation, parish or group of worshippers or members of any religious group or institution on any subject, topic or theme as may be specified in the order without the prior permission of the Minister;
> (b) restraining him from printing, publishing, editing, distributing or in any way assisting or contributing to any publication produced by any religious group without the prior permission of the Minister;

[116] Under section 411(d)(2), 'lashes' is defined as 'the symbolic punishment of striking an offender's back with a short length of rope in a manner not designed to cause bodily injury', with the lashes being inflicted only by the movement of the wrists and without the use of any other part of the arm or movement of the shoulders, hips, back, legs or torso.

[117] Penal Code (Amendment) Act 2007, Act 51 of 2007.

[118] Maintenance of Religious Harmony Act (Cap 167A, Rev Ed Sing 2001).

[119] ibid s 8(1).

(c) restraining him from holding office in an editorial board or a committee of a publication of any religious group without the prior permission of the Minister.[120]

The penalty for breaching a restraining order is a fine of up to $10,000 or imprisonment for up to two years for the first offence, and a fine of up to $20,000 or imprisonment for up to three years for a second or subsequent offence.[121] Between the Act's enactment in 1995 and 2019, no restraining order was ever issued.

In 2019, the Act was substantially amended for a number of broad purposes, two of which are relevant to our discussion. The first was to extend the application of restraining orders to religious groups, 'to pre-empt, prevent or reduce any foreign influence affecting the religious groups which may undermine religious tolerance between different religious groups in Singapore and present a threat to the public peace and public order in Singapore'; and the second was to 'consolidate offences involving religious vilification'.[122] Pursuant to the second object, Parliament inserted new sections 17E and 17F into the Act. These two sections essentially repeat the offences under sections 295, 296 and 297 of the Penal Code, and these have accordingly been repealed. Section 74 of the Penal Code – which provides for enhanced penalties for racially or religiously aggravated offences – was also amended to empower the courts to sentence a person to twice the amount of punishment for which he or she would otherwise have been liable under the Code.

F. Sri Lanka

Sri Lanka, formerly Ceylon, declared its independence from Great Britain in 1948, becoming a Dominion. In 1972, it proclaimed itself an independent republic. A new Constitution was promulgated in 1978, which among other things proclaimed the primacy of Buddhism among all religions. Article 9 of the Constitution provides that the state 'shall give to Buddhism the foremost place and accordingly it shall be the duty of the State to protect and foster the Buddha *Sasana*, while assuring to all religions the rights granted by Article 10 and 14(1)(e)'.[123] This move did not help the already fractured relations between the majority Sinhalese (who are overwhelmingly Buddhist) and the Tamil minority (who are mainly Hindu but also Christian and Muslim). Racial, religious and regional

[120] ibid s 8(2).
[121] ibid s 16.
[122] Explanatory Statement, Maintenance of Religious Harmony (Amendment) Bill, Bill No 25/2019, 62–63.
[123] Art 10 guarantees to every person 'freedom of thought, conscience and religion, including the freedom to have or to adopt a religion or belief of his choice', while Art 14(1)(e) guarantees every citizen 'the freedom by himself or in association with others, and either in public or in private, to manifest his religion or belief in worship, observance, practice and teaching'.

politics led to a 30-year civil war, which only ended in 2009. Despite all this, the religious penal provisions that were adopted in 1972 have not been amended or augmented.

V. CONCLUSION

Our brief survey of the evolution of religious penal clauses in Commonwealth Asia has shown that the development of these laws went through three distinct phases. The first phase involved the creation of the offence of blasphemy by the common law courts and its subsequent codification for use in India. As recounted, blasphemy originated as a religious offence that was dealt with by the old ecclesiastical courts in England, but was later made a common law offence by Chief Justice Matthew Hale in the landmark case of *Rex v Taylor*. The offence was primarily to prevent the denial of or attacks on the Christian faith, and it was in this mode that the offence travelled to Britain's settled colonies like America, Canada, Australia and New Zealand, where most of the settlers were white and Christian. But such a common law offence could not practically be transplanted to territories that had previously been settled and where the native populations already had long-standing religious traditions of their own. This was certainly the case in India, where a predominantly Hindu population had for centuries been dominated by Muslim rulers. The object of any blasphemy law would no longer be to protect a dominant or privileged religion from insult or derision but instead to prevent religious feelings from being inflamed to the point where public order and safety might be jeopardised.

The second phase sees the development and enhancement of penal provisions during the drafting of the Indian Penal Code and its subsequent additions, and its export to different parts of the British Empire. Macaulay and the rest of the Indian Law Commissioners knew well the dangers of allowing one group of religious zealots to demean or, worse still, attack or destroy the religious icons, buildings or ceremonies of another. This explains why the provisions creating offences against religion were couched in terms of insults and attacks that were likely to provoke a violent response. Under the Indian Penal Code, the offence of blasphemy had morphed from one that protected a particular religion and its tenets, to one that prevented one religious group from provoking the ire of another; a religious offence had become a public order offence. It was in this form that the offence of blasphemy was exported to various other British territories, including those in Commonwealth Asia.

The blasphemy offences in the Penal Code were supplemented by the later inclusion of what was also formerly a common law offence – sedition. The objective of sedition was to protect the state against attacks and subversion, but it was soon expanded to outlaw attacks that would foment 'disaffection' or conflict between different classes and groups within society. Jurisdictions like the Straits Settlements, the Federated Malay States and Brunei took this one step further by enacting separate Sedition Acts or Ordinances that were drafted in terms that made it much easier for the state to prosecute individuals for fomenting conflict between different classes or groups – which would necessarily include religious groups – in society. This happened in 1948 with the passage of the Straits Settlements Sedition Ordinance and the Federated Malay States Sedition Enactment.

The third phase of development takes place after these former colonies attained their independence. With the exception of India and Singapore, the other six Asian states adopted state religions, and accordingly took steps to either create more religious offences, or augment existing ones with increased punishments. However, both Sri Lanka, which made Buddhism its main religion, and Bangladesh, which made Islam its state religion, did not alter any of the religious penal clauses they inherited from their colonial past. All the others – Pakistan, Malaysia, Brunei and the Maldives – took steps to strengthen their penal legislation to create more offences or make older ones broader and more severe. Of these, Brunei has gone the furthest, with its Syariah Penal Code Order sitting cheek-by-jowl with the old Penal Code. For these states, the offence of blasphemy has gone full circle and returned to its roots, except that this time, instead of Christianity, it is Islam that has become the subject of the law's protection.

BIBLIOGRAPHY

—— An Act for the More Effectual Prevention and Punishment of Blasphemous and Seditious Libels 1819 (60 Geo III and 1 Geo IV, c 8)

—— Blasphemy Act 1697 (9 Will III 3, c 35)

—— Charter Act 1833 (3 & 4 Will 4, c 85)

—— Constitution of Brunei Darussalam 1959, Arts 3(2), 3(3)

—— Criminal Law (Amendment) Act 1927 s 2

—— Constitution of the Maldives 2008, arts 10, 16

—— 'Decisive Action Being Prepared' *Straits Times* (Singapore, 17 June 1948) 1

—— Enactment No 13 of 1939 (Federated Malay States)

—— Enactment 3 of 1948 (Brunei)

—— Explanatory Statement, Maintenance of Religious Harmony (Amendment) Bill, Bill No 25/2019, 62–63

—— 'Freedom of Speech' *Sunday Tribune* (Singapore, 15 May 1938) 12

—— HC Deb, 28 June 1831, vol 4, col 436

—— HC Deb, 17 April 1833, vol 17, cols 205–44

—— HC Deb, 10 July 1833, vol 19, col 531

—— HC Deb, 22 June 1938, vol 337, cols 1117–1232

—— HC Deb, 4 July 1938 vol 338, cols 59–104

—— Maldives Penal Code 1961 (Act No 1/81)

—— Maintenance of Religious Harmony Act (Cap 167A, Rev Ed Sing 2001)

—— Ordinance 11 of 1915 (Straits Settlements)

—— Ordinance 18 of 1938 (Straits Settlements)

—— Ordinance 19 of 1938 (Straits Settlements)
—— Pakistan Penal Code (Amendment) Ordinance 1 of 1982
—— Penal Code (Amendment) Bill 1938 (Straits Settlements)
—— Penal Code and Criminal Procedure Code (Amendment) Act 1983 (Act A549)
—— Penal Code (Amendment) Act 2007, Act 51 of 2007.
—— 'Penal Code Amendment Protest' *Singapore Free Press* (Singapore, 30 May 1938) 9
—— *Rex v Taylor* [1676] 1 Vent 293; [1676] 3 Keb 607
—— '"Savours of Fascism" Comments Opposition' *Singapore Free Press* (Singapore, 20 June 1938) 9
—— 'Sedition Act extended' *Straits Times* (Singapore, 30 May 1964) 1
—— Sedition Ordinance 1938 (Straits Settlements), ss 4(1), 10
—— 'Speech of Attorney-General GA Goodman, First Reading of the Seditious Publications (Prohibition) Bill, 25 June 1915' in *Proceedings of the Legislative Council of the Straits Settlements for the Year 1915* (Singapore, Government Printing Office, 1916) B40
—— 'Speech of Attorney-General CG Howell, First Reading of the Penal Code (Amendment) Bill, 25 April 1938' in *Proceedings of the Legislative Council of the Straits Settlements for the Year 1938* (Singapore, Government Printing Office, 1939) B25
—— 'Speech of Attorney-General CG Howell on the Sedition Bill, 13 June 1938' in *Proceedings of the Legislative Council of the Straits Settlements for the Year 1938* (Singapore, Government Printing Office, 1939) B46
—— 'Speech of the Acting Attorney-General EPS Bell, Second Reading of the Sedition Bill, 1948, 6 July 1948' in *Proceedings of the Legislative Council of the Federation of Malaya for the Period (First Session) February 1948 to February 1949* (Kuala Lumpur, Government Press, 1951) B351–52
—— Syariah Criminal Offences (Federal Territories) Act 1997 (Act 559)
—— Syariah Penal Code Order 2013 (Brunei), ss 69, 210(1), 210(2), 212, 217, 219, 220, 230
—— 'The Sedition Bill' *Singapore Free Press* (Singapore, 11 June 1938) 8
—— 'The "Sedition" Bill' *Malaya Tribune* (Singapore, 18 June 1938) 10
—— Undesirable Publications Ordinance 1938 (Ordinance 19) (Straits Settlements)
Al Suood, H, *The Maldivian Legal System* (Maldives Law Institute, 2014)
Baker, JH, *An Introduction to English Legal History*, 5th edn (Oxford University Press, 2009)
Bodia, AR, 'Genesis of Blasphemy Laws in Colonial India' (2017) 38(2) *Pakistan Journal of History and Culture* 139
Pillai, KNCh (ed), *Essays on the Indian Penal Code* (New Delhi, Indian Law Institute, 2005)
Chung, YC, 'Parliament, the Heresy Ordinance of 1648, and the Religious Toleration in Civil War England' (2015) 57 *Journal of Church and State* 119
Ellens, GFS, 'The Ranters Ranting: Reflections on a Ranting Counter Culture' (1971) 40(1) *Church History* 91
Ethirajan, A, 'Bangladesh PM Sheikh Hasina Rejects Blasphemy Law' (*BBC News*, 8 April 2013) at www.bbc.com/news/world-asia-22058462
Firth, CH, and Rait, RS, *Acts and Ordinances of the Interregnum, 1642–1660*, vol 1 (HM Stationery Office, 1911)
Gaur, KD, *Textbook on the Indian Penal Code*, 4th edn (Universal Law Publishing, 2009)
Harding, AJ, 'Malaysia: Religious Pluralism and the Constitution in a Contested Polity' (2012) 4 *Middle East Law and Governance* 356

Hussainmiya, BA, '"Manufacturing Consensus": The Role of the State Council in Brunei Darussalam' (2000) 31(2) *Journal of Southeast Asian Studies* 321

Indian Law Commission, *A Penal Code Prepared by The Indian Law Commissioners* (Calcutta, Bengal Military Orphan Press, 1837)

Jain, MP, *Outlines of Indian Legal and Constitutional History*, 6th edn (LexisNexis, 2012) 417

Kenny, C, 'The Evolution of the Law of Blasphemy' (1922) 1(2) *Cambridge Law Journal* 127

Kolsky, E, 'Codification and the Rule of Colonial Difference: Criminal Procedure in British India' (2005) 23 *Law and History Review* 631

Law Library of Congress Global Legal Research Directorate, 'Blasphemy and Related Laws' (*The Library of Congress*, 3 March 2017) at www.loc.gov/law/help/blasphemy/index.php.

Levy, LW, *Blasphemy: Verbal Offense against the Sacred from Moses to Salman Rushdie* (University of North Carolina Press Books, 1995)

Lindsey, T, and Steiner, K, 'Islam, the Monarchy and Criminal Law in Brunei: The Syariah Penal Code Order, 2013' (2016) 25(4) *Griffith Law Review* 552

Manning, RB, 'The Origins of the Doctrine of Sedition' (1980) 12(2) *Albion: A Quarterly Journal Concerned with British Studies* 99

Müller, DM, 'Sharia Law and the Politics of "Faith Control" in Brunei Darussalam: Dynamics of Socio-Legal Change in a Southeast Asian Sultanate' (2015) 46 *Internationales Asienforum* 313

Musrun, ZM, Nasohah, Z, Samuri, MA-A, and Zain, MNM, 'Legal Provisions and Restrictions on the Propagation of Non-Islamic Religions Among Muslims in Malaysia' (2013) 31(2) *Kajian Malaysia* 3

Read, JS, 'Criminal Law in the Africa of Today and Tomorrow' (1963) 7(1) *Journal of African Law* 5

Robinson, PH, et al, *Final Report of the Maldivian Penal Law & Sentencing Codification Project*, vol 2 (University of Pennsylvania Carey Law School, 2006)

Rumi, R, 'Unpacking the Blasphemy Laws of Pakistan' (2018) 49(2) *Asian Affairs* 319

Sandberg, R, and Doe, N, 'The Strange Death of Blasphemy' (2008) 71(6) *Modern Law Review* 971

Setalvad, MC, *The Common Law in India* (Stevens & Sons, 1960)

Skuy, D, 'Macaulay and the Indian Penal Code of 1862: The Myth of the Inherent Superiority and Modernity of the English Legal System Compared to India's Legal System in the Nineteenth Century' (1998) 32(3) *Modern Asian Studies* 513

Stephen, JF, *History of the Criminal Law of England*, vol 3 (Macmillan, 1883)

——, *A Digest of the Criminal Law (Crimes and Punishments)*, 4th edn (Macmillan, 1877)

Visconsi, E, 'The Invention of Criminal Blasphemy: *Rex v Taylor* (1676)' (2008) 103(1) *Representations* 30

Wright, B, 'Macaulay's Indian Penal Code: Historical Context and Originating Principles' in Chan Wing-Cheong, Barry Wright and Stanley Yeo (eds), *Codification, Macaulay and the Indian Penal Code: The Legacies and Modern Challenges of Criminal Law Reform* (Ashgate, 2011) 34

Yeo, S, 'Giving Precedence to the Indian Penal Code' in Mahendra Pal Singh and Niraj Kumar (eds), *The Indian Yearbook of Comparative Law 2018* (Springer, 2019) 341

2

Apollonian Restraint and Dionysian Impulse: Law, Freedom and Religious Feelings

LI-ANN THIO

I. INTRODUCTION

MANY FORMER BRITISH colonies in Asia have retained and renovated the religious offences penal code (RPC) provisions that had their origins in the 1860 Indian Penal Code ('On the Chapter of Offences Relating to Religion and Caste'); these deal with offences involving the wounding of religious feelings or religious insult, and promoting ill-will and hostility between religious groups, through words, gestures, trespass and defiling places of worship. More recently, countries like Russia have adopted variants of such 'religious insults' laws that criminalise actions and behaviour that insult the religious feelings of believers.[1] Such laws have been criticised as tools used to suppress political dissent[2] and harass religious minorities. While sometimes described as 'hate speech' laws, a distinction should be drawn between hurtful and hateful speech, where the latter involves incitement of discrimination,

[1] 'Holy Slight: How Russia Prosecutes for "Insulting Religious Feelings"' *Radio Free Europe Radio Liberty* (15 August 2017) at www.rferl.org/a/russia-prosecuting-insults-to-religious-feelings/28678284.html. This 2013 law has been applied against people for acts like posting social media memes that allegedly contain hate speech and insult religious believers: 'Mail.Ru Calls for changes to Russian Hate Speech Legislation' *Radio Free Europe Radio Liberty* (6 August 2018) at www.rferl.org/a/russian-woman-faces-prison-over-insulting-religious-feelings/29415163. html. See Mikhail Antonov and Ekaterina Samokhina, 'The Realist and Rhetorical Dimensions of the Protection of Religious Feelings in Russia' (2015) 40 *Review of Central and East European Law* 229.

[2] In Russia, some have called for the criminal prosecution of a regional lawmaker under these laws for insulting the religious feelings of communists in suggesting that Lenin's preserved body, on public display at a mausoleum in Red Square, be buried in 2024: 'Communists' Religious Feelings were Violated by Proposal to Replace Lenin's Body, Party Officials Say' *The Moscow Times* (Moscow, 27 November 2018) at www.themoscowtimes.com/2018/11/27/ communists-religious-feelings-were-violated-by-proposal-replace-lenins-body-party-official-says-a63619.

hostility or violence towards a religious group,[3] as distinct from being merely offensive.[4]

The framers of the 1860 Code (in relation to clause 282)[5] stated that they wished to allow 'all fair latitude to religious discussions', while preventing the abuse of this as a pretext to issue 'intentional insults to what is held sacred by others'.[6] What would fall outwith the ambit of this offence included a 'warm expression dropped in the heat of controversy' or an argument advanced in good faith to vindicate one's own creed, not to insult and annoy adherents of another creed.[7] Legislation is a site where competing tensions are negotiated in a field of human activity. Lord Thomas Macaulay, the architect of the Penal Code, said the underlying principle, 'that every man should be suffered to profess his own religion, and that no man should be suffered to insult the religion of another', was a desirable universal principle, and one from which the British Government in India 'cannot depart without risking the dissolution of society'.[8] The intent was to protect religious and expressive freedoms, while affording some protection from religious insult or wounding to protect social cohesion, which implicates communal identity and solidarity.

These 'religious insult' laws address emotions in the form of feelings of offence as a sort of moral damage. The compatibility of such laws within secular states committed to religious freedom and religious pluralism, where in general all religions are treated impartially, comes into question, as does their impact on expressive and religious freedoms. There is an unresolved tension between the French trinity of values: of *liberty* in the form of expressive and religious freedoms, of *equality* in terms of how the state treats religion, whether preferentially or similarly, and of *fraternity or solidarity*, where laws guarding against religious wounding speak to ideas of community tolerance and identity. The RPC laws, which in their roots bear some affiliation to blasphemy laws while departing from certain presuppositions underlying such laws, implicate the

[3] International Covenant on Civil and Political Rights (adopted 16 December 1966, entered into force 23 March 1976) 999 UNTS 171 (ICCPR), Art 20(2): 'Any advocacy of national, racial or religious hatred that constitutes incitement to discrimination, hostility or violence shall be prohibited by law.' See Jocelyn Maclure, 'The Regulation of Hateful and Hurtful Speech: Liberalism's Uncomfortable Predicament' (2017) 63(1) *McGill Law Journal* 133.

[4] A distinction was drawn between offensive and hate speech in *Mariya Alekhina v Russia* App No 38004/12 (ECtHR, 17 July 2018), para 225.

[5] Indian Penal Code, cl 282: 'Whoever, with the deliberate intention of wounding the religious feelings of any persons utters any word or makes any sound in the hearing of that person, or makes any gesture in the sight of that person, or places any object in the sight of that person, shall be punished with imprisonment of either description for a term which may extend to one year, or fine, or both.'

[6] Thomas B Macaulay, *The Complete Works of Thomas Babington Macaulay (Illustrated)*, 1st edn (Delphi Classics, 2016) note J.

[7] Thomas B Macaulay, *A Penal Code Prepared by the Indian Law Commissioners, and Published by Command of the Governor General of India in Council* (The Lawbook Exchange, 2002) 43.

[8] Macaulay, *The Complete Works* (n 6), note J.

broader question of how religion and religiously committed citizens are treated within secular democracies.

This chapter examines the role, rationale and assumptions of laws that regulate religious feelings, whether through targeting the manner of expression or the material content of 'offensive' speech and action. It considers the implications this has for freedoms or liberties, particularly free conscience, speech and religious liberty, and the extent to which law or cognate 'soft law' methods can promote liberty, nurture tolerant self-restraint and resilience, and secure effective pluralism and social cohesion. It examines the object the law seeks to protect – 'religious feelings' – and the vision this assumes of the citizen as a religious person. Rather than the reasonable person who acts rationally, with deliberation, laws protective of religious feelings and religious harmony address the 'emotional man' who reacts with passion, impulsively. The goals of securing liberty and protecting religious feelings foreground both the Apollonian restraint and the Dionysian impulse, where Apollo (the Greek god of light) and Dionysus (the Greek god of wine) are used as metaphors for the struggle between two forces that define the human condition. The Apollonian predilection is for individualistic rationality, thought before action, self-restraint, and maintaining a critical intellectual distance. The Dionysian impulse is towards irrationality, passion, a diminished sense of responsibility to the collective, immersion in a more primitive state of being and primordial tribal unit. Examining the law on religious offences provides insight into how law, viewed as embodying right reason and rationality, relates to emotions in the form of religious feelings.

Section II of this chapter examines the idea of 'religious feelings'. Laws that protect against the insult or 'wounding' of religious feelings beg the question of what the nature of this harm is, why it is privileged against non-religious feelings, whether the degree of hurt can be measured or quantified, and why and to what extent the law should protect the feelings or emotions of its subjects. Section III addresses the question of how and why law regulates religious sensitivities, the role of law in relation to preventing public disorder, promoting religious harmony as a facet of community identity, and protecting the equality of religions as an application of the principle of secularity, tolerance and religious pluralism. In particular, how does law regulate religious feelings within the context of rights protection? Does it rest on a right not to be religiously offended, which is at odds with liberal precepts but which may be accommodated more comfortably in communitarian settings that prize honour and dignity? How are the competing interests conceptualised, weighted and accommodated within a secular democracy? If a chief object of RPC laws is to preserve civil peace, aside from the 'command and control' model of law, do they play an integrative role in solidifying community norms by identifying and punishing anti-social and unlawful behaviour? How different are RPC laws from blasphemy laws, in which is located their genealogical root? Section IV offers concluding observations on the necessity and peril of RPC laws within plural secular states in Asia, which have religious societies and religious diversity, and where both the private and social dimensions of religion are apprehended as a constant feature in the socio-politico landscape.

II. RELIGIOUS FEELINGS

A. Law and Emotions

The deployment of law to regulate how religious feelings are treated is based on a particular vision of the subject, the religious person, and the duties other members of a secular polity might owe to said person. While the common law deploys the device of the 'reasonable person' to set standards for personal interactions and transactions,[9] the rational man is not the only occupant in this village of legal personages.[10] Laws protective of religious feelings and religious harmony address the 'emotional man', who responds to challenges or insults against his religious beliefs with passion and excess, which may engender chaos, even violence. Contrast this with the equanimity and epidermal density that a 'rational' man would display in tolerating viewpoints critical of his own, as he values free speech as an aid to goals and goods such as the pursuit of truth, self-development or facilitating democratic government. This raises the question of how law deals with feelings in general, and with religious feelings specifically.

We feel emotions. While closely interconnected, feelings are different from emotions. Emotions come before feelings, and are responses occurring in the amygdala (in the subcortical region of the brain) that trigger biochemical reactions in the body, altering the physical state and bringing about such physical reactions as 'fight or flight'. Emotions are universal to humans but may be particularly expressed. Feelings are 'mental associations and reactions to emotions', and are shaped by subjective factors such as memory, experience and personal belief.[11] Mortimer Seller asserts that 'reason differs from emotion as a motive

[9] The 'reasonable man' plays a standard-setting role in many areas of the law, such as cases involving constitutional rights like free speech and political defamation (whether an ordinary reasonable person hearing a defamatory statement would think less of a person) and in administrative law, in relation to the *Wednesbury* test and the 'reasonable public authority' or the rule of bias, which asks whether a 'reasonable and fair-minded person' sitting in court and knowing the relevant facts would harbour a 'reasonable suspicion' that a fair trial would not be possible. The reasonable man is the rational man, who makes decisions on an objective basis, able to perceive the greater good. He thinks through the consequences before taking action, acts in a deliberate and measured fashion, and displays an Apollonian self-restraint.

[10] At common law, the 'reasonable man' is one of the chief residents of 'the select group of personalities who inhabit our legal village and are available to be called upon when a problem arises that needs to be solved objectively': *Helow v Advocate General* [2008] 1 WLR 2416 (HL), 2417–18 (Lord Hope).

[11] Neuroscience professor at the University of Southern California, Antonio Damasio distinguished between 'feelings' and 'emotions' thus, 'Feelings are mental experiences of body states, which arise as the brain interprets emotions, themselves physical states arising from the body's responses to external stimuli. (The order of such events is: I am threatened, experience fear, and feel horror.)': Jason Pontin, 'The Importance of Feelings' *MIT Technology Review* (17 June 2014) at www.technologyreview.com/2014/06/17/172310/the-importance-of-feelings/. See Marinella Coco

to action, because reason begins with axioms, asserted as true, while emotions begins with feelings, accepted as real'.[12] In other words, while emotions express a 'personal condition', reason seeks an 'external reality',[13] and in seeking, truth is 'always subject to revision in the face of better evidence'.[14] While action shaped by 'reason' is reflective and deliberate, that shaped by emotion is impulsive, spontaneous, unrestrained – at least, that is the stereotypical account.

Passion or emotions are conventionally viewed in the Enlightenment tradition as the antithesis of reason, rationality and objectivity, a product of the unconscious or uncontrollable impulses, such that 'emotions are impervious to argument or reason', being more a matter of taste or preference.[15] This worldview, which is challenged by the 'law and emotions' school,[16] inhabits the realm of a concept of law that casts religion as law's pre-modern 'other', rather than as law's interlocutor. That law is seen as purely rational is viewed by some as a product of modernity, as the history of the West 'is the history of increasing emotional restraint. The modern period brought with it self-discipline, control and suppression.'[17] This dichotomised vision of 'law as reason'/'emotion as passion' has been shown to be an 'unhelpful myth',[18] not in accord with more scientific understandings of emotions beyond feeling and affect. However, this binary stereotype continues to exert a dominant influence in the legal imagination when it comes to the criminalisation of religious offences. A more nuanced perspective would see reason and emotion as responses lying along a continuum, rather than reductively as 'a set of quick intense, uneducable and unreflexive bursts of feeling'.[19] Plato, for example, embraced the interconnection between feeling and thinking: 'Emotions, after all, are things that we feel; at the same time, emotionally is how we often think.'[20] This appreciates the role of emotions in legal decision-making, as integral to practical reasoning, and in establishing legitimacy, as well as the role of reason in determining when emotions 'are useful or appropriate, and when they are not',[21] aligning emotional responses with 'reason and reality'.[22]

et al, 'Emotions Are the Rudder of Our Lives: Intensity and Duration in Young Adults' (2017) 1 *Proceedings* 867.

[12] Mortimer NS Sellers, 'Law, Reason and Emotion' in Mortimer NS Sellers (ed), *Law, Reason and Emotions* (Cambridge University Press, 2017) 19.

[13] ibid.

[14] ibid 30.

[15] Patricia Mindus, 'The Wrath of Reason and the Grace of Sentiment: Vindicating Emotion in Law' in Sellers (ed), *Law, Reason and Emotions* (n 12) 216.

[16] See, eg, Kathryn R Abrams and Hila Keren, 'Who's Afraid of Law and the Emotions?' (2009-2010) 94 *Minnesota Law Review* 1997; Jennifer Schweppe and John Stannard, 'What is So Special About Law and Emotions?' (2013) 64(1) *Northern Ireland Legal Quarterly* 1.

[17] Andras Sajo, 'The Constitutional Domestication of Emotions' in Sellers (ed), *Law, Reason and Emotions* (n 12) 57.

[18] ibid 58.

[19] Mindus, 'The Wrath of Reason' (n 13) 225.

[20] Anthony W Price, 'Emotions in Plato and Aristotle' in Peter Goldie (ed), *Oxford Handbook of Philosophy of Emotion* (Oxford University Press, 2009) 140.

[21] Sellers, 'Law, Reason and Emotion' (n 12) 12.

[22] ibid.

Laws, which serve human persons, are shaped by assumptions about human beings and how they act and react to their environment. It is clear that societies are 'full of emotions which affect collective action', whether this be empathy, happiness, sadness, indignation, shame, anger, repulsion, fear, remorse.[23] It is also clear that law does deal with the reality found in 'the architecture of human emotions'.[24] For example, 'anger' is relevant to the defence of provocation; tortious and contractual damages are awarded for harassment, nervous shock and mental distress. Even the separation of powers as a constitutional law doctrine is based on the fear of autocratic government and concentrated powers.[25] In countries with histories of racial and religious riots, fear may also be directed at the prospect of a lack of order and weak or biased government unable to protect religious minorities.

B. Religious Feelings: What Stuff' Tis Made Of, Whereof it is Born

Emotions and feelings are a part and parcel of human life. To speak in terms of wounding religious feelings is to presume an emotional harm, a form of intangible damage suffered by one, afflicted through words, sounds or gestures.

A range of emotions may be involved in a 'wounding religious feelings' incident, and the law decides which to penalise and which to protect, as the best legislation 'will take our human emotions into account'.[26] Loyalty (*pietas*) to one's religion or love (*caritas*) for one's god makes one sad when one's religious beliefs are criticised or mocked, as well as angry towards or disgusted with the offender, which is an emotion directed at another. If one is a member of a minority group, the constant ridicule of one's faith, which touches one's deepest feelings, especially where personal identity is closely bound up with religious identity and ethnicity,[27] may injure one's sense of self. This may provoke emotions directed at the self, such as shame, a sense of inferiority, guilt or embarrassment.[28] This may inhibit the ability of these persons to participate as full members of society, presenting a democratic rationale for restraining religiously offensive speech.[29]

[23] Daniel Mendoca, 'Rights, Reason and Emotion: Conflict and Balance of Rights' in Sellers (ed), *Law, Reason and Emotions* (n 12) 140. See Kathryn R Abrams, 'The Progress of Passion' (2002) 100 *Michigan Law Review* 1602, 1603–07.

[24] Sellers, 'Law, Reason and Emotion' (n 12) 21.

[25] Andras Sajo, 'Emotions in Constitutional Design' (2010) 8(3) *International Journal of Constitutional* Law 354.

[26] Sellers, 'Law, Reason and Emotion' (n 12) 15.

[27] eg, for Sikhs and Sikhism.

[28] For a discussion of the range of emotions and feelings, see Jonathan Haidt, 'The Moral Emotions' in Richard J Davidson, Klaus R Scherer and HH Goldsmith (eds), *Handbook of Affective Sciences* (Oxford University Press, 2003) 852.

[29] In the aftermath of the *Jylland Posten* cartoons of the Prophet Muhammad of 30 September 2005, some suggested that the cartoons discriminated against Muslims in Western societies and hindered their integration into society: Meital Pinto, 'What are Offences to Feelings Really About? A New Regulative Principle for the Multicultural Era' (2010) 30(4) *OJLS* 695, 696.

Conceptually speaking, what then are 'religious feelings'? In criminalising the wounding of religious feelings, how do we know when such feelings are insulted or wounded? Is there a way of measuring feelings precisely, or is there no need to distinguish between grave and serious harms in this respect? Between the temporary quality of feelings that come and go and the degree of intangible harm inflicted? In normative terms, how much weight should be accorded to hurt religious feelings in making political and legal decisions that restrict the behaviour of others – should they be protected as a human right, public good, solidarity interest?

Statman suggests that religious feelings 'express the believers' attitude towards God and towards the various laws and institutions of their religion'.[30] This may involve a sense of awe, reverence or piety in the worshipper, or devotion in obeying dietary laws, religious holy days, fasting obligations, etc. To be religiously offended when another person shows contemptuous disrespect for the victim's belief system and religious practices, or denigration through derogatory words, reflects the strong sense of attachment to sacred values and institutions that inform one's personal identity; the action of the offender is seen to somehow harm or weaken religious feelings. Such critical expressive acts may range from even-tempered academic inquiry, to mocking, satire and ridicule and other forms of provocative speech, including vulgar invective. If my car runs over your leg, your leg will certainly be weakened, and one can easily distinguish between the gravity of harm in the form of a superficial scratch and a broken bone. However, while my critical words against your religion may hurt your feelings, they may actually fortify your religious commitments and strengthen your religious feelings, even invoke a depth or intensity of feelings that was 'quite latent, if not dormant, until the perceived hurting behavior took place'.[31] Statman suggests that it is best to understand 'wounding' religious feelings as generating 'painful feelings', in the same way that individuals who run a corporate entity may be 'emotionally affected' by allegations of impropriety or words of insult against that corporate entity, which constitute a nuisance.[32] People are made to feel bad, particularly where their cherished beliefs, value system and sacred symbols are trashed, which may engender a sense of humiliation and insult that affects their sense of value and self-respect. It shows a dependency on the views of others.

Not all feelings are protected by law. Statman distinguishes between wounded religious feelings caused 'by merely thinking about the behavior of others' and cases where 'feelings are hurt by the deliberately offensive behavior of others'.[33] An example of the former might be the anger an Orthodox Jew might feel towards other Jews who do not keep kosher; leading pigs in front of a mosque

[30] Daniel Statman, 'Hurting Religious Feelings' (2000) 3 *Democratic Culture* 199, 200.
[31] ibid 201.
[32] *Chee Siok Chin v Ministry of Home Affairs* [2006] 1 SLR (R) 582 (HC), paras 65–66.
[33] Statman, 'Hurting Religious Feelings' (n 30) 205.

or burning a cross on a church lawn are examples of the latter. An intermediate scenario may be where a person in a restaurant orders a pork dish and is seated next to a Muslim or Jew whose religious feelings might be hurt, even if this is not the customer's intent. Statman describes this as 'incidental hurting'.[34] He adds that claims about hurt feelings are 'wholly parasitic' on claims that the offender's behaviour is wrong and unfair and therefore send a message of disrespect for the victim.[35]

Perhaps the most fruitful approach is to take a historical and 'harm'-oriented approach rather than to attempt abstract definitions of hurt religious feelings. One could enquire as to the typical cases where religious feelings are hurt and posit reasons why religious feelings seem to be hurt more often or more deeply (if this is the case in warranting a criminal offence) than other sorts of feelings. This could stem from the vulnerability of a religious minority group within a multi-religious setting where the dominant religious group wields political power, or the 'special sensitivity' of a formerly dominant religious group now threatened by a secular government and materialist culture.

Examples of cases where religious feelings were offended include:

- Singapore – parodying a halal logo and displaying it next to a pig's head on a web blog;[36]
- Malaysia – inviting Muslims to break fast with *Bak Kut Teh* (pork bone soup) during Ramadan was considered an insult to Muslims;[37]
- Philippines – disrupting a service in Manila Cathedral to protest the Catholic Church's stance on reproductive rights by holding a sign with the words 'Damaso', referring to a villainous priest in a novel by Jose Rizal, *Noli Me Tangere*;[38]
- Nepal – some persons were arrested for preaching Christianity and allegedly attempting to secure converts, thereby 'hurting religious sentiments';[39]
- Austria – holding a seminar where it was stated that Muhammad was a paedophile as he had a 9-year-old wife;[40]

[34] ibid 205.

[35] ibid 207.

[36] *Public Prosecutor v Koh Song Huat Benjamin* [2005] SGDC 272, para 11.

[37] *Tan Jye Lee & Anor v Public Prosecutor* [2014] 1 LNS 860 (Court of Appeal). The s 298A(1) charge was dropped on grounds that it did not apply to non-Muslims and Tan was convicted under the Sedition Act.

[38] *Carlos Celdran y Pamintuan v People of the Philippines* GR No 220127 (Supreme Court, 21 March 2018). Celdran was found guilty of violating s 133 of the Penal Code, which provides a crime is committed by 'anyone who, in a place devoted to religious worship or during the celebration of any religious ceremony, shall perform acts notoriously offensive to the feelings of the faithful'.

[39] 'Nepal's Criminalisation of Conversion a 'Direct Infringement' of Religious Freedom' *World Watch Monitor* (20 September 2018).

[40] *ES v Austria* App No 38450/12 (ECtHR, 25 October 2018). Art 188 of the Austrian Criminal Code ('Disparagement of religious doctrine') provides that 'Whoever, in circumstances where his or her behaviour is likely to arouse justified indignation, publicly disparages or insults a person who, or an object which, is an object of veneration of a church or religious community established

- Russia – insulting religious feelings by playing Pokemon Go on a smartphone in church, photo-shopping the face of Jesus on an SS uniform, and lighting a cigarette from a candle in a Russian Orthodox Church and posting a public online photo of this;[41] an atheist was charged with 'insulting the religious feelings of believers' by posting 'There is no God' in the comments section of a website;
- Israel – traffic running through an Orthodox Jewish neighbourhood in Jerusalem on the Sabbath, disrupting the desired Sabbath atmosphere the residents wanted;[42]
- Muslim-majority countries like Indonesia and Malaysia – the claim by minority groups like Ahmadis that they are Muslims, contrary to mainstream Islam, which holds that Muhammad is the final prophet, not Mirza Ghulam Ahmad.

Clearly, instances of invoking religious offence present a threat to the enjoyment of religious freedom; this includes the right to propagate faith, which would include challenging the veracity of any other faith, given the mutual exclusivity of competing truth-claims. The difficulty then is to decide when religiously offended feelings should be protected. Are restrictions to be based on content or manner of expression? Whether conceptualised as a right, duty or public good, 'freedom from offence' cannot be absolute, as other competing principles and rights are at stake. For example, a person of religious faith cannot in a democratic society expect to enjoy immunity from all criticism but must tolerate opposing views hostile to his faith; this is part of the price of living in a plural society, provided it does not rise to the level of incitement to religious intolerance or hatred.

The RPCs do not purpose to guide or shape emotions by law but to vindicate and thereby validate the injury done to religious feelings. In associating 'religion' with 'feeling', this appears to buttress the dichotomised understanding of 'law as reason' and 'religion as passion'. In secularising societies, where religious groups cannot directly protect their values, invoking laws on hurt religious feelings becomes an 'alternative resource'[43] to justify demands for restricting the behaviour of others.

within the country, or a dogma, a lawful custom or a lawful institution of such a church or religious community, shall be liable to up to six months' imprisonment or a day-fine for a period of up to 360 days.' In 2010, an Austrian man was convicted for disparaging religious symbols because he yodelled while mowing his lawn, apparently mocking the call of the muezzin and ridiculing the beliefs of his Muslim neighbours: Alex Hall, 'Austrian Man Convicted for Yodelling while Muslim Neighbours Prayed' *The Telegraph* (16 December 2010) at www.telegraph.co.uk/news/ worldnews/ europe/austria/8207015/Austrian-man convicted-for-yodelling-while-Muslim-neighbours-prayed.html.

[41] Art 148 of the Russian Criminal Code relates to the illegal obstruction of the activity of religious organisations or the performance of religious rites: see n 1.

[42] *Horev v Minister of Transportation* [1997] IsrLR 153 (Supreme Court); Statman, 'Hurting Religious Feelings' (n 30) 201.

[43] Statman, 'Hurting Religious Feelings' (n 30) 214.

III. LAW, FREEDOM AND RELIGIOUS FEELINGS

One of the functions of law is to regulate, which may be described as 'the employment of legal instruments for the implementation of social-economic policy objectives',[44] where the relevant actors may be compelled by legal sanction to comply with the prescribed behaviour. It is about bringing to bear a legal framework upon a sphere of social activity.

To have legislation dealing with 'feelings', which relate to emotions, is to identify a species of vulnerability ('religious feelings') and make it a trait of a category of persons (religious persons) whom everyone should know and have responsibilities towards. The law thereby imputes a certain trait to a class of people, whether or not members of that class actually have that trait, that is, a sensitivity that results in hurt religious feelings. Claims based on offence to religious feelings require legal intervention to either prohibit, regulate or limit religiously offensive communications. Beyond a 'control and command' Hobbesian vision of law, laws that protect religious feelings must, to have legitimacy, be accepted as an expression of right reason in permitting or prohibiting conduct in service of the common good.[45] Such laws must be viewed as making society better off. The premise of religious offences in the Penal Code is that law should protect 'religious believers from outrage to their feelings from relevantly offensive material being in circulation, in the interest of a social value of maintaining respect for a sense of reverence for the sacred'.[46] This relates to the ideal of community, one where religion is taken seriously and protected. The strength of support for such law, which impacts constitutional liberties, is related to the 'social status of religion'.[47]

Contemporary 'hate speech' or 'religious insult' laws trace their origins to blasphemy laws but depart from them in distinct ways. Indeed, in jurisdictions where religion does not enjoy the high public status it once did, formerly powerful religious groups can no longer invoke blasphemy laws to restrict the behaviour of others against their religion. Resort is thus had to a new basis to restrict the behaviour of others, to control the narrative of a religion in the face of alternative claims by 'deviant' sects. The following section briefly examines the nature of blasphemy law in common law countries, and how it has evolved over time from a law about heresy[48] to a law about civility that serves to promote

[44] Johan A den Hertog, 'General Theories of Regulation' in Johan A den Hertog (ed), *Encyclopedia of Law and Economics* (Utrecht University, 1999) 223.

[45] Sellers, 'Law, Reason and Emotion' (n 12) 21.

[46] Clive Unsworth, 'Blasphemy, Cultural Divergence and Legal Relativism' (1995) 58(5) *Modern Law Review* 658, 666.

[47] ibid.

[48] In *Taylor's Case* (1676) 3 Keb 607, 621, Sir Matthew Hale CJ said '[S]uch kind of wicked blasphemous words were not only an offence to God and religion, but a crime against the laws, State and Government, and therefore punishable in this Court. For to say, religion is a cheat, is to dissolve all those obligations whereby the civil societies are preserved, and that Christianity is parcel of the laws of England; and therefore to reproach the Christian religion is to speak in subversion of the law.' These cases dealt with attacks against the Christian religion.

pluralism and counter religious extremism through nurturing social solidarity. The point of continuity and rupture with 'hate laws' and 'insult laws' can then be brought into sharper focus.

A. Antecedent: Blasphemy Law

Together with defamatory, seditious and obscene libel, blasphemy was historically one of four forms of criminal libel. In this context, libel refers to the desecration of sacred or respected objects, institutions or personages, with the historical focus being on 'the phenomenon traduced rather than injury to the audience'.[49] Later, words were considered blasphemous if they constituted 'an outrage upon the religious feelings of [the blasphemer's] fellow citizens' within the context of a plural society.[50]

Blasphemy laws date back to a pre-modern era when the law upheld the absolute truth of one particular religion, when there was no strict separation of state and religion and no entrenched right of religious freedom for all faiths. In England, this was the Christian religion and the rituals and doctrines of the Church of England. Originally a spiritual offence handled by ecclesiastical courts, it eventually came under the purview of secular courts and flows in the stream of moral authoritarianism through the state's role in policing morals, where the law took a clear position on what is right and wrong and privileged one religious worldview as being inherently right. The Church of England as the established church was considered a public institution, indeed part of the constitutional framework, and came under the protection of sedition law, which addresses incitement against government institutions. This shows the link between sedition and blasphemy law and, in certain Asian states, between sedition law and religious insult laws that address 'ill-will and hostility' against 'races and classes' and 'racial and religious groups'.[51] They share in common the instrumental role of reasserting 'traditional social discipline'.[52]

Blasphemy is irreverent or outrageous speech of a strongly offensive character that is against and vilifies the sacred. The offence of blasphemy does not require an intent to blaspheme, only the mental element of the intent to publish the offending words. The law against blasphemy criminalises speech that does not require a context of immediate unlawful violence. Lord Scarman in *Whitehouse v Lemon* did not consider a breach of the peace to be an element of the offence,[53] as opposed to a reminder of the character of the offence.[54] It evolved away from

[49] Unsworth, 'Blasphemy' (n 46) 663.
[50] *Whitehouse v Lemon* [1979] AC 617 (HL) 665 E–F (Lord Scarman).
[51] Sedition Act (Cap 290, Rev Ed 2013), s 3(1)(e); Penal Code (Cap 224, Rev Ed 2008), ss 298, 298A.
[52] Unsworth, 'Blasphemy' (n 46) 664.
[53] *Whitehouse v Lemon* (n 50) 656 (Lord Russell), 662 (Lord Scarman).
[54] The Law Commission, *Criminal Law: Offences against Religion and Public Worship* (HM Stationery Office, 1985) 3.

a focus on public order, where the established religion was considered to have a critical role in maintaining social morality as part of public order, to focus on the vilification of belief and protecting the feelings of Christians.[55] The harm was intangible in nature, the offence being so great as to cause mental distress that required criminal sanctions. Blasphemy was described as 'an act of violence to the mind and spirit and deeply spiritual feelings' of the millions of people 'capable of entertaining such feelings. It is an assault upon the mind and spirit just as much as mayhem is an assault upon the body.'[56] What distinguishes religious beliefs from other beliefs, necessitating special treatment for the former, was the 'special reverence' for the sacred, which made people more susceptible to offence for their religious as opposed to political beliefs.[57] Thus abusive attacks against God constitute 'the verbal equivalents of acts of desecration'.[58] For a believer, the sacred is 'identified primarily as the divine' and 'only incidentally in terms of his feelings towards it'.[59]

Furthermore, not all religiously contemptuous matters 'relating to God, Jesus Christ, or the Bible, or the formularies of the Church of England' were blasphemous. Opinions that were hostile to the Christian religion and denied the existence of God were not blasphemous, provided the publication 'is couched in decent and temperate language'.[60] The more outrageous or scurrilous the language used, the more likely it was to wound or outrage people's feelings than sober arguments, precipitating discord and even violence. If the tone in religious discussion were to be not sober, temperate and decent but became one of insult and ridicule, it would not be an appeal to judgement but 'an appeal to the wild and improper feelings of the human mind', particularly in 'the younger part of the community',[61] which would attract criminality.

[55] Lord Scarman in *Whitehouse v Lemon* (n 50, 658) argued that the blasphemy law should be kept and extended to 'protect the religious beliefs and feelings of non-Christians'. He later stated, extra-judicially, '[l]et us consign blasphemy to the legal historian and concentrate on public order': Leslie G Scarman, 'Letter' *The Daily Telegraph* (London, 14 April 1990) 12. Lord Diplock stated in *Whitehouse v Lemon* (n 50, 632D–E) that a blasphemous libel must be likely 'to shock and arouse resentment among believing Christians'. Lord Scarman identified the predominant rationale as material 'calculated … to outrage and insult the Christian's religious feelings' (ibid 662D).

[56] HL Deb, 23 February 1978, vol 389, col 290 (Earl of Halsbury, John AH Giffard).

[57] While religious belief frequently concerns a person, political beliefs are concerned with policy. Thus, while holding religious beliefs 'entails an unqualified reverence for God on the part of believers, the holding of particular political beliefs … does not usually entail a similar unqualified reverence for a person connected with or expounding those beliefs. Reverence for God may differ from reverence from a person not in kind but degree.' The Law Commission, *Criminal Law* (n 54) 22, para 2.41.

[58] Dinah Shelton and Alexandre Kiss, 'A Draft Model Law on Freedom of Religion with Commentary' in Johan David Van der Vyver and John F Witte (eds), *Religious Human Rights in Global Perspective: Legal Perspectives* (Kluwer Law, 1996) 591.

[59] Peter Jones, 'Blasphemy, Offensiveness and Law' (1980) 10 *British Journal of Political Science* 138.

[60] Lewis F Sturge, *Stephen's Digest of the Criminal Law*, 9th edn (Sweet & Maxwell, 1950), art 214, approved by Lord Scarman in *Whitehouse v Lemon* (n 50) 665F–H.

[61] *R v Hetherington* (1841) 4 St Tr NS 563 (HL) 590–91 (Lord Denman CJ).

The test related not to doctrinal substance but to 'the manner in which the doctrines are advocated'.[62] This protected religious freedom insofar as it left room for civilised religious debate, as, 'if the decencies of controversies are observed, even the fundamentals of religion may be attacked without the writer being guilty of blasphemy'.[63] And so blasphemy in England came to concern itself not primarily with religious truth and protecting the religious deity, personages and doctrine, but with good manners in promoting civility and tolerance to minimise incidents of religious offence-taking, to sustain the good order and the public tranquility of society

B. Religious Feelings in a Plural and Secular Age

Blasphemy laws operate within religious constitutional orders, which may be confessional rather than theocratic states, where a religion receives preferential treatment. This is essentially about protecting the truth of one religion, rather than protecting religious freedom; such laws suppress the views of minority religious groups or anti-theistic speech. A commitment to religious pluralism within religiously diverse societies is necessary to serve religious freedom, which is a pillar of civil peace, if not solidarity – both key public goods.

With the advance of the forces of secularism, pluralism and liberalism, blasphemy law was seen to be redundant. The dangers it sought to contend with, once imminent, had become negligible given the decline in public prestige of established religion and the view that the moral basis of society rested on religious grounds.[64] Calls came for its abolition[65] and replacement with an 'incitement to hatred' law,[66] or legislative expansion to protect other religions from 'scurrility, vilification, ridicule and contempt' as befitted an 'increasingly plural society such as that of modern Britain'.[67] Indeed, Lord Macaulay declared in Parliament, 'If I were a judge in India, I should have no scruple punishing a Christian who should pollute a mosque.'[68] When he became a legislator in India, a plural society, he took care to ensure 'the law protected the religious feelings of all'.[69] The focus shifted from defending the faith from criticism to maintain respect for religious truth in a way that privileged the feelings of one set of

[62] Sturge, *Stephen's Digest* (n 60) art 214, approved by Lord Scarman in *Whitehouse v Lemon* (n 50).

[63] *R v Boulter* (1908) 72 JP 188 (HC).

[64] US blasphemy laws administered by civil magistrates did not punish blasphemy as 'sins or offences against God, but crimes injurious to and having a malignant influence on society'. *Updegraph v Commonwealth* (1824) 11 Ser & Rawls 394, 409 (Supreme Court of Pennsylvania).

[65] The Law Commission, *Criminal Law* (n 54).

[66] See, eg, Racial and Religious Hatred Act 2006 on 'stirring up hatred against persons on religious grounds'.

[67] *Whitehouse v Lemon* (n 50) 658B–C (Lord Scarman).

[68] Thomas B Macaulay, *Speeches* (Redfield, 1922) 116, quoted by Lord Scarman in *Whitehouse v Lemon* (n 50) 658E–F.

[69] *Whitehouse v Lemon* (n 50) 658F (Lord Scarman).

religious people, to defending the religious feelings of all against deep disrespect and grave offence, through public order offences. The equal protection of religions rested on principles of secularism and pluralism.

Two ideas guided the laws protecting religious feelings: first, the degree of pain caused to the offended. Lord Macaulay considered the law that sanctioned insults to religion independent of the veracity of that religion. The object of protection was not religious truth but the 'real' pain given to professors of that religion, which was 'as acute a pain' as that caused by 'almost any offence against the person, against property, or against character'.[70] Second, the degree of resentment it would spawn where insults were traded as insults, which, unlike discussion, had no tendency to 'elicit truth'. Instead, the nature of religious debate was such that where insults, rather than discussion, were directed at 'erroneous opinions', these tended to entrench the views of those holding to these opinions. They tended 'to give a character of particular ferocity to theological dissension. Instead of eliciting truth, they only inflame fanaticism.'[71] Macaulay considered the fact of strong religion within religiously diverse societies and the religious excitement stirred, given the mutual exclusivity of faiths, noting the strong attachment of Muslims and Christians to their faiths and how they 'join in reprobating' Hindu doctrine and rites.[72] This state of affairs was 'pregnant with danger', which could only be 'averted by firm adherence to the true principles of toleration'.[73]

Blasphemy laws have been replaced or complemented by 'religious insults' or 'religious wounding' laws, or by 'incitement to hatred' laws, which requires the state to prohibit the advocacy of religious hatred that constitutes incitement to discrimination, hostility or violence, as under Article 20(2) of the ICCPR. Indeed, the Human Rights Committee has noted that 'prohibitions of displays of lack of respect for a religion … including blasphemy laws' were incompatible with the ICCPR, except for in the specific circumstances listed in Article 20(2). It was not permissible for such prohibitive laws to discriminate in favour of or against any religion or belief system, or to 'prevent or punish criticism of religious leaders or commentary on religious doctrine and tenets of faith'.[74] The Rabat Plan of Action (5 October 2012), authored by experts at workshops convened by the UN High Commissioner for Human Rights, on the prohibition of advocacy of national, racial or religious hatred that constitutes incitement to discrimination, hostility or violence, urges the repeal of blasphemy laws, as these 'have a stifling impact on the enjoyment of freedom of religion or belief, and healthy dialogue and debate about religion'.[75]

[70] Macaulay, *The Complete Works* (n 6), note J.
[71] ibid.
[72] ibid.
[73] ibid.
[74] UNHRC, 'General Comment No 34' (12 September 2011) CCPR/C/GC/34.
[75] 'Rabat Plan of Action' in UNHCR, 'Annual Report: Addendum – Report of the UN High Commissioner for Human Rights on the expert workshops on the prohibition of incitement to national, racial or religious hatred' (11 January 2013) A/HRC/22/17/Add.4, 11, para 25.

'Insult' and 'incite' laws are often used inter-changeably under the rubric of 'hate speech', though they can be distinguished. The latter relates to violence. In relation to the former, the rationale for RPC laws relates primarily to protecting public order and protecting the religious feelings of all from mental distress, where securing respect for religion and religious beliefs (as constitutional liberties) is a way of securing the fundamental decencies and mutual respect necessary for social cohesion. This is because allowing total freedom to offend religious feelings or insult religion would have a negative effect on harmony between racial, religious and non-religious groups, damaging community stability. Nonetheless, RPC provisions may restrict speech in a way that inhibits the search for religious truth and interests in individual self-determination. In relation to 'incite' laws, the Rabat Plan of Action advocated seeking guidance from Principle 12 of the Camden Principles on Freedom of Expression and Equality.[76] This identifies 'hatred' and 'hostility' as terms referring to 'intense and irrational emotions of opprobrium, enmity and detestation towards the target group'.[77] 'Incitement' concerns 'statements about national, racial or religious groups which create an imminent risk of discrimination, hostility or violence against persons belonging to those groups'.[78]

If blasphemy laws sought to control religious narrative through an interpretive monopoly held by a dominant religious group, both between and within religious faiths, the termination of one religion or religious sect as sole spiritual authority underwritten by state power, consonant with liberal state neutrality, opened the door to a multiplicity of religious narratives.[79] These narratives challenged and conflicted with the dominant one. This opens up another fault-line of religious conflict and outraged feelings, which is likely to continue given the longevity and continuing faith in the transcendent, even in secular states. The RPC laws may be weaponised by a majority religion claiming to be offended by a minority religion or sect and demanding government prosecution of the offender.

The criminalisation of offences against religion may be directed at the singular person whose religious feelings may be wounded, or corporately, in terms of causing 'disharmony' and feelings of enmity, hatred or ill-will between religious groups, which can escalate into the distinct problem of inciting violence against religious groups. The rationale for laws protecting religious feelings may

[76] 'The Camden Principles on Freedom of Expression and Equality' (*Article 19: Global Campaign for Free Expression*, April 2009) at www.article19.org/data/files/pdfs/standards/the-camden-principles-on-freedom-of-expression-and-equality.pdf. These principles were included in UNHRC, 'Draft General Comment No 34' (29 January 2010) UN Doc CCPR/C/GC/34/CRP.2, Art 19, para 53, and later deleted.

[77] 'The Camden Principles' (n 76) principle 12.1.

[78] ibid principle 12.3.

[79] Salman Rushdie argued that the row over *The Satanic Verses* 'was at bottom an argument about who should have power over the grand narrative, the Story of Islam, and that that power must belong equally to everyone': Salman Rushdie, 'Excerpts from Rushdie's Address: 1,000 Days "Trapped Inside a Metaphor"' *New York Times* (12 December 1991) at www.movies2.nytimes.com/books/99/04/18/specials/rushdie-address.html.

be variously viewed as efforts to preserve civil peace, to protect personal and group identity where informed by strong religious commitments, and to ensure harmony between multiple religious groups, facilitating healthy community relations. It may also relate to curtailing the influence of religious extremism and glorification of terrorism, which preys on a sense of social alienation or the siege mentality that is spawned when suspicion and hatred are fomented against a religious group; this may compromise the position of individual group members as members of broader society in good standing.

Lately, there have been efforts to legislatively insulate a religion from being questioned or disrespected, in the form of the problematic idea of 'defamation of religion', which arguably seeks to reintroduce blasphemy laws through the backdoor. This is anathema to freedom of critical inquiry and other human rights, as protection from religious hatred must not insulate religious discourse from critical opposition.[80] This necessitates a balance of the competing interests, such as whether other rights, like the right to evangelism, are affected, the extent and degree of offence given, whether premeditation or malice was involved or whether something is said carelessly or in the spur of the moment, incidentally rather than intentionally, whether the expression is sober and temperate or abusive and provocative, the degree to which public order is imperiled and whether sufficient protection is accorded to the cultural integrity of vulnerable minority groups.

C. The Impact of Religious Offences on Rights, Duties and Public Goods

One of the primary functions of law is to secure freedom, such as through the mechanism of rights that are balanced against competing rights, duties and goods. While free speech is not a primary right and may be restricted, human rights standards require that states wishing to proscribe speech must 'demonstrate in specific and individualised fashion the precise nature of the threat, and the necessity and proportionality of the specific action taken, in particular by establishing a direct and immediate connection between the expression and the threat'.[81]

The RPC laws are often riddled with vague, subjective terms that address threats to good order in an over-broad fashion, requiring no strong evidential basis to link the expression or conduct to the threat, leaving it in the realm of the pre-emptive and speculative. A plural society with a track record of riots seen to be caused by religious and racial offence provides the context to justify taking action against conduct that may or may not give rise to the danger but

[80] Niraj Nathwani, 'Freedom of Expression and Religious Feelings' (2012) 1 *Yearbook of Muslims in Europe* 507.
[81] UNHRC, 'General Comment No 34' (n 74) para 35.

which has the capacity to. For example, section 298 of the Singapore Penal Code is intention-based and does not require any actual wounding of religious feelings, provided there is a 'deliberate' intention to engage in the relevant conduct. Section 298A criminalises the use of words by a person to 'knowingly' promote disharmony on grounds of religion or race, or the commission of acts he knows is prejudicial to racial and religious harmony or that disturb or are likely to disturb public tranquility, which requires some objective proof of the requisite intent.

In seeking to protect religious sensitivities, RPC laws impact other public values, such as liberties like expressive freedoms. Restricting conduct or speech in this respect involves the legal imposition of a certain moral view associated with the offended people, contrary to the liberal principle of individual freedom.[82] What value, then, is to be assigned to protecting religious feelings, and does this give rise to an independent or parasitic right or interest not to be religiously offended?

i. Right of Free Expression, Freedom of Thought and Religious Freedom

If religious sensitivities are the proper object of legal protection and a restraint on freedom of speech, it cannot be sufficient just to advance 'religious sensitivities' *in abstracto* to justify the restraint; the necessity of interference must be shown, as opposed to assumed.[83] If being offended is an absolute justification for limiting free speech, this crushes free speech, which as a basic right should remain a right rather than an exception. Such claims must be limited to accepted grounds of derogation, such as inciting hate and tests of reasonableness or proportionality. Any RPC laws relating to religious feelings require either the objective element of having a tendency to bring about an undesirable state of affairs, and/or the subjective test of a certain intention that is deliberate, malicious, rather than careless.[84]

Free speech, if not given primacy, must not be unduly restricted, even if certain forms of speech are prohibited without requiring actual disorder or a causative

[82] Pinto, 'What are Offences to Feelings Really About? (n 29) 707.

[83] The Rabat Plan of Action suggests a list of factors to help identify whether the high threshold of 'the most severe and deeply felt form of opprobrium' is met, justifying restriction of speech that involves 'incitement to hatred': 'Rabat Plan of Action' (n 75) 11, para 29. This includes the context, status of the speaker, the requisite intent, the content and form of the speech such as the nature of arguments used, the extent of the speech or act such as the means of dissemination and size of potential audience, and the likelihood of risk of harm.

[84] In *Mahendra Singh Dhoni v Yerraguntla Shyamsunder* (2017) 7 SCC 760, a cricketer was charged with hurting religious sentiments under s 295A of the Penal Code for appearing on a 2013 magazine cover where he was portrayed as Lord Vishnu. The Indian Supreme Court (at para 7) said that not all 'insults' against a religion are offences, only those perpetrated with 'the deliberate and malicious intention of outraging the religious feelings of that class of citizens. Insults to religion offered unwittingly or carelessly or without any deliberate or malicious intention to outrage the religious feelings of that class do not come within the Section.'

element, depending on their character. In order to think freely and give voice to this, one assumes the risk of being offensive; as Rushdie puts it, 'freedom of thought is precisely freedom from religious control, freedom from accusations of blasphemy'.[85] Blasphemy laws 'may result in *de facto* censure' of all inter- and intra-religious beliefs, 'dialogue, debate and criticism, most of which could be constructive, healthy and needed'.[86] Furthermore, there are no human rights standards that include within religious freedom the right to have a religion or belief 'that is free from criticism or ridicule'.[87] The same applies for RPC laws. The symbiotic relationship between expressive and religious freedoms is seen in that freedom of speech is necessary in order to have 'constructive discussion about religions matters', as 'free and critical thinking in an open debate' is 'the soundest way to probe whether religious interpretations adhere to or distort the original values that underpin religious belief'.[88] This open scrutiny and debate of any and all belief systems is permissible, provided it does not involve advocating hatred that incites violence, hostility or discrimination against an individual or group, connoting a certain level of vehemence and intensity.

Part of religious freedom includes the freedom to teach religious doctrine and to propagate faith, within the usual constraints of public order. Social tensions may arise where, for example, an Ahmaddiya claims to be a Muslim, incensing mainstream Muslims and causing religious persecution in countries like Pakistan and Indonesia, where the Ahmadis are considered a deviant sect by the mainstream Muslim community.[89]

Within religiously diverse societies, it is intrinsic to religious belief to deem all contradictory, unorthodox or otherwise deviant religious doctrine and manifestations 'heretical' or at least misguided and erroneous.[90] The beliefs of one religion may malign or be extremely critical of another. As such, evangelism is seen to challenge the truth-claim of another religion, such that the mere act of propagating a faith to a person from another faith may impact religious

[85] Rushdie, 'Excerpts from Rushdie's Address' (n 79).

[86] 'Rabat Plan of Action' (n 75) 9, para 19.

[87] ibid.

[88] ibid 7, para 10.

[89] Krithika Varagur, 'Bleak outlook for Indonesia's Long Persecuted Ahmadiyya' *VOA News* (21 November 2017) at www.voanews.com/east-asia-pacific/bleak-outlook-indonesias-long-persecuted-ahmadiyya. In Pakistan, cases have been launched against Ahmadis for having minarets on their mosques or for reading the Quran or printing Quranic verses on wedding invitations. Mujib-ur-Rehman, an Ahmadi and lawyer, noted '[Outraging the sentiments of Muslims] is something that I am not doing, it is something that [the other person] is feeling. Now if I am sitting at home and reading the Quran, your sentiments are outraged. If I am watching a TV programme, your sentiments are outraged … Using this as a basis, anyone can do anything … I don't even know what the criminal actions are!' 'Pakistan's Ahmadiyya: An "Absence of Justice"' *Al Jazeera* (8 August 2014) at www.aljazeera.com/indepth/features/2014/08/pakistan-ahmadiyya-an-absence-justice-20148616414279536.html.

[90] Jeroen Temperman, 'Freedom of Expression and Religious Sensitivities in Pluralist Societies: Facing the Challenge of Extreme Speech' (2011) 3 *Brigham Young University Law Review* 729.

sensitivities, where every religious disagreement is disrespectful and hurtful.[91] For example, the antipathy towards religious propagation is captured in a statement by Bhutan Prime Minister Jigmi Yoser Thinley in 2011:

> The first premise [of seeking conversion] is that you believe that your religion is the right religion, and the religion of the convertee is wrong – what he believes in is wrong, what he practices is wrong, that your religion is superior and that you have this responsibility to promote your way of life, your way of thinking, your way of worship … It's the worst form of intolerance. And it divides families and societies.[92]

If the exercise of the right of religious propagation is viewed as an act of disrespect or hostile challenge that wounds religious feelings, the right would be rendered illusory. This highlights the problem with the idea of 'religious feelings', which has no clear definition and can mean almost anything where subjectively and contextually interpreted. Such open-textured clauses are open to government abuse.

ii. The Right Not to be Religiously Offended

In framing law, the first step is to 'understand what they want and feel, as determined by human emotion'.[93] Where one's religious beliefs are mocked or insulted, this is experienced as offensive, one of the most grave forms of ridicule, an attack against the sacred to whom one owes a duty of allegiance.[94] Citizens may desire that the law protect them from being religiously offended, by conferring rights and duties and some means of redress. If not, their complaints are reduced to expressions of distress, where they, like 'whining children',[95] may elicit pity but not respect. The language of rights and legal interests may help avoid the need to compare who is more wounded, or who whines more loudly. If the law provided no protection for deeply felt slights or injustices, it would stand to lose legitimacy, although in seeking to restrict the liberty of others for causing painful feelings, the victims of offence should consider why 'they think their feelings are justified, what claims about rights, equality and fairness underline their bad feelings'.[96]

It is not clear that the 'right' not to be offended has an independent legal value, though there have been judicial instances of a court's balancing the

[91] 'It is clear that a missionary or teacher, bona fide pursuing his calling, could not be indicted for any offence he might give to others.' John D Mayne, *Commentaries on the Indian Penal Code*, 10th edn (Higginbotham & Co, 1878) 244.

[92] 'Religious Conversion Worst Form of "Intolerance", Bhutan PM says' *Christian Post* (14 April 2011) at www.christianpost.com/news/religious-conversion-worst-form-of-intolerance-bhutan-pm-says.html.

[93] Sellers, 'Law, Reason and Emotion' (n 12) 30.

[94] Arthur Dobrin, 'Insulting Another's Religion and Free Speech' *Psychology Today* (21 September 2012) at www.psychologytoday.com/sg/blog/am-i-right/201209/insulting-anothers-religion-and-free-speech.

[95] Statman, 'Hurting Religious Feelings' (n 30) 208, 211.

[96] ibid 209.

constitutional right of free speech against 'the right of another's freedom from offence', the latter having no specified juridical status.[97] Such claims may be seen as adjuncts to existing rights, either as part of them or as limits to them, or as integral to the public order.

a. Part of Religious Freedom and the State Duty to Promote Tolerance

Claims have been articulated to the effect that religious freedom includes a demand that you respect my religion (as opposed to respecting religious freedom), that religiously offensive speech prevents a religious believer from freely exercising her right to religious freedom through breaching the right not to be insulted in their religious beliefs. In *ES v Austria*, the European Court of Human Rights found that states under the religious freedom guarantee in Article 9 of the European Convention on Human Rights had the positive obligation 'to ensure the peaceful co-existence of religious and non-religious groups and individuals under their jurisdiction by ensuring an atmosphere of mutual tolerance'.[98] Presenting objects of religious worship 'in a provocative way capable of hurting the feelings' of that religion's followers 'could be conceived as a malicious violation of the spirit of tolerance, which was one of the bases of a democratic society'.[99] If to be tolerant one must present one's views in a less provocative way, then this broad framing can encompass and suppress every instance of religious satire as being grossly displeasing, deeply hurtful and psychologically harmful. Freedom of religion, based on free conscience, does not require one to respect another's religion or belief, as the 'tenets of one man may seem the rankest error to his neighbour'.[100]

b. The Rights of Others as Limitation

The right not to be religiously offended has also been read into the 'rights of others' as a limit on expressive rights imposed by 'duties and responsibilities' on specified grounds, as is 'necessary in a democratic society', under Article 10(2) of the European Convention on Human Rights. In *ES v Austria*, the applicant was charged under Article 188 of the Austrian Criminal Code, which criminalises disparagement of religious doctrine.[101] She had at several public seminars made statements about Islam and the Prophet Muhammad; an undercover

[97] *Public Prosecutor v Koh* (n 36) para 8.

[98] *ES v Austria* (n 40) para 53.

[99] ibid.

[100] *Cantwell v Connecticut* 310 US 296 (1940) (Roberts J).

[101] Art 188 of the Austrian Criminal Code reads: 'Whoever, in circumstances where his or her behavior is likely to arouse justified indignation, publicly disparages or insults a person, who, or an object which, is an object of veneration of a church or religious community established within the country, or a dogma, a lawful custom or a lawful institution of such a church or religious community, shall be liable for up to six months imprisonment or a day-fine for a period of up to 360 days.'

journalist launched a criminal complaint for these statements, in which the applicant described Muhammad as a paedophile for marrying Aisha when she was six years old and consummating the marriage when she was nine. The Court noted the function of Article 188 was to prevent disorder 'by safeguarding religious peace as well as protecting religious feelings, which corresponds to protecting the rights of others' under Article 10(2).[102] The Court endorsed the Government's formulation of the aims of Article 188, concluding that the criminal conviction served the legitimate aim of 'maintaining order (protecting religious peace) and protecting the rights of others (namely their religious feelings)'.[103] Religious peace was related to the vague idea of peaceful co-existence,[104] and not having one's religious feelings hurt was deemed a right. While believers were to tolerate criticism against their faith, this crossed the line when gratuitous offence was given, which would violate the right not to have one's religious feelings hurt, which is open-ended. Reading Article 9 against Article 10(2), to ensure the peaceful enjoyment of Article 9 rights, the state owes a duty 'to avoid as far as possible an expression that is in regard to objects of veneration, gratuitously offensive to others and profane'.[105] It is not clear how to identify when religious criticism is protected speech that contributes to public debate, does not jeopardise public order or violate the rights of others through abusive attacks that incite hatred and religious intolerance.

Is there in any event a right to be religiously offensive, to use satire and ridicule as a tool to critique religion? Dworkin argued that in a democracy, no one, 'however powerful or important',[106] has a right not to be insulted or offended; from the liberal tradition that does not elevate religion over any ideology, the law should not protect mere insult to feelings, even if this is related to sacred things. Truth can be offensive, but in the interests of free speech as justified by the argument from truth, civil peace cannot, without more, trump truth. Indeed, if religious sensitivities are pandered to, will greater deference need to be paid to religious communities that are more sensitive to slights, whether because they are a vulnerable minority or because of the high degree of honour with which they hold their gods, canons and prophets, which makes them more intolerant of criticism and susceptible to taking offence? Is there an expectation that some degree of tolerance, of mature personal and social resilience within a faith community should be demonstrated in the face of critique and insults? Or should law assume the view of a more 'sensitive' person towards slights to his religion, as to what constitutes an offensive attack on that religion?

[102] *ES v Austria* (n 40) para 41.
[103] ibid para 36.
[104] Religious peace was to be understood as the peaceful co-existence of the various churches and religious communities with each other, as well as with those who did not belong to a church or religious community: ibid.
[105] *ES v Austria* (n 40) para 43.
[106] Ronald M Dworkin, 'The Right to Ridicule' (2006) 53(5) *New York Review of Books* 44.

Some might argue that it is good to harm religious sensitivities, that there may be some value to ridicule as 'a distinct kind of expression' whose 'substance cannot be repackaged in a less offensive rhetorical form without expressing something very different from what was intended'.[107] This is based on the liberal idea that imposing views on people who dissent without giving them an opportunity to express that dissent undermines human dignity and equal citizenship within a democracy. Mocking religiously venerated objects might be a way of protesting against a dominant religion or religious fundamentalism, or the coercive imposition of ideas of sacredness on others and demands to respect a religion;[108] a counter-objection is that this might not further understanding of human affairs, and the animosity provoked could escalate into a public order threat, where religious sensitivities are grossly discounted.

IV. BETWEEN OLYMPIAN RATIONALITY AND IMPASSIONED EMOTION, HUMAN CIVILITY

If man were possessed of an Olympian rationality, there would be no need for religious insult laws because he would appreciate the Millian arguments for free speech, particularly with respect to the search for religious truth. This would fuel an Apollonian restraint, even in the face of offence, in the interests of the greater good of intellectual and expressive freedoms. The motivating fear here is a fear of government oppression; and the antidote, rights as bulwarks against autocratic rule, whether of the theocratic or secular variety. This assumes that an individual's truth commitments are to be weighed more heavily than social harmony considerations, that unrestricted discussion is better than state-regulated discussion.

However, at the other end of the spectrum is the view of the religious man who experiences an attack on his religion as an attack on the adherents of that faith for the views they hold, threatening both personal and corporate identity. His response is not restraint but passionate, impulsive, emotional, the stuff that fuelled past and present tribalism and religious wars that fractured solidarity and peace. The state's response may be to protect religious feelings from being wounded. This is a problematical idea at the best of times given the definitional difficulties in relation to what a 'religion' is, and the practical difficulties of measuring the requisite degree of woundedness of feelings, whether of the elite or the rank and file of a faith community, with feelings being a temporary phenomenon. In this endeavour, rather than valuing a statement on the basis of its truth, the metric is altered to the question of whether such truth is likely to

[107] ibid.

[108] It was argued that the duty not to mock certain historical figures who founded a religion 'amounts to a duty to show respect for these personalities and arguably constitutes a duty to participate in a religious practice': Nathwani, 'Freedom of Expression and Religious Feelings' (n 80) 520.

offend minority groups who are perceived as somehow 'victimised'. This favours 'good manners' rather than robust, material debate in truth-seeking, which has fallen out of fashion in a postmodern age where there is no truth, only many personal truths.

An over-emphasis on protecting religious sensitivities by restricting the conduct of others as a curative to the fear of disorder and societal breakdown in the event distinct religious and ethnic groups cannot pacifically co-exist, is inimical to the enjoyment of fundamental liberties, a key aspect of constitutionalism. One might argue that within rights-respecting democracies, the only permissible limit on free speech is that found in Article 20(2) of the ICCPR, that is, insult likely to provoke violence or public disorder. Otherwise, one person's incisive comment on a religion is another's hate speech, where resentment drives one to violent action. If expression is too readily curtailed, there is no pressure then on the part of religionist to develop a higher degree of impulse control, pursuant to the requirements of a tolerant society. Anyone can then be offended by anything when the question of whether a statement is objectively offensive is replaced by the question of whether a statement is subjectively offensive to anyone.

Freedom, peace and solidarity are all public goods. Racial and religious harmony cannot be tackled by law alone; it requires inter-faith and inter-cultural dialogue, education and other non-legislative measures, and a conciliatory ethos in the face of social disputes, as an aggressive legalism can exacerbate agonistic social relations. In non-homogeneous societies, law has to negotiate ethnic and religious differences, and it is clear that that the government has a role to play in deploying law to keep the peace, and to foster civility, tolerance and restraint amongst its citizens. In regulating offensive speech, attention must be had to context and particularities, as the words that endanger societies vary across times, depending on whether 'society is stable or insecure' or whether 'its reasonable members' believe it to be 'open to assault'.[109] Whether a given opinion, no matter how religiously offensive, endangers society 'is a question of the times and is a question of fact'.[110] Writing in 1917, Lord Sumner considered that reasonable men 'do not apprehend the dissolution or downfall of society because religion is publicly assailed by methods not scandalous'.[111]

It seems there is both a necessity for and a peril in laws protecting religious feelings. Prudence would appreciate the power of offensive speech and of religious commitment, and accept the need for a legal response to expressions of hostility to religion in a world where religion is 'sociologically ineradicable'[112] and will continue to be an important feature of human life and of many conceptions of the human flourishing. Principle would guard against the erosion of expressive and religious freedoms. In this complex task, law can play a civilising

[109] *Bowman v Secular Society Ltd* [1917] AC 406 (HL), 466–67 (Lord Sumner).
[110] ibid 467.
[111] ibid.
[112] Unsworth, 'Blasphemy' (n 46) 673.

force, in punishing offensive speech that is premeditated, deliberate, malicious or provocative, while protecting sober, respectful rational and temperate speech. However, while disrespectful speech that is entirely insulting can have adverse social effects, temperately delivered destructive analysis or criticism of a religion can also bring about social harm.[113]

While laws protecting wounded religious feelings and insulted religious beliefs are important to avoid public disorder, this is 'not a sufficient answer' as 'the true reason is respect for other people's bona fide religious beliefs. Religious freedom is a human right. Interference with it is not to be tolerated.'[114] Religious and expressive freedom may well affect religious feelings, and communicating with civility helps to keep the conversation calm. While manners matter, ultimately truth matters more, and to serve that we cannot afford to think with our feelings. In seeking truth as part of religious freedom, we ought to communicate with decency and civility to ward off Dionysian impulses, as 'discarding reason undermines virtue by replacing virtue with emotion-based reactivity; discarding virtue undermines the social fabric necessary to undergird the effectiveness of reason'.[115]

BIBLIOGRAPHY

—— *Alekhina v Russia* App No 38004/12 (ECtHR, 17 July 2018), para 225
—— *Bowman v Secular Society Ltd* [1917] AC 406 (HL) 466-67 (Lord Sumner)
—— *Cantwell v Connecticut* [1940] 310 US 296 (Roberts J)
—— *Carlos Celdran y Pamintuan v People of the Philippines* GR No 220127 (Supreme Court, 21 March 2018)
—— *Chee Siok Chin v Ministry of Home Affairs* [2006] 1 SLR (R) 582 (HC), paras 65–66
—— Criminal Code of the Republic of Austria, Art 188
—— Criminal Code of the Russian Federation (No 63-Fz, 13 June 1996), Art 148
—— *ES v Austria* App No 38450/12 (ECtHR, 25 October 2018), paras 36, 41, 43, 63
—— *Helow v Advocate General* [2008] 1 WLR 2416 (HL), 2417–18 (Lord Hope)
—— HL Deb, 23 February 1978, vol 389, col 290 (Earl of Halsbury, John AH Giffard)
—— *Horev v Minister of Transportation* [1997] IsrLR 153 (Supreme Court)
—— Indian Penal Code, cl 282
—— International Covenant on Civil and Political Rights (adopted 16 December 1966, entered into force 23 March 1976) 999 UNTS 171 (ICCPR), Art 20(2)
—— *Mahendra Singh Dhoni v Yerraguntla Shyamsunder* (2017) 7 SCC 760
—— Penal Code (Cap 224, Rev Ed 2008), ss 298, 298A
—— *Public Prosecutor v Koh Song Huat Benjamin* [2005] SGDC 272, paras 8, 11
—— *R v Boulter* [1908] 72 JP 188 (HC)
—— *R v Hetherington* (1841) 4 St Tr NS 563 (HL) 590–91 (Lord Denman CJ)

[113] The Law Commission, *Working Paper No 79: Offences Against Religion and Public Worship* (HM Stationery Office, 1981) para 7.9.

[114] Lord Scarman, interviewed in Unsworth, 'Blasphemy' (n 46) 674.

[115] Ben Shapiro, 'What Right Not to be Offended?' *National Review* (24 January 2018) at www.nationalreview.com/2018/01/jordan-peterson-interview-offending-people/.

—— Racial and Religious Hatred Act 2006
—— Sedition Act (Cap 290, Rev Ed 2013), s 3(1)(e)
—— *Tan Jye Lee & Anor v Public Prosecutor* [2014] 1 LNS 860 (Court of Appeal)
—— *Taylor's Case* (1676) 3 Keb 607, 621 (Sir Matthew Hale CJ)
—— 'The Camden Principles on Freedom of Expression and Equality' (*Article 19: Global Campaign for Free Expression*, April 2009) at www.article19.org/data/files/pdfs/standards/the-camden-principles-on-freedom-of-expression-and-equality.pdf
—— The Law Commission, *Working Paper No 79: Offences Against Religion and Public Worship* (HM Stationery Office, 1981), para 7.9
—— The Law Commission, *Criminal Law: Offences against Religion and Public Worship* (HM Stationery Office, 1985) 3, 22
—— UNHRC, 'Rabat Plan of Action' in *Annual Report: Addendum – Report of the UN High Commissioner for Human Rights on the expert workshops on the prohibition of incitement to national, racial or religious hatred* (11 January 2013) A/HRC/22/17/Add.4, paras 10, 19, 25, 29
—— UNHRC, 'General Comment No 34' (12 September 2011) CCPR/C/GC/34, para 35
—— UNHRC, 'Draft General Comment No 34' (29 January 2010) UN Doc CCPR/C/GC/34/CRP.2, Art 19, para 53
—— *Updegraph v Commonwealth* (1824) 11 Ser & Rawls 394, 409 (Supreme Court of Pennsylvania)
—— *Whitehouse v Lemon* [1979] AC 617 (HL) 632D–E (Lord Diplock), 656 (Lord Russell), 662, 665, 658 (Lord Scarman)
Abrams, KR, 'The Progress of Passion' (2002) 100 *Michigan Law Review* 1602
—— and Keren, H, 'Who's Afraid of Law and the Emotions?' (2009-2010) 94 *Minnesota Law Review* 1997
Al Jazeera 'Pakistan's Ahmadiyya: An "Absence of Justice"' (8 August 2014) at www.aljazeera.com/indepth/features/2014/08/pakistan-ahmadiyya-an-absence-justice-20148616414279536.html
Antonov, M, and Samokhina, E, 'The Realist and Rhetorical Dimensions of the Protection of Religious Feelings in Russia' (2015) 40 *Review of Central and East European Law* 229
Christian Post, 'Religious Conversion Worst Form of "Intolerance", Bhutan PM says' (14 April 2011) at www.christianpost.com/news/religious-conversion-worst-form-of-intolerance-bhutan-pm-says.html
Coco, M, et al, 'Emotions Are the Rudder of Our Lives: Intensity and Duration in Young Adults' (2017) 1 *Proceedings* 867
den Hertog, JA, 'General Theories of Regulation' in Johan A den Hertog (ed), *Encyclopedia of Law and Economics* (Utrecht University, 1999) 223
Dobrin, A, 'Insulting Another's Religion and Free Speech' *Psychology Today* (21 September 2012) at www.psychologytoday.com/sg/blog/am-i-right/201209/insulting-anothers-religion-and-free-speech
Dworkin, RM, 'The Right to Ridicule' (2006) 53(5) *New York Review of Books* 44
Haidt, J, 'The Moral Emotions' in Richard J Davidson, Klaus R Scherer and HH Goldsmith (eds), *Handbook of Affective Sciences* (Oxford, Oxford University Press, 2003) 852
Hall, A, 'Austrian Man Convicted for Yodelling while Muslim Neighbours Prayed' *The Telegraph* (16 December 2010) at www.telegraph.co.uk/news/worldnews/europe/austria/8207015/Austrian-man-convicted-for-yodelling-while-Muslim-neighbours-prayed.html

Jones, P, 'Blasphemy, Offensiveness and Law' (1980) 10 *British Journal of Political Science* 138

Macaulay, TB, *Speeches* (Redfield, 1922)

——, *A Penal Code Prepared by the Indian Law Commissioners, and Published by Command of the Governor General of India in Council* (The Lawbook Exchange, 2002)

——, *The Complete Works of Thomas Babington Macaulay (Illustrated)*, 1st edn (Delphi Classics, 2016)

Maclure, J, 'The Regulation of Hateful and Hurtful Speech: Liberalism's Uncomfortable Predicament' (2017) 63(1) *McGill Law Journal* 133

Mayne, JD, *Commentaries on the Indian Penal Code*, 10th edn (Higginbotham & Co, 1878)

Mendoca, D, 'Rights, Reason and Emotion: Conflict and Balance of Rights' in Mortimer NS Sellers (ed), *Law, Reason and Emotions* (Cambridge University Press, 2017) 138

Mindus, P, 'The Wrath of Reason and the Grace of Sentiment: Vindicating Emotion in Law' in Mortimer NS Sellers (ed), *Law, Reason and Emotions* (Cambridge University Press, 2017) 202

Nathwani, N, 'Freedom of Expression and Religious Feelings' (2012) 1 *Yearbook of Muslims in Europe* 507

Pinto, M, 'What are Offences to Feelings Really About? A New Regulative Principle for the Multicultural Era' (2010) 30(4) *OJLS* 695

Pontin, J, 'The Importance of Feelings' *MIT Technology Review* (17 June 2014) at www.technologyreview.com/2014/06/17/172310/the-importance-of-feelings/

Price, AW, 'Emotions in Plato and Aristotle' in Peter Goldie (ed), *Oxford Handbook of Philosophy of Emotion* (Oxford University Press, 2009) 121

Radio Free Europe Radio Liberty, 'Mail.Ru Calls for changes to Russian Hate Speech Legislation' (6 August 2018) at www.rferl.org/a/russian-woman-faces-prison-over-insulting-religious-feelings-/29415163.html

——, 'Holy Slight: How Russia Prosecutes for "Insulting Religious Feelings"' (15 August 2017) at www.rferl.org/a/russia-prosecuting-insults-to-religious-feelings/28678284.html

Rushdie, S, 'Excerpts from Rushdie's Address: 1,000 Days "Trapped Inside a Metaphor"' *New York Times* (12 December 1991) at www.movies2.nytimes.com/books/99/04/18/specials/rushdie-address.html

Sajo, A, 'The Constitutional Domestication of Emotions' in Mortimer NS Sellers (ed), *Law, Reason and Emotions* (Cambridge University Press, 2017) 55

——, 'Emotions in Constitutional Design' (2010) 8(3) *International Journal of Constitutional* Law 354

Scarman, LG, 'Letter' *Daily Telegraph* (London, 14 April 1990) 12

Schweppe, J, and Stannard, J, 'What is So Special About Law and Emotions?' (2013) 64(1) *Northern Ireland Legal Quarterly* 1

Sellers, MNS, 'Law, Reason and Emotion' in Mortimer NS Sellers (ed), *Law, Reason and Emotions* (Cambridge University Press, 2017) 11

Shapiro, B, 'What Right Not to be Offended?' *National Review* (24 January 2018) at www.nationalreview.com/2018/01/jordan-peterson-interview-offending-people/

Shelton, D, and Kiss, A, 'A Draft Model Law on Freedom of Religion with Commentary' in edited by Johan David Van der Vyver and John F Witte (eds), *Religious Human Rights in Global Perspective: Legal Perspectives* (Kluwer Law, 1996) 559

Statman, D, 'Hurting Religious Feelings' (2000) 3 *Democratic Culture* 199

Sturge, LF, *Stephen's Digest of the Criminal Law*, 9th edn (Sweet & Maxwell, 1950)

Temperman, J, 'Freedom of Expression and Religious Sensitivities in Pluralist Societies: Facing the Challenge of Extreme Speech' (2011) 3 *Brigham Young University Law Review* 729

The Moscow Times, 'Communists' Religious Feelings were Violated by Proposal to Replace Lenin's Body, Party Officials Say' (Moscow, 27 November 2018) at www.themoscowtimes.com/2018/11/27/communists-religious-feelings-were-violated-by-proposal-replace-lenins-body-party-official-says-a63619

Unsworth, C, 'Blasphemy, Cultural Divergence and Legal Relativism' (1995) 58(5) *Modern Law Review* 658 Varagur, K, 'Bleak outlook for Indonesia's Long Persecuted Ahmadiyya'

VOA News (21 November 2017) at www.voanews.com/east-asia-pacific/bleak-outlook-indonesias-long-persecuted-ahmadiyya

World Watch Monitor 'Nepal's Criminalisation of Conversion a 'Direct Infringement' of Religious Freedom' (20 September 2018)

3

Making Islamic Penal Clauses: Translation, Transformation and Transmogrification

ARIF A JAMAL

I. INTRODUCTION

THE PENAL OR criminal aspects of Islamic law attract a lot of headline-grabbing attention, largely because they are seen as allowing, even mandating, harsh and cruel punishments, and doing so in an uncompromising and mechanical manner. Such attention, however, oversimplifies how Islamic criminal law provisions have been understood and practised, both in their classical formulation and certainly under the influence of colonialism and the advent of the modern state.

In this chapter, I will first discuss the context of how Islamic penal clauses have developed by drawing on studies of the application of these clauses historically. This discussion will show that there has been much debate about penal clauses, which betrays a simple narrative regarding both the content of these provisions, as well as their application. Second, I go on to consider the impact of the colonial experience and reformulation of Islamic penal clauses by examining two case studies of recent experiences in Pakistan and Malaysia. I conclude with a set of reflections about what these narratives tell us about Islamic penal clauses, which highlights how these clauses have been subject to a great deal of translation and transformation and a considerable process of transmogrification, especially through the agency of the state.

II. THE CLASSICAL CONTEXT

Discussion about almost any topic in Islamic law typically begins with reference to the text of the Qur'an, which is held by Muslims to be the word of God as revealed to the Prophet Muhammad. A second basic source of Muslim legal normativity is the Sunna; the traditions associated with Muhammad, usually recording what he did or said when faced with certain situations or questions. The Sunna is regarded as significant because of the special and unique position occupied by Muhammad as an exemplar for Muslims.

Within the corpus of the Sunna and the text of the Qur'an in particular, certain offences are delineated. These offences are referred to as the hudud offences. *Hudud* is the plural of the word *hadd*, which means a boundary or limit. There is rough consensus that there are six such *hudud* offences. The six *hudud* offences (and their corresponding penalties) are: theft (amputation of the hand), illicit sexual relations (death by stoning or 100 lashes), making unproven accusations of illicit sex (80 lashes), drinking intoxicants (80 lashes), apostasy (death or banishment) and highway robbery (death).[1] *Hudud* offences are the most consequential of the offences articulated within the Islamic framework because they are conceived of as 'crimes against God' broadly speaking, or violating the rights of God *(huquq Allah)* with punishments prescribed in the Qur'an.

The words *hadd* and *hudud* are used in several places within the text of the Qur'an. However, they are often not used in a penal sense. For instance, the Qu'ran says:

> These are the *limits* [set by] Allah, and whoever obeys Allah and His Messenger will be admitted by Him to gardens [in Paradise] under which rivers flow, abiding eternally therein; and that is the great attainment.
>
> And whoever disobeys Allah and His Messenger and transgresses His *limits* – He will put him into the Fire to abide eternally therein, and he will have a humiliating punishment.[2]

In both cases the emphasised word translated as 'limits' is in fact the term *hudud*, but not in a criminal law sense.[3]

At the same time, interestingly, the terms *hadd* or *hudud* are not used with respect to several of the so-called *hudud* offences. Hence, the Qur'an states the following when speaking about theft and its punishment:

> [As for] the thief, the male and the female, amputate their hands in recompense for what they committed as a deterrent [punishment] from Allah. And Allah is Exalted in Might and Wise.
>
> But whoever repents after his wrongdoing and reforms, indeed, Allah will turn to him in forgiveness. Indeed, Allah is Forgiving and Merciful.[4]

The words *hadd* or *hudud* are not found in the Qur'anic verses above, notwithstanding that theft and the accompanying punishment of amputation are firmly

[1] John L Esposito, 'Hadd' in John L Esposito (ed), *The Oxford Dictionary of Islam* (Oxford Islamic Studies Online 2020) at www.oxfordislamicstudies.com/article/opr/t125/e757 accessed 1 July 2020.

[2] Qur'an 4:13–14 (emphasis added) at https://quran.com/4.

[3] See a discussion of this point in Mohammed Khalid Masud, *Hudood Ordinance 1979: A Critical Report* (Council of Islamic Ideology, Government of Pakistan, 2007) 136–38.

[4] Qur'an 5:38–39 at https://quran.com/5.

in the category of what is considered to be a *hadd* offence. The issue of theft and the punishment have been mentioned in the Sunna materials, with *hadith* of the Prophet Muhammad confirming the punishment.

Similarly, when addressing the consumption of intoxicants, the most significant Qur'anic verses on this topic state:

> O you who have believed, indeed, intoxicants, gambling, [sacrificing on] stone altars [to other than Allah], and divining arrows are but defilement from the work of Satan, so avoid it that you may be successful.
>
> Satan only wants to cause between you animosity and hatred through intoxicants and gambling and to avert you from the remembrance of Allah and from prayer. So will you not desist?[5]

Again, while the consumption of intoxicants is considered a *hadd* matter, the Arabic terms *hadd* or *hudud* are not used in the above Qur'anic text. Additionally, using the above verses as an example, the Qur'anic text notably mentions three matters – *viz*, intoxicants, gambling and sacrificing other than to God. However, it is only the consumption of intoxicants that has been regarded as a *hadd* crime.

When one looks at the other major source of Islamic normativity, the Sunna, the context becomes even more complex. I refer to Sunna as the Prophetic Sunna – that is, the traditions of what was said or done that are attributed to the Prophet Muhammad. It is this Sunna, especially in the majority Sunni tradition of Islam, that has become a salient source of legal normativity, including that about the *hudud*. The terms *hadd* and *hudud* do appear in the Sunna. Thus, Mohamed Hashim Kamali notes several themes related to the discussion of *hadd* and *hudud* in the Sunna. These include the sense of *hadd* or *hudud* as transgressing the limits, as well as crime and punishment.[6] Nonetheless, overall, Kamali observed:

> Exploring these various aspects of the *hadith* literature relating to *hudud* will serve to show that a degree of diversity is present in the language of *hadith* on *hudud*. One does not, in other words, see the kind of predominantly punitive stress and lack of flexibility in the language of *hadith*, as one later finds developing in the juristic doctrine of the leading schools on *hudud*.[7]

Indeed, Kamali points out that in both the Qur'an and *hadith*, there is the mention of 'stricture as well as forgiveness', and that the Prophet 'tried, whenever he noted signs of remorse on the part of the culprit, to turn a blind eye to instances of *hudud*'.[8] In fact, there are several reports that the Prophet forgave the commission of a *hadd* act in the face of contrition. Moreover, in the face of uncertainty or doubt, with respect to a *hadd* act, it is recorded that the Prophet would suspend the *hudud* punishment.

[5] Qu'ran 5:90–91 at https://quran.com/5.

[6] Mohamed Hashim Kamali, *Crime and Punishment in Islamic Law* (Oxford University Press, 2019) 41.

[7] ibid.

[8] ibid 41–42.

The point to make in considering these accounts is simply that there has been an interpretive process of determining and stipulating *hudud* offences, and of using the term *hudud* for them, because of the sense of certain actions as violating the limits of God. In other words, the category of *hudud* offences or of *hudud*-meaning defined crimes is one that has been developed and constructed over time, drawing not only from the Qu'ran and Sunna but from other influences as well.

In terms of breaching the limits prescribed by God (*huquq Allah*), *hudud* offences may be distinguished from violations of the rights of people (*huquq adami*), which are also known to the tradition. Understandably for a legal system premised on the existence of God, violations of the rights of God are the most serious offences and accordingly attract the most serious penalties. However, it should be said that the *hudud* offences are not the only expressions of criminal offences understood in Islamic law. In addition to the *hudud*, there are also offences in non-*hudud* categories. These encompass retribution crimes or *qisas* (offences against persons) such as homicide, wounding and battery, *diya* (the possibilities for compensation for such injuries), *ta'zir* (discretionary punishments that may be imposed by the state both for acts that are sinful or forbidden), as well as *siyasa* (breaches of public order or state security). *Qisas* offences are based on retributive justice, and punished through just retaliation on a generally 'eye for eye' basis. *Ta'zir* offences are any other offences that should be deterred in society and call for discretionary punishments other than those prescribed for *hudud*. The focus in this discussion will largely be on the *hudud*.

Before talking further about the *hudud* as 'criminal' offences, the first question that must be dealt with is whether the categories of criminal or penal law are even appropriate when dealing with Islamic law. While it is certainly the case that Islamic law has known offences, both those considered severe and those considered less severe, some may question whether these offences known in Islamic law can be categorised as akin to the systems of criminal or penal law that are generally understood and practised today. Hence, Wael Hallaq has stated that it would be a mischaracterisation to label offences under the branch of the *shari'a* as 'criminal' or 'penal', since 'far from all [*shari'a*] infractions can be dealt with under modern notions of criminality'.[9] More significantly, Hallaq also asserts that the offences discussed in classical Islamic law 'served epistemic imperatives that fundamentally differed from those enshrined in and by the modern state and its systems'.[10] Of course, there are certainly books that are happy to use the idea of crime in Islamic law and articles that are content to refer to 'Islamic Criminal Law'.[11] Nevertheless, Hallaq's observations highlight an

[9] Wael Hallaq, *Shari'a: Theory, Practice, Transformations* (Cambridge University Press, 2009) 308.
[10] ibid.
[11] See, for instance, Kamali, *Crime and Punishment in Islamic Law* (n 6); Rudolf Peters, *Crime and Punishment in Islamic Law* (Cambridge University Press, 2005); Silvia Tellenbach, 'Islamic Criminal Law' in Markus D Dubber and Tatjana Hornle (eds), *The Oxford Handbook of Criminal Law* (Oxford University Press, 2014) 248.

important matter that will be germane to our discussion, namely, the (perhaps awkward) fit of classical offences, especially the *hudud*, with the modern state and their application in state-based criminal law or penal law systems.

III. FORMULATING ISLAMIC OFFENCES – THE CLASSICAL CONTEXT

We can turn now to consider how offences, including *hadd* offences, were developed in Muslim societies before the establishment of the modern nation state. We can begin this discussion by noting, once again, that there was an interpretive process even in classical works to delineate and define the *hudud*. This is unsurprising, and is in fact part and parcel of what Rudolph Peters calls the 'rich and variegated' legal discourses that have been a perennial feature of Muslim legal discourses since the early days of Islam.[12] Doctrines were neither static nor immutable, and over time there ended up being many differences, even on essential legal issues, and so a great variety of opinions ensued. Even when the *madhahib* (schools of law) emerged, there were still differences between the schools as well as within them, where one might find varying and even contradictory opinions.[13]

This interpretive diversity also applied to penal clauses and the *hudud*. Thus, when coming to define the *hudud*, there were different formulations, generating different listings of *hudud* crimes. For instance, in their review of a range classical works, the Council of Islamic Ideology of Pakistan reported that three crimes are listed as *hudud* in the *Muwatta*, one of Malik b. Annas' works and a classical book of the Maliki school (or *madhhab*) that was named after him. However, five crimes are listed as *hudud* in the equally classical work, the *Kitab al-Umm*, written by Muhammad bin Idris al-Shafi'i, after whom the Shafi'i school is named.[14] Other scholars of classical studies placed varying numbers of crimes in their chapters on *hudud*, and sometimes varying crimes. However, in the case of Ibn Rush (Averroes), who served as judge in Seville and Cordoba in the twelfth century when these areas were under the Almohad dynasty and part of Muslim Spain (al-Andalus), his handbook for judges, the *Bidayat al-Mujtahid*,[15] contained no chapter on *hudud*. Rather, he dealt with *hudud* crimes under different categories (*viz*, crimes against property, honour, sex and the human body).

As we have noted, these types of variations are part of the inherent structure of Islamic law generally, and in this respect diversity of opinion about *hudud* is simply one manifestation. Moreover, given the importance of *hudud* in the sense

[12] Rudolph Peters, *Crime and Punishment in Islamic Law: Theory and Practice from the Sixteenth to Twenty-first Century* (Cambridge University Press, 2005) 6.

[13] ibid 1–2 and 6.

[14] Masud, *Hudood Ordinance 1979* (n 3) 153–54.

[15] Ibn Rushd, *The Distinguished Jurist's Primer: A Translation of Bidāyat Al-Mujtahid*, trs Imran Ahsan Khan Nyazee, Muhammad Abdul Rauf (Garnet Publishing, 1996).

of violations of the rights of God or limits prescribed by God, it is only to be expected that there would be particularly serious debates about the contours of the *hudud*.

In addition to debates about how to categorise the *hudud*, the issues of uncertainty or doubt and their impact on application of *hudud* mentioned above in the context of Prophetic practice tradition were also significant matters in the juristic consideration. Uncertainty and doubt conditioned the way the jurists would assess '*hadd* events' and the way in which punishments were applied. In fact, as suggested by Intisar Rabb in her study of doubt in Islamic law, it may well be that the identification and canonisation of Prophetic *hadith* regarding doubt with respect to *hadith* came after the development of the jurists development of 'doubt canon' about the *hudud*.[16] This means that for instances in which there may have been doubt, jurists would use this doubt not to apply *hudud* punishments.

An illustrative example comes in the following account where the *hadd* offence of consumption of intoxicants (in this case, wine) was suggested. The example involves Abu Hanifa, the eponymous founder of the Hanafi *madhhab*:

> Question:
>
> [What happens] if a wine jar is found in Zeyd's possession?
>
> Answer:
>
> It is related that Abu Hanıfa (may God have mercy on him) went on a Pilgrimage and that he, upon entering Medina, saw the people gathered around a man. They said: 'We found him with a wine-skin, and we wish to inflict the fixed [ie *hadd*] punishment on him.' Abu Hanıfa replied: 'He's got the instrument of fornication with him, too. So stone him.' And they left the man and scattered.'[17]

Rabb's extensive study constructs a narrative that highlights the significance of the doubt canon from the beginning of Islamic legal discourses and as a part of the development of Islamic legal schools and their normativity. Thus, there has been a 'jurisprudence of doubt' that has developed in Muslim legal traditions conditioning the interpretation, understanding and application of, particularly, the *hudud*. In this respect, Rabb's analysis is fundamentally about correcting the historical record. She makes clear that the issue of doubt has early roots, saying:

> [N]o student of Islamic law should be fooled by the relatively late appearance of treatises on legal maxims into thinking that those maxims were not devised or deployed until the fourteenth century … The doubt canon was there from the beginning of Islamic law.[18]

Moreover, no less significant was the institutionalisation of the modalities of legal normativity. Rabb notes, as has been discussed in other studies, that in the classical situation, Muslim jurists, and thus definitions of Islamic law, were

[16] Intisar Rabb, *Doubt in Islamic Law* (Cambridge University Press, 2015) ch 2, 318.
[17] Colin Imber, *Ebu's-Su'ud: the Islamic legal tradition* (Edinburgh University Press, 1997) 211.
[18] Rabb, *Doubt in Islamic Law* (n 16) 319.

neither integrated into nor controlled by the state in the way that modern states exert monopoly over law. Jurists were legal scholars distinct from a separate class of state-appointed judges, even though some jurists wore both hats. Thus, there was an interplay between jurists, who articulated the *shari'a*, ruling authorities who enforced law, and judges, who looked to jurists for definitions of law and to rulers for enforcement of their decisions.[19]

The implications of this historical narrative reach into the contemporary period and will be discussed in what follows.

IV. APPLYING 'CRIMINAL LAW'

The foregoing discussion helps us to see that in the classical period, the formulation of Islamic 'criminal law' was part of a hermeneutical process that involved different actors and was conditioned by the moderating effect of doubt, in its application.

It is also important to understand that because the jurists-scholars were not, or at least not always and sometimes not often, part of the machinery of the 'state', the *hudud* was not a part of a penal code and did not operate as penal law in the modern sense of the term. In other words, there was a difference between at least two senses of 'law'. On one hand, there was the classical juristic (one might say '*fiqh*') discourses, with *fiqh* here understood to be the work product of the jurists, or their best-effort attempts to articulate the *shari'a* norms. On the other hand, there were the positive and posited laws of the state (or probably, more appropriately for the time, of the empire). This sort of 'state law' also existed in Muslim contexts.

Perhaps the best expression of this comes in the so-called *siyasa* (political) jurisdiction, ie, the early general recognition of the legitimate role of the government to make and apply law to run society. *Siyasa* could be used to address matters that may not have been well articulated in the *shari'a* schema – for instance, administrative law or fiscal law (which the *shari'a* was generally held to have less to say about than family law or dietary law). It could also be used to allow for governing authorities to make other rules for addressing topics that were discussed in the classical *shari'a* sources, though perhaps not in the level of detail that was felt to be required, if they felt the need to supplement provisions in the *shari'a*.

Political officials, and most particularly for our purposes judges, would be expected to apply the *siyasa* rules. The legitimacy of the *siyasa* was recognised in classical doctrine. For instance, Ann Lambton cites al-Ghazzali (d 1111CE), one of the most prominent intellectual figures in Muslim history, who claimed that

[19] ibid 17.

'God has singled out two groups of men and given them preference over others, one prophets; the other kings'.[20]

Thus, in criminal law there were different sources of normativity that could be at play: *shari'a* norms as well as state-set *siyasa* norms, and there were different legal actors. This resulted in a measure of normative fluidity. In fact, there is nothing new here in the story of Islamic law. It is a well-known part of the development of Muslim legal traditions that there were different legal actors exercising different 'normativities'. Thus, there were the jurist-scholars – the *'ulama* – who developed and defined the schools of law, but there were also the *qadis* (judges) who settled cases in courts by drawing upon the *shari'a* inspired norms, and also state-sanctioned prescripts – the administrators (local governors and the like). As a result, criminal law was handled via different modalities. These in turn presented a model at significant variance from the default, standard contemporary criminal law model in which the state looms both large and virtually supreme in determining the contours of criminal law. This plurality was accompanied by a certain amorphousness of roles typical of pre-modern Muslim legal discourses. As Carl Brown has put it:

> Certain ulama could resist the blandishments of government office, others could accept, and all could accommodate in a system where no one – not even the caliph – presumed to speak ex cathedra (to use the Catholic term) on religious dogma ... The early Muslim community developed in a way that facilitated compartmentalization, isolation, and, thus, *non-resolution of potentially explosive issues involving religion and politics ... Muslims found it easier to rock along with a certain indeterminacy.*[21]

Part of this indeterminacy in the area of criminal law was the availability of *ta'zir* and *qisas*, which were mentioned in section II. *Ta'zir* punishments could be applied when *hudud* standards were not met, and their application was often set by political authorities because of their discretionary nature. This was part of the *siyasa* or political jurisdiction. In criminal law, *siyasa* authority allowed the political leadership to deal with discretionary matters and to make laws and regulations to supplement the *shari'a* norms.[22] Naturally, *siyasa* did not have the same moral force as the *hudud*, but it was still part of the criminal law or penal law structure. While *ta'zir* was a sub-theme of *siyasa*, Kamali notes that the political authority or judge did not create the *ta'zir* offence, which rested on scriptural authority akin to *hudud*, but did have discretion as to the application of punishment because the punishment did not have scriptural sanction, unlike *hudud*.[23]

[20] Ann KS Lambton, *Theory and Practice in Medieval Persian Government* (Vaorium Reprints, 1954) 105.

[21] L Carl Brown, *Religion and State: The Muslim Approach to Politics* (Columbia University Press Brown, 2000) 53 (emphasis added). I have discussed this context with more elaboration in Arif A Jamal, *Islam, Law and the Modern State* (Routledge, 2018) 58–83.

[22] For a longer discussion of *siyasa sharia* under the idea of state law as Islamic law, see Clark Lombardi, *State Law as Islamic Law in Modern Egypt: The Incorporation of the Sharī'a into Egyptian Constitutional Law* (Brill, 2006).

[23] Kamali, *Crime and Punishment in Islamic Law* (n 6) 191.

As for *qisas*, these 'retributions' could be satisfied by *diya* (monetary compensation) or by forgiveness at the option of the offended party, such as an individual or a family. Indeed, the Qur'an itself urges, though does not insist upon, forgiveness.

Importantly, Rabb argues that the use of doubt was not suspended when it came to *ta'zir* and *qisas*. Doubt was also used to delimit the application of these penalties, hence the maxim 'Avoid imposing criminal sanctions in cases of doubt: idrau l-hudud bi'l-shubahat' ran through all of the criminal law.[24] Moreover, and most interestingly, Rabb also asserts that

> the avoidance imperative of the doubt canon was the inverse of the enforcement imperative of the foundational texts, yet the former took precedence over the latter: whenever jurists feared divergence from the criminal law texts, even inadvertently, doubt cautioned avoidance of punishment.[25]

Thus, in the classical schema, religion-inspired penal clauses exhibited an amount of diversity in interpretation both in general and due to the impact of doubt concerns, and there was flexibility in punishments with the role of *ta'zir*, *siyasa* and *diya*. But this classical schema was not going to persist.

V. MODERNITY, TRANSFORMATION AND TRANSLATION

> The transition from a jurist's law to a written state law has transformed the traditional Islamic legal culture and diluted its distinctive features. Ever since this major transformation of the established and longstanding Islamic legal tradition, calls for Islamization have often focused almost exclusively on the reinstatement of the Islamic penal system … This, in turn, has created a disconnect between these modern constructions and their historical origins. These modern constructions have had a significant impact on the understanding of Islamic law in terms of its nature and mode of application. Most remarkably, the certainty with which these penal ordinances are implemented breaks with a well-established classical tendency to subject penal cases to extraordinary measures of verification and to exhaust every possibility through which the severe canonical punishments can be avoided.[26]

Ayman Shaybana's words reflect a theme in contemporary scholarship about Islamic law. It is a theme of rupture – in his words, disconnect – between the classical tradition and modernist forms and expressions.[27] This process significantly affected criminal law and the *hudud*. Earlier, it was noted that the framework

[24] Rabb, Doubt in Islamic Law (n 16) 38.

[25] ibid.

[26] Ayman Shabana, '*Doubt in Islamic Law: A History of Legal Maxims, Interpretation, and Islamic Criminal Law*, written by Intisar A. Rabb, 2014' (2017) 24(3) *Islamic Law and Society* 290, 290–91.

[27] For a more elaborate discussion of the rupture between the past and present, see Wael Hallaq, 'What is Sharia?' (2005) 12 *Yearbook of Islamic and Middle Eastern Law* 15.

of criminal law and religious penal clauses was rather ill-fitting, at least in the minds of some scholars, to the *shari'a* and its criminal aspects. This mismatch is based on an understanding of the classical schema of the *shari'a* including the interaction of jurists, judges and political rulers, with their different normativities and agency, on the interplay of *hudud*, *ta'zir* and *qisas*, and on the high evidentiary standards required for conviction and the mitigating force of doubt.

For many Muslim contexts, the encounter with modernity was not a benign experience. Modernity and the modern state were often foisted upon these environments through the processes of colonial domination. Mohamed Arkoun called this a 'a brutal eruption into the "living space of Islam"' and noted that 'Colonial endeavours of 19th century Europe sought justification in what was called a civilising mission. It was a matter of raising "backward" peoples to the level of a "universal" culture and civilisation.'[28] In this process, Islamic laws, including penal laws, were 'adulterated',[29] not least in the process of codification. Indeed, this process was especially significant for penal law. In effect, codification was the means by which the classical tradition was significantly transformed into 'modern law' and made to fit into the paradigm of criminal law and penal codes. And it must be emphasised what a major transformation this was. Thus, in the view of some, the previous dynamic, which gave a prominent role to the jurist-scholars in identifying with different schools of law and, even within such schools, exhibiting interpretational variation and locating themselves outside of the folds of the state, was largely given over to a state-centric, judge-defined structure. Penal codes were structured and organised, but also stylised and de-pluralised. This had a profound effect on the traditional *shari'a* schema, and on Muslim understanding of *shari'a*. Hence, as Anver Emon says, the colonial treatment of Islamic law, in terms of redefining its structure, scope and modalities, 'rendered the *shari'a* reified and static in application and conceptual coherence'.[30] One might say that a sort of caricature of the traditional schema emerged from this process: the organic, varied and diverse was transformed to the static and fixed. Emon argues that additionally, there was a loss of conceptual coherence in this transformation because of the different principal actors and modes of application of the criminal provisions.[31] Several moves have been identified in the transition from classical to

[28] Mohammed Arkoun, 'The State, the Individual, and Human Rights: A Contemporary View of Muslims in a Global Context' in Azim Nanji (ed), *The Muslim Almanac: A Reference Work on the History, Faith and Culture and Peoples of Islam* (Gale Research Inc, 1995) 453.

[29] Javaid Rehman, Islamic State Practices, International Law and the Threat from Terrorism (Hart Publishing, 2005) 24.

[30] Anver Emon, 'Conceiving Islamic Law in a Pluralistic Society: History, Politics and Multicultural Jurisprudence' (July 2006) *Singapore Journal of Legal Studies* 331, 349.

[31] ibid. For more discussion in the same vein, see Abdullahi An-Nai'm, 'Shari a in the Secular State: a Paradox of Separation and Conflation' in Peri Bearman, Wolfhart Heinrichs and Bernard G Weiss (eds), *The Law Applied: Contextualizing the Islamic Shari'a* (IB Tauris, 2008) 321; Tim Lindsey and Jeremy Kingsley, 'Talking in Code: Legal Islamisation in Indonesia and the MMI Shari'a Criminal Code' in Peri Bearman, Wolfhart Heinrichs and Bernard G Weiss (eds), *The Law Applied: Contextualizing the Islamic Shari'a* (IB Tauris, 2008) 295.

modern. The transition was a transformation that entailed bureaucratisation, the abolition of *siyasa* or discretionary criminal justice in favour of the rule of law, the establishment of a secular judiciary, sometimes alongside the traditional judiciary (that is the *qadis*), and the integration of the classical *shari'a* system into the national legal and court system.[32]

Accordingly, as part of this narrative, the upshot of this process was to politicise the criminal provisions, especially the *hudud*. By this I mean that the way the criminal law was dealt with became expressive of the state's political values. Under colonial administrators, on the one hand, Islamic criminal law was often considered too variable and uncertain because *siyasa* rules and *ta'zir* punishments could be different. On the other hand, the *hudud* punishments were thought too severe and culturally unacceptable.[33] Thus, the colonial administrators felt the political need to reform the classical law. In North Africa, the reform was effected by installing Western (French) style codes to replace *shari'a* rather quickly. In British colonies, the process was more gradual, with the Islamic norms initially applied, though in moderated form, until later replaced by codes. Interestingly, in British India, while British judges commuted sentences imposing amputation as unacceptable, other aspects of Islamic (in this case, Hanafi) criminal law were considered too lenient because capital punishment, used then in Britain and in British India, was difficult to apply. The classical *shari'a* schema seemed to offer too many possibilities of avoiding capital punishment for offences such as manslaughter, rape and theft, and so the colonial judges worked to align Hanafi law with the stricter British standards.[34] Even in Muslim-controlled states – notably the Ottoman Empire – a dual system emerged, with *siyasa* being formalised and codified, while *shari'a* courts continued to use the traditional norms, though eventually more and more of the criminal law was removed from the *shari'a* jurisdiction and brought under the state's courts.[35]

Taking these developments in the round, an overall pattern can be seen to emerge, wherein the traditional schema was effectively supplanted by Western-style codes. This was a transformation as well as a translation. The transformation has already been discussed, but it was the translation that may have been more subtle, and also more deeply-rooted.

The translation involved altering the morality of the *hudud* (and *ta'zir* and *qisas*). Recall that the term *hudud* had a sense of transgressing the limits of God, which was what made it so consequential, and why one had to be cautious in ensuring that the standards were met before enacting *hudud* punishments.

[32] Muhammad Khalid Masud, Rudolph Peters, and David Powers, 'Qadis and their courts: an historical survey' in Muhammad Khalid Masud, Rudolph Peters and David Powers (eds), *Dispensing Justice in Islam: Qadis and their Judgments* (Brill, 2005) 1, 32–33.

[33] Peters, *Crime and Punishment in Islamic Law* (n 12) 104.

[34] Masud, Peters and Powers, 'Qadis and their courts: an historical survey' (n 32) 38. Masud et al note (ibid 40) that the same approach was also taken by British judges in Nigeria, where they would have encountered Mailki law.

[35] Peters, *Crime and Punishment in Islamic Law* (n 12) 104–05.

The moral sense of the *hudud* was so strong, at least among some, that there are accounts of people confessing to a *hadd* act and asking for the punishment to be applied to them. For instance, Kamali quoted a *hadith* (account of what the Prophet Muhammad did or said) from the collection of Bukhari – one of the most famous *hadith* compilers – in which a man came to Muhammad and said 'O Messenger! I have committed a legally punishable [*hadd*] act, please apply the punishment on me'. Before the Prophet could respond, the time for the prayer fell. After the prayer, the man again made his confession and asked for the punishment 'according to the Book of God'. As it turned out, the Prophet is reported to have said to the man that since he had prayed together with him, God had forgiven the *hadd* act.[36] In another *hadith*, which was conveyed via the Prophet's wife Aisha, Muhammad reportedly said:

> Avoid condemning the Muslims to hudud whenever you can, in all instances of doubt, and when you can find a way out for a Muslim then clear his way. If the Imam [roughly 'leader', though in this case also the one who would decide the case and punishment] errs, it is better that he errs on the side of forgiveness than on the side of punishment.[37]

Undergirding these *hadiths* is the Qur'anic verse from the chapter of repentance (Sura Taubah), 'But if they repent, establish prayer, and give *zakah*, then they are your brothers in religion; and We detail the verses for a people who know.'[38]

Even from these short excerpts, one can discern the moral fabric in which the *hudud* were embedded, and hence the flexibility with which they were endowed. The move to codification translated this moral character into a legal character. Of course, even codified criminal law has interpretive room and flexibility, but the moral registers of state law are very different from the moral registers of the traditional schema where the state was less significant.

Thus, the emergence of penal codes had the effect of having the state translate the criminal provisions by occupying the hermeneutic space of the traditional criminal law. The texts of the codes shifted the debate from the classical sources to the statutory provisions and language. It was a different debate, and one that suggested, indeed asserted, that the tradition could be fit into codified forms. As Rabb notes, the popular notion of Islamic law as a divinely revealed textual idea endowed with certainty (and so amenable to codification)

> seems not only ahistorical and incorrect but also an unfortunately pervasive way of approaching Islamic law in the modern world. In pursuit of clarity, that notion tends to produce legal doctrines that are far more rigid, explicitly harsh, and resistant to change than Islam's historical tradition would have it – especially in criminal law.[39]

[36] Muhammad Muhsin Khan (tr), *Sahih al-Bukhari*, 6th edn (Kazi Publications, 1983) 8:533–534, hadith no 821; cited in Kamali, *Crime and Punishment in Islamic Law* (n 6) 42.

[37] Kamali, *Crime and Punishment in Islamic Law* (n 6) 44, fn 34; see also various hadith sources, including Abu Isa al-Tirmidhi, *Sunan al-Tirmidhi* (Dar al-Fikr, 1980) 2:439, hadith no 1477.

[38] Qur'an 9:11 at https://quran.com/9/11.

[39] Rabb, *Doubt in Islamic Law* (n 16) 321.

VI. CONTEMPORARY APPLICATION: CASE STUDIES

We can now turn to look at a couple of contemporary case studies to explore the manifestations of the transformation and translation processes. The case studies show a picture in which the tradition is changed, though not without continuing debate, even though the terms and space of the debate have shifted significantly from those that are hermeneutic to those that are legally formalised.

The first study comes from Pakistan and the case of Asia Bibi, who was accused of blasphemy. The offences relating to religion were first codified by India's British rulers in 1860, and were expanded in 1927. The law enacted by the British made it a crime to disturb a religious assembly, trespass on burial grounds, insult religious beliefs, or intentionally destroy or defile a place or an object of worship. Pakistan inherited these laws when it came into existence after the partition of India in 1947. Between 1980 and 1986, a number of clauses were added to the laws by the military Government of General Zia-ul Haq as part of its 'Islamization' initiative.[40] Some of the changes included making derogatory remarks against Islamic personages an offence in 1980, carrying a maximum punishment of three years in jail. Another change was the legislation of life imprisonment for 'wilful' desecration of the Koran in 1982. In 1986, for blasphemy against the Prophet Muhammad, the Penal Code penalties were amended to recommend 'death, or imprisonment for life', in that order. As part of this same process, Zia ul-Haq's Government enacted the Hudood Ordinances.[41]

Asia Bibi was Christian farm labourer, a 47-year-old mother of five, and was sentenced to hang for blasphemy in 2010, under section 295C of the Pakistan Penal Code (1860).[42] However, in 2018, a three-member bench of the Supreme Court of Pakistan, led by the Chief Justice Saqib Nisar, struck down the death sentence for blasphemy and ordered Aisa Bibi's release. In fact, Pakistan has never executed anyone for the offence of blasphemy,[43] despite the popular perception arising from international news media coverage.

Both the Hudood Ordinances specifically and the larger project of the Islamisation of Pakistan's criminal law, including the changes in the blasphemy laws, were part of a move to establish what is perceived by the supporters of these laws as an 'Islamic' system of justice in the country.[44] However, these have

[40] For a discussion of the actions of the Zia Government with a focus on criminal law and the hudud, see Martin Lau, 'Twenty-Five Years of Hudood Ordinances: A Review' (2007) 64(4) *Washington and Lee Law Review* 1292.

[41] There are four hudud ordinances: The Offences Against Property (Enforcement Of Hudood) Ordinance (VI of 1979), The Offence of Zina (Enforcement of Hudood) Ordinance (VII of 1979), The Offence of *Qazf* (Enforcement of Hudood) Ordinance of 1979, and The Prohibition (Enforcement of Hadd) Order of 1979.

[42] Pakistan Penal Code (Act XLV of 1860) (Oct 6 1860).

[43] '10 Things you need to know about Pakistan's Blasphemy Law' *The Nation* (14 October 2016) at https://nation.com.pk/14-Oct-2016/10-things-you-need-to-know-about-pakistan-s-blasphemy-law accessed 1 July 2020.

[44] Hudood Laws at www.pakistani.org/pakistan/legislation/hudood.html.

been highly contested and controversial moves. As Muhammad Taqi Usmani noted:

> Pakistan has been in the grip of a raging debate on the issue of the *Hudud* Laws ever since they were introduced in 1979. There are some who ask for complete repeal of these laws, others who insist on keeping them as they are, and a third group call for amending and reforming these laws to make them more responsive to human and social conditions.[45]

In fact, Taqi Usmani reported that no *hadd* punishments have been applied in Pakistan under the Ordinances.[46]

Indeed, the earlier-mentioned report on the Hudood Ordinances by Pakistan's own Council of Islamic Ideology, called 'A Critical Report', stipulated several objections to the Hudood Ordinances. These included: (i) that the definition of *hadd* in the Ordinances is not derived from the Quran and Sunna, nor does it agree with the opinions of the classical jurists; (ii) the concept of *hadd* in the Ordinances varies from the classical tradition – and specifically in that in the Prophetic *hadith*, *hadd* is used in a general sense rather than the technical sense of the Ordinances; (iii) that the identification of *hudud*, *qisas* and *ta'zir* was the work of the jurists and varied with interpretation; (iv) that the Ordnances applied the *fiqh* definitions of *hudud* 'selectively and arbitrarily'; and (v) that not all Muslim countries apply *fiqh*-derived *hudud* provisions.

Asia Bibi's case was one salient example of the type of issue that helps to concentrate the mind in thinking through the contemporary debate about religious penal clauses in Muslim majority contexts. For instance, Tehreek-e-Labbaik (TLP) party leader Khadim Hussain Rizvi and several senior figures shut down major cities in protest at the acquittal of Bibi.[47] On the other hand, Prime Minister Imran Khan issued stark warnings to religio-political groups who were agitating against the Asia Bibi acquittal, saying that Pakistan was founded 'in the name of Islam' and the verdict given by the Supreme Court was in accordance with the Constitution, which is in line with the teachings of the Holy Quran and Sunna.[48]

Another example comes from Malaysia and involves the case of the caning of two women in the state of Terengganu in 2018. On 12 August 2018, the Kuala

[45] Muhammad Taqi Usmani, 'The Islamization of Laws in Pakistan: The Case of *Hudud* Ordinances' (2006) 96(2) *Muslim World* 287.

[46] This should not be confused with convictions. Masud, *Hudood Ordinance 1979: A Critical Report* (n 3) notes several convictions under the various Hudood Ordinances, but whether the *hadd* punishments were actually enforced is not clear.

[47] Eventually, Rizvi and others were given jail sentences for these actions. See Reuters, 'Terrorism charges for Pakistan cleric who led protests against Asia Bibi, woman acquitted of blasphemy' *South China Morning Post* (South Asia, 2 December 2018) at www.scmp.com/news/asia/south-asia/article/2175993/terrorism-charges-pakistan-cleric-who-led-protests-against-asia accessed 1 July 2020; 'Khadim Rizvi's brother, nephew handed 5 year sentences' *Daily Times* (Pakistan, 17 January 2020) at https://dailytimes.com.pk/541158/khadim-rizvis-brother-nephew-handed-55-year-sentences/ accessed 1 July 2020.

[48] '"Do not clash with the state": PM Khan issues stern warning to agitators after Assia Bibi verdict' *Dawn* (31 October 2018) at www.dawn.com/news/1442630 accessed 1 July 2020.

Terengganu Syariah (ie *shari'a*) High Court fined two women, aged 32 and 22, RM3,300, and ordered that they be caned six times each for committing *musahaqah* (sexual relations between women)[49] under sections 30 and 59(1) of the Syariah Criminal Offences Enactment (Takzir) (Terengganu).[50] This Act, as its name implies, purports to address shari'a criminal offences. As a legislated set of religious penal clauses, it clearly falls into the category of the modern codes discussed earlier, with all stylisation and transformation of *shari'a* norms previously mentioned. Interestingly, and similar to the Pakistani legislation regarding blasphemy, the Terengganu enactment includes many provisions that go well beyond the classical *hudud*. Thus, while *hudud* acts, like consumption of intoxicants and illicit sexual relations, are mentioned in the legislation, other acts include 'collection of *zakat* or *fitrah* without authority', 'abuses of *halal* sign' and 'secrecy'. It is not self-evident that all of these, and other matters mentioned in the enactment, would have been considered 'shari'a criminal offences' in the pre-modern schema. Further, they are outside of *hudud* in its classical definitions. Thus, the Terengganu enactment represents an expansion and formalisation of Islamic law's criminal norms.

As with Asia Bibi's situation in Pakistan, the caning of the two women in Terengganu was controversial, with different perspectives being reported in the Malaysian media. On one hand, it was reported that Presiding Judge, Amarul Azmi, told the courtroom that the execution of the sentence was intended as a reminder and deterrent to members of society. This was later reiterated at a press conference by Saiful Bahri Mamat, the Terengganu executive councillor in charge of Syariah implementation. It added that the execution was to demonstrate to the public how Syariah caning is supposedly 'kinder' compared to caning executed under civil law.[51] However, the same media source, on the same day, also carried a commentary, which said:

> Malaysia's first public caning held in a courtroom at the Terengganu Syariah High Court today marks a dark chapter in this nation's history … The caning proceeded despite huge protests by diverse actors in civil society, and clear recommendations by human rights and legal advocates to end the practice of whipping and caning in the criminal justice system as they are forms of cruel, inhumane or degrading treatment …

Other social media sources also carried commentary:

> Youth and Sports Minister @SyedSaddiq has condemned the act of public caning, saying it's a step backward for the country[52]

[49] 'Two women whipped six times in Terengganu Syariah High Court' *Borneo Post Online* (Kuala Terengganu, 3 September 2018) at www.theborneopost.com/2018/09/03/two-women-whipped-six-times-at-terengganu-syariah-high-court/ accessed 1 July 2020.

[50] Syariah Criminal Offenses (Takzir) (Terengganu) Enactment 2001 (Enactment No 7 of 2001).

[51] Reported in astro awani, 3 September 2018.

[52] *Astro Radio News* (6 September 2018) at https://t.co/duXWyjarPa; pic.twitter.com/Y5BK8UhBTv accessed 1 July 2020.

> Banyak lagi cara untuk menangani isu LGBT. Walaupun termaktub dalam undang2, tak wajar dilaksanakan sebatan di khalayak ramai. Islam teaches us to look after the dignity of every human being. And that mercy is preferable to punishment.[53]

One news source distilled the debate into an accurate but rather curt summary: 'Some were against it; Some were for it.'[54] Indeed, this case has become one of several that serve as a site of contestation between secular law and Islamic law in Malaysia.

VII. CONCLUSION: TRANSMOGRIFICATION

Religiously-inspired criminal law has been part and parcel of Muslim legal traditions. The *hudud* is an especially prominent manifestation of this law, though not its only expression.

As we have seen from the preceding discussion, there has been much classic and contemporary debate concerning both definition and application, and therefore about how Islamic criminal law (if one can use this term) is to be understood. These debates are not unexpected and reflect the inherent structure of Islamic law in general, characterised as it is by interpretational diversity and internal pluralism. With respect to criminal law, important cautionary principles, such as a concern about doubt, the avoidance of error and the preference for erring in favour of forgiveness, have been invoked. These concerns have moderated the application of the *hudud*. One of the important upshots of the classical contexts in our discussion is that this tradition shows that one cannot construct a simple 'orthodoxy' from the diversity of considerations and sources that were employed. It is simple orthodoxy that is too often presented as a caricature of Islamic penal provisions.

A second major insight is that, indeed, the colonial experience had a large impact on the classical tradition through the impact of modernity and most specifically of the codification of Islamic criminal law. Codification, whether done under the aegis of Muslim-run states such as the Ottoman Empire or more dramatically in colonial environments, had the effect of presenting Islamic penal norms through a lens of distorting simplicity and reduction. The criminal law normativity was transformed by being separated from its moral and hermeneutical contexts – especially with respect to interpretations and opinions – and made into a device of the state. While this has not meant an end to debates about the application of Islamic penal clauses, it has engendered a different schema within which the debates take place, and the modern debates are traceable to the reforms that took place widely in Muslim societies in the nineteenth

[53] Khairy Jamaluddin (3 September 2018) at https://t.co/FqkTqeoZeA accessed 1 July 2020.

[54] Jessica Chua, 'What did the Terengganu Public Caning Trigger Across Malaysia?' *Rojak Daily* (6 September 2018) at https://rojakdaily.com/news/article/5751/what-did-the-terengganu-public-caning-trigger-across-malaysia accessed 1 July 2020.

and twentieth centuries under European colonisation, with the development of legal codes that emulated European models. In this respect, modernity and the colonial (and neo-colonial?) experience has resulted in the transmogrification of Islamic penal clauses, altering them fundamentally. Practically, including in most jurisdictions that have a Muslim majority, *hudud* (much less so for *ta'zir* and *qisas*) are not heavily applied, but debates around them are now conducted in a different register – translated, transformed and transmogrified.

BIBLIOGRAPHY

—— Syariah Criminal Offenses (Takzir) (Terengganu) Enactment 2001 (Enactment No 7 of 2001)

An-Nai'm, A, 'Shari a in the Secular State: a Paradox of Separation and Conflation' in Peri Bearman, Wolfhart Heinrichs and Bernard G Weiss (eds), *The Law Applied: Contextualizing the Islamic Shari'a* (IB Tauris, 2008) 321

Astro Radio News (6 September 2018) at https://t.co/duXWyjarPa;pic.twitter.com/Y5BK8UhBTv accessed 1 July 2020

Borneo Post Online, 'Two women whipped six times in Terengganu Syariah High Court' (Kuala Terengganu, 3 September 2018) at www.theborneopost.com/2018/09/03/two-women-whipped-six-times-at-terengganu-syariah-high-court/ accessed 1 July 2020

Brown, LC, *Religion and State: The Muslim Approach to Politics* (Columbia University Press Brown, 2000)

Chua, J, 'What did the Terengganu Public Caning Trigger Across Malaysia?' *Rojak Daily* (6 September 2018) at https://rojakdaily.com/news/article/5751/what-did-the-terengganu-public-caning-trigger-across-malaysia accessed 1 July 2020

Daily Times, 'Khadim Rizvi's brother, nephew handed 5 year sentences' (Pakistan, 17 January 2020) at https://dailytimes.com.pk/541158/khadim-rizvis-brother-nephew-handed-55-year-sentences/ accessed 1 July 2020

Dawn, '"Do not clash with the state": PM Khan issues stern warning to agitators after Assia Bibi verdict' (31 October 2018) at www.dawn.com/news/1442630 accessed 1 July 2020

Emon, A, 'Conceiving Islamic Law in a Pluralistic Society: History, Politics and Multicultural Jurisprudence' (2006) *Singapore Journal of Legal Studies* 331, 349

Esposito, JL, 'Hadd' in John L Esposito (ed), *The Oxford Dictionary of Islam* (Oxford Islamic Studies Online 2020)

Hallaq, W, *Shari'a: Theory, Practice, Transformations* (Cambridge University Press, 2009)

——, 'What is Sharia?' (2005) 12 *Yearbook of Islamic and Middle Eastern Law* 15

Imber, C, *Ebu's-Su'ud: the Islamic legal tradition* (Edinburgh University Press, 1997)

Isa al-Tirmidhi, A, *Sunan al-Tirmidhi* (Dar al-Fikr, 1980)

Jamal, AA, *Islam, Law and the Modern State* (Routledge, 2018)

Jamaluddin, K, 3 September 2018 at https://t.co/FqkTqeoZeA accessed 1 July 2020

Kamali, MH, *Crime and Punishment in Islamic Law* (Oxford University Press, 2019)

Khan, MM (tr), *Sahih al-Bukhari* (6th edn, Lahore: Kazi Publications, 1983)

Lambton, AKS, Theory and Practice in Medieval Persian Government (Vaorium Reprints, 1954)

Lau, M, 'Twenty-Five Years of Hudood Ordinances: A Review' (2007) 64(4) *Washington and Lee Law Review* 1292

Lindsey, T, and Kingsley, J, 'Talking in Code: Legal Islamisation in Indonesia and the MMI Shari'a Criminal Code' in Peri Bearman, Wolfhart Heinrichs and Bernard G Weiss (eds), *The Law Applied: Contextualizing the Islamic Shari'a* (IB Tauris, 2008) 321

Lombardi, C, State Law as Islamic Law in Modern Egypt: The Incorporation of the Sharī'a into Egyptian Constitutional Law (Brill, 2006)

Masud, MK, *Hudood Ordinance 1979: A Critical Report* (Council of Islamic Ideology, Government of Pakistan, 2007)

Masud, MK, Peters, R, and Powers, D, 'Qadis and their courts: an historical survey' in Muhammad Khalid Masud, Rudolph Peters and David Powers (eds), *Dispensing Justice in Islam: Qadis and their Judgments* (Brill, 2005)

Peters, R, *Crime and Punishment in Islamic Law* (Cambridge University Press, 2005)

Rabb, IA, *Doubt in Islamic Law* (Cambridge University Press, 2015)

Reuters, 'Terrorism charges for Pakistan cleric who led protests against Asia Bibi, woman acquitted of blasphemy' *South China Morning Post* (South Asia, 2 December 2018) at https://www.scmp.com/news/asia/south-asia/article/2175993/terrorism-charges-pakistan-cleric-who-led-protests-against-asia accessed 1 July 2020

Rushd, *The Distinguished Jurist's Primer: A Translation of Bidāyat Al-Mujtahid*, trs Imran Ahsan Khan Nyazee and Muhammad Abdul Rauf (Garnet Publishing, 1996)

Shabana, A, '*Doubt in Islamic Law: A History of Legal Maxims, Interpretation, and Islamic Criminal Law*, written by Intisar A. Rabb, 2014' (2017) 24(3) Islamic Law and Society 290

Tellenbach, S, 'Islamic Criminal Law' in Markus D Dubber and Tatjana Hornle (eds), *The Oxford Handbook of Criminal Law* (Oxford University Press, 2014) 248

The Nation, '10 Things you need to know about Pakistan's Blasphemy Law' (14 October 2016) at https://nation.com.pk/14-Oct-2016/10-things-you-need-to-know-about-pakistan-s-blasphemy-law accessed 1 July 2020

Usmani, MT, 'The Islamization of Laws in Pakistan: The Case of *Hudud* Ordinances' (2006) 96(2) *Muslim World* 287

4

Between Religious Coexistence and Religious Hierarchy: Divergent Developments in Religious Offence Laws in Common Law Asia

JACLYN L NEO

I. INTRODUCTION

THE 1870 INDIAN Penal Code (IPC) and its transplantation to the rest of the British colonies in Asia represent one of the most transformative acts of legislation in the common law world. The IPC was a criminal code designed for the colonies, albeit drawn from English common law. This transplantation,[1] or perhaps more accurately the imposition, of a written code of criminal law changed ideas about crime and criminality, reshaping modes of thinking about culpability as well as limits of speech and conduct. Like most legal interventions, the criminal code displaced pre-existing legal systems, some of which were oral and flexible, and replaced them with more formal systems supported by established procedures and bureaucratic systems of administration.[2] It led to a social and legal transformation of the colonies.

Among the many provisions in the Code is a chapter criminalising offences relating to religion. These religious penal clauses, or religious offences as they are more broadly called, are distinctive because they are criminal provisions implicating religion, religious ideologies, or a person or group identified specifically

[1] On the legal transplant debate generally, see Alan Watson, *Legal Transplants: An Approach to Comparative Law* (University of Georgia Press, 1993); Pierre Legrand, 'The Impossibility of "Legal Transplants"' (1997) 4 *Maastrict Journal of European and Comparative Law* 111; and Harding's intervention in the debate: Andrew Harding, 'The Legal Transplants Debate: Getting Beyond the Impasse?' in Vito Breda (ed), *Legal Transplants in East Asia and Oceania* (Cambridge University Press, 2019) 13.

[2] See generally, Sally Engle Merry, 'Law and Colonialism' (1991) 25 *Law and Society Review* 889, 917.

by their religion. A broad range of conduct may be prohibited as religious offences; behaviours that 'discredit the religious convictions of the population or a segment thereof',[3] disrupt the practice of religion, cause damage to a place of worship, etc. Historically, religious offences were crimes of blasphemy, which overlapped with crimes of apostasy and heresy. Blasphemy is strictly speaking concerned with the 'disrespectful or offensive treatment' of sacred material.[4] It is closely associated with heresy, which in Western Christendom includes a denial of Jesus or attribution of his miracles to satanic forces.[5]

Today, religious penal clauses include religious denigration or defamation of religion as well as religious hate speech. Such laws shift the subject of protection to individuals who are part of vulnerable groups and target denigration with intent to harm the subject of speech. Such laws have been justified as necessary to protect the dignity of persons who are identified as part of a community.[6] Alternatively, hate speech laws are justified as necessary for harm-prevention, whereby harm is conceptualised more broadly as including the psychological and emotional health of persons belonging to the group.[7] One may therefore see a broad dichotomy between religious penal clauses aimed at protecting religious sacredness and those aimed at protecting religious persons.

This dichotomy is embedded within the religious penal clauses in the IPC and its progenies. On the one hand, these laws can trace their genealogy to blasphemy laws in England. On the other, by the time they were written, the philosophical foundations of the laws had shifted from upholding a state religion to protecting social cohesion in an increasingly disenchanted post-Enlightenment England. Accordingly, the drafters were explicit in stating that their chief concern was not to uphold the boundaries of orthodoxy in support of a national religion. Instead, the stated intent for these provisions was the maintenance of public order and peaceful coexistence among different groups in an ethnically and religiously plural society. They were aimed at sanctioning conduct that could affect peaceable relations among groups.

Developments in these post-British colonial countries show that the religious penal clauses have continued to remain relevant and have been employed over the years to address different inter-religious and even intra-religious disputes. These developments show that despite the IPC's initial focus on public order

[3] Henning Radtke, 'Religious Offenses' in Hans Dieter Betz et al (eds), *Religion Past and Present Online* (Brill, 2011) at referenceworks.brillonline.com /entries/religion-past-and-present/religious-offenses-SIM_ 124602.

[4] Neville Cox, 'Pourquoi Suis-Je Charlie? Blasphemy, Freedom of Religion, and the Nature of "Offensive" Cartoons' (2015) 4 *Oxford Journal of Law and Religion* 343, 351.

[5] John C Knechtle, 'Blasphemy, Defamation of Religion and Religious Hate Speech: Is There a Difference that Makes a Difference?' in András Koltay and Jeroen Temperman (eds), *Blasphemy and Freedom of Expression: Comparative, Theoretical, and Historical Reflections after the Charlie Hebdo Massacre* (Cambridge University Press 2017) 199, 200.

[6] Jeremy Waldron, *The Harm in Hate Speech* (Harvard University Press, 2012).

[7] Katharine Gelber, 'The False Analogy between Vilification and Sedition' (2009) 33 *Melbourne University Law Review* 270, 285.

as maintenance of inter-religious peace, the blasphemy roots of these laws have re-emerged in some jurisdictions. Accordingly, while some countries have retained the public order orientation of these provisions as the maintenance of inter-religious harmony, others have 'transformed' the law effectively into blasphemy laws, that is, as laws to protect sacred symbols, persons, objects, or even doctrines within a religion. In a way, both orientations can be said to be aimed at preserving public order, peace and tranquility. The key distinguishing factor, I argue, is that public order or, more properly speaking, religious coexistence envisages coequality of religion, that is, of coexistence of *religions of more or less equal status*. In contrast, anti-blasphemy legislation is a way to police religious orthodoxy so as to preserve *religious hierarchy* both within the dominant religion as well as vis-à-vis the dominant religion.

This chapter thus employs these two concepts – *religious coexistence* and *religious hierarchy* – as marking two extremes on a spectrum that can serve as a legal framework to think about legal developments surrounding religious penal clauses. These two concepts can also assist in thinking more deeply about divergences and the underlying vision of pluralities in society – whether as coequal or as hierarchical. I further argue that there are at least three factors for different jurisdictions to diverge in their application of the religious penal clauses: the first is the degree of identification between state and religion in the constitutional text; the second is the religious demography of the country; and the third is the extent to which the government relies on religion to legitimise its power. In examining the development of these laws, this chapter aims to reflect further on the role of legal transplants and the process of legal transformation. In particular, it suggests that colonies are not merely passive receptors of legal ideas but do exercise their social and political agency in re-transforming colonial laws to respond to local conditions. Accordingly, the legal legacies of colonialism must be examined contextually and contemporarily.

Section II provides a historical overview to illuminate the original intent of the religious offence clauses in the IPC. This historical discussion will be brief, as Kevin Tan's chapter in this volume (chapter 1) goes into greater depth into the historical genesis of the IPC and its links to the common law offence of blasphemy. Section III discusses developments in three countries – Singapore, Pakistan, and Myanmar – to illustrate how the three factors play a role in the development of law and thereby the divergence in approaches. In particular, one can see how Singapore has maintained the original intent of the religious penal clauses as maintaining religious coexistence, while Pakistan and Myanmar have employed the laws in a way that preserves the hierarchy of the religious majority over others. The two latter case studies illustrate two focal points in the maintenance of religious hierarchy – one emphasising the singularity of the majority religion vis-à-vis a minority within the majority, and the other maintaining the singularity of the majority religion vis-à-vis minority religions. In other words, the laws regulate inter- and intra-religious relations.

II. RELIGIOUS OFFENCE: INTERTWINING RELIGIOUS FEELINGS AND PUBLIC ORDER

An examination of the drafting history of the chapter in the IPC on religious offences clearly shows that the primary motivating factor for the British in introducing the religious penal clauses was to ensure 'communal harmony' within the context of a multicultural society.[8] This is represented by two planks in the thinking behind the religious penal clauses. The first is a recognition that insults to one's religion can generate intangible but real feelings of harm to adherents. In explanatory note J, the drafters stated that the thinking behind offences relating to religion and caste in the IPC is encapsulated by this principle, 'that every man should be suffered to profess his own religion, and that no man should be suffered to insult the religion of another'.[9] Further, it was observed:

> The question whether insults offered to a religion ought to be visited with punishment does not appear to us at all to depend on the question whether that religion be true or false. The religion may be false, but the pain which such insults give to the professors of that religion is real. It is often, as the most superficial observation may convince us, as real a pain, and as acute a pain, as is caused by almost any offence against the person, against property, or against character.[10]

The second plank is the recognition that such 'hurt' feelings can give rise to acts that may threaten public order and the maintenance of peaceful coexistence among different groups.

Even though the IPC criminalises speech deliberately wounding the religious feelings of person by words, gestures or exhibitions under the pretext of religious discussion, the drafters suggested that this retains 'fair latitude' in religious discussion. This is because what are criminalised are 'intentional insults to what is held sacred by others'.[11] Religious insults were not considered part of legitimate discussion since they have no tendency to persuade and elicit truth. As an example, it was said that insults directed against erroneous opinions 'seldom have any other effect than to fix those opinions deeper, and to give a character of peculiar ferocity to theological dissension'. Accordingly, '[i]nstead of eliciting truth they only inflame fanaticism'.[12] Even then, the drafters were adamant that the religious offence provisions, at their core, provide an appropriate balance between freedom of religious profession, which itself implicates both freedom of religion and freedom of speech, and a protection against harm arising from insult. This is partly because there is no 'compensating good whatsoever to be

[8] Akhtar Rasool Bodla, 'Genesis of Blasphemy Laws in Colonial India' (2017) XXXVIII(2) *Pakistan Journal of History and Culture* 140, 152.

[9] JM Macleod, 'Note J on the Chapter of Offences Relating to Religion and Caste' in *Notes on the Report of the Indian Law Commissions on the Indian Penal Code* (W Clowes, 1848) 87.

[10] ibid.

[11] ibid.

[12] ibid.

set off against [the] pain [of insults]'.[13] Furthermore, as the drafters emphasised, not all forms of offensive speech would fall within the scope of the law, and words spoken in the heat of a moment or in defence of one's religion may be exempted.[14]

Understandably, from the start, there were concerns that these laws would be overly intrusive. Members of the British Parliament raised specific concerns about the religious penal clauses. For instance, one parliamentarian argued that the provisions were 'a dangerous novelty liable to extensive abuse, that a man should be subjected to criminal prosecution for every gesture or sound that he may utter, offensive to the religious feelings or prejudices of another'.[15] Nonetheless, the Penal Code drafters were adamant that the laws were necessary to preserve public peace and order in a religiously diverse society. In recognising the peculiarity of the social condition in India, Macaulay's concern was in ensuring public order among the different peoples. He noted, 'There is perhaps no country in which the Government has so much to apprehend from religious excitement among the people.'[16] Thus, in providing for punishment for the intentional destroying or defiling of places of worship or of objects held sacred, for instance, the drafters explained that '[n]o offence in the whole Code is so likely to lead to tumult, to sanguinary outrage, and even to armed insurrection'. This intertwining of hurt religious feelings with public order concerns in the IPC gives great importance to protecting religious feelings as a basis for action, which can itself serve to preserve the legitimacy of the state.

This focus on public order indicates that these initial provisions were not meant to function as 'blasphemy' laws. Blasphemy is *inherently religious*, in that it is proscribed because it attacks sacredly-held persons, objects or doctrines within religion.[17] The drafters of the IPC were clear that the religious penal clauses were meant to substitute the need for blasphemy laws. Macaulay's draft shows a shift in the purpose from protection of deity or Christianity to the protection of religious sensibilities of believers from scurrilous attack.[18] This is also reflected in how religious offences are categorised under the chapter on 'Offences Relating to Religion and Caste', rather than Blackstone's title of 'Offences against God and Religion'. As Wright notes, the provisions in the Penal Code were a huge advance on existing common law and 'reflected toleration while addressing intangible harms in a manner that minimised contested moral and ethical criteria'.[19] The provisions sought to strike a balance between

[13] ibid.

[14] ibid.

[15] James C Melville, *Copies of the Special Reports of the Indian Law Commission* (East India House, 1847) 51.

[16] Macleod, 'Note J' (n 9).

[17] Knechtle, 'Blasphemy, Defamation of Religion and Religious Hate Speech' (n 5).

[18] ibid 206.

[19] Barry Wright, 'Macaulay's Indian Penal Code: Historical Context and Originating Principles' in Chan Wing-Cheong, Barry Wright and Stanley Yeo (eds), *Codification, Macaulay and the Indian Penal Code: The Legacies and Modern Challenges of Criminal Law Reform* (Ashgate, 2011) 47.

allowing fair latitude for religious freedom and restraining proselytisers from exploiting religious tolerance to intentionally insult what others hold sacred.[20]

Clarifying the public order justification for religious offence is important as it determines the content of the offence. Whether the law is meant to protect religious orthodoxy or to ensure public order affects the elements of the offence, particularly whether the focus should be on an objective assessment of its potential impact or on the intention of the speaker. If the focus is on offence against god(s) or religion then the crime may be established simply on the basis of publication of material adjudged to be offensive (*actus reus*). Whether the material is offensive is to be determined by the judge on an objective basis and does not depend on whether the speaker subjectively intended the material as offensive or if the religious group, in fact, views the material as offensive. The *mens rea* is established by a mere intent to publish the material (as opposed to negligent publication). There is no additional need for the speaker to (subjectively) intend to offend. In some instances, the offence may even be one of strict liability; there would be no need to prove the *mens rea* as it is presumed. Indeed, in one of the last few blasphemy cases prosecuted in the United Kingdom, it was held that blasphemy did not require a subjective intention to blaspheme, merely an intention to publish the offensive material. Whether the material is offensive is to be objectively determined.[21]

However, where the law is meant to protect public order, that is, to prevent potential threats to public order, the focus should be on the impact of the material. This brings in more difficult concepts like feelings and offence, and their relationship with order. This is because the analysis of whether particular speech could threaten public order depends on how it is received by the recipients or targets of the speech. The *actus reus* requirement may still be the same in terms of the mere publication of material adjudged to be offensive. However, the determination of whether a material is offensive should be linked to its potential impact on public order, which itself is premised upon the effect of the speech on the feelings of adherents and the actions that they are likely to undertake as a result of those feelings. In other words, there is a need to determine the speech-action nexus.

The move away from blasphemy, *stricto sensu*, was necessary for the provisions to operate meaningfully within a context of great religious diversity, rather than in a dominant Christian context where the primary divisions are sectarian (intra-religious) rather than inter-religious. Macaulay's provisions in the Penal Code have been described as a concession to the realities of cultural diversity.[22] Blasphemy laws make little sense in such a pluralistic setting, since there is no consensus on what is sacred or orthodox. Laws against blasphemy serve to protect the dominant values and norms of society and to ensure its continuing

[20] ibid. See also Macleod, 'Note J' (n 9).
[21] *Whitehouse and Lemon v Gay News Ltd* [1979] AC 617 (HL), 618.
[22] Wright, 'Macaulay's Indian Penal Code' (n 19) 47.

cohesion. That blasphemy laws tend to be specific to the dominant religion is ironically reflected in the 1991 blasphemy case in England against Salman Rushdie for his book, *The Satanic Verses*. In rejecting the case, the British courts held that the book insulted Islam, not Christianity, and as such did not fall within the scope of its blasphemy laws.[23]

Practice also shows that blasphemy laws could be and have been used to control a religious population; since religion is a useful means of ensuring obedience to the law, offensive speech could undermine the foundation of law.[24] Where the legitimacy of the state is closely tied to a particular religion, either because there is a state religion or when the state strongly identifies itself with a particular religion, religious offences may be viewed as attacks on the state itself, and accordingly threatened with severe penalties that may extend to the death penalty.[25] In this regard, blasphemy has been regarded as akin to treason.[26] Indeed, according to Blackstone, blasphemy was justified in England because 'Christianity is part of the laws of England.'[27] In one of the major cases on the criminal offence of blasphemy in England, *R v Taylor*, the King's Bench held that the accused's utterance was 'not only an offence to God and to religion, but a crime against the laws, state and Government'.[28] This represents a subtle but sure shift from a focus on protecting religion to protecting religious believers. Notably, it is around this time that Macaulay prepared the IPC. It is perhaps unsurprising that instead of codifying the 'arcane common law of blasphemy', Macaulay replaced it with provisions that 'recognised cultural plurality and anticipated modern measures against cultural denigration'.[29] There was a change in focus from 'You shall not revile God' to 'You shall not revile individuals because of their religion'.[30]

There are disagreements about whether the religious penal clauses went too far to accommodate local cultural diversity, or not far enough.[31] At the same time, it would be a mistake to think that religious penal clauses were only meant to ensure peaceable inter-group relations. In colonial India, power differentials had a religious dimension. The British were identified with Christianity and were in possession of all the highest posts in government, in the judiciary and in the army. They ruled over Muslims (then identified as Mohammedans) and Hindus. As Macaulay observes, 'Such a state of things is pregnant with

[23] *R v Chief Metropolitan Stipendiary Magistrate, ex parte Choudhury* [1991] 1 QB 429, 447.
[24] Greg Taylor, 'Austria's Law Against Defamation of Religion: A Case Study' (2015) 30(1) *Journal of Law and Religion* 80.
[25] Radtke, 'Religious Offenses' (n 3).
[26] Knechtle, 'Blasphemy, Defamation of Religion and Religious Hate Speech' (n 5) 203.
[27] William Blackstone, *Commentaries on the Laws of England* (University of Chicago Press, 1979) bk IV, ch 4.
[28] *R v Taylor* (1676) 1 Vent 293 (KB).
[29] Wright, 'Macaulay's Indian Penal Code' (n 19) 48.
[30] Knechtle, 'Blasphemy, Defamation of Religion and Religious Hate Speech' (n 5) 211.
[31] Wright, 'Macaulay's Indian Penal Code' (n 19) 48.

dangers which can only be averted by a firm adherence to the true principles of toleration.'[32] One impact of the religious penal clauses was that they changed the terms of inter-religious relations and installed the British colonial authorities as the determiner of the parameters of inter-religious engagement. Law was a powerful tool used by colonialists to create new legal relations in order to reinforce colonial rule and capitalist expansion.[33] As Merry points out, 'Law often serves as the handmaiden for processes of domination, helping to create new systems of control and regulation.'[34] Indeed, the religious penal clauses had a double function of preserving public order and legitimating the role of the ruling British class as the supposedly neutral arbiter of inter- and intra-communal conflict.

III. DIVERGING NORMS: CONSTITUTIONAL ARRANGEMENT, RELIGIOUS DEMOGRAPHY AND POLITICAL POWER

While common law countries in Asia trace the genealogy of their religious penal provisions to the IPC, there is divergence in how these have been applied in the different jurisdictions. These divergences reflect differing understanding of the aims of these provisions, the socio-political place of religion as well as the function of criminal law. That these provisions have been employed differently is not surprising. Laws develop differently in response to different constitutional and political contexts. Legal transplants create path dependencies, but these paths may still diverge depending on the conditions in which these transplants find themselves. In relation to the religious penal clauses, there are at least three factors influencing whether a jurisdiction tends towards using the religious offence provisions to police public order or to police religious orthodoxy. The first is the degree of *identification* between state and religion in the constitutional text. The closer a constitution identifies religion as a basis of state identity, or declares a majority religion deserving of special protection, the more likely the law could be captured by a religious majority to advance its objective of policing the boundaries of orthodoxy. This is consistent with Durham's insight that positive identification (alongside negative identification) correlates with low levels of religious freedom. This is because state identification means that the state adopts a 'sharply defined attitude toward one or more religions, leaving little room for dissenting views'.[35] Accordingly, the laws are more likely to be interpreted as preserving a religious hierarchy within society, and therefore operate in a way that is more akin to blasphemy laws.

[32] Macleod, 'Note J' (n 9), 87.
[33] Merry, 'Law and Colonialism' (n 2) 917.
[34] ibid 917.
[35] W Cole Durham Jr, 'Perspectives on Religious Liberty: A Comparative Framework' in Johan D Van der Vyver and John Witte Jr (eds), *Religious Human Rights in Global Perspectives: Legal Perspectives* (Martinus Nijhoff Publishers, 1996) 18.

A second factor is the *religious demography* of the country. Interestingly, the more religiously diverse a country is, such that there is no single dominant majority, the less likely it would be for the laws to be captured for policing religious orthodoxy. In contrast, where there is a dominant religious majority existing within a religiously divided society, it is more likely that offences against religion would be used like blasphemy laws in favour of the majority religion. Religious penal clauses would therefore serve to preserve a double religious hierarchy – the first is a hierarchy between the majority religion and the minority religion; and the second is a hierarchy within the majority religion (in policing the boundaries between orthodoxy and heresy).

The third factor is the extent to which the government relies on religion to legitimise its power. The weaker the government, the more likely it is to depend on religion to legitimise its position, and thus the use of the provisions as blasphemy laws can enhance the government's position vis-à-vis its religious constituents. At the very least, the weakness of the government means that it is often not in a position to oppose religious extremism. Accordingly, a weak government is more likely to be pressured to employ religious penal clauses to preserve religious hierarchy.

I will now discuss key developments in the jurisprudence on religious penal clauses in three countries – Singapore, Pakistan, and Myanmar. In showing the divergence in jurisprudential developments, I will point to the role that the three factors – *state-religion identification*, *religious demography* and *religious legitimation* – play in influencing these developments.

A. Singapore and the Maintenance of Religious Harmony

Singapore's penal provisions under its 'Offences Against Race and Religion' chapter in the Penal Code were infrequently employed until more recent times. The stated aim of these prosecutions was to ensure racial and religious harmony. In most instances, the case was dealt with summarily. There is, however, one case where extensive treatment was given to a provision in that chapter, *Public Prosecutor v Amos Yee Pang Seng*.[36] In this case, the accused was charged under section 298 of the Penal Code, alongside section 292(1)(a) (criminalising the transmission of obscene materials). The offending material was a YouTube video that he had made, entitled 'Lee Kuan Yew is finally dead'. Section 298 is a provision adopted directly from the IPC, which criminalises speech made with deliberate intent to wound the religious or racial feelings of any person. The full provision states:

> Whoever, with deliberate intention of wounding the religious or racial feelings of any person, utters any word or makes any sound in the hearing of that person, or

[36] *Public Prosecutor v Amos Yee Pang Seng* [2015] SGDC 215 (District Court).

> makes any gesture in the sight of that person, or places any object in the sight of that person, or causes any matter however represented to be seen or heard by that person, shall be punished with imprisonment for a term which may extend to 3 years, or with fine, or with both.

The section 298 charge specifically related to the portion of the video that compared Lee Kuan Yew with Jesus, whom the accused called both 'power hungry and malicious, but deceive others into thinking that they are compassionate and kind', and further claimed that 'Their impact and legacy will ultimately not last as more and more people find out that they're full of bull.' The accused further stated that

> Lee Kuan Yew's followers are completely delusional and ignorant and have absolutely no sound logic or knowledge about him that is grounded in reality, which Lee Kuan Yew very easily manipulates, similar to the Christian knowledge of the Bible and the work of a multitude of priests.

The requirement of deliberate intent in section 298 addresses intentional racial or religious disparagement. However, it does not look to the impact of the speech, which raises the question of whether this provision as currently interpreted is conceptually consistent with the objectives of public order. This is especially since the court held that the offence 'does not require proof that the religious feelings were in fact wounded'.[37] Nonetheless, it is clear that the District Court had in mind that religious offence should be linked to public order concerns. In the same judgment, the Court stated:

> Religion is a very sensitive and passionate subject. We pride ourselves on our multi-ethnic and multi-religious society where everyone is free to practice his religion. This achievement is the result of much hard work over the years and is an on-going effort. Pejorative remarks have the potential to cause social disorder.[38]

The subject of protection is the feelings of adherents as linked to public order considerations, rather than the policing of the boundaries of religious orthodoxy. This is further emphasised in the High Court's reasoning affirming the decision. The High Court stated in a summary of the grounds of the decision:

> All this was done in the noble disguise of freedom of speech and a purported desire to generate genuine discussions and debate. [The accused's] deliberate use of vulgarities and crude language and obscene depiction to provoke reaction seems like someone throwing stones at the windows of a neighbour's flat to force the neighbour to notice him, come out to quarrel or even to fight. This does not sound like freedom of speech at all. It is a licence to hate, to humiliate others and to totally disregard their feelings or beliefs by using words to inflict unseen wounds.[39]

[37] ibid [40].
[38] ibid [81].
[39] 'Justice Tay Yong Kwang's Oral Judgement for Magistrate's Appeal No 9108 of 2015 *Amos Yee v Public Prosecutor*', [9] (Singapore, *Attorney-General's Chambers*, 9 October 2015) at www.agc.gov.sg/home/justice-tay-yong-kwang%27s-oral-judgement-for-magistrate-s-appeal-no.-9108-of-2015-amos-yee-v-public-prosecutor accessed 28 May 2019.

The public order objective is even clearer in the new provision added in 2007 by the Singapore Parliament. A new section 298A was introduced to criminalise the deliberate promotion of enmity, hatred or ill-will between different racial and religious groups on grounds of race or religion. It is meant to complement section 298. The provision states:

> Whoever—
>
> (a) by words, either spoken or written, or by signs or by visible representations or otherwise, knowingly promotes or attempts to promote, on grounds of religion or race, disharmony or feelings of enmity, hatred or ill-will between different religious or racial groups; or
>
> (b) commits any act which he knows is prejudicial to the maintenance of harmony between different religious or racial groups and which disturbs or is likely to disturb the public tranquility,
>
> shall be punished with imprisonment for a term which may extend to 3 years, or with fine, or with both.

Section 298A thus makes it clear that the law is aimed at protecting public order linked to peaceful inter-religious and inter-racial relations. Like the Penal Code's original drafters, the Singapore Parliament sees the provision as striking a balance between the right to freedom of religion and freedom of speech and the need to maintain public order that could be affected by religious offence.[40]

As I have previously argued, 'feelings are an unreliable basis upon which to find a constitutional violation'.[41] This means that a criminal provision that depends on the subjective feelings of a subject group would be highly problematic, as this could allow highly sensitive segments of particular groups to hold others hostage to their feelings.[42] As such, a much better test is to consider the potential threat to public order. This is more justifiable from the perspective of free speech as a constitutional right, since public order is an explicit basis upon which speech could be circumscribed in the Singapore Constitution. Furthermore, while many scholars have argued against a right not to be offended in one's religious beliefs as a justifiable reason for freedom of speech, many nonetheless acknowledge that there may be other legitimate reasons to restrict speech.[43] Public order is one such legitimate aim. Notably, the Singapore Parliament recently extracted these provisions, insofar as they relate to religion,

[40] 'Penal Code (Amendment) Bill', Singapore Parliamentary Debates: Official Reports, 22 October 2007, vol 83, col 2175 (Senior Minister of State for Home Affairs, Associate Professor Ho Peng Kee) (describing the expansion of s 298 and introduction of s 298A as responses to a greater need for sensitivity, amidst the threat of religious extremism and terrorism to the new global security climate).

[41] Jaclyn L Neo, 'Seditious in Singapore! Free Speech and the Offence of Promoting Ill-Will and Hostility between Different Racial Groups' [2011] *Singapore Journal of Legal Studies* 351.

[42] ibid.

[43] See, eg, George Letsas, 'Is There a Right Not to be Offended in One's Religious Beliefs?' in Lorenzo Zucca and Camil Ungureanu (eds), *Law, State and Religion in the New Europe: Debates and Dilemmas* (Cambridge University Press, 2012) 243.

from the Singapore Penal Code, and incorporated these religious penal offences into the Maintenance of Religious Harmony Act. Li-ann Thio's chapter (chapter 2) provides a closer examination of these changes, but what is crucial for our discussion here is that these legislative changes have made it clear that the aim of these provisions is to maintain public order through the management of inter-religious relations.

Based on the three factors identified above, it is perhaps not surprising that Singapore is the jurisdiction that has best kept to the original intent of the provisions as a way to maintain public order as peaceful coexistence among different groups, rather than to preserve one religion's dominance. On *state-religion identification*, Singapore has always proclaimed itself to be a secular state. This of course can mean many things. However, what is crucial is that the Singapore state does not identify positively (or even negatively) with any religion. Indeed, courts have held that the Constitution of the Republic of Singapore does not forbid the establishment of religion,[44] but that the state practises accommodative secularism.[45] This is understood as ensuring that the protection of freedom of religion under our Constitution is premised on removing restrictions to one's choice of religious belief.[46] Secularism here is further conceptualised as state neutrality and even-handed treatment of all religions.[47] Accordingly, Singapore eschews any state identification with any particular religion and is not interested in applying the religious penal clauses specifically to benefit one particular religious majority. The Singapore Government has always emphasised that it is not interested in matters of theology but only in ensuring public order and peace.

This brings us to the second factor – *religious demography*. The Pew Research Centre identified Singapore as the most religiously diverse country of the 232 countries it studied.[48] Its high score reflects the spread of religions across its population. About one-third of Singapore's population is Buddhist (34 per cent), while 18 per cent are Christian, 16 per cent are religiously unaffiliated, 14 per cent are Muslim, 5 per cent are Hindu, less than 1 per cent are Jewish, with the remainder belonging to folk or traditional religions (2 per cent) or to other religions

[44] *Chan Hiang Leng Colin v Public Prosecutor* [1994] 3 SLR 662 (High Court) (Yong Pung How CJ).

[45] *Nappalli Peter Williams v Institute of Technical Education* [1999] 2 SLR(R) 529, [28]; see also Thio Li-ann, 'The Secular Trumps the Sacred: Constitutional Issues Arising from Colin Chan v Public Prosecutor' (1995) 16 *Singapore Law Review* 26.

[46] *Nappalli* (ibid) [28].

[47] Dr Tony Tan Keng Yam, 'Teaching of Religious Knowledge in Schools (Statement by the Minister of Education)', Singapore Parliamentary Debates: Official Reports, 6 October 1989, vol 54, col 574. See also 'Govt is secular, not atheistic: BG Yeo' *The Straits Times* (Singapore, 8 October 1992).

[48] Singapore scored the highest on the Religious Diversity Index, which looks at the percentage of each country's population that belongs to the eight major religious groups as of 2010. The closer a country comes to having equal shares of the eight groups, the higher its religious diversity score. 'Global Religious Diversity: Half of the Most Religiously Diverse Countries are in Asia-Pacific Region' (*Pew Research Center*, 4 April 2014) at www.pewforum.org/2014/04/04/global-religious-diversity/ accessed 26 November 2018.

(making up 10 per cent as a group).[49] In other words, while Singaporean society is religiously diverse, there is no one dominant religion. Furthermore, religious division is carefully managed and often sought to be transcended by emphasising commonality. Lastly, Singapore is a dominant party state, where the ruling party has held supermajorities in Parliament since independence. The Government does not depend on *religious legitimation* to buttress its political legitimacy but instead has relied on economic success and good governance to create performance legitimacy. This goes to the third factor: since there is no need to depend on religious legitimation, the Government sees its function as ensuring peaceful coexistence among fairly coequal religious communities. There is no need for it to appeal to any one single group to buttress its political legitimacy. If any, it sees the need to treat all groups equally (to the extent possible) in order to ensure that no major religious group feels permanently excluded or maltreated.

B. Pakistan and Religious Orthodoxy of the Majority

In contrast, in Pakistan, which calls itself an Islamic Republic, the justification for the religious penal clauses has shifted to protecting religious orthodoxy, with the law increasingly used against religious minorities, including minorities within the religious majority. Part of this stemmed from significant legislative changes to the Penal Code, which effectively introduced blasphemy-type provisions to police the boundaries of religious orthodoxy. The military regime enacted Ordinances in the early 1980s and inserted section 295-B[50] into the Pakistani Penal Code, which made defiling the Holy Quran punishable with life imprisonment. The provision states:

> Whoever willfully defiles, damages or desecrates a copy of the Holy Quran or of an extract therefrom or uses it in any derogatory manner or for any unlawful purpose shall be punishable with imprisonment for life.

In addition, a new section 298A criminalised the use of derogatory remarks in respect of holy personages. The provision states:

> Whoever by words, either spoken or written, or by visible representation, or by any imputation, innuendo or insinuation, directly or indirectly, defiles the sacred name of any wife (Ummul Mumineen), or members of the family (Ahle-bait) any of the righteous Caliphs (Khulafa-e-Rashideen) or companions (Sahaaba) of the Holy Prophet

[49] The Pew Survey closely tracks, though not identically, the breakdown in the 2010 Population Census, which records the following statistics: Buddhism (33.3%), Christianity (18.3%), no religion (17.0%), Islam (14.7%), Taoism (10.9%), Hinduism (5.1%), and other religions (0.7%). 'Key Findings – Census of Population 2010 Statistical Release 1: Demographic Characteristics, Education, Language and Religion' (*Singapore Department of Statistics*, 26 February 2016) at www.singstat.gov.sg/docs/default-source/default-document-library/publications/publications_and_papers/cop2010/census_2010_release1/ findings.pdf accessed 26 November 2018.

[50] The provision was inserted by the Pakistan Penal Code (Amendment) Ordinance (Ordinance 1 of 1981) to the Pakistan Penal Code on 18 March 1981.

> (peace be upon him) shall be punishable with imprisonment of either description for a term which may extend to three years, or with fine, or both.[51]

The Penal Code has specifically been used to target the Ahmadi minority, especially after 1984 when two further provisions were added to Chapter XV of the Pakistani Penal Code. Section 298B specifically targets the Ahmadis by criminalising the 'misuse' of epithets, descriptions and titles reserved for Muslim holy personages or places. The provision states:

> (1) Any person of the Quadiani group or the Lahori Group (who call themselves 'Ahmadis' or by any other name) who by words, either spoken or written, or by visible representation,
>
> (a) refers to or addresses, any person, other than a Caliph or companion of the Holy Prophet Muhammad (PBUH), as 'Ameerul-Mumineen,' 'Khalifa-tul-Muslimeen', 'Sahaabi' or 'Razi Alah Anho';
> (b) refers to, or addresses, any person, other than a wife of the Holy Prophet Muhammad (peace be upon him), as 'Ummul-Mumineen';
> (c) refers to, or addresses, any person, other than a member of the family (Ahle- bait) of the Holy Prophet Muhammad (peace be upon him) as Ahle-bait; or
> (d) refers to, or names, or calls, his place of worship as 'Masjid';
>
> shall be punished with imprisonment of either description for a term which may extend to three years, and shall also be liable to fine.
>
> (2) Any person of the Qadiani group or Lahori group (who call themselves 'Ahmadis' or by any other name) who by words, either spoken or written, or by visible representation, refers to the mode or form of call to prayers followed by his faith as 'Azan', or recites Azan as used by the Muslims, shall be punished with imprisonment of either description for a term which may extend to three years, and shall also be liable to fine.

Furthermore, the new section 298-C makes it an offence for Ahmadis to call themselves Muslims and preach their faith. The provision states:

> Any person of the Quadiani group or Lahori group (who call themselves 'Ahmadis' or by another name), who, directly or indirectly, poses himself as a Muslim, or calls, or refers to, his faith as Islam, or preaches or propagates his faith, or invites others to accept his faith, by words, either spoken or written, or by visible representation, or in any manner whatsoever outrages the religious feelings of Muslims, shall be punished with imprisonment of either description for a term which may extend to three years and shall also be liable to fine.

In 1985, another new section 295-C was added, which criminalised the use of derogatory remarks made with respect to the Prophet. The provision states:

> Whoever by words, either spoken or written, or by visible representation, or by any imputation, innuendo, or insinuation, directly or indirectly, defiles the sacred name of the Holy Prophet Muhammad (peace be upon him) shall be punishable with death, or imprisonment for life, and shall also be liable to fine.

[51] The provision was inserted by Pakistan Penal Code (Second Amendment) Ordinance (Ordinance XLIV of 1980) to the Pakistan Penal Code on 17 September 1980.

The wording of this section is general and vague, and does not require deliberate or malicious intent, even though it is a harsh provision that could attract the death penalty. Legislative changes to religious offences in the Pakistani Penal Code continued under the democratic government. In 1991, section 295-A of the Pakistani Penal Code was revised to raise the maximum punishment from two to 10 years' imprisonment.

Despite the apparent violation of the Ahmadis' freedom of religion, the Pakistan Supreme Court has upheld the law, thus preserving both a distinction between the Ahmadis and mainstream Muslims, and a hierarchy between them. The case of *Zaheeruddin v The State*[52] is instructive, as this is an instance where the Ahmadiyyas had challenged the constitutional validity of the Anti-Islamic Activities of the Quadiani Group, Lahori Group and Ahmadis (Prohibition and Punishment) Ordinance 1984, which added new sections 298B and 298C to the Pakistan Penal Code 1860.[53] A number of Ahmadis had been charged with and convicted of offences under the new sections added by the Ordinance. They claimed that the convictions violated their constitutionally guaranteed fundamental right to freedom of religion as provided in Article 20 of the 1973 Constitution. Article 20 states:

> Subject to law, public order and morality,—
>
> (a) every citizen shall have the right to profess, practice and propagate his religion; and
>
> (b) every religious denomination and every sect thereof shall have the right to establish, maintain and manage its religious institutions.

The Supreme Court upheld the Ordinance on the basis that it did not violate the freedom of religion as guaranteed under Article 20. The bulk of the majority opinion was devoted to establishing that Ahmadis are not Muslims, because their beliefs and theological doctrines are at variance with the beliefs of the majority of Muslims. The Court equated the regulation of religious epithets and terms with other statutes that regulate commercial activity, target deceptive trade practices, and protect trademarks and copyright. In doing so, the Court treated religious symbols and words as a form of property.[54] This raises questions of who owns that property, and who decides how to differentiate the owners from the 'thieves'. One of the Court's grounds was that the Ahmadis are religious frauds, and that they were engaging in deceptive practices in using those Islamic epithets.[55]

[52] *Zaheeruddin v The State* (1993) 26 SCMR 1718.

[53] The Ordinance also amended s 99A of the Code of Criminal Procedure 1898 and s 24 of the West Pakistan Press and Publications Ordinance 1963.

[54] The Court noted, 'For example, the Coca Cola company would not permit anyone to sell, even a few ounces of his own product in his own bottles or other receptacles, marked Coca Cola, even though its price may be a few cents. Further, it is a criminal offense carrying sentences of imprisonment and also fine. The principles involved are: do not deceive and do not violate the property rights of others.' *Zaheeruddin* (n 52) 1753–54.

[55] Interestingly, the majority erroneously quoted from the US Supreme Court judgment in *Cantwell v Connecticut*, 310 US 296 (1940), 306, which supposedly stated that 'the cloak of religion

While acknowledging that religious freedom extends beyond beliefs to religious practices, the Supreme Court held that this was limited to 'essential and integral' practices.[56] It then concluded that the Ahmadis had not demonstrated how the prohibited epithets and public rituals formed an essential part of their religion.[57] The Court stated that the use of the epithets by the Ahmadis created a law and order issue because it would potentially mislead Muslims:

> The Ahmadis have been desecrating [Islamic epithets] and using them for their own leaders and practices etc., to deceive the people that they are also of the same type status and the calibre. This practice not only deceived innocent, simple and not-well-informed people but also created law and order situation [*sic*] throughout the period. The legislation was, therefore, necessary, which in any way does not interfere with the religious freedom of the Ahamadis; for it only prohibits them from using those epithets etc., on which they have no claim of any nature. It does not prohibit them from coining their own.

By framing the issue as a question of balancing competing religious rights (the religious rights of Muslims versus the religious rights of the Ahmadis), the Court could justify supporting the state's position. The Ahmadis' request was couched as seeking to 'violate or take away the fundamental rights of others'.[58] Thus, the Court remarked:

> Can then anyone blame a Muslim if he loses control of himsel[f] on hearing, reading or seeing such blasphemous material as has been produced by Mirza Sahib? … It is in this background that one should visualize the public conduct of Ahmadis, at the centenary celebrations and imagine the reaction that it might have attracted from the Muslims. So, if an Ahmadi is allowed by the administration or the law to display or chant in public, the Shaair-e-Islam', *it is like creating a [Salman] Rushdi' out of him.* Can the administration in that case guarantee his life, liberty and property and if so at what cost? Again, if this permission is given to a procession or assembly on the streets or a public place, it is like *permitting civil war.*[59]

or religious belief does not protect anybody in committing fraud upon the public'. The correct quote was in fact more ambiguous, ie 'Nothing we have said is intended even remotely to imply that, under the cloak of religion, persons may, with impunity, commit frauds upon the public.' In *Cantwell*, father and son Jehovah's Witnesses had been charged for violating a local ordinance requiring a permit for solicitation, and for inciting a breach of peace after they travelled door-to-door proselytising in a predominantly Catholic neighbourhood. They argued that the solicitation statute and the breach of peace ordinance violated their First Amendment free-speech and free-exercise rights. The Court held unanimously in their favour. The Cantwells' message, while offensive, did not entail any threat to 'bodily harm' and was protected religious speech. In fact, the Court opined, 'No one would contest the proposition that a State may not, by statute, wholly deny the right to preach or to disseminate religious views.' The majority opinion in *Zaheeruddin* wholly and rather disingenuously misconstrued *Cantwell*; there is no doubt that Ordinance XX would not have been upheld under the standards applied in *Cantwell*.

[56] *Zaheeruddin* (n 52) 1762.

[57] ibid 1763.

[58] ibid 1765.

[59] ibid 1777–78 (emphasis added).

The decision situates the problem of Ahmadi practices within sectarian discussions concerning doctrines of Islamic morality and Islamic law, rather than strictly with considerations of public order and safety.[60] This is a distinctly pro-majoritarian approach since it relies on '*local public opinion*' to determine the parameters of the religious minorities' free exercise of religious liberties.[61] This nuanced distinction is important to note. A judgment based on religious orthodoxy limits the possibility of change, and on the range of persons who can permit this change. The acceptability of the Ahmadis becomes dependent on religious scholars, whereas the question of public order depends mainly on public opinion and political elites.[62] Religious penal clauses thus have been deployed to maintain a religious hierarchy within Muslim-majority Pakistan.

To contextualise, this jurisprudential shift in the use of the religious penal clauses as blasphemy provisions to preserve religious hierarchy may seem inevitable since Pakistan is a state that has at its core an identity seemingly inextricable from religion. It was created as a separate nation for Muslims in the subcontinent in contradistinction to India's secular (though Hindu-dominated) state. The Preamble to its 1973 Constitution declares that 'Pakistan would be a democratic State based on Islamic principles of social justice', and Article 1 of the Constitution states that 'Pakistan shall be a Federal Republic to be known as the Islamic Republic of Pakistan'. Article 2 of the Constitution further states that 'Islam shall be the State religion of Pakistan'. This establishes a strong *identification* between the state and Islam.

On religious demography, Pakistan has very low levels of religious diversity. About 96 per cent of its population are Muslims, with about 1.6 per cent Christians and 1.9 per cent Hindus.[63] The religious dominance of Muslims is expected to remain fairly stable in the coming decades.[64] Nevertheless, this religious dominance belies a religiously divided society where sectarianism is a deep source of division in the country. Religious penal clauses have served to preserve religious hierarchy. One can see this in the number of cases filed against Christians, for instance, for alleged blasphemy. The Asia Bibi case is only one of the most high-profile blasphemy cases involving the Christian minority.[65] Furthermore, as already seen, besides preserving the priority of Islam over other

[60] See also Jeffrey A Redding, 'Constitutionalizing Islam: Theory and Pakistan' (2004) 44(3) *Virginia Journal of International Law* 759, 794–95.

[61] ibid 795.

[62] The Ahmadis may perhaps be compared with the Mormon Church in the United States. It was only recently, during the 2012 campaign, that some Christian leaders started to accept Mormonism as compatible with Christianity and stopped calling it a cult.

[63] Pew Research Centre Report, 'Table: Religious Diversity Index Scores by Country' (4 April 2014), at www.pewforum.org/2014/04/04/religious-diversity-index-scores-by-country/.

[64] ibid.

[65] 'How blasphemy still remains Pakistan's notorious law a year after Asia Bibi's acquittal' *WION* (New Delhi, 27 February 2020) at www.wionews.com/south-asia/how-blasphemy-still-remains-pakistans-notorious-law-a-year-after-asia-bibis-acquittal-283051; *Deustche Welle*, 'The case of Asia Bibi in Pakistan' at www.dw.com/en/the-case-of-asia-bibi-in-pakistan/a-46263524. For more, please see Syed Ali Raza's contribution to this book (ch 6).

minority religions, the religious penal clauses have also served to preserve a distinction between the majority Muslims and the minority Ahmadis.

Lastly, it bears emphasising that *religious legitimation* has become crucial in Pakistan, which has a generally unstable political climate, having undergone cycles of democratic government and military dictatorships. Since its independence in 1947, Pakistan has had three constitutions,[66] multiple military coups and various regime changes.[67] The provisions added to the Pakistani Penal Code that serve to police the boundaries of religious orthodoxy were introduced under the military regime of Zia-ul-Haq, who pursued a clear Islamisation policy to bolster his legitimacy.[68] The political instability of Pakistan further means that civilian governments are weak and are never in a sufficiently strong position to eschew religious legitimation. They are also often in such a precarious political situation that any attempts to limit the use of the religious penal clauses as anti-blasphemy provisions to preserve religious hierarchy would be met with strong and sometimes violent resistance from certain sectors in society. For instance, in 2011, the governor of Punjab, the country's wealthiest and most populous province, was shot dead by one of his own guards, who said he was angry with the politician's public opposition to blasphemy laws.[69] The increasing use of the religious penal clauses in ways akin to anti-blasphemy laws must therefore be understood as an outcome of a confluence of these three factors on state-religious identification, religious demography and religious legitimation.

C. Myanmar

The religious penal clauses have been periodically used in Buddhist-majority Myanmar, though Frydenlund points out that British legal records indicate that 'religious offence' cases were not frequent. This suggests that, unlike in India, the religious penal clauses were 'not an important legal instrument for either the

[66] The first two constitutions were adopted in 1956 and 1962. The 1956 Constitution was drafted by the first Pakistani Constituent Assembly, which was elected in 1947 and adopted the first indigenous constitution nine years later. The 1962 Constitution was drafted under the General Ayub Khan's regime and abrogated by him in 1969 before he handed power to the Army Commander-in-Chief, General Agha Mohammad Yahya Khan. The present constitution was approved by the legislative assembly on 10 April 1973 under the Zulfikar Ali Bhutto Government. It was adopted in the aftermath of the 1971 civil war in Pakistan, which led to the creation of Bangladesh (formerly East Pakistan).

[67] Since independence in 1947, Pakistan has experienced three successful military coups. In 1958, the first Pakistani President, Major General Iskander Mirza, was deposed by General Ayub Khan. In 1977, General Zia-ul-Haq successfully deposed Prime Minister Zulfikar Ali Bhutto in a coup d'état. In 1999, senior officials loyal to army chief General Pervez Musharraf arrested Prime Minister Nawaz Sharif and took over the ruling of Pakistan. There were also other unsuccessful coup attempts.

[68] Martin Lau, *The Role of Islam In The Legal System of Pakistan* (Brill, 2006) 121. See also generally, Redding, 'Constitutionalizing Islam: Theory and Pakistan' (n 60).

[69] 'Pakistani governor opposing blasphemy law killed' *CTV News* (4 January 2011) at www.ctvnews.ca/pakistani-governor-opposing-blasphemy-law-killed-1.592093 accessed 26 November 2018.

British or the Burmese Buddhists in the larger schemes of contestation and negotiation over the status of religion in the colony'.[70] Burma was annexed to British India in three stages (1825 to 1885), and was administered as part of British India until 1937 when it became a separate administrative unit.[71] The IPC, which had applied to Burma, was now recast as the Burma Penal Code and has been in continuous application since. Like Pakistan, Myanmar has also experienced tumultuous periods of political instability. The initial 1947 Constitution marked Myanmar's independence as a parliamentary democracy, but since then Myanmar has experienced long periods of military rule, peppered with democratic elections in between. Scholars like Cheeseman have pointed to the profound and damaging effects on legal institutions as a result of half a century of military rule in Myanmar, where the criminal justice system has at times been instrumentalised for political control.[72] The current 2008 Constitution was drafted under military supervision, and was meant to 'guide' Myanmar's transition to a democracy.[73]

The religious penal clauses continue to have salience in Myanmar, having been occasionally used by the military regime to curb monastic opposition and dissent.[74] They have increasingly been employed against alleged insults to Buddhism in response to pressure from Buddhist nationalists during the current period of democratic transition, thus being used as a form of 'blasphemy' law to secure Buddhism's status as a national religion.[75] This is even though the 2008 Constitution does not establish Buddhism as the state religion but merely points to its special status. One recent case that has garnered widespread international attention was the conviction of bar manager, Phillip Blackwood (a New Zealander), and his two associates, Tun Thurein and Htut Ko Ko Lwin (Myanmar nationals), in 2015 for having insulted Buddhism.[76] The controversial case stemmed from an online advertisement that showed a psychedelic depiction of Buddha wearing headphones on the bar's Facebook page as part of a promotional campaign.[77] This caused outrage after the image was shared online, and

[70] Iselin Frydenlund, 'The rise of religious offence in transitional Myanmar' in Paul Rollier, Kathinka Frøystad and Arild Engelsen Ruud (eds), *Outrage: The Rise of Religious Offence in Contemporary South Asia* (University of Chicago Press, 2020) 84.

[71] See Melissa Crouch, *The Constitution of Myanmar: A Contextual Analysis* (Hart Publishing, 2019) on the complex constitutional history of and developments in Myanmar.

[72] Nick Cheesman, 'Thin Rule of Law or Un-Rule of Law in Myanmar?' (2009/2010) 82(4) *Pacific Affairs* 597.

[73] Crouch, *The Constitution of Myanmar* (n 71).

[74] Frydenlund, 'The rise of religious offence in transitional Myanmar' (n 70) 89.

[75] ibid.

[76] Elizabeth LaForgia, 'Myanmar court jails New Zealand man for insulting Buddha' *Jurist* (17 March 2015) at www.jurist.org/news/2015/03/myanmar-court-jails-new-zealand-man-for-insulting-buddha/.

[77] 'Burma Jails New Zealand Bar Manager over "Insulting" Buddha Images' *The Guardian* (Rangoon, 17 March 2015) at www.theguardian.com/world/2015/mar/17/burma-jails-new-zealand-bar-manager-over-insulting-buddha-images.

the bar was ordered to be shut down.[78] The three were charged under sections 295 and 295A of the Myanmar Penal Code. There was also another charge under section 188 of the Penal Code for disobeying the direction of a civil servant. Section 295 provides that

> [w]hoever destroys, damages or defiles any of worship, or any object held sacred by any class or person with the intention of thereby insulting the religion of any of person or with the knowledge that any class of likely to consider such destruction, damage or defilement as insult to their religion, shall be punished with either description for a term which may extend to two years or with fine, or with both.

Section 295(A) states that

> [w]hoever, with deliberate and malicious intention of outraging the religious feelings of any class of [persons in the Union] by words, either spoken or written, or by visible representations, insults or attempts to insult the religion or the religious beliefs of that class, shall be punished with imprisonment of either description for a term which may extend to two years, or with fine, or with both.

The Bahan Township Court Judge sentenced each defendant to two and a half years in prison with hard labour. The Judge held that Blackwood 'intentionally plotted to insult religious belief' when he posted the defamatory picture of the Buddha.[79] It was deemed insufficient that Blackwood removed the image and posted an apology. The Judge said that 'ignorance of the law is not an excuse', and that in any case, Blackwood should be well aware of the culture in Myanmar because he had stayed in Myanmar for more than three years.[80] As for the bar-owner, the judge stated that he should have but failed to instruct his foreign staff about the culture and traditions of the country. Blackwood was released in a presidential amnesty on 22 January 2016, but not his two co-defendants.[81]

Like in Pakistan, the religious penal clauses have become the tool for prosecuting blasphemy. There is a close association between the Myanmar state and the Buddhist monastic order, and this is reflected, for instance, in how the religious penal clauses have been used to punish heretics. The military regime had asserted strong state control of the Sangha (the monastic order) by strengthening the Buddhist courts (vinicchaya) and creating the State Sangha Mahanayaka Committee (referred to as the MaHaNa) in 1980. The MaHaNa oversees the regulation and conduct of the Sangha, and together with the Buddhist courts has served to institute a particularly conservative and scripturalist strand of elite

[78] 'New Zealand Bar Manager Held in Burma over "Buddha" Drinks Promotion' *The Guardian* (11 December 2014) at www.theguardian.com/world/2014/dec/11/new-zealand-bar-manager-held-in-burma-over-buddha-drinks-promotion.

[79] See 'Myanmar court jails three for insulting Buddhism', Al Jazeera (17 March 2015) at www.aljazeera.com/news/2015/03/17/myanmar-court-jails-three-for-insulting-buddhism/.

[80] See 'Myanmar court jails three for insulting Buddhism', Al Jazeera (17 March 2015) at https://globalfreedomofexpression.columbia.edu/cases/the-case-of-v-gastro-bar-philip-blackwood-htut-ko-ko-lwin-and-tun-thurein/.

[81] '"They can Arrest You at Any Time": The Criminalization of Peaceful Expression in Burma' *Human Rights Watch* (29 June 2016) at www.hrw.org/report/2016/06/30/they-can-arrest-you-any-time/criminalization-peaceful-expression-burma.

monasticism.[82] The religious penal clauses have buttressed this control over the Sangha. In the case of *Shin Nyana (aka) Shin Moe Pya (Monk) v Republic of the Union of Myanmar*,[83] a monk was alleged to have rejected the supervision of the State Sangha Council by establishing his own religious order commonly known as 'Moe Pya'. He was punished with three years' imprisonment under the Law relating to the Sangha Organisation No 20/1990, which provides that if a monk establishes a 'new sect' or organisation that is not under the supervision of the State Sangha Council (sections 8–9) then he is liable to a term of imprisonment of between six months and three years (section 12). In a subsequent case, he was sentenced to two years' imprisonment for defiling a religious place of worship under section 295, and an additional two years' imprisonment under section 295 (A) of the Penal Code. In the third case before a court, he was sentenced to five years' imprisonment under section 6 of the Law Relating to Forming of Organisations No 6/1988, for insulting the Sangha and promoting ideology that was said to be inconsistent with the teachings of Buddhism. His appeals against these cases were all dismissed.[84]

The use of religious penal clauses in a manner akin to blasphemy laws has the aim of preserving religious hierarchy vis-à-vis religious minorities. As in Pakistan, this includes maintaining religious orthodoxy within the dominant religion so as to ensure the integrity of that religion. The three factors all serve to contribute to this direction. On state-religion identification, it is notable that while the earlier 1974 Constitution did not grant special recognition to Buddhism, the 2008 Constitution expressly recognises the 'special position of Buddhism as the faith professed by the great majority of the citizens of the Union'.[85] While this does not necessarily mean that Myanmar is a Buddhist state, this special position provides a strong impetus for strong positive identification between the state and Buddhism. By doing so, the policing of boundaries of orthodoxy between religious majorities and religious minorities becomes crucial in upholding this special relationship. This is further aggravated by the second factor on religious demography. Myanmar society comprises 80.1 per cent Buddhists, 7.8 per cent Christians, and 4 per cent Muslims.[86] This means that Buddhists are the overwhelming majority in the country, though in a slightly lower proportion than for Muslims in Pakistan.

This goes to the third factor, which is that the Government has seen a need to legitimate its political power through religion, or at least is unable to resist pressure from religious groups, particularly religious nationalist groups, which have been very active in Myanmar.[87] Two of the most prominent Buddhist nationalist

[82] Frydenlund, 'The rise of religious offence in transitional Myanmar' (n 70) 78.
[83] *Shin Nyana (aka) Shin Moe Pya (Monk) v Republic of the Union of Myanmar* 2011 MLR P 126.
[84] With thanks to Professor Thi Thi Lwin for reference to this case.
[85] Section 368 of the Constitution of the Republic of the Union of Myanmar (2008).
[86] Again, using the Pew Research Centre Report, 'Table: Religious Diversity Index Scores by Country' (4 April 2014) at www.pewforum.org/2014/04/04/religious-diversity-index-scores-by-country/.
[87] *Keeping the Faith: A Study of Freedom of Thought, Conscience, and Religion in ASEAN* (Human Rights Resource Centre, 2015).

groups are the *Amyo Ba-tha Tha-tha-na Ka-kwaè-saung-shauk-ye Apwè* (abbreviated to *Ma-Ba-Tha*) (literally translated as Organisation for Protection of Race, Religion and Sāsanā, although its official English translation is Patriotic Association of Myanmar (PAM)) and the 969 monks movement. *Ma-Ba-Tha* was responsible for promoting the package of Race and Religion Protection Laws, comprising four laws – one against religious conversion, one against interfaith marriage, one on monogamy and another on population control.[88] The motivation behind these laws is to supposedly protect Buddhism, which both *Ma-Ba-Tha* and 969 claim is under threat from Islam and Islamisation.[89]

The role of the *Ma-Ba-Tha* in championing prosecutions under the religious penal clauses has been clear in some cases. It was *Ma-Ba-Tha* that complained about Blackwood's Facebook advertisement and pressured the Government to prosecute. It was also *Ma-Ba-Tha* that pressured the Government to prosecute the writer Htin Lin Oo under section 295(A) of the Penal Code for criticising the radical racist rhetoric of some monks, saying it was not consistent with Buddhist teaching.[90] The current National League of Democracy Government, while democratically elected in a landslide, remains politically weak. Even if it may not be actively seeking religious legitimation, it is also not in a sufficiently strong position to resist political pressure from Buddhist nationalist groups. Accordingly, whether directly or indirectly, religious legitimation or, at least, the lack of direct opposition from the religious majority, is seen as crucial to strengthen political legitimacy and regime stability.

IV. CONCLUSION

Religious penal clauses may well continue to have a place in societies divided by religious differences. However, the evolving use of such provisions to police religious orthodoxy will be problematic as it tends to be used to control religious minorities, which includes minorities within the religious majority, so as to preserve the hierarchical religious status quo. In contrast, one might suggest that the way in which Singapore has employed its religious penal clauses hews most closely to the original intent of the laws. The laws are primarily used by a government assuming for itself the role of a neutral arbiter to control and manage inter-religious relations.

[88] Iselin Frydenlund, 'A new formatting: Myanmar's 2015 "race and religion laws"' in Marius Timmann Mjaaland (ed), *Formatting Religion: Across Politics, Education, Media, and Law* (Taylor & Francis, 2019) ch 3 (detailing how *Ma-Ba-Tha* circulated drafts of these four laws, and claimed that its nationwide mobilisation and pressure led to the Government's eventually enacting them).

[89] ibid.

[90] ibid.

Ultimately, the relationship between religious offence and religious pluralism needs to be better interrogated. A purely individualistic view of religion and religious practice would not provide an adequate lens through which to understand religious offence and religious dignity. As Martínez-Torrón argues, 'Democracy and pluralism could be more endangered by a possible abuse of the power to restrict free speech than by the potential harm that abusive forms of expression cause to religious beliefs.'[91] While the religious penal clauses can and have been abused, arguments based on expansive free speech and religious freedom claims coming from a historically embedded intellectual and cultural tradition are unlikely to be persuasive if the particular context is not taken into account. Legal interventions do shape and reshape society, and legal reforms are necessary to pursue certain objectives in society.[92] Contextualised approaches are, however, more likely to be persuasive and effective. Lastly, legal 'intervention' can also take the form of forbearance. Indeed, when it comes to religious offences, it may be that 'law should only play a limited role'.[93] Even without prosecution and active enforcement, law can play an expressive role in setting out the terms of the debate, and signalling good from bad behaviour.[94]

Whatever approach one takes, it should be borne in mind that the law of each society must be understood within its historical, cultural, economic, moral/religious and jurisprudential/intellectual tradition.[95] Watson once said that a 'successful legal transplant … will grow in its new body, and become part of that body just as the rule or institution would have continued to develop in its parent system'.[96] Not quite a 'legal irritant',[97] the religious penal clauses have adapted to local contexts and transformed these legal and political systems. After all, legal transplants bring 'legal transformation'.[98] The extent of that transformation is not entirely detached from its original intent, however, and in some contexts one might see a reversion to, and even an augmentation of, the original purpose of the law. In this regard, one might see these developments in religious penal clauses in common law Asia as both old and new.[99]

[91] Javier Martínez-Torrón, 'Freedom of Expression Versus Freedom of Religion in the European Court of Human Rights' in András Sajó (ed), *Censorial Sensitivities: Free Speech and Religion in a Fundamentalist World* (Eleven International Publishing, 2007) 269.

[92] Sally Falk Moore, *Law as Process: An Anthropological Approach* (Routledge and K Paul, 1978) 343.

[93] George Baylon Radics and Poon Yee Suan, 'Amos Yee, Free Speech, and Maintaining Religious Harmony in Singapore' (2016) 12(2) *University of Pennsylvania Asian Law Review* 186, 241.

[94] On how laws on the maintenance of religious harmony in Singapore have an expressive function, see Jaclyn Neo, 'Dimensions of Religious Harmony as Constitutional Practice: Beyond State Control' (2019) 20(7) *German Law Journal* 966.

[95] Knechtle, 'Blasphemy, Defamation of Religion and Religious Hate Speech' (n 5) 217.

[96] Watson, 'Legal Transplants' (n 1) 27.

[97] Gunther Teubner, 'Legal Irritants: Good Faith in British Law, or How Unifying Law Ends up in New Divergences' (1998) 61 *Modern Law Review* 11.

[98] Watson, *Legal Transplants* (n 1) 116.

[99] ibid.

BIBLIOGRAPHY

—— 'Table: Religious Diversity Index Scores by Country' (4 April 2014) www.pewforum.org/2014/04/04/religious-diversity-index-scores-by-country/

Al Jazeera, 'Myanmar court jails three for insulting Buddhism' (17 March 2015) at https://www.aljazeera.com/news/2015/3/17/myanmar-court-jails-three-for-insulting-buddhism.

Blackstone, W, *Commentaries on the Laws of England* (University of Chicago Press, 1979)

Bodla, AR, 'Genesis of Blasphemy Laws in Colonial India' (2017) XXXVIII(2) *Pakistan Journal of History and Culture* 140

Cheesman, N, 'Thin Rule of Law or Un-Rule of Law in Myanmar?' (2009/2010) 82(4) *Pacific Affairs* 597

Cox, N, 'Pourquoi Suis-Je Charlie? Blasphemy, Freedom of Religion, and the Nature of "Offensive" Cartoons' (2015) 4 *Oxford Journal of Law and Religion* 343

Crouch, M, *The Constitution of Myanmar: A Contextual Analysis* (Hart Publishing, 2019)

CTV News, 'Pakistani governor opposing blasphemy law killed' (4 January 2011) at www.ctvnews.ca/pakistani-governor-opposing-blasphemy-law-killed-1.592093 accessed 26 November 2018.

Deustche Welle, 'The case of Asia Bibi in Pakistan' at www.dw.com/en/the-case-of-asi a-bibi-in-pakistan/a-46263524

Durham, WC Jr, 'Perspectives on Religious Liberty: A Comparative Framework' in Johan D Van der Vyver and John Witte Jr (eds), *Religious Human Rights in Global Perspectives: Legal Perspectives* (Martinus Nijhoff Publishers, 1996) 18

Gelber, K, 'The False Analogy between Vilification and Sedition' (2009) 33 *Melbourne University Law Review* 270

Global Freedom of Expression, 'The Case of V Gastro Bar (PHilip Blackwood, Htut Ko Ko Lwin, and Tun Thurein' (17 March 2015) at https://globalfreedomofexpression.columbia.edu/cases/the-case-of-v-gastro-bar-philip-blackwood-htut-ko-ko-lwin-and-tun-thurein/

Harding, A, 'The Legal Transplants Debate: Getting Beyond the Impasse?' in Vito Breda (ed), *Legal Transplants in East Asia and Oceania* (Cambridge University Press, 2019) 13

Human Rights Resource Centre, *Keeping the Faith: A Study of Freedom of Thought, Conscience, and Religion in ASEAN* (2015)

Human Rights Watch, '"They can Arrest You at Any Time": The Criminalization of Peaceful Expression in Burma' (29 June 2016) at www.hrw.org/report/2016/06/30/they-can-arrest-you-any-time/criminalization-peaceful-expression-burma

Knechtle, JC, 'Blasphemy, Defamation of Religion and Religious Hate Speech: Is There a Difference that Makes a Difference?' in Andras Koltay and Jeroen Temperman J (eds), *Blasphemy and Freedom of Expression: Comparative, Theoretical, and Historical Reflections after the Charlie Hebdo Massacre* (Cambridge University Press, 2017) 199

LaForgia, E, 'Myanmar court jails New Zealand man for insulting Buddha' *Jurist* (17 March 2015) at www.jurist.org/news/2015/03/myanmar-court-jails-new-zealand-man-for-insulting-buddha/

Lau, M, *The Role of Islam In The Legal System of Pakistan* (Brill, 2006)

Legrand, P, 'The Impossibility of "Legal Transplants"' (1997) 4 *Maastrict Journal of European and Comparative Law* 111

Letsas, G, 'Is There a Right Not to be Offended in One's Religious Beliefs?' in Lorenzo Zucca and Camil Ungureanu (eds), *Law, State and Religion in the New Europe: Debates and Dilemmas* (Cambridge University Press, 2012) 243

Macleod, JM, 'Note J on the Chapter of Offences Relating to Religion and Caste' in *Notes on the Report of the Indian Law Commissions on the Indian Penal Code* (W Clowes, 1848) 87

Martínez-Torrón, J, 'Freedom of Expression Versus Freedom of Religion in the European Court of Human Rights' in András Sajó (ed), *Censorial Sensitivities: Free Speech and Religion in a Fundamentalist World* (Eleven International Publishing, 2007) 269

Melville, JC, *Copies of the Special Reports of the Indian Law Commission* (East India House, 1847)

Merry, SE, 'Law and Colonialism' (1991) 25 *Law and Society Review* 889

Moore, SF, *Law as Process: An Anthropological Approach* (Routledge and K Paul, 1978)

Neo, JL, 'Dimensions of Religious Harmony as Constitutional Practice: Beyond State Control' (2019) 20(7) *German Law Journal* 966

——, 'Seditious in Singapore! Free Speech and the Offence of Promoting Ill-Will and Hostility between Different Racial Groups' [2011] *Singapore Journal of Legal Studies* 351

Pew Research Center, 'Global Religious Diversity: Half of the Most Religiously Diverse Countries are in Asia-Pacific Region' (4 April 2014) at www.pewforum.org/2014/04/04/global-religious-diversity/ accessed 26 November 2018

Radics, GB, and Poon, YS, 'Amos Yee, Free Speech, and Maintaining Religious Harmony in Singapore' (2016) 12(2) *University of Pennsylvania Asian Law Review* 186

Radtke, H, 'Religious Offenses' in Hans Dieter Betz et al (eds), *Religion Past and Present Online* (Brill, 2011) at referenceworks.brillonline.com/entries/religion-past-and-present/religious-offenses-SIM_124602

Redding, JA, 'Constitutionalizing Islam: Theory and Pakistan' (2004) 44(3) *Virginia Journal of International Law* 759

Singapore Department of Statistics, 'Key Findings – Census of Population 2010 Statistical Release 1: Demographic Characteristics, Education, Language and Religion' (26 February 2016) at www.singstat.gov.sg/docs/default-source/default-document-library/publications/publications_and_papers/cop2010/census_2010_release1/findings.pdf accessed 26 November 2018

Taylor, G, 'Austria's Law Against Defamation of Religion: A Case Study' (2015) 30(1) *Journal of Law and Religion* 80

Teubner, G, 'Legal Irritants: Good Faith in British Law, or How Unifying Law Ends up in New Divergences' (1998) 61 *Modern Law Review* 11

The Guardian, 'Burma Jails New Zealand Bar Manager over "Insulting" Buddha Images' (Rangoon, 17 March 2015) at www.theguardian.com/world/2015/mar/17/burma-jails-new-zealand-bar-manager-over-insulting-buddha-images

——, 'New Zealand Bar Manager Held in Burma over "Buddha" Drinks Promotion' (11 December 2014) at www.theguardian.com/world/2014/dec/11/new-zealand-bar-manager-held-in-burma-over-buddha-drinks-promotion

The Straits Times, 'Govt is secular, not atheistic: BG Yeo' (Singapore, 8 October 1992)

Thio Li-ann, 'The Secular Trumps the Sacred: Constitutional Issues Arising From Colin Chan v Public Prosecutor' (1995) 16 *Singapore Law Review* 26

Waldron, J, *The Harm in Hate Speech* (Harvard University Press, 2012)

Watson, A, *Legal Transplants: An Approach to Comparative Law* (University of Georgia Press, 1993)

WION, 'How blasphemy still remains Pakistan's notorious law a year after Asia Bibi's acquittal' (New Delhi, 27 February 2020) at www.wionews.com/south-asia/how-blasphemy-still-remains-pakistans-notorious-law-a-year-after-asia-bibis-acquittal-283051

Wright, B, 'Macaulay's Indian Penal Code: Historical Context and Originating Principles' in Chan Wing-Cheong, Barry Wright and Stanley Yeo (eds), *Codification, Macaulay and the Indian Penal Code: The Legacies and Modern Challenges of Criminal Law Reform* (Ashgate 2011) 47

Part II

Religious Penal Clauses in Context: Country Studies in Common Law Asia

5

Religious Penal Clauses in India

MRINAL SATISH

I. INTRODUCTION

> The State, in India, is secular and does not take sides with one religion or other prevalent in our pluralistic society. It has no direct concern with the faiths of the people but is deeply obligated not merely to preserve and protect society against breaches of peace and violations of public order, but also to create conditions where sentiments and feelings of people of diverse or opposing beliefs and bigotries are not so molested by ribald writings or offensive publications as to provoke or outrage groups into possible violent action. Essentially, good government necessitates peace and security and whoever violates by bombs or books societal tranquillity will become target of legal interdict by the State.[1]

This paragraph from the judgment of the Supreme Court of India in *State of Uttar Pradesh v Lalai Singh Yadav*,[2] aptly captures the justification provided by the Indian state (and the judiciary) for the necessity of religious penal clauses in the Indian Penal Code of 1860 (IPC). Chapter XV of the IPC, entitled, 'Of Offences Relating to Religion', when enacted in 1860 contained four sections – sections 295, 296, 297 and 298. Section 295A was added to Chapter XV in 1927. Two other sections in the IPC – section 153A and sections 505(2) and (3) – may also be classified as 'religious penal clauses'. These were inserted into the IPC by amendments in 1898. In addition, a set of procedural provisions are also relevant. Section 196 of the Code of Criminal Procedure, 1973 (CrPC) requires the prior sanction of the State or Central Government before a court takes cognisance[3] of an offence under section 153A or 295A of the IPC. Section 95 of the CrPC empowers State governments to forfeit books, newspapers and documents that 'appear to contain' any matter whose publication is punishable under sections 153A or 295A of the IPC.

[1] *State of Uttar Pradesh v Lalai Singh Yadav* (1976) 4 SCC 213, 217.
[2] ibid.
[3] Cognisance means taking judicial notice of a criminal case. A case begins in court only after a Magistrate takes cognisance of the offence, using their powers under s 190, IPC.

In this chapter, I trace the history, interpretation and contemporary application of religious penal clauses in India. I argue that the contemporary application of religious penal clauses has a chilling effect on free speech and expression, and is being used as a tool to curtail dissent and differing points of view. I demonstrate how a few provisions have been actively used in order to prosecute articulation of counter-majoritarian thoughts and views. Analysing contemporary usage of religious penal clauses, I argue that the criminal process is the punishment intended, and that there is no serious effort to take cases filed to their logical end.

This chapter is divided into six further sections. In section II, I discuss the context of religious penal clauses, focusing on the religious composition of Indian society, constitutional provisions in the context of religion, and laws on the interface between law and religion. In section III, I discuss the legislative history of religious penal clauses. In section IV, I analyse how religious penal clauses have been interpreted. I examine whether the interpretation broadens the scope of the legal provisions, and provide a critique of the decided cases. Section V deals with the provisions in the 1973 CrPC relevant to religious penal clauses. I discuss and analyse safeguards to invoking religious penal clauses, as well as procedural provisions, such as provisions providing for forfeiture of material, which leads to these clauses impacting free speech. In section VI, I discuss the interface between the Constitution of India and religious penal clauses. I discuss Constituent Assembly Debates in relation to free speech, restrictions to free speech, as well as specific discussions of sections 153A and 295A. I also discuss constitutional challenges to religious penal clauses. Finally, in section VII, I discuss the contemporary application of religious penal clauses. Section VIII concludes.

II. CONTEXT

As per the census of 2011, India had a population of 1,210,854,977.[4] The census also asked people to identify themselves by their religions. The data indicate that people identified themselves as Hindus, Muslims, Christians, Sikhs, Buddhists, Jains, and those belonging to 'other religions and persuasions'. Some opted not to answer the question. The majority of Indians identified themselves as Hindus (966,257,353), followed by Muslims (172,245,158), Christians (27,819,588) and Sikhs (20,833,116).[5] With these many diverse religions, India has faced challenges with communal violence. Communal riots were common in pre-independence India,[6] and continue to be a challenge today. Several attempts have been made,

[4] Office of the Registrar General and Census Scans Commissioner, 'Religion PCA' (India, Ministry of Home Affairs, 2011) at www.censusindia.gov.in/2011census/Religion_PCA.html.

[5] In percentages, this amounts to the following: Hindus (79.79%), Muslims (14.22%), Christians (2.29%) and Sikhs (1.72%).

[6] Gopal Krishna, 'Communal Violence in India: A Study of Communal Disturbance in Delhi' (1985) 20(2) *Economic and Political Weekly* 61, 61–62.

albeit unsuccessfully, to enact legislation to curb and punish communal violence.[7] In the past few years, mob-lynching has emerged as a major issue in India, with most linked to cow protection. Vigilante mobs, consisting generally of Hindus, have turned to violence in objecting to people ostensibly consuming beef, and to cattle being transported ostensibly for slaughter, etc.[8] People suspected of consuming beef have been lynched to death,[9] as well as persons transporting cattle.[10] Hence, religion continues to be a sensitive issue, with law and order strategies focused on ensuring that communal riots are prevented.

This communal violence takes place against the backdrop of the Constitution of India, which guarantees the right to freedom of religion as a Fundamental Right.[11] Article 25(1) of the Constitution provides the right 'freely to profess, practice and propagate religion'. This right is, however, subject to 'public order, morality and health', as well as other Fundamental Rights guaranteed by Part III of the Constitution. Article 25(2) provides another set of caveats; it empowers the State to enact laws that are meant for 'social welfare and reform' or laws for 'throwing open … Hindu religious institutions of a public character to all classes and sections of Hindus'. The Supreme Court in *Ramji Lal Modi v State of UP*,[12] dealing with section 295A of the IPC, ruled that it is clear from a reading of the Constitution that the freedom of religion is subject to public order, morality and health. Hence, a law may be enacted creating an offence relating to practice of a person's religion if it is in the interest of 'public order'. In addition, in *Lily Thomas v Union of India*,[13] the Supreme Court held that the freedom guaranteed by Article 25 is a 'freedom which does not encroach upon a similar freedom of other persons'.[14] As such, the Court ruled that the exercise of the freedom of religion should not 'infringe the religious right and personal freedom of others'.[15]

Article 26 of the Indian Constitution further guarantees religious denominations the freedom to manage religious affairs, subject to 'public order, morality and health'. This includes the right to establish and maintain institutions for religious and charitable purposes, the right to manage their own affairs in

[7] See Sunil Prabhu, 'After fierce debate, anti-communal violence bill is dropped. Here's why' *NDTV* (5 February 2009) at www.ndtv.com/cheat-sheet/after-fierce-debate-anti-communal-violence-bill-is-dropped-heres-why-549881.

[8] See generally Human Rights Watch, *Violent Cow Protection in India: Vigilante Groups Attack Minorities* (2019) at www.hrw.org/report/2019/02/18/violent-cow-protection-india/vigilante-groups-attack-minorities.

[9] ibid.

[10] ibid.

[11] Arts 25–28, Constitution of India.

[12] *Ramji Lal Modi v State of UP* AIR 1957 SC 620. See also *Rev Stainislaus v State of Madhya Pradesh* (1977) 1 SCC 677 (where the Supreme Court held that 'public order' signifies a 'state of tranquillity which prevails among the members of a political society as a result of internal regulations enforced by the Government which they have established').

[13] *Lily Thomas v Union of India* (2000) 6 SCC 224.

[14] ibid 254.

[15] ibid.

matters of religion, to own and acquire movable and immovable property, and to administer such property in accordance with the law. Article 27 prohibits a person from being compelled to pay taxes specifically for religious purposes. In addition, Article 28 prohibits religious instruction from being provided in any educational institution wholly maintained out of 'State' funds. However, this prohibition does not extend to institutions administered by the 'State' but that were established under an endowment or trust that requires that religious instruction be imparted in the institution. The Article also guarantees the freedom to a person attending an educational institution recognised by the 'State' or receiving 'State' funds, not to take part in any religious instruction imparted in the institution or attend any religious worship in the institution, unless they consent to such participation. In the case of minors, the consent of their guardian is required.

The Preamble to the Constitution declares India to be a 'secular' Republic. The word 'secular' was not originally in the Preamble – it was added by amendment in 1976. The Supreme Court, in *SR Bommai v Union of India*,[16] noted that although the term 'secular' was not mentioned in the Constitution, secularism was 'embedded in [Indian] constitutional philosophy'.[17] What was implicit was made explicit by the amendment.[18] The Court held that secularism means a prohibition on the establishment of a theocratic State, and prohibition of the State from identifying with one religion, sect or denomination. It implies equal treatment to all religions.[19] The Court further ruled that 'positive secularism' connotes values of 'freedom, equality, and fellowship'.[20] It is a mode to ensure establishment of an 'egalitarian social order'.[21] The Court importantly held that secularism is a part of the 'basic structure' of the Indian Constitution (and as such a part of immutable constitutional identity), and that it is a constitutional goal.

Justice Ruma Pal, in her dissent in part in *TMA Pai Foundation v State of Karnataka*,[22] noted that 'secular' in the Indian context implies that the State has no official religion, and is not theocratic.[23] Justice Pal ruled that India does not subscribe to non-interference of the State in religious organisations, but by declaring itself to be 'secular' it strives to provide respect for all.[24] In *Aruna Roy v Union of India*,[25] the Supreme Court noted that 'secularism' means non-discrimination by the State of people on the basis of different religious

[16] *SR Bommai v Union of India* (1994) 3 SCC 1.
[17] ibid 77.
[18] ibid.
[19] ibid 144.
[20] ibid 166.
[21] ibid 170.
[22] *TMA Pai Foundation v State of Karnataka* (2002) 8 SCC 481.
[23] ibid 651
[24] ibid 654.
[25] *Aruna Roy v Union of India* (2002) 7 SCC 368.

practices,[26] but does not mean 'negation of all religions'.[27] In *Bal Patil v Union of India*,[28] the Court held that the concept of secularism in the Indian Constitution implied that the state has no religion.[29] The State has to 'treat all religions and religious groups equally and with equal respect without in any manner interfering with their individual rights of religion, faith and worship'.[30] Noting these features, Rajeev Bhargava argues that the Indian conception of secularism implies the state's maintaining a 'principled distance' from all religions for the sake of certain values – 'peace, worldly goods, dignity, equality and fraternity'.[31] He argues that this model separates state and religion in the context of ends and institutions, but not policy and law.[32]

There are various laws that are at the interface between law and religion in India. The most prominent amongst these are personal laws that deal with issues relating to marriage, divorce, succession, maintenance, adoption and other issues with respect to family relations. Indian personal laws are both codified and uncodified. Citizens are by default governed by their personal laws, but in certain aspects they have the option of being governed by secular laws.[33] Laws have been enacted to govern the function of religious endowments,[34] and to prohibit 'forced conversion' from one religion to another.[35]

In addition to penal provisions in the Indian Penal Code dealing with offences against religion (discussed in section III), seeking votes or asking people to refrain from voting using religion as a ground is defined as a 'corrupt practice' under the Representation of the People Act, 1951.[36] Similarly, promoting enmity between different classes of people on account of religion for furthering one's prospects in an election or prejudicially affecting another's prospects is also defined as a 'corrupt practice'.[37] A finding that a candidate has indulged in a 'corrupt practice' may lead to disqualification from contesting elections.[38] Further, section 125 of the Act criminalises promoting enmity between groups of persons on grounds of religion, in the context of an election, and provides for a maximum sentence of a period of three years on conviction. Hence, the legal framework strives to ensure that religion is not used as a ground to create differences between people.

[26] ibid.

[27] ibid 407.

[28] *Bal Patil v Union of India* (2005) 6 SCC 690.

[29] ibid 704.

[30] ibid.

[31] Rajeev Bhargava, 'Reimagining Secularism: Respect, Domination and Principled Distance' (2013) 48(50) *Economic and Political Weekly* 79, 86.

[32] ibid.

[33] For instance, a Hindu may get married under the Special Marriage Act, 1954 instead of the Hindu Marriage Act, 1955, and be governed by the provisions of the former.

[34] Tahir Mahmood, 'Religion, Law, and Judiciary in Modern India' (2006) *Brigham Young University Law Review* 755, 762–63.

[35] Faizan Mustafa and Jagteshwar Singh Sohi, 'Freedom of Religion in India: Current Issues and Supreme Court Acting as Clergy' (2017) *Brigham Young University Law Review* 915, 939–43.

[36] The Representation of the People Act, 1951, s 123(3).

[37] The Representation of the People Act, 1951, s 123(3A).

[38] The Representation of the People Act, 1951, s 8A.

III. PENAL PROVISIONS: LEGISLATIVE HISTORY

A. Chapter XV

Chapter XV of the IPC, in its first draft of 1837, was originally entitled 'Of Offences Relating to Religion and Caste'. It initially contained a provision criminalising an act that made a person lose their caste,[39] which was dropped when the Code was enacted in 1860. In their Notes to the Indian Penal Code, the Law Commissioners explained that Chapter XV was based on the principle of freedom for everyone to profess the religion of their choice, and a prohibition against insulting the religion of another person.[40] They noted that this was an essential principle, which was required to ensure against dissolution of society. Considering India's religious diversity, they wrote that the situation in India was 'pregnant with dangers',[41] which could only be avoided by ensuring religious tolerance.[42] Among the offences created was the intentional destroying or defiling of places of worship, or of objects held sacred by a group of people.[43] The Law Commissioners opined that no other act criminalised by the Code had as much potential for causing public disorder and 'armed insurrection'.[44] They pointed to the killing of a cow in Benares and the pollution of a mosque in Bangalore as examples of incidents that caused violent reactions.[45] They also criminalised the intentional insulting of another person's religion, in the garb of religious discussions.[46] Words, gestures or exhibitions through which the religious feelings of others were intentionally insulted were also criminalised.[47]

In their Second Report to the Governor General in Council, submitted in 1846, the Law Commissioners addressed objections to Chapter XV. They noted that many people had objected to the Chapter, but those objections impugned the general principle on which the chapter was based – religious tolerance.[48] Primary objections were to clause 282 (what is now section 298, IPC) and to the clauses relating to deprivation of caste.[49] Many of the commentators pointed out that due to intra-religious differences, it is likely that clause 282 would be regularly invoked.[50] The Commissioners, however, did not accept the suggestion

[39] Indian Law Commission, *The Indian Penal Code, As Originally Framed in 1837, With Notes by TB Macaulay, JM Macleod, GW Anderson, and F Millett, And the First and Second Reports Thereon by CH Cameron and D Elliott: A Verbatim Reprint* (Higginbotham & Co, 1888) 136.
[40] ibid.
[41] ibid.
[42] ibid.
[43] ibid 137.
[44] ibid.
[45] ibid.
[46] ibid.
[47] ibid.
[48] ibid 409.
[49] ibid 409–17.
[50] ibid 409–14.

to remove this clause, and decided to retain it with a few changes.[51] Missionaries objected to clause 282, amongst others, which they believed would interfere in their work.[52] In their Second Report, the Law Commissioners finally recommended that clauses 283–286, those dealing with offences related to losing caste, be omitted.[53] They also opined that there was no need to have a separate chapter on offences relating to religion, and that the provisions could be included in the chapter on criminal intimidation and annoyance.[54] However, this was not to be. As mentioned in section I, a separate chapter entitled 'Of Offences Relating to Religion' was included in the Penal Code when it was eventually enacted in 1860. Sorabjee notes that the Chapter was included in the Code with the objective of maintaining peace and tranquillity, as well as to prevent religious riots.[55] Sorabjee further argues that the chapter was 'not inspired by any antipathy to free speech as such'.[56]

B. Section 153A

Section 153A was added to the IPC in 1898. It was placed in Chapter VIII of the Code, entitled 'Of Offences Against Public Tranquillity'. The section originally criminalised promoting enmity or hatred between different classes of 'Her Majesty's Subjects'.[57] The immediate cause for adding the provision was hate speech that had been used to instigate religious agitations in British India.[58] The justification provided was the need for a legal framework to deal with sectarian and caste-based feuds and riots.[59] The Select Committee that recommended the insertion of section 153A noted that 'stirring up class hatred' differs from the offence of sedition.[60] Such 'stirring up class hatred', the Committee noted, would encourage people to indulge in acts that disturb public tranquillity.[61]

A few members in the Viceroy's Council spoke against introduction of the provision. One of the members opined that the provision could be used

[51] ibid 413–14.
[52] ibid 410–14.
[53] ibid 417.
[54] ibid.
[55] Soli J Sorabjee, 'Freedom of Expression and Censorship: Some Aspects of the Indian Experience' (1994) 45 *Northern Ireland Legal Quarterly* 327, 334.
[56] ibid.
[57] Abhinav Chandrachud, *Republic of Rhetoric: Free Speech and the Constitution of India* (Penguin India, 2017) 226.
[58] Abhinav Chandrachud argues, however, that the incidents referred to by Mr Chalmers, the Law Member of the Governor General in Council, in fact had nothing to do with hate speech (see ibid 227).
[59] ibid 227.
[60] Siddharth Narrain, 'The Harm in Hate Speech Laws: Examining the Origins of Hate Speech Legislation in India' in Rina Ramdev, Sandhya Devesan Nambiar and Debaditya Bhattacharya (eds), *Sentiment, Politics, Censorship: The State of Hurt* (Sage, 2016) 44.
[61] ibid 44–45.

against social reformers, especially those trying to end practices such as widow remarriage.[62] Concerns were expressed about potential abuse of the law.[63] To assuage these concerns, an Explanation was added to the section. The Explanation sought to exclude from the purview of the section instances where a person pointed out matters that had the tendency to produce feelings of enmity or hatred, without having malicious intention, and with an 'honest' view to removing such matters.[64] Further, sanction of the local government would be required to commence prosecutions under the section.[65]

Section 153A was amended twice again in the 1960s. I will discuss this in detail later.

C. Section 505

Another section introduced in 1898, along with section 153A, was a newer version of section 505. The amendment substituted the existing section 505 in Chapter XXII, dealing with 'Criminal Intimidation, Insult and Annoyance'. The existing section dealt with circulating mischievous reports.[66] The revised section sought to punish statements creating or promoting enmity, hatred or ill-will between classes.

IV. COURT CASES AND POLITICAL USE: INTERPRETATION OF RELIGIOUS PENAL CLAUSES

A. Section 295

Chapter XV of the IPC begins with section 295, which reads as follows:

> **Injuring or defiling place of worship with intent to insult the religion of any class** – Whosoever destroys, damages or defiles any place of worship, or any object held sacred by any class of persons with the intention of thereby insulting the religion of any class of persons or with the knowledge that any class of persons is likely to consider such destruction, damage or defilement as an insult to their religion, shall be punishable …

The crux of the section is the intent to insult the religion, or the knowledge that the proscribed act would be considered by a class of person to be an insult to their religion. Hence, the *mens rea* of the accused has to be proved to be able to convict a person under this section.

[62] Chandrachud, *Republic of Rhetoric* (n 57) 227.
[63] Narrain, 'The Harm in Hate Speech Laws' (n 60) 45.
[64] ibid.
[65] ibid.
[66] ibid 45–46.

Two judgments are of importance: one which restricted the scope of section 295, and one that broadened it. A Full Bench (five judges) of the Allahabad High Court was called upon in *Queen Empress v Imam Ali*,[67] to decide whether killing a cow in a place within a few yards of a public road, exposed to public view, would constitute an offence under section 295. The question was whether a cow is 'an object' for the purposes of the section. All five judges held that it is not. They held that the word 'object' should be read *ejusdem generis* with 'place of worship'.[68] So done, the word 'object' would imply an inanimate object, and not an animal.[69] Justice Brodhurst further held that killing of a cow as sacrifice would not fall within the ambit of the section.[70] Justice Mahmood, while concurring with the rest of the judges and convicting the accused, made a plea for tolerance and sensitivity between religious groups.[71] He noted that till 'somewhat recent times', Hindus and Muslims were considerate towards and respected each other, and did not have reckless disregard for each other's feelings.[72] He lamented that he had come across multiple cases where this sentiment had changed.[73] He opined that Chapter XV had been introduced into the IPC by the British to encourage religious tolerance.[74] He further said that any difficulties in the law did not indicate a problem with the law, but that a section of the population did not appreciate 'religious toleration and individual liberty'.[75] This commentary by a judge (presumably the only Indian on the bench) is interesting, since he justifies the existence of religious penal clauses on the grounds of the 'civilising' function of 'wise' British laws.[76]

The other important case on section 295 is the Supreme Court's decision in *S Veerabadran Chettiar v EV Ramaswami Naicker*.[77] It is an interesting commentary on regional religious practices, as it is of the Court's broadening the scope of section 295. In this case, the accused, Naicker, was the leader of a political group that, inter alia, aimed to stop idol worship. In that context, Naicker had announced that he would break the idol of Lord Ganesha, a revered Hindu God. He ultimately did so in public, and allegedly gave a speech thereafter. A criminal complaint was filed by the appellant under sections 295 and 295A, IPC. The Magistrate dismissed the complaint on the ground that 'the mud figure alleged to have been broken … [was] not an object held sacred or worshipped by any class of persons'.[78] The Magistrate reasoned that a mud figure that resembled

[67] *Queen Empress v Imam Ali* (1888) 10 ILR All 150.
[68] See ibid 152–54.
[69] See ibid. See also *Ramesh Chandra Sanyal v Hiru Mondal* (1890) 17 Cal 852; *Ali Muhammad*, AIR 1918 Lah 365.
[70] *Queen Empress v Imam Ali* (n 67) 153.
[71] ibid 155–59.
[72] ibid 156.
[73] ibid.
[74] ibid 158.
[75] ibid.
[76] ibid.
[77] *Veerabadran Chettiar v EV Ramaswami Naicker* AIR 1958 SC 1032.
[78] ibid para 2.

Lord Ganesha would not fall within the scope of section 295. A petition filed by the complainant before the Sessions Court was also dismissed. The Court agreed with the Magistrate's order and ruled that the object that Naicker broke was his private property. It held that it was not an object held sacred by a group of persons.[79] The High Court too agreed with both the lower courts. The Court held that section 295 was confined to cases where an idol in a temple, or one that is taken out in a procession, is sought to be destroyed. The Court likened the idol destroyed by Naicker to a doll. A doll that resembles a deity, the Court ruled, cannot be considered as an 'object' for the purposes of section 295.[80] It appears from the tenor of the three judgments that the anti-idol movement in the Madras State (as it then was) impacted the decision of the three courts. Consequently, they sought to confine section 295 to idols in temples or processions, and not beyond.

The Supreme Court, however, disagreed. It ruled that it is a 'well known fact' that the image of Lord Ganesha, or 'any objective representation of a similar kind', is considered sacred by Hindus, irrespective of whether it is consecrated or not. It ruled that the High Court, by restricting the scope of the word 'object' in section 295 only to idols in temples, had unnecessarily restricted the scope of the section.[81] The Court did not stop there. It further held that a sacred book is also within the scope of section 295. It observed that if the interpretation of the lower courts were to be accepted, a person burning a sacred book could not be punished under section 295 either.[82] It held that 'any object, however trivial or destitute of real value in itself, if regarded sacred by a class of persons' would be covered by the section.[83] It was also not necessary that the object destroyed had ever been worshipped.[84] The Supreme Court warned that '[c]ourts have … to be very circumspect in [matters of religion] and to pay due regard to the feelings and religious emotions of different classes of persons with different beliefs, irrespective of … whether or not they share those beliefs, or whether they are rational or otherwise in the opinion of the court'.[85] Thus, the Court gave a wide scope to section 295, extending it to objects that resembled deities and to objects considered sacred by a class of persons (even if never worshipped).[86] By giving an example of burning of holy books, the Court also brought holy books within the scope of the section, although that was not an issue in the case.[87]

[79] ibid para 3.
[80] ibid para 4.
[81] ibid para 7.
[82] ibid.
[83] ibid.
[84] ibid.
[85] ibid.
[86] For a critique of the case, and the implications that it had for Indian law, see Rina Ramdev et al, 'Introduction: Sentimental Sovereignties: Hurt and the Political Unconscious' in Ramdev, Nambiar and Bhattacharya (eds), *Sentiment, Politics, Censorship: The State of Hurt* (n 60) xv, xxiv–xxvi.
[87] In *Chandmal Chopra v State of West Bengal*, 1988 Cri LJ 739 (Cal), a writ of mandamus was filed before the Calcutta High Court seeking forfeiture of the Quran on the grounds that it incites violence on grounds of religion. A Single Judge of the Court, relying on *Chettiar v Naicker* ruled

B. Section 296

Section 296 of the IPC reads as follows:

> **Disturbing religious assembly** – Whoever voluntarily causes disturbance to any assembly, lawfully engaged in the performance of religious worship, or religious ceremonies, shall be punished …

Unlike section 295, section 296 does not expressly use the words 'intention' or 'knowledge'. It requires the prosecution to prove that the act was done 'voluntarily'. The term 'voluntarily' is defined in section 39 of the IPC.[88] The manner in which 'voluntarily' is defined brings in requirements of intent or knowledge in causing disturbance to an assembly.

Two cases are useful to understand the scope of section 296. The first is *Emperor v Masit*.[89] In this case, the accused attacked a group of persons who were carrying flags to a temple in a procession, for which they had obtained the required permission. The accused argued that until the flags were consecrated, the offence under section 296 would not be constituted, since up to that point, religious worship or a religious ceremony would not have been performed. The Court rejected this argument. It held that the group carrying flags considered their taking the flags to the temple as a religious ceremony, for which they had received permission from the relevant authorities.[90] Hence, the focus of the interpretation is on voluntarily causing disturbance, which the accused had done, in addition to proof that the disturbance was caused to an assembly lawfully engaged in what they perceived to be a religious ceremony.

The second case is *Kolimi Mahbub Sahib & Others v Sri Sidheswaraswami Temple*.[91] There, the Madras High Court held that mere playing of music near a mosque would not by itself constitute an offence under section 296. Although a deliberate intention to disturb the worship is not necessary, it must be found on facts that there was a 'substantial and not merely fanciful disturbance of the worship'.[92]

C. Section 297

Section 297 of the IPC criminalises trespassing into designated places – a place of worship, a place of sepulture, a place set apart of the performance of funeral

that the Quran is a holy book and is held sacred by a class of persons, which consequently takes it out of the purview of sections 153A and 295A, IPC. A Division Bench of the High Court dismissed the writ on multiple grounds.

[88] Section 39, IPC states as follows: 'A person is said to cause an effect 'voluntarily' when he causes it by means whereby he intended to cause it, or by means which, at the time of employing those means, he knew or had reason to believe to be likely to cause it'.

[89] *Emperor v Masit* (1911) 34 ILR All 78.

[90] ibid 79.

[91] *Kolimi Mahbub Sahib & Others v Sri Sidheswaraswami Temple* (1945) 58 LW 409 (Mad).

[92] ibid 411.

rites or as a depository of remains of the dead – with the intention of wounding the feelings or religion of any person, or with the knowledge that the feelings are or the religion of a person is likely to be wounded. It also criminalises offering indignity to a human corpse, or causing disturbance to any persons assembled for the purpose of performance of funeral ceremonies.

The only noteworthy issue that has arisen in the context of section 297 is how the term 'trespass' should be interpreted. In *Emperor v Maqsud Hussain*,[93] the accused were found engaging in sexual acts inside a mosque and were prosecuted under section 297. Interpreting the word 'trespass', the Allahabad High Court reiterated decisions of other courts, which had held that trespass should be given its 'original meaning' and not be interpreted as 'criminal trespass', as the term defined in the IPC would be.[94] Although no discussion in detail on the point of *mens rea* took place in the case, it is clear that engaging in sexual acts inside the mosque was considered as wounding the religious feelings of a person, and knowledge was accordingly presumed.

D. Section 298

Section 298 criminalises uttering words or making gestures with the intention of wounding religious feelings. It reads as follows:

> **Uttering words, etc, with deliberate intent to wound religious feelings** – Whoever, with the deliberate intention of wounding the religious feelings of any person, utters any word or makes any sound in the hearing of that person or makes any gesture in the sight of that person or places any object in the sight of that person, shall be punished ...

As noted earlier, at the time of drafting of the IPC, a lot of discussion took place regarding this provision, and it was included despite objections against its inclusion. The nub of the section is the requirement of deliberate intention. The prosecution have to prove this element to be able to secure a conviction under this section.

The interpretation of this section was subject to discussion in a relatively recent case in the Punjab and Haryana High Court. In *Harbhajan Singh @ Bhajji v Arvind Thakur*,[95] the complaint against the accused was that he dressed up as Ravana,[96] and uttered objectionable words to a woman who was dressed up as Sita. The complainant alleged that the religious sentiments of Hindus were hurt by these actions of the accused. The High Court quashed the complaint. In doing so, it ruled that the sensitivity of every individual is not relevant, but

[93] *Emperor v Maqsud Hussain* AIR 1924 All 9.
[94] ibid.
[95] *Harbhajan Singh @ Bhajji v Arvind Thakur* (2010) 3 RCR 100.
[96] In the epic *Ramayana*, Ravana is the King of Lanka who kidnaps Rama's wife, Sita.

.'[97] It further held that words, gestures, etc should be ...rspective and not out of context.[98] Ultimately, the inten- ., the court held, is the 'paramount factor' to bring the case ...e of section 298. Unless the act is intended to hurt the religious st ...of a person, the section will not be attracted.[99]

E. Section 153A

As noted earlier, section 153A was added to the IPC in 1898.[100] The first authoritative decision interpreting section 153A came only in 1926, in *PK Chakravarty v The King Emperor*.[101] The Calcutta High Court held that the words 'promote or attempt to promote feelings of enmity' in section 153A are important. They imply that promoting feelings of enmity or hatred must have been the 'purpose or part of the purpose of the accused'.[102] Hence, merely the fact that the words, signs, etc may have a tendency to lead to feelings of enmity was held not to be sufficient.[103] The Court further held that the intention of the accused could be inferred from the words used by him/her, although other evidence could also be adduced.[104]

The Calcutta High Court had another occasion a few months later to interpret section 153A in *Hemendra Prasad Ghose v King Emperor*.[105] The court reiterated its holding in *Chakravarty*, ruling that 'malicious intention' is a *sine qua non* for section 153A to be attracted.[106] Interpreting the Explanation to the section, the Court held that if there is no malicious intention on the part of the publisher, 'honesty of purpose may safely be inferred'.[107] Commenting on the duties of the editor of a newspaper, the Court said that publishing matters that are of public interest is one such duty. If such publication were done honestly then the editor would not be liable under section 153A.[108]

[97] *Harbhajan Singh @ Bhajji v Arvind Thakur* (n 95) para 26.

[98] ibid para 25.

[99] ibid para 30. See also *Sheikh Amjad v King Emperor* AIR 1942 Pat 471 (holding that deliberate intention is a prerequisite to attract s 298).

[100] The Section originally read as follows: 'Whoever by words, either spoken or written or by signs, or by visible representations, or otherwise, promotes or attempts to promote feelings of enmity or hatred between different classes of citizens of India, shall be punished …' It also had an Explanation, which read as follows: 'It does not amount to an offence within the meaning of this section to point out without malicious intention and with an honest view to their removal, matters which are producing or have a tendency to produce, feelings of enmity or hatred between different classes of Her Majesty's subjects.'

[101] *PK Chakravarty v The King Emperor* 30 CWN 953 (1926).

[102] ibid 956.

[103] ibid 956–57.

[104] ibid 957.

[105] *Hemendra Prasad Ghose v King Emperor* 31 CWN 168 (1926).

[106] ibid 171.

[107] ibid.

[108] ibid 170.

The most important (and controversial) case on section 153A, which ultimately led to the insertion of section 295A in the IPC, is the Lahore High Court's decision in *Raj Paul v Emperor*.[109] Raj Pal, an *Arya Samajist*, published a tract titled *Rangeela Rasool (The Colourful Prophet)*.[110] The tract was in the nature of a satire against the Prophet Mohammad,[111] and mocked his marriages and sex life.[112] One thousand copies of the tract were sold, and a second edition was also ordered.[113] The contents of the tract led to protests against it by the Muslim community.[114] Mahatma Gandhi too opined that the objective of the publication appeared to have been to inflame passions.[115] Raj Pal was ultimately prosecuted under section 153A,[116] based on a complaint filed in July 1924.[117] The Magistrate convicted Raj Pal of the offence under section 153A, which was upheld by the Sessions Court. Raj Pal then appealed this decision to the Punjab High Court, where the matter came up before Justice Dalip Singh.

In convicting Raj Pal, the Magistrate had held that the accused had the intention to 'make a wanton attack'[118] on the Prophet Mohammed. He further ruled that the objective of the accused was to 'hold [the Prophet] up to ridicule and contempt, to ridicule his religion, and thus to wound the feelings of his followers'.[119] Since such intent was proved, the accused was convicted under section 153A.[120] The Sessions Judge, in upholding the Magistrate's decision, had further held that the contents of the pamphlet were 'intentionally offensive, scurrilous, and wounding to the religious feelings of the Mahomedan community'.[121] He ruled that the intention was clearly to wound and insult the feelings of the community.[122]

The first argument made by Raj Pal before the High Court, which was rejected by the Court, was that the term 'classes' used in section 153A means 'races' and not religious denominations.[123] He further argued that the objective of the

[109] *Raj Paul v Emperor* AIR 1927 Lah 590.
[110] Narrain, 'The Harm in Hate Speech Laws' (n 60) 46. Richa Raj argues that *rangila/rangeela* 'could have a wide range of meaning from jovial to libertine'. See Richa Raj, 'A Pamphlet and its (Dis)contents: A Case Study of *Rangila Rasul* and the Controversy Surrounding it in Colonial Punjab 1923–29' (2015) 9(2) *History and Sociology of South Asia* 146, 150.
[111] Raj, 'A Pamphlet and its (Dis)contents' (n 110) 150.
[112] Nishant Kumar, 'Laws and Colonial Subjects: The Subject-Citizen Riddle and the Making of Section 295(A)' in Guneel Cederlöf and Sanjukta Das Gupta (eds), *Subjects, Citizens and Law* (Routledge, 2017) 78.
[113] Neeti Nair, 'Beyond the "Communal" 1920s: The Problem of Intention, Legislative Pragmatism, and the Making of Section 295A of the Indian Penal Code' (2013) 50(3) *The Indian Economic and Social History Review* 317, 318.
[114] Narrain, 'The Harm in Hate Speech Laws' (n 60) 47.
[115] See Nair, 'Beyond the "Communal" 1920s' (n 113) 318.
[116] Narrain, 'The Harm in Hate Speech Laws' (n 60) 47.
[117] Raj, 'A Pamphlet and its (Dis)contents' (n 110) 151.
[118] *Raj Paul v Emperor* (n 109) 591.
[119] ibid.
[120] ibid.
[121] ibid.
[122] ibid.
[123] ibid.

light the evils of polygamy and marriage between people ne High Court rejected this explanation and held that the ilous satire'[125] on the Prophet. However, it did not appear c the Muslim community.[126] The Court, controversially, then held that section 153A was meant to punish attacks on a particular community, and not 'polemics against deceased religious leaders, however scurrilous and in bad taste such attacks might be'.[127] The Judge warned that interpreting the section to include attacks against deceased religious leaders would lead to a situation where historians might be prosecuted under section 153A if they adversely commented on the life or character of a deceased religious leader.[128] The High Court acquitted Raj Pal. However, the judge noted that a separate section in the IPC might be required to deal with pamphlets of the nature published by Raj Pal.[129]

Another argument relevant to the discussion on religious penal clauses made in this case by the Government was that the Muslim community is 'more fanatical on the question of religion'[130] in comparison to others.[131] Hence, an attack on the founder of Islam is likely to ignite passions more than an attack on the founder of another religion.[132] The Court rejected this argument, and held that this not a relevant factor in the interpretation of section 153A.[133]

The judgment of the Lahore High Court led to widespread protests by the Muslim community.[134] The *Muslim Outlook* called for an enquiry against Justice Dalip Singh, and also sought his resignation.[135] Contempt proceedings were initiated against the editor and the publisher of the newspaper.[136] The two were found guilty and punished for the same.[137]

Another case on section 153A came up before the Allahabad High Court in 1927 – *Kali Charan Sharma v King Emperor*.[138] The book involved, *Vichitra Jiwan* (*Strange Life*), was also ostensibly on the life of Prophet Mohammed.[139] The *Raj Paul* case was cited before the Allahabad High Court as precedent that attacks on deceased founders of the religion do not constitute an offence under

[124] ibid.
[125] ibid.
[126] ibid.
[127] ibid 592.
[128] ibid.
[129] ibid.
[130] ibid.
[131] ibid.
[132] ibid.
[133] ibid.
[134] Narrain, 'The Harm in Hate Speech Laws' (n 60) 48.
[135] Nair, 'Beyond the "Communal" 1920s' (n 113) 320.
[136] *Re Muslim Outlook, Lahore*, AIR 1927 Lah 610. For a detailed discussion of the case, see Nair, 'Beyond the "Communal" 1920s' (n 113) 321–22.
[137] ibid 613.
[138] *Kali Charan Sharma v King Emperor* AIR 1927 All 654.
[139] ibid 655.

section 153A. The Court disagreed, however, holding that it did not see the 'i. distinction'.[140] The Court held that the test would be whether, when placed in 'the position of a Mahomedan who honours his prophet',[141] the ridiculing of the Prophet would have any impact on his feelings.[142] The Court ruled that such a book would 'certainly promote feelings of enmity and hatred between Hindus and Mahomedans'.[143]

Neeti Nair notes how the Governor of Punjab informed a delegation of Muslims who met him after the *Raj Paul* case that the Government was considering amending the law.[144] She also notes that the Government was also hoping for another 'test case' in the Lahore High Court on the issue.[145] This test case was *Devi Sharan Sharma v Emperor*.[146]

The case involved an article in a journal called *Risala-i-Vartaman*.[147] The article itself was entitled 'Sair-i-Dozakh' ('A Trip to Hell').[148] It caused 'considerable excitement' in the Muslim population of the city of Amritsar.[149] The government ordered seizure of the book and the prosecution under section 153A of the author of the piece, Devi Sharan Sharma.[150] One of the questions before the Special Bench of the Lahore High Court was whether section 153A could be invoked in this case.[151] Justice Broadway, writing for the Court, noted that 'the article [was] in extremely bad taste, scurrilous in nature and [was] a disgusting satire on certain incidents in the life of the holy Prophet of Islam'.[152] The Court first ruled that it agreed with the interpretation of section 153A in *PK Chakravarty*.[153] Taking the ruling a step forward, the Court held that the intention of the author could be inferred not only from the wording of the article, but also from 'the general policy of the paper … persons for whom it was written, and the state of feeling between the two communities at the time of publication'.[154] The Court further ruled that when the words of an article are likely to produce hatred, it should be presumed that that was the intention of the author, unless proved to the contrary.[155] The Court rejected the contention of the accused that the hatred and enmity between classes needs to be reciprocal.[156]

[140] ibid.
[141] ibid.
[142] ibid.
[143] ibid 656.
[144] Nair, 'Beyond the "Communal" 1920s' (n 113) 320.
[145] ibid 321. The Allahabad High Court had already delivered its judgment in *Kali Charan Sharma* by the time the delegation had met the Governor.
[146] *Devi Sharan Sharma v Emperor* AIR 1927 Lah 594.
[147] ibid 594.
[148] ibid.
[149] ibid.
[150] The publisher, Gian Chand Pathak, was also prosecuted.
[151] *Devi Sharan Sharma v Emperor* (n 146) 597.
[152] ibid.
[153] ibid 598.
[154] ibid.
[155] ibid 599.
[156] ibid.

The next argument made was the one upheld in *Raj Paul* – the attack on the Prophet individually did not amount to an attack on a 'class' of people, that is, the Muslims. The Court held that scurrilous depiction of the founder of a religion 'was bound to inflame' the followers of that religion against the author, the class perceived to be behind the article.[157] It ruled that a scurrilous attack on a religion or its founder would prima facie fall within the purview of section 153A.[158]

The Government ultimately decided to enact new law to cover the type of situations encountered in *Raj Paul*, *Kali Charan Sharma* and *Devi Sharan Sharma*. This was done by enacting section 295A in the IPC, which I discuss later in this chapter.

Multiple decisions followed *PK Chakravarty* on the question of *mens rea* in section 153A.[159] Another question that arose was regarding what constituted a 'class' for the purposes of the section.[160] In *Emperor v Miss Maniben L Kara*,[161] the Bombay High Court ruled that the people constituting a group should be easily ascertainable, and should be well-defined.[162] There should be an element of stability or permanence in the group, and the group should be 'sufficiently numerous and widespread' to be defined as a class.[163]

The constitutionality of section 153A was challenged in *Master Tara Singh v The State*.[164] The Punjab High Court struck down the section as being in violation of Article 19(1)(a) of the Constitution.[165] I discuss this later in this chapter, and also the amendment made to Article 19 to restore the constitutionality, inter alia, of section 153A.

In 1961, the Indian Parliament substituted 'classes' in the original wording of section 153A[166] with religious and other groups. It also criminalised committing any act prejudicial to the maintenance of harmony between religions and

[157] ibid 600.

[158] ibid 601.

[159] See *Satya Ranjan Bakshi v Emperor*, 56 ILR (Cal) 1090 (1929); *Chamupati v The Crown* (1931) 13 ILR Lah 152.

[160] See *Emperor v Gautam* (1937) ILR All 69 (where the court held that for the purposes of the section, 'class' would constitute two sections of people that can be classified as groups opposed to each other).

[161] *Emperor v Miss Maniben L Kara* (1932) 57 ILR Bom 253.

[162] ibid 265.

[163] ibid. See also *Narayan Vasudev Phadke v Emperor*, AIR 1940 Bom 379 (on the question of identifying a group of people as a class); *Vishambar Dayal Tripathi v King Emperor*, 1940 Oudh Weekly Notes 965 (defining 'class' and questions of evidence).

[164] *Master Tara Singh v The State* (1950) 4 ILR Pun 193.

[165] The right to speech and expression.

[166] The substituted section read as follows: 'Whoever (a) by words, either spoken or written or by signs or by visible representations or otherwise, promotes, or attempts to promote, on grounds of religion, race, language, caste, or community or any other ground whatsoever, feelings of enmity or hatred between religious, racial, or language groups or caste or communities, or (b) commits any act which is prejudicial to the maintenance of harmony between different religious, racial, or language groups or castes, or communities and which disturbs or is likely to disturb the public tranquillity, shall be punished …'

other categories defined in the section. The section was amended again in 1969, adding subsection (2), providing for increased punishment if the acts proscribed in subsection (1) were committed in a place of worship or in an assembly engaged in performance of religious worship or religious ceremonies. In 1972, another set of circumstances were added to subsection (1). Section 153A(1)(c) proscribed organising any exercise, movement, drill or other similar activity with the intention that the participants in such activity shall use or be trained to use criminal force or violence against a religious group, amongst others, or to cause fear in a religious group. No amendments to the section have taken place since then.

The question of the *mens rea* requirement in the amended section 153A arose before the Supreme Court in *Balwant Singh v State of Punjab*.[167] The Court held that 'the intention to cause disorder or incite people to violence is the *sine qua non* of the offence under section 153A, IPC'.[168] This was reiterated by the Supreme Court in *Bilal Ahmed Kaloo v State of AP.*[169] In *Manzar Sayeed Khan v State of Maharashtra*,[170] the Supreme Court, while reiterating the issue of *mens rea*, also held that in the case of a book, the intention may be judged 'primarily by the language of the book, and the circumstances in which the book was written and published'.[171] It further held that the matter alleged to be within the scope of section 153A should be read as a whole.[172] Isolated strong words, sentences or paragraphs, or sentences from 'here and there', cannot be threaded together to infer intention.[173]

F. Section 295A

Section 295A was inserted into the Indian Penal Code in 1927, to deal with the type of situation that arose in *Raj Paul*, *Kali Charan Sharma* and *Devi Charan Sharma*. It punishes deliberate and malicious acts intended to outrage the religious feelings of any class of Indian citizens[174] by insulting their religion or religious beliefs. Section 295A reads as follows:

> Whoever, with deliberate and malicious intention of outraging the religious feelings of any class of citizens of India, by words, either spoken or written, or by signs or by visible representations or otherwise, insults or attempts to insult the religion or the religious beliefs of that class, shall be punished …

[167] *Balwant Singh v State of Punjab* (1995) 3 SCC 214.
[168] ibid 219.
[169] *Bilal Ahmed Kaloo v State of AP* (1997) 7 SCC 431.
[170] *Manzar Sayeed Khan v State of Maharashtra* (2007) 5 SCC 1.
[171] ibid 9.
[172] ibid.
[173] ibid.
[174] It was 'Her Majesty's subjects' at the time of enactment in 1927. This was replaced with 'Indian citizens' in 1950.

The Religious Insults Bill, which proposed adding section 295A to the IPC, was introduced in the Central Legislative Assembly in August 1927.[175] The objective of the Bill was to strengthen the existing provisions of the IPC with regard to insulting/outraging the feelings of classes of people.[176] The perceived shortcomings of the existing provision – section 153A – consequent to the judgment in *Raj Paul* were also highlighted when the Bill was introduced.[177] It was viewed as 'a measure to make a scurrilous attack upon religion as a substantive matter'.[178] The prosecution would no longer have to prove that the publication had led to feelings of enmity between classes of people; an act with the intent of outraging the religious feelings was sufficient.[179]

When the Bill was first discussed in the Council, concerns were raised about the implications for free speech and expression.[180] Legislators wanted to protect valid criticism of religion, religious reform and historical works.[181] The Bill was ultimately sent to a Select Committee of the Council.[182] The Select Committee recommended changing a few words in the section.[183] Notes of dissent were made on three issues by a few members.[184] The main note of dissent was on providing safeguards for honest publishers and printers.[185] The focus was on protecting valid criticism by academic writers, as well as the press.[186] Noteworthy is the warning by Pandit Nilakantha Das that the section would end up being used against 'free thinkers'.[187] Finally, only one of these suggestions of the dissenters – to make the offence non-bailable – was accepted.[188] The Bill was passed and section 295A was added to the IPC.[189]

In *Shri Shiv Ram Dass Udasi Chakravarti v The Punjab State*,[190] a Full Bench of the Punjab High Court, discussing the scope of section 295A, ruled that the manner of discourse, and not the matter, is relevant.[191] It held that 'the words used must be such as are bound to be regarded by any reasonable man as grossly

[175] Kumar, 'Laws and Colonial Subjects' (n 112) 89.
[176] ibid.
[177] ibid.
[178] Nair, 'Beyond the "Communal" 1920s' (n 113) 331.
[179] ibid.
[180] Kumar, 'Laws and Colonial Subjects' (n 112) 90. See also Nair (n 113) 332 (noting Hari Singh Gour's comments).
[181] Kumar (n 112) 90. See also Nair (n 113) 331 (noting Lala Lajpat Rai and MA Jinnah's objections).
[182] Kumar (n 112) 91.
[183] ibid. See also Nair (n 113) 334 (discussing the debates that led to change in the words).
[184] Kumar (n 112) 91.
[185] Nair (n 113) 335.
[186] ibid.
[187] ibid 337.
[188] Kumar (n 112) 93.
[189] ibid.
[190] *Shri Shiv Ram Dass Udasi Chakravarti v The Punjab State* (1954) 7 ILR Pun 1020.
[191] ibid 1028.

offensive and provocative'.[192] They should be accompanied by the malicious and deliberate intention to outrage the feelings of a class of Indian citizens.[193]

The High Court of Mysore, in *The State of Mysore v Henry Rodrigues*,[194] was called upon to rule whether truth is a defence to section 295A. The Court first referred to the Allahabad High Court's decision in *Khalil Ahamad v State*,[195] where the Court had held that the word 'malicious' in section 295A is not used in the 'popular sense'.[196] The prosecution do not have to prove that the accused had ill-will or enmity towards specific persons; they only need to show that the act was done voluntarily, without lawful excuse – malice can then be presumed.[197] In *Ahamad*, the Court had also noted that 'a true statement may [also] outrage religious feelings'.[198] Following *Ahamad*, the Mysore High Court ruled that just because the statement happens to be true, it will not be a valid defence to section 295A if it falls within the mischief that the section was enacted to remedy.[199]

More recently, the Supreme Court, in *Mahendra Singh Dhoni v Yerraguntla Shyamsundar*,[200] ruled that section 295A only penalises those acts that are done with a deliberate and malicious intention to outrage the religious feelings or beliefs of a class of citizens.[201] Hence, insults to religious sentiment done 'unwittingly or carelessly'[202] will not be covered.

G. Section 505(2) and (3)

Sections 505(2) and (3) were inserted into the IPC in 1969. Section 505(2) penalises the making of statements with the intent to create or promote enmity, hatred or ill-will between classes of people. It reads as follows:

> Whoever makes, publishes or circulates any statement or report containing rumour or alarming news with intent to create or promote or which is likely to create or promote, on grounds of religion, race, place of birth, residence, language, caste, or community or any other ground whatsoever, feelings of enmity, hatred, or ill-will between different religious, racial, language or regional groups or castes or communities, shall be punished …

Section 505(3) is an aggravated form of the offence defined in section 505(2). It provides for an enhanced sentence if the offence specified in section 505(2) is

[192] ibid.
[193] ibid.
[194] *The State of Mysore v Henry Rodrigues* (1961) ILR Mys 1099.
[195] *Khalil Ahmad v State* 1960 All LJ 481.
[196] *The State of Mysore v Henry Rodrigues* (n 194) 1106.
[197] ibid.
[198] *Ahamad* (n 195) 485.
[199] *The State of Mysore v Henry Rodrigues* (n 194) 1106.
[200] *Mahendra Singh Dhoni v Yerraguntla Shyamsundar* (2017) 7 SCC 760.
[201] ibid 764.
[202] ibid.

committed in a place of worship, or in an assembly engaged in the performance of religious worship or ceremonies.

Section 505 has an Exception, which provides for truth as a defence if the person who makes, publishes or circulates the statement has reasonable grounds for believing that the statement is true. If such person acts in good faith and without the requisite intent, they will not come within the purview of the provision.

In *Bilal Ahmed Kaloo v State of AP*,[203] the Supreme Court, distinguishing section 153A from section 505(2), held that publication is the *sine qua non* for section 505(2) to be attracted.[204] It ruled that the words 'makes, publishes, or circulates' should not be constructed disjunctively but as supplementary to each other.[205] It further held that like section 153A, *mens rea* is an essential requirement to prove section 505(2).[206]

V. PROCEDURAL PROVISIONS RELATING TO RELIGIOUS PENAL CLAUSES

Chapter XIV of the 1973 CrPC deals with conditions for the initiation of criminal proceedings. A Magistrate takes cognisance of an offence, after which the criminal process commences in the court.[207] For certain offences, the CrPC places limitations on the power of a Magistrate to take cognisance of an offence. Sections 153A, 295A, 505(2) and 505(3) of the IPC are some of the offences on which a limitation is placed on taking cognisance.

Section 196(1) of the CrPC mandates that a court shall not take cognisance of an offence punishable under sections 153A or 295A, except with the prior sanction of the Central Government or State government.[208] Prior sanction of the Central Government or the State government or a District Magistrate is also required before cognisance is taken of an offence punishable under sections 505(2) or 505(3) of the IPC.[209] These provisions' requiring sanction was viewed as a safeguard for these sections when they were being introduced into the Penal Code.

Offences punishable under sections 153A, 295, 295A, 296, 297, 505(2) and 505(3) of the IPC are all cognisable offences.[210] It is only section 298 that is

[203] *Bilal Ahmed Kaloo v State of AP* (1997) 7 SCC 431.

[204] ibid 436.

[205] ibid.

[206] ibid.

[207] Section 190, CrPC.

[208] s 196(1)(a), CrPC. Conspiracy to commit the offence, or abetment is also covered. See ss 196(1)(b) and (c).

[209] s 196(1A)(a), CrPC. Conspiracy to commit the offence is also covered. See s 196(1A)(b), CrPC.

[210] Cognisable offences are those where the police can investigate the case without the prior permission of the Magistrate. Police are also permitted to arrest without warrant in these cases. For a general introduction to the Indian criminal process, see Mrinal Satish, *Discretion, Discrimination and the Rule of Law: Reforming Rape Sentencing in India* (Cambridge University Press, 2016) 13–26.

non-cognisable.[211] Further, sections 153A, 295, 295A, 505(2) and 505(3) of the IPC are non-bailable offences. Sections 296, 297 and 298 are bailable offences. Offences being cognisable and non-bailable have an impact on the manner in which these religious penal clauses are put to use, which I discuss later in this chapter.

An important procedural provision that is generally invoked when cases under sections 153A or 295A are filed is section 95 of the CrPC. Where a newspaper, book or document *appears* to the State government to contain any matter, the publication of which is punishable, inter alia, under section 153A or 295A of the IPC, it may order forfeiture of such a book, newspaper or document.[212] The government is required to issue a notification to this effect, stating grounds for arriving at such opinion.[213] On issuance of such a notification, police officers are authorised to seize such book, newspaper or document, and magistrates are empowered to issue warrants authorising police officers to enter and search premises for any such document, newspaper or book.[214] Section 96 of the CrPC provides the procedure to be followed for setting aside a declaration of forfeiture made under Section 95. A person may make an application to the High Court seeking the setting aside of the order of forfeiture.[215] The ground on which the person may request the setting aside of the order is that the book, newspaper or document does not contain matter the publication of which is punishable, inter alia, under section 153A or 295A of the IPC.[216] The case has to be mandatorily heard by a special bench of the High Court of three judges or more.[217] The court has the power to set aside the order of forfeiture if it finds that the book, document or newspaper does not contain any such matter as is referred to in Section 95(1).[218] Hence, State governments have immense power to order forfeiture of books, newspapers or documents. This is seen as a preventative function, in order to ensure that religious passions are not inflamed.

Justice Krishna Iyer, in *State of UP v Lalai Singh Yadav*,[219] noted that the spirit of section 99A of the 1898 CrPC[220] (now section 95) is as follows:

> In the interests of public order and public peace, public power comes into play not because the heterodox few must be suppressed to placate the orthodox many but because everyone's cranium must be saved from mayhem before his cerebrum can have chance to simmer. Hatred, outrage and like feelings of large groups may have

[211] Prior permission of a Magistrate is required before the police investigate a non-cognisable offence.
[212] Section 95(1), CrPC.
[213] ibid.
[214] ibid.
[215] s 96(1), CrPC.
[216] ibid.
[217] s 96(2), CrPC.
[218] s 96(3), CrPC.
[219] *State of UP v Lalai Singh Yadav* (1976) 4 SCC 213.
[220] The Code of Criminal Procedure of 1898 was repealed and replaced by a new code in 1973.

crypto-violent proneness and the State, in its well-grounded judgment, may prefer to stop the circulation of the book to preserve safety and peace in society. No enlightened State would use this power to suppress advanced economic views, radical rational criticisms or fearless exposure of primitive obscurantism but ordered security is a constitutional value wisely to be safeguarded if progressives and regressives are to peacefully coexist.[221]

The Supreme Court discussed the nature and scope of section 95 in *Baragur Ramachandrappa v State of Karnataka*.[222] It ruled that the objective of sections 95 and 96 is pre-emptive and is to ensure that public order is not disturbed.[223] The Court recognised that the forfeiture of a publication is a serious encroachment on the rights of a citizen. It ruled, however, that forfeiture for public interest would override individual interests.[224]

The wide power that section 95 provides the State government is evident from the wording of the section. The section uses the word 'appear', in the context of the matter falling inter alia within the scope of sections 153A or 295A. As the Supreme Court ruled in *Baragur Ramachandrappa*, it only needs to *appear* to the State government that the requirements of the penal provisions (such as sections 153A or 295A) have been met. It need not be *proved* that the requirements are met.[225] The Court also ruled that section 95 is not in violation of Article 19(1)(a)[226] of the Constitution of India, on the grounds that it is a preventative measure and that an 'extremely efficacious' remedy to challenge the forfeiture is provided in section 96.[227]

In *State of Maharashtra v Sangharaj Damodar Rupawate*,[228] the Supreme Court summarised guidelines drawn up in various cases on notifications of forfeiture under section 95 of the CrPC. Some of the guidelines include:

(a) The intention of the author 'has to be gathered from the language, contents, and import of the offending material'.[229]
(b) In cases of section 153A of the IPC, the fact that the writing is a 'truthful account of past events' or is supported by authority is not a defence.[230] The Court noted that '[a]dherence to the strict part of history is not by itself a complete defence to a charge under section 153A, IPC'.[231]

[221] *State of UP v Lalai Singh Yadav* (n 219) 219.
[222] *Baragur Ramachandrappa v State of Karnataka* (2007) 5 SCC 11.
[223] ibid 22.
[224] ibid.
[225] ibid 22–23.
[226] Art 19(1)(a) provides the right to speech and expression.
[227] ibid 23.
[228] *State of Maharashtra v Sangharaj Damodar Rupawate* (2010) 7 SCC 398.
[229] ibid 414.
[230] ibid.
[231] ibid.

(c) Since section 95 uses the word 'appear', it only needs to appear to the government that the ingredients of the offences mentioned in section 95 will be attracted.[232] It need not be proved that they are in fact attracted.[233]

(d) The burden of proving that the matter does not fall within the purview of the offences mentioned in section 95 is on the person challenging the Notification.[234]

(e) On the question of from whose perspective the material should be judged, the Court ruled that the perspective of 'reasonable, strong-minded, firm and courageous men' should be considered.[235] The class of readers for whom the book is primarily meant, and the probable consequence in their minds, also needs to be considered.[236]

VI. CONSTITUTIONAL IMPLICATIONS

An important question that arises in the context of religious penal clauses is whether they are constitutional, especially whether they violate the right to speech and expression, and the right to practise and profess a religion of one's choice. All the sections classified as religious penal clauses were enacted before the Constitution of India came into force in 1950. By virtue of Article 372 of the Constitution, these provisions continued in force. However, if a provision were to be found repugnant to the Constitution, it would not survive.[237] The constitutionality of some religious penal clauses has been challenged in courts. In this section of the chapter, I discuss and analyse these constitutional challenges. I also discuss debates in the Constituent Assembly about these provisions.

One of the questions before the Constituent Assembly was whether the Constitution should impose any restrictions on the right to free speech.[238] The Assembly decided that restrictions were necessary, and decided to enumerate particular exceptions to the right to free speech.[239] The Advisory Committee on Fundamental Rights, a sub-committee of the Constituent Assembly, proposed multiple exceptions to the right of free speech, which included public order, morality, sedition, obscenity, blasphemy and defamation.[240] There was concern amongst many members in the Assembly about having multiple exceptions to free speech.[241] However, most members were agreeable to certain

[232] ibid 415.
[233] ibid.
[234] ibid.
[235] ibid.
[236] ibid.
[237] Mahendra Pal Singh, *VN Shukla's Constitution of India*, 12th edn (Eastern Book Company, 2013) 1110–12.
[238] Chandrachud, *Republic of Rhetoric* (n 57) 55.
[239] ibid 59.
[240] ibid.
[241] ibid 60.

exceptions, such as defamation, libel and slander.[242] Early drafts prepared by the Advisory Committee on Fundamental Rights included blasphemy as one of the restrictions.[243] However, it was removed in subsequent drafts.[244] There was a proposal to introduce 'public order' as a restriction, which ultimately was not accepted.[245] Sir Alladi Krishnaswami Ayyar specifically noted the presence of section 153A in the IPC, and the need to ensure that speech that would be punished by that section should not be protected by the right to speech and expression.[246] Other members also recommended restricting speech that promoted feelings of enmity and hatred amongst classes of persons.[247] There was opposition to this, however, particularly from Syama Prasad Mookerjee, KM Munshi and Bakshi Tek Chand.[248] Ultimately, this too was not included, which led to section 153A's being promptly struck down by the Punjab High Court in *Master Tara Singh v The State*,[249] where the constitutionality of section 153A was challenged in the Punjab High Court.

The argument made in *Master Tara Singh* was that section 153A violated Article 19(1)(a) of the Constitution of India, which provides for freedom of speech and expression, subject to limitations enumerated in Article 19(2). At the time of the coming into force of the Constitution in 1950, limitations under Article 19(2) were restricted to the making of laws relating to libel, slander, defamation, contempt of court, or any other matter that offended against decency or morality, or which undermined the security of the State or tended to overthrow the State. The Court in *Master Tara Singh* held that section 153A was an unwarranted restriction on the freedom of speech and expression,[250] since it was not a law relating to one of the limitations in Article 19(2). Hence, the Court declared the section to be unconstitutional.[251]

Section 153A was not the only provision struck down by courts as a restriction on the rights in Article 19(1). In fact, in *Master Tara Singh*, section 124A of the IPC, which punishes sedition, was also struck down by the Court. *Master Tara Singh* followed cases where the Supreme Court struck down laws that curtailed free speech on the basis of 'public order' – a limitation that was not enumerated in Article 19(2).[252] There was also a judgment of the Patna High Court, in which one of the judges had observed that even if a person incited murder

[242] ibid 61.
[243] ibid.
[244] ibid.
[245] ibid 62–63.
[246] ibid 64.
[247] ibid.
[248] ibid 64–65.
[249] *Master Tara Singh v The State* (n 164).
[250] ibid 201.
[251] ibid 201.
[252] *Romesh Thapar v State of Delhi*, AIR 1950 SC 124; *Brij Bhushan v State of Delhi*, AIR 1950 SC 129. See Chandrachud, *Republic of Rhetoric* (n 57) 73–74.

through his speech, he could seek the protection of Article 19(1)(a).[253] These cases, and multiple other events, including false press reports of communal riots, led Parliament to amend Article 19(2) and include three new restrictions on Article 19(1)(a) – public order, friendly relations with foreign states, and incitement to an offence.[254] The First Amendment also retrospectively restored the constitutional validity of provisions, including section 153A, that had been struck down by courts.

After the First Amendment to the Indian Constitution came into force, the constitutionality of section 295A was challenged in *Ramji Lal Modi v State of UP*.[255] The petitioner argued that the section contravened Article 19(1)(a) of the Constitution. His contention was that only 'public order' in Article 19(2) could protect section 295A. He argued that a law that seeks to restrict speech on the grounds of public order, will be saved only if causing public disorder is an ingredient of the offence. Section 295A could be invoked even if the actions did not lead to public disorder. Hence, the petitioner argued that the section contravened Article 19(1)(a), although the section could also be invoked in cases where public disorder did occur. He argued that the constitutionally impermissible part of the section was not severable, and hence the entire section should be struck down.[256]

The Court did not agree with the arguments of the petitioner and upheld the constitutionality of section 295A. The Court made a distinction between the terms 'in the interests of public order' and 'for the maintenance of public order'. Noting that Article 19(2) uses the former term, it held that the ambit of the former is wider than the latter. Consequently, a law may not have been designed to maintain public order but may have been enacted in the interests of public order.[257] Hence, section 295A is constitutional. The Court also pointed out that Articles 25 and 26 of the Constitution, which deal with the right to religion, are also subject to public order.[258] The Court held that the deliberate and malicious intent required in section 295A indicates an intent to disrupt the public order. The section consequently is protected by Article 19(2).[259]

The next challenge was to section 153A, whose constitutionality had been restored by the First Amendment to the Indian Constitution. The constitutionality

[253] *Bharati Press v Chief Secretary*, AIR 1951 Pat 12. See Chandrachud (n 57) 76–77.

[254] For a detailed discussion of the history behind the First Amendment to the Indian Constitution, see Chandrachud, *Republic of Rhetoric* (n 57) 72–97. For a detailed analysis, see Arudra Burra, 'Freedom of Speech in the Early Constitution: A Study of the Constitution (First Amendment) Bill' in Udit Bhatia (ed), *The Indian Constituent* Assembly: *Deliberations on Democracy* (Taylor & Francis, 2017) 130.

[255] *Ramji Lal Modi v State of UP* AIR 1957 SC 620.

[256] ibid para 3.

[257] ibid para 7. For a critique, see Gautam Bhatia, 'The Conservative Constitution: Freedom of Speech and the Constituent Assembly Debates' in Udit Bhatia (ed), *The Indian Constituent Assembly: Deliberations on Democracy* (Taylor & Francis, 2017) 121; Gautam Bhatia, *Offend, Shock and Disturb* (Oxford India Paperback, 2018) 54–55.

[258] *Ramji Lal Modi v State of UP* (n 255) para 8.

[259] ibid para 9. See also Bhatia, 'The Conservative Constitution' (n 257) 121.

of the section was challenged before the Bombay High Court in *Gopal Vinayak Godse v Union of India*.[260] The High Court upheld the constitutionality of the section, stating that acts proscribed by section 153A, although impinging on the rights to speech and expression, fell within the limitations to Article 19(1)(a) prescribed in Article 19(2). The Court held that 'the limitations imposed by section 153A are in the interests of public order'.[261] The constitutionality of section 505(2) of the IPC too has been upheld, on the ground that the acts proscribed fall within the 'public order' exception to free speech provided in Article 19(2).[262]

VII. CONTEMPORARY USAGE OF RELIGIOUS PENAL CLAUSES

As is evident from the discussion of decisions of the High Courts and Supreme Court of India, there seem to be very few decisions on sections in Chapter XV of the IPC. This is also the case with section 295A of the IPC, about which there has been a lot of debate and discussion. Section 153A, which is also a 'religious penal clause', has seen relatively more cases in the High Courts and the Supreme Court. However, the number is not too large when compared to decisions relating to other sections of the Penal Code. Does that indicate that religious penal clauses are not being applied? That is certainly not so. Three instances that arose in late 2018 illustrate this. Abhijit Iyer-Mitra, a defence analyst and journalist, was at the centre of a controversy in late 2018. On 16 September 2018, Iyer-Mitra tweeted, posting a video blog of his visit to the famous Konark temple in the State of Orissa, which is known for its erotic sculptures. He referred to the temple as a 'humple', and said that such erotic sculptures are against Hindu tradition.[263] He also said that the temple was a Muslim conspiracy against Hindus. He clarified in his next tweet that his remarks were made jokingly.[264] However, he was arrested for committing offences punishable under sections 153A, 295A and 298 of the IPC, and spent 43 days in prison.[265]

In November 2018, Jack Dorsey, the CEO of Twitter during his visit to India, met a few female journalists to discuss the trolling that women face on Twitter.[266]

[260] *Gopal Vinayak Godse v Union of India* AIR 1971 Bom 56.

[261] ibid 72.

[262] See *Kedar Nath Singh v State of Bihar* AIR 1962 SC 955.

[263] See Debabrata Mohanty, 'Journalist Abhijit Iyer-Mitra arrested for "derogatory remarks" on Konark temple, released on Bail' *Hindustan Times* (India, 20 September, 2018) at www.hindustantimes.com/india-news/journalist-abhijit-iyer-mitra-arrested-for-derogatory-remarks-on-konark-temple-released-on-bail/story-EqzL9k9PsAUzUFSm4r71sM.html.

[264] ibid.

[265] Debabrata Mohanty, 'After 43 days in Odisha prison, Abhijit Iyer-Mitra walks free' *Hindustan Times* (India, 7 December 2018) at www.hindustantimes.com/india-news/after-43-days-in-odisha-prison-abhijit-iyer-mitra-walks-free/story-e7xdZfYYEQfBMNB0KxsV4H.html.

[266] 'Smash Brahminical Patriarchy outrage: Barkha Dutt counters Twitter executive, says it wasn't a "private photo"' *DNA* (20 November 2018) at www.dnaindia.com/india/report-smash-brahminical-patriarchy-outrage-barkha-dutt-counters-twitter-version-says-it-wasn-t-a-private-photo-2687637.

In a photograph that was taken after the meeting, and circulated on Twitter, Dorsey was seen holding a poster that read 'Smash Bhramanical Patriarchy'. The content of the poster outraged certain groups of people, who threatened the journalists in the photograph, and also Jack Dorsey, Twitter and Twitter India with legal action.[267] A senior officer of the Indian Administrative Service tweeted, saying that 'prosecution under section 295A is "fully in order"'.[268] On 22 November, a complaint under section 295A was filed against Dorsey.[269] A few days prior to this incident, a journalist in the State of Karnataka was arrested under section 295A, for saying that an eighteenth-century Muslim ruler committed 'terrorist acts' because of Prophet Mohammed's ideologies.[270]

The three incidents mentioned all occurred over a period of one month (November–December 2018). The National Crime Records Bureau (NCRB) maintains statistics of crime in India, and annually publishes a report on the number of First Information Reports (FIRs),[271] charge sheets,[272] arrests and convictions/acquittals, amongst other data. It does not record data specifically for section 295A, although from 2017 it began publishing data on 'Offences Against Religion'.[273] Hence, there are no official statistics available about the number of cases filed under section 295A. Anecdotal evidence, through press reports and court cases, indicates regular use of the section. In the past, cases under the section have been filed against a former cricketer for saying that he loves a beef dish,[274] a famous painter for painting nudes of a Hindu goddess,[275] a novelist for allegedly insulting religion in her books,[276] and a respected academic

[267] Nandita Singh, 'Jack Dorsey wants to "smash Brahminical patriarchy", triggers Twitter outrage' *ThePrint* (New Delhi, 20 November 2018) at www.theprint.in/culture/jack-dorsey-wants-to-smash-brahminical-patriarchy-triggers-twitter-outrage/151764/.

[268] ibid.

[269] 'Brahmin Body files defamation case against Twitter CEO Jack Dorsey' *Scroll.in* (23 November 2018) at www.scroll.in/latest/903156/brahmin-body-files-defamation-case-against-twitter-ceo-jack-dorsey.

[270] 'Karnataka Journalist arrested for Hate Speech Against Prophet Mohammed, Tipu Sultan' *The Wire* (13 November 2018) at www.thewire.in/media/Karnataka-journalist-arrested-infalmmatory-speech-prophet-mohammed-tipu-sultan.

[271] One of the methods (the most common one) of initiating a criminal case is by filing a FIR with the police (Section 154, CrPC).

[272] After the investigation is completed, the police file a 'charge sheet' before a Magistrate. The charge sheet details the offences for which the person ought to be prosecuted.

[273] Data for 2017 were published by the National Crime Records Bureau in October 2019.

[274] Rasheed Kidwai, 'Town that 'courts' celebs – From Ravi to Rai, Indore's petition brigade spares none' *The Telegraph* (Indore, 28 December 2006) at www.telegraphindia.com/india/town-that-courts-celebs-from-ravi-to-rai-indore-s-petition-brigade-spares-none/cid/746832.

[275] Madhu Jain, 'MF Husain's 20-year-old painting of nude deity raises questions about artistic freedom' *India Today* (31 October 1996) at www.indiatoday.in/magazine/society-the-arts/story/19961031-m-f-husain-20-year-old-painting-of-nude-deity-raises-questions-about-artistic-freedom-833984-1996-10-31.

[276] Swati Sharma, 'Right or wrong, Wendy Doniger's "The Hindus" should be published' *The Washington Post* (20 February 2014) at www.washingtonpost.com/blogs/post-partisan/wp/2014/02/20/right-or-wrong-wendy-donigers-the-hindus-should-be-published/?noredirect=on.

for writing a book on a Hindu King,[277] parts of which offended people, amongst others.[278]

As noted earlier, the NCRB did not maintain or report statistics with respect to offences against religion till 2017. Its reports published in 2019 (with data for 2017 and 2018), indicated that 1,808 FIRs were registered for offences against religion in 2017[279] and 1,942 in 2018.[280] In 2017, 1,914 individuals were arrested,[281] 2,090 in 2018.[282] Charge sheets were filed in 66.2 per cent of cases in 2017,[283] and in 67.5 per cent of cases in 2018.[284] The conviction rate was 21.9 per cent in 2017[285] and 35.1 per cent in 2018.[286]

The NCRB began collecting and reporting statistics on section 153A from 2014, with the report published in 2019 (with data for 2018) being the latest. In 2014, 323 FIRs were registered under section 153A.[287] This increased to 378 FIRs in 2015,[288] to 447 FIRs in 2016[289] to 934 FIRs in 2017[290] and 1,076 in 2018.[291] The charge-sheeting rate for 'offences promoting enmity between different groups', which consists of cases under both sections 153A and 153B, was 60.2 per cent in 2014.[292] It increased to 80.9 per cent in 2015,[293] fell to 65.4 per cent in 2016,[294] and fell further to 34.58 per cent in 2017.[295] It increased to 67.9 per cent, however, in 2018.[296] In 2014, 637 individuals were arrested for committing offences punishable under section 153A.[297] This number increased

[277] Pranesh Prakash, 'Adding Insult to Injury' *Outlook* (Bangalore, 19 November 2012) at www.outlookindia.com/website/story/adding-insult-to-injury/283033.

[278] Mukund Padmanabhan, 'How Far Can you Go?' in Rina Ramdev, Sandhya Devesan Nambiar and Debaditya Bhattacharya (eds), *Sentiment, Politics, Censorship: The State of Hurt* (Sage, 2016) 6.

[279] National Crime Records Bureau, *Crime in India 2017* (India, Ministry of Home Affairs, 2019) Table 1A.4, p 54.

[280] National Crime Records Bureau, *Crime in India 2018*, vol 1 (India, Ministry of Home Affairs, 2019) Table 1.2, 5.

[281] National Crime Records Bureau, *Crime in India, 2017* (n 279) Table 19A.1, 1174.

[282] National Crime Records Bureau, *Crime in India 2018*, vol 3 (India, Ministry of Home Affairs, 2019) Table 19A.5, 1196.

[283] National Crime Records Bureau, *Crime in India, 2017* (n 279) Table 17A.1, 1016.

[284] National Crime Records Bureau, *Crime in India 2018*, vol 3 (n 282) Table 17A.1, 1016.

[285] National Crime Records Bureau, *Crime in India, 2017* (n 279) Table 18A.1, 1096.

[286] National Crime Records Bureau, *Crime in India, 2018*, vol 3 (n 282) Table 18A.1, 1096.

[287] National Crime Records Bureau, *Crime in India 2014* (India, Ministry of Home Affairs, 2015) Table 1.6.

[288] National Crime Records Bureau, *Crime in India 2015* (India, Ministry of Home Affairs, 2015) Table 1.6.

[289] National Crime Records Bureau, *Crime in India 2016* (India, Ministry of Home Affairs, 2017) Table 1A.4, 24.

[290] National Crime Records Bureau, *Crime in India 2017* (n 279) Table 1A.4, 39.

[291] National Crime Records Bureau, *Crime in India 2018*, vol 1 (n 280) Table 1.2, 4.

[292] National Crime Records Bureau, *Crime in India 2014* (n 287) Table 4.1.

[293] National Crime Records Bureau, *Crime in India 2015* (n 288) Table 4.1.

[294] National Crime Records Bureau, *Crime in India 2016* (n 289) Table 17A.1, 543.

[295] National Crime Records Bureau, *Crime in India 2017* (n 279) Table 17A.1, 1011. Note that for 2017 and 2018, data were provided separately for sections 153A and 153B.

[296] National Crime Records Bureau, *Crime in India 2018*, vol 3 (n 282) Table 17A.1, 1012.

[297] National Crime Records Bureau, *Crime in India 2014* (n 287) Table 12.1.

to 888 in 2015,[298] to 966 in 2016[299] and to 1,795 individuals in 2017.[300] In 2018, 1,716 individuals were arrested.[301] The conviction rate for 'offences promoting enmity between different groups' was 21.1 per cent in 2014.[302] It fell to 13.8 per cent in 2015,[303] increased to 15.3 per cent in 2016[304] and fell again to 11.5 per cent in 2017.[305] It increased to 20.9 per cent in 2018.[306] Noteworthy is that the conviction rate for this category of offences was the sixth lowest amongst all IPC crimes in 2014, the *lowest* in 2015, the third lowest in 2016 and the *lowest* in 2017, when the data were desegregated between sections 153A and 153B. It was fourteenth from the bottom in 2018.[307] The conviction rate in 2017 for offences in Chapter XV, IPC was the ninth lowest amongst all IPC crimes. This itself tells a story – that the police arrest individuals and file charge sheets against them in a substantially large number of cases involving section 153A, and for offences against religion. Courts, on the other hand, acquit most of these individuals, with the conviction rate's being amongst the lowest for all IPC crimes.[308]

The Supreme Court, in *Mahendra Singh Dhoni v Yerraguntla Shyamsundar*,[309] cautioned magistrates not to take cognisance of offences routinely but to apply their minds and determine whether the basic ingredients of the offence were constituted.[310] The Court in multiple cases has also noted that Indian police have a tendency to make unnecessary arrests, and have issued guidelines many times to curb this.[311] When offences are cognisable and non-bailable, arrest becomes routine, and bail is often denied. Discussing hate speech laws, including section 295A, Siddharth Narrain argues that courts have become more strict over the years, and have dismissed accusations if they find them to be frivolous.[312] The same is definitely the case with section 153A, and for offences in Chapter XV of the IPC. However, the process itself amounts to punishment, and may deter

[298] National Crime Records Bureau, *Crime in India 2015* (n 288) Table 12.1.
[299] National Crime Records Bureau, *Crime in India 2016* (n 289) Table 19A.1, 610
[300] National Crime Records Bureau, *Crime in India 2017* (n 279) Table 19A.1, 1171.
[301] National Crime Records Bureau, *Crime in India 2018*, vol 3 (n 282) Table 19A.5, 1194.
[302] National Crime Records Bureau, *Crime in India 2014* (n 287) Table 4.5.
[303] National Crime Records Bureau, *Crime in India 2015* (n 288) Table 4.5.
[304] National Crime Records Bureau, *Crime in India 2016* (n 289) Table 18A.1, 567.
[305] National Crime Records Bureau, *Crime in India 2017* (n 279) Table 18A.1, 1092. Note that for 2017 and 2018, data were provided separately for sections 153A and 153B.
[306] National Crime Records Bureau, *Crime in India 2018*, vol 3 (n 282) 1092.
[307] Note that in 2018, data were provided for specific subsections of the IPC; for instance, whereas earlier, 'Causing Death by Negligence' was a general category for which data were provided, in 2018, data were provided for specific professions, such as medical negligence. Similarly, whereas earlier consolidated data were provided for the offence of 'grievous hurt', for 2018, data were provided for specific subsections of the IPC dealing with the manner in which the grievous hurt was inflicted.
[308] In 2014, 2015, 2016, and 2017, the other two crimes for which the conviction rates were as low were section 498A (matrimonial cruelty) and for the offence of preparing to commit dacoity (robbery committed or attempted to be committed by five or more people).
[309] *Mahendra Singh Dhoni v Yerraguntla Shyamsunda* (2017) 7 SCC 760.
[310] ibid 766.
[311] See *Joginder Kumar v State of Uttar Pradesh* (1994) 4 SCC 260; *Arnesh Kumar v State of Bihar* (2014) 8 SCC 273; *Social Action Forum for Manav Adhikar v Union of India* (2018) 10 SCC 443.
[312] Narrain, 'The Harm in Hate Speech Laws' (n 60) 52.

free speech. Added to this is section 95 of the CrPC, which gives the Government power to forfeit books, documents and newspapers if it *appears* that the matter constitutes an offence under section 153A or 295A of the IPC. The existence of such a provision is in itself a deterrent to free speech, as Narrain argues.[313] Dissent, or different points of view, also ends up being penalised in the name of offences against religion or intent to bring disharmony between groups.[314]

There have been multiple instances over the past few years where publishers have withdrawn books when threatened with legal action under sections 153A or 295A. One of the most conspicuous of these was Penguin India's decision to withdraw all copies of Wendy Doniger's *The Hindus: An Alternative History*.[315] Penguin India released a statement that section 295A of the IPC places severe restrictions on free speech.[316] In 2014, Orient Blackswan withdrew Megha Kumar's *Communalism and Sexual Violence: Ahmedabad Since 1969*, after being threatened with legal action.[317] Hence, although criminal cases may not be filed, people may self-censor, and publishers may insist that lawyers approve books (fiction, non-fiction, academic and poetry) before they publish them. If books are eventually published, they may be forfeited by a State Government. As Mukund Padmanabhan terms it, India seems to have become a 'republic of hurt sentiments'.[318] Religious penal clauses, the introduction of which in the Penal Code was justified on the grounds that they were designed to ensure religious tolerance, now appear to have become a tool for propagating religious intolerance.

It would appear, then, that public sentiment would call for the repeal of these clauses. However, there is no such movement. In fact, there are efforts to introduce more blasphemy laws. The government in the State of Punjab[319] proposed adding a section 295AA to the IPC to punish desecration of holy books – the Guru Granth Sahib, the Bhagvad Gita, the Quran and the Bible – with imprisonment for life.[320] Opinion pieces in newspapers and web-magazines[321] criticised

[313] ibid.

[314] See, for instance, *Baragur Ramachandrappa v State of Karnataka* (2007) 5 SCC 11 (where the author of a fictional work was not permitted to take a point of view with which the majority of the followers of a particular sect disagreed).

[315] Rina Ramdev, Sandhya Devesan Nambiar and Debaditya Bhattacharya, 'Sentimental Sovereignties: Hurt and the Political Unconscious' in Rina Ramdev, Sandhya Devesan Nambiar and Debaditya Bhattacharya (eds), *Sentiment, Politics, Censorship: The State of Hurt* (Sage, 2016) xvii.

[316] ibid xx.

[317] ibid xix. See also at www.meghakumar.org/news.html (accessed on 22 November 2018), where Kumar documents this withdrawal, along with correspondence and news reports.

[318] Padmanabhan, 'How Far Can You Go?' (n 278) 6.

[319] The Congress Party, which is currently the main opposition party in the country, is in power in Punjab. It is one of the few States in India that have a non-Bharatiya Janata Party (BJP) government. The BJP is the party in power at the Centre and in most States.

[320] 'Punjab's effort to criminalise blasphemy further is dangerous' *Hindustan Times* (India, 24 August 2018) at www.hindustantimes.com/editorials/punjab-s-effort-to-criminalise-blasphemy-further-is-dangerous/story-7eKE57Ub71fjP9hUIWjGoL.html.

[321] See, for instance, Jagrup Singh Sekhon, 'Blasphemy Law Sounds Warning Bell Not Just for Punjab But All of India' *The Wire* (Haryana, 12 September 2018) at www.thewire.in/law/punjab-blasphemy-law-amarinder-singh-congress; Gautam Bhatia, 'How the Blasphemy Law Could

this move, but there does not seem to be any perceptible public discomfort against adding section 295AA. The only time that there has been public discourse on a legal provision similar to religious penal clauses has been in the context of section 66A of the Information Technology Act. Many people had been prosecuted under that section (which came into force in 2009) for their posts on social media. Given the impact on social media, there were protests against this provision, which was ultimately struck down by the Supreme Court as being unconstitutional.[322]

VIII. CONCLUSION

This contribution was originally written and presented at a workshop at the National University of Singapore in December 2018. The incidents discussed in the preceding sections have been updated to that point. Many developments have taken place since, which can be argued to manifest the increased religious polarisation in India. The most controversial among them are amendments to the Citizenship Act, 1955, made in December 2019. A proviso was added to section 2(1) of the Citizenship Act, 1955, which defined 'illegal immigrant' to state that any Hindu, Sikh, Buddhist, Jain, Parsi or Christian from Afghanistan, Bangladesh or Pakistan, who entered India on or before 31 December 2014 would not be treated as an illegal immigrant, subject to the meeting of a few other conditions. Further, section 6B was added to the Act, whereby the category of people mentioned above could apply for and be granted Indian citizenship on an accelerated basis. All legal proceedings against this category of individuals would also abate.[323] As is evident, Muslims were excluded from this category. There was apprehension that the Government would also go ahead with its proposal to create a 'National Register of Citizens' (NRC).[324] It was apprehended that the NRC, in conjunction with amendments to the Citizenship Act, would lead to a large of number of Muslims being rendered stateless.[325]

Transform Punjab into a Theocratic State' *Hindustan Times* (Punjab, 21 September 2018) at www.hindustantimes.com/analysis/how-the-blasphemy-law-could-transform-punjab-into-a-theocratic-state/story-DnPOeSdaD5yPGFhUKTijmI.html; Pratap Bhanu Mehta, 'A Blasphemous Law' *The Indian Express* (Punjab, 25 August 2018) at https://indianexpress.com/article/opinion/columns/blasphemy-law-punjab-government-article-295-imprisonment-for-causing-damnage-religious-scriptures-5323736/.

322 *Shreya Singhal v Union of India* (2015) 5 SCC 1.

323 Section 6B(3), Citizenship Act, 1955.

324 See Zoya Hasan, 'An Anatomy of anti-CAA protests' *The Hindu* (India, 1 January 2020) at www.thehindu.com/opinion/op-ed/an-anatomy-of-anti-caa-protests/article30446145.ece. See also Amitabh Kundu and PC Mohanan, 'Citizenship (Amendment) Act: How Do We Move Forward?' (2020) 50 (12) *Economic and Political Weekly* 15.

325 Nayanima Basu, 'CAA, NRC could render huge number of Indian Muslims stateless, says Ashutosh Varshney' *The Print* (India, 5 March 2020) at https://theprint.in/india/caa-nrc-could-render-huge-numbers-of-indian-muslims-stateless-says-ashutosh-varshney/376008/. See also Barkha Dutt, 'How Citizenship Act, NRC will alter the idea of India, writes Barkha Dutt' *Hindustan Times* (New Delhi, 14 December 2019) at https://www.hindustantimes.com/columns/how-the-amended-citizenship-act-and-nrc-will-alter-the-idea-of-india/story-Qti007fZz8HIsqFn8NmTKL.html.

Widespread protests broke out all over India against amendments to the Citizenship Act and the proposed NRC. The most prominent amongst these was a women-led protest that began on 15 December 2019 in Shaheen Bagh, a Muslim-dominated area of New Delhi.[326] Protests at this site continued for 101 days without a break, until protestors were forced to leave due to the COVID-related lockdown in India.[327] These protests were also viewed as an assertion of constitutional rights by Muslim women, who spearheaded the movement.[328] In the midst of these protests, communal riots broke out in Delhi in late February 2020, in which 53 people were killed.[329] Thereafter, in March 2020, when COVID 19 cases started surging in India, a congregation of a Muslim sect in New Delhi accounted for nearly one-third of India's cases at that time.[330] The sect was alleged to have violated orders restricting the number of people that could assemble in one place.[331] This group was considered a super-spreader, and this led to a wave of Islamophobic reactions,[332] where Muslims were blamed for the spread of the disease in India.[333] The 'ruling classes' were accused of polarising society along communal lines.[334] Noted historian Ramachandra Guha opined that bureaucrats of the Health Department, in their daily media briefings on the pandemic, were 'inciting polarisation'.[335]

As I have argued earlier, offences against religion have also been used by governments to stifle dissent. In the recent past, the number of criminal cases filed against journalists has increased. In 2020, India dropped two places in the

[326] Somya Lakhani, 'Hours into Delhi lockdown, on 101st day of sit-in, Shaheen Bagh cleared, police cite curbs' *The Indian Express* (New Delhi, 25 March, 2020) at https://indianexpress.com/article/cities/delhi/delhi-lockdown-coronavirus-shaheen-bagh-cleared-6330360/.

[327] ibid.

[328] Rafia Kazim, 'At Shaheen Bagh, Muslim Women Take Their Place as Heroes of the Movement' *The Wire* (India, 30 January 2020) at https://thewire.in/women/shaheen-bagh-muslim-women.

[329] Scroll Staff, 'Explainer: What do we know about the communal violence that left 53 dead in Delhi in February 2020?' *Scroll.in* (India, 6 March 2020) at https://scroll.in/article/955251/explainer-what-do-we-know-about-the-communal-violence-that-left-47-dead-in-delhi-in-february-2020.

[330] Akash Bisht and Sadiq Naqvi, 'How Tablighi Jamaat event became India's worst coronavirus vector' *AlJazeera* (India, 7 April 2020) at www.aljazeera.com/news/2020/04/tablighi-jamaat-event-india-worst-coronavirus-vector-200407052957511.html.

[331] Saurabh Trivedi, 'Coronavirus: The story of India's largest COVID-19 cluster' *The Hindu* (India, 11 April 2020) at www.thehindu.com/news/national/coronavirus-nizamuddin-tablighi-jamaat-markaz-the-story-of-indias-largest-covid-19-cluster/article31313698.ece.

[332] See Joanna Slater, Niha Masih and Shams Irfan, 'India confronts its first coronavirus super-spreader – a Muslim missionary group with more than 400 members infected' *The Washington Post* (Asia Pacific, 2 April 2020) at www.washingtonpost.com/world/asia_pacific/india-coronavirus-tablighi-jamaat-delhi/2020/04/02/abdc5af0-7386-11ea-ad9b-254ec99993bc_story.html.

[333] Rohini Chatterji, 'Tablighi Jamat: News Channels Are Spreading Hate in the Name of Reporting' *Huffpost* (2 April 2020) at www.huffingtonpost.in/entry/news-channels-coronavirus-tablighi-jamaat_in_5e859b09c5b692780507aeab.

[334] D Raja, 'Covid-19 pandemic has shown up inequities and injustices of the old order' *The Indian Express* (New Delhi, 11 June 2020) at https://indianexpress.com/article/opinion/columns/coronavirus-pandemic-modi-government-failure-health-emergency-6452917/.

[335] Karan Thapar, 'Media and Top Central Leaders are Complicit in Communalising COVID-19' *The Wire* (New Delhi, 26 April 2020) at https://thewire.in/communalism/media-and-top-central-leaders-are-complicit-in-communalising-covid-19.

World Press Freedom Index, and is now ranked 142nd.[336] The organisation that undertakes this exercise of ranking noted that criminal prosecutions against journalists with the objective of gagging them, were one of the reasons that indicated the lack of press freedom in India.[337] Cases have been filed against multiple journalists for their COVID-related reporting, including under section 505 of the IPC, when they have attempted to hold governments to account.[338] Concerned about this, the Editors Guild of India has issued statements condemning the use of criminal laws against journalists.[339] The Guild has expressed concern about the increasing frequency of such use, and has cautioned that such action destroys 'a key pillar of India's democracy'.[340]

The amendments to the Citizenship Act, the protests thereafter, the Delhi riots and, ironically, COVID too, are further manifestations of increased religious polarisation in India. This, along with the increasing attempts of the state to stifle dissent, make it but natural that the state is more likely to expand its powers with respect to offences against religion, rather than curtail them.

BIBLIOGRAPHY

Basu, N, 'CAA, NRC could render huge number of Indian Muslims stateless, says Ashutosh Varshney' *The Print* (India, 5 March 2020) at https://theprint.in/india/caa-nrc-could-render-huge-numbers-of-indian-muslims-stateless-says-ashutosh-varshney/376008/

Bhargava, R, 'Reimagining Secularism: Respect, Domination and Principled Distance' (2013) 48(50) *Economic and Political Weekly* 79

[336] Reporters Without Borders, 'Modi tightens his grip on the media', (2020) at https://rsf/org/en/india.

[337] ibid.

[338] *The Wire* Staff, '55 Indian Journalists Arrested, Booked, Threatened for Reporting on COVID-19: Report' *The Wire* (India, 16 June 2020) at https://thewire.in/media/covid-19-journalists-arrested-booked-report. See also Arushi Thapar, 'FIR Against Scroll Editor Latest in Series of Police Cases Against Indian Journalists' *Article 14* (India, 18 June, 2020) at www.article-14.com/post/fir-against-scroll-editor-latest-in-series-of-police-cases-against-indian-journalists; *The Wire* Staff, 'UP Police FIR Against The Wire an Attack on the Freedom of Press' *The Wire* (India, 1 April, 2020) at https://thewire.in/media/up-police-fir-against-the-wire-an-attack-on-freedom-of-the-press; Abhishek Saha, 'Man who Alleged Corruption in Nagaland Covid Handling Held, *The Indian Express* (Guwahati, 11 June 2020) at https://indianexpress.com/article/north-east-india/nagaland/man-who-alleged-corruption-in-nagaland-covid-handling-held-6453100/; *The Wire* Staff, 'Tamil Nadu Police Jails News Portal Founder for Stories on Lockdown Shortcomings' *The Wire* (New Delhi, 24 April 2020) at https://thewire.in/media/coimbatore-founder-of-news-portal-arrested-for-reporting-on-governments-handling-of-covid-19.

[339] Editors Guild of India, 'Statement: The Editors Guild of India is deeply concerned over registration of a First Information Report (FIR) at Varanasi's Ramnagar police station against Scroll Executive Editor Supriya Sharma' (India, 19 June 2020) at https://editorsguild.in/statements-issued/. See also Editors Guild of India, 'Statement: The Editors Guild of India notes with concern a growing pattern of misuse of criminal laws to intimidate journalists in different parts of the country' (India, 13 May 2020) at https://editorsguild.in/statements-issued/.

[340] Editors Guild of India, 'Statement: The Editors Guild of India is deeply concerned' (India, 19 June 2020) (n 339).

Bhatia, G, 'How the Blasphemy Law Could Transform Punjab into a Theocratic State' *Hindustan Times* (Punjab, 21 September 2018) at www.hindustantimes.com/analysis/how-the-blasphemy-law-could-transform-punjab-into-a-theocratic-state/story-DnPOeSdaD5yPGFhUKTijmI.html

—— *Offend, Shock and Disturb* (Oxford India Paperback, 2018)

—— 'The Conservative Constitution: Freedom of Speech and the Constituent Assembly Debates' in Udit Bhatia (ed), *The Indian Constituent Assembly: Deliberations on Democracy* (Taylor & Francis, 2017) 121

Bisht, A, and Naqvi, S, 'How Tablighi Jamaat event became India's worst coronavirus vector' *AlJazeera* (India, 7 April 2020) at www.aljazeera.com/news/2020/04/tablighi-jamaat-event-india-worst-coronavirus-vector-200407052957511.html

Burra, A, 'Freedom of Speech in the Early Constitution: A Study of the Constitution (First Amendment) Bill' in Udit Bhatia (ed), *The Indian Constituent* Assembly: *Deliberations on Democracy* (Taylor & Francis, 2017) 130

Chandrachud, A, *Republic of Rhetoric: Free Speech and the Constitution of India* (Gurgaon, Penguin India, 2017)

Chatterji, R, 'Tablighi Jamat: News Channels Are Spreading Hate in the Name of Reporting' *Huffington Post* (2 April 2020) at www.huffingtonpost.in/entry/news-channels-coronavirus-tablighi-jamaat_in_5e859b09c5b692780507aeab

DNA, 'Smash Brahminical Patriarchy outrage: Barkha Dutt counters Twitter executive, says it wasn't a "private photo"' (20 November 2018) at www.dnaindia.com/india/report-smash-brahminical-patriarchy-outrage-barkha-dutt-counters-twitter-version-says-it-wasn-t-a-private-photo-2687637

Dutt, B, 'How Citizenship Act, NRC will alter the idea of India, writes Barkha Dutt' *Hindustan Times* (New Delhi, 14 December 2019) at www.hindustantimes.com/columns/how-the-amended-citizenship-act-and-nrc-will-alter-the-idea-of-india/story-Qti007fZz8HIsqFn8NmTKL.html

Hasan, Z, 'An Anatomy of anti-CAA protests' *The Hindu* (India, 1 January 2020) at www.thehindu.com/opinion/op-ed/an-anatomy-of-anti-caa-protests/article30446145.ece

Hindustan Times, 'Punjab's effort to criminalise blasphemy further is dangerous' (India, 24 August 2018) at www.hindustantimes.com/editorials/punjab-s-effort-to-criminalise-blasphemy-further-is-dangerous/story-7eKE57Ub71fjP9hUIWjGoL.html

Human Rights Watch, 'Violent Cow Protection in India: Vigilante Groups Attack Minorities' (2019) at www.hrw.org/report/2019/02/18/violent-cow-protection-india/vigilante-groups-attack-minorities

Indian Law Commission, *The Indian Penal Code, As Originally Framed in 1837, With Notes by TB Macaulay, JM Macleod, GW Anderson, and F Millett, And the First and Second Reports Thereon by CH Cameron and D Elliott: A Verbatim Reprint* (Higginbotham & Co, 1888)

Jain, M, 'MF Husain's 20-year-old painting of nude deity raises questions about artistic freedom' *India Today* (31 October 1996) at www.indiatoday.in/magazine/society-the-arts/story/19961031-m-f-husain-20-year-old-painting-of-nude-deity-raises-questions-about-artistic-freedom-833984-1996-10-31

Kazim, R, 'At Shaheen Bagh, Muslim Women Take Their Place as Heroes of the Movement' *The Wire* (30 January 2020) at https://thewire.in/women/shaheen-bagh-muslim-women

Kidwai, R, 'Town that 'courts' celebs – From Ravi to Rai, Indore's petition brigade spares none' *The Telegraph* (Indore, 28 December 2006) at www.telegraphindia.com/

india/town-that-courts-celebs-from-ravi-to-rai-indore-s-petition-brigade-spares-none/cid/746832

Krishna, G, 'Communal Violence in India: A Study of Communal Disturbance in Delhi,' (1985) 20(2) *Economic and Political Weekly* 61

Kumar, N, 'Laws and Colonial Subjects: The Subject-Citizen Riddle and the Making of Section 295(A)' in Guneel Cederlöf and Sanjukta Das Gupta (eds), Subjects, Citizens and Law (Routledge, 2017) 78

Kundu, A, and Mohanan, PC, 'Citizenship (Amendment) Act: How Do We Move Forward?' (2020) 50 (12) *Economic and Political Weekly* 15

Lakhani, S, 'Hours into Delhi lockdown, on 101st day of sit-in, Shaheen Bagh cleared, police cite curbs' *The Indian Express* (New Delhi, 25 March, 2020) at https://indianexpress.com/article/cities/delhi/delhi-lockdown-coronavirus-shaheen-bagh-cleared-6330360/

Mahmood, T, 'Religion, Law, and Judiciary in Modern India' (2006) *Brigham Young University Law Review* 755

Mehta, PB, 'A Blasphemous Law' *The Indian Express* (Punjab, 25 August 2018) at https://indianexpress.com/article/opinion/columns/blasphemy-law-punjab-government-article-295-imprisonment-for-causing-damnage-religious-scriptures-5323736/

Mohanty, D, 'After 43 days in Odisha prison, Abhijit Iyer-Mitra walks free' *Hindustan Times* (India,7December2018)atwww.hindustantimes.com/india-news/after-43-days-in-odisha-prison-abhijit-iyer-mitra-walks-free/story-e7xdZfYYEQfBMNB0KxsV4H.html

—— 'Journalist Abhijit Iyer-Mitra arrested for "derogatory remarks" on Konark temple, released on Bail' *Hindustan Times* (India, 20 September, 2018) at www.hindustantimes.com/india-news/journalist-abhijit-iyer-mitra-arrested-for-derogatory-remarks-on-konark-temple-released-on-bail/story-EqzL9k9PsAUzUFSm4r71sM.html

Mustafa, F, and Sohi, JS, 'Freedom of Religion in India: Current Issues and Supreme Court Acting as Clergy' (2017) *Brigham Young University Law Review* 915

Nair, N, 'Beyond the "Communal" 1920s: The Problem of Intention, Legislative Pragmatism, and the Making of Section 295A of the Indian Penal Code' (2013) 50(3) *The Indian Economic and Social History Review* 317

Narrain, S, 'The Harm in Hate Speech Laws: Examining the Origins of Hate Speech Legislation in India' in Rina Ramdev, Sandhya Devesan Nambiar and Debaditya Bhattacharya (eds), *Sentiment, Politics, Censorship: The State of Hurt* (Sage, 2016) 44

National Crime Records Bureau, *Crime in India 2018* (India, Ministry of Home Affairs, 2019)

——, *Crime in India 2017* (India, Ministry of Home Affairs, 2019)

——, *Crime in India 2016* (India, Ministry of Home Affairs, 2017)

——, *Crime in India 2015* (India, Ministry of Home Affairs, 2015)

—— *Crime in India 2014* (India, Ministry of Home Affairs, 2015)

Office of the Registrar General and Census Scans Commissioner, 'Religion PCA' (India, Ministry of Home Affairs, 2011) at www.censusindia.gov.in/2011census/Religion_PCA.html

Padmanabhan, M, 'How Far Can you Go?' in Rina Ramdev, Sandhya Devesan Nambiar, Debaditya Bhattacharya (eds), *Sentiment, Politics, Censorship: The State of Hurt* (Sage, 2016) 6

Prabhu, S, 'After fierce debate, anti-communal violence bill is dropped. Here's why' *NDTV* (5 February 2009) at www.ndtv.com/cheat-sheet/after-fierce-debate-anti-communal-violence-bill-is-dropped-heres-why-549881

Prakash, P, 'Adding Insult to Injury' *Outlook* (Bangalore, 19 November 2012) at www.outlookindia.com/website/story/adding-insult-to-injury/283033

Raj, R, 'A Pamphlet and its (Dis)contents: A Case Study of *Rangila Rasul* and the Controversy Surrounding it in Colonial Punjab 1923–29' (2015) 9(2) *History and Sociology of South Asia* 146

Raja, D, 'Covid-19 pandemic has shown up inequities and injustices of the old order' *The Indian Express* (New Delhi, 11 June 2020) at https://indianexpress.com/article/opinion/columns/coronavirus-pandemic-modi-government-failure-health-emergency-6452917/

Ramdev, R et al, 'Introduction: Sentimental Sovereignties: Hurt and the Political Unconscious' in Rina Ramdev, Sandhya Devesan Nambiar and Debaditya Bhattacharya (eds), *Sentiment, Politics, Censorship: The State of Hurt* (Sage, 2016) xv

——, Nambiar, SD, and Bhattacharya, D, 'Sentimental Sovereignties: Hurt and the Political Unconscious' in Rina Ramdev, Sandhya Devesan Nambiar and Debaditya Bhattacharya (eds), *Sentiment, Politics, Censorship: The State of Hurt* (Sage, 2016) xvii

Saha, A, 'Man who Alleged Corruption in Nagaland Covid Handling Held, *The Indian Express* (Guwahati, 11 June 2020) at https://indianexpress.com/article/north-east-india/nagaland/man-who-alleged-corruption-in-nagaland-covid-handling-held-6453100/

Satish, M, *Discretion, Discrimination and the Rule of Law: Reforming Rape Sentencing in India* (Cambridge, Cambridge University Press, 2016)

Scroll.in, 'Brahmin Body files defamation case against Twitter CEO Jack Dorsey' (23 November 2018) at www.scroll.in/latest/903156/brahmin-body-files-defamation-case-against-twitter-ceo-jack-dorsey

Scroll Staff, 'Explainer: What do we know about the communal violence that left 53 dead in Delhi in February 2020?' *Scroll.in* (6 March 2020) at https://scroll.in/article/955251/explainer-what-do-we-know-about-the-communal-violence-that-left-47-dead-in-delhi-in-february-2020

Sekhon, JS, 'Blasphemy Law Sounds Warning Bell Not Just for Punjab But All of India' *The Wire* (Haryana, 12 September 2018) at www.thewire.in/law/punjab-blasphemy-law-amarinder-singh-congress

Sharma, S, 'Right or wrong, Wendy Doniger's "The Hindus" should be published' *The Washington Post* (20 February 2014) at www.washingtonpost.com/blogs/post-partisan/wp/2014/02/20/right-or-wrong-wendy-donigers-the-hindus-should-be-published/?noredirect=on

Singh, MP, *VN Shukla's Constitution of India*, 12th edn (Eastern Book Company, 2013)

Singh, N, 'Jack Dorsey wants to "smash Brahminical patriarchy", triggers Twitter outrage' *ThePrint* (New Delhi, 20 November 2018) at www.theprint.in/culture/jack-dorsey-wants-to-smash-brahminical-patriarchy-triggers-twitter-outrage/151764/

Slater, J, Masih, N, and Irfan, S, 'India confronts its first coronavirus super-spreader – a Muslim missionary group with more than 400 members infected' *The Washington Post* (Asia Pacific, 2 April 2020) at www.washingtonpost.com/world/asia_pacific/india-coronavirus-tablighi-jamaat-delhi/2020/04/02/abdc5af0-7386-11ea-ad9b-254ec99993bc_story.html

Sorabjee, SJ, 'Freedom of Expression and Censorship: Some Aspects of the Indian Experience' (1994) 45 *Northern Ireland Legal Quarterly* 327

Thapar, A, 'FIR Against Scroll Editor Latest in Series of Police Cases Against Indian Journalists' *Article 14* (India, 18 June, 2020) at www.article-14.com/post/fir-against-scroll-editor-latest-in-series-of-police-cases-against-indian-journalists

Thapar, K, 'Media and Top Central Leaders are Complicit in Communalising COVID-19' *The Wire* (New Delhi, 26 April 2020) at https://thewire.in/communalism/media-and-top-central-leaders-are-complicit-in-communalising-covid-19

The Wire, '55 Indian Journalists Arrested, Booked, Threatened for Reporting on COVID-19: Report' (India, 16 June 2020) at https://thewire.in/media/covid-19-journalists-arrested-booked-report

——, 'Tamil Nadu Police Jails News Portal Founder for Stories on Lockdown Shortcomings' (New Delhi, 24 April 2020) at https://thewire.in/media/coimbatore-founder-of-news-portal-arrested-for-reporting-on-governments-handling-of-covid-19

——, 'UP Police FIR Against The Wire an Attack on the Freedom of Press' (India, 1 April 2020) at https://thewire.in/media/up-police-fir-against-the-wire-an-attack-on-freedom-of-the-press

——, 'Karnataka Journalist arrested for Hate Speech Against Prophet Mohammed, Tipu Sultan' (13 November 2018) at www.thewire.in/media/Karnataka-journalist-arrested-infalmmatory-speech-prophet-mohammed-tipu-sultan

Trivedi, S, 'Coronavirus: The story of India's largest COVID-19 cluster' *The Hindu* (India, 11 April 2020) at www.thehindu.com/news/national/coronavirus-nizamuddin-tablighi-jamaat-markaz-the-story-of-indias-largest-covid-19-cluster/article31313698.ece

6

Forbidden Discourse: Evaluating the Transformation of Colonial-era Religious Penal Offences into Contemporary Pakistan's Blasphemy Laws

SYED ALI RAZA*

At every utterance, you say, 'What art thou?'
You yourself tell me, what is this manner of discourse?
Not remained is the strength to speak, but even if were there
With what hope would we say what is our longing?

Ghalib[1]

I. INTRODUCTION

On 31 October 2018, a full bench of the Supreme Court of Pakistan ordered the acquittal of Ms Asia Bibi, a Christian woman who had earlier been sentenced to death by both a trial court and a provincial High Court.[2] The woman was previously convicted for allegedly uttering derogatory remarks against the Holy Prophet (Peace Be Upon Him) during a heated conversation with Muslim women in a small and poor district of the

* Excellent research assistance was provided by Ms Zaira Anwar, final year law student at Pakistan College of Law. Credit also goes to Mr Kevin Leong for looking over the draft of this chapter.

[1] Mirza Asadullah Khan Ghalib was a renowned 19th-century Urdu Poet of Indian subcontinent. These verses are from Mirza Asadullah Khan Ghalib, *Wine of Passion: The Urdu Ghazals of Ghalib*, tr Sarfaraz K Niazi (Ferozsons, 2009) 179.

[2] *Mst Asia Bibi v The State* (Crl A 39-L of 2015, Supreme Court of Pakistan, Full Bench) at www.supremecourt.gov.pk/web/user_files/File/Crl.A._39_L_2015.pdf.

Province of Punjab. The decision of the Supreme Court led to a great hue and cry, and in subsequent days the whole country came to a total standstill, with massive rioting taking place in every major city.[3] A leading religious group rejected the judgment and made open calls for assassination of the Supreme Court judges. They accused the judges of wrongly interpreting the divine law, and also pronounced them guilty of blasphemy by siding with Bibi. Her defence lawyer had to flee the country along with his family, and the Government ended up signing a truce with protestors.[4] The Government ceded to demands of not creating obstacles to the filing of a review petition to the Supreme Court against the acquittal, and agreed to prevent Bibi from leaving Pakistan until the final decision.[5] Nonetheless, in May 2019, it was reported that Bibi had silently left Pakistan for Canada after spending nearly eight years on death row.[6] The review petition made by the religious groups and local mullah of the district against the acquittal order was also subsequently rejected by the Supreme Court.[7]

The sort of backlash and rioting that occurred after the *Asia Bibi* judgment would not surprise those who have a basic understanding of the socio-political and legal complexion of the country. Pakistan inherited religious penal offences from the time of the British Raj, and went on to expand them in a manner that has now crippled the ability of the state to bring about any meaningful change to these provisions. The academic discussions on the subject remain within careful bounds and public debates are nearly non-existent. Even with one of the harshest blasphemy laws in the world, incidents of religious vigilantism are on the rise, and a mere criminal charge permanently jeopardises the lives of the accused. This makes Pakistan a dangerous state for open voices and a free press. Freedom of speech is interpreted conservatively, with many restrictions that make it incompatible with contemporary global understanding. Therefore, the democratic credentials of the state stand compromised by religious taboos and sets of puritanical beliefs.

This chapter will examine the legal background, developments and present-day practice of penal offences against religion in Pakistan. It will analyse various cases to explain the approaches adopted and interpretations made by the higher

[3] Memphis Barker and Aamir Iqbal, 'Asia Bibi: anti blasphemy protests spread across Pakistan' *The Guardian* (Islamabad, 1 November 2018) at www.theguardian.com/world/2018/nov/01/asia-bibi-anti-blasphemy-protests-spread-across-pakistan.

[4] 'Defence Lawyer in Pakistan in blasphemy case flees country' *Associated Press* (Islamabad, 3 November2018) at www.washingtonpost.com/world/asia_pacific/protests-in-pakistan-over-christian-womans-acquittal-end/2018/11/03/43f4f046-df30-11e8-8bac-bfe01fcdc3a6_story.html?noredirect=on&utm_term=.652bce45087e.

[5] 'TLP ends sit in after agreement with government' *Pakistan Today* (Lahore, 3 November 2018) at www.pakistantoday.com.pk/2018/11/02/tlp-ends-sit-in-after-agreement-with-government/.

[6] Michael Safi and Shah Meer Baloch, 'Asia Bibi arrives in Canada after leaving Pakistan' *The Guardian* (Islamabad, 8 May 2019) at www.theguardian.com/world/2019/may/08/asia-bibi-arrives-in-canada-after-leaving-pakistan.

[7] 'Pakistan's Supreme Court upholds Asia Bibi acquittal' *The Economist* (2 February 2019) at www.economist.com/asia/2019/02/02/pakistans-supreme-court-upholds-asia-bibis-acquittal.

courts on the subject of religious penal offences. It will also assess how the constitutional guarantees of free speech, religious freedoms and minority rights should be weighed vis-à-vis these religious penal provisions. This chapter will outline the social and political contexts in which these religious offences were expanded and then in many instances deliberately allowed by the state to be abused for political purposes. In the end, as a part of an overarching reflection, this chapter also proposes some pragmatic legal, policy and administrative solutions that could lead to reducing the intensity of the misuse, if not abolition or amendment, of these provisions. This chapter specifically does not intend to debate the theological arguments on the issue of blasphemy from the perspective of Islamic jurisprudence, nor does it offer reflections on any divinely ordained perspective.

II. CONSTITUTIONAL CONTEXT

A. The Initial Struggle for a Constitution in the Muslim Homeland

The 1973 Constitution of the Republic of Pakistan declares Islam to be the state religion. The majority of Pakistanis are Sunni Muslims, though there is a sizeable and assertive Shia Muslim population as well. According to a recent survey, 96.28 per cent of the total population is Muslim; 1.59 per cent is Christian; 1.6 per cent is Hindu; 0.22 per cent belong to the Ahmadi Community; and 0.07 per cent consists of other groups.[8] The overall literacy rate in the country is abysmally low at 58 per cent.[9] The role of Islam is central in public discourse, and no political party in the country can avoid becoming embroiled in religious debate during political campaigns. There are several ethnic groups in the country and only a few political parties with national outreach. The federating units, also called provinces, remain at odds with one another with regard to resource distribution and financial spoils. The sectarian tensions in the society are well known, and the country has a violent history involving radical religious groups. Pakistan has a large military whose continued existence is justified on the basis that it is necessary in a violent and conflict-ridden society. The state has to heavily rely on foreign aid and loans to fulfil its economic requirements and address problems of abject poverty. The predominantly rural and semi-urban population of Pakistan surged to more than 200 million as per last census of 2017, making the state the fifth largest in the world.[10]

[8] Pakistan Bureau of Statistics, *Population By Religion* (23 April 2019) at www.pbs.gov.pk/sites/default/files//tables/POPULATION%20BY%20RELIGION.pdf.

[9] Mumtaz Alvi, 'Pakistan's literacy rate stands at 58%' *The News* (Islamabad, 27 April 2018) at www.thenews.com.pk/print/309542-pakistan-s-literacy-rate-stands-at-58pc.

[10] Pamela Constable, 'A disaster in the making: Pakistan's population surges to 207.7 million' *The Washington Post* (Rawalpindi, 9 September 2017) at www.washingtonpost.com/world/asia_pacific/a-disaster-in-the-making-pakistans-population-has-more-than-doubled-in-20-years/2017/09/08/4f434c58-926b-11e7-8482-8dc9a7af29f9_story.html?noredirect=on&utm_term=.19880fbde791.

The genesis of the idea of Pakistan lay in a strong inclination amongst the Muslims of India towards having an Islamic state where their political, social and religious rights could, presumably, be better protected. Interestingly, the most right-wing Islamic parties opposed the creation of Pakistan and deemed Jinnah, the founder of Pakistan, an infidel. The religious parties were of the view that in an undivided India, the combined Muslim population made them a potent political force. The creation of a separate Muslim homeland would thus segregate and divide this combined body. Jinnah, on the other hand, wanted a homeland where the political and social rights of the vulnerable Muslim community of the subcontinent could be autonomously exercised. Thus, soon after the creation of this new country, religious groups became its most significant beneficiaries. The first legal instrument of Pakistan, known as the Objectives Resolution of 1949, attached a strong Islamic front to the new Republic.[11] The emotions of common Muslims were roused by interest groups, and the legal design of the state was muddled with farcical arguments on the vague concept of an Islamic state where *Sharia'h* could be enforced. The struggle to seize power within the new state of Pakistan led to the fanning of sectarian differences among Muslims, and the first community that faced violent wrath were the Ahmadis.[12] Anti-Ahmadi Muslim sentiments were instigated in 1952 by the fiery rhetoric of Ulemas (religious scholars).[13] This worked and violence erupted in Punjab, the largest province of Pakistan, where Ahmadis were publicly murdered, looted and humiliated by mobs. The public hate speeches against Ahmadis were supplemented with a demand for an Islamic Constitution. As a result, on 6 March 1952, martial law was imposed in Lahore to quell religious riots. This event also opened the gate for the military to brazenly seize direct control of political power and impose legislation of their choice, without any need for parliamentary or public debate. The inept political parties and timid civilian regimes have mostly kept their focus on staying in office instead of spending any political capital towards this matter of blasphemy laws. Parliament has never been allowed to gain any supremacy, and civilian rulers have always been beholden to

[11] The first constituent assembly passed it with a view that the prospective Constitution should be in line with this framework. The Islamic portions of the Objectives Resolution, 1949 include: 'In the name of Allah, the Beneficent, the Merciful: Whereas sovereignty over the entire universe belongs to God Almighty alone and the authority which He has delegated to the state of Pakistan through its people for being exercised within the limits prescribed by Him is a sacred trust ... Wherein the principles of democracy, freedom, equality, tolerance, and social justice as enunciated by Islam shall be fully observed; Wherein the Muslims shall be enabled to order their lives in the individual and collective spheres in accordance with the teachings and requirements of Islam as set out in the Holy Quran and Sunnah.'

[12] Ahmadis, also known as Mirzais or Qadianis, believe that Mirza Ghulam Ahmad (1835–1908) was a prophet or *nabi*, though subservient to Prophet Muhammad (PBUH). This belief is regarded as blasphemous by the Muslims who regard finality of the prophethood of Hazrat Muhammad (PBUH) as a cardinal principle of Islam.

[13] Hamid Khan, *Constitutional and Political History of Pakistan*, 2nd edn (Oxford University Press, 2004) 117–22.

the military. Thus, the social issues and national agenda have never been entirely in the hands of political parties right from the day of the inception of Pakistan on 14 August 1947.

The country had its first hard-earned but short-lived Constitution on 23 March 1956, which declared it the Islamic Republic of Pakistan. However, after just two years, the Constitution was abrogated and a long period of military rule began. A minor amendment was made to the religious penal clauses in 1961, replacing the phrase 'His Majesty's subjects' with 'the citizens of Pakistan' in the penal code.[14]

B. The Islamic Constitution

In 1971, the two wings of Pakistan were dismembered and East Pakistan became Bangladesh. After the ignoble Decca Debacle,[15] there was a realisation in the military and political quarters that Pakistan needed to accommodate divergent societal views. On 14 August 1973, 26 years after the creation of Pakistan, the present Constitution was promulgated.[16] It was a politically compromised document that reflected a broader consensus between all the key interest groups, including mainstream political parties, the military, religious leaders, bureaucrats and proponents of provincial autonomy. Such broad political consensus did not happen in earlier constitutions that Pakistan had in the past. Through this Constitution, Islam was declared the state religion of the country.[17] A directive principle of state policy included enabling Muslims to order their lives according to their faith.[18] The Constitution also required the President of Pakistan to be a Muslim.[19] A separate chapter on Islamic Provisions was also added to the Constitution to ensure that no proposed law that conflicts with the Quran and Sunnah may be passed.[20] A Council of Islamic Ideology was formed, whose purpose was to forward recommendations to the legislature to bring existing laws into conformity with the injunctions of Islam.[21] Nonetheless, a detailed

[14] Shayan Malik, 'Blasphemy: A Crime in Pakistan Penal Code versus the Traditional Perspective' (2017) 8 *Pakistan Law Review* 23, 36.

[15] At the time of Independence, Pakistan comprised an East Wing and West Wing. In 1971, the East Wing became an independent state called Bangladesh. This is colloquially known in Pakistan as the 'Decca Debacle'.

[16] The Constitution of Islamic Republic of Pakistan, 1973 (the '1973 Constitution').

[17] ibid, Art 2.

[18] Art 31 of the 1973 Constitution reads as follows: '*Steps to be taken to enable Muslims to order their lives in accordance with the Holy Quran and sunnah*. The state should endeavour to facilitate learning of Arabic, to promote observance of Islamic moral standards, and to secure the proper organization of zakat, auqaf and mosques.'

[19] ibid, Art 41.

[20] Art 227 of the 1973 Constitution reads as follows: 'No law shall be enacted which is repugnant to the injunctions of Islam as laid down in the Holy Quran and the sunnah and that existing laws shall be brought into conformity with injunctions of Islam as laid down in the Holy Quran and sunnah.'

[21] ibid, Arts 228 and 230.

list of secular fundamental rights not only became part of this Constitution, but were also given an overriding effect. The strength of subsequent religious penal clauses should be assessed in the light of these fundamental rights. In its original form, the Constitution was a unique document, as it represented an awkward albeit politically pragmatic fusion of religion and modern-day human rights.

The religious features of the Constitution would have an imperative role in shaping the prevailing religious penal laws of the country. Despite the concessions, religious parties were still not satisfied with the extent to which the new Constitution would establish an Islamic State. Soon after the Constitution took effect, anti-Ahmadi agitation intensified again. Mosques became propaganda units and sermons served to fan the flames of religious hostilities among ordinary Muslims, many of whom were illiterate. Prime Minister Zulfiqar Bhutto, otherwise well known to have modern and progressive views, was ineffective in managing this religious aggravation. As an unfortunate consequence, Ahmadis were declared a non-Muslim minority under the Second Constitutional Amendment in 1974.[22] This constitutional discrimination against one religious group sowed the seeds for the fierce abuse of blasphemy laws in times to come. The manner in which this amendment was passed also gave significant power to religious groups to dictate to parliament from the outside without holding any electoral representation, or without need to obtain support from the politically-manifested will of the people.

C. Usage of Religious Penal Clauses in Pakistan

Despite the growing prominence of the Islamic faith in state structures, the first few decades after partition did not see many religious penal clause cases. The first major case brought under section 295-A of the present Pakistan Penal Code (PPC) was in 1954, against an Ahmadi for writing a book that allegedly contained objectionable remarks against the Christian faith.[23] However, the court acquitted the accused for lack of deliberate or malicious intent.[24] Similarly, in another case, in response to allegations that certain material in a book entitled *Development of Muslim Theology, Jurisprudence and Constitutional Theory* was offensive, the Court stated that the research value of the book should instead be preserved.[25] It is worthwhile to point out that prosecution of

[22] Art 260(3) was the part of second amendment brought about in the 1973 Constitution, which defined non-Muslim as follows: 'A person who does not believe in the absolute and unqualified finality of the Prophethood of Muhammad (PBUH) as the last of the Prophets or claims to be a Prophet, in any sense of the word or of any description whatsoever, after Muhammad (PBUH), or recognizes such a claimant as a prophet or a religious reformer, is not a Muslim for the purposes of the constitution or law.'

[23] *The Working Muslim Mission and Literary Trust, Lahore and of The Civil & Military Gazette Limited v The Crown* [1954] PLD Lahore 724 (Full Bench).

[24] ibid.

[25] *Muhammad Khalil v The State* [1962] PLD Lahore WP 850 (Full Bench).

an offence under section 295-A requires the prior sanction of the Government in accordance with the Code of Criminal Procedure, 1898.[26] This procedural requirement provides a necessary check on the potential abuse of section 295-A by any person. This was an effective way of relying on legal procedure in order to prevent abuse of law and still uphold free speech, as courts would generally dismiss these cases because of absence of governmental authorisation.[27]

D. Approach of Courts in Dealing with Religious Offences from 1947 till 1978

As such, the socio-political environment of the country remained religiously charged though the judiciary demonstrated abundant caution, at least in the first three decades, in dealing with religious offences. In a particular case, it even went on to say that in a conflict between two sects, the matter should have been handled administratively to preserve the national interest and societal interests.[28] In another case, when a senior governmental officer was charged under a religious offence clause, the court dismissed the case because of a lack of prior government authorisation.[29] A 15-year-old juvenile was charged under section 295-A in 1979, but the Court dismissed that case as well.[30] It is worth noting that after independence, fewer than 10 cases[31] were reported in the country. This was until stringent amendments were introduced during the 1980s.[32] Another startling fact is that most of these cases were filed by Muslims against Muslims, or were filed by non-Muslims against Muslims.[33] However, at the end of the 1970s, this was about to change completely.

E. Zia's Coup and Blasphemy Laws in Pakistan

On 5 July 1978, the country once again came under direct military rule. The military dictator Zia-ul-Haq was well aware that to avoid questions of legitimacy, it was necessary to keep public sentiment on his side. He therefore chose to systematically escalate religious fervour in Pakistani society, and within Pakistan's state agencies. He took steps to include the Constitution's Objectives

[26] The Code of Criminal Procedure, 1898 (Act V of 1898) (CRPC) regulates the trial and procedure of penal offences. As per s 196 of the CRPC, no court is allowed to take cognisance of s 295-A without permission of the Government.

[27] *Abdul Karim v The State* [1963] PLD Karachi 669.

[28] *Shafiqur-Rehman v The State* [1976] PCrLJ 1456 (Single Bench, Ferozewala, Punjab).

[29] *Fazal-e-Raziq, Chairman, WAPDA v Riaz Ahmad* [1978] PLD Lahore 1082.

[30] *Qaisar Raza v the State* [1979] PCrLJ 758.

[31] Reported judgments only include those of the decisions of High Courts and Supreme Court. The cases were prosecuted under ss 295, 295-A, and 297 of the Penal Code.

[32] Center for Research and Security Studies (CRSS), *Blasphemy Laws in Pakistan: A Historical Overview* (2010) at crss.pk/wp-content/uploads/2010/07/Report-on-Blasphemy-Laws-.pdf, 21.

[33] ibid.

Resolution,[34] which contained assertions on the religious character of the state, in the main part of the Constitution, thus placing it on a par with fundamental rights. The Federal Shariat Court (FSC) was given constitutional recognition, with powers to examine any law and assess its validity in accordance with Islamic injunctions.[35] Zia also introduced a constitutional definition of a Muslim and revised the earlier definition of non-Muslim introduced under the previous Bhutto administration.[36] The era of Zia also coincided with final battle of the Cold War between the US and USSR that took place in Afghanistan. Zia created a narrative that portrayed Islamists as the foot soldiers of the free world, who defeated the godless communists with the help of the country's authoritarian regime and with the generous funding of the western world. This national narrative was peddled by Zia to fuel religiosity in society. It was the context in which the social acceptability of having the strictest blasphemy laws was made possible.

The Zia amendments to the Constitution were all made arbitrarily and in the absence of any representative input. This would have a far-reaching impact. The notion of bringing religious provisions into the constitutional scheme made a rights-restrictive interpretation of all Pakistani legislation possible. As a result, the social makeup of society was reconditioned and the drift towards radicalisation was well-supported by the law. The Zia-ul-Haq regime, through Ordinances in the early 1980s, initially inserted section 295-B into the PPC, which made defiling of the Holy Quran punishable with life imprisonment.[37] Through section 298-A, it made usage of derogatory remarks, etc in respect of holy personages of Islam punishable with imprisonment for up to three years along with a fine.[38] This later provision was structured in such a way that it allowed further schism between mainstream sects of Muslims based on their variant understanding of Islamic history. In particular, the religious practices of

[34] In the 1973 Constitution (n 16), the Objectives Resolution was a preamble. However, it was later made a substantive part of the instrument by the insertion of Art 2(A) into the Constitution.

[35] As per Art 203-D, the Federal Shariat Court can examine and decide the question, whether or not any law or provision of law is repugnant to the injunctions of Islam.

[36] Arts 260(3)(a)–(b) provide 'Muslim means a person who believes in the Unity and Oneness of Almighty Allah, in the absolute and unqualified finality of the Prophethood of Muhammad (PBUH) the last of the prophets, and does not believe in, or recognize as, a prophet or religious reformer, any person who claimed or claims to be a prophet, in any sense of the word or of any description whatsoever, after Muhammad (PBUH) … Non-Muslim means a person who is not a Muslim and includes a person belonging to the Christian, Hindu, Sikh, Buddhist, or Parsee community, a person of the Quadiani group or the Lahori group (who call themselves "Ahmedis" or by any other name), or a Bahai and a person belonging to any of the scheduled castes.'

[37] The provision was inserted by Pakistan Penal Code (Amendment) Ordinance, 1981 (Ordinance 1 of 1981, dated 18 March 1981). It states that 'Whoever willfully defiles, damages or desecrates a copy of the Holy Quran or of an extract therefrom or uses it in any derogatory manner or for any unlawful purpose shall be punishable with imprisonment for life.'

[38] The provision was inserted by the Pakistan Penal Code (Second Amendment) Ordinance, 1980 (Ordinance XLIV of 1980, dated 17 September 1980). It states 'Whoever by words, either spoken or written, or by visible representation, or by any imputation, innuendo or insinuation, directly or indirectly, defiles the sacred name of any wife (Ummul Mumineen), or members of the family

Shias and annual rituals followed by them could be conveniently criminalised. A clear preference was shown by Zia towards one brand of Muslim sect at the cost of others. Both additions to Chapter XV of PPC took away its general applicability, which earlier had provided protection to all faiths and sects. During this time, Zia's Pakistan found itself next door to the Shia Iranian Revolution, the decade-long Iran-Iraq War, the start of the Soviet invasion of Afghanistan and the burgeoning influence of Saudi Arabia. The geo-political situation thus further allowed the regime to brazenly carry out the process of state-approved Islamisation.

The ongoing state assault against the Ahmadis also continued unabated. In 1984, two additional provisions were inserted in Chapter XV of the PPC.[39] Section 298-B barred them from conducting any rituals that generally are attributable to Muslims, thus practically criminalising their religious worship and practices.[40] Similarly, section 298-C provided that it would be a penal offence for Ahmadis to call themselves Muslims and preach their faith, as this would outrage the religious feelings of 'real' Muslims.[41] The religious antagonism that was framed by Hindu-Muslim conflict in British India now reframed itself into a sectarian conflict between Ahmadis and mainstream Muslims in the Islamic Republic of Pakistan, despite the fact that both communities jointly struggled

(Ahle-bait), any of the righteous Caliphs (Khulafa-e-Rashideen) or companions (Sahaaba) of the Holy Prophet (peace be upon him) shall be punishable with imprisonment of either description for a term which may extend to three years, or with fine, or both.'

[39] Anti-Islamic Activities of Quadiani Group, Lahori Group and Ahmadis (Prohibition and Punishment) Ordinance, 1984 (Ordinance XX of 1984, dated 26 April 1984).

[40] As amended by Anti-Islamic Activities Ordinance (n 39), s 298-B of the PPC (Act XLV of 1860) provides:

Misuse of epithets, descriptions and titles, etc reserved for certain holy personages or places.

(1) Any person of the Quadiani group or the Lahori Group (who call themselves 'Ahmadis' or by any other name) who by words, either spoken or written, or by visible representation,

(a) refers to or addresses, any person, other than a Caliph or companion of the Holy Prophet Muhammad (PBUH), as 'Ameerul-Mumineen,' 'Khalifatul-Mumineen', 'Khalifa-tul-Muslimeen', 'Sahaabi' or 'Razi Allah Anho';
(b) refers to, or addresses, any person, other than a wife of the Holy Prophet Muhammad (peace be upon him), as 'Ummul-Mumineen';
(c) refers to, or addresses, any person, other than a member of the family (Ahle-bait) of the Holy Prophet Muhammad (peace be upon him) as Ahle-bait; or
(d) refers to, or names, or calls, his place of worship as 'Masjid';

shall be punished with imprisonment of either description for a term which may extend to three years, and shall also be liable to fine.

(2) Any person of the Quadiani group or Lahori group (who call themselves 'Ahmadis' or by any other name) who by words, either spoken or written, or by visible representation, refers to the mode or form of call to prayers followed by his faith as 'Azan', or recites Azan as used by the Muslims, shall be punished with imprisonment of either description for a term which may extend to three years, and shall also be liable to fine.

[41] ibid, s 298-C: '*Person of Quadiani group, etc, calling himself a Muslim or preaching or propagating his faith.* Any person of the Quadiani group or Lahori group (who call themselves 'Ahmadis' or by another name), who, directly or indirectly, poses himself as a Muslim, or calls, or refers to,

for an independent homeland.[42] These amendments removed the freedom of speech to profess one's faith in the Ahmadi community and legally reduced their socio-political status within the mainstream Pakistani population. As a result, this community has been socially ostracised and forced to live in ghettos, with no sign of efforts to address their deprivations, insecurities and legally marginalised status.

F. Punishment of Death for Blasphemy

The aggressive Islamisation of Pakistan can therefore be understood as serving Zia's singular aim of prolonging his rule. He conducted the elections in February 1985 on a non-party basis, which were boycotted by many mainstream political parties; this established a subservient civilian rule of hand-picked political leaders and thus a manufactured legislative assembly. On 9 July 1986, the assembly of Zia pushed for the addition of another anti-blasphemy provision in Chapter XV of the PPC.[43] Section 295-C was added.[44] It called for punishment by death or life imprisonment for the use of derogatory remarks in respect of the Holy Prophet (PBUH). There were merely six parliamentarians in Zia's Assembly who proactively took part in the debate. Ironically, all were religious mullahs who had angry religious discussions on the subject. One of the speakers stated that if the amendment was not passed, there would be 250,000 people who would surround the parliament. Another vociferously stated that they would not leave the floor of the assembly until the bill was passed. Except for one speaker who urged that the bill not be passed in a hasty manner and without verifying religious dictum, all other voices were pushing to get it through without any delay. The minority voice also pressed for some definition of 'derogatory remarks', concerned that it would otherwise be an absurd and unclear law. Another lonely voice also pressed for a provision that in the event that a complainant failed to prove the charges against someone for blasphemy, he or she should be given the same punishment of death. The bill was nevertheless passed by this assembly with virtually no meaningful debate or extensive deliberation. On passing of the

his faith as Islam, or preaches or propagates his faith, or invites others to accept his faith, by words, either spoken or written, or by visible representation, or in any manner whatsoever outrages the religious feelings of Muslims, shall be punished with imprisonment of either description for a term which may extend to three years and shall also be liable to fine. / 'Real' Muslims refers to a cardinal principle in mainstream Islam that there will be no other divine revelation after the Quran and no other prophet after Prophet Muhammad (PBUH), who is the last and 'seal' of all prophets.'

[42] CRSS, *Blasphemy Laws in Pakistan* (n 32) 24.

[43] Malik, 'Blasphemy' (n 14) 39.

[44] PPC, s 295-C: '*Use of derogatory remarks, etc, in respect of the Holy Prophet*. Whoever by words, either spoken or written, or by visible representation, or by any imputation, innuendo, or insinuation, directly or indirectly, defiles the sacred name of the Holy Prophet Muhammad (peace be upon him) shall be punishable with death, or imprisonment for life, and shall also be liable to fine.'

bill, the religious members congratulated each other and expressed their view that now the blessings of God would be on Pakistan.[45]

The framers of this amendment did not feel the need to add the requirement of deliberate or malicious intention to this provision. It was in stark contrast to the colonial-era religious penal provisions, which placed great emphasis on the intention of the accused. The wording of section 295-C is general, vague, and is linked to the sole assessment of the complainant. Moreover, unlike section 295-A, which required the prior sanction of the Government before a court could take cognisance, section 295-C did not have any such procedural prerequisites. Thus, this allowed any private complainant to arbitrarily decide that his or her own idea of religious belief had been disrespected according to his or her own view of what constituted an innuendo or insinuation, and to lodge a police report. On the procedural side, another amendment was simultaneously brought about that required the judge trying a section 295-C case to be a Muslim.[46] The qualification of faith to try this offence signifies the intensity with which religiosity and religious agendas were being pushed and enacted as state instruments. More importantly, in the event that the charges against the accused were found to be incorrect, false or malicious, no consequences were provided for under the law against the complainant. Thus, there was no corresponding check or punishment provided for wrong allegations and complaints.

Legally speaking, there was also no yardstick to determine what would constitute derogatory remarks or how the holy name could be defiled. In an attempt to uphold respect of the Prophet Muhammad (PBUH), the state ended up creating an atmosphere of fear and social anxiety.

G. Revisions in Religious Penal Offences during Democratic Eras

Zia died suddenly in August 1988 when a Pakistani Air Force plane carrying him, some senior army officers and the United States Ambassador to Pakistan crashed in eastern Pakistan.[47] After Zia, Pakistan had successive democratic governments that were unfortunately weak and with fragmented mandate. The long era of military rule and its policy of forced Islamisation had already tilted society towards radicalisation. The use of faith-based legislation and the politics of religion was becoming a norm. In 1991, without any substantive need, the government of the day decided to revise section 295-A of the PPC. The original two years' punishment introduced by the British in 1927 for deliberate actions

[45] The National Assembly Debates of Pakistan of 9 July 1986 are in the Urdu language, and can be accessed at www.scribd.com/document/327051790/9th-July-Parliamentary-Debate-on-295C.

[46] sch II to the CRPC (n 26) requires that the Court of Session can try the offence under s 295(C), and the judge has to be Muslim.

[47] Elaine Sciolino, 'Zia of Pakistan Killed as blast downs plane' *New York Times* (18 August, 1988) at www.nytimes.com/1988/08/18/world/zia-of-pakistan-killed-as-blast-downs-plane-us-envoy-28-others-die.html.

to insult religions or beliefs was increased to 10 years. This also changed the offence to a non-bailable one.[48]

In 1997, the Government also introduced a separate law for the prevention of terrorism, violence and sectarian offences.[49] It referred to section 295-A of the PPC, which deals with insulting or outraging religious feelings of others, as a scheduled offence of terrorism that requires trial by special courts. The law provides for separate procedures and hands powers to investigation agencies and courts in dealing with such offences. The scope of bail in offences falling under this statute is limited.

As a consequence, Pakistan became a country with one of the harshest religious penal clauses in the world. Any talks pertaining to religion or open faith-related discussion had to be curtailed. The likelihood of a person's being executed for uttering wrongful words even by mistake or inadvertently was now very much real and legal. The religious parties became primary interest groups in this matter, and controlled the narrative and public agenda each time any complaint was lodged under this provision. The rampant illiteracy, extreme poverty and crippled criminal legal system provided a lethal combination, in which abuse of this law became the order of the day.

III. RELIGIOUS PENAL CLAUSES IN THE PAKISTAN PENAL CODE

A. Historical Origins

The origin of the PPC, which is the main criminal legislation of the land and contains its religious offences, lies in the country's colonial past. It would be worthwhile to briefly evaluate the legal history underlying the introduction of the Penal Code to contextualise its present-day usage and practice. The history of the English criminal justice system in British India starts around the time of the establishment of the East India Company.[50] The Great Indian Revolt of 1857 marked the end of the administration of the Company, with the removal of the last Mughal King Bahadur Shah Zafar.[51] Control was formally transferred to the

[48] As per s 4(b) of the CRPC (n 26), bailable and non-bailable offences under the PPC are provided for in sch II, which notes that any offence under any law punishable with imprisonment for a term not exceeding three years or with fine or both is bailable unless specifically made non-bailable.

[49] The definition of 'terrorism' as per s 6 of the Anti-Terrorism Act, 1997 (Act XXVII of 1997) includes inciting hatred and contempt on a religious, sectarian or ethnic basis to stir up violence or cause internal disturbance; and firing on religious congregations, mosques, imambargahs, churches, temples and all other places of worship, or random firing to spread panic, or involves any forcible takeover of mosques or other places of worship.

[50] The East India Company was incorporated in England by the Crown's Charter of 1600. For more details, see Kailash Rai, *Indian Legal and Constitutional History* (Allahabad Law Agency, 2004) 1.

[51] The great Indian Revolt is also known as 'The Indian Mutiny' and 'The First War of Independence' by historians. The violent uprising by both Hindus and Muslims of the Indian subcontinent

British Crown by virtue of the Government of India Act 1858.[52] Prior to this, the drafting of a comprehensive penal code to maintain law and order in the subcontinent had already been done by the First Law Commission of India.[53] The criminal code was mainly the work of Lord Thomas Babington Macaulay, and it is still sometimes referred to as Macaulay's Code.[54] On 6 October 1860, the Indian Penal Code[55] was enacted after receiving approval from the Indian Legislative Council and subsequent assent from the Governor General of India. However, this Code did not come into operation until 1 January 1862, to allow for local translations and for judges and officers to become acquainted with it.[56] The Code comprehensively provided for a range of offences, with corresponding punishments ranging from a fine to the death penalty. To date, this Code exists as the basic criminal legislation for all the major states that evolved from the former British India.

Chapter XV of the Penal Code was originally entitled 'Of Offences Relating to Religion and Caste'. It is currently headed 'Of Offences Relating to Religion'. The rationale for including this Chapter in the Penal Code was stated by the First Law Commission of India, 'that there is perhaps no [other] country in which the Government has so much to apprehend from religious excitement among the people'.[57] It appeared obvious to the authors of the Penal Code that the religious plurality of the Indian subcontinent could have the potential to trigger violence, and there could be a risk of dissolution of its society.[58] The protection of religious sentiments of the subjects was deemed imperative from the viewpoint of the colonial administration, for law and order considerations. The provisions of Chapter XV were thus kept broad and applicable to all faiths without any specification or discrimination. In the absence of any constitution that could guarantee rights or representation to the locals, the religious clauses of Penal Code were drafted solely by the colonial masters to consolidate their rule over the religiously volatile subcontinent.

The four provisions[59] of Chapter XV, from sections 295 to 298, criminalised injuring or defiling a place of worship with intent to insult others' faiths;[60]

started when a rumour spread that the Enfield rifle bullet cartridges, which needed to be ripped open by the mouths of sepoys, used grease made from cows and pigs. This outraged the sepoys, hence they revolted against their British masters. The uprising lasted a year and was put down in 1858. For further details, see Nigel Smith, *Pakistan: History, Culture and Government*, 1st edn (Oxford University Press, 2007) 34.

[52] Khan, *Constitutional and Political History of Pakistan* (n 13) 9.

[53] The First Law Commission was appointed in 1835 to prepare drafts of various civil and criminal laws for India that also proposed the Indian Penal Code. For details see Rai, *Indian Legal and Constitutional History* (n 50) 153.

[54] ibid.

[55] Act XLV of 1860.

[56] Shahid Hussain Qadri, *Pakistan Penal Code (XLV of 1860)* (Mansoor Law Book House, 2003) 32.

[57] WMH Allen and Co, 'Penal Code of British India' in (1838) 27 *The Asiatic Journal and Monthly Register for British and Foreign India, China and Australasia* 87, note J, at https://books.google.com.pk/books?id=wjk9AQAAMAAJ.

[58] ibid, 87.

[59] The religious penal provisions initially placed in penal code were from ss 295 to 298.

[60] PPC, s 295: '*Injuring or defiling place of worship, with intent to insult the religion of any class:* Whoever destroys, damages or defiles any place of worship, or any object held sacred by any class

disturbing a religious assembly;[61] trespassing on burial places;[62] and uttering words to deliberately hurt religious feelings.[63] A basic ingredient of all these provisions was the presence of the deliberate intention of the accused. This necessary requirement of intent originally envisaged in these religious provisions became the fundamental difference that distinguished them from a subsequent amendment that was brought about in Chapter XV after the independence of Pakistan. This amendment to section 298 was meant to cover incidents of hate speech, albeit in a limited way. In creating a balance between free speech and hateful utterances, the Law Commission stated that it wished to allow fair religious discussions but not intentional insults in the garb of free speech.[64] The Commission emphasised that warm expressions or arguments in a heated discussion, which did not annoy others having a different creed or faith, did not fall under the mischief criminalised by this provision.[65]

B. Usage of Religious Penal Clauses and Amendments During British Era

Between 1860 and 1927, there were 70 communal riots due to politico-religious issues related to the performance of religious rituals or conflicts between various revivalist movements.[66] During the 1920s, in the midst of heightened Hindu-Muslim confrontation, an Urdu booklet entitled *Colourful Prophet*,

of persons with the intention of thereby insulting the religion of any class or persons or with the knowledge that any class of persons is likely to consider such destruction, damage or defilement as an insult to their religion, shall be punished with imprisonment of either description for a term which may extend to two years, or with fine, or with both.'

[61] ibid, s 296: '*Disturbing Religious Assembly*: Whoever voluntarily causes disturbance to any assembly lawfully engaged in the performance of religious worship, or religious ceremonies, shall be punished with imprisonment of either description for a term which may extend to one year, or with fine, or with both.'

[62] ibid, s 297: '*Trespassing on burial places, etc*: Whoever, with the intention of wounding the feelings of any person, or of insulting the religion of any person or with the knowledge that the feelings of any person are likely to be wounded, or that the religion of any person is likely to be insulted thereby, commits any trespass in any place of worship or on any place of sculpture, or any place set apart for the performance of funeral rites or as a depository for the remains of the dead, or offers any indignity to any human corpse or causes disturbance to any persons assembled for the performance of funeral ceremonies, shall be punished with imprisonment of either description for a term which may extend to one year, or with fine, or with both.'

[63] ibid, s 298: '*Uttering words, etc, with deliberate intent to wound religious feelings*: Whoever, with the deliberate intention of wounding the religious feelings of any person, utters any word or makes any sound in the hearing of that person or makes any gesture in the sight of that person or places any object in the sight of that person, shall be punished with imprisonment of either description for a term which may extend to one year or with fine, or with both.'

[64] WMH Allen and Co, 'Penal Code of British India' (n 57) 88.

[65] ibid.

[66] Malik, 'Blasphemy' (n 14) 35.

comically depicting the life of the Prophet Muhammad, was published by Mahashay Rajpal. It was translated into several South Asian languages and was spread across India.[67] As a result violent communal protests erupted. The publisher was arrested and, due to the inadequacy of the Chapter XV offences, was charged under another provision relating to committing acts prejudicial to the maintenance of harmony between different religions.[68] The High Court acquitted Rajpal, stating that the law as it stood did not treat satirisation of saints and prophets as a legal offence.[69] The judgment specifically pointed out that there was an absence of such a provision in the Penal Code that could directly address the accused's activity. Consequently, demand for change in the law was vociferously made by Muslims. In 1927, a new provision, section 295-A, was added in the religious offences of the Penal Code, which related to speech, writings or signs that insult the religion or beliefs of any class of citizens.[70] The Select Committee proposing this new clause also cited Jinnah,[71] who emphasised that the words 'deliberate and malicious intention' should be made part of this new provision.[72]

In 1929, the publisher Rajpal was stabbed to death by a young Muslim carpenter, Ilam Din. Another reported incident in Karachi in 1935 occurred when a Hindu writer, Nathuramal Sharma, was murdered by Abdul Qayyum for publishing a religiously insulting pamphlet.[73] These assassinations by ordinary Muslims, and their subsequent executions by the Colonial Government, turned them into heroes in the eyes of the community. These 'sacrifices' became synonymous with martyrs protecting the honour of the Prophet (PBUH). The famous national poet of Pakistan, Allama Iqbal, is said to have called Ilam Din superior to others for having defended the faith.[74] Jinnah also appeared before the High Court as a lawyer on behalf of Ilam Din and, despite his unsuccessful defence, ended up solidifying his credentials as the undisputed leader

[67] Shahan Mufti, 'What Gandhi Understood About Inflammatory Depictions of Muhammad' *The New Republic* (22 January 2015) at newrepublic.com/article/120819/muhammad-images-used-provoke-muslims-what-gandhi-understood.

[68] PPC, s 153A is about promoting enmity between different groups on the grounds of religion, race, place of birth, residence, language, etc, and doing acts prejudicial to the maintenance of harmony.

[69] Girja Kumar, *The Book on Trial, Fundamentalism and Censorship in India*, 1st edn (Har-Anand Publications 1997) 58.

[70] PPC, s 295-A: '*Deliberate and malicious acts intended to outrage religious feelings of any class by insulting its religion or religious beliefs*: Whoever with deliberate and malicious intention of outraging the religious feelings of His Majesty's subjects, by words, either spoken or written, or by visible representations, insults or attempts to insult the religion or religious beliefs of that class, shall be punished with imprisonment of either description for a term which may extend to two years, or with fine, or with both.'

[71] Muhammad Ali Jinnah, also known as Quaid-e-Azam, is the founding father of Pakistan.

[72] Soli Sorabjee, 'Insult to Religion' *The Indian Express* (25 June 2006) at archive.indianexpress.com/news/insult-to-religion-/7214/.

[73] BR Ambedkar, *Pakistan or Partition of India*, 2nd edn (Thackers Publishers, 1943).

[74] Raza Rumi, 'Blasphemy it was not' *The Friday Times* (30 October 2015) at thefridaytimes.net/blasphemy-it-was-not/.

of Muslims of the subcontinent.[75] The extra-judicial killings of Rajpal and Sharma were the two reported incidents of heinous offence that were committed from the time of introduction of section 295A in 1927 until the time of the emergence of Pakistan.[76] Violent communal tension continued to increase, however. Numerous incidents of religious rioting were fuelled and mismanaged by the Colonial Raj, provoking a strong sense of faith-based identity in Indian Muslims. It also led to concerns that in a Hindu majority subcontinent, the honour of Islam and the Prophet Muhammad would always be at risk. The horrific events leading to the partition of India in 1947 contributed to building a strong narrative of persecution that also subsequently allowed for introduction of several new religious penal offences in Pakistan.[77]

C. Judicial Interpretations of Blasphemy Laws from the 1980s to the 1990s

The unconstitutional steps that followed the military coup of Zia included the removal of undesirable, independent judges and the elevation of like-minded individuals into the higher judiciary. The Ahmadis were the worst hit by this wave of Islamisation. During Zia's era, their petitions to courts for protection were not only unsympathetically received, but the courts on several occasions also gave strong judgments against them, and further restricted their religious freedoms and civil rights.[78] From the time of independence in 1947 to the late 1970s, the judicial approach towards religious penal offences was focused on securing public order and achieving social harmony. However, the new provisions introduced in Chapter XV during the 1980s were inherently restrictive, textually inadequate, provided narrow room for interpretation and did not contain established elements of criminalising actions (ie *actus reus* and *mens rea*). This, coupled with a submissive judiciary, created a lethal mix. Nonetheless, the judicial approaches towards these offences kept on changing over time, and one can also note some occasional, progressive judgments appearing on the subject. The rise of public interest litigation and the rising trend to expand the scope of fundamental rights then also later influenced the judicial understandings of these offences.

The first-instance courts in blasphemy offences are the sessions courts where trials take place. It is not possible to accurately estimate the number of times religious offences may have been taken up at the level of the subordinate judiciary. However, one of the first cases that reached the higher courts dealt with the

[75] ibid.

[76] CRSS, *Blasphemy Laws in Pakistan* (n 32).

[77] The Indian Partition is known to have displaced 15 million people and killed more than a million. For details, see William Dalrymple, 'The Great Divide' *The New Yorker* (29 June 2015) at www.newyorker.com/magazine/2015/06/29/the-great-divide-books-dalrymple.

[78] Khan, *Constitutional and Political History of Pakistan* (n 13) 520.

question of bail for a person accused under the new religious offences introduced during the time of Zia. In 1989, while deciding a matter in which an Ahmadi was accused of writing Quranic verses on the wall, the Karachi High Court stated that it was difficult to ascertain the meaning of the inscribed verses and what they were meant to convey, hence it granted bail.[79] In a similar matter, the full bench of the Supreme Court decided a question of confirmation of bail for a person charged with several religious penal offences. The accused was an Ahmadi who allegedly wrote on the wedding card of his daughter some expressions that were exclusive to Muslims; thus he was culpable under Chapter XV. The Full Bench of the Court confirmed the bail, though it stated the offences were severe and required authoritative pronouncement.[80] It also emphasised the necessity of looking into the background, intention and object of the person as well.

The broader questions involving the validity of these stringent religious penal clauses came to judicial attention in 1991. The FSC was endowed with the specific constitutional mandate that determined the religious validity of section 295-C in a precedent-setting case.[81] This court ended up declaring the penalty of death for derogatory remarks made with respect to the Holy Prophet to be in accordance with principles of Islam, but not life imprisonment, and suggested the Parliament delete the option of life imprisonment.[82] The judgment also stated that the same acts or things when said about other Prophets should also be made an offence with similar punishment. This was suggested perhaps to offer some protection to followers of Abrahamic faiths. The judgment did identify problematic aspects of this clause, and emphasised that the offence of blasphemy involves an intentional or reckless wrong and requires *mens rea* or intention and purpose as a valid prerequisite. It also discussed the relevance of penitence to this offence. The FSC held in the end that if the President did not take any action to amend the law, the provision would be automatically amended. Could it therefore be presumed that, as the FSC's judgment is binding, despite the inclusion of the punishment of life imprisonment under section 295-C, it does not have any effect or relevance, such that only the death penalty or a fine applies? An independent opinion argues otherwise, asserting that the FSC does not possess authority to enact legislation that in effect has been drafted by the court as a result of this judgment.[83]

In 1995, the Lahore High Court was faced with the question of whether to confirm the death penalty for a mentally disabled person convicted by trial

[79] *Rasheed Ahmed Khan v The State* [1988] PCrLJ 1595 (Single Bench).
[80] *Nasir Ahmad v The State* [1993] SCMR 153 (Full Bench).
[81] *Muhammad Ismail Qureshi v Pakistan through Secretary, Law and Parliamentary Affairs* [1991] PLD 10.
[82] ibid.
[83] The views of a jurist Abid Hassan Minto are mentioned in this authoritative article on the subject. See Osama Siddique and Zahra Hayat, 'Unholy Speech and Holy Laws: Blasphemy Laws in Pakistan – Controversial Origins, Design Defects and Free Speech Implications' (2008) 17(2) *Minnesota Journal of International Law* 380.

court under section 295-C. He allegedly declared himself to be Jesus, and in a provocative speech declared that the *Satanic Verses* was correct.[84] The court held that mental abnormality is a valid defence and *mens rea* is a condition precedent to establishing criminal liability.[85]

An important case that marked the turning point in the legal history of religious penal offences was decided in 1995. The case involved a Christian who allegedly wrote some objectionable words in the toilet of the mosque and received punishment by the trial court.[86] The Court applied the standard of proof beyond reasonable doubt and made an acquittal order. Not long after the judgment, the High Court judge was murdered by religiously motivated individuals.[87]

In another case, a mosque on government land was being demolished by state officials for public use. The Court went into lengthy arguments discussing and corroborating the religious basis of the Chapter XV penal provisions.[88] The Court also went on to state that the original offence envisaged in section 295 about defiling a place of worship insufficiently provides a period of punishment of up to two years only. It proposed that the punishment be increased to death or life imprisonment.[89] The Government was given instructions to reconstruct the mosque at the same site within six months, and to undertake an appropriate investigation against the relevant public officials. This case was in sharp contrast to a similar case that was adjudicated by a different judge of the same provincial court, in which a man was accused of turning his house into a mosque where religious views derogatory of Islam were being preached. The Court stated that fanaticism and extremism are permeating society and that the religious views of adversaries are unnecessarily deemed blasphemous without regard to the personal views of others.[90] It emphasised the need for tolerance of puritanical views in an enlightened society.

The word 'defiling' has been used in section 295-B in relation to the Holy Quran. The provision criminalises defiling, damaging or desecrating the holy book, and requires wilfulness in this regard. In a 1994 case, the court expanded the meaning of 'defile' to include not only a spiritual aspect but also the need to physically show respect and honour to the book, which is a legal, religious and moral duty placed on a person. It did not accept the plea of insanity and upheld the imprisonment.[91]

[84] A book by Salman Rushdie that portrayed the life of Prophet Muhammad (PBUH) in a derogatory manner. It was banned in Pakistan upon its publication in 1989, and in several other countries.

[85] *The State v Muhammad Arshad Javed* [1995] MLD Lahore 667 (Double Bench).

[86] *Salamat Masih v The State* [1995] PCrLJ Lahore 811 (Double Bench).

[87] Rana Yasif, '1990s blasphemy acquittal: Judge's murder case put in hibernation'*The Tribune* (Lahore, 29 November 2012) at tribune.com.pk/story/472495/1990s-blasphemy-acquittal-judges-murder-case-put-in-hibernation/.

[88] *Haq Nawaz and Other vs. Province of Punjab* [1997] MLD Lahore 299 (Single Bench).

[89] ibid.

[90] *Abdul Rahim aka Kaka v The State* [1997] P CrLJ Lahore 1617 (Single Bench).

[91] *Ijaz Hussain v The State* [1994] MLD Lahore 15 (Single Bench).

The minority Ahmadi community continually found themselves in court, mostly as victims, seeking bail or demanding their right to profess their faith as secured under the Constitution. It was a tall order for them. In 1989, when they were preparing to hold their centenary celebrations in a certain district, the Government issued a prohibition order under the pretext of law-and-order considerations. The Ahmadis approached the Court seeking a suspension of the order. However, the decision insinuated that section 295-C might be used if the celebrations were to be carried out as planned.[92] The Court did not accept the Ahmadis' claim, and stated that if they decided to proceed with the celebration and display certain banners, it might be tantamount to defiling the name of Prophet Muhammad (PBUH).[93] The judge concluded that their activities were found objectionable by other people, and to keep the faith of Muslims pure, the Government was well within its rights to prohibit the celebrations.

The very next year, the Supreme Court also endorsed the constitutional validity of section 298-C, which relates to penalising the usage of Muslim epithets by Ahmadis.[94] The reasoning provided by that Court clearly reflected the will of state to exclude the Ahmadi community from mainstream Islam and criminalise any attempt at their inclusion.[95] The scope of constitutional freedom to profess religion was narrowed down by the highest court quite emphatically to appease the religious groups, keeping in line with the popular national mood.[96]

The analysis of the initial cases on religious offences in the 1980s indicates that the higher courts of Pakistan could not become the torchbearers of freedom. They decided not to go against the popular public mood, nor expand minority rights for fear of public disorder. The hue and cry surrounding issues involving Ahmadis, and their constitutional degradation by a popular political party, did not allow the judiciary to champion their rights as an independent state institution. The judicial benches that emerged as a result of state-sponsored Islamisation under the Zia regime had overbearing religious tendencies and strong beliefs. In many instances, individual judges tried to provide narrow relief to petitions filed before them and mentioned the propensity to misuse the rigid religious clauses. However, the overall judicial approach was that of complete acquiescence. By the 1990s, Chapter XV of the PPC had a completely different complexion from its original colonial shape and content. The vaguely worded religious penal clauses with the harshest punishments would now be a permanent part of the legal jurisprudence of Pakistan.

[92] *Mirza Khurshid Ahmad v Government of Punjab* [1992] PLD Lahore 1 (Single Bench).

[93] ibid.

[94] *Zaheeruddin v State* [1993] SCMR 1718 (Full Bench).

[95] Malik, 'Blasphemy' (n 14) 42.

[96] Art 20 of the 1973 Constitution (n 16) protects freedom to profess religion and to manage religious institutions. It states that subject to law, public order and morality, '(a) every citizen shall have the right to profess, practice and propagate his religion; and (b) every religious denomination and every sect thereof shall have the right to establish, maintain and manage its religious institutions'.

D. Inconsistent Jurisprudence on Religious Penal Clauses in the Twenty-first Century

At the end of the twentieth century, Pakistan found itself under yet another military dictatorship led by General Musharraf. Another set of higher judiciary members subservient to the new dictator would now occupy the judicial benches. Ironically, Musharraf portrayed himself as benevolent and progressive to perpetuate his rule. Nonetheless, with a significant rise in the number of cases brought under Chapter XV, problems and complications concerning prosecution and enforcement increased alarmingly. Every case registered under religious penal clauses would have law and order complications for its particular area. The police were mostly compelled to register cases without ascertaining the basic facts, just to appease protesters. Cases would sometimes be lodged to save the lives of the accused from angry mobs. Judicial handling of these matters has also been put to question, as mixed judgments on similar points of law and nearly the same factual situations were being pronounced throughout the country, seemingly based on the personal disposition of the judges.

In a 2002 case heard by a Division Bench of the Lahore High Court, allegations that section 295-C was violated were made against the accused for pasting a derogatory advertisement against the Prophet Muhammad (PBUH) on the walls of a mosque.[97] Justice Chowhan highlighted the dilemmas of using and enforcing the religious provisions. He stated that there was a complete failure, inefficiency and incompetence of investigation officers in handling blasphemy cases.[98] He also highlighted the poor quality of previous judicial decisions, by stating that judges also think they are earning divine favour by upholding charges under this law, amounting to religious zeal sanctioned by law and cloaked in self-righteousness.[99] The court ended up advancing that the accused would enjoy the presumption of the 'benefit of doubt' in acquitting him of charges under section 295-C, and also stated that a Muslim cannot commit blasphemy because, if he does, that would amount to apostasy which cannot be repented.

The presumption of the benefit of doubt was also highlighted in another prominent case in the Supreme Court, where a Christian man was accused of blasphemy.[100] In this case, during the trial, the accused escaped life-threatening attacks twice and his Christian village was set on fire. It was later discovered that the complainant wanted to get hold of property belonging to the accused. The conviction was set aside by the Supreme Court.[101]

It was in 2005 that the first conviction of the twenty-first century under section 295-C was confirmed by the High Court.[102] An accused made several

[97] *Muhammad Mahboob v The State* [2002] PLD Lahore 587 (Double Bench).
[98] ibid.
[99] ibid.
[100] *Ayub Masih v The State* [2002] PLD Supreme Court 1048.
[101] ibid.
[102] *Haji Basir Ahmed v The State* [2005] YLR 985 (Lahore).

blasphemous statements, which were recorded on audio cassette. The Court said that for such an offence, the statement of a single witness even inside the house could be sufficient to incur imposition of the death penalty.[103] This was in contrast to another case in which the court stated that if any Muslim denies the charge and claims he is a true Muslim, the person cannot be convicted under section 295-C.[104]

For section 295-B, which is about the defiling of the Holy Quran, the Court emphasised that mental incapacity is an essential factor to take into account in punishing a person, and wilful intention is a necessary ingredient to punish someone.[105] In taking this point further, in another case the Court stated that it would not succumb to pressure tactics or fears to deny justice to an insane person charged under this offence.[106] In another case involving a minor and mentally handicapped girl accused of blasphemy, she was also not found to have committed the offence.[107] The language of section 295-B at least included the element of *mens rea* in it, which afforded some protection to those charged under this provision.

The sectarianism deeply rooted in society had also led to the filing of charges under Chapter XV between people of different sects. The courts in several cases showed restraint and discouraged the practice of criminal complaints under religious penal clauses on the basis of sectarian differences. It has been held that sectarian hatred and differences are not per se offences under the ambit of Chapter XV.[108] The court reasoned that sectarian differences and hate did not fall within the scope of a penal offence.

Perhaps the most important case of blasphemy to date in Pakistan is that of Asia Bibi, discussed in the introduction to this chapter.[109] Her conviction under section 295-C was for allegedly uttering that Jesus Christ died on the cross for the sins of mankind and questioning what the Prophet Muhammad ever did to save mankind. This led to the involvement of an enlightened Governor, who met the lady in prison and raised her plight in the public forum by allegedly calling the offence a bad law that should be changed. As a result, he was assassinated by his own police guard, who accused the Governor of grave and sudden provocation, and who thus claimed that he was motivated to commit the murder by faith and duty towards the Prophet (PBUH). The conviction of the police guard became a complex political and religious issue. The matter went up to the Supreme Court, and the Court stated that the straightforward case of a self-confessed murderer had been transformed into an existential and metaphysical battle involving religious beliefs and philosophical reflections.[110] The Court

[103] ibid.
[104] *Hazrat Ali Shah v The State* [2014] PLD Peshawar 122.
[105] *Shahbaz Masih v The State* [2007] MLD 1040 (Lahore).
[106] *Saifullah Khan alias Turab v the State* [2006] PLD Peshawar 140 (Single Bench).
[107] *Rimsha Masih v The State* [2013] PLD Islamabad 1.
[108] *The State v Muhammad Azam* [2012–14] GBLR 10 (Supreme Appellate Court, Full Bench).
[109] *Mst Asia Bibi v The State* (n 2).
[110] *Malik Muhammad Mumtaz Qadri v The State* (Crl A 210 of 2015, Supreme Court of Pakistan) at www.supremecourt.gov.pk/web/user_files/file/crl.a._210_2015.pdf.

established that any criticism of the blasphemy provision was not blasphemous itself, and no legal or factual justification allowed the killer to commit this act of terrorism.[111] It also stated that a false allegation regarding blasphemy is detestable and the state should ensure that no innocent person faces a trial on the basis of trumped-up allegations.

In the *Bibi* case, the Supreme Court stated that only the state has the authority to bring the machinery of law into operation if incidents of blasphemy take place.[112] This emphasis that only the state can punish arose because of consistent cries from religious leaders that if the state did not protect the honour of the Prophet, followers could also avenge his honour by punishing the blasphemer. The Court asserted that the burden of proving the guilt of the accused rests upon the prosecution. One of the judges also wrote a concurring opinion, and stated that the insult of another's faith and then mixing truth with falsehood in the name of the Prophet (PBUH) is itself a form of blasphemy.[113]

Over the course of several decades, contradictory case law has been produced by the higher courts in Pakistan on the matter of religious penal offences. The personal dispositions of judges towards religion have played a significant role in determining the outcomes of cases. The shortcomings of the law and procedural problems add up to a complicated environment for the adjudication of religious penal offences. There is an evident arbitrariness in practice, and wavering jurisprudence has developed on the subject; coupled with the vague language of the legal text, this presents a dangerous prospect for the accused. The lower courts, owing to capacity and security constraints, have shifted the burden to the higher courts to resolve such cases. Of late, the higher court judges have shown a strong realisation that the law is often misused. Moreover, in many prominent cases that were closely followed by religious groups, the judges did show courage and ended up acquitting innocent people at the cost of threats to their own lives. One must recognise the courage of the judges who penned these judgments.

E. Staggering Statistics, Social Responses and International Image

There is a plethora of empirical evidence that clearly shows a significant increase in the registration of cases under religious penal clauses after the 1980s. The largest number of blasphemy-related cases litigated between 2000 and 2011 were brought specifically under section 295-C; however, only one conviction was upheld.[114] From 1986 till the year 2015, 25 cases were decided on their merits in relation to section 295-C offences, out of which six convictions were upheld. For the same period, out of 12 reported cases in relation to sections 295-A and 295-B,

[111] ibid.
[112] *Mst Asia Bibi v The State* (n 2).
[113] ibid.
[114] Malik, 'Blasphemy' (n 14) 45.

only one conviction has occurred.[115] There were three cases reported in the 1979–86 period, while 44 cases were registered between 1987 and 1999.[116] Since 1987, 633 Muslims, 494 Ahmedis, 187 Christians and 21 Hindus have been accused under various clauses of blasphemy law.[117] In the year 2000 alone, 52 cases were registered.[118] As per the analysis carried out by the International Commission of Jurists on blasphemy cases in the higher courts of Pakistan, it was deduced that in 60 per cent of the cases, complaints were made in a *mala fide* manner and for political interests or personal rivalries against the accused persons.[119] There are already concerns that those convicted of these offences may not have received a fair trial or due process. One of the striking statistics is that religious minorities in Pakistan constitute only 4 per cent of the total population but they make up at least 50 per cent of the total number of persons accused of these offences.[120]

The UN Special Rapporteur found that these religious penal laws serve the vested interests of extremist religious groups and are contrary to the Constitution of Pakistan and international human rights norms.[121] International voices have consistently called for the repeal of the religious penal clauses, in particular the death sentence provided for under section 295-C. The defence lawyers who end up defending blasphemy cases face constant threats to their lives from the legal community and society. Rashid Rehman was killed in May 2014 for defending one such accused person.[122]

The mere news of a religious offence has led to mob violence and the destruction of public property on several occasions. In March 2013, the houses of Christians in Joseph Colony of Lahore were set ablaze after an allegation of blasphemy by a Christian person.[123] The lives of those who are accused of blasphemy remain threatened in all places and at all times. As at 2012, some 51 people had been murdered before the conclusion of their trials, including those who were killed by fellow inmates in prison.[124] From 2012 to date, 11 more people accused of blasphemy have lost their lives.

[115] International Commission of Jurists (ICJ), *On Trial: The Implementation of Pakistan's Blasphemy Laws* (2015) 6, at www.refworld.org/pdfid/565da4824.pdf.

[116] *Muhammad Mahboob v The State* (n 97).

[117] 'What are Pakistan's Blasphemy Laws?' *BBC News* (6 November 2014) at www.bbc.com/news/world-asia-48204815.

[118] *Muhammad Maboob v the State* (n 97).

[119] ICJ, *On Trial* (n 115) 25.

[120] Omar Khan, 'In the Name of God: Problems with Pakistan's Blasphemy Laws' (2016) 4 *Cornell International Online Journal* 1.

[121] Gabriela Knaul, *Report of the Special Rapporteur on the Independence of Judges and Lawyers* A/HRC/23/43/Add.2 (United Nations, 2012).

[122] Andrew Buncombe and Umair Aziz, 'Pakistani lawyer Murdered' *The Independent* (8 May 2014) at www.independent.co.uk/incoming/pakistani-lawyer-rashid-rehman-murdered-after-taking-on-blasphemy-case-9341021.html.

[123] 'Christian Houses Torched' *Dawn* (Lahore, 9 March 2013) at www.dawn.com/news/791408/mob-attacks-christian-neighbourhood-in-lahore.

[124] 'Timeline: Accused under the Blasphemy Law' *Dawn* (19 September 2012) at www.dawn.com/news/750512/timeline-accused-under-the-blasphemy-law.

F. Implications of Religious Penal Laws on Fair Trial and Free Speech

The Constitution of Pakistan provides for the rights of individuals to be dealt with in accordance with law.[125] In addition, the rights to freedom of speech and religion are also comprehensively enshrined in the Constitution.[126] However, in Pakistan, the Constitution and constitutional culture have been influenced by religion.[127] The question of free speech has never been discussed by the courts while adjudicating blasphemy matters.[128] This simply entails either wilful reluctance or plain ignorance on the part of the courts regarding their duty to protect constitutional freedoms.

There has never been any official assessment of bias in the bench. The hostility of judges and their pre-disposition in such cases places the accused in a compromised position. Moreover, poor legislative construction of the religious offences has given the courts undue discretion in deciding the matter. Hence, we find similar factual cases yielding varying outcomes, with far-reaching consequences for the accused. The UN Rapporteur also observed that the vague language of these laws makes no reference to an offender's psychological state or intention, and provides an open door for abuse and the persecution of minorities by religious or sectarian groups.[129]

In 2010, Pakistan ratified the International Covenant on Civil and Political Rights, which provides for freedom of religion and expression, and demands equality before the law without discrimination.[130] There has been a clear understanding that the religious offences provisions come into direct conflict with the international obligations of the country. Pakistan presented a resolution before UN Human Rights Council in Geneva in 2009 condemning the defamation of religion as a human rights violation. Pakistan asserted that a delicate balance needs to be struck between freedom of expression and respect for religion.[131] There were reservations that such a resolution would lead to further persecution of minorities in Muslim countries.

On several occasions, Pakistan has also restricted digital space and banned the use of social media networks.[132] Facebook was also blocked as it promoted

[125] Art 4 of the 1973 Constitution (n 16).

[126] See ibid Arts 4 and 19.

[127] Siddique and Hayat, 'Unholy Speech and Holy Laws' (n 83).

[128] ibid.

[129] Knaul, *Report of the Special Rapporteur* (n 121).

[130] Art 18(1) of the International Covenant on Civil and Political Rights states that 'Everyone shall have the right to freedom of thought, conscience and religion. This right shall include freedom to have or to adopt a religion or belief of his choice, and freedom, either individually or in community with others and in public or private, to manifest his religion or belief in worship, observance, practice and teaching.'

[131] Laura MacInnis, 'UN Body adopts resolution on religious defamation' *Reuters* (Geneva 26 March 2009) at www.reuters.com/article/us-religion-defamation-idUSTRE52P60220090326.

[132] Jahanzaib Haque and Saba Imtiaz, 'Pakistan's list of blocked websites swells' *The Tribune* (Karachi, 21 March 2010) at tribune.com.pk/story/15015/pakistans-list-of-blocked-websites-swells.

'Everybody Draw Muhammad Day' before the page was made inaccessible in the country. An extremely unfortunate event occurred in April 2017 when Mashal Khan, a student of Abdul Wali Khan University, was lynched by a mob within the campus, based on the allegation that he posted blasphemous content online.[133] Another high-profile murder was that of sitting Minister of Minorities, Shahbaz Bhatti, who also made a public statement in support of changes in blasphemy laws.[134] Pakistan is also far from any real prospect of abolishing the death penalty. An attempt was made to limit its use by placing a moratorium on it that lasted for several years, before it was lifted again due to continued incidents of terrorism and heinous offences.[135]

IV. CONCLUSION AND PLAUSIBLE WAY FORWARD

The colonial-era religious penal clauses as originally drafted did consider the principles of proper criminal liability with a focus on hate speech and malicious intention, that is *mens rea*, and then the *actus reus* itself. This was done to assert and assist colonial rule; however, from an administrative viewpoint they also provided discretion to the prosecution over whether to pursue such charges. Moreover, earlier courts would ascertain the intention of the accused rather than focus on actions. As a result, there were not many cases registered under the religious penal clauses introduced during the British era.

On the other hand, revisions introduced during the era of military dictatorship in Pakistan had the purpose of perpetuating power and seeking popular legitimacy through a process of state-sponsored Islamisation. Ahmadis, Christians and other religious minorities have been gravely affected by the religious penal clauses introduced by Zia. In addition, these provisions have fanned sectarianism in the country. The letter of the law and consequential implementation have both created a complex social problem. There does not exist any valid and legally plausible room for an accused person to repent, and certain utterances cannot be retracted. The strong influence of religious groups in shaping legislation from outside parliament is something that places serious doubts on the strength of Pakistani democracy. It is likely to remain so in the foreseeable future; indeed, the mainstream parties do not feel politically compelled to raise this issue in their electoral agendas. There is no viable left-wing secular political party in Pakistan. On an ideological spectrum, political agendas are mostly of the centre or religious right. In the recent past, popular political parties have also

[133] Ali Akbar and Hassan Farhan, 'Mardan university student lynched by mob over alleged blasphemy' *Dawn* (13 April 2017) at www.dawn.com/news/1326729.

[134] 'Minorities Minister Shahbaz Bhatti assassinated in Islamabad' *Dawn* (Islamabad, 2 March 2011) at www.dawn.com/news/610105/minorities-minister-attacked-in-islamabad.

[135] 'Death penalty moratorium lifted completely in Pakistan' *Dawn* (Islamabad, 10 March, 2015) at www.dawn.com/news/1168652.

occasionally played the religious card by questioning the allegiance to the faith and love of the Prophet of their political opponents.

At minimum, what might possibly be done to improve matters is to amend Chapter XV offences to make them non-cognisable – that is, warrants from courts should be required before arrests are made. The assertion that the presence of these laws does not allow ordinary citizens to take the law into their own hands and kill alleged blasphemers themselves is not tenable or supported by any plausible data. In fact, the empirical evidence suggests that the presence of this legislation has only instigated non-state violence. The police end up arresting people under the religious offences as an administrative measure to avoid confrontation with the violent mobs. In many instances, policemen themselves have been found to have religiously-charged opinions that marred the investigations and handling of the accused in custody.

On the criminal procedure front, section 295-A and other religious offences such as section 295-C should require the prior permission of the Government before any trial commences. This would help prevent mischievous complainants from misusing the law. If the courts feel persuaded that complainants and witnesses in such cases are involved in perjury, strict legal action should follow to deter malicious complainants. At least for section 295-C offences, the investigation should be carried out by senior police officials strictly in accordance with section 156-A of the Criminal Procedure Code.

The courts should continually look into pleas of unsoundness of mind and lunacy of the accused. At present, the state at all formal and informal levels is unable to demonstrate neutrality towards the accused in such offences. The lawyers who defend the accused also face harassment at the hands of the legal fraternity and the unfavourable attitude of court staff. The inability of lower trial courts to try these offences independently without adequate security should be addressed administratively. Perhaps the High Courts should try these offences directly, despite depriving the accused of one level of appellate forum. There is barely any social or political appetite to carry forward the cause of amending these penal clauses. The ability or desire of any political party to prioritise this matter would be an extremely far-fetched hope.

Pakistan has turned into a legally hostile and intolerant republic due to the severity of punishment of religious offences. These laws give rise to a reputational crisis for the state. While it is not the only country in the world with blasphemy laws, in other countries such laws are either dormant or rarely applied. Only Saudi Arabia and Iran have similarly stringent blasphemy laws. There are many measures discussed here that can address procedural processes and improve the judicial environment in which judgments relating to religious offences are made. At a bare minimum, immediate efforts are needed to prevent their misuse and the perpetual victimisation of minorities.

BIBLIOGRAPHY

Akbar, A, and Farhan, H, 'Mardan university student lynched by mob over alleged blasphemy' *Dawn* (13 April 2017) at www.dawn.com/news/1326729

Alvi, M, 'Pakistan's literacy rate stands at 58%' *The News* (Islamabad, 27 April 2018) at www.thenews.com.pk/print/309542-pakistan-s-literacy-rate-stands-at-58pc

Ambedkar, BR, *Pakistan or Partition of India*, 2nd edn (Thackers Publishers, 1943)

Associated Press, 'Defence Lawyer in Pakistan in blasphemy case flees country' (Islamabad, 3 November 2018) at www.washingtonpost.com/world/asia_pacific/protests-in-pakistan-over-christian-womans-acquittal-end/2018/11/03/43f4f046-df30-11e8-8bac-bfe01fcd c3a6_story.html?noredirect=on&utm_term=.652bce45087e accessed 17 November 2018

Barker, M, and Iqbal, A, 'Asia Bibi: anti blasphemy protests spread across Pakistan' *The Guardian* (Islamabad, 1 November 2018) at www.theguardian.com/world/2018/nov/01/asia-bibi-anti-blasphemy-protests-spread-across-pakistan

BBC News, 'What are Pakistan's Blasphemy Laws?' (6 November 2014) at www.bbc.com/news/world-asia-48204815

Buncombe, A, and Aziz, U, 'Pakistani lawyer Murdered' *The Independent* (8 May 2014) at www.independent.co.uk/incoming/pakistani-lawyer-rashid-rehman-murdered-after-taking-on-blasphemy-case-9341021.html

Center for Research and Security Studies, *Blasphemy Laws in Pakistan: A Historical Overview* (2010) at crss.pk/wp-content/uploads/2010/07/Report-on-Blasphemy-Laws-.pdf, 21

Constable, P, 'A disaster in the making: Pakistan's population surges to 207.7 million' *The Washington Post* (Rawalpindi, 9 September 2017) at www.washingtonpost.com/world/asia_pacific/a-disaster-in-the-making-pakistans-population-has-more-than-doubled-in-20-years/2017/09/08/4f434c58-926b-11e7-8482-8dc9a7af29f9_story.html?noredirect=on&utm_term=.19880fbde791

Dalrymple, W, 'The Great Divide' *The New Yorker* (29 June 2015) at www.newyorker.com/magazine/2015/06/29/the-great-divide-books-dalrymple

Dawn, 'Death penalty moratorium lifted completely in Pakistan' (Islamabad, 10 March, 2015) at www.dawn.com/news/1168652

——, 'Christian Houses Torched' (Lahore, 9 March 2013) at www.dawn.com/news/791408/mob-attacks-christian-neighbourhood-in-lahore

——, 'Timeline: Accused under the Blasphemy Law' (19 September 2012) at www.dawn.com/news/750512/timeline-accused-under-the-blasphemy-law

——, 'Minorities Minister Shahbaz Bhatti assassinated in Islamabad' (Islamabad, 2 March 2011) at www.dawn.com/news/610105/minorities-minister-attacked-in-islamabad

Haque, J, and Imtiaz, S, 'Pakistan's list of blocked websites swells' *The Tribune* (Karachi, 21 March 2010) at tribune.com.pk/story/15015/pakistans-list-of-blocked-websites-swells

International Commission of Jurists, *On Trial: The Implementation of Pakistan's Blasphemy Laws* (2015) at www.refworld.org/pdfid/565da4824.pdf

Khan, H, *Constitutional and Political History of Pakistan*, 2nd edn (Oxford University Press, 2004)

Khan, O, 'In the Name of God: Problems with Pakistan's Blasphemy Laws' (2016) 4 *Cornell International Online Journal* 1

Knaul, G, *Report of the Special Rapporteur on the Independence of Judges and Lawyers* A/HRC/23/43/Add.2 (United Nations, 2012)

Kumar, G, *The Book on Trial, Fundamentalism and Censorship in India*, 1st edn (Har-Anand Publications 1997)
MacInnis, L, 'UN Body adopts resolution on religious defamation' *Reuters* (Geneva, 26 March 2009) at www.reuters.com/article/us-religion-defamation-idUSTRE52P602 20090326
Malik, S, 'Blasphemy: A Crime in Pakistan Penal Code versus the Traditional Perspective' (2017) 8 *Pakistan Law Review* 23
Mufti, S, 'What Gandhi Understood About Inflammatory Depictions of Muhammad' *The New Republic* (22 January 2015) at newrepublic.com/article/120819/muhammad-images-used-provoke-muslims-what-gandhi-understood
Pakistan Bureau of Statistics, *Population by Religion* (23 April 2019) at www.pbs.gov.pk/sites/default/files//tables/POPULATION%20BY%20RELIGION.pdf
Pakistan Today, 'TLP ends sit in after agreement with government' (Lahore, 3 November 2018) at www.pakistantoday.com.pk/2018/11/02/tlp-ends-sit-in-after-agreement-with-government/
Qadri, SH, *Pakistan Penal Code (XLV of 1860)* (Mansoor Law Book House 2003)
Rai, K, *Indian Legal and Constitutional History* (Allahabad Law Agency, 2004)
Rumi, R, 'Blasphemy it is not' *The Friday Times* (30 October 2015) at thefridaytimes.net/blasphemy-it-was-not/
Safi, M, and Baloch, SM, 'Asia Bibi arrives in Canada after leaving Pakistan' *The Guardian* (Islamabad, 8 May 2019) at www.theguardian.com/world/2019/may/08/asia-bibi-arrives-in-canada-after-leaving-pakistan
Siddique, O, and Hayat, Z, 'Unholy Speech and Holy Laws: Blasphemy Laws in Pakistan – Controversial Origins, Design Defects and Free Speech Implications' (2008) 17(2) *Minnesota Journal of International Law* 380
Smith, N, *Pakistan: History, Culture and Government*, 1st edn (Oxford University Press, 2007) 34
Sorabjee, S, 'Insult to Religion' *The Indian Express* (25 June 2006) at archive.indianexpress.com/news/insult-to-religion-/7214/
The Economist, 'Pakistan's Supreme Court upholds Asia Bibi acquittal' (2 February 2019) at www.economist.com/asia/2019/02/02/pakistans-supreme-court-upholds-asia-bibis-acquittal
WMH Allen and Co, 'Penal Code of British India' in (1838) 27 *The Asiatic Journal and Monthly Register for British and Foreign India, China and Australasia* 87
Yasif, R, '1990s blasphemy acquittal: Judge's murder case put in hibernation' *The Tribune* (Lahore, 29 November 2012) at tribune.com.pk/story/472495/1990s-blasphemy-acquittal-judges-murder-case-put-in-hibernation/

7

Bangladesh: Public Law, Religious Freedom and Regulating 'Religious Sentiment'

SM MASUM BILLAH

I. INTRODUCTION

BANGLADESH IS A South Asian country having an overall population of 163 million.[1] Apparently, Bangladesh seems to be a nation with practically no diversity. In fact, about 98 per cent of the population identifies themselves with a single ethnicity: Bengali.[2] The Muslims constitute the majority in terms of religious composition, the Hindus, Christians and Buddhists being the other major religions.[3] Bengali Islam has its own cultural distinctiveness because of the way it was introduced here. Wright observes that there is a strong tradition of harmony among the religious communities of Bangladesh, and the religion practised in this part of the globe is largely liberal in outlook.[4] It shares a British colonial history with India and Pakistan. As such, it carries a legacy of common law traditions conditioned by personal law systems and fashioned by Anglo-Indian jurisprudence and post-independence developments.[5] Having emerged

[1] 'Bangladesh Population 2020 (Live)' *World Population Review* (undated) at worldpopulation review.com/countries/ bangladesh-population/.

[2] Although the other 2% make up a small fraction of the population, there are at least 27 other distinct ethnic groups in Bangladesh formally recognised by the Government; independent researchers, however, claim that the number is closer to 75. See Bangladesh Ethnic Groups, at https://study.com/academy/lesson/bangladesh-ethnic-groups.html. The groups prefer to identify themselves as *adivasis* (indigenous communities); the Constitution of Bangladesh, however, uses the phrase 'tribes, minor races, ethnic sects and communities' to refer to them. See Art 23A.

[3] The religious composition is: Muslims 89.1%, Hindus 10%; and Others (Buddhists, Christians) 0.9%: 'Bangladesh Population 2020 (Live)' (n 1). See also Ali Riaz, 'The Politics of Islamization in Bangladesh' in Ali Riaz (ed), *Religion and Politics in South Asia* (Routledge, 2010) 47.

[4] Denis Wright, 'Islam and Bangladeshi Polity' (1987) 10(2) *South Asia* 15.

[5] Ridwanul Hoque, *Judicial Activism in Bangladesh: A Golden Mean Approach* (Cambridge Scholars Publishing, 2011) 99.

as an independent, sovereign country in 1971 when it seceded from Pakistan, Bangladesh adopted a Constitution in 1972 based on a secular ethos and religious freedom. The Constitution embodied four fundamental principles: nationalism, socialism, democracy and secularism.[6] The constitutional journey in Bangladesh has not been a smooth one, however, and the country was placed under martial law twice.[7] The use of religion as a form of power politics by Bangladeshi political leaders has been a common phenomenon.

The desirability of incorporating secularism as a state principle was widely debated during the drafting of the 1972 Constitution. The framers decided to adopt a moderate interpretation of secularism, with emphasis on respect and tolerance towards religious beliefs.[8] In 1979, during President Ziaur Rahman's regime, the Fifth Amendment[9] was enacted, which removed secularism as a constitutional principle. The Fifth Amendment also allowed religion-based political parties to function, and characteristically added the Arabic words *Bismillah-ar-Rahman-ar-Rahim* (In the Name of God, the Most Merciful, Benevolent) as the opening words of the Constitution.[10] The process of Islamisation of the Constitution culminated into the Eighth Amendment, which elevated Islam to the status of 'state religion' in 1988.[11] In 2005, the High Court Division of the Supreme Court of Bangladesh declared the Fifth Amendment illegal, which was upheld by the Appellate Division in 2010.[12] In a drive to make the Supreme Court ruling stronger, the secularity principle was entrenched in the Constitution by the Fifteenth Amendment in 2011.[13] However, this time, as opposed to the 1972 ideals, the secularism clause was refashioned, leaving the

[6] Preamble to the Constitution of the People's Republic of Bangladesh.

[7] The First Martial Law spanned from 1975 to 1979, the Second Martial Law from 1982 to 1986. See, eg, Mustafa Kamal, *Bangladesh Constitution: Trends and Issues* (Dhaka University Press, 1994). See also Shahdeen Malik, 'Bangladesh' in Andrew Harding and John Hatchard (eds), *Preventive Detention and Security Law: A Comparative Study* (Martinus Nijhoff, 1993) 55.

[8] Santanu Majumder, 'Secularism and Anti-Secularism' in Ali Riaz and Mohammad Sajjadur Rahman (eds), *Routledge Handbook of Contemporary Bangladesh* (Routledge, 2016) 40. In the Constituent Assembly debate, Maulana Abdur Rashid Tarkobagish, a senior Lawmaker of Awami League, delivered an intellectually compelling speech on Bangladeshi secularism, terming the concept a process of attaining religious tolerance, social justice and economic democracy. See Abdul Halim, *The Constituent Assembly Debate* (CCB Foundation, 2014) 444. Huque and Akhter think that although Bangladesh was *constitutionally* secularised in 1972, the nature of the society remained unaltered, except for the momentary spirit of Bengali resurgence. See AS Huque and MY Akhter, 'The Ubiquity of Islam: Religion and Society in Bangladesh' (1987) 60(2) *Pacific Affairs* 203.

[9] The Constitution (Fifth Amendment) Act 1979.

[10] 'Secularism is back in Bangladesh, rules High Court' *Deccan Herald* (5 October 2010) at www.deccanherald.com/ content/102192/secularism-back-bangladesh-rules-high.html.

[11] 'Islamisation' as a process assumes a wider scope and perspective. I use the term as an historic process of religious orientation and application of Islamic beliefs, traditions and thought processes. See, eg, Surendra Nath Kaushik, *Politics of Islamization in Pakistan: A Study of Zia Regime* (South Asian Publishers, 1993) 8.

[12] *Bangladesh Italian Marble Works Ltd v Bangladesh* (2006) 14 BLT (Special) (HCD) 1 (29.08.2005); *Khondker Delwar Hossain v Bangladesh Italian Marble Works Ltd and Others* (2010) 62 DLR (AD) 298.

[13] The Constitution (Fifteenth Amendment) Act 2011 (Act No XIV of 2011).

'Islam as State Religion' position of 1988 unchanged. The new brand of secularism was couched in a more inclusive language taking note of the presence of different religions in the country. From this perspective, it can be said that Bangladesh by now understands secularism as a process that seeks to accommodate religious freedom both as a social reality as well as a legal principle.

Religiosity is omnipresent in the country's public affairs and in private life.[14] The penal system, an offshoot of the British colonial regime, also did not ignore the importance of establishing offences that address the upsetting of the religious sentiments of the people. The Penal Code of 1860, a brainchild of famous English historian TB Macaulay, is still the governing criminal law of Bangladesh, with certain modifications. The Macaulay Code arguably maintained a balance between religious pluralism and the need to introduce a modernised criminal law. While the Code criminalised several offences relating to religious feelings in its Chapter XV, it importantly omitted any rigid blasphemy provisions. However, the religion-centric politics in the post-independence era posed a challenge to the penal norms based on secular premises. There have been frequent incidents where publications have been banned, or persons have been exiled or harassed for allegedly violating religious sentiments. The country has also witnessed two attempts – in 1994 and 2004 – by the more religiously conservative section of the politicians to enact a rigorous blasphemy law, which was doomed to failure due to the re-emergence of pro-secular politics and the progressive role played by the judiciary in the early 1990s.

In this chapter, I will examine the Bangladesh's colonial and post-colonial legal approach in dealing with 'religious sentiments' and its ramifications within the socio-cultural-political context. One of the central planks of my argument is that there are struggles in Bangladesh in relation to the constitutional status of theocracy and secularism. This struggle has seen three waves: (i) the 1972 original wave that wanted to achieve the goal of a society free from religious bigotry by taking lessons from past history; (ii) the theocratic wave featuring martial law and religious politics to establish a constitutional theocracy; and (iii) the mixed approach after 2009, which seeks to march forward by construing secularism and religious freedom in the same way, in a harmonious manner. These three-dimensional struggles have affected the functioning of the religious penal clauses and posed challenges for Bangladeshi society, to prevent their use as a political tool by individuals and entities with theocratic aspirations.

My main motivation in investigating this issue is to understand the relation between secularism and constitutionalism, and to identify the place of 'religious feelings' in public law. This chapter proceeds in six sections. After this introduction as section I, section II gives a general overview of the Bangladeshi penal law

[14] Granville Austin, 'Religion, Personal Law and Identity in India' in Gerald J Larson (ed), *Religion and Personal Law in Secular India: A Call to Judgment* (Indiana University Press, 2011) 16. See also Md Nazrul Islam and Md Saidul Islam, 'Islam, Politics and Secularism in Bangladesh: Contesting the Dominant Narratives' (2018) 7 *Social Science* 39.

and its formation. Section III focuses on the criminal law offences relating to religious feelings and examines judicial approaches to those offences. Section IV explains the situation in which the scope of religious penal clauses was extended by the British during the political turmoil of the 1920s. Section V considers the shift in legal and political thinking with respect to the way of addressing religious offences in the post-colonial and post-independence era. It illuminates how secularism and religiously driven politics formed a complex web, which shaped and reshaped the legal understanding of religious liberty in Bangladesh. Section VI offers concluding remarks.

II. LEGAL CONTEXT: THE CRIMINAL LAW OF BANGLADESH

The Bangladesh Penal Code (BPC) was modelled after the Indian Penal Code (IPC), which is the longest-serving criminal code in the common law world.[15] The IPC entirely obliterated the criminal laws that preceded it. According to George Rankin, the efforts of the British to improve criminal law were so widespread that Indian indigenous law had fallen out of the picture.[16]

Today, one reflects with some surprise that it was not until 1862 that English criminal law, operating over the greater part of British India, become detached from its base in Mohamedan jurisprudence.[17] Rankin wondered if Mohamedan criminal law could have lasted for much longer even if the IPC was not adopted to extensively amend and modernise criminal law in Bangladesh.[18] Indeed, Stephen found that pre-1833 Mohamedan criminal law was weak, defective, confusing, and lacked certainty and uniformity in almost every respect.[19] Campbell termed the reforms made to the native criminal law from time to time as a 'patchwork made up of pieces'.[20] Before 1833, all the main topics had been dealt with by 'Regulations'. Rankin noted that British India before 1833 was the India of 'Regulations' – laws passed by the separate legislatures of Bengal, Madras and Bombay before the Charter of 1833 had set up one unified legislature for the whole of India, having authority over all the inhabitants, whether British,

[15] Stanley Yeo and Barry Wright, 'Revitalising Macaulay's Indian Penal Code' in Chan Wing Cheong, Barry Wright and Stanley Yeo (eds), *Codification, Macaulay and the Indian Penal Code: The Legacies and Challenges of Modern Criminal Law Reform* (Routledge, 2011) 3.

[16] GC Rankin, *Background to Indian Law* (Cambridge University Press, 1946) 161. See also VD Kulshreshtha, *Landmarks in Indian Legal and Constitutional History* (Eastern Book Company, 2016) 257.

[17] On the introduction of English criminal law principles in India, Sir James Stephen found in 1883 that the IPC reflected the criminal law of England in a systematic way devoid of technicality and superfluity. See JF Stephen, *A History of the Criminal Law of England*, vol III (Macmillan & Co, 1883) 300.

[18] Rankin, *Background* (n 16) 161.

[19] Stephen, *History* (n 17) 295–97.

[20] George Campbell, *Modern India: A Sketch of the System of Civil Government with Some Accounts of the Natives and Native Institutions* (John Murray, 1853) 465. For an analysis of the 'Regulations', see also John Herrington, *Analysis of the Laws and Regulations of Bengal* (The Honorable Company's Press, 1805).

Indians, Europeans or others. In 1832, non-Muslims ceased to be subjected in Bengal to the Mohamedan criminal law, and in 1827, Bombay was given a statutory criminal code. However, Mohamedan criminal law was never cast aside altogether until the IPC of 1860, drafted by Macaulay in 1837,[21] the Evidence Act of 1872 and the Criminal Procedure Code of 1898 (CrPC) came into force.

Macaulay attached due importance to the qualities of precision, comprehensibility, accessibility and legislative law-making in drafting the Code.[22] According to Macaulay, 'the principle is simply this; uniformity when you can have it; diversity when you must have it; but, in all cases certainty'.[23] It seems that a reference to this statement is a must whenever Macaulay is studied, 'probably because it encapsulates so elegantly the basic criticisms of Indian law'.[24]

Although David Skuy doubts the purpose of the British in introducing a Penal Code for India,[25] there is a consensus among the scholars that these principles have stood the test of time and have remained as progressive general aims for law reform in the twenty-first century.[26]

III. THE OFFENCES RELATING TO RELIGION

A. The Law on Religious Sentiments

Chapter XV of the BPC criminalises conduct intended to insult another's religion. Macaulay recognised a range of intersecting forms of harm that transcend mere physical harm, such as intangible harm to honour, dignity, status, feelings and reputation. This was a radical departure from the English criminal law.[27] Macaulay, however, justified this variance on grounds of addressing acts of private revenge and vigilantism, which were prevalent in British India at the time.[28]

[21] The Charter Act of 1833 mandated that the Indian Law Commission rectify the discrepancies in the legal system at the time. With the support of James Mill, Macaulay was appointed to the Commission, and set sail for India soon after. See George Trevelyan, *Life and Letters of Lord Macaulay* (Oxford University Press, 1978) 244.

[22] TB Macaulay, *A Penal Code Prepared by the Indian Law Commission* (Pelham Richardson, 1838) v.

[23] TB Macaulay, *Complete Works of Thomas Babington Macaulay* (Longmans, Green & Co, 1898) 579.

[24] David Skuy, 'Macaulay and the Indian Penal Code of 1862: The Myth of the Inherent Superiority and Modernity of the English Legal System Compared to India's Legal System in the 19th Century' (1998) 32(3) *Modern Asian Studies* 513, 517.

[25] ibid 513–57. David Skuy wrote (at 514) 'The Indian Penal Code did not represent Britain's attempt to modernize India's primitive criminal justice system; but rather reflected Britain's attempt to modernize its *own* primitive criminal justice system.'

[26] Yeo and Wright, 'Macaulay's Indian Penal Code' (n 15) 21.

[27] David Skuy, to the contrary, shows that even English law had a tradition of treating offences against religion as criminal acts. Macaulay simply adopted that tradition and applied it to India, making those changes dictated by common sense. See Skuy, 'Macaulay' (n 24) 517.

[28] Ian Leader-Elliot, 'Provocation' in Cheong, Wright and Yeo (eds), *Codification, Macaulay and the Indian Penal Code* (n 15) 291.

Nevertheless, Macaulay proved to have foresight in establishing these offences ahead of future modern legislation against hatred and disparagement.[29]

Although the Code was formally enacted in 1860, it underwent several amendments in later years, and was retained by various countries, such as Bangladesh, India, Sri Lanka, Pakistan, Malaysia, Singapore and Brunei, either upon decolonisation or on attaining independence. According to Macaulay, the religious penal clauses were based on the principle that 'every man should be suffered to profess his own religion, and that no man should be suffered to insult the religion of another'.[30] Macaulay claimed that if the government failed to comply with this principle, social order would be at stake. Macaulay also held the view that any insult to religion would 'inflame fanaticism', and that in India, such dangers could 'only be averted by a firm adherence to the true principles of toleration'.[31] From that perspective, Macaulay suggested providing a punishment of 'great severity' for religious offences so as to avoid 'tumult', 'sanguinary outrage' and 'armed insurrection'.[32] Macaulay in the long run seemed to believe that the religious penal clauses would still 'allow all fair latitude to religious discussion'.[33]

The Bangladesh Constitution guarantees, on the one hand, the freedom of expression, and on the other hand, the right to religion; both being subject to reasonable restrictions imposed by law. Article 39 makes one's freedom of expression conditional upon 'any reasonable restrictions imposed by law in the interests of the security of the state, friendly relations with foreign states, public order, decency or morality, or in relation to contempt of court, defamation or incitement to an offence'. Such a broad mandate confers a wider discretionary power upon the state to define 'public order', 'decency', 'morality' and, by default, 'religious sentiment'. Thus, the jurisprudence of reasonable restrictions swims in a grey area, and consequently, freedom of religion reigns over freedom of expression, and statutory laws commonly place the latter under the threshold of hurting religious sentiments.[34] A couple of offences relating to religion can be found in section 153 (provocation to communal riot) and section 153A (promoting sectarian enmity) of the BPC. However, the main provisions relating to the religious offences are dealt with in sections 295 to 298 of the BPC, as follows:

- Defiling a place of worship – section 295;
- Intentional disturbances to assemblies held for religious worship or for the performance of religious ceremonies – section 296;[35]

[29] ibid.

[30] TB Macaulay, *The Miscellaneous Writings, Speeches and Poems of Lord Macaulay*, vol IV (Longmans, Green & Co, 1880) 104.

[31] ibid 105.

[32] ibid 106.

[33] ibid.

[34] The Digital Security Act 2018 (Act XLVI of 2018) is one such law that makes provision to prosecute people who offend the religious values and feelings of citizens by publishing or broadcasting any information in social media or electronic devices and so on (s 28).

[35] In *Panagganti Parthasarathy Pallikapu v Venkataswami Reddi* (1910) 11 CrLJ 400 (High Court), Miller J observed that mere absence of 'intention' does not exonerate the accused from the charge under this section if the crime is caused with knowledge.

- Trespasses in place of worship and insults to the rite of sepulture and the remains of the dead – section 297;
- Speech or gestures advisedly and deliberately intended to wound the religious feelings of some persons – section 298.[36]

B. Judicial Approaches

John Mayne maintains that the provisions take into account not merely contemplation or mischief, but also intentional insult to religion.[37] Mahmood J, in an earlier case,[38] noted religious pluralism as an underlying philosophy of preventing offences relating to religion. In that case, the Allahabad High Court pragmatically viewed the sacrifice of a cow by a member of the Muslim community in an open place, and held that such act did not offend the religious feelings of the neighbouring Hindu community. Mahmood J, while writing the concurring opinion with John Edge CJ, observed as follows:

> I have no doubt that the Legislature in framing Chapter XV of the Indian Penal Code has made a great advance in the direction of the religious toleration which civilised methods of thoughts enjoin, and if difficulties arise in connection with such matters, they are due not to any defect of the law but to the inconsiderate and reckless behaviour of the various sections of a population which does not fully appreciate the blessings of religious toleration and individual liberty which the British rule by framing wise laws has accorded to the people of this country.[39]

In the Madras High Court decision of *Veerabhadran Chettia*,[40] Somasundaram J considered the scope of section 296 of the IPC (corresponding to the same clause of the BPC) in examining an allegation that the respondent had broken a mud image of Lord Ganesa in public. The Court identified two ingredients of the offence: (i) a person must destroy, damage or defile any place of worship or any object held sacred by any class of persons; and (ii) one must have the intention or knowledge that any class of persons is likely to consider such destruction, damage or defilement an insult to their religion. According to this formula, the Court noted that 'if one of the ingredients is not present, then the offence is not made out'. The Dhaka High Court endorsed this view in *Okil Ali v Bohari Lal Paul*.[41] In *Shunku Sheethiah*,[42] the accused crossed a mosque with a public rally playing music during a prayer hour. The court considered

[36] William Morgan and AG Macpherson, *Indian Penal Code* (GC Hay & Co, 1863) 218.
[37] John Mayne, *Commentaries on the Indian Penal Code* (Higginbotham and Co, 1874) 218.
[38] *Queen Empress v Imam Ali* (1888) ILR 10 (High Court).
[39] ibid 12.
[40] *Veerabhadran Chettiar v EV Ramaswami Naicker* (1955) AIR Mad 550 (High Court).
[41] *Okil Ali v Bohari Lal Paul* (1961) 13 DLR 305 (High Court).
[42] *The Public Prosecutor v Sunku Seethiah* (1911) ILR 34 Mad 92 (High Court).

the accused's knowledge sufficient for conviction. Munro and Sankaran Nair JJ held:

> It is not necessary for the purpose of s 296 of the Penal Code that the accused should have had an active intention to disturb religious worship, it is sufficient, if knowing they were likely to disturb it by their music they took the risk and did actually cause disturbance.[43]

In *Manzur Hassan*,[44] the Privy Council refused to interfere with the longstanding tradition of holding a religious procession by the *Shia* Muslims. In this case, the *Shias*, a Muslim sect, claimed their right to process during the holy *Moharram*. In particular, the *Shias* conduct a procession along with various emblems in memory of the martyrdom of Imam Husain, and as the procession proceeds, from time to time, they perform a ceremony called *Matam*, which means that they stop for a little while and wail. The *Sunnis*, another Muslim sect, also revere the martyrdom of Husain but worship in a different way. The *Sunnis* interfered with the procession and alleged that it disturbed their devotions in the mosque. On the failure of several interim arrangements, the issue came for judicial determination under section 296 of the IPC (corresponding to the same section of the BPC). The Magistrate's Court ruled for the *Shias*; however, the Bombay High Court reversed the decision. On appeal, the Privy Council affirmed the Magistrate's decision on the ground that the *Shias*' procession was of a religious character and barring them (the *Shias*) from exercising the right would convey the wrong message to religious groups in India.[45]

Judicial decisions on religious penal clauses are numerous and exhibit the constant development of penal jurisprudence in relation to dealing with religious sentiments in the Indian subcontinent. The main problem, however, is not with the provisions mentioned above. The main concern, rather, relates to a later addition to the BPC, made in the form of section 295A (hurting religious sentiments) in 1927.[46] Section 295A represents the Bangladeshi variant of 'blasphemy law' in a loose sense, as a legacy of British, Indian and Pakistani religious penal clauses. It needs to be examined how 'religious sentiment' is understood and applied in a new state within a context of religious and cultural pluralism and political divisions. In the later part of this chapter, I will focus my discussions primarily on the ramifications of section 295A of the BPC.[47]

[43] ibid 92.

[44] *Saiyid Manzur Hasan v Muhammad Zaman* (1925) 27 BOMLR 170 (High Court).

[45] Per Dunedin J.

[46] See section IV.

[47] I will, however, make cross-references to other relevant laws relating to religious offences in proper places. For example, s 99A of the Code of Criminal Procedure 1898, another criminal statute of the colonial era, empowers the government to declare any publication forfeited if that publication promotes communal animosity or hurts religious feelings.

IV. EXPANSION OF RELIGIOUS PENAL CLAUSES

In 1924, the publication of an offensive book by Mahashe Rajpal, provocatively entitled *Rangila Rasool* ('Playboy Prophet') agitated the Muslims, and they lodged a criminal case.[48] This was a time when communal tensions in Punjab were at their peak, given certain political and religious events. In this tense situation, Dilip Singh J at the Lahore High Court acquitted Rajpal in June 1927.[49] Rajpal was tried under section 153A of the IPC, which criminalised the causing of communal hatred between various religious communities through wanton attacks on religious beliefs and faiths. Singh J noted that 'the nature of the act cannot be determined by the reaction of a particular class', and attempted to view the matter from an historical perspective, holding that if Rajpal's work was criminalised, this being a satire, in the future the door would be open for serious historical works implicating religious issues to be attacked for causing communal hatred. Singh J also found that the criminal law at the time fell short and did not cover works of satire, and observed that 'the law as it stood then did not treat the satirisation of the saints and prophets as a legal offence'.[50] Rajpal's 'judicial exoneration' made the situation more explosive.

In 1926, Muhammad Iqbal, a poet and philosopher of Pakistan, entered politics and was elected as a member of the Punjab Legislative Council. 'Wearing a politician's hat,' Ayesha Jalal observes, 'Iqbal joined the Muslim delegation which met the Punjab Governor to demand a judicial review or failing that an amendment in the criminal law'.[51] The Government agreed to reopen Rajpal's case, and Iqbal led the drafting of a resolution prohibiting the publication of anything that would hurt religious sensibilities. In the criminal review, the Lahore High Court convicted Rajpal for wounding Muslim religious sentiments. On 6 April 1929, however, Rajpal was murdered in Lahore by a young, illiterate carpenter named Ilmuddin. Ilmuddin was given the title of *ghazi* (warrior for the faith) by Islamist political groups, and was unsuccessfully defended in court by Muhammad Ali Jinnah, who would later become the founder of Pakistan. It was in the midst of these developments that the British amended the IPC in 1927, to add punishment for hurting religious sentiments and incitement of religious hatred.[52] The amended provision, now section 295A of the BPC, reads as follows:

> Whoever, with deliberate and malicious intention of outraging the religious feelings of any class of citizens of India, by words, either spoken or written, or by signs or by

[48] *Rajpal v Emperor* AIR (1927) Lahore 591.

[49] The Magisterial Court and the Sessions Judges' Court in Lahore, however, found Rajpal guilty of offending the religious sensitivity of the Muslims by ridiculing the Prophet of Islam, and sentenced Rajpal to six months' imprisonment. See, eg, Girja Kumar, *The Book on Trial: Fundamentalism and Censorship in India* (Har-Anand Publications, 1997) 56.

[50] *Rajpal* (n 48) 591–92.

[51] Ayesha Jalal, *Self and Sovereignty: Individual and Community in South Asian Islam Since 1850* (Routledge, 2000) 295.

[52] Criminal Law Amendment Act 1927, s 2.

> visible representations or otherwise, insults or attempts to insult the religion or the religious beliefs of that class, shall be punished with imprisonment of either description for a term which may extend to three years, or with fine, or with both.

A subsequent judicial decision following *Rangila Rasool* seemed to be sceptical of the legislative intention of section 295A and tried to adopt a lenient view of the offence of hurting religious feelings. Thus, in *Ambalal Paragji*,[53] Baker J held:

> The violently abusive and obscene diatribe against the offender or prophet of a religion or against a system of religion may amount to an attempt to stir up hatred or enmity against the persons who follow that religion. To attribute to the Mohamedan religion the teachings of the doctrine of Dawood, a heretic, is insulting to that religion, and if done, deliberately and maliciously, would fall under Section 295A. There is a further reference to God, who, according to the Mohamedan, is a celibate, having given permission to Mohamedan males to have as many as four wives to boot and have as many non-Mohamedan women as they like and other liberties with regard to women. I agree with the Sessions Judge as regarding this as insulting to the Mohamedan religion and if the insult is malicious and deliberate with the intention of outraging the feeling of Mohamedan the publication would be an offence under Section 295A.

The history of section 295A shows that writers, filmmakers and scholars have borne the brunt of censorship in British India and beyond. The *Rangila Rasool* controversy polarised Hindu-Muslim relations in India in general, and in Punjab in particular. The region eventually had to be parcelled out between the two religious communities in the 1947 Partition, and the two Punjabs suffered the most brutal communal violence of that horrific time.[54] Pakistani leaders have cited the book's publication as an example of how the Islamic faith would have been threatened under non-Muslim rule had the British left the subcontinent undivided. The argument holds political overtones, and seems very poorly articulated, as there are roughly as many Muslims today in India as there are in Pakistan.[55] This historical development suggests that a tougher stance would not help the countries in the subcontinent in establishing communal harmony. Mahatma Gandhi himself expressed disappointment in these terms:

> Government protection will not make us tolerant of one another. Each hater of the other religion will under a stiffer law seek secret channels of making vicious attacks on his opponent's religion or writing vilely enough to provoke anger but veiled enough to avoid the penal clause of the law.[56]

The distinction between the political sphere and religious identity had been blurred to the point of being largely indistinguishable, further exacerbating

[53] *Ambalal Paragji* (1929) Criminal Appeal Nos 17 and 18 of 1929 (High Court).

[54] Neeti Nair, 'Beyond the "Communal" 1920s: The Problem of Intention, Legislative Pragmatism, and the Making of Section 295A of the Indian Penal Code' (2013) 50(3) *The Indian Economic and Social History Review* 317.

[55] Husain Haqqani, 'Muslim Rage is About Politics, Not Religion' *Hudson Institute* (1 October 2012) at www.hudson.org/research/9280-muslim-rage-is-about-politics-not-religion.

[56] Mahatma Gandhi, quoted in Gene Thursby, *Hindu-Muslim Relations in British India: A Study of Controversy, Conflict and Communal Movements in Northern India 1923–1928* (Brill, 1975) 9.

tensions during this period. The colonial administration contributed to this process by perpetuating the gaps between religious communities, such as through the establishment of communally defined electorates, which strengthened the divide between the Hindu and Muslim communities, and challenged any lingering perceptions of the separation between religion and politics.[57]

V. THE COLONIAL LEGACY

A. The East Pakistan Period (1947–71)

Bangladesh formed the east wing of Pakistan upon independence from the British in 1947. Pakistan had waited nine years for a Constitution, and enacted it in 1956. Although the necessity of separation between religion and politics was felt in late colonial India,[58] Pakistan developed its constitutional principles based on Islamic thought, broadly a by-product of the Partition between India and Pakistan in 1947, adopting an approach that would put Bengali cultural identity and Islamic religious identity into contest with one another.

The principles of criminal law are largely conditioned by the kind of constitution a country adopts. As such, it will be pertinent to examine the constitutional psyche of Bangladesh to form an understanding of its approach to the concepts of crime, social values and personal liberty. Independent Bangladesh adopted its own Constitution in 1972, nine months after it became separated from Pakistan through the 1971 Bangladesh Liberation War. The Founding Fathers of the Bangladesh Constitution considered the misuse of Islam they had witnessed during the Pakistani regime (1947–71). After nine years of protracted deliberations, the Constituent Assembly adopted the first Constitution of Pakistan, proclaiming the state to be an 'Islamic Republic'.[59] Thus, it ignored the distinctive Bengali linguistic and cultural orientation of the people of East Pakistan (Bangladesh). This Islamisation of the Republic encouraged the Pakistani Government in suppressing the Bengalis on the pretext of preserving Muslim unity against the so-called 'Hindustani (Indian) intrusion'.[60]

[57] Erica McLachlan, 'The Story of Section 295A: A Law and Literature Approach' (MA Thesis, University of Calgary, 2017) 11, at www.prism.ucalgary.ca/bitstream/handle/11023/3967/ucalgary_2017_mclachlan_erica.pdf?sequence=1 &isAllowed=y.

[58] Julia Stephens, 'The Politics of Muslim Rage: Secular Law and Religious Sentiment in Late Colonial India' (2014) 77(1) *History Workshop Journal* 46.

[59] Under this 'Islamic Republic' concept, people were asked to order their lives according to Quran and Sunnah, the position of the head of the state was reserved to Muslims, legislatures were obliged not to make any laws inconsistent with Islamic law, *riba* (interest) in the economic system was abolished and the state was obliged to develop healthy relationships with Muslim countries, etc. For an illuminating discussion of the framing of Pakistan's 1956 Constitution, see GW Chowdhury, *Constitutional Development in Pakistan* (Institute of Pacific Relations, 1959).

[60] SM Masum Billah, 'Can Secularism and State Religion Go Together' in Mizanur Rahman and Rahmat Ullah (eds), *Human Rights and Religion* (Empowerment through Law of the Common People, 2014) 32, 33–34.

A couple of interesting examples of how state formation was conditioned by Islamic fervour can be mentioned here. In 1961, the centenary of the birth of Rabindranath Tagore, the Nobel Laureate Bengali poet, was celebrated throughout Bengal, India and East Pakistan. The West Pakistani Government attempted to frustrate this celebration on the pretext that Tagore, who composed the Indian National Anthem, was characterised as a Hindu poet, which could not be accommodated in Pakistan. In another attempt in 1967, a ban was imposed on broadcasting Tagore's songs on the government-controlled Radio Pakistan, which caused discontent amongst Bengalis. Further, Bina D'Costa cites the example of the alteration of song lyrics written by the most celebrated Muslim poet, Kazi Nazrul Islam, by the Central Government of Pakistan, to demonstrate the extent to which the Central Government of Pakistan wanted East Pakistan (Bangladesh) to be 'purged' of 'Hinduism'.[61] The song title 'Kheliche jolodebi sunilo sagoro joley' ('The Goddess of the Water is Playing in the Blue Water of the Ocean') was changed to 'Kheliche jolopori' ('The Fairies of the Water') since the idea of a Goddess was not permissible in Islam.[62]

The birth of independent Bangladesh was inevitable not only because of the differences between the Bengalis and the West Pakistanis in terms of ethnicity and historical memory, but also because of Bengali resentment towards the disparate and inferior economic and political treatment they received at the hands of the West Pakistan Central Government.[63] In addition, the common ground of 'Muslim identity' faded in the face of rising Bengali nationalism which primarily focused on culture and religion.

Interestingly, the judicial application of section 295A during this period was mainly confined to Punjab and Lahore (West Pakistan). Nazir notes several religious sentiment challenges relating to the *Qadianis*, an Islamic sect known for its doctrinal peculiarities and religious publications or speeches disposed of by the Lahore and Punjab High Courts.[64] In contrast, there is no reported leading case on the point decided by the Dhaka High Court, East Pakistan's highest judicial forum in the same period. One may wonder what might have been the reasons for not applying the provision widely in East Bengal in an environment where the idea of Islamisation was at the root of Pakistan's state formation. Religious polarisation as a historical process was there from the developments that had taken place during the British period. It has been mentioned that West Pakistani leaders, including Muhammad Ali Jinnah and poet Allama Iqbal, had arguably made contributions to toughening the penal law on offending religious sentiments following the 1927 *Rangila Rasool* controversy.

[61] Bina D'Costa, *Nation Building, Gender and War Crimes in South Asia* (Routledge, 2011) 87.

[62] ibid.

[63] Habibul Hoque Khandaker, 'Nationalism and the Politics of National Identity' in Riaz and Rahman (eds), *Routledge Handbook of Contemporary Bangladesh* (n 8) 34.

[64] FA Nazir, *The Evolution of Legislation on Religious Offences* (Langham Publishing, 2019).

The non-recognition of Bangla as a state language and undermining Bengali values from a religious point of view, the making of separate suffrage for the Hindus, declaring Pakistan an Islamic Republic without considering the cultural distinctiveness of East Bengal, the banning of Tagore – all these together defined the theocratic nature of the state. Excepting *Jamaat-e-Islami*, the leading political parties of the time, that is the Awami League (AL) and the Communist Parties, were progressive in their political aspirations, believing in a state polity harmonised by Bengali cultural values and a liberal religious ethos. The Bangladesh movement under the leadership of these parties, among others, had been opposing the religious expansionism of the Islamabad Government.[65] As such, from a broader point of view, the practice of individuals litigating under section 295A was marred by the uneasy blend of politics and religion at the state level. The post-independence polity in Bangladesh, would, however, start to exhibit the consequences of the approach taken during the Pakistan regime.

B. The Bangladesh Period (1972–Present)

Religion was a significant factor in the Bangladesh Liberation War of 1971. The Pakistani army carried out a massacre against Bengali Hindus – arguably tantamount to genocide – using the preservation of the unity and sanctity of Islam and Pakistan as justification. In response to this act, where religion motivated the oppression of religious minorities, the founding fathers of the Bangladeshi Constitution of 1972 incorporated 'secularism' as one of the guiding principles of the new state, with the text itself omitting any religious words. Moreover, the Father of the Nation, Bangabandhu Sheikh Mujibur Rahman, envisioned that independent *Sonar Bangla* (Golden Bengal) would be a place free from religious bigotry.[66] As a reflection of Bangabandhu's political vision, the principles of nationalism, secularism, democracy and socialism were adopted as the four basic pillars of the Constitution. Its preamble declared the national identity of the Bengalis in the following terms:[67]

> The high ideals of nationalism, socialism, democracy and secularism, which inspired our heroic people to dedicate themselves to, and our brave martyrs to sacrifice their lives in, the national liberation struggle, shall be the fundamental principles of the Constitution.[68]

[65] ibid, ch 4. Nazir mentions that President Ayub Khan took some initiatives to separate the state and religion by reforming Muslim Family Law, declaring Pakistan a 'Republic'; however, Ayub himself started to promote the cause of Islam during the election campaign in 1964.

[66] On Bangabandhu's secular political philosophy, see especially Sheikh Mujibur Rahman, *The Unfinished Memoirs*, tr Fakrul Alam (Penguin Books, 2012).

[67] Restored third paragraph of the 1972 Constitution of the People's Republic of Bangladesh.

[68] Preamble to the Constitution of the People's Republic of Bangladesh; Constitution (Fifteenth Amendment) Act 2011.

The 1972 Constitution entrenched these four principles by describing them as 'the fundamental principles of state policy' as well as 'the guiding principles of interpreting the Constitution and other laws of the country'.[69] These four fundamental principles of state policy formed the basis of the governance of the country. Furthermore, Article 12 of the Constitution guaranteed religious freedom and prohibited the abuse of religion for political ends. In line with this, Articles 38 and 41 carefully guaranteed the right to association and religion, with certain qualifications. Article 38 allowed citizens to form associations or unions subject to any reasonable restrictions imposed by law in the interests of morality or public order. It sought to prohibit religion-driven politics, and the formation of any association that (i) destroys the religious, social and communal harmony among citizens; (ii) creates discrimination among citizens on the ground of religion, race, caste, sex, place of birth or language; (iii) organises terrorist acts or militant activities against the country or the citizens or any other country; and (iv) thwarts the objectives of the Constitution. Article 41 guaranteed freedom of religion subject to law, public order and morality.[70] Thus, Articles 8, 12, 38 and 41 read conjunctively conveyed the meaning of secularism in Bangladesh as maintaining neutrality amongst religions and the prohibition of discrimination on religious grounds.

In 1976, Islamic religious expressions such as *Bismillah-ar-Rahman-ar-Rahim* and 'Absolute Faith and Trust to Almighty Allah' were inserted into the Constitution by General Ziaur Rahman through martial law proclamations.[71] The four principles of the Constitution including secularism were annulled and Article 12, which defined the meaning of secularism, and the proviso to Article 38, which prohibited religion-based politics, were removed.[72] Article 25(2) emphasised the importance of establishing good relations with the Muslim world. General Zia allowed the religion-based political parties to operate again, despite the existence of credible evidence that these parties were involved in atrocities that took place during the 1971 Liberation War and were active in propagating religious hatred in society.[73]

In 1988, General Ershad elevated Islam to be the 'state religion' through the Eighth Amendment to the Constitution.[74] The provision read as follows: 'The

[69] Constitution of the People's Republic of Bangladesh, Art 8.

[70] Further, the proviso to Art 41 guaranteed individuals the right to refuse to practise a religion or to be compelled to be educated in a religion other than their own. The provision does not state whether a person has the freedom 'not to believe' in any religion. This raises the important question on the extent to which an alleged 'non-believer' could be condemned on the ground of offending 'religious feelings', 'public morality or decency' and so on. The Constitution refrains from saying anything on this.

[71] Political analysts in their commentaries describe this as 'political Islam'. Thus, Ali Riaz writes, 'Their (Zia and Ershad) goal was to construct a "statist Islam" through the production of an emergent Islamic discourse that, it was hoped, marginalised all other discourses, including that of democracy'. See Ali Riaz, *God Willing: The Politics of Islamism in Bangladesh* (Rowman and Littlefield Publishers, 2004) 139.

[72] Proclamation Order No I of 1977; Second Proclamation Order No IV of 1978.

[73] Masum Billah, 'Can Secularism and State Religion Go Together' (n 60) 33–34.

[74] See the Constitution (Eighth Amendment) Act 1988 (Act XXX of 1988).

state religion of the Republic is Islam, but other religions may be practised in peace and harmony in the Republic.'[75] Thus, General Ershad made a classification based on religious criteria, which effectively placed non-Muslims (Hindu, Christians, Buddhists and others) at the mercy of the state in relation to the right to profess, practise and propagate their religion, which was qualified by the requirement of maintaining 'peace and harmony'.

Under this theocratic constitutional scheme, post-1991 Bangladesh saw politico-legal tensions relating to the de facto application of section 295A of the BPC in a blasphemous way. As discussed later, attempts by the conservative sects of politicians to enact a blasphemy law did not succeed, first, in 1994 and, second, in 2004. Following the *5th Amendment Ruling*,[76] in 2011 the Parliament restored the original provisions of the 1971 Constitution, including the term 'secularism'.[77] However, at the same time, the amended Constitution retained the reference to *Bismillah*, the Muslim expression, as the opening word of the preamble, and the recognition of Islam as the state religion.

Bangladesh's current approach to penalising religious offences needs to be accentuated in the context of these most recent developments. Sara Hossain underscores the relationship between post-independence constitutional developments and the criminal law relating to religious sentiments in the following manner:

> While the impact of post-independence incursion into constitutional guarantees of secularism has not been critically assessed to date, it seems evident that if nothing else, it enables, in particular, the rightist and obstructionist forces to articulate the demands within a constitutional framework. The amended Constitution's reference to the primacy of Islam as the state religion is treated as a mandate by the religious right to argue in favour of the marginalisation of other religious practices and indeed their eradication from national life.[78]

While Hossain's view carries some weight, it fails to appreciate the fact that removing the constitutional reference to Islam would be perceived as a sudden denial of religion as a way of life, which in turn bears the potential of producing havoc in Bangladeshi society. The rest of this section of the chapter discusses the notable cases and events that took place in the post-1971 era involving issues relating to religious offences.

i. The Daud Haider Case

The 1973–74 period saw the first wave of incidents involving the question of religious feelings, prosecuted under the Bangladeshi variant of religious blasphemy

[75] Constitution of the People's Republic of Bangladesh, Art 2A.

[76] *Khondker Delwar Hossain* (n 12) 298.

[77] The Constitution (Fifteenth Amendment) Act 2011.

[78] Sara Hossain, 'Apostate, Ahmadis and Advocate: Use and Abuse of the Offences Relating to Religion in Bangladesh' in Ayesha Imam, Jenny Morgan and Nira Yuval-Davis (eds), *Warning Signs of Fundamentalisms* (Women Living Under Muslim Laws Publications, 2004) 93.

offences (section 295A). These incidents showed the strength of the otherwise weak Islamist groups, like the *Jamaat-e-Islami* and so on, which had been sidelined for their support of Pakistan during the 1971 War.

In 1973, Daud Haider, a famous poet, published a poem in the daily *Sangbad*. A college teacher filed a complaint against Haider for allegedly insulting the Prophet of Islam, Jesus Christ and Gautama Buddha. This led to Dhaka's seeing its first post-1971 demonstration by Islamist groups. Haider received death threats and was imprisoned 'for his own protection' after he was beaten by a religious mob. His ancestral home was burnt, and his family members were also attacked by mobs, resulting in the loss of one relative.[79] Haider left Bangladesh for India, his passport was impounded in 1979 and later he went into permanent exile in Germany. Soon afterwards, in 1974, social worker and engineer Enamul Haq published a leaflet that contained a reference to the Prophet's wives. Although Haq denied any malicious intent, religious processions took place and death threats were chanted to Haq. However, the Government was able to establish control over the situation, as the negative popular perception of the action taken by the Islamists in 1971 remained strong. Haq was offered protective custody and ultimately released.

Thus, it can be argued that in the first half of the 1970s, in these two cases, where an attack on religious sentiment was alleged, the Government addressed the issues beyond the precincts of the Court. One may assume that the Government did not want to antagonise the religious sentiments of the people, and handled matters in a manner that signalled a bad omen for the future fate of secularism in Bangladesh.[80] The two events also symbolised the reality and resistance of Muslim politics and culture that did not wither away with the emergence of Bangladesh.

ii. Islamism, Constitutionalism and Criminal Law

As previously mentioned, the initiatives of General Zia and General Ershad in amending the Constitution and altering state religion arrangements created a legal basis for the primacy of Islam over other religions in the lives of citizens. This shift furnished later prosecutions for hurting religious sentiments.[81] The evidence for a change of attitude of the Government may be deduced from its action in seizing the 3 April 1989 issue of *Newsweek*, for allegedly carrying an image of the Holy Prophet.[82] More regrettably, the move by the progressive

[79] Karen Kinnerly et al, 'The Case of Daud Haider: A Letter to Rajiv Gandhi' *The New York Review of Books* (New York City, October 1985).

[80] Paul Rollier, Kathinka Frøystad, and Arild Engelsen Ruud (eds), *Outrage: The Rise of Religious Offence in Contemporary South Asia* (UCL Press, 2019) 18.

[81] Naeem Mohaiemen, 'We Wish to Inform You: A History of Censorship in Bangladesh (1972–2012)' *Naeem Mohaiemen* (1 April 2013) at www.blogs.cuit.columbia.edu/nm2678/2013/04/01/censorship-1972-2012.

[82] ibid.

factions of civil society to challenge the constitutional validity of according Islam its place as the 'state religion' failed due to political turmoil and the conservative attitude of the judiciary.[83] There was no further effective civil society engagement in questioning the state religion principle. Nor was there any citizens' movement to demand the repeal of section 295A of the BPC.

An analogy taken from relevant Indian jurisprudence will be useful, as both Bangladesh and India share the British legal heritage on the point. The constitutionality of section 295A was questioned in the case of *Ramji Lal Mody*,[84] where the Court upheld the law on the ground that the statute only contemplated punishing aggravated forms of insult to religion perpetrated with deliberate and malicious intention.

iii. A Failed Attempt to Enact Blasphemy Law

Bangladesh re-established parliamentary democracy in 1991 after the fall of General Ershad's government through a mass uprising. Khaleda Zia-led Bangladesh Nationalist Party (BNP) formed a coalition government with *Jamaat-e-Islami* after winning the General Election of 1991. To form the coalition, Begum Zia, the widow of late President General Zia, obtained support from *Jamaat-e-Islami*, the party criticised for its controversial role in the 1971 Liberation War. Arguably, religion played a bigger role in the party politics of this time, and it will be seen that 'hurting religious sentiments' was used as a political weapon by the Government to gain popularity. An earlier manifestation was *Ahmad Sharif*,[85] where Professor Sharif, an eminent academic, faced a criminal case under section 295A of the BPC, reportedly for criticising Islam in a seminar.[86]

By 1993, a sharp increase was seen in prosecutions for the hurting of religious sentiments, as section 99A of the CrPC 1898, another statutory power in the hands of the Government for safeguarding the religious sentiments of the people, was invoked by the Government to ban a book that contained verses from Sufi mystic Lalon Fakir. Another case was brought in the Subordinate

[83] Therese Saliba, Carolyn Allen and Juditha Howard (eds), *Gender, Politics and Islam* (Orient Longman, 2002) 265. A civil society group called the Committee for Resistance against Autocracy and Communalism lodged a petition with the High Court Division (HCD) questioning the validity of the state religion clause. Incredibly, the matter became apparently frozen in the courts for more than two decades. In 2016, in a new wave of political developments, there was a revived hearing of the 28-year-old petition before the HCD, resulting in its summary dismissal for lack of standing of the petitioners. See, eg, Eusef Robin Huq, 'The Legality of a State Religion in a Secular Nation' (2018) 17 *Washington University Global Studies Law Review* 245; and Ridwanul Hoque, 'Constitutional Challenge to the State Religion Status of Islam in Bangladesh: Back to Square One' (27 May 2016) at www.iconnectblog.com/2016/05/islam-in-bangladesh.

[84] *Ramji Lal Mody v State of UP* (1957) 1 SCR 860 (Supreme Court).

[85] *Dr Ahmed Sharif v State and Others* (1994) 23 CLC (High Court Division).

[86] The pro-Government daily *Inqilab* published the news without specifically mentioning what Professor Sharif actually had said in the seminar.

Court to halt the publication of a book entitled *Islam e Nabuyat*, brought out by the *Ahmadiyya* community, an Islamic sect having its origins in the *Qadian* city of Punjab in 1889. The petitioner unsuccessfully asked the High Court Division to declare the *Ahmadiyyas* non-Muslims, following the precedent established in Pakistan.[87] The Division's ruling was a temporary success, which would soon evaporate with the rise of the debate over having a 'blasphemy law' at the national stage.

iv. The Taslima Nasreen *Case*

The early 1990s developments on religious sentiment issues featured in the events surrounding the controversial writings of feminist author Taslima Nasreen. The 'Taslima events' represented the tension between the secular and religion-based politics of Bangladesh at the time.

Taslima Nasreen became a known name in the literary fraternity of Dhaka in the early 1990s. Her bold language of self-expression, and strong critiques of patriarchy and fanaticism earned her a place in the minds of the readers. Religious fanatical groups, however, kept a sharp eye on her writings. Problems started specifically with two publications: first, with her novel *Lajja* (shame); and, second, with her remarks about the Quran in a newspaper interview.

In *Lajja*, Nasreen portrayed the atrocities perpetrated against the Hindu minorities of Bangladesh by Muslim extremist groups as a response to the demolition of the *Babri* mosque in India by Hindu fanatics. In the novel, a Hindu family in Bangladesh, the Sudhamays, is caught up in the communal violence that had stained the nation-state. The persecuted family is set to leave for India, with the parting words 'Bangladesh was no longer home to non-Muslims'.[88] These words 'demonizing Bangladesh' hit at the heart of the religious intolerance of which Nasreen was critical.[89]

Lajja drew a huge amount of attention, nationally and globally, and the issue of minority repression in Bangladesh came to the fore. Embarrassed, the Government, led by the right-wing political party BNP, banned the book six months after its publication. That did not ease the situation, however. An extremist group calling itself *Sahaba Sainik Parishad* (Fighters for Prophet's Camaraderie) announced a bounty on Nasreen's head, evoking parallels with the Iranian *fatwa* (religious opinion) against Salman Rushdie.

Fuel was added to the fire when Nasreen, in an interview with an Indian newspaper, allegedly said that the Quran was written by human beings and

[87] Pakistan declared the *Ahmadiyyas* non-Muslim in 1984 by bringing an amendment to the Constitution.

[88] Ali Riaz, 'Constructing Outraged Communities and State Responses: The Taslima Nasreen Saga in 1994 and 2007' (2008) 2 *South Asia Multidisciplinary Academic Journal* 1.

[89] Manmay Zafar, 'Under the Gaze of the State: Policing Literature and the Case of Taslima Nasrin' (2005) 6(3) *Inter-Asia Cultural Studies* 410.

requires revision given its 'discriminatory' prescriptions against women. Nasreen, in a rejoinder to the newspaper, vigorously denied the allegation. To Nasreen's surprise, a Dhaka-based English daily published her interview without the permission of the Indian newspaper, and even without the rejoinder. In such a published form, the interview outraged Bangladeshi readers once again.

The police then filed a complaint under section 295A of the BPC, alleging that Nasreen had hurt the religious sentiments of Muslims.[90] This was followed by a court warrant, which forced Nasreen into hiding. She eventually fled abroad, probably with official connivance, and obtained Swedish citizenship after her Bangladeshi passport was revoked.[91] Nasreen has been living in exile since then. In the sensitive political and religious climate of Bangladesh, Nasreen's work was considered offensive to religious feelings, mainly because it sharply criticised the silence of religiously polarised Bangladesh.

The events invited further legal ramifications. The ruling BNP's political ally *Jamaat-e-Islami* (*Jamaat*) pressed the Government for the introduction of *Sharia* law, especially capital punishment, for blasphemy. *Jamaat* was encouraged by the apparent success of the *Taslima* outcome. Moreover, as Ali Riaz[92] mentioned, *Jamaat* became morally inspired by the decision of the Supreme Court in the citizenship controversy case filed against its *Amir* (party chief), Ghulam Azam. After a long-drawn-out legal battle, the Appellate Division, in *Professor Ghulam Azam*,[93] confirmed Azam's citizenship. With double euphoria, thus, *Jamaat* started to claim that section 295A of the BPC was not fully capable of protecting people's religious interests and the *Taslima* affair had proved the need for a stringent blasphemy law.[94] Matiur Rahman Nizami, the Secretary-General of *Jamaat* and then a Member of Parliament (MP), revived a Bill he had introduced in the House in 1993, suggesting the addition of two new clauses to section 295A of the BPC, proposing capital punishment for defiling the Holy Quran or the sacred name of the Holy Prophet by means of written or spoken words or conduct. This was a serious departure from the existing punishment threshold prescribed by section 295A.[95]

While introducing the Bill in the House, Nizami stated that the move was intended to 'halt the increasing trend of causing disrespect to the Holy Quran'

[90] *Nurul Alam, Officer in Charge, Motijheel Police Station v Taslima Nasreen*, Complaint Case No 1315 of 1994 (unreported).

[91] Manmay notes that international media and personalities intervened in the affair and helped Nasreen achieve safe refuge in Sweden. See Manmay Zafar, 'Under the Gaze of the State' (n 89) 412. See also Mohammad Rashiduzzaman, 'The Liberals and the Religious Right in Bangladesh' (1994) 34(2) *Asian Survey* 974.

[92] Ali Riaz, 'Constructing Outraged Communities' (n 88) 2.

[93] *Bangladesh v Professor Golam Azam* (1994) 46 DLR 146 (AD).

[94] Ali Riaz, *God Willing* (n 71) 102. *Jamaat* had been advocating the passing of such a law since 1993. However, they had been waiting for a favourable political environment to press the BNP, their political ally, to pass the law.

[95] Under the existing provision, a person could be sentenced to imprisonment for up to two years with or without fine. The amendment motion proposed a death sentence instead, and specifically made reference to the defiling of the Quran and the Prophet.

and 'defiling the Holy Prophet Muhammad', which caused great hurt to the Muslim people of Bangladesh and thereby had 'given rise to the possibility of a disruption of law and order'.[96] The proposed Bill resembled the Pakistani blasphemy laws made in the 1980s. Ali Riaz argues that the Bill was 'self-explanatory' and to a great extent 'superfluous', as the prescribed crimes would come under the ambit of the existing section 295A.[97] The Bill was never passed, partly due to the BNP's retreat with the advent of new political issues and partly due to the protests of secular forces. The move nonetheless suggested how the politicisation of Islam could create an environment of fear and anarchy, and in many respects cause minority repression. It was also indicative of the fact that the primacy of Islamic traditions and sentiments, cast aside by the Bengalis to fight the Pakistani crackdown in 1971, returned once again as the widely felt phenomenon of 'political Islam' and a broader quest for Muslim identity.

v. Subsequent Developments

As Nasreen had left the country, the demonstrations demanding her execution calmed down. The pro-blasphemy groups then changed their strategies. In 1995, Humayun Azad's book *Naari* (woman) was banned on the basis of complaints that it insulted Islamic principles on women's rights. Azad, however, successfully challenged the ban. The Court held that the author and publisher had a constitutional right of thought and conscience, which could not be taken away arbitrarily.[98]

The Court, however, displayed considerable latitude in two other cases, namely, *Jahangir Beiman al-Shuresari*[99] and *Sadruddin Ahmad Chisty*,[100] which concerned the banning of books containing well-known *baul* (mystic folk singer) verses by the Sufi mystic Lalon Fakir. The High Court Division held that 'if deliberate and malicious acts, either spoken or written or by visible representation are done intending to outrage religious feelings of any class of citizens, they would constitute an offence under s 295A of the Penal Code'.[101] On the observance of procedural formalities for banning a book under the CrPC, the Court took a rigid view and stated that the notification of proscription may not record the reasons for the Government's *satisfaction* as to the ban.[102] In the separate earlier case of *Anjuman e Ahmadiyya*, a longstanding publication of the *Ahmadiyya* community was called into question for a possible violation of

[96] Ali Riaz, *God Willing* (n 71) 102.

[97] ibid 102–03.

[98] *Humayun Azad and Others v Secretary, Ministry of Home Affairs and Others*, Writ Petition No 2553 of 1995 (unreported).

[99] *Dr [Homeo] Baba Jahangir Beiman al-Shuresari v The State* (1993) 16 BLD 140 (HCD).

[100] *Sadruddin Ahmed Chisty v Bangladesh and Others* (1996) 16 BLD 141 (HCD), partly upheld in *Sadruddin Ahmed Chisty v Bangladesh and Others* (1998) 18 BLD 210 (Appellate Division).

[101] *Sadruddin Ahmed Chisty* (1998) 18 BLD 210.

[102] ibid.

section 295A. Sultan Hossain Khan J dismissed the contention by holding that since the *Ahmadiyyas* were also Muslims, they could not outrage the feelings of Muslims.[103]

Sara Hossain wrote that the judiciary, in holding a person responsible for creating religious bigotry, did not follow a hard-and-fast rule.[104] However, Hossain assumed that the Court displayed a lenient view when such an allegation was made against a religious figure. For example, when the *khatib* (a person who delivers sermons) of the National Mosque, also a protagonist of anti-*Ahmadiyya* movement, was charged under section 501 of the BPC for allegedly defaming the freedom fighters of 1971 by terming them *gaddar* (traitors), the Court rejected the plea on the ground of fair comment. The case, however, was not about offending religious feelings.

In the *Janakantha* case,[105] the petitioner alleged that the defendant wrote a feature in the *Daily Janakantha* under the title '*ei bolod amin-er, marhaba, marhaba*!' ('This bull belongs to Amin, bravo!) and under the pseudonym '*klantho pathik*', which is a distorted meaning of *Surah At-tin* of the Holy Quran (Chapter 95), and thus affected the religious feelings and sentiments of the Muslims, constituting an offence under section 295A of the BPC. This time, the Court took a liberal view on religious feelings by taking the published text of the feature in question into account and then referring to the freedom of religion clauses of the Constitution. Abu Sayeed Ahmed J observed:

> The intention of the publication was to make the real Muslims aware of the false interpretation given by the so-called half-educated preachers of Islam. The allegation does not come within the ambit of the offence of s 295A of the Penal Code.[106]

The Court relied on the decision of the Lahore High Court, where MR Kayani J stated:

> Section 295A [of the Penal Code] or its language is applicable to those insults to religious beliefs which in addition to being deliberate and malicious are intended to outrage the religious feelings of the followers of that religion.[107]

Janakantha was being decided by the judiciary at a time when Awami League, the pro-secular party in many respects, was in power (1996–2001). In a subsequent event, Taslima Nasreen again made headlines when the BNP returned to power in 2001. This was once more a time marked by post-election violence against

[103] *Bangladesh Anjuman e Ahmadiyya v Bangladesh* (1993) 45 DLR 185 (HCD). Earlier in 1993, a lawyer unsuccessfully sought a declaration from the HCD that the *Ahmadiyyas* were non-Muslims. See *Alhaj ABM Nurul Islam v Government of Bangladesh*, Case No 298 of 1993 (unreported), cited in Sara Hossain, 'Use and Abuse' (n 78). Interestingly, however, in 2004, human rights organisations represented by Sara Hossain were temporarily successful in obtaining a stay order on the government ban on *Ahmadiyya* publications.

[104] Hossain, 'Use and Abuse' (n 78) 92.

[105] *Shamsuddin Ahmed and Others v State and Others* (2000) 52 DLR 497 (HCD).

[106] ibid 499.

[107] ibid 498.

minority communities, that is, Hindus. The Home Ministry ordered the police to confiscate all copies of volume II of Nasreen's autobiography *Utal Hawa* (Wild Wind).[108] The Indian edition was seized under section 99A of the CrPC, and the ban was extended to future editions published in Dhaka.[109] In another case, the members of an amateur theatre group of Faridpur, a number of whom were prominent in the Hindu community, were arrested under section 295A of the BPC for performing a play that was causing hurt to 'religious sentiment'; the decision is unknown.[110]

In 2004, Abdul Mannan, one of the BNP lawmakers, indicated that he would introduce a Private Member's Bill on *dhormo obomanona* (insults to religion). Mannan reportedly gave up the idea after being advised by his fellow members on grounds of political expediency.[111] Sara Hossain mentions that the proposed Bill was pervasive in its mandate, and included all conceivable insults against *Shariah* (Islamic law and practice), the Quran and Sunnah.[112] During this time, certain authors published works that were critical of Islamist politics, precipitating an angry backlash from some politicians.

In 2003, for example, author Humayun Azad published excerpts from his forthcoming novel, *Pak Sar Jamin Sad Bad* (Blessed Be the Sacred Land – the first line of Pakistan's National Anthem). In 2004, a *Jamaat-e-Islami* lawmaker, Delwar Hossain Sayeedi, demanded in Parliament that the book be banned. A week later, Azad was stabbed by unknown assailants outside the Ekushey Book Fair, but eventually recovered from his wounds in hospital. Six months after the attack, Azad went to Germany to begin research for a forthcoming book on Heinrich Himmler, a leading member of the Nazi Party. A week later, Azad's body was found in a Munich apartment. Although his family demanded an investigation, the official explanation was that Azad had died of a heart attack brought on by the stress of his earlier injuries.[113]

In September 2007, *Alpin*, the satirical weekly magazine of the newspaper *Prothom Alo*, published a cartoon by Arifur Rahman depicting a fictional chat between a religious leader and a young boy about the proper use of the honorific 'Mohammad'. In the punchline, the boy called his cat 'Mohammad Biral' (Mohammad Cat). Many considered this to be insulting to the Prophet, and after public demonstrations, the Government banned the edition. Cartoonist Arifur was immediately arrested and the editor of *Alpin* fired. The Dhaka Magistrate's Court ordered that the publication of *Alpin* be suspended. Arifur was acquitted after languishing in jail for seven months.[114]

[108] Hossain, 'Use and Abuse' (n 78) 96.
[109] *Mesbahuddin Ahmed v Bangladesh and others*, Case No 681 of 2003 (unreported).
[110] Hossain, 'Use and Abuse' (n 78) 96.
[111] ibid 92.
[112] ibid.
[113] Mohaiemen, 'History of Censorship' (n 81).
[114] ibid.

The experiences of the 1970s appeared to revisit Bangladesh in 2007. Following the *Alpin* controversy, *Shaptahik 2000*, a weekly periodical, published an article by Daud Haider, the Bangladeshi poet who had been living in exile in Germany since 1974, in which he allegedly ridiculed Islam. The Government confiscated all copies of the weekly and the editor apologised.[115] In another incident, members of *Islami Chatra Shibir*, the student wing of *Jamaat-e-Islami*, threatened to burn alive members of the theatre group *Udichi*, as well as a Hindu playwright, for staging the allegedly blasphemous play *Mandar* at Rajshahi University.[116] The University authorities responded by banning the play and another related local theatre group, *Dhumketu Natya Sangsad*. As the national elections of 2009 drew near, *Jamaat-e-Islami* announced its manifesto, which contained a promise to enact a Blasphemy Law, which *Jamaat* had been seeking to do since 1993. *Jamaat-e-Islami* and its political ally, BNP, could not get elected to power in 2009, one of the reasons being the popular dislike of misuse of religious feelings. One such example was translated into reality when an Islamist group pulled down Mrinal Haq's in-progress sculpture of *baul* musicians near the Dhaka Airport; there was intense mobilisation of cultural activists to defend *baul* cultural icons.[117]

vi. Secularism and the State Religion Interface

In 2009, with the return of the Awami League to power, the principle of secularism returned to the Constitution, first, as a consequence of the judicial ruling in the *5th Amendment* and, second, as an amendment to the Constitution.[118] This was done in a qualified manner in an attempt to adhere to the tenets of religious freedom and tolerance.[119] Since 2009, in particular from 2013 onwards, however, there has developed a culture of excessive regard for 'hurt sentiments', particularly in response to the content of many online blogs.

During this time, Bangladesh saw systematic and targeted attacks on free thinkers and religion dissidents. While there were demands to enact a separate blasphemy law, the Government took a moderate approach by not condemning the attacks in unequivocal terms, nor bowing down to the demands to enact a hard blasphemy law.[120] While this approach may appear balanced, it does little

[115] US Department of State Department Bureau of Democracy, Human Rights, and Labour, 'Bangladesh: Country Reports on Human Rights Practices for 2007' (11 March 2008) at https://20092017.state.gov/j/drl/rls/hrrpt/2007/100612.htm.

[116] 'Theatre Group Banned at RU under Pressure' *The Daily Star* (Dhaka, 20 November 2008).

[117] Mohaiemen, 'History of Censorship' (n 81).

[118] Jahid Hossain Bhuiyan, 'Secularism in the Constitution of Bangladesh' (2017) 49(2) *The Journal of Legal Pluralism and Unofficial Law* 204.

[119] Orrin Hatch, 'Keynote Address at the 21st International Law and Religion Symposium, Brigham Young University, J Reuben Clark Law School, 5 October 2014' (2016) 2015 *Brigham University Law Review* 585. The same line of argument has been made in the Bangladesh context. See, eg, Jahid Hossain Bhuiyan, 'Law and Religion in Bangladesh' (2018) 2017 *Brigham University Law Review* 839.

[120] Anbarasan Athirajan, 'Bangladesh PM Sheikh Hasina Rejects Blasphemy Law' *BBC News* (Dhaka, 2 April 2013).

to help when coordinated acts of violence are dismissed by the state as an inevitable result of extremely hurt religious feelings. It is argued, however, that the concept of free thinking and its expression, though firmly wedded to the idea of liberty, must be exercised with judicious self-restraint, to avoid the outcome of a limitless freedom, particularly in a pluralist society where the hurt religious sentiment may translate into physical violence.[121] The inherent weakness of the present balance between secularism and state-endorsed religion is that while expecting a person not to criticise the religion of another, it fails to address the need for insulted religionists to demonstrate restraint and tolerance, and not to overreact to criticism.[122] The law cannot compel people to love one another, but at least the law should be able to prevent people from spreading hatred and intolerance that leads to violence.[123]

VI. CONCLUDING REFLECTIONS

On examining the journey of the religious penal clauses of the BPC and how these have been applied since the colonial era, one may end up with varied conclusions. The first and foremost feature of the Bangladeshi penal law relating to religious offences – that is, section 295A of the BPC – is that although there have been identical incidents relating to offences dealing with 'religious sentiment' in the colonial and post-colonial era, nevertheless the Bengali people have demonstrated their ability to resist any attempt to enact a radical blasphemy law, such as that adopted elsewhere in the subcontinent, such as in Pakistan. This perhaps flows from the inner cultural strength of Bengali society and its values.

Second, it may be observed that the religious penal law operates more politically than legally. What is meant by this, is that the leading post-1971 incidents regarding hurting 'religious sentiments' have been dealt with not only in the courts but also in political spaces. An aspect of this politicised use of religious penal law is that none of the reported cases dealt with the hurting of the 'religious sentiments' of minority groups;[124] this is so, despite the existence of allegations of attacks on the places of worship of minority communities.

[121] Mahmudul Hasan, 'Free Speech, Ban and Fatwa: A Study of the Taslima Nasreen Affair' (2010) 46(5) *Journal of Postcolonial Writing* 540, 549.

[122] See, eg, Cassie Adcock, 'Violence, Passion and the Law: A Brief History of Section 295A and Its Antecedents' (2016) 84(2) *Journal of the American Academy of Religion* 337.

[123] But see the *State v Shariat Boyati* (2020) GR Case No 10 of Mirzapur Station, where a *baul* (mystic) folk singer was arrested and put in jail under s 28 of the Digital Security Act 2018, a controversial law that broadly mandated the restriction of freedom of expression on the ground of offending religious sentiments.

[124] An exceptional incident was the arrest of poet Henry Sawpon, a Bangladeshi Christian, for allegedly hurting the religious sentiments of the Christians. A priest had made a complaint against Sawpon under the controversial Digital Security Act 2018, for allegedly making a slanderous post on Facebook. See 'Bangladesh Christian Poet Arrested for Allegedly Hurting Religious Sentiments & Defaming Priests' *News 18* (14 May 2019) at www.news18.com/news/ world/bangladesh-christian-poet-arrested-for-allegedly-hurting-religious-sentiments-defaming-priests2141357.html.

Third, the judiciary has not developed a consistent jurisprudence in cases that involve religious penal clauses; they have at times come up with different findings on identical issues, depending on which political actor is involved.

Fourth, an accused under section 295A cases suffers more than what is contemplated by the law, due to procedural harassments (ie arrest, detention, delay in dispensing justice, etc) embedded in the Bangladeshi legal system.

Lastly, although section 295A penalises those acting with the malicious intention of hurting the religious feelings of people in general, in practice the clause is predominantly used to penalise acts that insult Islam.[125]

Criminal law manifests the most direct relationship between a state and its citizens. Therefore, as a matter of constitutional principle, this relationship should be clearly stated in the Code.[126] In light of the cases decided and developments since the colonial era, it can be observed that the public disorder and violence that section 295A pre-emptively seeks to check is in fact escalated by social, religious, cultural and political specificities. The whole journey of 'religious offence' jurisprudence vis-à-vis public law represents the three-wave tussle indicated in the introduction to this chapter, that is, liberal secularism, mixed secularism and theocratic extremism.

In 1927, section 295A was enacted to extend the circumstances in which 'wounding religious feelings' by verbal acts could be prosecuted. The purpose was to curb religious violence by restricting provocative speech. However, the law operated in a manner different from that envisaged, enhancing in political terms the strategic value of demonstrating that passions had been aroused that threatened the public peace, in order to induce the Government to take legal action against one's opponents. Political havoc between the pro-secular and anti-secular forces has disrupted policy continuity, as the various power-holders tend to reframe the rules of the game in relation to the relationship between politics and religion, which has implications for legal approaches towards regulating and protecting religious belief and rights. Section 295A thus gave impetus to the politics of religious sentiment.

As Bangladesh is still undergoing an experimental phase in relation to how the Constitution negotiates the pull of secularism at one end of the divide and theocracy at the other, the theory and practice of the criminal law on religious offences will continue to be affected by these broader struggles.

BIBLIOGRAPHY

—— Constitution (Fifth Amendment) Act 1979

—— Constitution (Eighth Amendment) Act 1988

—— Constitution (Fifteenth Amendment) Act 2011

[125] Jeroen Temperman, *State-Religion Relationships and Human Rights Law: Towards a Right to Religiously Neutral Governance* (Martinus Nijhoff, 2010).

[126] Yeo and Wright, 'Macaulay's Indian Penal Code' (n 15) 21.

—— Constitution of the People's Republic of Bangladesh
—— Criminal Law Amendment Act 1927
—— Digital Security Act 2018
—— Proclamation Order No I of 1977
—— Second Proclamation Order No IV of 1978
—— *Alhaj ABM Nurul Islam v Government of Bangladesh*, Case No 298 of 1993 (unreported)
—— *Ambalal Paragji* (1929) Criminal Appeal Nos 17 and 18 of 1929 (High Court)
—— *Bangladesh Anjuman e Ahmadiyya v Bangladesh* (1993) 45 DLR 185 (HCD)
—— *Bangladesh v Professor Golam Azam* (1994) 46 DLR 146 (AD)
—— *Chisty v Bangladesh and Others* (1998) 18 BLD 210 (AD)
—— *Dr Ahmed Sharif v State and Others* (1994) 23 CLC (HCD)
—— *Dr [Homeo] Baba Jahangir Beiman al-Shuresari v The State* (1993) 16 BLD 140 (HCD)
—— *Humayun Azad and Others v Secretary, Ministry of Home Affairs and Others*, Writ Petition No 2553 of 1995 (unreported)
—— *Khondker Delwar Hossain v Bangladesh Italian Marble Works Ltd and Others* (2010) 62 DLR 298 (AD)
—— *Mesbahuddin Ahmed v Bangladesh and others*, Case No 681 of 2003 (unreported)
—— *Nurul Alam, Officer in Charge, Motijheel Police Station v Taslima Nasreen*, Complaint Case No 1315 of 1994 (unreported)
—— *Okil Ali v Bohari Lal Paul* (1961) 13 DLR 305 (High Court)
—— *Panagganti Parthasarathy Pallikapu v Venkataswami Reddi* (1910) 11 CrLJ 400 (High Court)
—— *Queen Empress v Imam Ali* (1888) ILR 10 (High Court)
—— *Rajpal v Emperor* AIR (1927) Lahore 591
—— *Ramji Lal Mody v State of UP* (1957) 1 SCR 860 (Supreme Court)
—— *Sadruddin Ahmed Chisty v Bangladesh and Others* (1996) 16 BLD 141 (HCD)
—— *Sadruddin Ahmed Chisty v Bangladesh and Others* (1998) 18 BLD 210 (AD)
—— *Saiyid Manzur Hasan v Muhammad Zaman* (1925) 27 BOMLR 170 (High Court)
—— *Shamsuddin Ahmed and Others v State and Others* (2000) 52 DLR 497 (HCD)
—— *State v Shariat Boyati* (2020) GR Case No 10 of Mirzapur Station
—— *The Public Prosecutor v Sunku Seethiah* (1911) ILR 34 Mad 92 (High Court)
—— *Veerabhadran Chettiar v EV Ramaswami Naicker* (1955) AIR Mad 550 (High Court)
Adcock, CS, 'Violence, Passion and the Law: A Brief History of Section 295A and Its Antecedents' (2016) 84(2) *Journal of the American Academy of Religion* 337
Athirajan, A, 'Bangladesh PM Sheikh Hasina Rejects Blasphemy Law' *BBC News* (Dhaka, 2 April 2013)
Austin, G, 'Religion, Personal Law and Identity in India' in Gerald J Larson (ed), *Religion and Personal Law in Secular India: A Call to Judgment* (Indiana University Press, 2011) 16
Bangladesh Ethnic Groups, at https://study.com/academy/lesson/bangladesh-ethnic-groups.html
Bhuiyan, JH, 'Secularism in the Constitution of Bangladesh' (2017) 49(2) *The Journal of Legal Pluralism and Unofficial Law* 204
——, 'Law and Religion in Bangladesh' (2018) 2017 *Brigham University Law Review* 839
Billah, SM Masum, 'Can Secularism and State Religion Go Together' in Mizanur Rahman and Rahmat Ullah (eds), *Human Rights and Religion* (ELCOP, 2014) 32

Campbell, G, *Modern India: A Sketch of the System of Civil Government with Some Accounts of the Natives and Native Institutions* (John Murray, 1853)
Chowdhury, GW, *Constitutional Development in Pakistan* (Institute of Pacific Relations, 1959)
Deccan Herald, 'Secularism is back in Bangladesh, rules High Court' (5 October 2010) at www.deccanherald.com/content/102192/secularism-back-bangladesh-rules-high.html
D'Costa, B, *Nation Building, Gender and War Crimes in South Asia* (Routledge, 2011)
Halim, A, *The Constituent Assembly Debate* (CCB Foundation, 2014)
Haqqani, H, 'Muslim Rage is About Politics, Not Religion' *Hudson Institute* (1 October 2012) at www.hudson.org/research/9280-muslim-rage-is-about-politics-not-religion
Hasan, M, 'Free Speech, Ban and Fatwa: A Study of the Taslima Nasreen Affair' (2010) 46(5) *Journal of Postcolonial Writing* 540
Hatch, O, 'Keynote Address at the 21st International Law and Religion Symposium, Brigham Young University, J Reuben Clark Law School, 5 October 2014' (2016) 2015 *Brigham University Law Review* 585
Herrington, J, *Analysis of the Laws and Regulations of Bengal* (The Honorable Company's Press, 1805)
Hoque, R, 'Constitutional Challenge to the State Religion Status of Islam in Bangladesh: Back to Square One' (27 May 2016) at www.iconnectblog.com/2016/05/islam-in-bangladesh
——, *Judicial Activism in Bangladesh: A Golden Mean Approach* (Cambridge Scholars Publishing, 2011)
Hossain, S, 'Apostate, Ahmadis and Advocate: Use and Abuse of the Offences Relating to Religion in Bangladesh' in Ayesha Imam, Jenny Morgan and Nira Yuval-Davis (eds), *Warning Signs of Fundamentalisms* (Women Living Under Muslim Laws Publications, 2004) 93
Huq, ER, 'The Legality of a State Religion in a Secular Nation' (2018)17 *Washington University Global Studies Law Review* 245
Huque, AS, and Akhter, MY, 'The Ubiquity of Islam: Religion and Society in Bangladesh' (1987) 60(2) *Pacific Affairs* 203
Islam, Md Nazrul, and Islam, Md Saidul, 'Islam, Politics and Secularism in Bangladesh: Contesting the Dominant Narratives' (2018) 7 *Social Science* 39
Jalal, A, *Self and Sovereignty: Individual and Community in South Asian Islam Since 1850* (Routledge, 2000)
Kamal, M, *Bangladesh Constitution: Trends and Issues* (Dhaka University Press, 1994)
Kaushik, SN, *Politics of Islamization in Pakistan: A Study of Zia Regime* (South Asian Publishers, 1993)
Khandaker, HH, 'Nationalism and the Politics of National Identity' in Ali Riaz and Mohammad Sajjadur Rahman (eds), *Routledge Handbook of Contemporary Bangladesh* (Routledge, 2016)
Kinnerly, K, et al, 'The Case of Daud Haider: A Letter to Rajiv Gandhi' *The New York Review of Books* (New York City, October 1985)
Kulshreshtha, VD, *Landmarks in Indian Legal and Constitutional History* (Eastern Book Company 2016)
Kumar, G, *The Book on Trial: Fundamentalism and Censorship in India* (Har-Anand Publications, 1997)
Leader-Elliot, I, 'Provocation' in Chan Wing Cheong, Barry Wright and Stanley Yeo (eds), *Codification, Macaulay and the Indian Penal Code: The Legacies and Challenges of Modern Criminal Law Reform* (Routledge, 2011) 291

Macaulay, TB, *Complete Works of Thomas Babington Macaulay* (Longmans, Green & Co, 1898)
——, *The Miscellaneous Writings, Speeches and Poems of Lord Macaulay*, vol IV (Longmans, Green & Co, 1880)
——, *A Penal Code Prepared by the Indian Law Commission* (Pelham Richardson, 1838)
Majumder, S, 'Secularism and Anti-Secularism' in Ali Riaz and Mohammad Sajjadur Rahman (eds), *Routledge Handbook of Contemporary Bangladesh* (Routledge, 2016)
Malik, S, 'Bangladesh' in Andrew Harding and John Hatchard (eds), *Preventive Detention and Security Law: A Comparative Study* (Martinus Nijhoff, 1993)
Mayne, J, *Commentaries on the Indian Penal Code* (Higginbotham and Co, 1874)
McLachlan, E, 'The Story of Section 295A: A Law and Literature Approach' (MA Thesis, University of Calgary, 2017) at www.prism.ucalgary.ca/bitstream/handle/11023/3967/ucalgary_2017_mclachlan_erica.pdf?sequence=1 &isAllowed=y
Mohaiemen, N, 'We Wish to Inform You: A History of Censorship in Bangladesh (1972–2012)' *Naeem Mohaiemen* (1 April 2013) at www.blogs.cuit.columbia.edu/nm2678/2013/04/01/censorship-1972-2012
Morgan, W, and Macpherson, AG, *Indian Penal Code* (GC Hay & Co, 1863)
Nair, N, 'Beyond the "Communal" 1920s: The Problem of Intention, Legislative Pragmatism, and the Making of Section 295A of the Indian Penal Code' (2013) 50(3) *The Indian Economic and Social History Review* 317
News 18, 'Bangladesh Christian Poet Arrested for Allegedly Hurting Religious Sentiments & Defaming Priests' (14 May 2019) at www.news18.com/news/world/bangladesh-christian-poet-arrested-for-allegedly-hurting-religious-sentiments-defaming-priests2141357.html
Rahman, Sheikh Mujibur, *The Unfinished Memoirs*, tr Fakrul Alam (Penguin Books, 2012)
Rankin, GC, *Background to Indian Law* (Cambridge University Press, 1946)
Rashiduzzaman, M, 'The Liberals and the Religious Right in Bangladesh' (1994) 34(2) *Asian Survey* 974
Riaz, A, 'The Politics of Islamization in Bangladesh' in Ali Riaz (ed), *Religion and Politics in South Asia* (Routledge, 2010)
——, 'Constructing Outraged Communities and State Responses: The Taslima Nasreen Saga in 1994 and 2007' (2008) *South Asia Multidisciplinary Academic Journal* 2
——, *God Willing: The Politics of Islamism in Bangladesh* (Rowman and Littlefield Publishers, 2004)
Rollier, P, Frøystad, K, and Ruud, AE (eds), *Outrage: The Rise of Religious Offence in Contemporary South Asia* (UCL Press, 2019)
Saliba, T, Allen, C, and Howard, J (eds), *Gender, Politics and Islam* (Orient Longman, 2002)
Skuy, D, 'Macaulay and the Indian Penal Code of 1862: The Myth of the Inherent Superiority and Modernity of the English Legal System Compared to India's Legal System in the 19th Century' (1998) 32(3) *Modern Asian Studies* 513
Stephen, JF, *A History of the Criminal Law of England*, vol III (Macmillan & Co, 1883)
Stephens, J, 'The Politics of Muslim Rage: Secular Law and Religious Sentiment in Late Colonial India' (2014) 77(1) *History Workshop Journal* 46
Temperman, J, *State-Religion Relationships and Human Rights Law: Towards a Right to Religiously Neutral Governance* (Martinus Nijhoff, 2010)

The Daily Star, 'Theatre Group Banned at RU under Pressure' (Dhaka, 20 November 2008)
Thursby, GR, *Hindu-Muslim Relations in British India: A Study of Controversy, Conflict and Communal Movements in Northern India 1923–1928* (Brill, 1975)
Trevelyan, GO, *Life and Letters of Lord Macaulay* (Oxford University Press, 1978)
US Department of State Department Bureau of Democracy, Human Rights, and Labour, 'Bangladesh: Country Reports on Human Rights Practices for 2007' (11 March 2008) at https://2009-2017.state.gov/j/drl/rls/hrrpt/2007/100612.htm
World Population Review, 'Bangladesh Population 2020' (undated) at worldpopulation review.com/countries/bangladesh-population
Wright, D, 'Islam and Bangladesh Polity' (1987) 10(2) *South Asia* 15
Yeo, S, and Wright, B, 'Revitalising Macaulay's Indian Penal Code' in Chan Wing Cheong, Barry Wright and Stanley Yeo (eds), *Codification, Macaulay and the Indian Penal Code: The Legacies and Challenges of Modern Criminal Law Reform* (Routledge, 2011) 3

8

Prosecuting Religious Violence in Sri Lanka

MARIO GOMEZ*

I. INTRODUCTION

IN AUGUST 2018, the Court of Appeal in Sri Lanka convicted a member of the Buddhist clergy to six years' imprisonment. This conviction is significant, because it is the first conviction of a radical nationalist Buddhist monk who has been accused of fanning escalating religious tensions and violence. The primary crime for which the monk was convicted was, however, not for damaging or defiling a place of worship, or for speech intended to wound religious feelings, or of any of the other religious offences in the Penal Code or in other laws. Rather, the Venerable Galagoda Aththe Gnanasara Thero, who leads the hardline Bodu Bala Sena (BBS) or 'Buddhist Power Force', was convicted for contempt of court under Article 105[1] of the Constitution, when he interrupted an inquiry into the disappearance of a journalist and hurled abuse at the presiding magistrate.[2] His conviction was subsequently confirmed by the Supreme Court.

* My thanks to Raaya Gomez and Panuga Pulenthiran for help with some of the early research, and to Tessa Martin for comments and help with the later research.

[1] Art 105(3) of the Constitution of the Democratic Socialist Republic of Sri Lanka states 'The Supreme Court of the Republic of Sri Lanka and the Court of Appeal of the Republic of Sri Lanka shall each be a superior court of record and shall have all the powers of such court including the power to punish for contempt of itself, whether committed in the court itself or elsewhere, with imprisonment or fine or both as the court may deem fit. The power of the Court of Appeal shall include the power to punish for contempt of any other court, tribunal or institution referred to in paragraph 1(c) of this Article, whether committed in the presence of such court or elsewhere: Provided that the preceding provisions of this Article shall not prejudice or affect the rights now or hereafter vested by any law in such other court, tribunal or institution to punish for contempt of itself.'

[2] *In re Galagoda Aththe Gnanasara* (Court of Appeal, 8 August 2018).

Gnanasara Thero had earlier been convicted for criminal intimidation and harassment in relation to the same incident.[3] When the judgment was delivered in 2018, it was thought that this might mark a shift in the way religious violence is addressed in Sri Lanka. Protests for his release continued on a regular basis, however, illustrating the deep religious divisions around ethnicity and religion that characterise Sri Lankan society. In May 2019, then President Maithripala Sirisena exercised his constitutionally derived presidential pardon to secure Gnanasara Thero's release. The presidential pardon was clearly effected with a view to appeasing groups that supported the radical monk, and sends a problematic signal that there will be few legal consequences for those who mobilise and agitate for violence using religious terms.

Religious identities thus continue to serve as points of political mobilisation, and this takes place against the backdrop of intense and intensifying competition for political power among political elites. The Easter Sunday bombings in April 2019 have further escalated religious tension in Sri Lanka. Within this context, this chapter looks at how the religious penal provisions have been used (or not used) to respond to increasing religious violence in Sri Lanka. Like many of its post-British colonial neighbours in Asia, Sri Lanka inherited a criminal code modelled after the Indian Penal Code, which contains the same chapter setting out offences against religion. However, unlike some Asian countries, such as India, Malaysia, and Singapore, Sri Lanka has not actively invoked these laws. I argue that the lack of punitive measures has contributed to the impunity with which radical actors have acted in attacking religious minorities, including Muslims and evangelical Christians. In addition to examining some of the sparse case law on the subject, this chapter also focuses on some recent constitutional jurisprudence that implicates religious identity and religious offences, to further demonstrate the general failure of the law to act as a restraint on religious violence and violence instigated by religious actors.

Section II looks at the background to Sri Lanka's ethnic and religious conflicts, and discusses the opportunities that the 2015 political transition presented for better ethnic and religious relations. Section III examines the constitutional framework and the application of the penal provisions, and discusses the case law in connection with those provisions. Other laws, such as the International Covenant on Civil and Political Rights Act (ICCPR Act) and the Prevention of Terrorism Act are also discussed, and their selective application identified. Section IV discusses some aspects of constitutional history and looks at some of the processes leading to the adoption of the 1972 and 1978 Constitutions, in which Buddhism was privileged, and discusses some relevant jurisprudence. I conclude by further examining whether the 19th Amendment to the Constitution, passed in 2015, has provided a more conducive environment

[3] 'Sri Lankan Buddhist Monk Sentenced Six Years' Jail In Contempt Case' *NDTV* (8 August 2018) at www.ndtv.com/world-news/sri-lankan-buddhist-monk-sentenced-six-years-jail-in-contempt-case-1897204.

for the courts to act independently and enforce the rule of law in relation to religious violence in the country.

II. BACKGROUND AND SOCIO-POLITICAL CONTEXT

A. Ethnic and Religious Cleavages

The 2012 Census on Population and Housing lists eight major ethnicities in Sri Lanka: Sinhalese, Sri Lankan Tamil, Indian Tamil (or Up country Tamil), Sri Lanka Moor (or Muslims), Burger, Malay, Sri Lanka Chetti and Bharatha, of which the Sinhalese comprised 74.9 per cent of the population; Tamils 11.2 per cent; Indian Tamils /Up country Tamils 4.1 per cent; Muslims or Moors 9.3 per cent; and other groups 0.5 per cent.[4] For the purposes of the Census, the ethnicity of the father determined the ethnicity of persons of mixed ethnicity. The Census also showed the following religious composition: Buddhists 70.1 per cent; Hindus 12.6 per cent; Muslims 9.7 per cent; Roman Catholics 6.2 per cent; and other Christians 1.4 per cent.[5] There is a slight discrepancy between those categorised as Moors and the followers of Islam. Notably, most Muslims in Sri Lanka adhere to the Sunni tradition, while the Christians are mainly Roman Catholics. There are small numbers of Baha'is, Shias (Bohras), Sufis, Ahmadis, Jehovah Witnesses, Methodists, Pentecostals and Evangelicals. There are also the Veddas, an indigenous community.

A major fault line in Sri Lanka has been the division between Sinhalese and Tamils. The primary Sinhalese grievance is that the Tamils had wielded a disproportionate amount of public power when Sri Lanka was a British colony (then known as Ceylon), as part of the deliberate British policy to 'divide and rule', to their detriment. As a result, Tamils held a disproportionate number of public service appointments. It is also alleged that the educational and other facilities in the Northern Province, which is almost 90 per cent Tamil, were at a better stage of development than other predominantly Sinhalese areas, under colonial rule. In contrast, Tamils allege a consistent policy of discrimination against them by Sinhalese-dominated governments since independence. Few government resources have been channeled into areas where Tamils reside, and they have been discriminated against regarding the use of the Tamil language, educational opportunities and access to public service jobs.[6]

[4] Department of Census and Statistics Sri Lanka, *Census of Population and Housing 2012 – Final Report* (undated) 140–41 at http://www.statistics.gov.lk/PopHouSat/CPH2011/Pages/Activities/Reports/FinalReport/FinalReportE.pdf.

[5] ibid 160.

[6] See John Richardson, *Paradise Poisoned: Learning about Conflict, Terrorism and Development from Sri Lanka's Civil Wars* (International Centre for Ethnic Studies, 2005); Nira Wickramasinghe, *Sri Lanka in the Modern Age: A History of Contested Identities* (Hurst, 2006) Rajan Hoole, Daya Somasundaram, KA Sritharan and Rajani Thiranagama, *The Broken Palmyra: The Tamil Crisis in Sri Lanka: An Inside Account* (Sri Lanka Studies Institute, 1990); KM de Silva, *Reaping the Whirlwind: Ethnic Conflict, Ethnic Politics in Sri Lanka* (Penguin Books, 2000); MR Narayan Swamy, *Tigers of Lanka: From Boys to Guerrillas* (Vijitha Yapa Publications, 2006).

This major fault line has framed several bouts of political violence over the past 50 years, though not all were ethnically inflected. In 1971, a Maoist-type party from the Sinhalese 'South', Janatha Vimukthi Peramuna (People's Liberation Front) or JVP, sought to capture state power through a violent struggle that was crushed ruthlessly by the Government at that time.[7] In 1987 the JVP staged a comeback. During a two-year period, it brought the country to a halt through a series of tactics that entailed intimidation and fear. The violence came to an end in November 1989, when most of the JVP leadership was killed. Some escaped, however, returned to Sri Lanka and formed a mainstream political party, which is now represented in Parliament.

In 1976, a Tamil political party adopted the 'Vaddukoddai Resolution', which called for the creation of 'a free, sovereign, secular, socialist state of Tamil Eelam' based on the right of self-determination inherent in every nation. The Resolution argued that the Tamils had tried to live together with the Sinhalese, but this was now not possible. The Vaddukodai Resolution marked the commencement of a struggle for the establishment of a separate state of Tamil Eelam. While there had been many demands for Tamil independence before, this Resolution articulated, for the first time, the demand for an independent state for the Tamil nation, based on Tamils' historical habitation of the Northern and Eastern provinces.[8]

The Resolution came four years after adoption of the 1972 Constitution. The 1972 Constitution made Sri Lanka a unitary state for the first time, gave 'foremost' place to Buddhism and made Sinhala the official language. It also expressly precluded the courts from reviewing the constitutional validity of legislation and removed an important safeguard for minorities that was in the previous Constitution.[9] At around this time, language-based 'standardisation' regarding entry to Sri Lankan universities had angered Tamil youth. The 1972 Constitution and Vaddukodai Resolution represented turning points in Sri Lankan politics, leading to the marginalisation of moderate forces and the emergence of radical forces among Tamils in Sri Lanka. It was during this time that Tamil groups began to embrace violence, and over time, the LTTE (Liberation Tigers of Tamil Eelam) emerged as the strongest group. In 1983, 13 army soldiers were killed by the LTTE in Jaffna, and soon after, ethnic riots erupted in Colombo. Many Tamils were killed, Tamil businesses were attacked and looted, and many Tamils lost their property. There was evidence to suggest that the state was involved in fuelling the riots, or at the very least was 'standing by' while the rioting and looting took place.[10]

[7] HAI Goonetillke, *The April 1971 Insurrection in Ceylon: A Bibliographical Commentary* (Centre de Recherches Socio-Religieuses, Université de Louvain, 1975).

[8] The Vaddukodai Resolution was adopted by the Tamil United Liberation Front (TULF) at its First National Convention held at Vaddukoddai on 14 May 1976 under the chairmanship of SJV Chelvanayakam.

[9] Constitution of the Dominion of Ceylon 1947, Art 29(2).

[10] Paul Sieghart, *Sri Lanka: A Mounting Tragedy of Errors – Report of a Mission on Sri Lanka in January 1984 on Behalf of the International Commission of Jurists and its British Section, JUSTICE* (International Commission of Jurists and JUSTICE, 1984).

Between 1983 and 2009, the state, the LTTE and, for a while, other Tamil groups fought a brutal civil war. Both sides attacked not only military targets, but also civilians and their property, and other places, including temples and places of historical and intellectual value. Human rights violations by both the state and non-state actors are well-documented.[11] During this civil war, the Muslim minority, many of whom have lived for years in the north and east, suffered particularly. Muslims villages were attacked and Muslim residents killed by the LTTE, who accused Muslims of collaborating with Sri Lankan armed forces. In 1990, about 70,000 Muslims were evicted overnight from the north by the LTTE. The eviction occurred despite a shared linguistic identity: both Muslims and Tamils share the same language, and a shared prior history of several years of coexistence.[12]

The conflict in Sri Lanka came to a sudden end in May 2009 when the Sri Lankan military decisively defeated the LTTE and eliminated its senior leadership. The United Nations, as well as other international organisations, and domestic organisations estimate that thousands of civilians died in the final phases of the war.[13] The Government and the military strenuously deny these claims. However, to date, there has been no proper accounting of the human costs of these final stages of civil war.[14]

Soon after the war ended, former President Mahinda Rajapaksa moved to consolidate his hold on political power. He called for an early Presidential Election in January 2010, and then followed this with a hurriedly passed constitutional amendment in September 2010 that strengthened his power.[15] This was followed by the impeachment of the Chief Justice in January 2013. Parliament proceeded with the impeachment despite rulings from the Court of Appeal and the Supreme Court that the proceedings were constitutionally flawed.[16]

[11] Mario Gomez, 'Keeping Rights Alive: Reform and Reconciliation in Post-War Sri Lanka' (2011) 17 *Asian Yearbook of International Law* 117.

[12] *The Quest for Redemption: The Story of the Northern Muslims – Final Report of the Citizens' Commission on the Expulsion of Muslims from the Northern Province by the LTTE in October 1990*, 2nd edn (Law & Society Trust, 2011) at www.lstlanka.org/wp-content/uploads/2017/12/The-Quest-for-Redemption-Book-English.pdf; Farah Mihlar, *Coming out of the Margins: Justice and Reconciliation for Conflict-Affected Muslims in Sri Lanka* (International Centre for Ethnic Studies, 2018).

[13] See US Department of State, *Report to Congress on Incidents During the Recent Conflict in Sri Lanka* (Washington DC, US Department of State, 2009) at www.reliefweb.int/sites/reliefweb.int/files/resources/4792D63B35FAD 909 492576580005B2E2-Full_Report.pdf; International Crisis Group, *War Crimes in Sri Lanka – Asia Report No 191* (International Crisis Group, 2010) at www.d2071andvip0wj.cloudfront.net/191-war-crimes-in-sri-lanka.pdf.

[14] Gomez, 'Keeping Rights Alive' (n 11).

[15] See Mario Gomez, 'Constitutional Change and Institutional Resilience in Sri Lanka' in Henning Glaser (ed), *Shifting to a New Constitutionalism: Changing Political Orders in Asia* (Nomos, forthcoming 2020); Rohan Edrisinha and Aruni Jayakody, *The Eighteenth Amendment to the Constitution: Substance and Process* (Centre for Policy Alternatives, 2011).

[16] ibid.

B. Escalating Tensions Since 2009

Religious tensions and attacks on religious minorities escalated after the war ended in 2009. Despite this escalation, few prosecutions of perpetrators of violence or hate speech have taken place.[17] Anti-Muslim violence occurred in June 2014, in the southern town of Aluthgama and its vicinity, in November 2017 in the town of Gintota, in February 2018 in and around the eastern town of Ampara, and in March 2018 in the Digana and Teldeniya areas in the central part of the country. In many cases Muslim businesses and other symbols of economic prosperity were targeted, highlighting the economic dimensions of these attacks.[18] There are reports of state complicity, as law enforcement officers stood by or participated in the attacks, thus underlying their political dimensions.[19] In 2014, there was a fear that the anti-Muslim violence could have spread throughout the country in the same manner as the anti-Tamil riots of 1983. This did not happen, however, and the violence was contained.[20] Other than Muslims, evangelical Christians have also been at the receiving end of violence, which includes physical attacks, attacks on places of

[17] For some recent writing on inter-religious violence in Sri Lanka, see Gehan Gunatilleke, *The Chronic and the Acute: Post-War Religious Violence in Sri Lanka* (International Centre for Ethnic Studies and Equitas, 2015); Gehan Gunatilleke, *The Chronic and the Entrenched: Ethno-Religious Violence in Sri Lanka* (International Centre for Ethnic Studies and Equitas, 2018); Dian AH Shah, *Constitutions, Religions and Politics in Asia: Indonesia, Malaysia and Sri Lanka* (Cambridge University Press, 2017); Benjamin Schonthal, 'Environments of Law: Islam, Buddhism, and the State in Contemporary Sri Lanka' (2016) 75(1) *The Journal of Asian Studies* 137; Benjamin Schonthal, 'Litigating Vinaya: Buddhist Law and Public Law in Contemporary Sri Lanka' (2018) 3 *Buddhism Law & Society* 1; Mohamed Faslan and Nadine Vanniasinkam, *Fracturing Community: Intra-Group Relations among the Muslims of Sri Lanka* (International Centre for Ethnic Studies, 2015); Mihlar, *Coming Out of the Margins* (n 12); Farzana Haniffa and Vijay Nagaraj, *Towards Recovering Histories of Anti-Muslim Violence in the Context of Sinhala-Muslim Tensions in Sri Lanka* (International Centre for Ethnic Studies, 2016); Ameer Ali, 'Four Waves of Muslim-Phobia in Sri Lanka: c.1880–2009' (2015) 35(4) *Journal of Muslim Minority Affairs* 486; Dhammika Herath and Harshana Rambukwella, *Self, Religion, Identity and Politics: Buddhist and Muslim Encounters in Contemporary Sri Lanka* (International Centre for Ethnic Studies, 2015); Neil Devotta, 'Religious Intolerance in Post-Civil War Sri Lanka' (2018) 49(2) *Asian Affairs* 278; National Christian Evangelical Alliance of Sri Lanka, *The Role of Religion in Transitional Justice in Sri Lanka: A Faith Exploration – Right to Truth, Justice and Human Dignity* (National Christian Evangelical Alliance of Sri Lanka, 2018); UN OHCHR, 'Report of the UN Special Rapporteur on Freedom of Religion or Belief, Dr Ahmed Shaheed, to the Human Rights Council, following a country visit to Sri Lanka in August 2019' (28 February 2020) UN Doc A/HRC/43/48/Add.2 at www.ohchr.org/EN/Issues/FreedomReligion/Pages/Visits.aspx; National Christian Evangelical Alliance of Sri Lanka, *Religious Freedom Violations in Sri Lanka: The Use of Right to Information Law to Assess the Response of Law Enforcement Authorities and the Judiciary, Phase 1,* (National Christian Evangelical Alliance of Sri Lanka, 2020); and Ranmini Vithanagama, *Tracking Coexistence: Understanding Perceptions of the Religious 'Other'* (International Centre for Ethnic Studies, 2020).

[18] See Kumari Jayawardene, 'Economic and Political Factors in the 1915 Riots' (1970) 29(2) *The Journal of Asian Studies* 223; Ali, 'Four Waves' (n 17).

[19] See Gunatilleke, *The Chronic and the Acute* (n 17); Gunatilleke, *The Chronic and the Entrenched* (n 17).

[20] See also Ali, 'Four Waves' (n 17).

worship, interruption of religious services and obstruction of religious rites, including burial ceremonies.[21]

Although violence against the Muslims escalated after 2009, this is not a new phenomenon. In 1915, anti-Muslim riots erupted in Kandy and spread to five of the country's nine provinces.[22] There were also attacks on Muslims in the 1970s and 1980s.[23] Haniffa and Nagaraj discuss three relatively unknown pogroms against the Muslims, in Puttalam (1976), Galle (1982) and in Mawanella (2001).[24] The 1976 violence was followed by anti-Tamil violence in 1977, and the violence in Galle in 1982 was followed by the violence of 1983 against the Tamils, which marked the commencement of the 26-year civil war. Haniffa and Nagaraj make two important points: on the economic and political dimensions of the violence, and the failure of law enforcement officials to act. They note:

> Puttalam, Galle and Mawanella must be understood not merely as randomly localised violence against Muslims but as reflective of competition over political (and) economic spaces … [C]entral to the mobilisation of the Sinhalese working class and poor, was the alliance or alignment, most visible in Puttalam and Mawanella, between the Sinhalese bourgeoisie and the temple or the Buddhist clergy buttressed by local Sinhalese political interests who commanded 'muscle power'. The involvement of the local Buddhist clergy was critical in both legitimising anti-Muslim sentiment as well as in providing a physical and spiritual/religious locus for such sentiment and its eventual translation into violence. Indeed, Buddhist temples, like any other socially embedded places of worship, thrive on the capital accumulated by local Sinhalese Buddhists and as such have a vested interest in its expansion. The involvement of the clergy, or the appearance that they condoned such acts just by turning a blind-eye or not condemning it, is crucial … it provided a particular sense of legitimacy by lending morality to anti-Muslim sentiment, especially when a monk led from the front as in the case of Puttalam … [I]t also facilitated an alignment across all sections of the local Sinhalese Buddhists, from those in institutions of state to local politicians and the bourgeoisie to the working class poor … [T]he clergy's involvement, even tacit, enabled the reproduction of a certain social and moral impunity for such acts that could be construed as safeguarding Sinhala Buddhist interests.

[21] See UN OHCHR, 'Report of the UN Special Rapporteur on Freedom of Religion or Belief, Dr Ahmed Shaheed, to the Human Rights Council, following a country visit to Sri Lanka in August 2019' (28 February 2020) UN Doc A/HRC/43/48/Add.2 at www.ohchr.org/EN/Issues/FreedomReligion/Pages/Visits.aspx; Gunatilleke, *The Chronic and the Entrenched* (n 17) 15–39.

[22] See Arthur C Dep, *Ceylon Police and Sinhala-Muslim Riots of 1915* (Sarvodaya Vishva Lekha, 2001); Michael Roberts, *Noise as Cultural Struggle: Tom-Tom Beating, the British and Communal Disturbances in Sri Lanka, 1880s–1930s* (Studies in Society and Culture, 1993); Michael Roberts, *Exploring Confrontation: Sri Lanka – Politics, Culture and History* (Harwood Academic Publishers, 1994); Michael Roberts, 'Hobgoblins, Low-Country Sinhalese Plotters, or Local Elite Chauvinists?: Directions and Patterns in the 1915 Communal Riots' (1981) 4 *Sri Lanka Journal of Social Sciences* 83; Jayawardene, 'Economic and Political Factors' (n 18); Ponnambalam Ramanathan, *Riots and Martial Law in Ceylon – 1915* (St Martin's Press, 1916). The 1915 riot is discussed in more detail in section III.B.

[23] See Ali, 'Four Waves' (n 17); Haniffa and Nagaraj, *Towards Recovering Histories* (n 17).

[24] Haniffa and Nagaraj, *Towards Recovering Histories* (n 17).

> …
>
> This leads us to the final crucial factor in understanding anti-Muslim violence in the context of Sinhala-Muslim tensions – the highly politicised and prejudiced nature of law enforcement and policing. Time after time policing and law enforcement failed or simply refused to protect Muslims and their property from attacks by Sinhalese mobs or even provoked the violence. Notwithstanding repeated demands, including in Parliament, there was little by way of credible investigation into the role of law enforcement agencies and no one was held to account for the violence in all Puttalam, Galle and Mawanella.[25]

The growing violence against religious minorities has been accompanied by the increasing presence of Buddhist symbols in public spaces. Since 2009, there has been a growth in Buddhist shrines and monuments, even in those areas with a very little Buddhist presence. Religious contests over archeological and religious sites have also escalated since the end of the war.

In his recent report on Sri Lanka, the UN Special Rapporteur on Freedom of Religion or Belief observes:

> While the legal framework in Sri Lanka guarantees the right to freedom of religion or belief for everyone, in practice there are several challenges to the enjoyment of this right. Religious minorities face restrictions in the manifestation of their religion or belief, their places of worship are desecrated while their religious activities such as worship sessions are disrupted by locals and the authorities. There is difficulty for the minority religious communities to build new places of worship while some places were forced to close down due to arbitrary registration requirements. Non-Roman Catholic Christians are also exposed to numerous incidents of violent attack due to a suspicion of 'unethical conversion' and limitations on their right to proselytise. Aggressive campaigns by militant nationalist and religious groups against ethnic, religious and other minorities, particularly Muslims, are particularly concerning.[26]

C. The Political Transition of 2015

There was great hope that greater protection for religious minorities would emerge after a change in government, after Sri Lankans voted out Mahinda Rajapaksa and elected Maithripala Sirisena in the January 2015 Presidential Elections. Sirisena had served as the Minister of Health in the Rajapaksa Government, but in 2015 he was the 'common candidate' supported by a multi-party coalition that campaigned against Rajapaksa. The electoral result came as a surprise to many, who thought that Rajapaksa could not be dislodged because of his role in winning the war against the LTTE. Rajapaksa gave up power reluctantly, and Sri Lanka showed that it could manage a transition peacefully within the framework of the country's Constitution. The Parliamentary Elections of

[25] ibid 41–42, 44.

[26] See UN OHCHR, 'Report of the UN Special Rapporteur' (n 21) para 90.

August 2015 consolidated President Sirisena's grip on power when his National Unity Coalition Government, consisting of traditional rivals the United National Party (UNP) and the Sri Lanka Freedom Party, secured a parliamentary majority.

The new regime promised many things, including increased security for religious minorities.[27] While there was an overall decline in the number of incidents of religious violence, attacks on evangelical Christians and Muslims continued during this period.[28] Even though many of the expectations of the political transition of 2015 have not been realised, especially with regard to constitutional reform and transitional justice, it is important to highlight three key developments with implications for religious freedom and the rule of law. The 19th Amendment to the Constitution, passed in May 2015, altered the balance of power between the executive and the legislature, and created a more balanced scheme of constitutional government. The Right to Information Act, passed in August 2016, has enabled the public to access government decisions that were previously not placed in the public domain.[29] However, the most important change has been the increase in democratic space, which has resulted in citizens and groups being able to challenge public policy and decisions without fear of sanctions.

D. The 2019 Easter Sunday Bombings and their Aftermath

The Easter Sunday bombings of 21 April 2019 added a new dimension to inter-religious relations in Sri Lanka. Three churches, two of which were Roman Catholic and the other Protestant, and three high-profile hotels were targeted in well-coordinated attacks on the morning of Easter Sunday, a day of high religious significance for Christians. Over 250 were killed and hundreds more were injured. Extensive damage was caused to the churches and hotels. One of the churches targeted, St Anthony's Kochikade, was a site of worship for several religious denominations, not only Roman Catholics. The perpetrators were Sri Lankan Muslims, including at least two from affluent backgrounds. It was the first time that members of the Muslim community had been involved in such high-profile killings including suicide attacks. It was also the first time that foreigners were specifically targeted as part of the country's many bouts of political violence. The Government declared a state of emergency under the Public Security Ordinance soon after, and security forces were given wide powers

[27] Mario Gomez, 'The Politics of Dealing with the Past in Deeply Divided Sri Lanka' (2017) Harvard Human Rights Journal Online Symposium on Transitional Justice, 3 October 2017 at www.ices.lk/wp-content/uploads/2017/10/TJ-Harvard-HR-3-Oct-2017.pdf.

[28] See National Christian Evangelical Alliance of Sri Lanka, *The Role of Religion* (n 17); Gunatilleke, *The Chronic and the Entrenched* (n 17).

[29] Right to Information Act (No 12 of 2016). See Mario Gomez, 'The Right to Information and Transformative Development Outcomes' (2019) *Law and Development Review* 837.

of arrest and detention for extended periods. The state of emergency lapsed in August 2019 and was not renewed.[30]

Since the April bombings, Muslims have been at the receiving end of a new series of attacks. This has occurred in the mainstream and social media, through thousands of arrests for suspected involvement in terrorism, and in anti-Muslim violence. It has also included a fast to death by a prominent Buddhist monk, close to the Dalada Maligawa, a well-known Buddhist temple in Kandy, calling for the resignations of Muslim ministers and governors, two days of rioting around 13 and 14 May 2019, when over a 100 Muslim houses and shops were attacked, and a ban on the wearing of the face veil.[31]

An unexpected consequence of the April bombings is that it has opened space to discuss reform of the Muslim personal law. Reform of the Muslim Marriage and Divorce Act of 1951 (MMDA) has been resisted by Muslim hardliners for many years. Since the bombings, Cabinet has recently been reported to have approved reform of the MMDA.[32] Currently Muslims are not allowed to opt out of the MMDA and marry under the General Marriages Registration Ordinance. Five key reforms are being contemplated: raising the minimum age of marriage to 18, in line with the general law, with the proviso that marriages of girls over 16 can take place with the permission of the *quazi*; the representation of women as *quazis* and on the Board of Quazis; the first forum of appeal under the MMDA; the mandatory consent of the woman, as evidenced by her signature or thumb print in the case of marriage; conditional polygamy; further, those that are appointed as *quazis* should be lawyers with a sound knowledge of Muslim law.[33]

III. AN OVERVIEW OF THE LEGAL AND CONSTITUTIONAL FRAMEWORK

A. The Constitutional Framework

In Sri Lanka, four legal regimes apply in the case of religious offences: the Penal Code; the ICCPR Act of 2007; the Police Ordinance; and the Prevention of Terrorism Act. All these regimes function independently of each other and have

[30] See GPV Somaratna, *Kotahena Riot 1883: A Religious Riot in Sri Lanka* (Deepanee Printers, 1991) for a discussion of a Christian-Sinhalese riot that occurred in 1883.

[31] 'Call for Action: Mapping Anti-Muslim Attacks in Sri Lanka' (August 2019), on file with the author.

[32] 'Cabinet Nod For Muslim Marriage Law Amendments, Puts Marriageable Age At 18' *Colombo Telegraph* (21 August 2019) at www.colombotelegraph.com/index.php/cabinet-nod-for-muslim-marriage-law-amendments-puts-marriageable-age-at-18/. See also UN OHCHR, 'Report of the UN Special Rapporteur' (n 21) para 48.

[33] See 'Muslim Personal Law Action Reforms Group (MPLRAG)' (MPLRAG, undated) at www.mplreforms.com/. *Quazis*, sometimes spelt *Qadis*, are judges administering the Muslim Personal Law.

seldom been employed to address religious violence. Penal Code offences have figured in fundamental rights litigation, as the state has sometimes sought to justify its actions on the basis that the petitioner has violated sections of the Penal Code.[34] This legal debate sits at the uneasy intersection of two seemingly contradictory provisions in the Constitution. On the one hand, Article 9 of the Constitution privileges Buddhism by providing:

> The Republic of Sri Lanka shall give to Buddhism the foremost place and accordingly it shall be the duty of the State to protect and foster the Buddha Sasana, while assuring to all religions the rights granted by Articles 10 and 14(1)(e).[35]

On the other hand, Article 10 of the Constitution guarantees freedom of thought, conscience and belief, and the freedom to have or adopt a religion or belief. It is an entrenched provision and cannot be restricted.[36] This is buttressed by Article 14(1)(e), which protects the right to manifest religion or belief in worship, observance, practice and teaching either alone or in association with others, and either in public or in private.[37] Unlike Article 10, the rights contained in Article 14(1)(e) can be restricted on the grounds of national security, public order and the protection of public health or morality, or for the purpose of securing due recognition and respect for the rights and freedom of others, or of meeting the just requirements of the general welfare of a democratic society.[38] As mentioned previously, the Sri Lankan Constitution currently does not permit judicial review of enacted legislation, and allows instead for pre-enactment review of bills placed on the order paper of Parliament.[39] The Constitution also protects past laws inconsistent with the Constitution, mainly to protect the sanctity of the personal laws that apply in limited circumstances.[40]

Constitutional arguments have arisen in relation to religious disputes. In *Sarath Lakshman v Premawathie*,[41] the High Court held, on appeal, that the magistrate at first instance had erred in preventing a woman from conducting a prayer service in her home, concluding that the magistrate had not conducted a proper examination of the facts. The High Court used Article 10 and Article 14(1)(e) of the Constitution to conclude that holding a prayer meeting with friends in a private residence did not amount to noise pollution or a disturbance of the peace under the law.

[34] See, eg, *Sisira Kumar v Jayantha Wickramaratne* (Supreme Court, Minutes of 5 November 2015), where the police relied on s 120 of the Penal Code, a sedition offence, to justify the arrest of the petitioners. The Supreme Court held that s 120 of the Penal Code did not apply and granted a remedy to the petitioners under Arts 12(1) and (2), 13(1) and 14(1)(a) of the Constitution. See also *Cokeman v Attorney General*, SC (FR) 136/2014 (Supreme Court, Minutes of 15 November 2017).

[35] Constitution of the Democratic Socialist Republic of Sri Lanka, Art 9.

[36] ibid Art 10.

[37] See also Jayampathy Wickremeratne, 'Fundamental Rights in Sri Lanka' in Asanga Welikala (ed), *The Sri Lankan Republic at 40: Reflections on Constitutional History, Theory and Practice* (Centre for Policy Alternatives, 2012).

[38] Constitution of the Democratic Socialist Republic of Sri Lanka, Art 15.

[39] ibid Art 121.

[40] ibid Art 16.

[41] *Sarath Lakshman v Premawathie* [2012] Case No 15/2009.

More recently, the case of *Cokeman v Attorney General* illustrates the connections between the penal provisions and constitutional law, where the state in a fundamental rights application pleaded in defence that Penal Code provisions were violated.[42] In *Cokeman*, a British woman was arrested at the airport because she was wearing a tattoo of the Buddha sitting on a lotus leaf on her arm. She was taken to a nearby police station first, and then to an immigration detention centre. She was produced by the police before a magistrate who ordered that she be deported. She was subjected to harassment and intimation during her arrest and detention. Cokeman subsequently challenged her arrest, detention and deportation in her fundamental rights application before the Supreme Court.[43] In her petition, she pleaded that she was a devout Buddhist and it was as a personal expression of this devotion to Buddhist teachings and as a mark of respect, that she displayed a tattoo of the Buddha on her right arm. She alleged a violation of Article 11 of the Constitution (the right against cruel, inhuman or degrading treatment), Article 12(1) of the Constitution (equality before the law and the right to equal protection of the law) and Article 13(1) (freedom from arbitrary arrest, detention and punishment).

The Supreme Court held that there was a violation of her fundamental rights under Articles 11, 12(1) and 13(1), and ordered compensation payable by the state and individually by the two police officers concerned. In its judgment, the Court observed that there was no intention to outrage religious feelings on the part of Cokeman, and therefore a charge under section 291B of the Penal Code could not be sustained to justify her arrest.[44] The police officer had also pleaded in defence of the arrest that he envisaged a breach of peace as a result of people in the vicinity seeing the tattoo. This was also rejected by the Court on the basis that credible evidence to this effect was not produced. The implication of this judgment is that where there is credible evidence to establish that there was an intention to outrage religious feelings, or there is an imminent threat of a breach of peace, then the arrest of a person as a preventive measure is permissible, and a violation of the right to equality before the law and the equal protection of the law would be difficult to establish.

B. Religious Clauses under the Penal Code and the Criminal Procedure Code

Like other criminal codes in Asia modelled after the Indian Penal Code, the Penal Code of Sri Lanka lists six offences dealing with religion.[45] These offences on religion are contained in Chapter XV:

> s 290: Whoever destroys, damages, or defiles any place of worship, or any object held sacred by any class of persons, with the intention of thereby insulting the religion

[42] *Cokeman* (n 34).
[43] Constitution of the Democratic Socialist Republic of Sri Lanka, Arts 17 and 126.
[44] See *Cokeman* (n 34).
[45] Penal Code, ss 290, 290A, 291A, 291B and 292. See also G.L.Peiris, *Offences Under the Penal Code of Sri Lanka* (Stamford Lake, 1976) 418–22.

of any class of persons or with the knowledge that any class of persons is likely to consider such destruction, damage, or defilement as an insult to their religion, shall be punished with imprisonment of either description for a term which may extend to two years, or with fine, or with both.

s 290A: Whoever does any act, in or upon, or in the vicinity of, any place of worship or any object which is held sacred or in veneration by any class of persons, with the intention of wounding the religious feelings of any class of persons of with the knowledge that any class of persons is likely to consider such act as an insult to their religion, shall be punished with imprisonment of either description for a term which may extend to one year, or with fine, or with both.

s 291: Whoever voluntarily causes disturbance to any assembly lawfully engaged in the performance of religious worship or religious ceremonies shall be punished with imprisonment of either description for a term which may extend to one year, or with fine, or with both.

s 291A: Whoever, with the deliberate intention of wounding the religious feelings of any person, utters any word or makes any sound in the hearing of that person, or makes any gesture in the sight of that person, or places any object in the sight of that person, shall be punished with imprisonment of either description for a term which may extend to one year, or with fine, or with both.

s 291B: Whoever, with the deliberate and malicious intention of outraging the religious feelings of any class of persons, by words, either spoken or written, or by visible representations, insults or attempts to insult the religion or the religious beliefs of that class, shall be punished with imprisonment of either description for a term which may extend to two years, or with fine, or with both.

s 292: Whoever, with the intention of wounding the feelings of any person, or of insulting the religion of any person, or with the knowledge that the feelings of any person are likely to be wounded, or that the religion of any person is likely to be insulted thereby, commits any trespass in any place of worship or on any place of sepulture or any place set apart for the performance of funeral rites, or as a depository for the remains of the dead, or offers any indignity to any human corpse, or causes disturbance to any persons assembled for the performance of funeral ceremonies, shall be punished with imprisonment of either description tor a term which may extend to one year, or with fine, or with both.

Three other provisions, two in the Penal Code and the other in the Criminal Procedure Code, are also relevant for the purposes of prosecuting religious violence:

s 483 of the Penal Code: Whoever threatens another with any injury to his person, reputation, or property, or to the person or reputation of any one in whom that person is interested, with intent to cause alarm to that person, or to cause that person to do any act which he is not legally bound to do, or to omit to do any act which that person is legally entitled to do, as the means of avoiding the execution of such threat, commits criminal intimidation.

s 120 of the Penal Code: Whoever by words, either spoken or intended to be read, or by signs; or by visible representations, or otherwise, excites or attempts to excite feelings of disaffection to the President or to the Government of the Republic, or excites or attempts to excite hatred to or contempt of the administration of justice,

> or excites or attempts to excite the People of Sri Lanka to procure, otherwise than by lawful means, the alteration of any matter by law established, or *attempts to raise discontent or disaffection amongst the People of Sri Lanka, or to promote feelings of ill-will and hostility between different classes of such People, shall be punished with simple imprisonment for a term which may extend to two years.*[46]

> s 81 of the Criminal Procedure Code: Whenever a Magistrate receives information that any person is likely to commit a breach of the peace or to do any wrongful act that may probably occasion a breach of the peace within the local limits of the jurisdiction of the court of such Magistrate, or that there is within such limits a person who is likely to commit a breach of the peace or do any wrongful act as aforesaid in any place beyond such limits the Magistrate may in manner hereinafter provided require such person to show cause why he should not be ordered to execute a bond with or without sureties for keeping the peace for such period not exceeding two years as the court thinks fit to fix.

Notably, radical Buddhist monk, Galagoda Aththe Gnanasara Thero, whose case is discussed in section I and section VI.A, was also convicted of criminal intimidation under the Penal Code.[47] According to a lawyer involved in cases of religious violence in the lower courts, magistrates tend to rely on section 81 of the Criminal Procedure Code in responding to cases on religious violence.[48]

In general, however, the case law on the religious penal clauses is scarce and old, as they have not been actively invoked to deal with cases of religious violence. There is a tendency for courts to prosecute such crimes through other laws, such as breach of peace.[49] This follows the pattern from colonial times. For instance, perpetrators of violence during the Sinhala-Muslim Riots of 1915, probably the most violent of the religious riots under British colonial rule, were charged with treason (under section 120 of the Penal Code) and other offences, including shop breaking and murder.[50] None of the rioters were prosecuted under any of the religious offences listed in the Penal Code.[51] This is despite the strong religious undertones of the riots, which began on 28 May 1915 during a procession on Vesak Day involving singing, dancing, drumming and firecrackers.[52] Citing Michael Roberts and Ameer Ali, Wettimuny contends that the British attempted to shield a mosque in Kandy from the noise of the procession. This angered the

[46] Emphasis added.

[47] 'Court finds Gnanasara Thero guilty of criminal intimidation' *Daily FT* (25 May 2018) at www.ft.lk/news/Court-finds-Gnanasara-Thero-guilty-of-criminal-intimidation/56-655906.

[48] Interview with National Christian Evangelical Alliance lawyer (on file with the author).

[49] ibid.

[50] Dep, *Ceylon Police* (n 22) 114–25; Roberts, 'Hobgoblins' (n 22) 98. See also Roberts, *Noise as Cultural Struggle* (n 22); Roberts, *Exploring Confrontation* (n 22); Jayawardene, 'Economic and Political Factors' (n 18); Ali, 'Four Waves' (n 17); Ramanathan, *Riots and Martial Law* (n 22).

[51] Dep, *Ceylon Police* (n 22) 114–25.

[52] Shamara Wettimuny, 'Regulating Religious Rites: Did British Regulation of "Noise Worship" Trigger the 1915 Riots in Ceylon?' (London School of Economic and Political Science, 31 March 3018) at www.blogs.lse.ac.uk/lseih/2018/03/31/regulating-religious-rites-did- british-regulation-of-noise-worship-trigger-the-1915-riots-in-ceylon/.

Sinhala-Buddhist crowd, which first attacked the mosque and then turned their fury on Muslim homes, businesses and places of worship. The violence engulfed five of the nine provinces in the country. Wettimuny observes:

> The riots lasted nine days. According to official estimates, violence resulted in at least 25 murders, the rape of four women and left 189 people wounded. Furthermore, over 4,000 Muslim shops were looted, and 350 houses and seventeen mosques were set on fire … The anti-Muslim riots of 1915 were the first of its [*sic*] kind. Moreover, such intense and widespread violence between Sinhala-Buddhists and Muslims has not been witnessed since.[53]

Notably, the riots were preceded by an attempt by the British colonial administration to regulate the 'noise' associated with many Buddhist rituals, including the beating of 'tom-tom' drums, a regular feature of many of these rituals. Section 96 of the Police Ordinance of 1865 prohibited the beating of tom-toms without a licence, with a punishment for breach of up to three months' imprisonment.[54] Citing Roberts, Wettimuny observes that there were at least 14 incidents between Sinhala-Buddhists and Muslims involving 'noise worship' that occurred between 1899 and 1915, culminating in the riots of 1915.[55] The prosecutorial choices after this event showed that the religious penal clauses tended not to be employed to sanction religious violence even during British rule. This could be because, as Jayawardene notes, that the 1915 riots were not entirely driven by religious factors but as part of a broader anti-colonial movement. By this period, political agitation against British colonial rule had gained significant traction in the preceding years. She contends that the working class (including railway workers who had organised a major strike in 1912) led the rioting in Colombo, capitalising on the outbreak of violence in Kandy to agitate for their political ends.[56]

For incidents that did not involve widespread violence, however, the religious penal clauses still served the purpose of sanctioning inappropriate behaviour towards other religious groups. In *Sevvanthinathan v Nagalingam*, the court had to decide whether the accused had defiled a Saivite temple by entering the flagstaff 'madapam' of the temple, thus breaching section 290 (defilement of a place of worship), as well as section 292 (wounding religious feelings) of the Penal Code.[57] A private prosecution was filed by the petitioner on the basis that the accused had defiled the Saivite temple, aware that the Vellala and other high castes would consider the intrusion of minority caste members into the inner courtyard of the temple an insult to their religion.[58] The magistrate found

[53] ibid.
[54] ibid.
[55] ibid.
[56] Jayawardene, 'Economic and Political Factors' (n 18).
[57] *Sevvanthinathan v Nagalingam* (1960) 69 NLR 419.
[58] See the discussion of this case in Jayantha de Almeida Guneratne, Kishali Pinto-Jayawardena and Gehan Gunatilleke, *The Judicial Mind in Sri Lanka: Responding to the Protection of Minority Rights* (Law & Society Trust, 2014) 141–46.

that while there had been trespassing, there was no defilement in terms of the Penal Code. The magistrate also held that the accused were denied their right to worship at the temple. On appeal, the Supreme Court held that there was no evidence to suggest any intention to insult the Saivite religion, or knowledge that the accuseds' entry into the inner courtyard constituted defilement of the temple.[59] At the same time, the Court also disagreed with the magistrate that there was a denial of the accuseds' right to worship. Implicit in the Court's judgment is support for the caste system by acknowledging that the accused did not have a right to worship in the inner courtyard, which was reserved for the Vellala and other high castes.

In another case, *Sri Mudali v Sabastian*, the court had to decide if a person who scribbled indecent and insulting pictures and words in charcoal on the wall of a mosque had committed an offence of defiling a place of worship under section 290.[60] The court found that the act fell short of the offence. To the court, defilement entailed more: it involved the doing of some act that would impair the sacredness of the building. The facts of this case may have fallen more easily within the scope of section 290A, which is more extensive in its application.[61]

On the offence of disturbing a religious assembly, there is at least one case. In *Sub-Inspector of Police, Bentota v Zoysa*, the Court held that religious worship or a religious ceremony should have been in progress at the time of intervention by the accused. Two Buddhist monks were in procession on the way to conduct a religious (*pirith*) ceremony at a private house. They were escorted by a person blowing a horn, four tom-tom beaters, and two others carrying relics and books. The accused intervened by physically attacking the horn blower, and broke up the procession. While the musicians fled, the priests and the others proceeded to the house. The accused then visited the house and prevented the religious ceremony from taking place. On appeal, the Supreme Court held that for a conviction to be entered under this section of the Penal Code, the accused should have intervened in a 'religious ceremony'. The procession did not amount to a religious ceremony and therefore there was no offence under this section. The acts of the accused in preventing the ceremony from taking place also did not constitute an offence under this section.[62] While the accused may have been guilty of other offences, he was not guilty of an offence under section 291 of the Penal Code. As a result the conviction was set aside.[63]

[59] *Sevvanthinathan* (n 57) 421: 'Having listened to the exhaustive arguments of counsel for both parties before me and having examined with care the evidence adduced by the petitioner and the expert before the learned Magistrate, I find myself unable to say with any confidence that the latter's finding that the prosecution failed to establish a defilement of the temple is unsupportable.'

[60] *Sri Mudali v Sabastian* [1898] 4 Bal Rep 133.

[61] Penal Code, s 290A: 'Whoever does any act, in or upon, or in the vicinity of, any place of worship or any object which is held sacred or in veneration by any class of persons, with the intention of wounding the religious feelings of any class of persons or with the knowledge that any class of persons is likely to consider such act as an insult to their religion, shall be punished with imprisonment of either description for a term which may extend to one year, or with fine, or with both.'

[62] *Sub-Inspector of Police, Bentota v Zoysa* (1921) 23 NLR 125.

[63] See also *Jayatilleke v Fernando* [1891] 6 CL Rev 25.

At other times, the religious penal clauses also became a focal point for inter-religious disputes. In *Pasmore v Francisku*, the accused, who was a Buddhist, buried his Buddhist wife in a place that was allegedly reserved for those belonging to the Wesleyan Congregation.[64] There was some evidence to suggest that other Buddhists, some of whom were relatives of the accused, had been buried there previously. The court found that there was no intention to insult the Wesleyan Congregation, or that he had knowledge that they were likely to feel insulted, and therefore the act did not constitute an offence under section 292.[65]

In her examination of some recent cases involving religious violence that were decided at the level of the Magistrate's Court, Sabrina Esufally notes certain problematic features in judicial reasoning.[66] In a case decided in 2004, the Magistrate's Court had to decide if vandalising and setting fire to a 'house church' amounted to a violation of the Penal Code.[67] The group of over 75 persons were initially charged with breaching sections 140 (unlawful assembly), 419 (mischief by fire or explosive substance with intent to cause damage) and 290 (injuring or defiling a place of worship with intent to insult the religion of any class) of the Penal Code. However, in the Court's final order, the charges were reduced to sections 434 (house-trespass) and 410 (committing mischief and thereby causing damage to the amount of 50 rupees) of the Penal Code. Further, only seven persons were actually found guilty.[68] The Court was unwilling to address the question of vandalism under section 290 of the Penal Code. Esufally observes that the 'Court's conservative approach to dealing with perpetrators of religious violence establishes a dangerous precedent and invites future perpetrators to act with impunity'.[69] Again, in another case Esufally discusses, where over 500 people interfered with the proceedings of a Christian service, the magistrate warned both parties not to disturb the peace but did not impose any punishment.[70] In a third case, Esufally notes that the Magistrate's Court had issued an interim order to prevent a worshipper of the Calvary Church from engaging in religious practices in public, following objections from members of a largely Buddhist community.[71] The order was affirmed on appeal by the High Court.

Based on her reading of these cases, Esufally contends:

> Notwithstanding a legal and policy framework that guarantees the freedom of religion, it appears that the lower courts have seldom endeavoured to protect minorities from religious violence … [J]udicial decision-making rarely deploys the language of

[64] *Pasmore v Francisku* [1900] 1 Br 94.

[65] See also *Noordeen v Arunasalam* [1911] 1 Bal N of C 7; *Kanapathy v Namasivayam* [1914] 1 Bal N of C 61; *Silva v Fernando* [1925] 6 CL Rev 71.

[66] Sabrina Esufally, 'Judicial Responses to Religious Freedom: A Case Analysis' (National Christian Evangelical Alliance of Sri Lanka and Verité Research, 2015).

[67] *State v Rathnayake* [2004] Case No 96107.

[68] ibid; Esufally, 'Judicial Responses' (n 66) 8.

[69] Esufally, 'Judicial Responses' (n 66) 8.

[70] *KBNP Rupasinghe and others v KCGA Perera and others* [2004] Case No 56189/C/81.

[71] *Panadura Police Commissioner v Thriangama Arachchige Sarath Chandalal* [2004] Case No 38946.

> 'freedom of religion' or 'freedom from religious violence' when resolving disputes that involve targeted violence against minority places of worship. The lower courts' failure to recognise the religious motivation behind the violence has certain serious connotations. Such failure serves to de-link the physical aspect of the violence from its actual motivations … [O]n the one hand, the courts have only been prepared to condemn physical violence; on the other, by virtue of their silence, they have tacitly condoned the intolerance of minority religious communities.[72]

C. Laws against Religious Violence

Besides the Penal Code, there are other laws that serve to proscribe religious violence. Section 3(1) of the ICCPR Act of 2007 provides that 'No person shall propagate war or advocate national, racial or religious hatred that constitutes incitement to discrimination, hostility or violence.' The law goes on to add:

> Every person who—
>
> (a) attempts to commit;
> (b) aids or abets in the commission of; or
> (c) threatens to commit,
>
> an offence referred to in subsection (1), shall be guilty of an offence under this Act.[73]

The High Court is given jurisdiction over this offence and the Court is required to give priority to the conduct of trials under this provision.[74] Under section 3(3) of the Act, a person found guilty of the above offence shall be punished with up to 10 years' rigorous imprisonment. The law adds that 'An offence under this section shall be cognisable and non-bailable, and no person suspected or accused of such an offence shall be enlarged on bail, except by the High Court in exceptional circumstances.'[75]

The implementation of the law has been problematic. In April 2019, Shakthika Sathkumara, an award-winning Sri Lankan writer, was arrested for writing a short story and sharing it on his Facebook profile. The fictional story he shared was about life in a Buddhist temple, and it hinted at homosexuality and child sexual abuse. He was arrested on the basis that his short story was derogatory of Buddhism, and he was charged under section 3(1) of the ICCPR Act and section 291B of the Penal Code of Sri Lanka, which deals with propagating hatred and incitement of racial or religious violence.[76] Amnesty

[72] Esufally (n 66) 8.
[73] ICCPR Act of 2007, s 3(2).
[74] ibid, s 3(5).
[75] ibid s 3(4).
[76] See also 'Sri Lanka: Release award-winning writer Shakthika Sathkumara' *Pen International* (20 June 2019) at www.pen-international.org/news/sri-lanka-release-award-winning-writer-shakthika-sathkumara.

International subsequently declared him a prisoner of conscience, observing that he was detained for peacefully exercising his right to freedom of expression.[77]

In May 2020, the UN Working Group on Arbitrary detention found that Sathkumara's short story fell within the boundaries of the right to freedom of thought, conscience and religion protected by the International Covenant on Civil and Political Rights and that his detention was arbitrary.[78]

Following the Easter Sunday bombings, there was a wave of arrests using the Emergency Regulations promulgated under the Public Security Ordinance.[79] Many of those arrested were charged under either the ICCPR Act or the Prevention of Terrorism, Act No 48 of 1979 (PTA).[80] One document citing a police spokesperson notes that 2,289 persons were arrested, of whom 1,655 were granted bail.[81] It is unclear if any of the prosecutions launched under the ICCPR Act have been completed. Subsequent to the outbreak of the COVID-19 pandemic too, there have been several arrests under the ICCPR Act and the PTA, including the arrest of a prominent Muslim lawyer and a Muslim blogger.[82]

In the absence of authoritative Sri Lankan jurisprudence on these provisions, the Human Rights Commission of Sri Lanka (HRC) issued a legal analysis of section 3 and its recommendations on how the provision should be applied.[83] The HRC's analysis was based on section 20 of the International Covenant on Civil and Political Rights, on which, it argued, section 3 of the ICCPR Act was based, and an analysis of the 'The Rabat Plan of Action'.[84] The HRC

[77] 'Amnesty declares Writer Shakthika a Prisoner of Conscience' *Economy Next* (30 July 2019) at www.economy next.com/amnesty-declares-writer-shakthika-a-prisoner-of-conscience-43906/.

[78] UNHRC Working Group on Arbitrary Detention, 'Opinion No 8/2020 Concerning Delankage Sameera Shakthika Sathkumara (Sri Lanka)' (1 May 2020) UN Doc A/HRC/WGAD/2020/8 at www.ohchr.org/Documents/Issues/Detention/Opinions/Session87/A_HRC_WGAD_2020_8_Advance_Edited_Version.pdf.

[79] 'Call for Action' (n 31) 11.

[80] See also the high-profile cases of Dr Siyabdeen Shafi, a Muslim doctor who was accused soon after the Easter bombings of sterilising hundreds of Sinhalese women: 'The Dr Shafi Siyabdeen Case' *Republic Next* (undated) at www.republicnext.com/series/dr-shafi-case/; and of Abdul Raheem Masaheena, a Muslim woman who was arrested on the pretext that she was wearing a religious symbol on her kaftan: Aanya Wipulasena, 'Abuse of ICCPR Act has "Chilling Effect" on Fundamental Freedoms' *Sunday Observer* (16 June 2019) at www.sundayobserver.lk/2019/06/19/news-features/abuse-iccpr-act-has-%E2%80%98chillingeffect%E2%80%99-fundamental-freedoms.

[81] 'Call for Action' (n 31) 11.

[82] See 'Repression of Dissent in Sri Lanka Before and During curfew 1st February 2020–30th April 2020' *INFORM* (30 May 2020) at www.inform.lk/repression-of-dissent-before-during-covid19-sl/; 'Repression of Dissent in May 2020' *INFORM* (24 June 2020) at www.inform.lk/repression-of-dissent-in-may-2020/.

[83] Human Rights Commission of Sri Lanka, 'The Human Rights Commission of Sri Lanka's (HRCSL) Analysis of the Scope of Section 3 of the ICCPR Act No 55 of 2007 and Attendant Guidelines' *Sri Lanka Brief* (29 August 2019) at www.srilankabrief.org/2019/09/sri-lankas-hrcsl-provides-its-analysis-of-the-scope-of-section-3-of-the-iccpr-act-in-the-context-of-recent-abuses-of-the-act/. The HRC was set up under statute in 1996. See Mario Gomez, 'Sri Lanka's New Human Rights Commission' (1998) 20 *Human Rights Quarterly* 281.

[84] UNGA, 'Annual Report of the United Nations High Commissioner for Human Rights: Addendum – Report of the United Nations High Commissioner for Human Rights on the Expert Workshops on the Prohibition of Incitement to National, Racial or Religious Hatred' (11 January 2013)

recommended that section 3 of the ICCPR Act be interpreted in the light of the international jurisprudence on the subject and the six-part threshold test contained in the Rabat Plan of Action. It further recommended that advocacy of hatred under section 3 should not be proscribed unless it constitutes incitement to discrimination, hostility or violence that is intentional. Section 3 is also not a standalone provision and should be interpreted in the light of the right to freedom of expression contained in the Constitution.[85]

Another law that, on the face of it, addresses religious violence is section 2(1)(h) of the PTA, which provides that:

> Any person by words either spoken or intended to be read or by signs or by visible representations or otherwise causes or intends to cause commission of acts of violence or religious, racial or communal disharmony or feelings of ill-will or hostility between different communities or racial or religious groups … shall be guilty of an offence.

When the PTA was passed in 1979, it was intended to be a temporary law for the purpose of responding to the extraordinary law-and-order situation brought about by the violence of the LTTE. Over the years, it has been criticised by human rights groups for its draconian provisions, including those that accept confessions made to a police officer of a certain rank, and its failure to conform to international standards.[86] It has been used to target not only LTTE suspects but also political opponents, whether Sinhalese, Tamil or Muslim. The previous Government had indicated on several occasions that it intended to replace the PTA with a law that conforms to international norms. Despite several public proclamations and several drafts, a new law has yet to be enacted and the PTA remains in force.[87]

Again, the implementation of the PTA has been problematic. The Act has not been used to prosecute hate speech, but instead has been used to target journalists and political opponents. In 2009, Tamil journalist JS Tissainayagam was convicted under section 2(1)(h) for accusing the Sri Lankan armed forces of committing war crimes against Tamil civilians in the Eastern Province.[88] The prosecution made the argument, which was accepted by the High Court, that Tissainayagam's accusation against the predominantly Sinhalese army

UN Doc A/HRC/22/L7/Add.4 at www.ohchr.org/Documents/Issues/Opinion/SeminarRabat/Rabat_draft_outcome.pdf.

[85] Constitution of the Democratic Socialist Republic of Sri Lanka, Art 14(1)(a).

[86] See Guneratne, Pinto-Jayawardena and Gunatilleke, *The Judicial Mind* (n 58). See also Visakesa Chandrasekaram, *One Confession, Two Confessors: A Forensic Linguistic Analysis of the Confessions Submitted in the High Court Cases of Nallaratnam Singarasa and Sellapulle Mahendran* (International Centre for Ethnic Studies, 2016).

[87] See 'Promoting Reconciliation, Accountability and Human Rights in Sri Lanka' UNHCR Res 30/1 (29 September 2015) UN Doc A/HRC/30/L.29, para 12, where the Government of Sri Lanka made a commitment to repeal this law and introduce new legislation in conformity with international standards.

[88] *The Democratic Socialist Republic of Sri Lanka v JS Tissainayagam* [2008] HC 4425/2008.

of war crimes against Tamil civilians would incite the commission of acts of violence by Sinhalese readers against Tamils, or lead to racial or communal disharmony.[89] In his article, Tissainayagam had written that it 'is fairly obvious that the government is not going to offer civilians any protection. In fact it is the state security forces that are the main perpetrators of the killings.'[90] The prosecution's argument was that by accusing a Sinhalese army of committing atrocities, he had intended to incite acts of violence by Sinhalese readers against Tamils. Tissainayagam was convicted, and then pardoned by the President while serving his sentence.

Further, in 2013, the same provision was used to arrest and detain Azath Salley, a Muslim politician who criticised the Government at that time for its failure to prosecute those involved in the attack on the Dambulla Mosque.[91] Gunatilleke observes that in contrast, in June 2014, no action was taken against a Buddhist monk, the Secretary of the BBS, who promised 'the end of Muslims in Sri Lanka should harm come to even a single Sinhalese person' in a provocative speech in Aluthgama in the south of Sri Lanka.[92] The speech was followed by a pogrom in Aluthgama, which caused extensive damage to Muslim-owned property.[93]

Furthermore, in June 2019, no prosecution followed statements made by the head of one of the leading Buddhist orders in Sri Lanka:

> I will say now, don't go to these Muslim owned shops, don't consume the food they offer … I overheard some Upaasaka Ammas here speaking of how these doctors must be stoned to death. I will not say it should happen, but that is what should happen.[94]

In this case too, no action was taken either under the PTA or the ICCPR Act.[95]

D. Law Reform

In 2015, the Minister of Justice presented two bills to amend the Penal Code and the Criminal Procedure Code. One of the bills sought to introduce a new offence into the Penal Code of advocacy of religious hatred and the 'causing of or instigating acts of violence, hostility', punishable by imprisonment for up to two years. The amendment proposed was almost identical in formulation to section 2(1)(h) of the PTA, discussed in section III.C. The second bill sought

[89] See Guneratne, Pinto-Jayawardena and Gunatilleke, *The Judicial Mind* (n 58) 243–44.
[90] ibid 243.
[91] ibid 262.
[92] Gunatilleke, *The Chronic and the Acute* (n 17).
[93] Farzana Haniffa, Harini Amarasuriya, Gehan Gunatilleke and Vishakha Wijenayake, *Where Have All the Neighbours Gone? Aluthgama Riots and its Aftermath* (Law & Society Trust, 2014).
[94] 'Call for Action' (n 31) 11.
[95] See also the cases discussed in National Christian Evangelical Alliance of Sri Lanka, *Religious Freedom Violations in Sri Lanka, Phase 1* (n 17).

to amend the Code of Criminal Procedure to enable prosecutions for the new offence. Gunatilleke has argued that the introduction of a new offence prohibiting advocacy on religious or racial lines would have given the impression this advocacy was not an existing offence despite the ICCPR Act and the Penal Code, and could have resulted in perpetuating immunity because the new laws would not have had retrospective effect.[96]

In December 2015, a group of civil society organisations and human rights practitioners issued a statement requesting the Government not to proceed with the proposed amendments. This group argued that the amendments sought to introduce an overbroad restriction on the freedom of expression, which was not permissible under the Constitution and the International Covenant on Civil and Political Rights. They observed that the amendment could have a chilling effect on freedom of expression and could be used to target political opponents, as illustrated by the *Tissainayagam* case. The Government then decided not to proceed with these legal amendments.[97] The thrust of the civil society statement was that it was not the lack of an appropriate legal framework that was preventing prosecution for hate speech. It was rather the selective application or the non-implementation of existing laws that had allowed impunity and hate speech to flourish.

The UN Special Rapporteur on Freedom of Religion or Belief reinforced this point in his recent report:

> Most interlocutors who spoke with the Rapporteur pointed out that perpetrators of hate speech are not prosecuted, not because of inadequacy of existing legal framework on hate speech, however, the implementation of these legislation [*sic*] is rather poor. The lack of accountability in these incidents illustrates an absence of political will, weak implementation of rule of law, low awareness of the available legal provisions, and possibly fears of public backlash.[98]

IV. CONSTITUTIONAL IMPLICATIONS

Like many other Asian societies, Sri Lanka remains deeply divided on some fundamental aspects of the nature of the state. The place of religion in the country's constitutional structure and scheme of government lies at the centre of these divisions, with implications for the status and autonomy of religious minorities. It bears noting that Sri Lanka's first post-independence constitution did not contain a bill of rights, but instead included a section protecting minority rights. Article 29(2) of the Soulbury Constitution (the country's first

[96] See Gehan Gunatilleke, 'Hate Speech in Sri Lanka: How a New Ban Could Perpetuate Impunity' *Oxford Human Rights Hub Blog* (11 January 2016) at www.ohrh.law.ox.ac.uk/hate-speech-in-sri-lanka-how-a-new-ban-couldper petuate-impunity.

[97] 'Joint Civil Society Statement on Amendment to Penal Code Criminalising Hate Speech' *Sri Lanka Brief* (15 December 2015) at www.srilankabrief.org/2015/12/joint-civil-society-statement-on-amendment-to-penal-code criminalizing-hate-speech/.

[98] UN OHCHR 'Report of the UN Special Rapporteur' (n 21) para 68.

post-independence constitution) restrained Parliament from making laws that would:

> (a) Prohibit or restrict the free exercise of any religion; or
> (b) Make persons of any community or religion liable to disabilities or restrictions to which persons of other communities or religions are not made liable; or
> (c) Confer on persons of any community or religion any privilege or advantage which is not conferred on persons of other communities or religions; or
> (d) Alter the constitution of any religious body except with the consent of the governing authority of that body; provided that in any case where a religious body is incorporated by law, no such alteration shall be made except on the express request of such body.[99]

In *Bribery Commissioner v Ranasinghe*, Lord Pearce of the Privy Council made the well-known comment that Article 29 represented 'the solemn balance of rights between citizens of Ceylon, the fundamental condition on which *inter se* they accepted the Constitution and these are unalterable under the Constitution'.[100]

Article 29(2) had its share of critics. Some argued that the provision did not go far enough in protecting religious freedom and that Sri Lanka required a comprehensive bill of rights. Others from the Sinhala-Buddhist end of the spectrum wanted the historical grievances against Buddhism to be addressed by the new constitution, and stronger provisions protecting Buddhism to be entrenched in the constitution. For example, the Ceylon National Congress, the All Ceylon Tamil Congress and the Communist Party of Ceylon called for greater protections and the adoption of a comprehensive bill of rights. The All Ceylon Buddhist Congress, on the other hand, said that Article 29 did not address the historical injustices that Buddhism had to endure under colonialism, and called for the greater protection of Buddhism.[101] Even though DS Senanayake, who was to become the first Prime Minister of independent Ceylon, favoured the inclusion of a bill of rights, constitutional architect Ivor Jennings had his way, and Ceylon did not get a bill of rights at independence.[102] The views of Jennings on the value and impact of a bill of rights are reflected in a later piece of writing:

> In Britain we have no Bill of Rights; we merely have liberty according to law, and we think – truly, I believe – that we do the job better than any country which has a Bill of Rights or a Declaration of the Rights of Man.[103]

[99] Constitution of the Dominion of Ceylon 1947, Art 29(2). Cooray, citing Jennings, suggests that this provision was modelled on s 5 of the Government of Ireland Act of 1920. See Joseph AL Cooray, *Constitutional and Administrative Law of Sri Lanka (Ceylon)* (Hansa Publishers, 1973) 509.

[100] *Bribery Commissioner v Ranasinghe* (1964) 66 NLR 73. For a discussion of this and related case law, see H. L. de Silva, 'Pluralism and the Judiciary in Sri Lanka' in Neelan Tiruchelvam and Radhika Coomaraswamy (eds), *The Role of the Judiciary in Plural Societies* (Frances Pinter, 1987) 87.

[101] See Benjamin Schonthal and Asanga Welikala, 'Buddhism and Regulation of Religion in the New Constitution: Past Debates, Present Challenges and Future Options' (2016) *Centre for Policy Alternatives Working Paper No 3*, 4; Rohan Edrisinha, Mario Gomez, VT Thamilmaran and Asanga Welikala, *Power-Sharing in Sri Lanka: Constitutional and Political Documents, 1926–2008* (Berghof Foundation for Conflict Studies & Centre for Policy Alternatives, 2008).

[102] Cooray, *Constitutional and Administrative Law* (n 99) 508–10.

[103] Ivor Jennings, *The Approach to Self-Government* (Cambridge University Press, 1956), cited in Cooray, *Constitutional and Administrative Law* (n 98) 509.

Jennings was to later regret his decision. In a talk over the British Broadcasting Corporation's Overseas Service in 1961, he stated that a bill of rights would have been desirable for a society like Ceylon. He noted, 'If I knew then, as much about the problems of Ceylon, as I do now, some of the provisions would have been different.'[104]

In the 1950s, a Joint Select Committee of Parliament proposed the adoption of a comprehensive bill of rights including dedicated provisions on freedom of religion, modelled largely on the Indian Constitution.[105] This was followed by a 'Buddha Sasana Commission' that recommended stronger institutional safeguards for Buddhism.[106] The assassination of Prime Minister Bandaranaike in September 1959 halted both these processes, even though the issues continued to be debated throughout the 1960s and 1970s.[107] Since then, Sri Lanka has had two Constitutions, first in 1972 and then in 1978. The current Constitution, adopted in 1978, has been amended 19 times. The 13th Amendment in 1987, which introduced a semi-federal system, and the 19th Amendment, adopted in May 2015, which made important changes to the scheme of constitutional government and reduced the power of the executive, are among the most significant.[108]

A bill of rights was finally included for the first time in the 1972 Constitution, but because there was no mention of specific remedies for violations, only one case was litigated under its provisions. The Constitutional Court that functioned for a brief period under the 1972 Constitution issued several pronouncements on the constitutional validity of bills, including on freedom of religion and belief.[109] A stronger bill of rights and explicit remedies for its enforcement were included in the current Second Republican Constitution of 1978.

Among the constitutional guarantees is Article 10, which protects freedom of thought, conscience and belief and the freedom to have or adopt a religion or

[104] Cooray, *Constitutional and Administrative Law* (n 98) 509.

[105] Schonthal and Welikala, 'Buddhism and Regulation of Religion' (n 101).

[106] ibid.

[107] See Shah, *Constitutions, Religions and Politics in Asia* (n 17) for detailed treatment of the constitutional drafting process, including the events leading up to the inclusion of the Buddhism clause in the 1972 Constitution and then again in an expanded form in the 1978 Constitution. See also Nihal Jayawickreme, 'Reflections on the Making and Content of the 1972 Constitution: An Insider's Perspective' in Asanga Welikala (ed), *The Sri Lankan Republic at 40: Reflections on Constitutional History, Theory and Practice* (Centre for Policy Alternatives, 2012) 44; Schonthal and Welikala, 'Buddhism and Regulation of Religion' (n 101).

[108] See Gomez, *Constitutional Change* (n 15) for a discussion of the impact of the 19th Amendment to the Constitution.

[109] See, eg, the opinions of the Constitutional Court on the 'The Places and Objects of Worship Bill' in *Decisions of the Constitutional Court of Sri Lanka*, vol 1 (Colombo, undated) 27, and on 'The Church of Sri Lanka (Consequential Provisions) Bill' in *Decisions of the Constitutional Court of Sri Lanka*, vol 3 (Colombo, undated) 7. The Constitutional Court does not exist under the current Constitution. The Constitutional Court was created by the 1972 Constitution to review the constitutionality of bills. The Supreme Court took on this role when the new Constitution was enacted in 1978.

belief. It is an entrenched provision and cannot be restricted. In *Premalal Perera v Weerasuriya*, the Supreme Court observed:

> Beliefs rooted in religion are protected. A religious belief need not be logical, acceptable, consistent, or comprehensible in order to be protected ... the courts are not arbiters of scriptural interpretation and should not undertake to dissect religious beliefs.[110]

This is reinforced by Article 14(1)(e), which protects the right to manifest religion or belief in worship, observance, practice and teaching, and which can be restricted on the grounds prescribed in Article 15.[111] Unlike Article 10, the rights contained in Article 14(1)(e) can be restricted on the grounds of national security, public order and the protection of public health or morality, or for the purpose of securing due recognition and respect for the rights and freedom of others, or of meeting the just requirements of the general welfare of a democratic society.

Besides Articles 10 and 14, Article 12 provides protection for religious groups, guaranteeing that no citizen shall be discriminated against on the grounds of race, religion, language, caste, sex, political opinion, place of birth or any such grounds; and Article 12(3) prevents persons, on the grounds of religion, being subject to any disability, liability, restriction, or condition with regard to accessing places of worship of their own religion.

The Directive Principles of State Policy contained in Article 27(5) provides that the 'state shall strengthen national unity by promoting cooperation and mutual confidence among all sections of the People of Sri Lanka, including the racial, religious, linguistic and other groups', and in Article 27(6) requires that the state 'ensure equality of opportunity to citizens, so that no citizen shall suffer any disability on the ground of race, religion, language, caste, sex, political opinion or occupation'.

Despite constitutional guarantees, religious minorities have often found their rights severely limited. This stems partly from constitutional design. At the same time that the 1972 Constitution included a bill of rights, it also strengthened protections for Buddhism in response to longstanding demands from Sinhala-Buddhist groups. In the 1972 Constitution, Buddhism was given explicit privileged status for the first time, and it has retained this privileged position in the current Constitution, which states:

> The Republic of Sri Lanka shall give to Buddhism the foremost place and accordingly it shall be the duty of the State to protect and foster the Buddha Sasana, while assuring to all religions the rights granted by Articles 10 and 14(1)(e).[112]

[110] *Premalal Perera v Weerasuriya* [1985] 2 Sri LR 177.
[111] See Wickremeratne, 'Fundamental Rights' (n 37).
[112] Constitution of the Democratic Socialist Republic of Sri Lanka, Art 9.

In her assessment of the events leading up to the adoption of the Buddhism clause in the 1972 Constitution, Shah observes:

> It is important to note that Colvin De Silva (who led the drafting process in 1972) could have opted to concede to the demands of those who demanded a stronger assertion for Buddhism ... there were, for example, demands to constitutionalise the requirement for the President and Prime Minister to be Buddhists.[113] Right-wing elements in the SLFP and several Buddhist organisations like the ACBC also demanded that Buddhism be made the state religion.[114] Instead, he strongly rejected these, arguing that no such protection was needed in a country where 74% of the population are Buddhists. Alternatively, he could have yielded to calls for a secular state (in fact, it was what he would have preferred) along the lines argued by Mr Dharmalingam and the Federal Party. He also rejected this proposal, owing to on-the-ground support for Buddhist protections and the majority sentiments in the popularly-elected Assembly. In a public speech in 1987, De Silva argued that the provision on Buddhism should be seen as a compromise of sorts between secularism and Buddhist majoritarianism. That the provision did not explicitly make Buddhism the state religion, according to De Silva, was in and of itself significant.[115]

It bears noting that despite Article 9, at least two opinions from the Supreme Court of Sri Lanka have adverted to the fact that Sri Lanka is a secular state.[116] In the Kapuwatta Mosque case for example, where a mosque was denied a loudspeaker permit to broadcast prayers, Chief Justice Sarath Silva stated:

> It has to be firmly born [*sic*] in mind that Sri Lanka is a secular State. In terms of Article 3 of the Constitution, Sovereignty is in the People at common [*sic*] devoid of any divisions based on perceptions of race, religion, language and the like. Especially in the area of preserving the environment and the protection of public health, being of immediate concern in this case, there could be no exceptions to accommodate perceived religious propensities of one group or another. No religion advocates a practice that would cause harm to another or worse still as would cause pollution of the environment, a health hazard or a public nuisance being an annoyance to the public.[117]

The case dealt with a dispute between the trustees of two mosques in the southern town of Weligama, and the refusal of the police officer in the area to issue a permit to one of the mosques to broadcast prayers, as it had previously done. The issue in the case related to the right of the trustees of the mosque to manifest their religion through amplified sound and the rights of the citizens living

[113] Colvin R De Silva, *Safeguards for the Minorities in the 1972 Constitution* (Young Socialist Publication, 1987) 11.

[114] Wickremeratne, 'Fundamental Rights' (n 37) 768.

[115] De Silva, *Safeguards* (n 113) 10–12; Shah, *Constitutions, Religions and Politics in Asia* (n 17) 50–51.

[116] See *Determination of the Supreme Court on the 19th Amendment to the Constitution* (Supreme Court Determination No 32/2004) and the 'Kapuwatta Mosque Case': *Ashik v Bandula* [2007] 1 Sri LR 191.

[117] *Ashik v Bandula* [2007] 1 Sri LR 191. See Schonthal, 'Environments of Law' (n 17) for a detailed analysis of this case.

in the vicinity to be protected from the harmful effects of noise pollution. The Supreme Court held that the broadcast of prayers amounted to a public nuisance in terms of section 261 of the Penal Code and issued a prohibition on the use of loudspeakers between 10 at night and 6 in the morning. The Supreme Court also referred to a previous judgment of the Court in 1895, where the Court had held that 'no religious body, whether Buddhist, or Protestant, or Catholic, is entitled to commit a public nuisance'.[118] In the older case, a trustee of a Buddhist temple was charged with creating noise at night and disturbing the residents in the vicinity.[119]

After Buddhism was explicitly privileged in the 1972 Constitution, some Buddhist groups and individuals used the clause in the Constitution on a regular basis to secure a privileged position for Buddhism through constitutional litigation. Other Buddhist groups sought to curtail state involvement in monastic life and to plead for greater monastic autonomy.[120] Schonthal reflects on this wide use of the law and litigation to protect Buddhist rights in Sri Lanka, and observes that this has not occurred in other Buddhist majority countries like Cambodia, Myanmar and Thailand. He argues that both the strong protection afforded to Buddhism in the Constitution coupled with the wide availability of public law remedies and a vibrant public law culture have resulted in a variety of organisations and individuals using the courts regularly to vindicate the privileged position of Buddhism.[121]

A. The *Gnanasara Thero Case*

Coming back to the case mentioned in the introduction to this chapter, the Venerable Galagoda Aththe Gnanasara Thero was a leading member of the BBS, a radical Sinhala-Buddhist nationalist organisation. He was well known for his anti-Muslim sentiments and his previous encounters with law enforcement officers, though none of them had attracted sanctions. Some commentators link his statements to the anti-Muslim violence that took place in Aluthgama in southern Sri Lanka in June 2014.[122] Although there had been some previous convictions of Buddhist monks, including one for the killing of a Prime Minister in the 1950s, this was the first conviction of a high-profile monk for his strong Sinhala-Buddhist nationalist views in recent times.

[118] *Marshall v Gunaratne Unnanse* (1895) 1 NLR 179.

[119] ibid.

[120] For a discussion of how the state intervenes in Buddhist monastic life, see Benjamin Schonthal, 'Securing the Sasana through Law: Buddhist Constitutionalism and Buddhist Interest-Litigation in Sri Lanka' (2016) 50(6) *Modern Asian Studies* 1966. See also Shah, *Constitutions, Religions and Politics in Asia* (n 17); Schonthal and Welikala, 'Buddhism and Regulation of Religion' (n 100).

[121] Schonthal, 'Securing the Sasana' (n 120).

[122] See Gunatilleke, *The Chronic and the Acute* (n 17).

Gnanasara Thero was convicted over a 2016 incident in which he interrupted a court hearing against military intelligence officials accused of involvement in the 2010 abduction and disappearance of journalist and cartoonist Prageeth Ekneligoda. During the hearing, Gnanasara Thero shouted at the judge and lawyers when the military officials were not given bail, and threatened Sandya Ekneligoda, Prageeth's wife, who had long campaigned to find out what happened to her husband, whose cartoons had lampooned the former President Mahinda Rajapakse.[123] In delivering the judgment, the President of the Court of Appeal said that Gnanasara Thero had 'intentionally committed the offence to undermine the judiciary', and found him guilty of all charges.[124] The Supreme Court affirmed his conviction in September 2018. Protests for his release by Buddhist monks and others, however, continued on a regular basis. Prior to that, the Magistrate's Court had held that Gnanasara Thero used abusive language and insulted Sandya Ekneligoda. In May 2019, the monk was released by way of a presidential pardon.

B. *Manjula v Pushpakumara*

The *Gnanasara Case* followed another Supreme Court decision that held that the detention of two Jehovah's Witnesses was illegal.[125] The petitioners were arrested on suspicion of the offences of 'criminal trespass' and 'criminal intimidation'. The Supreme Court found that both criminal intimidation and criminal trespass were not established, and therefore the arrests were unconstitutional under Article 13(1) of the Constitution, which states that 'No person shall be arrested except according to procedure established by law. Any person arrested shall be informed of the reason for his arrest.'

The Court also held that the police officers had acted arbitrarily, unfairly and unlawfully, and therefore had violated the petitioners' right to equal protection under the law.[126] However, the Court was not willing to hold that there had been a violation of the petitioners' right under Article 14(1)(e) to manifest their religion in worship, observance, practice or teaching. House-to-house visits to evangelise and the discussions that ensued, the Court found, did not fall within the meaning of Article 14(1)(e) of the Constitution. The Court further observed that there was no constitutional right to propagate one's religion.[127]

The case is also interesting for the connection between fundamental rights and the Penal Code. The police sought to justify the arrests on the basis that

[123] 'Court finds Gnanasara Thero guilty' (n 46).
[124] 'Sri Lankan Buddhist Monk Sentenced' (n 3).
[125] *Manjula v Pushpakumara*, SC FR 241/14 (Supreme Court, Minutes of 18 July 2018).
[126] Constitution of the Democratic Socialist Republic of Sri Lanka, Art 12(1).
[127] See also *Ashik* (n 117); Schonthal and Welikala, 'Buddhism and Regulation of Religion' (n 101) for discussion of some of the other constitutional litigation.

there had been a violation of the Penal Code. However, the Court found that there was no infringement of the sections of the Penal Code on 'criminal intimidation' or 'criminal trespass', and therefore the arrests were unlawful.

An earlier case involved protests by residents against the construction of a mosque in a suburb of Colombo. Residents, including some members of the Buddhist clergy, alleged that the board of trustees of the mosque had obtained permission from the local authority for the construction of a school, but what they in fact had proceeded to construct was a mosque. The local authority suspended the construction as a result of these protests, and the trustees of the mosque lodged a fundamental rights application alleging violations of Article 10, Article 12(1) and (2), and Article 14(1)(e). The Supreme Court observed that the local authority had acted legitimately in suspending construction of the building in order to avert a breach of peace in the area. The Court also held that approval had not been obtained from the Ministry of Religious Affairs for the construction of the school.[128] The case is important also because it challenged the legality of a circular published by the then Ministry of Buddha Sasana and Religious Affairs that required prior approval for the construction of new places of worship. In this case Supreme Court upheld the legality of circular. The Special Rapporteur on Freedom of Religion or Belief observes, however:

> Law enforcement and local Government officials allegedly use the Circular to discriminate against religious minority groups and curtail their right to worship. It is also used retroactively to close non-mainline churches. Since 2015, at least 57 Protestant Christian churches have been instructed to obtain registration. Evangelical Christian churches in particular continue to report pressure and harassment by local authorities to close down places of worship because they were not registered, their prayer meetings and worship activities are also routinely denied permission to take place. Moreover, intimidation and attacks against clergy and church members; desecration of Evangelical churches and interference with religious activities are also perpetrated by local villagers and Buddhist monks.[129]

In an older case, a private member's bill was challenged under Article 121 of the Constitution, where the petitioner argued that certain clauses in the bill violated the Constitution, including Articles 9 and 10.[130] In that case, the Supreme Court held that the Constitution did not contain a right to propagate one's religion. Although it was permissible for a person to manifest his or her religion, propagation of a religion would not be permissible as the Constitution does not contain such a guarantee.[131]

[128] *Faril, President of the Board of Trustees Wekada Jumma Mosque v Bandaragama Pradeshiya Sabha*, SC FR Application No 92/2016 (Supreme Court, Minutes of 28 June 2017).

[129] UN OHCHR 'Report of the UN Special Rapporteur' (n 21) para 36.

[130] *Provincial of the Teaching Sisters of the Holy Cross of the Third Order of Saint Francis in Menzingen of Sri Lanka (Incorporated), In the Matter of a Petition under Article 121 of the Constitution* (Supreme Court Special Determination No 19/2003).

[131] ibid. See Shah, *Constitutions, Religions and Politics in Asia* (n 17) 143–47 for discussion of the case.

V. CONCLUSION

Despite legal provisions on 'religious offences' in the Penal Code and in other legislation, such as the Police Ordinance and the ICCPR Act, little has been done to enforce these laws in cases of religious violence. There has been a lack of political will to implement existing laws, and an inability on the part of law enforcement officers to quell religious violence. The privileged position accorded to Buddhism has not remained a mere constitutional value; it is part of the lived social and political reality of Sri Lanka. The 'politics of Buddhism' and the privileged position accorded to the Buddhist clergy, even to those involved in orchestrating violence or hate speech, have diluted the rule of law and provided impunity to perpetrators of religious violence.

On the other hand, there has been a plethora of cases initiated by Buddhist organisations and individuals since the early 1970s that have sought to vindicate the privileged position of Buddhism in the Constitution.[132] At the same time, those who have been at the receiving end of unfair state action, have used the fundamental rights jurisdiction in an endeavour to protect their rights to freedom of religion or belief, or their right to manifest such a freedom, with some degree of success.

Sri Lanka's attempt to use the law to respond to religious violence has largely been a failure. While there were some prosecutions after the 1915 anti-Muslim riots, the penal law and other laws have only been used sporadically to respond to inter-religious tensions and violence. This must be contrasted with Malaysia and Singapore, where there has been a larger commitment on the part of the state to control religious violence. In Sri Lanka, the silence of the law has promoted a culture of impunity and allowed radical actors to flourish and engage in hate speech and acts of intimidation and violence. Radical actors have been most active where they have received tacit support from the state. The current legal framework does enable prosecution in cases of hate speech, acts of defilement of places of worship and other religious offences. Yet the case law suggests that these legal provisions have been seldom used, despite an escalating and tense environment. In recent years, as we have seen, where they have been used, they have been used selectively, to target religious minorities.

Sri Lanka is also an example of the failure of law enforcement. Law enforcement officers who have acted impartially during presidential and parliamentary elections, and facilitated peaceful political transitions, have been unwilling to exercise their writ at moments of religious violence. At times, they have been instigators and participants.

[132] See Schonthal, 'Securing the Sasana' (n 120); Shah, *Constitutions, Religions and Politics in Asia* (n 17); Schonthal and Welikala, 'Buddhism and Regulation of Religion' (n 101).

Law enforcement officers have unfortunately not been animated by the values contained in the recent judgment of the Supreme Court in *Manjula*:

> The police officers were probably motivated by a desire to prevent disharmony in their community and, even perhaps, a desire to protect their own religion from what they saw as incursions of another faith. Those motives are human traits and are understandable. However, police officers must act lawfully and also act respectfully of the rights of all persons in the country including persons who profess different beliefs or who are different in some other way, even where those different beliefs or ways are distasteful to the police officers. Zealotry and harassment in its cause by police officers, are not to be countenanced.[133]

A wide range of Sinhala-Buddhist actors have used the Constitution and the law since the early 1970s to advance their interests and to argue for enhanced protection for Buddhism in line with the constitutional provision on Buddhism in both the 1972 and 1978 Constitutions. The responses of the Supreme Court have been mixed, with some judicial decisions advancing Sinhala-Buddhist interests, while others have adopted a more cautionary approach and even held that Sri Lanka is a secular state. These cases have also highlighted divisions among Sinhala-Buddhist groups and among the clergy, with some favouring less state control over monastic life and others looking at closer control over the clergy.

It is in constitutional litigation before the Supreme Court (and occasionally in writs before the Court of Appeal) that the contests over religion have mainly been fought. Those who feel they have not had the protection of the state in cases of religious violence have resorted to fundamental rights litigation to seek redress.[134] Others who have feared a dilution of the place accorded to Buddhism have challenged provisions in proposed legislation on the basis that they conflict with constitutional provisions.

The inability of the law and law enforcement to act evenly in protecting Tamils, Muslims and Christians from ethno-religious violence illustrates the deep divisions that continue to pervade Sri Lankan society over 10 years after the end of the war and 70 years since independence. It illustrates the point that it is politics, mobilisation around religion and fear of a public backlash, that drives law enforcement in situations of ethno-religious violence. The fissures have widened following the Easter bombings in April 2019. On the other hand, the 19th Amendment to the Constitution, passed in 2015, has enabled the courts to act independently, and has fostered a more tolerant constitutional culture. Recent judgments from the Supreme Court, which suggest a more balanced approach, offer a glimmer of hope.

Sri Lanka will struggle to manage its deep social divisions and rein in violence. Yet it is important that these divisions are managed within the framework of the Constitution and the law if the country is to move to a safer and more inclusive space that respects and promotes ethnic and religious diversity.

[133] *Manjula* (n 125) 24–25 (Prasanna Jayawardena J).
[134] Constitution of the Democratic Socialist Republic of Sri Lanka, Arts 17 and 126.

The constitutional crisis of 2018 reflected these deep divisions and is due, at least in part, to differences on the place and role of Buddhism, the role of the President, divisions around the need for constitutional reform and social polarisation on the need to deal with Sri Lanka's violent past.

Tolerant political elites could create conditions that would enable legal institutions to act in a bold and principled way, foster diversity and protect religious liberties. This has been one of the lessons of the political culture that emerged during 2015 and 2019. Tolerant political elites could also provide clear directions to law enforcement officers in cases of ethno-religious violence, to ensure that violence against ethno-religious groups is prevented and, where it occurs, prosecuted immediately. Despite deep divisions, a combination of tolerant political elites, bold legal institutions and principled law enforcement could help manage the country's divisions and effectively respond to the violence of radical actors and violent extremism within a framework of the Constitution and the law.

BIBLIOGRAPHY

—— *Ashik v Bandula* [2007] 1 Sri LR 191

—— *Bribery Commissioner v Ranasinghe* (1964) 66 NLR 73

—— 'Call for Action: Mapping Anti-Muslim Attacks in Sri Lanka' (August 2019), on file with the author

—— *Cokeman v Attorney General*, SC (FR) 136/2014 (Supreme Court, Minutes of 15 November 2017)

—— Constitution of the Democratic Socialist Republic of Sri Lanka, Arts 9, 10, 12(1), 14(1)(a), 15, 16, 17, 105(3), 121, 126

—— Constitution of the Dominion of Ceylon 1947, Art 29(2)

—— *Determination of the Supreme Court on the 19th Amendment to the Constitution* (Supreme Court Determination No 32/2004)

—— *Faril, President of the Board of Trustees Wekada Jumma Mosque v Bandaragama Pradeshiya Sabha*, SC FR Application No 92/2016 (Supreme Court, Minutes of 28 June 2017)

—— Human Rights Commission of Sri Lanka, 'The Human Rights Commission of Sri Lanka's (HRCSL) Analysis of the Scope of Section 3 of the ICCPR Act No 55 of 2007 and Attendant Guidelines' *Sri Lanka Brief* (29 August 2019) at www.srilankabrief.org/2019/09/sri-lankas-hrcsl-provides-its-analysis-of-the-scope-of-section-3-of-the-iccpr-act-in-the-context-of-recent-abuses-of-the-act/

—— *In re Galagoda Aththe Gnanasara* (Court of Appeal, 8 August 2018)

—— International Covenant on Civil and Political Rights Act 2007, ss 3(1), 3(2), 3(4), 3(5)

—— Interview with National Christian Evangelical Alliance lawyer (on file with the author)

—— *Jayatilleke v Fernando* [1891] 6 CL Rev 25

—— *Kanapathy v Namasivayam* [1914] 1 Bal N of C 61

—— *KBNP Rupasinghe and others v KCGA Perera and others* [2004] Case No 56189/C/81

—— *Manjula v Pushpakumara*, SC FR 241/14 (Supreme Court, Minutes of 18 July 2018), 24–25

—— *Marshall v Gunaratne Unnanse* (1895) 1 NLR 179
—— *Noordeen v Arunasalam* [1911] 1 Bal N of C 7
—— *Panadura Police Commissioner v Thriangama Arachchige Sarath Chandalal* [2004] Case No 38946
—— *Pasmore v Francisku* [1900] 1 Br 94
—— Penal Code, ss 290, 290A, 291A, 291B and 292
—— *Premalal Perera v Weerasuriya* [1985] 2 Sri LR 177
—— 'Promoting Reconciliation, Accountability and Human Rights in Sri Lanka' UNHCR Res 30/1 (29 September 2015) UN Doc A/HRC/30/L.29, para 12
—— *Provincial of the Teaching Sisters of the Holy Cross of the Third Order of Saint Francis in Menzingen of Sri Lanka (Incorporated), In the Matter of a Petition under Article 121 of the Constitution* (Supreme Court Special Determination No 19/2003)
—— Right to Information Act (No 12 of 2016)
—— *Sarath Lakshman v Premawathie* [2012] Case No 15/2009
—— *Sevvanthinathan v Nagalingam* (1960) 69 NLR 419, 421
—— *Silva v Fernando* [1925] 6 CL Rev 71
—— *Sisira Kumar v Jayantha Wickramaratne* (Supreme Court, Minutes of 5 November 2015)
—— *Sri Mudali v Sabastian* [1898] 4 Bal Rep 133
—— *State v Rathnayake* [2004] Case No 96107
—— *Sub-Inspector of Police, Bentota v Zoysa* (1921) 23 NLR 125.
—— *The Democratic Socialist Republic of Sri Lanka v JS Tissainayagam* [2008] HC 4425/2008
—— 'The Church of Sri Lanka (Consequential Provisions) Bill' in *Decisions of the Constitutional Court of Sri Lanka*, vol 3 (Colombo, undated) 7
—— 'The Places and Objects of Worship Bill' in *Decisions of the Constitutional Court of Sri Lanka*, vol 1 (Colombo, undated) 27
—— UNGA, 'Annual Report of the United Nations High Commissioner for Human Rights: Addendum – Report of the United Nations High Commissioner for Human Rights on the Expert Workshops on the Prohibition of Incitement to National, Racial or Religious Hatred' (11 January 2013) UN Doc A/HRC/22/L7/Add.4, at www.ohchr.org/Documents/Issues/Opinion/Seminar Rabat/Rabat_draft_outcome.pdf
—— UN OHCHR, 'Report of the UN Special Rapporteur on Freedom of Religion or Belief, Dr Ahmed Shaheed, to the Human Rights Council, following a country visit to Sri Lanka in August 2019' (28 February 2020) UN Doc A/HRC/43/48/Add.2, at www.ohchr.org/EN/Issues/Freedom Religion/Pages/Visits.aspx, paras 36, 48, 68, 90
—— UNHRC Working Group on Arbitrary Detention, 'Opinion No. 8/2020 Concerning Delankage Sameera Shakthika Sathkumara (Sri Lanka)' (1 May 2020) UN Doc A/HRC/WGAD/2020/8 at www.ohchr.org/Documents/Issues/Detention/Opinions/Session87/A_HRC_WGAD_2020_8_Advance_Edited_Version.pdf
Ali, A, 'Four Waves of Muslim-Phobia in Sri Lanka: c.1880–2009' (2015) 35(4) *Journal of Muslim Minority Affairs* 486
Chandrasekaram, V, *One Confession, Two Confessors: A Forensic Linguistic Analysis of the Confessions Submitted in the High Court Cases of Nallaratnam Singarasa and Sellapulle Mahendran* (International Centre for Ethnic Studies, 2016)
Colombo Telegraph, 'Cabinet Nod For Muslim Marriage Law Amendments, Puts Marriageable Age At 18' (21 August 2019) at www.colombotelegraph.com/index.php/cabinet-nod-for-muslim-marriage-law-amendments-puts-marriageable-age-at-18/
Cooray, JAL, *Constitutional and Administrative Law of Sri Lanka (Ceylon)* (Hansa Publishers, 1973)

Daily FT, 'Court finds Gnanasara Thero guilty of criminal intimidation' (25 May 2018) at www.ft.lk/news/Court-finds-Gnanasara-Thero-guilty-of-criminal-intimidation/56-655906

Department of Census and Statistics Sri Lanka, 'Census of Population and Housing 2012 – Final Report' (undated) at http://www.statistics.gov.lk/PopHouSat/CPH2011/Pages/Activities/Reports/FinalReport/FinalReportE.pdf

Dep, AC, *Ceylon Police and Sinhala-Muslim Riots of 1915* (Sarvodaya Vishva Lekha, 2001)

De Silva, Colvin R, *Safeguards for the Minorities in the 1972 Constitution* (Young Socialist Publication, 1987)

De Silva, HL, 'Pluralism and the Judiciary in Sri Lanka' in Neelan Tiruchelvam and Radhika Coomaraswamy (eds), *The Role of the Judiciary in Plural Societies* (Frances Pinter, 1987) 87

De Silva, KM, *Reaping the Whirlwind: Ethnic Conflict, Ethnic Politics in Sri Lanka* (Penguin Books, 2000)

Devotta, N, 'Religious Intolerance in Post-Civil War Sri Lanka' (2018) 49(2) *Asian Affairs* 278

Economy Next, 'Amnesty declares Writer Shakthika a Prisoner of Conscience' (30 July 2019) at www.economynext.com/amnesty-declares-writer-shakthika-a-prisoner-of-conscience-43906/

Edrisinha, R, Gomez, M, Thamilmaran, VT, and Welikala, A, *Power-Sharing in Sri Lanka: Constitutional and Political Documents, 1926–2008* (Centre for Policy Alternatives, 2008)

——, and Jayakody, Aruni, *The Eighteenth Amendment to the Constitution: Substance and Process* (Centre for Policy Alternatives, 2011)

Esufally, S, *Judicial Responses to Religious Freedom: A Case Analysis* (National Christian Evangelical Alliance of Sri Lanka and Verité Research, 2015)

Faslan, M, and Vanniasinkam, N, *Fracturing Community: Intra-Group Relations among the Muslims of Sri Lanka* (International Centre for Ethnic Studies, 2015)

Gomez, M, 'Constitutional Change and Institutional Resilience in Sri Lanka' in Henning Glaser (ed), *Shifting to a New Constitutionalism: Changing Political Orders in Asia* (Nomos, forthcoming 2020)

——, 'The Right to Information and Transformative Development Outcomes' (2019) *Law and Development Review* 837

——, 'The Politics of Dealing with the Past in Deeply Divided Sri Lanka' (2017) *Harvard Human Rights Journal Online Symposium on Transitional Justice* (3 October 2017) at www.ices.lk/wp-content/uploads/2017/10/TJ-Harvard-HR-3-Oct-2017.pdf

——, 'Keeping Rights Alive: Reform and Reconciliation in Post-War Sri Lanka' (2011) 17 *Asian Yearbook of International Law* 117

——, 'Sri Lanka's New Human Rights Commission' (1998) 20 *Human Rights Quarterly* 281

Goonetillke, HAI, *The April 1971 Insurrection in Ceylon: A Bibliographical Commentary* (Centre de Recherches Socio-Religieuses, Université de Louvain, 1975)

Gunatilleke, G, *The Chronic and the Entrenched: Ethno-Religious Violence in Sri Lanka* (International Centre for Ethnic Studies and Equitas, 2018)

——, 'Hate Speech in Sri Lanka: How a New Ban Could Perpetuate Impunity' *Oxford Human Rights Hub Blog* (11 January 2016) at www.ohrh.law.ox.ac.uk/hate-speech-in-sri-lanka-how-a-new-ban-could-perpetuate-impunity

——, *The Chronic and the Acute: Post-War Religious Violence in Sri Lanka* (International Centre for Ethnic Studies and Equitas, 2015)

Guneratne, J de A, Pinto-Jayawardena, K, and Gunatilleke, G, *The Judicial Mind in Sri Lanka: Responding to the Protection of Minority Rights* (Law & Society Trust, 2014)
Haniffa, F, Amarasuriya, H, Gunatilleke, G, and Wijenayake, V, *Where Have All the Neighbours Gone? Aluthgama Riots and its Aftermath* (Law & Society Trust, 2014)
——, and Nagaraj, Vijay, *Towards Recovering Histories of Anti-Muslim Violence in the Context of Sinhala-Muslim Tensions in Sri Lanka* (International Centre for Ethnic Studies, 2016)
Herath, D, and Rambukwella, H, *Self, Religion, Identity and Politics: Buddhist and Muslim Encounters in Contemporary Sri Lanka* (International Centre for Ethnic Studies, 2015)
Hoole, R, Somasundaram, D, Sritharan, KA, and Thiranagama, R, *The Broken Palmyra: The Tamil Crisis in Sri Lanka: An Inside Account* (Sri Lanka Studies Institute, 1990)
INFORM, 'Repression of Dissent in May 2020' (24 June 2020) at www.inform.lk/repression-of-dissent-in-may-2020/
——, 'Repression of Dissent in Sri Lanka Before and During curfew 1st February 2020–30th April 2020' (30 May 2020) at www.inform.lk/repression-of-dissent-before-during-covid19-sl/
International Crisis Group, *War Crimes in Sri Lanka – Asia Report No 191* (Brussels, International Crisis Group, 2010) at www.d2071andvip0wj.cloudfront.net/191-war-crimes-in-sri-lanka.pdf
Jayawardene, K, 'Economic and Political Factors in the 1915 Riots' (1970) 29(2) *The Journal of Asian Studies* 223
Jayawickreme, N, 'Reflections on the Making and Content of the 1972 Constitution: An Insider's Perspective' in Asanga Welikala (ed), *The Sri Lankan Republic at 40: Reflections on Constitutional History, Theory and Practice* (Centre for Policy Alternatives, 2012) 44
Jennings, I, *The Approach to Self-Government* (Cambridge University Press, 1956)
Mihlar, F, *Coming out of the Margins: Justice and Reconciliation for Conflict-Affected Muslims in Sri Lanka* (International Centre for Ethnic Studies, 2018)
MPLRAG, 'Muslim Personal Law Action Reforms Group (MPLRAG)' (undated) at www.mplreforms.com/
National Christian Evangelical Alliance of Sri Lanka, *Religious Freedom Violations in Sri Lanka: The Use of Right to Information Law to Assess the Response of Law Enforcement Authorities and the Judiciary, Phase 1* (National Christian Evangelical Alliance of Sri Lanka, 2020)
National Christian Evangelical Alliance of Sri Lanka, *The Role of Religion in Transitional Justice in Sri Lanka: A Faith Exploration – Right to Truth, Justice and Human Dignity* (National Christian Evangelical Alliance of Sri Lanka, 2018)
NDTV, 'Sri Lankan Buddhist Monk Sentenced Six Years' Jail In Contempt Case' (8 August 2018) at www.ndtv.com/world-news/sri-lankan-buddhist-monk-sentenced-six-years-jail-in-contempt-case-1897204
Peiris, GL, *Offences Under the Penal Code of Sri Lanka* (Stamford Lake, 1976)
Pen International, 'Sri Lanka: Release award-winning writer Shakthika Sathkumara' (20 June 2019) at www.pen-international.org/news/sri-lanka-release-award-winning-writer-shakthika-sath ku mara
Ramanathan, P, *Riots and Martial Law in Ceylon – 1915* (St Martin's Press, 1916)
Republic Next, 'The Dr Shafi Siyabdeen Case' (undated) at www.republicnext.com/series/dr-shafi-case/
Richardson, J, *Paradise Poisoned: Learning about Conflict, Terrorism and Development from Sri Lanka's Civil Wars* (International Centre for Ethnic Studies, 2005)

Roberts, M, *Exploring Confrontation: Sri Lanka – Politics, Culture and History* (Harwood Academic Publishers, 1994)

——, *Noise as Cultural Struggle: Tom-Tom Beating, the British and Communal Disturbances in Sri Lanka, 1880s – 1930s* (Studies in Society and Culture, 1993)

——, 'Hobgoblins, Low-Country Sinhalese Plotters, or Local Elite Chauvinists?: Directions and Patterns in the 1915 Communal Riots' (1981) 4 *Sri Lanka Journal of Social Sciences* 83

Schonthal, B, 'Litigating Vinaya: Buddhist Law and Public Law in Contemporary Sri Lanka' (2018) 3 *Buddhism Law & Society* 1

——, 'Securing the Sasana through Law: Buddhist Constitutionalism and Buddhist Interest-Litigation in Sri Lanka' (2016) 50(6) *Modern Asian Studies* 1966

——, 'Environments of Law: Islam, Buddhism, and the State in Contemporary Sri Lanka' (2016) 75(1) *The Journal of Asian Studies* 137

——, and Welikala, A, 'Buddhism and Regulation of Religion in the New Constitution: Past Debates, Present Challenges and Future Options' (2016) *Centre for Policy Alternatives Working Paper No 3*, 4

Shah, DAH, *Constitutions, Religions and Politics in Asia: Indonesia, Malaysia and Sri Lanka* (Cambridge University Press, 2017)

Sieghart, P, *Sri Lanka: A Mounting Tragedy of Errors – Report of a Mission on Sri Lanka in January 1984 on Behalf of the International Commission of Jurists and its British Section, JUSTICE* (International Commission of Jurists and JUSTICE, 1984)

Somaratna, GPV, *Kotahena Riot 1883: A Religious Riot in Sri Lanka* (Deepanee Printers, 1991)

Sri Lanka Brief, 'Joint Civil Society Statement on Amendment to Penal Code Criminalising Hate Speech' (15 December 2015) at www.srilankabrief.org/2015/12/joint-civil-society-statement-on-amendment-to-penal-code-criminalizing-hate-speech/

Swamy, MRN, *Tigers of Lanka: From Boys to Guerrillas* (Vijitha Yapa Publications, 2006)

The Quest for Redemption: The Story of the Northern Muslims – Final Report of the Citizens' Commission on the Expulsion of Muslims from the Northern Province by the LTTE in October 1990, 2nd edn (Colombo, Law & Society Trust, 2011) at www.lstlanka.org/wp-content/uploads/2017/12/The-Quest-for-Redemption-Book-English.pdf

US Department of State, *Report to Congress on Incidents During the Recent Conflict in Sri Lanka* (Washington DC, US Department of State, 2009) at www.reliefweb.int/sites/reliefweb.int/files/resources/4792D63B35FAD909 492576580005B2E2-Full_Report.pdf

Vithanagama, R, *Tracking Coexistence: Understanding Perceptions of the Religious 'Other'* (International Centre for Ethnic Studies, 2020)

Wettimuny, S, 'Regulating Religious Rites: Did British Regulation of "Noise Worship" Trigger the 1915 Riots in Ceylon?' (London School of Economic and Political Science, 31 March 3018) at www.blogs.lse.ac.uk/lseih/2018/03/31/regulating-religious-rites-did-british-regulation-of-noise-worship-trigger-the-1915-riots-in-ceylon/

Wickremeratne, J, 'Fundamental Rights in Sri Lanka' in Asanga Welikala (ed), *The Sri Lankan Republic at 40: Reflections on Constitutional History, Theory and Practice* (Centre for Policy Alternatives, 2012) 768

Wickramasinghe, N, *Sri Lanka in the Modern Age: A History of Contested Identities* (Hurst, 2006)

Wipulasena, A, 'Abuse of ICCPR Act has "Chilling Effect" on Fundamental Freedoms' *Sunday Observer* (16 June 2019) at www.sundayobserver.lk/2019/06/19/news-features/abuse-iccpr-act-has-%E2%80%98chillingeffect%E2%80%99-fundamental-freedoms

9

Offences against Religion in Malaysia: Navigating the 'Secular' Federal Constitution and the Salience of Islam in the Constitutional Order

DIAN AH SHAH

I. INTRODUCTION

As in most former British colonies, Malaysia's Penal Code is a colonial legacy, modelled on and transplanted – almost in its entirety – from the Indian Penal Code of 1860.[1] A set of clauses on 'offences relating to religion' number among those provisions adopted verbatim from the Indian Code. These provisions have been reshaped and redefined through subsequent amendments, as the Government sought to enhance their deterrent effect.[2]

With regard to religious offences, in particular, section 298A was introduced by an amendment to the Code in February 1983. In essence, this provision criminalises speech (either spoken or written) or actions that may be prejudicial to harmony and unity in the context of religion and religious relations. For instance, section 298A(2) specifies that if a person from a particular religion alleges that another person has ceased to profess that religion, or if he or she defies or undermines actions by a religious official and claims that those actions do not comport with the doctrines of the religion, then he or she 'shall be presumed to have contravened' the provision. The primary motivation behind the introduction of section 298A appears to rest in the protection of public order in the context of Malaysia's multi-ethnic and multi-religious social fabric and, by extension, to 'ensure the protection of religious freedom' for all citizens.[3]

[1] See generally, Ahmad Ibrahim, *Towards A History of Law in Malaysia and Singapore*, 2nd edn (Dewan Bahasa dan Pustaka, Ministry of Education Malaysia, 1992).

[2] Norbani M Nazeri, 'Criminal Law Codification and Reform in Malaysia: An Overview' (Dec 2010) *Singapore Journal of Legal Studies* 375, 384.

[3] Parliamentary Debates, Sixth Parliament, First Session, 11 January 1983 (Dato Haji Mohamed Suhaimi bin Dato Haji Kamaruddin) 2175.

This clearly links the maintaining of public order and harmony amongst different religious groups to the freedom of religion. In addition, the Government expressed concern that if there were no laws to control conduct or speech implicating religion, there would be a risk of religious discord not just among different religious groups, but also within a particular religious group in society. Part of this is reflected in section 298A(5), which prohibits a person who is not an appointed religious official (ie not appointed by the state) from performing any functions 'of a religious character'.

However, the amended provisions did not emerge in a vacuum. To understand these amendments, it is first important to appreciate the constitutional, social and political contexts that surround them. I explain these dynamics in greater detail in sections II and III of this chapter, but at this juncture, it suffices to mention that Malaysia is a Muslim-majority country and the Federal Constitution provides that Islam is the 'religion of the Federation' (Article 3). Although this provision did not change the secular character of the country (in the sense that laws and governing institutions are not derived from religious texts), nor did it trump constitutional rights guarantees (Article 3(4)), it has subsequently evolved to take on a greater significance. The role of Islam has extended beyond ceremonial uses and, in some cases, it has been invoked to determine the boundaries of constitutional rights protection. All this is linked to the political salience of religion and religious identities in the country.

In this regard, consider again section 298A(5) of the Penal Code, which was a product of the 1983 amendments. Even though it does not specifically address Islam, this provision appears to be motivated by concerns over the activities of unauthorised religious individuals who may be using their influence and position in anti-government propaganda. In addition, in a context where religion – particularly Islam – is highly regulated by the state, there has always been some disquiet about the spread of doctrines or practices that 'diverge' from the 'official' Islamic denomination (ie Sunni) endorsed by the state. What I mean by 'official' is essentially the doctrines and practices that are deemed by state religious authorities and bodies to be the correct interpretation of Islamic laws and principles. To put it in more concrete terms, the practice and teaching of Shiism is prohibited, as are other movements or organisations whose doctrines, philosophies and ideas do not conform to the state's version of Islam, such as the Qadiani, *Al-Arqam* (they were deemed to be a cult and subsequently disbanded in the 1990s) and Sisters in Islam (they are deemed as proponents of liberal thought, and the Selangor State Fatwa Committee has declared them deviant). From the perspective of the state, Muslim deviancy, as well as the lack of uniformity in Islamic doctrines and praxis and conformity to the state's brand of Islam, risks religious conflict and disharmony within the Muslim community.[4] However, as this chapter demonstrates later, in the context of intra-Muslim relations,

[4] See Mohd Faizal Musa, 'The Malaysian Shi'a: A Preliminary Study of Their History, Oppression, and Denied Rights' (2013) 6(4) *Journal of Shi'a Islamic Studies* 411, 412.

enforcing uniformity and conformity under the pretext of 'public order' and 'religious harmony' is also underpinned by important political considerations. This is tied to the continuing dominance of the then-ruling coalition, which – for reasons I shall explain in section III – faced the perennial challenge of maintaining its Malay-Muslim electoral support base amidst the growing influence of the Islamic opposition party, *Parti Islam Se-Malaysia* (PAS).

The foregoing explanation demonstrates that both intra-religious and inter-religious aspects are important in analysing public order and religious harmony in Malaysia. Nevertheless, it is also interesting to note that despite the justifications offered for the enactment of these clauses, they have been used sparsely. So far, they have been invoked as the basis for police investigations against acts deemed prejudicial to both inter- and intra-religious harmony, but in the end, they have only reached the courts three times, with all cases involving section 298A prosecutions. Building on the brief contextual discussion above, this chapter raises and assesses three issues that are crucial to understanding how religious penal clauses have been employed and developed in Malaysia. First, section II situates the discussion within the constitutional and legal contexts of the country. More specifically, I will explain the constitutional recognition of Islam in Article 3 of the Constitution, the civil–*syariah* court division of powers in matters implicating Islam, and the federal–State division of powers with regard to Islam and religion more broadly. The second issue, which will be dealt with in sections III and IV, focuses on the evolution of religious penal clauses in Malaysia. Aside from examining the jurisprudential patterns in the three cases that have emerged in Malaysia's civil courts, I shall engage with the broader political contexts that underlie the development of such clauses. Finally, section V will consider the constitutional implications of the use and development of religious offences in Malaysia.

My arguments are three-fold. The first rests in the constitutional and legal contexts of the country. The federalised arrangement in managing and administering Islam has led to some overlapping laws and regulations dealing with religion. Religious offences against Muslims (section 298), or actions that cause disharmony or enmity on the ground of religion (section 298A(1)) could also be prosecuted under the blasphemy provision in State *syariah* enactments. In addition, there are – as this chapter will show – various other laws (such as the Sedition Act) that have been invoked to address or prosecute criminal offences implicating religion. My second argument is anchored in the political salience of religion in Malaysia: the emergence of religious penal clauses and the jurisprudential developments are constantly shaped (and re-shaped) by competition among Malay-Muslim parties for political support from the mainstream Malay-Muslim electorate. However, there is yet another facet to this political dynamic, which is the federal–State division of power on Islamic matters. This has proved to be significant where the federal and State governments are controlled by different political parties. Finally, although maintaining inter-religious harmony has always been a pressing concern in Malaysia's deeply divided, multi-ethnic and multi-religious society, it is worth noting that there appears to be a tendency to enact and invoke laws on offences relating to religion – be they at federal or State (*syariah*) levels – to regulate intra-religious (ie intra-Muslim) issues. In all these three arguments, as we shall see in this chapter, a recurring issue is the rather amorphous concept of religious disharmony or public disorder, which – in the Malaysian context – renders it susceptible to politicisation and selective enforcement.

II. BACKGROUND: LEGAL AND CONSTITUTIONAL CONTEXTS

The Federation of Malaysia comprises 13 States – 11 of which make up the Federation of Malaya, and the two Borneo States of Sabah and Sarawak. This territorial diversity is accompanied by a diverse social fabric. According to the latest official data, the population is estimated to have reached 28.4 million people, of which 63.6 per cent are *Bumiputra*, 23.4 per cent are Chinese and 7 per cent are Indians. There are 179 officially defined ethnic groups, but the term *Bumiputra* (literally translated as 'the sons of the soil') typically encompasses those from the Malay ethnic group (about 60 per cent of the population), the *Orang Asal* (original inhabitants) and the native tribes from Sabah and Sarawak. Ethnic cleavages, though most prominent, are only one of the many divisions that define Malaysia's deeply divided society. Religion is also a politically salient social marker – Islam is the dominant religion (about 61 per cent of the population), followed by Buddhism (19 per cent) and Christianity (9 per cent) – and there are overlapping cleavages across territorial, linguistic and cultural lines. These national-level statistics largely comport with the religious demography in Peninsula Malaysia (ie Federation of Malaya) and Sabah,[5] but the demography in Sarawak is significantly different. There, the Christians comprise about 44 per cent of the population, while Muslims make up 30 per cent.

In view of the religious make-up of the country, Article 3(1) of the Federal Constitution of Malaysia recognises Islam as the 'religion of the Federation'.[6] Indeed, during the pre-Independence constitution-making process, it was the multi-ethnic, multi-religious Alliance Party (a coalition of ethnic Malay, Chinese and Indian parties) that pushed for special constitutional recognition for Islam. This was done in response to demands from sections of the Malay electorate, who feared the erosion of the significance of Malay and Islamic culture and traditions in the country post-Independence, given – among other things – the impending grant of *jus soli* citizenship to the non-Malays.[7] From a political perspective, the constitutional privileging of Islam was therefore thought to be

[5] Christianity is the next biggest religion in Sabah after Islam. Christians comprise 26% of the population in Sabah, while Buddhists comprise 6% of the population.

[6] Art 3(1) of the Federal Constitution.

[7] Dian AH Shah, *Constitutions, Religion and Politics in Asia: Malaysia, Indonesia and Sri Lanka* (Cambridge University Press, 2017) 33, 43–45.

symbolically and psychologically important for the Malays.[8] Having said that, it is important to note that the same provision that privileges Islam also guarantees that other religions may be 'practised in peace and harmony'. In this regard, during the constitution-making debates, the Constitutional Commission stressed that the privileging of Islam shall not affect the civil rights of non-Muslims, and in the same vein, the leader of the Alliance Party (who went on to become the first Prime Minister in independent Malaya) – Tunku Abdul Rahman – gave assurance that the provision does not create a theocratic state.[9] This is in fact reflected in the Constitution: Article 3(4) provides that the establishment of Islam shall not derogate from other provisions in the Constitution, including the fundamental rights guarantees.

The fundamental rights chapter in the Constitution further guarantees protection for the right to profess, practise and propagate one's religion under Article 11.[10] This same provision also guarantees the rights of religious *communities* to manage their own affairs. However, in addition to the standard, permissible restrictions on religious freedom on the grounds of safeguarding public order, health and morality, Article 11(4) qualifies the right to propagate one's religion. This essentially allows State legislatures to restrict the propagation of any religious doctrine or belief among Muslims.

Pursuant to this provision, at least 10 State legislatures in Malaysia have passed laws that criminalise acts to persuade, influence or instigate a Muslim to follow another religion; 'subjecting' Muslim minors to influences of a non-Islamic religion; and the distribution and delivery of certain religious publications to Muslims. These laws are clearly aimed at curbing proselytisation activities, because the provisions render it an offence to use 'words and expressions of Islamic origin' and to 'approach' a Muslim person to subject him or her to 'any speech on or display of any matter concerning a non-Islamic religion'.[11] All this, perceived as actions that could offend Muslim religious sensitivities, is packaged as the 'Non-Islamic Religions (Control of Propagation Amongst Muslims) Enactment'. Only the Federal Territories (which are under the jurisdiction of the federal legislature) and the states of Penang, Sabah and Sarawak have not enacted similar laws. In 1999, Abdul Hadi Awang (then Vice-President of the Islamic party, PAS) attempted to table the 'Control and Restriction of Propagation of Non-Muslim Religions (Federal Territories) Bill' as a private member's bill in the federal parliament, but this fell through. Apart from these enactments, there are State-level *syariah* criminal enactments that, as I shall explain, are applicable and enforceable only against Muslims. These enactments target unauthorised proselytising activities within the Muslim community in

[8] ibid 45.

[9] ibid 46.

[10] Art 11(1) of the Federal Constitution.

[11] These words are laid out in the Schedule to the enactments. They include words such as 'Allah', 'Ilahi', 'Fatwa', 'Solat', 'Nabi', 'Rasul' and 'Dakwah', and expressions such as 'Alhamdulillah', 'Insya Allah' and 'Allahu Akbar'.

order to control the spread of doctrines that the State deems 'heretical' or those that fall outside the mainstream Sunni Islam doctrine.

As with the Article 3(1) clause on Islam, there are distinct contextual factors behind the constitutional provision that permits restrictions on propagation, and they can be traced to underlying apprehensions about the integrity of the Malay-Muslim identity and community. The first is that restrictions on propagation have their roots in British colonial policy. When the Treaty of Pangkor paved the way for British imperialism in Malaya in 1874, there were no specific injunctions against churches proselytising Muslims. However, the colonial government recognised that such practice would offend local sensitivities, and it subsequently introduced regulations restricting proselytising of Muslim school children and prohibiting Muslim children from attending religious services of other religions, even with parental consent.[12] The Constitutions of individual Malay States had also preserved the right of State governments to restrict proselytisation of Muslims. Second, during the pre-Independence constitution-making exercise, there was considerable anxiety amongst the Malay-Muslims about the activities of Christian missionaries. This was compounded by the Malay Rulers (the Sultans in the nine Malay States), who were concerned about the possibility that it would no longer be illegal to proselytise Muslims if the right to propagate received constitutional protection.[13]

This brings us to the third crucial aspect of the constitutional framework governing religion–state relations in Malaysia: the federal–State division of power. The Constitution, by design, creates a strong central Government, with limited autonomy for the States. Article 74(1) of the Constitution authorises Parliament to enact laws on any of the matters provided in the Federal List or the Concurrent List, while Article 74(2) empowers the State legislatures to enact laws with respect to any of the matters enumerated in the State List or the Concurrent List. These lists are set out in the Ninth Schedule: the 'Federal List' includes matters of internal security (including the regulation of public order) and criminal law and procedure. Matters implicating Islam have traditionally been under the purview of the individual States. In other words, the Constitution devolves autonomy on certain Islamic matters to individual States because, historically, matters relating to Islam were under the prerogative of the Sultans in their respective States. Thus, in addition to their political role, the Sultans, as the *Khalifahs* (God's Regents on Earth),[14] also maintained a spiritual role – they were the heads of religion for their Malay subjects.

Nevertheless, the sphere of *syariah* or Islamic matters on which States can legislate is limited, and its contours are explicitly spelled out in List II of the

[12] Hearing of the Malayan Christians' Council before the Constitutional Commission (23 August 1956), CO889/6.

[13] Minutes of the First Meeting of the Working Party (22 February 1957), CO941/25.

[14] See, eg, Anthony C Milner, 'Islam and Malay Kingship' (1981) 1 *The Journal of the Royal Asiatic Society of Great Britain and Ireland* 46, 52.

Ninth Schedule. These matters mainly revolve around personal and family law issues for 'persons professing the religion of Islam', but the Constitution also empowers State legislatures to create and spell out punishments for 'offences against the precepts of Islam'. To promulgate, administer and enforce Islamic laws and policies, as well as advise the Heads of Islam (be they hereditary monarchs or appointed Heads of State) in the State, each State has its own religious council, religious department and a system of *syariah* courts. However, at the federal level, there is the Department of Islamic Development (JAKIM), which is set up under and overseen by the Prime Minister's Department. Despite the existence of State-level religious departments, JAKIM has the crucial role of carrying out the Federal Government's policies and agenda on Islam across State lines. Aside from its inter-State coordinating role, JAKIM has led efforts to standardise Islamic laws nationwide, and it monitors and controls the kinds of Islamic doctrines and teachings that are developed and practised in the Muslim community.

States across Malaysia have enacted statutes regulating *syariah* criminal offences, and these exist alongside federal laws on religious offences. With regard to the State-level statutes, there are similarities and divergences in their content (ie the kinds of offences that are spelled out in the statutes). They are applicable only to Muslims (this is typically stated in section 1 of the statutes, and *syariah* courts do not have jurisdiction over non-Muslims). The criminalisation of intra-religion propagation (eg propagation of Shia or Ahmadiyah doctrines) is also common across all State (and Federal Territories) *syariah* criminal enactments: this is categorised under 'offences relating to "*aqidah*" (Islamic creed)'[15] and 'offences relating to the sanctity of the religion of Islam and its institutions'.[16]

The differences in content can be further categorised into major and minor divergences. The former concerns differences between *syariah* criminal codes in Kelantan and Terengganu on the one hand, and *syariah* criminal enactments in the 10 remaining States (including the Federal Territories) on the other. In particular, the Kelantan and Terengganu codes – which were promulgated by the PAS State Government – provide punishments for *hudud* offences (including amputation for theft offences and stoning for adultery or same-sex sexual conduct). These punishments, however, could not be implemented because of the limitations set by the 1965 *Syariah* Courts (Criminal Jurisdiction) Act. This federal-level law only authorises *Syariah* Courts to impose a maximum of three years' imprisonment, a fine not exceeding RM5,000, and/or six strokes of the cane. Thus, the provisions on *hudud* offences and punishments remain on the statute books but are unenforceable. For States other than Kelantan and Terengganu, their *syariah* criminal enactments are almost identical (except for

[15] See, eg, *Syariah* Criminal Offences (Selangor) Enactment 1995 (Enactment No 9 of 1995) s 7; and *Syariah* Criminal Offences (Federal Territories) Act 1997, s 4. Both provisions deal with the 'false doctrine'.

[16] See, eg, 1995 Selangor Enactment, ss 13 and 16; and 1997 Federal Territories Act, ss 12 and 13.

minor differences in the wording and organisation of the provisions) to the *Syariah* Criminal Offences (Federal Territories) Act 1997. However, a recent exception to this is Sabah's *Syariah* Criminal Offences Enactment. In August 2019, the Sabah State Legislative Assembly passed an amendment that appears to narrow the scope of acceptable Islamic doctrine to that of the Sunni school. The amendment does so by defining the 'religion of Islam' as 'Islam *Ahli Sunnah Waljama'ah*' and by criminalising the propagation of 'false doctrine' (ie doctrines that deviate from Islamic law or *fatwa* in force in the State).[17]

At the federal level, aside from the Penal Code's 'offences relating to religion', which are examined in greater detail in the next section, there are various general laws that affect religion and religious practice. For instance, there is the Sedition Act 1948 – another law inherited from the colonial period – that criminalises any act, speech or publication that brings into hatred or contempt the Rulers (ie the King, Sultans or Heads of State) of any State in Malaysia. This is particularly significant because the Rulers are the traditional heads of Islam in their respective States. In addition, religion is now explicitly implicated – particularly after the Act was amended in 2015 – because it prohibits acts, speeches or publications that promote feelings of ill-will and hostility or hatred between persons or group of persons on the ground of religion. Previously, the Act only specifically addressed hate speech implicating race.

The force of the Sedition Act is buttressed by the Printing Presses and Publications Act 1984. Under this Act, the Minister possesses 'absolute discretion' to prohibit or issue conditions for the printing, publication and distribution of publications that are prejudicial (or are *likely* to be prejudicial) to public order, morality, security or public interest or contrary to any law.[18] Although it is not explicitly drafted to covers matters relating to religion, this provision has been used in several cases implicating religion. One of them is the 'Allah' case, where the Ministry of Home Affairs granted the Catholic Church a publication permit for its weekly publication (*The Herald*), subject to a prohibition on the use of the word 'Allah' in the Malay language edition of the periodical.[19] From the Government's perspective, the restriction was justified to avoid 'religious confusion' among Muslims and to prevent potential public disorder from the aggravation of Muslim religious sensitivities. The Court of Appeal agreed with these assertions as it overturned an earlier High Court decision in 2010 that had declared the prohibition on the use of 'Allah' to be unconstitutional.[20] In another case under the 1984 Act, the Ministry of Home Affairs banned four books written by a Muslim writer and academic, on the basis that the books, which included references to Shiism, were potentially prejudicial to public order

[17] Syariah Criminal Offences Enactment (Sabah) 1995, ss 2 and 52A.

[18] Printing Presses and Publications Act 1984 (DR 15/1984), s 7(1).

[19] *Titular Roman Catholic Archbishop of Kuala Lumpur v Menteri Dalam Negeri & Anor* [2009] 2 MLJ 78 (High Court, Kuala Lumpur) (*Titular*).

[20] *Menteri Dalam Negeri & Ors v Titular Roman Catholic Archbishop of Kuala Lumpur* [2013] 6 MLJ 468 (Court of Appeal, Putrajaya).

and national security, as they contained elements that could lead to 'confusion' amongst Muslims.[21] The Ministry had reached this conclusion after consulting the Department of Islamic Development (JAKIM). However, the ban was subsequently quashed by the Court of Appeal in January 2018.[22]

These two cases demonstrate, again, patterns of apprehension against religious propagation both toward and between Muslims, and the concern that uncontrolled propagation and proselytisation activities could trigger public disorder. In some cases, these activities have also explicitly been framed as a national security issue, prompting the use of the now-repealed Internal Security Act 1960 (ISA). In a seminal case, however, the Supreme Court held that propagation of Christianity among Muslims and the alleged conversion of Malays – even it were true – could not be deemed as a national security threat that justified detention under the ISA.[23]

III. THE PENAL CODE'S 'OFFENCES RELATING TO RELIGION': PROVISIONS AND CONTEXTS

As mentioned in section I, federal-level religious penal clauses are modelled after provisions in the Indian Penal Code 1860. An amendment in 1983 introduced section 298A, which criminalises acts that cause, attempt to cause or are likely to cause disharmony or feelings of enmity *on the grounds of religion* (either between persons professing the same religion, or between persons of different religions). Other 'offences relating to religion' under Chapter XV of the Penal Code are adopted almost word for word from the Indian Penal Code, and they include: (i) injuring or defiling a place of worship; (ii) disturbing a religious assembly; (iii) trespassing on burial places or funeral ceremonies; and (iv) acts deliberately intended to wound religious feelings of a person.

Apart from concerns over public order, more specific reasons for introducing section 298A are not immediately obvious from the parliamentary debates on the 1983 amendment. It is also worth noting that it is common to see the reference to 'public order' as a justification for amending laws that may have an impact on religion. For instance, when the Government amended the Sedition Act in April 2015 to include – within the definition of 'seditious tendency' – acts that promote ill-will, hostility or hatred on the ground of religion, the Minister of Home Affairs referred to the need to 'ensure the protection of safety and public order'.[24]

[21] *Mohd Faizal Musa v Minister of Home Affairs* [2017] 7 CLJ 352 (High Court, Kuala Lumpur).

[22] *Titular* (n 20).

[23] *Menteri Dalam Negeri v Jamaluddin bin Othman* [1989] 1 MLJ 418 (Supreme Court, Kuala Lumpur).

[24] Parliamentary Debates, Thirteenth Parliament, Third Session, First Meeting, 9 April 2015 (Dato' Seri Dr Ahmad Zahid bin Hamidi) 34.

However, with regard to section 298A, there was some suggestion – in parliamentary debates *after* the 1983 amendment was passed – that the Government had amended the Penal Code to target anti-government propaganda delivered through *fatwa*, sermons and other forms of religious propagation.[25] These acts were deemed a threat to national security. Yet the specific forms of conduct that are prohibited under section 298A do not appear to implicate national security concerns. For instance, the provision prohibits any allegation that a person or a group of persons has ceased to profess his/her religion, or should not be accepted as professing his/her religion, or does not believe or profess his/her religion anymore. It also prohibits any allegation that an established or officially appointed religious authority has – in the course of his duties – done something that contravened the requirements of the religion.

In view of all this, the drafting (and subsequent enactment) of section 298A must be understood within the then-prevailing political contexts. Of particular significance here was the political competition between UMNO (the Malay-Muslim nationalist party, which was the dominant party in the ruling coalition until 2018) and PAS. In the late 1970s and 1980, the religious overtones of social and political movements in Malaysia intensified. *Dakwah* (religious preaching) movements proliferated throughout the country, calling for stronger adherence to Islamic ideals and principles in public life.[26] These organisations espoused various interpretations of Islam, and some had sought to achieve their objectives through more radical and militant means, while others maintained active participation in politics and the civil society sphere.[27] Along with these developments, PAS became closely linked with some of the *dakwah* groups that emerged from the Islamic revival movement, and they rose to become UMNO's prime competitor for votes within the Malay-Muslim electorate. In response to UMNO's political rhetoric that the party was the most capable and committed protector of Malay-Muslim rights and interests, PAS campaigned, among others, on the premise that the UMNO-led Government lacked the capacity and motivation to pursue the fundamental principles of Islam. In the battle to demonstrate who best championed Islamic causes, it was common to hear PAS leaders (or PAS-linked religious preachers and movements) labelling the Government and its leaders as un-Islamic or *kafir* (infidel), and even prohibiting their supporters from attending government-sponsored mosques or religious events.

All this lends credence to the view that section 298A was enacted to address – at least in part – the politicisation of religion to fuel anti-government propaganda. Parliamentary debates in 1985, for instance, referred to individuals or groups who derided and belittled the religious practices and observance of other

[25] Parliamentary Debates, Sixth Parliament, Third Session, First Meeting, 24 April 1985 (Tuan Haji Shaharom bin Haji Maasom) 1299–1300.

[26] Gordon P Means, *Malaysian Politics: The Second Generation*, 2nd edn (Oxford University Press, 1991) 71.

[27] ibid 72.

Muslims individuals, or groups who mocked the Government's efforts in building mosques and *madrasahs* or in 'implementing Islamic values in administration'.[28] These kinds of conduct were deemed by the Government to be prejudicial to social harmony and public order. It is unsurprising, therefore, that the sub-provisions presume a person to have contravened section 298A where he or she alleges, for example, that another person 'has ceased to profess that religion'[29] or 'does not believe, follow, profess, or belong to, that religion'.[30] Similarly, a person is also presumed to have acted in a manner likely to cause disharmony or feelings of enmity between persons professing the religion, if he or she instigates another person 'not to use for worship any place which is lawfully used for such purpose by persons professing that religion'.[31] In addition, there is also a sub-provision that affords the Government the means to control the religious discourse, especially pertaining to Islam: section 298A(5) states that a person is presumed to have contravened the Penal Code if he or she exercises duties or functions that could only be performed by a (state-approved) religious official or authority.

In spite of the Penal Code's detailed regulation of religious offences through section 298A, these offences, as well as those that pertain to religious insult (section 298), have rarely been prosecuted in court, at least until 2019. By contrast, there have been several prosecutions pursuant to section 295 (where the sanctions are lighter than those involving section 298 or section 298A offences). These cases involve the damaging or defiling of places of worship for both Islamic and non-Islamic faiths. For instance, in 2015, a man was prosecuted and found guilty of damaging statues of deities at a Siamese Buddhist temple in Penang.[32] This was followed by the indictment of a man who pleaded guilty to throwing pork into a mosque compound in Penang.[33] There have also been instances where an act or conduct could have been prosecuted under the religious penal clauses, but it was instead prosecuted under other Penal Code provisions. One striking example of this is the arson attack against the Metro Tabernacle Church in Kuala Lumpur at the height of the 'Allah' case in 2010. In this case, two men were prosecuted for causing 'mischief by fire' under section 436 of the Penal Code. They were subsequently convicted and sentenced to a five-year jail term. In this respect, it is worth noting that section 436 provides more stringent punishment as compared to section 295: the term of imprisonment under the

[28] Parliamentary Debates 24 April 1985 (Tuan Haji Shaharom bin Haji Maasom) 1299–1302.

[29] Malaysian Penal Code 2015, s 298A(3)(a)(i).

[30] Malaysian Penal Code 2015, s 298A(3)(a)(iii).

[31] Malaysian Penal Code 2015, s 298A(4)(b)(iii).

[32] 'Man fined RM3,000 for damaging diety statues in Siamese temple' *The Malaysian Insider* (13 January 2015) at sg.news.yahoo.com/man-fined-rm3-000-damaging-diety-statues-siamese-034834415.html.

[33] Priya Pubalan, 'Three months in prison for mechanic who threw pork into mosque' *The New Straits Times* (Malaysia, 9 July 2015) at www.nst.com.my/news/2015/09/three-months-prison-mechanic-who-threw-pork-mosque.

former provision may extend to 20 years, whereas the term under section 295 may only extend to two years.

With regard to sections 298 and 298A, there used to be only a handful of reported prosecutions, as discussed in the next section. This changed, however, in the first few months of 2019, when there was a surge in prosecutions under these provisions, most of which dealt with insults against Prophet Muhammad on social media. Prior to that, the most recent conviction was in December 2017, where a housewife was convicted under section 298 of the Penal Code for deliberately wounding religious feelings, and was sentenced to a six months' imprisonment and a RM15,000 fine. She had been accused of insulting Prophet Muhammad while in the prayer hall of a mosque, and was overheard by three individuals.[34] Then, in March 2019, the Inspector-General of Police announced that 929 police reports had been lodged involving insults against Islam, Prophet Muhammad and his wife, and the police had begun investigations in 16 cases, though the cases were being investigated under the Multimedia and Communications Act 1998.[35] This rise in police reports lodged against speech allegedly insulting of Islam or the Prophet emerged in the wake of criticisms from a senior PAS leader that the new *Pakatan Harapan* (PH) Government was too lenient toward cases concerning insults against Islam.[36] In the same post, the PAS leader also threatened to rally the masses to force the Government to act against such cases. Two weeks later, the Sessions Court in Kuching, Sarawak, sentenced a man to an unprecedented 10 years and 10 months jail term, after he pleaded guilty to 10 charges of insulting Islam and Prophet Muhammad.[37] He was charged alongside three other individuals, who have also subsequently been found guilty.

Muslims, too, have not escaped investigations under these religious penal clauses for conduct deemed prejudicial or insulting to Islam or the Muslim community. In 2010, for example, the Selangor Islamic Religious Council (*Majlis Agama Islam Selangor* or MAIS) filed a police report against Sisters in Islam for criticising the caning of three women who were convicted of committing pre-marital sex under Selangor's *syariah* criminal offence enactment. The MAIS saw the criticism as an insult against Islam and *syariah* law. Sisters in Islam were subsequently investigated under section 298A. In 2016, a former journalist who tweeted a comment criticising Haron Din (a deceased PAS spiritual leader)

[34] Shaarani Ismail, 'Housewife sentenced to 6 months prison and fine for insulting Prophet Muhammad' *The New Straits Times* (Ipoh, 15 December 2017) at www.nst.com.my/news/crime-courts/2017/12/314760/housewife-sentenced-6-months-prison-and-fine-insulting-prophet.

[35] 'Police begin investigating reports on insult to Prophet' *The Star* (Kuala Lumpur,6 March 2019) atwww.thestar.com.my/news/nation/2019/03/06/police-begin-investigating-reports-on-insult-to-prophet/.

[36] 'PAS says govt too lenient with those who insult Islam' *The Straits Times* (Singapore, 26 February 2019) at www.straitstimes.com/world/pas-says-govt-too-lenient-with-those-who-insult-islam.

[37] 'Facebook user jailed 10 years for insulting Islam and prophet' *The Star* (Kuala Lumpur, 10 March 2019) at www.thestar.com.my/news/nation/2019/03/10/facebook-user-jailed-10-years-for-insulting-islam-and-prophet/.

was arrested under section 298 for causing religious disharmony. His tweet – in which he stated that 'Someone who made his career out of selling *air jampi* (water that has been blessed with Quranic verses) for any illness succumbed to his illness in a modern hospital in San Francisco' – was deemed to have insulted Islam. The Attorney General's Chambers, however, did not prosecute him. A year before that, a journalist, Aisyah Tajuddin, who produced a satirical video on *hudud*, was investigated under section 298. While the Inspector-General of Police commented that her video had poked fun at Islam, the investigations in the 2016 case did not end up with any prosecution. In any event, these cases illustrate just how broadly the offence of religious insult could be construed, and how it can be used to suppress dissent against religious personalities and authorities. By extension, they appear to support the argument that religious penal clauses could be used by state authorities (including religious authorities) as a tool to control and discipline Muslims.[38] Indeed, this appeared to have been mooted by the Minister of Law in 2000, who suggested that section 298 could be used against those who 'disunite' Muslims.[39]

In any case, amidst the growth of prosecutions for religious insults against Islam under section 298A, questions have emerged as to whether and how the Government would react against insults to non-Islamic religions. The concern about the arbitrary enforcement of the provision against religious minorities had already been raised by Sisters in Islam in 2017, following the conviction of a housewife for insulting the Prophet.[40] This appears to be a valid concern, as there have been relatively fewer – if not non-existent – prosecutions under the Penal Code in cases implicating minority religions. In March 2019, a man was charged for insulting Hinduism on social media. The trial is reportedly still ongoing, but it is worth noting that he was charged not under the Penal Code, but rather under section 233(1)(a) of the Multimedia and Communications Act 1998. The decision to invoke laws other than the Penal Code in addressing religious insults was also evident in the *Makkal Osai* case. In 2007, *Makkal Osai* – a Tamil daily newspaper – published a picture of Jesus with a cigarette and a can of beer in his hands. The Ministry of Home Affairs subsequently suspended *Makkal Osai*'s publication permit for a month. That said, it remains the case that thus far, there have been no successful prosecutions under section 298 or section 298A for insults against a minority religion. In April 2019, a Muslim preacher was investigated under section 298A for comments he had made about Hinduism, but in September 2019 the Attorney General's Chambers decided to drop the charges. Prior to that, in August 2019, then Prime Minister Mahathir and several Cabinet Ministers criticised a foreign preacher from India

[38] Patricia A Martinez, 'The Islamic State or the State of Islam in Malaysia' (2001) 23(3) *Contemporary Southeast Asia* 474, 480.

[39] ibid.

[40] 'Press Statement: Arbitrary Use of Law is Oppressive to Society' *Sisters in Islam* (Malaysia, 18 December 2017) at www.sistersinislam.org.my/news.php?item.1497.98.

(who is banned from preaching in seven States) for comments he made against the Chinese and Indian communities in the country.[41]

IV. ENFORCING OFFENCES AGAINST RELIGION

At this juncture, it is important to recall that religious offences are regulated not only by federal laws, but also by State laws. In fact, religious offences appear to be more widely regulated by State *syariah* criminal enactments, which are only applicable to Muslims. Given the dual-track civil and *syariah* systems in Malaysia, Muslims are subjected to two sets of laws when it comes to 'offences relating to religion'. In most State enactments (I say 'most' because the States of Kelantan and Terengganu have *syariah* criminal codes that differ from other States in Malaysia), there at least 35 types of 'offences', ranging from insulting Islam and disobeying religious authorities, to engaging in homosexual conduct, failure to perform Friday prayers and failure to observe fasting in the month of Ramadan. It is interesting to note, however, that the regulation of some of these offences dates back to the colonial period. For instance, the British introduced religious enactments that spelled out offences such as apostasy, adultery and failure to perform Friday prayers.[42]

Although *hudud* punishments in Kelantan and Terengganu are unenforceable due to federal law restrictions on the punitive powers of the *syariah* courts, data from the (federal-level) *Syariah* Judiciary Department still show that the broad range of *syariah* offences have not been so widely enforced or prosecuted in the States. The first ever 'successful' criminal prosecution for prostitution and *musahaqah* (female–female sexual relations) only emerged in the State of Terengganu in September and October 2018. The offenders in both cases were sentenced to four to six strokes of the cane after pleading guilty to the charges against them. Prior to that, in February 2010, three individuals prosecuted and convicted for extra-marital sex under Selangor's *syariah* criminal laws became the first women in the country to be caned under *syariah* law.[43] Aside from extra-marital sexual relations, the next highest number of prosecutions involves alcohol consumption. One well-known case was that of Kartika Sari Dewi Shukarno, who was sentenced to be caned for drinking beer in public in 2010. Like the women in Terengganu, Kartika pleaded guilty and did not appeal

[41] Bhavan Jaipragas, 'Malaysia's Mahathir toughens stance against controversial Indian Muslim preacher Zakir Naik' *South China Morning Post* (Hong Kong, 19 August 2019) at www.scmp.com/week-asia/politics/article/3023427/malaysias-mahathir-toughens-stance-against-controversial-indian.

[42] Shamrahayu A Aziz, 'Islamic Criminal Law in the Malaysian Federal Structure: A Constitutional Perspective' (2012) 15(1) *International Islamic University of Malaysia Law Journal* 101, 106. See also Muslim Law Enactment 1904 (Pahang), Muslim Offences Order in Council 1938 (Negeri Sembilan, and Muhammadan (Offences) Enactment 1939.

[43] David Kloos and Ward Berenschot, 'Citizenship and Islam in Malaysia and Indonesia' in Ward Berenschot et al (eds), *Citizenship and Democratization in Southeast Asia* (Brill, 2017) 178.

against her sentence. She would have been the first woman to be caned under *syariah* law in Malaysia, but she was later spared from the punishment after receiving a commutation from the Sultan of Pahang. The Sultan ordered her to perform three weeks of community service instead.

Leaving aside these 'morality' cases, *syariah* enactments addressing blasphemy offences have been routinely enforced against minority Muslims (such as the Shias and the Ahmadis). For instance, in 2014, hundreds of Shia Muslims who gathered for a religious event were arrested by religious authorities in Perak.[44] In the same year, three men were prosecuted for violating a *fatwa* in the State of Perak, which provides that Muslims in Malaysia are bound by the Sunni branch of Islam. They were prosecuted in the *syariah* court but acquitted on technical grounds. There have been occasions when Friday prayer sermons issued by State religious authorities have carried anti-Shia messages that could be deemed an incitement of hatred against Shias.[45] In 2013, the Director-General of JAKIM asserted that Shia teachings in Malaysia had deviated from true Islamic teachings, and likened such teachings to 'cancer that needs to be prevented from spreading' as they threatened Muslim unity.[46] Yet none of these have been deemed or prosecuted as offences under the Penal Code.

The anti-Shia persecution in Malaysia is laced with political considerations, especially when one takes into account the fact that harassment was largely absent prior to 2000.[47] There are two interrelated aspects to the political explanation, and both could also explain why many of the investigations and prosecutions under Chapter XV of the Penal Code have involved insults against the majority religion and religious community. The first aspect, to which I have alluded in the discussion of the emergence of section 298A, concerns the growing politicisation of Islam in order to bolster the state's (ie the Federal Government's) political power and its control over religious discourse. These, in turn, are related to the second aspect, which involves maintaining and strengthening the then ruling Government's support base within the Malay-Muslim electorate. Under the Mahathir premiership, the Government began a series of 'Islamisation' initiatives in the 1980s, which spanned sectors such as finance and education. These initiatives began with the more symbolic and ritualistic aspects

[44] Mandates of the Special Rapporteur on the promotion and protection of the right to freedom of opinion and expression; the Special Rapporteur on the rights to freedom of peaceful assembly and of association; the Special Rapporteur on freedom of religion or belief; and the Independent Expert on minority issues to the Office of the UN High Commissioner for Human Rights (28 March 2014) at spcommreports.ohchr.org/TMResultsBase/DownLoadPublicCommunicationFile?gId=17611.

[45] See Mohd Faizal Musa and Tan Beng Hui, 'State-backed discrimination against Shia Muslims in Malaysia' (2017) 49(3) *Critical Asian Studies* 308.

[46] 'Jakim: All branches of Shiah in Malaysia violate Islamic law' *Malaymail* (Putrajaya, 13 December 2013) at malaymail.com/news/malaysia/2013/12/13/jakim-all-branches-of-shiah-in-malaysia-violate-islamic-law/581217.

[47] Musa and Tan, 'State-backed discrimination against Shia Muslims' (n 45) 310. Musa and Tan explained four factors that have contributed to the discrimination against Muslim minorities (ie the Shias) in Malaysia. See ibid 310–13.

of Islam.[48] Later, they morphed into more substantive efforts as the Government strengthened religious institutions, particularly at the federal level, by endowing them with huge amounts of funds. This was influenced by calls from both state and non-government actors for a greater formal role for Islamic laws and principles in governance.[49] This was also to some extent driven by the view that Islam's special constitutional position meant that the religion ought to be protected and prioritised, and that Islamic principles and precepts ought to become the basis for law-making and policy-making in the country. In short, maintaining political power and appealing to the Malay-Muslim electorate hinged on the Government's ability to show that it was fully committed to championing Islam above other considerations.

These considerations were reflected in the Government's response to two prominent cases involving religious hatred or insult. The first was the infamous 'cow's head protest' in Shah Alam, where 50 Malay-Muslim residents placed a cow's head at the gates of the Selangor State government's office and stamped on it as a form of protest against the decision to relocate a Hindu temple to their (predominantly Muslim) neighbourhood. The then Minister of Home Affairs, Hishammuddin Hussein, defended the protestors, claiming they had no intention to provoke racial or religious sentiments and only wanted their voices to be heard. Several of the protestors were subsequently prosecuted under the Sedition Act – one of them was sentenced to a week in jail and a RM3,000 fine.[50] In another case, which occurred in the midst of the 'Allah' dispute in 2014, a leader of a Malay-Muslim non-governmental organisation reportedly called for the burning of Malay-language Bibles. However, he was not charged, as the Attorney General's Chambers decided that he had no intention to trigger religious disharmony and that he was only defending the sanctity of Islam.[51]

A recent incident in November 2018, involving a riot at a Hindu temple in Selangor, raised questions as to whether the 'offences relating to religion' clauses in the Penal Code would be invoked. In that incident, a mob comprising 50 individuals (all of whom were allegedly Malay-Muslim) attacked a Hindu temple. This triggered a two-day riot at a temple that had been under the spotlight for several months for refusing to relocate, despite being provided with an alternative plot of land and compensation by the developers who own the land on which the temple stands. Four men were charged, not under section 295 of the Penal Code (involving acts that defile or damage a place of worship) but

[48] ibid 310.

[49] This is what Musa and Tan refer to as the 'Syariah lobby' – lobbyists comprising both state and non-state actors 'whose primary goal has been to turn Islam into the reference point for all matters – public and private – in the nation'. See ibid 310.

[50] 'Cow-head protest: 12 fined RM1,000 each for illegal assembly (Updated)' *The Star* (Shah Alam, 27 July 2010) at thestar.com.my/news/nation/2010/07/27/cowhead-protest-12-fined-rm1000-each-for-illegal-assembly-updated/.

[51] Tan Yi-Lian, 'A-G: Ibrahim Ali's bible-burning remark not of "seditious tendency"' *The Star* (Petaling Jaya, 27 October 2014) at thestar.com.my/news/nation/2014/10/27/attorney-general-ibrahim-ali-bible-burning-speech-not-seditious.

under section 148 (involving the offence of taking part in a riot and possessing dangerous weapons while participating in the riot). One way to read this series of events is to see it as a reflection of the Government's 'official' position that the two-day fracas was a mere land dispute between a developer and the temple authorities. Given the heightened ethnic and religious tensions in Malaysia since the political transition in May 2018, the Government has been very quick to suppress the ethnic undertones of public disorders. What this might suggest is that the enforcement of religious penal clauses could well be a politically-loaded affair tied to the interests and agenda of the government of the day.

Having considered the various examples discussed so far, we may surmise that the use of criminal provisions on 'offences relating to religion' is politicised and selective, and they are also invoked expansively, when we reflect on cases involving insults to Islam and Muslims. As I have demonstrated in the previous section, criticising religious figures and authorities (or even the implementation of *syariah* law) has been deemed as insulting Islam. In the following discussion of three prominent cases that reached the superior courts in Malaysia, the expansive, selective and political use of section 298A of the Penal Code will be even more apparent.

The first case involved four individuals who were charged for 'acting in a manner likely to prejudice the maintenance of unity on grounds of religion' under section 298A. The impugned conduct involved their acting as a *Bilal* (a person who performs the call to prayer), an *Imam* (a person who leads congregational prayer and a *Khatib* (a person who delivers Friday prayer sermons) during Friday prayers in the State of Terengganu, without prior State authorisation.[52] They were convicted at the High Court of Kuala Terengganu, but instead of receiving custodial sentences, the trial judge bound them to 'keep the peace and be of good behaviour' for three years. The Government appealed against the sentence on the basis that it lacked sufficient deterrent effect for an issue that implicated public interest and the interest of the Muslim community, but this was rejected by the Supreme Court.

In 1987, the Supreme Court was again called upon to consider a similar situation: the petitioners in that case were also charged under section 298A for acting as unauthorised *Bilal*, *Khatib* and *Imam* at a Friday prayer in Kuala Terengganu.[53] As in *Mohamed Nor*, the petitioners were charged under section 298A on the basis that they were engaging in an 'act which is likely to prejudice unity among persons professing the Islamic religion'. Again, the charge illustrates how the provision – particularly with regard to the offence of 'prejudicing unity' on the grounds of religion – can be attributed an expansive meaning. In understanding these cases – *Mohamed Nor* and *Mamat bin Daud* – one cannot ignore the then prevailing social and political contexts. Apart from

[52] *Public Prosecutor v Mohamed Nor & Others* [1985] 2 MLJ 200 (Kota Baru).
[53] *Mamat bin Daud v Government of Malaysia* [1988] 1 MLJ 119 (Kuala Lumpur, Supreme Court).

the groundswell of Islamic revivalism in society, the opposition party PAS had begun to make inroads in the conservative and predominantly Malay States of Kelantan and Terengganu in the 1982 general elections. In Kelantan, PAS had won 10 State legislative assembly seats (compared to two seats in the 1978 general elections) and in Terengganu, they won five seats (they failed to win any seats in the previous elections).

Unlike *Mohamed Nor*, the petitioners in *Mamat bin Daud* went further and challenged the validity of section 298A. They argued that section 298A was unconstitutional, as the provision concerns a matter (ie causing religious disunity) that ought to be regulated by State as opposed to federal legislature. In other words, the issues governed by section 298A – which specifies prohibited acts that are presumed to amount to causing religious disunity – ought to be legislated by the State assemblies because they concerned the Islamic religion. The Supreme Court held in favour of the petitioners, holding that section 298A is, in pith and substance, a law relating to the Islamic religion which should be under the purview of State legislatures. In particular, the majority opinion thought that section 298A aimed to ensure that practices relating to the Islamic religion must conform to the tenets, precepts and practices of Islam spelled out by the States.[54] In doing so, the majority rejected the Government's contention that the provision was enacted to pursue public order and internal security objectives.[55] In fact, Chief Justice Salleh Abas went further by expressing his scepticism about the Government's stated aims – he saw the provision as an 'attempt to hide the reality of legislating upon an impermissible subject or matter behind the general façade of constitutionality'.[56] This was echoed by Justice Mohamed Azmi, who argued that the prohibited acts under section 298A had 'nothing to do with "public order"'; rather, they were concerned with the regulation of religious matters.[57]

Despite the declaration that section 298A was null and void, the provision continues to be used as a basis for arrests, charge and prosecution in cases involving religious insults. In *Tan Jye Yee v Public Prosecutor*,[58] two individuals were charged under the section 4(1) of the Sedition Act 1948 and section 298A(1)(a) of the Penal Code for posting on Facebook a *Hari Raya* greeting, alongside photographs of them enjoying a pork dish while displaying a '*Halal*' logo. They appealed against a High Court decision that dismissed their application to strike out the charge under section 298A, arguing that the provision had already been declared illegal in *Mamat bin Daud*. The Court of Appeal upheld the appeal, holding that the Supreme Court's decision in *Mamat bin Daud* stands, that is, that section 298A was illegal.

[54] ibid 122.
[55] ibid 120.
[56] ibid 121.
[57] ibid 125.
[58] *Tan Jye Yee & Anor v Public Prosecutor* [2014] 6 MLJ 609 (Putrajaya, Court of Appeal).

V. CONSTITUTIONAL ISSUES AND IMPLICATIONS

The foregoing discussion highlights several important constitutional issues with regard to the application and operation of Chapter XV of the Penal Code. One striking issue concerns what may be seen as a continuing rule-of-law problem in Malaysia. Section 298A was declared invalid and unconstitutional by the Supreme Court in 1987 and, subsequently, by the Court of Appeal in 2014. Yet, as seen in the various examples presented throughout this chapter, the provision is still being used not only to arrest, charge and prosecute individuals deemed to have committed the offences covered by the provision, but also as a basis to convict and sentence those individuals.

The second issue concerns the boundaries of fundamental rights protections such as the freedom of expression and the freedom of religion, and this also implicates questions on how the state conceives of 'public order' for the purposes of restricting such freedoms. It is obvious by now that the Government's desire to control the religious discourse and exert its authority over religion is, in part, reflected in the sub-provisions of section 298A. Although the provisions do not mention Islam specifically, the context surrounding the enactment of section 298A and the detailed sub-provisions regarding the authority of religious officials, the imputation that a person has ceased to profess his or her religion and the use of places of worship, all appear to point toward the regulation of Islam. The creation of offences concerning the authority of religious officials or the performance of a religious function, in particular, have constricted the space for religious practice and interpretation for Muslims. Even if a person argues that his or her speech or conduct was done based on an honest belief in, or an honest interpretation of, the precepts of the religion, this cannot be used as a defence under the scheme of section 298A. All this gives great latitude to the Federal Government to define and enforce (through the heavy hand of JAKIM) what it deems as acceptable religious doctrines or practices. This must also be considered in light of the Federal Government's preoccupation with standardising and expanding the corpus of Islamic laws throughout the country since the 1980s.[59] Furthermore, sections 298 and 298A, as drafted and as applied, create a chilling effect on free speech. They insulate religion (particularly the dominant religion) from being debated, discussed and criticised, because this may be perceived by some Muslims as insulting to the religion and seen by the Government as a potential trigger for religious conflict.

The state has routinely invoked 'public order' as a justification for criminalising offences relating to religion and for enacting other laws aimed at protecting religious harmony. While 'public order' is a constitutionally-approved limit on the rights to free speech and religious freedom, the religious penal clauses and

[59] See Maznah Mohamed, 'The Ascendance of Bureaucratic Islam and the Secularization of the Sharia in Malaysia' (2010) 83(3) *Pacific Affairs* 505; Shah, *Constitutions, Religion and Politics* (n 6) 87–88.

the ways in which they have been applied reveal a broad conception of public order that potentially undermines the full benefit and value of those rights. In this regard, the subjectivity of (and the arbitrary nature of deciding) what amounts to an 'insult' or 'causing religious disharmony' allows the state a very broad latitude in determining the parameters of public order.[60] In cases involving these religious penal clauses, even the courts have demonstrated willingness to adopt a broad conception of public order. In *Mohamed Nor*, for instance, the Supreme Court took the position that conduct need not involve violence for it to pose a threat to public order, and it acknowledged that the activities in question (ie acting as unauthorised *Bilal*, *Khatib* and *Imam*) were 'likely to have [a] far-reaching effect' that could prejudice public order and national security.[61] The Court upheld the sentence meted out by the High Court, as it did not want to interfere with the sentencing decision of the lower courts. The case of *Mamat bin Daud* also demonstrates the broad conception of public order and the adverse implications this may have for religious practice. Chief Justice Salleh Abas, for instance, opined that 'to allow any Muslim or groups of Muslims to adopt divergent practices and entertain differing concepts of Islamic religion may well be dangerous and could lead to disunity among Muslims and, therefore, could affect public order'.[62] All in all, regardless of whether it is the right to religious freedom or the right to free speech that is implicated, the breadth of the term 'insult' and the wording of sections 298 and 298A, as well as the broad conception of public order, render the application and enforcement of these religious penal clauses prone to inconsistency and unpredictability. This is because enforcement appears to hinge upon populist sentiments as well as the political imperatives of the state.

In addition, the overlaps between State religious penal clauses and federal penal clauses raise questions about the constitutionality of State-level religious penal laws. One striking example of this overlap is the criminalisation of same-sex (both male and female) sexual intercourse. Almost all State legislatures criminalise and distinguish sodomy (*liwat*) and *musahaqah*[63] offences, except

[60] This point comports with Justice Mohamad Azmi's comment in *Mamat bin Daud* that the wording of s 298A(1) 'is so wide that it comprehends almost every act which can be construed as causing or likely to cause disharmony or disunity, or prejudicing the maintenance of harmony or unity on ground of religion'.

[61] *Mohamed Nor* (n 52) 202.

[62] *Mamat bin Daud* (n 53) 121.

[63] Syariah Criminal Offences Enactment (Johor) 1997; Syariah Criminal Offences Enactment (Kelantan) 2015; Syariah Criminal Offences Enactment (Kedah) 2014; Syariah Criminal Offences Enactment (Negeri Sembilan) 2004; Syariah Criminal Offences Enactment (Penang) 1996; Criminal Offences in Syarak Enactment (Perlis) 1991; Syariah Criminal Offences Ordinance (Sarawak) 2001; Syariah Criminal Offences (Hudud and Qisas) Enactment (Terengganu) 2002; and Syariah Criminal Offences (Takzir) Enactment (Terengganu) 2001; Syariah Offences Enactment (Melaka) 1991. Pahang is the only State without provisions criminalising same-sex sexual relations. Perak criminalises same-sex sexual relations between women (*musahaqah*), but has no provisions on sodomy. In Sabah, while *musahaqah* is explicitly prohibited, the Syariah Criminal Offences Enactment 1995 also prohibits 'intercourse against the order of nature'.

for Selangor, which packages both offences as 'intercourse against the order of nature'. In addition, in the northeastern States of Kelantan and Terengganu, theft, robbery and homicide are criminalised in the States' *syariah* criminal offences enactments, and these offences are subject to *hudud* and *qisas* punishments. There are also clear overlaps with the Penal Code's provisions on offences relating to religion. As I have illustrated in the foregoing sections, the Penal Code governs crimes such as defiling a place of religion (Section 295), wounding the religious feelings of any person (section 298) and causing disharmony or feelings of ill-will or hatred on the grounds of religion (section 298(A)). Yet State-level enactments regulating *syariah* offences also criminalise similar conduct under chapters on 'Offences Relating to the Sanctity of the Religion of Islam and Its Institutions'. Consider, as an example, the Selangor Enactment: there are provisions on destroying or defiling Islamic places of worship,[64] acting in contempt of religious authorities[65] and propagating or disseminating opinions contrary to any *fatwa* in force in the State.[66] There are also broadly-worded provisions criminalising insults against Islam. This offence covers acts or speeches that 'ridicule' Islamic practices and ceremonies, as well as those that 'degrade' any laws relating to Islam that are in force in the State.[67]

These examples demonstrate that State legislatures have routinely (mis)used the constitutional dispensation in the Ninth Schedule (List II) that allows them to enact laws on 'offences against the precepts of Islam' in order to create and regulate particular offences, even if such offences are covered by federal law. In other words, we are faced with the problem of State legislatures encroaching into the federal parliament's field of legislative competence on criminal and public order matters, despite the clear delineation of legislative powers in Article 74 of the Constitution. Viewed in its entirety, Malaysia's constitutional scheme – especially when we consider the federal–State dynamics and division of powers – does not vest State legislatures with unfettered powers to legislate on any or all offences against the precepts of Islam as the lawmakers deem fit. This is reinforced by the fact that Article 75 of the Constitution provides that federal law shall prevail over State law where the latter conflicts with the former.

Thus far, State *syariah* criminal offences enactments have not been invalidated on the basis that such enactments violate the Constitution's federal–State legislative divisions of power. In the most recent case, *Sulaiman Takrib*, a Muslim man was arrested and charged for defying or disobeying a *fatwa* in the State of Terengganu, and for possessing a VCD with contents that were deemed contrary to the precepts of Islam.[68] He argued that the offences with which he

[64] Syariah Criminal Offences (Selangor) Enactment 1995 s 11.

[65] ibid s 12.

[66] ibid s 13.

[67] ibid s 10.

[68] He was charged under ss 10 and 14 of the Syariah Criminal Offences (Takzir) Enactment (Terengganu) 2001, respectively. See *Sulaiman bin Takrib v Kerajaan Negeri Terengganu and Other Applications* [2009] 6 MLJ 354 (Putrajaya, Federal Court).

was charged under the Terengganu Enactment were criminal in nature, and these fell within the jurisdiction of the federal parliament. Thus, the provisions were ultra vires the Constitution.[69] The Federal Court, however, upheld the validity of the provisions on the grounds that the offences spelled out in the Terengganu Enactment were offences against the precepts of Islam enforceable only against Muslims, and that these kinds of offences were not provided for in federal law.[70] In other words, the Court opined that these two characteristics meant that the offences were not 'criminal law' for the purposes of Article 74 and the Ninth Schedule.

This conclusion appears thin and simplistic for several reasons. First, it fails to consider the fact that despite implicating 'Islamic precepts', the offences in question in pith and substance pertain to criminal law in so far as they seek to regulate or criminalise speech and expression. Second, one could question whether disobedience against a *fatwa* (or acting in contempt of State religious authorities, more generally) is indeed a crime against the 'Islamic precepts'. Finally, a careful reading of section 10 of the Terengganu Enactment, which deals with acts in contempt of, or defiance or disobedience against religious authorities, indicates that there is in fact a comparable offence in the Penal Code. section 298A(3)(b), in particular, presumes that a person has caused or is likely to cause disharmony or feelings of enmity on the ground of religion if he or she challenges the conduct of religious authorities or alleges that such conduct does not comport with the requirements of the religion. That said, it remains to be seen how courts in Malaysia would treat other provisions in State enactments covering offences for which the Penal Code explicitly provides.

VI. CONCLUSION

By way of conclusion, there are several ways in which we can attempt to understand the development and enforcement of religious penal clauses in Malaysia. The first is by looking at the legal and constitutional framework, particularly the federal–State division of power. The federalised approach to regulating Islam and the recognition that the States may legislate and administer certain aspects of Islamic law for persons professing the religion of Islam have led to significant overlaps between federal and State laws governing religious offences. The implication of this is that Muslims are subjected to two sets of laws on religious offences, and the existence of overlaps mean that they could, for instance, be charged for blasphemy or deviancy under the Penal Code or the State-level *syariah* criminal enactments. This might explain why – at least when it comes to offences against the Islamic religion committed by Muslims – prosecutions under the Penal Code have been few and far between. The other pertinent

[69] *Sulaiman bin Takrib* (n 68) 375.
[70] ibid 377.

point is that despite the existence of specific provisions on offences relating to religion in the Penal Code, Malaysia maintains a jungle of different laws that could potentially be applied to such offences. As we have seen in the preceding sections, conduct that could have been prosecuted pursuant to the religious penal clauses has been pursued instead under other laws (such as the Multimedia and Communications Act), or even under other provisions in the Penal Code. In other words, the public order aim that the state pursues could also be served by laws other than the Penal Code.

Finally, the development and implementation of the clauses are – in the context of Malaysia's social and political dynamics – a politically-charged affair. The examples offered throughout this chapter illustrate that the primary site of contestation has related to the doctrines and practice of Islam. While the state has sought to regulate minority religions, these have been in the context where the practice of Islam itself has been implicated. The dominant pattern is that the State is not only quicker to react against issues where the majority religion (Islam) is implicated, but it also tends to be more proactive in prosecuting conduct that involves the majority religion.

BIBLIOGRAPHY

Mamat bin Daud v Government of Malaysia [1988] 1 MLJ 119 (Kuala Lumpur, Supreme Court)

Menteri Dalam Negeri & Ors v Titular Roman Catholic Archbishop of Kuala Lumpur [2013] 6 MLJ 468 (Court of Appeal, Putrajaya)

Mohd Faizal Musa v Minister of Home Affairs [2017] 7 CLJ 352 (High Court, Kuala Lumpur)

Menteri Dalam Negeri v Jamaluddin bin Othman [1989] 1 MLJ 418 (Supreme Court, Kuala Lumpur)

Public Prosecutor v Mohamed Nor & Others [1985] 2 MLJ 200 (Kota Baru)

Sulaiman bin Takrib v Kerajaan Negeri Terengganu and Other Applications [2009] 6 MLJ 354 (Putrajaya, Federal Court)

Tan Jye Yee & Anor v Public Prosecutor [2014] 6 MLJ 609 (Putrajaya, Court of Appeal)

Titular Roman Catholic Archbishop of Kuala Lumpur v Menteri Dalam Negeri & Anor [2009] 2 MLJ 78 (High Court, Kuala Lumpur)

Aziz, SA, 'Islamic Criminal Law in the Malaysian Federal Structure: A Constitutional Perspective' (2012) 15(1) *International Islamic University of Malaysia Law Journal* 101

Ibrahim, A, *Towards A History of Law in Malaysia and Singapore*, 2nd edn (Dewan Bahasa dan Pustaka, Ministry of Education Malaysia, 1992)

Ismail, S, 'Housewife sentenced to 6 months prison and fine for insulting Prophet Muhammad' *The New Straits Times* (Ipoh, 15 December 2017) at www.nst.com.my/news/crime-courts/2017/12/314760/housewife-sentenced-6-months-prison-and-fine-in sulting-prophet

Jaipragas, B, 'Malaysia's Mahathir toughens stance against controversial Indian Muslim preacher Zakir Naik' *South China Morning Post* (Hong Kong, 19 August 2019) at www.scmp.com/week-asia/politics/article/3023427/malaysias-mahathir-toughen s-stance-against-controversial-indian

Kloos, D, and Berenschot, W, 'Citizenship and Islam in Malaysia and Indonesia' in Ward Berenschot et al (eds), *Citizenship and Democratization in Southeast Asia* (Brill, 2017) 178

Malay Mail, 'Jakim: All branches of Shiah in Malaysia violate Islamic law' (Putrajaya, 13 December 2013) at malaymail.com/news/malaysia/2013/12/13/jakim-all-branches-of-shiah-in-malaysia-violate-islamic-law/581217

Mandates of the Special Rapporteur on the promotion and protection of the right to freedom of opinion and expression; the Special Rapporteur on the rights to freedom of peaceful assembly and of association; the Special Rapporteur on freedom of religion or belief; and the Independent Expert on minority issues to the Office of the UN High Commissioner for Human Rights (28 March 2014) at spcommreports.ohchr.org/TMResultsBase/DownLoadPublicCommunicationFile?gId=17611

Martinez, PA, 'The Islamic State or the State of Islam in Malaysia' (2001) 23(3) *Contemporary Southeast Asia* 474

Means, GP, *Malaysian Politics: The Second Generation*, 2nd edn (Oxford University Press, 1991)

Milner, AC, 'Islam and Malay Kingship' (1981) 1 *The Journal of the Royal Asiatic Society of Great Britain and Ireland* 46

Mohamed, M, 'The Ascendance of Bureaucratic Islam and the Secularization of the Sharia in Malaysia' (2010) 83(3) *Pacific Affairs* 505

Musa, MF, 'The Malaysian Shi'a: A Preliminary Study of Their History, Oppression, and Denied Rights' (2013) 6(4) *Journal of Shi'a Islamic Studies* 411

——, and Tan, BH, 'State-backed discrimination against Shia Muslims in Malaysia' (2017) 49(3) Critical Asian Studies 308

Nazeri, NM, 'Criminal Law Codification and Reform in Malaysia: An Overview' (Dec 2010) *Singapore Journal of Legal Studies* 375

Pubalan, P, 'Three months in prison for mechanic who threw pork into mosque' *The New Straits Times* (Malaysia, 9 July 2015) at www.nst.com.my/news/2015/09/three-months-prison-mechanic-who-threw-pork-mosque

Shah, DAH, *Constitutions, Religion and Politics in Asia: Malaysia, Indonesia and Sri Lanka* (Cambridge University Press, 2017)

Tan, YL, 'A-G: Ibrahim Ali's bible-burning remark not of "seditious tendency"' *The Star* (Petaling Jaya, 27 October 2014) at thestar.com.my/news/nation/2014/10/27/attorney-general-ibrahim-ali-bible-burning-speech-not-seditious

The Malaysian Insider, 'Man fined RM3,000 for damaging deity statues in Siamese temple' (Malaysia, 13 January 2015) at sg.news.yahoo.com/man-fined-rm3-000-damaging-diety-statues-siamese-034834415.html

The Star, 'Facebook user jailed 10 years for insulting Islam and prophet' (Kuala Lumpur, 10 March 2019) at www.thestar.com.my/news/nation/2019/03/10/facebook-user-jailed-10-years-for-insulting-islam-and-prophet/

——, 'Police begin investigating reports on insult to Prophet' (Kuala Lumpur, 6 March 2019) www.thestar.com.my/news/nation/2019/03/06/police-begin-investigating-reports-on-insult-to-prophet/

——, 'Cow-head protest: 12 fined RM1,000 each for illegal assembly (Updated)' (Shah Alam, 27 July 2010) at thestar.com.my/news/nation/2010/07/27/cowhead-protest-12-fined-rm1000-each-for-illegal-assembly-updated/

The Straits Times, 'PAS says govt too lenient with those who insult Islam' (Singapore, 26 February 2019) at www.straitstimes.com/world/pas-says-govt-too-lenient-with-those-who-insult-islam

10

Religious Offences Penal Clauses and the Singapore Constitutional Order: Secular, Sensible but Sensitive to the Sacred?

LI-ANN THIO

THE ORIGINS OF Chapter XV of the Singapore Penal Code ('Offences Relating to Religion or Race') are rooted in the 1860 Indian Penal Code 'Offences Relating to Religion' provisions. These provisions relate to insult and wounding religious feelings through words or deeds, which entails regulating emotions. They operate within a secular democratic context and are designed to serve public order considerations, not protect religious orthodoxy. Singapore's founding fathers maintained an antipathy towards the emotionalism and divisive forces associated with the 'primordial pull of ancestry, race, language and religion',[1] the last of which is heightened within the multi-racial context of Singapore,[2] the world's most religiously diverse state.[3]

In aversive contrast to the Malaysian Federal Constitution, which recognises Islam as the official religion, the Singapore Constitution does not formally identify with any religion: Articles 152(1) and (2) respectively oblige the Government

[1] Vivian Balakrishnan (Minister for Foreign Affairs), 'Speech by Minister for Foreign Affairs Dr Vivian Balakrishnan During The Committee of Supply Debate' (Singapore, Ministry for Foreign Affairs, 1 March 2018) at www.mfa.gov.sg/Newsroom/Press-Statements-Transcripts-and-Photos/2018/03/Min-COS-2018-Speech.

[2] As of 2015, the ethnic composition of the population was Chinese (74.3%), Indian (13.3%), Indian (9.1%); the remaining 3.2% are Eurasians and other communities: 'Singapore at a Glance' (Singapore, National Integration Council, 28 November 2019) at www.nationalintegrationcouncil.gov.sg/living-in-singapore/singapore-at-a-glance.

[3] The Pew Research Centre ranked Singapore first on the Religious Diversity Index in 2014. It stated that 'About a third of Singapore's population is Buddhist (34%), while 18% are Christian, 16% are religiously unaffiliated, 14% are Muslim, 5% are Hindu and <1% are Jewish. The remainder of the population of 5 million people belongs to folk or traditional religions (2%) or other religions considered as a group (10%).' Pew Research Center, 'Global Religious Diversity' (4 April 2014) at www.pewforum.org/2014/04/04/global-religious-diversity/.

to protect racial and religious minorities and to secure the interests of Malays as the indigenous people, including their religious interests.[4] Article 153 endorses legal pluralism in mandating legislation to regulate Muslim religious affairs, without correlating any religion with an ethnicity.

Singapore's political leaders failed in their attempt to promote a 'Malaysian Malaysia' as opposed to a 'Malay' Malaysia based on privilege and hierarchy; after secession from Malaysia in 1965, energies were redirected towards engendering a 'Singaporean Singapore' based on equal opportunity and multi-racialism.[5] Rather than recognising group rights or privileges predicated on 'exclusiveness of race, language, religion', the Singapore Constitution protects the equal rights of all citizens; Prime Minister Lee Kuan Yew hoped this individualistic approach founded on a rational *sensibility* seeking to defuse religious tensions by not grounding citizenship on religious identity, would assist Singapore's neighbours 'in reaching similar rational adjustments in their own domestic arrangements' concerning 'problems of language and culture'.[6] Apparently, race-based group rights or privileges nurture a sense of entitlement, evoking emotional reactions when threatened. This was evident when Malaysia reversed its decision to ratify the UN Convention against All Forms of Racial Discrimination, in response to fears that race riots might erupt owing to perceived threats to Malay privilege and Islam's pre-eminent position as the official religion.[7]

While technocratic and pragmatic in style of governance, the Singapore Government has demonstrated solicitude for religious *sensitivities* given that 80 per cent of Singapore's citizens bear a religious affiliation and some sort of relationship to the *Sacred* or divine. While recognising that religion is for many Singaporeans a 'constructive social force' and 'the source of their sense of morality, social duty and concern for their fellow citizens',[8] the Government fears that civil peace might be imperilled where religion is used to pursue political causes or where incidents of disrespect and insult may precipitate religious disharmony. To that end, it maintains a legal framework to manage religious harmony through punitive and deterrent legal sanctions; in regulating religion, the state also deploys pre-emptive restraining orders and utilises hortatory soft constitutional norms, such as those contained in the Declaration of Religious

[4] Art 152(2) requires the Government 'to protect, safeguard, support, foster and promote their political, educational, religious, economic, social and cultural interests and the Malay language'.

[5] Lee Hsien Loong, 'Race, multiracialism and Singapore's place in the world' *The Straits Times* (Singapore, 30 September 2017) at www.straitstimes.com/opinion/race-multiracialism-and-singapores-place-in-the-world. See Lee Kuan Yew, 'Transcript of a Press Conference Given by the Prime Minister' (Singapore, Television Singapura Studio, 22 May 1965) at www.nas.gov.sg/archivesonline/data/pdfdoc/lky19650522.pdf.

[6] Lee Kuan Yew, 'Yang di-Pertuan Negara's Speech (Debate on the Address)', Singapore Parliamentary Debates: Official Reports, 14 December 1965, vol 24, col 115.

[7] 'Why Malaysia backpedaled on ICERD Ratification' *New Straits Times* (Malaysia, 24 November 2018) at www.nst.com.my/news/nation/2018/11/434078/why-malaysia-backpedalled-icerd-ratification.

[8] Prime Minister's Office, *Shared Values White Paper* (Cmd 1 of 1991) para 45.

Harmony (2003), to promote the internalisation of religious harmony-orientated norms and conciliatory methods of resolving 'disharmony' disputes, to secure relational welfare and solidarity.[9] The retention and renovation of the religious offences penal clauses (RPCs) are part of a broader arsenal of 'hard' and 'soft law' tools deployed to handle threats to racial and religious harmony.

Section I of this chapter contextualises the RPCs by setting forth the general legal framework and rationale in addressing race and religion issues. It considers how past race-religious riots have scarred the national psyche, accounting for the acute contemporary concern towards managing racial and religious sensitivities. It considers the 2007 renovation of section 298 by the inclusion of section 298A, and the porting over of these offences to the Maintenance of Religious Harmony Act (MRHA) when it was amended in October 2019. Section II examines the cases prosecuted under these legal provisions, particularly the RPCs, and 'stern warnings' issued in lieu of prosecution; it considers how practice impacts constitutional rights, civic duties such as civility and tolerance, and public goods, including communal morality and social solidarity. Section III considers the rationale for retaining and renovating the RPCs within a secular state, given that the English tradition of treating offences against religion as criminal acts dates back to a time when blasphemy laws were linked to sedition and the church was entangled with the state. This allows insight into the ordering of religion–state relations within Singapore, the particularities of its history and political culture, the interrelationship between law and the emotional or dignitary harm of wounded religious feelings, and how best to contain and defuse religious disharmony.

I. LEGAL FRAMEWORK AND SOCIAL CONTEXT – OFFENCES RELATING TO RELIGION (AND RACE)

A. Legal Framework in Relation to Religion and Public Order

The RPCs seek to maintain civil peace rather than to protect religious orthodoxy. Unlike the Malaysian Federal Constitution,[10] the Singapore Constitution

[9] Li-ann Thio, 'Relational Constitutionalism and the Management of Religious Disputes: The Singapore "Secularism with a Soul" Model' (2012) 1(2) *Oxford Journal of Law and Religion* 446.

[10] Art 160 defines a 'Malay' as 'a person who professes the religion of Islam, habitually speaks the Malay language, conforms to Malay custom'. In relation to the Group Representation Constituency Scheme, which requires the identification of a 'person belonging to the Malay community' Art 39(A)(4) of the Singapore Constitution provides for a subjective element in the form of someone, 'whether of the Malay race or otherwise who considers himself to be a member of the Malay community', and an objective element in that a person is 'generally accepted as a member of the Malay community by that community'. During a 2017 public forum, an academic made the contested contention that contemporary ground sentiments 'require Malays to be Muslims'. As such, it may be that 'a person who has an Indian father and a Malay mother is more Malay than a whole-hearted Malay who happens to be a Christian'. Siau Ming En and Kelly Ng, 'Community committee 'able to deal with

does not attribute a specific religion to a specific ethnic group. While freedom to choose religious identity is guaranteed,[11] and although no ethnic group professes a single[12] religion, policies[13] and judicial attitudes[14] are influenced by the sociological reality that Malays overwhelmingly profess Islam.

Article 15(1) guarantees the right of every person 'to profess and practise his religion and to propagate it'. This is limited by section 15(4), which does not authorise 'any act contrary to any general law relating to public order, public health or morality'. There is no bar to the participation of citizens with religiously influenced convictions in public policy debates, as a facet of the equal democratic rights of citizens and free speech, guaranteed under Article 14 but subject to broad limitations.

While religious free conscience is absolute, the need to regulate external expressions of religious practice, such as propagation, is related to the 'conflicts arising from religious differences', since what is 'self-evident religious truth' to one can be 'rank heresy or dangerous fanaticism' to another.[15] This reflects the fear of roiling emotions stirred by inter-religious conflicts, or cases where third-party conflict entrepreneurs act to stir disquiet between religious groups.[16]

Other than the RPCs, there is a range of laws addressing religious disharmony. Publications dealing with 'matters of race or religion in such a manner that the availability of the publication is likely to cause feelings of enmity, hatred, ill-will or hostility between different racial or religious group' may attract fines or imprisonment under section 4(b) of the Undesirable Publications Act.[17]

evolving concept of race' *Today* (Singapore, 9 September 2017) at www.todayonline.com/singapore/community-committee-able-deal-evolving-concept-race.

[11] The Court of Appeal held that 'religious freedom 'is premised on removing restrictions to one's choice of religious belief': *Nappalli v Institute of Technical Education* [1999] 2 SLR 569 [28].

[12] Adam Ibrahim, a Malay Christian pastor, testified before the 1966 Constitutional Commission, urging that the Constitution should not define Malays as those professing the Muslim faith. He considered it possible to practise Malay traditions and customs without being Muslim, as he celebrated Hari Raya with his family as a matter of culture 'without following the religious implications': 'The right to choose one's religion – by a padre' *The Straits Times* (Singapore, 9 March 1966) 6. For insight into the social pressures Malays converting out of Islam face, see 'I converted to Christianity and My Muslim friends and family condemned me' *Millennials of SG* (5 January 2017) at millennialsofsg.com/2017/01/05/christian-muslim-family/.

[13] For example, Lee Kuan Yew's exhortations to Christians not to evangelise Malays because 'I think there are 60 to 70 per cent of people who are in need of some form of religious and moral guidance': 'Transcript of the Prime Minister's statement to Religious Representatives and Members of the Inter-Religious Council' (Singapore, 30 September 1965) at www.nas.gov.sg/archivesonline/data/pdfdoc/lky19650930a.pdf.

[14] *Public Prosecutor v Ong Kian Cheong* [2009] SGDC 163 [48], where Neighbour DJ noted that '[i]n the Singapore context, the Muslim population mainly comprises people of the Malay race'.

[15] Chan Hiang Leng Colin v Minister for Information and the Arts [1995] SGHC 159.

[16] For example, a church made a complaint against an article by a christophobic secularist, alleging that the contents stirred up religious tensions and had a 'seditious tendency' to promote feelings of ill-will and hostility between Christians and Muslims: Jeanette Tan, 'Church in S'pore make police report against Rice Media for "scurrilous attack" in article' (Singapore, *Mothership.sg*, 27 March 2018) at mothership.sg/2018/03/preacher-lou-engle-cornerstone-church-anti-islam/.

[17] Cap 338, 1998 Rev Ed.

The MRHA,[18] enacted in 1990 and later amended in 2019, empowers the Minister to pre-emptively make non-justiciable restraining orders against a religious leader (section 8(1)) or 'any person' (section 9(1)) inciting or instigating religious groups to do the following acts:

(a) causing feelings of enmity, hatred, ill-will or hostility between different religious groups;
(b) carrying out activities to promote a political cause, or a cause of any political party while, or under the guise of, propagating or practising any religious belief;
(c) carrying out subversive activities under the guise of propagating or practising any religious belief; or
(d) exciting disaffection against the President or the Government while, or under the guise of, propagating or practising any religious belief.

Only section 8(1)(a) applies horizontally between religious groups; the remaining three heads relate to the 'vertical' relationship between someone acting in the name of religion against a public authority or national society at large.

The restraining orders prohibit their subject from addressing, orally or in writing, members of a religious group, for example, without prior ministerial permission. The President has to confirm this order within a set period after receiving the recommendations of the Presidential Council for Religious Harmony. Breach of this order may incur a fine of up to $10,000 or a two-year term of imprisonment.[19] No restraining order has ever been issued during the almost 30 years' existence of the MRHA;[20] the Government has lauded the MRHA's deterrent effect and Buddhist groups have referenced the MRHA as a safeguard against unwanted proselytisation.[21]

The wording of section 8(1)(a) MRHA shares some similarities with a provision in the Sedition Act,[22] which dates back to the 1948 Sedition Ordinance.[23] Section 3(1) identifies five types of 'seditious tendency', one of which departs

[18] Cap 167A, 2001 Rev Ed.

[19] MRHA, ss 8, 9, 12,16, 17.

[20] 'Maintenance of Religious Harmony Act (Number of Restraining Orders issued)', Singapore Parliamentary Debates: Official Reports, 12 February 2007, vol 82, col 1319. Under the 2019 amendments, the restraining orders under s 8(1A) authorise the Minister to issue restraining orders against religious groups to 'pre-empt, prevent or reduce any foreign influence' affecting the religious group that might undermine inter-religious group tolerance or threaten public peace and order in Singapore. Restraining orders may require a person to 'stop undertaking any communications activity' or printing or editing any religious publication without prior ministerial permission, to require a religious group not to accept certain donations, and/or to ensure every member of the governing body of a religious group is a Singapore citizen.

[21] This would probably fall under s 8(1)(a). *Agree to Disagree: Conversations on Conversions* (Singapore, *conversion.buddhists.sg*, 2010) 18, at conversion.buddhist.sg/wp-content/uploads/2016/02/Agree-to-Disagree-Conversations-on-Conversion.pdf. Buddhists comprise the religious majority in Singapore.

[22] Cap 290.

[23] Tan Yock Lin, 'Sedition and its New Clothes in Singapore' [2011] *Singapore Journal of Legal Studies* 212; Jaclyn Neo, 'Seditious in Singapore! Free Speech and the Offence of Promoting Ill-Will and Hostility between Different Racial Groups' [2011] *Singapore Journal of Legal Studies* 351; Thio Li-ann, *A Treatise on Singapore Constitutional Law* (Academy Publishing, 2012) 774–92.

sharply from the common law conception of sedition,[24] which entails insurrection against state institutions. Section 3(1)(e) includes the tendency 'to promote feelings of ill-will and hostility between different races or classes of the population of Singapore', which does not directly involve the state, although one may rationalise it as an assault on the state's multi-racial character.[25] The purpose of section 3(1)(e) has been described as protecting 'racial and national cohesion in Singapore'.[26] Under section 3(3), the intention of the person making a seditious publication is irrelevant where that publication in fact had a 'seditious tendency'. Quentin Loh J noted this had been treated as 'an offence of strict liability' in *Ong Kian Cheong*,[27] but that even absent mens rea of a seditious intention, there remained 'the check of the offending article of expression having a "tendency" to cause the outcomes'[28] under section 3(1). Both section 8(1) MRHA and section 3(3) Sedition Act focus on the vague, subjective term 'causing feelings' or 'promoting feelings', which may constitute an emotional, psychological or dignitary harm, rather than actual physical violence.[29] The direct harm it relates to is causing relations between 'different religious groups' or 'different races or classes' in Singapore to deteriorate, endangering civil peace. The constitutionally protected act of religious propagation was found to have a 'seditious tendency' in *Ong Kian Cheong*, which involved a Christian couple who were distributing Christians tracts like 'The Little Bride' or 'Who is Allah' to people 'with a Muslim name'.[30] This limits religious and expressive freedoms. The tracts were considered 'seditious and objectionable for having offensive and denigratory content[31] dealing with religion or race in such a manner as to promote feelings of enmity, hatred, ill-will or hostility between different racial or religious groups'[32] – specifically, between Christians and Muslims. 'Race' under

[24] As Quentin Loh J noted in *Public Prosecutor v Yue Mun Yew Gary* [2013] 1 SLR 39 [27], the concept of 'seditious intention' at common law is 'a concept allied to an incitement to violence'. At common law, sedition is directed against subverting state institutions: *Boucher v R* [1951] 2 DLR 369, 383–84; *R v Chief Metropolitan Stipendiary Magistrate, ex parte Choudhury* [1990] 3 WLR 986, 1004.

[25] Multi-racialism as a constitutional commitment is further underscored by the race-based reserved presidential elections: Art 19B, Singapore Constitution.

[26] *Public Prosecutor v Ai Takagi* (District Court, MAC 903124-2015 to MAC 903131-2015) [5].

[27] *Ong Kian Cheong* (n 14).

[28] *Yue Mun Yew Gary* (n 24) [20].

[29] Other laws addressing emotions include s 13A of the Miscellaneous Offences (Public Order and Nuisance) Act (Cap 184, 1997 Rev Ed), where the use of 'threatening, abusive or insulting words or behavior' to 'cause harassment, alarm or distress' to a person is an offence. See also the Protection from Harassment Act (Cap 256A).

[30] *Ong Kian Cheong* (n 14) [35].

[31] While it may be permissible to 'talk about the glory of your own race or language', the Law and Home Affairs Minister K Shanmugam stated that 'the moment you run down somebody else, the moment you say that religion or that race or that language is no good, we come after you. In other countries, freedom of speech allows you to do that. We do not.' K Shanmugam, 'Inter-Agency Aftercare Group Youth Forum on "Dangers of Extremism in the Cyber World: Building Resilience in Youth"' (Ministry of Home Affairs, speech delivered on 11 August 2018) at www.mha.gov.sg/newsroom/speeches/news/inter-agency-aftercare-group-youth-forum-on-dangers-of-extremism-in-the-cyber-world-building-resilience-in-youth.

[32] *Ong Kian Cheong* (n 14) [84].

section 3(3) is used interchangeably with 'religion'. This conflation is evident in that a Muslim tract recipient, one Isa Bin Rafee, gave evidence that the publication had '10 segments' that, 'in promoting Christianity, denigrated his religion, Islam', such that the publication was 'offensive because it could provoke or incite racial hatred'.[33] The cases prosecuted in the twenty-first century have involved inter-group relations rather than exciting disaffection against the Government.

The *Maintenance of Religious Harmony White Paper*, a source of non-binding but influential, executive-authored and -published 'soft constitutional law' norms, provides examples of perceived threats to religious harmony. These standards, which must operate within constitutional parameters, speak to how constitutional religious freedoms are to be exercised. This includes respecting the right of individuals to accept or not accept any religion, acknowledging religious sensitivities and exercising the liberty to propagate religious faith 'very sensitively', without denigrating other religions; religious leaders must not allow their followers or clergy to act disrespectfully towards other religious groups, or incite members to hostility or violence towards other groups. Religious groups are urged not to compete for political influence, though individuals from any group may participate *qua* individual citizens in democratic processes.[34]

The external expression of religious freedom is unsurprisingly not absolute. The courts have upheld restrictions on religious freedom, such as prohibition orders barring religious publications from the de-registered Jehovah's Witnesses' publishing arm. Religious freedom was subject to a categorical statist public order trump extra-textually fashioned by the High Court in *Colin Chan v Public Prosecutor*, identifying the 'sovereignty, integrity and unity of Singapore' as the constitutional 'paramount mandate', such that anything that tended to run counter to this trump had to be 'restrained'.[35] In contrast, an attempt to actually balance religious freedom against public order considerations was evident in *Vijaya Kumar v AG*,[36] where the constitutionality of a police permit with conditions regulating the use of music during a Hindu Thaipusam foot procession was challenged, given the general policy of proscribing singing, music and using drums during religious processions. The ban on music was not complete, as musical instruments could be played on temple grounds at the start and end of the procession, and religious hymns could be sung throughout the procession and broadcast from three locations from public address systems. The High Court found that the police conditions relating to 'legitimate public order considerations'[37] were reasonably imposed: the police had access to ground intelligence, had considered the scale, duration and route of the procession, including its religious dimension; the police had liberalised their approach over

[33] ibid [10].
[34] Ministry of Home Affairs, *Maintenance of Religious Harmony White Paper* (Cmd 21 of 1989).
[35] *Colin Chan v Public Prosecutor* [1994] 3 SLR 662, 684F–G.
[36] *Vijaya Kumar v AG* [2015] SGHC 244.
[37] ibid [35].

time in consultation with the Hindu community, in permitting some music to be played at points during specified times, at a specified volume. This 'calibrated approach' demonstrated that 'due regard' had been accorded to the Article 15 rights of the applicants, as the police 'sought to balance these rights against the exigencies of public order'.[38] The police were entitled to consider the heightened public order considerations religious processions posed, compared to 'cultural' processions celebrating Chingay and St Patrick's Day, where music was allowed, and to factor in the potential for communal disturbance, which was not 'unreal',[39] in formulating permit conditions, given Singapore's history of racial riots and its multi-religious make-up. This demonstrates solicitude for religious feelings and underscores the 'premium' accorded to public order in the adjudicatory process in relation to cognate rights like the right to public assembly, which has to be exercised 'responsibly' and within the 'confines of law' – specifically, the law of nuisance in the form of threatening, abusive and insulting speech.

Quite apart from religious feelings, expressive rights have been curtailed where the law has protected other sorts of feelings, as in the case of allegations of impropriety or words of insult directed at a public institution. The High Court, in *Chee Siok Chin v MHA*, stated that insults or abuse directed at a body that contravene public nuisance laws, 'can create feelings of distress, harassment or alarm amongst the directors and officers responsible for it'; this applied to unincorporated bodies, 'where the individuals who are running the organization can also similarly be emotionally affected'.[40] Free speech is clearly not a primary right in the Singapore context, qualified by heavily weighted public order considerations that encompass the maintenance of the quasi-constitutional values of 'racial and religious harmony'. The latter term, in relating to 'harmony', goes beyond the absence of disorder to the quality of a relationship, whether it is durable and sustainable, as a facet of relational welfare.

B. Section 298 and Section 298A Penal Code

i. Section 298

Aside from devoting a chapter to Offences relating to Religion or Race, section 74 of the Penal Code, introduced in 2007, provides for enhanced penalties (one and a half times the amount of punishment) for racially or religiously aggravated offences, together with crimes against foreign domestic workers, a vulnerable category of persons. This amendment to the sentencing regime, in tandem with developments in other Commonwealth countries like New Zealand,

[38] ibid [38].

[39] ibid [49]. The police had pointed out that religious foot processions were 'fundamentally different' from non-religious ones; in 1964, riots arose out of a religious foot procession, and the current one passed by three places of worship – a mosque and two churches: ibid [33].

[40] *Chee Siok Chin v Minister for Home Affairs* [2006] 1 SLR (R) 582 [65].

Canada and the UK, underscores the seriousness of such crimes and the threat posed to the multi-religious and multi-racial nature of the body politic. This includes offences relating to rioting (section 147), communicating and distributing documents or electronic records containing any incitement to violence or counselling disobedience to the law (section 276C), and intentional insult with intent to provoke a breach of the peace (section 504).

Chapter XV of the Penal Code houses the 'Offences Relating to Religion and Race'. Section 295 relates to offensive acts of desecration of places of worship with intent to insult the religion of any class of persons, while sections 296 and 297 relate to the disruption of religious assemblies and funeral rites. Section 298 of the Penal Code belongs to the class of legislation that 'proscribe[s] free expression for similar public policy reason',[41] comparable to provisions like section 504. It reads:

> Whoever, with deliberate intention of wounding the religious or racial feelings of any person, utters any word or makes any sound in the hearing of that person, or makes any gesture in the sight of that person, or places any object in the sight of that person, or causes any matter however represented to be seen or heard by that person, shall be punished with imprisonment for a term which may extend to 3 years, or with fine, or with both.

Two key points may be raised. First, the section 298 offence requires mens rea in the form of 'deliberate intention'. It does not on the face require proof of any violence or physical harm in the form of a more objective requirement pertaining to likelihood of, or actual harm to society. It appears, then, to enforce a norm of civility as a community standard. Second, the harm done is not physical but more psychological, in terms of wounding religious feelings, a vague concept, implicating questions like what sorts of feelings there are, how 'woundedness' is measured, etc. The focus is on harm done to 'feelings', but are the feelings of all persons similarly affected, to the same degree? Is this relevant given the offender's subjective intent? To wound a person's religious feelings may involve insulting the god a person worships, or respected religious personages or even contesting religious doctrine. When should such wounds be shielded, and when might one demand that fellow citizens show a degree of resilience and tolerance when it comes to debates over dogma, such as over who is the final prophet or which school of religious law is most authoritative? The vagueness of the term does not promote certainty in apprehension or application.[42]

[41] *Yue Mun Yew Gary* (n 24) [16].

[42] Section 17F of the amended MRHA requires that a person 'knowingly' engages in certain conduct, knowing that feelings of enmity, ill-will or hostility towards the targeted religious group are 'likely to occur'. If a religious leader knowingly engages in conduct that insults another person's religious belief or wounds a person's religious feelings, knowing the target person is 'likely' to be insulted, an offence is committed. If a non-religious leader acts similarly, the additional requirement is that these feelings, insults or wounds must pose a threat to public peace or order in Singapore or any part thereof.

ii. 2007 Amendments: 'Racial Feelings'

In amending section 298 of the Penal Code in 2007, Parliament described the law as one that helped to preserve 'religious and racial harmony in the new global security climate'.[43] It could serve as both a prophylactic and a punitive instrument. The term 'racial' was added to expand the scope of section 298.[44] The rationale was to provide for 'greater prosecutorial discretion', stemming from the prosecution of two racist bloggers, Benjamin Koh and Nicholas Lim, under section 3(1)(e) of the Sedition Act, which idiosyncratically defines a seditious tendency as one that promotes ill-will and hostility 'between different races or classes' of Singaporeans. This speaks to the 'horizontal' relationship between races or classes, which indirectly implicates the state insofar as it injures the state's 'multi-racial' character. While sedition goes to the life of the state or government, a crime that goes to public order rather than national survivability is a lesser threat. Nonetheless, the sense that there was some disjoint in attributing the character of sedition to acts that upset inter-group feelings is evident, in that questions were raised 'whether there was a need to prosecute the offenders under such a high signature Act'.[45]

The insertion of 'racial feelings' reflects the de facto close correlation of Malay ethnicity with the Muslim religion (over 99 per cent), where words that insult Islam are taken to wound 'racial feelings' rather than 'religious feelings', given that not all Malays are Muslims, and not all Muslims are Malays. This near-conflation of race and religion as a sociological reality does not exist for any other ethnic group; it would be unprincipled and unconstitutional for the law to attribute a particular religion to an entire ethnic group, as freedom of conscience is guaranteed.

Presumably, a racial feeling has to do with denigrating a race as inferior, which wounds the sense of esteem and self-identity of the offended person; hurt pride is a form of dignitary or moral harm. When this disables participation in the democratic process through discrimination, it raises a justification for limiting free speech in the interests of democratic participation as equal citizens. This has not been an argument raised before courts or in general political discourse.

Apparently, the fear is that disquiet, escalating into riots, may be provoked where the racial feeling of a person or a group is offended. However, section 298 is not explicitly concerned with this; in addressing 'wounding of religious feelings', section 298 is distinct from what is usually called 'hate speech'. To avoid depleting the category of meaningful content through overly broad invocations, hate speech should be understood not as disagreement over doctrine or criticism of conduct, but as something akin to the advocacy of 'national, racial or religious hatred that constitutes incitement to discrimination, hostility

[43] Ho Peng Kee (Senior Minister of State for Home Affairs), 'Penal Code (Amendment) Bill', Singapore Parliamentary Debates: Official Reports, 22 October 2007, vol 83, cols 2181 et seq.

[44] The clause now exclusively refers to 'racial' feelings, with the porting over of offences against religious feelings to the MRHA in 2019.

[45] Ho Peng Kee, 'Penal Code (Amendment) Bill' (n 43) cols 2175 et seq.

or violence'.[46] In other contexts, hate speech laws play a symbolic function in creating specific offences that attract grave penalties; such laws seek to promote the esteem of a minority or 'victim' group through a process of state-directed remoralisation, which challenges prejudice towards a protected class.[47]

Law Minister Shanmugam described 'hate speech' as a 'precursor to violence'; in urging society to reject hate speech as part of free speech, he noted that if the routine utterance of hate speech is permitted, 'it pollutes the discourse and normalises extremist behaviour'.[48] The danger, of course, is who gets to define hate, and using what criteria? If an extreme position is taken that 'speech is violence', then what critique is immunised from curtailment? It is a legitimate objective to regulate 'incitement' to hatred and to avoid unduly curtailing expressive freedoms. Hence, the term 'incitement' cannot be understood too laxly to mean 'to persuade or suggest ... to stir up or to arouse'. To incite means 'to instigate, to move to action, to rouse, to spur or to stimulate vigorously into action by, as a prime example, making an inflammatory speech'.[49]

iii. 2007 Amendments – The New Offence under Section 298A

A new section 298A was introduced in 2007, creating an offence punishable by a fine, imprisonment for up to three years, or both. It provides:

> Whoever—
>
> (a) by words, either spoken or written, or by signs or by visible representations or otherwise, knowingly promotes or attempts to promote, on grounds of religion or race, disharmony or feelings of enmity, hatred or ill-will between different religious or racial groups; or
>
> (b) commits any act which he knows is prejudicial to the maintenance of harmony between different religious or racial groups and which disturbs or is likely to disturb the public tranquility,
>
> shall be punished with imprisonment for a term which may extend to 3 years, or with fine, or with both.

This 'disharmony' amendment to section 298 sprang from what was characterised as a more volatile global security climate, with a greater likelihood of

[46] Art 20(2), International Covenant on Civil and Political Rights, UNGA Res 2200A (XXI) (16 December 1966, entered into force 23 March 1976).

[47] Gail Mason, 'The symbolic purpose of hate crime law: Ideal victims and emotion' (2014) 18(1) *Theoretical Criminology* 75.

[48] Danson Cheong, 'Boundaries must be drawn to prevent hate speech: K Shanmugam' *The Straits Times* (Singapore, 25 August 2017) at www.straitstimes.com/politics/hate-speech-boundaries-must-be-drawn-says-shanmugam. See K Shanmugam, 'Ministerial Statement on Restricting Hate Speech to Maintain Racial and Religious Harmony in Singapore' (Singapore, Ministry of Home Affairs, 1 April 2019) at www.mha.gov.sg/newsroom/in-parliament/parliamentary-speeches/news/ministerial-statement-on-restricting-hate-speech-to-maintain-racial-and-religious-harmony-in-singapore-speech-by-mr-k-shanmugam-minister-for-home-affairs-and-minister-for-law.

[49] *Yue Mun Yew Gary* (n 24) [24].

'extremists stirring up enmity or ill-will in a religious setting and fanning racist flames', which would 'yield graver consequences than before'.[50] This is through the phenomenon of 'terrorism driven by religious extremism', where 'a particular race or religion' comes 'under fire' after a terrorist attack; this fuels increased racism and xenophobia, highlighting the need to 'tend carefully' to expressions of religious and racial sentiment.[51] The continuing priority is 'maintaining religious and racial harmony' through sustaining tolerance, moderation, sensitivity and mutual respect between the different races and religions which had been 'painstakingly nurtured over the past decades'.[52] Section 298A would complement section 298, and was considered to 'go a long way in safeguarding racial and religious harmony in Singapore today',[53] by preserving the 'social fabric of the country'.[54]

Section 298A 'plugs a gap' as, prior to its adoption, the Penal Code did not criminalise 'actions that are likely to cause racial or religious disharmony between different racial and religious groups'. Section 298A(a) requires the satisfaction of subjective intent where one 'knowingly promotes' by words a certain state of affairs, independent of whether this eventuates. The inclusion of 'knowingly promotes' was a response to feedback concerns over the 'seemingly broad' scope of the offence; the intent is that it should mirror the section 298 requirement of 'deliberate intention of wounding', sending a 'clear signal that the bar set for these offences is a high one'.[55]

Section 298A(b) refers to conduct the offender 'knows' is prejudicial to the maintenance of religious and racial harmony; it posits an objective element in the form of the actual or likely disturbance of public tranquillity. This requires an evidential basis beyond mere speculation, although the threshold might not be very high given the social matrix in which this sort of predictive calculus operates: the reaction is pegged to that of the 'emotional man' with heightened religious sensitivities acting out of tribal instincts, rather than the 'reasonable man' who keeps an eye to the common good. The reference in section 298A(a) to 'ill-will' and 'feelings' reflects an attempt to manage the 'emotional man', positing a reason/passion dichotomy.

Certain parliamentarians considered that the section 298 amendment played an educative function in setting '[Out-of-Bounds] markers for people who have ill intention to cause frictions among races or religions';[56] this goes to establishing community identity as a tolerant, multi-racial and religiously diverse society, while applying legal sanctions to anti-social behaviour. There were concerns that this penal clause would unduly undermine expressive and religious liberties,

[50] Ho Peng Kee, 'Penal Code (Amendment) Bill' (n 43) cols 2175 et seq.

[51] ibid.

[52] ibid col 2181.

[53] ibid col 2434.

[54] Lim Biow Chuan, 'Penal Code (Amendment Bill)', Singapore Parliamentary Debates: Official Reports, 23 October 2007, vol 83, col 2416.

[55] Ho Peng Kee, 'Penal Code (Amendment) Bill' (n 43) cols 2175 et seq.

[56] Dr Teo Ho Pin, 'Penal Code (Amendment Bill)', Singapore Parliamentary Debates: Official Reports, 22 October 2007, vol 83, col 2208.

particularly in relation to the right to evangelise, which soft constitutional law norms have instructed should be done sensitively and respectfully.[57]

In speaking of prosecutorial discretion, four examples were identified of what would not come under the ambit of the new section 298 and 298A offences. First, carelessly spoken words, such as where friends made casual jokes about race and religion without deliberate intent to cause insult, or where jokes and remarks are made 'purely for entertainment purposes'[58] during arts and cultural performances. The bar for this offence 'is set high',[59] with both sections 298 and 298A serving the purpose of 'protecting individuals and targeting people who promote enmity, ill will, hatred between religious groups'.[60] The context of friendship or humour apparently negates the need to protect individuals or sanction potential offenders in the absence of deliberate intent to wound; however, it is not always easy to distinguish the thin line between gentle satire and robust, rude ridicule. Further, there are variable degrees of sensitivity with respect to how one receives jokes about one's race and/or religion. This sense of indeterminacy compels one to trust in the public prosecutor's discretion, an unattractive proposition for some. In light of the *Jylland-Posten* Muhammad cartoon controversy,[61] it may be difficult to ascertain whether a situation in which cartoons or pictures are drawn 'innocently, ignorantly or under the guise of freedom of expression without deliberate intention to provoke nor knowledge that it will lead to disharmony'[62] is caught by the penal clauses.[63]

Second, fact-based articles written by journalists would not be caught even if racially or religiously sensitive; this presumably operates on the premise that journalism in Singapore is based on accurate reporting rather than descending into political advocacy or grandstanding to serve an ideological agenda.[64] Journalistic bias may be expressed not just through misrepresentation and 'fake news', but also through tone and over/under-coverage of an issue in such a way as to subtly cultivate ill-will towards a religious or racial group. A mix of fact and opinion may also compound the difficulty in exercising prosecutorial discretion prudently, in balancing free speech against religious sensitivities concerns.

Third, a distinction appears to have been made between matter and manner, insofar as a 'critical but rational and objective discussion of religion and religious

[57] Ministry of Home Affairs, *Maintenance of Religious Harmony White Paper* (n 34) paras 15–18.

[58] Dr Teo Ho Pin, 'Penal Code (Amendment Bill)' (n 56) col 2209.

[59] Ho Peng Kee, 'Penal Code (Amendment) Bill' (n 43) col 2434.

[60] ibid.

[61] See, eg, Ian Cram, 'The Danish Cartoons, Offensive Expression and Democratic Legitimacy' in Ivan Hare and James Weinstein (eds), *Extreme Speech and Democracy* (Oxford University Press, 2009) 311.

[62] Ong Kian Ming, 'Penal Code (Amendment Bill)', Singapore Parliamentary Debates: Official Reports, 23 October 2007, vol 83, col 2377.

[63] If the focal point is on the subjective frame of mind rather than the effect of the publication, presumably this falls beyond the scope of ss 298/298A.

[64] 'The media has no special role beyond reporting the news and giving its views on matters of public interest fairly and accurately', ie the courts and political leadership do not view the media as having a watchdog role or engaging in investigative journalism: *Review Publishing Co Ltd v Lee Hsien Loong* [2009] SGCA 46 [277].

principles will also not likely be caught'.[65] This permits scrutiny of religious tenets and their real-world effect, with the understanding that rationality and objectivity are able to facilitate dialogue and the search for religious truth and understanding; speech that contains false statements or misinformation is of low value and unworthy of protection on the basis of theoretical justifications for free speech, such as the argument from truth or from democracy.[66]

Lastly, there were concerns that the penal clauses would unduly restrict the constitutional right to religious propagation, as Singaporeans should be free to choose their religious beliefs, although a thin line existed 'between promoting religion and promoting enmity between different groups of people on grounds of religion'. This flows from the view that aggressive proselytism would result in 'unhealthy competition',[67] causing inter-religious tensions, disrupting national unity. Religious organisations were exhorted to appreciate that religious belief should be 'a "draw" instead of a "push" initiative by individuals'.[68] Home Affairs Senior Minister of State Ho Peng Kee affirmed that Article 15 provided 'that everyone has the right to hold his own religious beliefs and to accept or not to accept any religion'.[69] Therefore, if a person were to share his testimony of his conversion from one religion to another on his personal Internet website, 'stating how he found fulfillment and meaning in life after he converted to the other religion, without denigrating another person's religion',[70] this would not be caught under section 298A. Instances involving the mocking of a faith would, minimally, attract a stern police warning.[71] Minister Ho emphasised that appreciating religious sensitivities should accompany religious propagation, distinguishing between people interested in hearing religious views from those someone tries to convert 'by denigrating his religion, especially when he has no desire to be converted'.[72] In effect, the executive is interpreting Article 15 in furnishing guidance on how to exercise a right responsibly.

Discussions on religious matters may potentially stir up disquiet and disagreement, but when does disagreement cross over into 'wounding' a religious feeling? For example, political leaders, in seeking to maintain public peace and good inter-group relations, regularly warn against 'Islamophobia' and urge that terrorism not be associated with any one religion.[73] However, to insulate any

[65] Ronald JJ Wong, 'Practising and professing your faith: Know your rights' *Salt & Light* (15 September 2018) at https://saltandlight.sg/faith/practising-and-professing-your-faith-know-your-rights/.

[66] Sundaresh Menon CJ (dissenting) in *AG v Ting Choon Meng* [2017] 1 SLR 373 [113]–[117].

[67] Dr Teo Ho Pin, 'Penal Code (Amendment Bill)' (n 56).

[68] ibid.

[69] Ho Peng Kee, 'Penal Code (Amendment) Bill' (n 43) col 2175.

[70] ibid.

[71] See the discussion on the Lighthouse evangelism case in Thio Li-ann, 'Contentious Liberty: Regulating Religious Propagation in a Religiously Diverse Secular Democracy' [2010] *Singapore Journal of Legal Studies* 484.

[72] Ho Peng Kee, 'Penal Code (Amendment) Bill' (n 43) col 2175 et seq.

[73] 'Islamophobia as bad and unacceptable as terrorism, says PM Lee' *The Straits Times* (Singapore, 21 June 2017) at www.straitstimes.com/singapore/islamophobia-as-bad-and-unacceptable-

religion from honest, temperate and reason-based criticism bears the danger of creating a new secular form of blasphemy inimical to a free society. There is a difference between accenting the positive in religions, and legally shielding any one religion (or ideology) from critique; the line between reasonable civil critique and abusive invective is not self-evident.

Given the state's secular disposition and constitutional religious freedom guarantees, religious discussions positing the veracity of one faith and the falsehood of another, however upsetting to adherents of that other religion, cannot *per se* fall within section 298A. This is unavoidable, given the mutual exclusivity of religious beliefs, and par for the course where religious discussion is concerned, which implicates the idea of truth. Part and parcel of living in a free society is that someone might disagree with your most deeply cherished religious or ideological views. It is not the business of the secular state to advance any one conception of religious truth and, thus, section 298A must serve the instrumental purpose of keeping the peace, not keeping the faith. To impose legal sanctions too readily to punish speech the religious may find offensive would unduly chill expressive freedom; this might perpetuate a 'thin-skinned' approach towards being religiously offended and not require the cultivation of tolerance and self-restraint. Conversely, failing to restrain speech that incites hatred, ill-will or violence towards a religious or ethnic group would be a dereliction of government duty to maintain civil peace. Law Minister Shanmugam argued that 'Islamophobia' increased the risk of violence not only from terrorists killing in the name of Islam, but also from 'those who want to attack Muslims'.[74] Laws are appropriate to punish acts of violence; however, more hortatory methods of persuasion and inculcation are better suited to cultivating a sense of civility,[75] if not solidarity and friendly relations.[76]

as-terrorism-says-pm-lee (citing an incident in London, where a Caucasian man drove his van into a crowd of Muslim worshippers leaving the mosque, killing one person, as an act of Islamophobia, ie an act of physical violence against Muslims). Law Minister K Shanmugam expressed his discomfort against Islamophobia, which had to be kept out of Singapore through strategies like promoting inter-faith harmony and addressing the need for non-Muslims to better appreciate 'the nature of Islam, the true essence, true philosophy and beauty of Islamic teachings' and the peaceful nature of most Muslims around the word. He insisted that Muslims who were extremist and intolerant, who 'make absurd, ridiculous propositions' about non-Muslims, women and other groups, are 'very few' in nature' and that 'you have such people in every religion': Faris Mokhtar, 'S'pore must continue to keep out of Islamophobia: Shanmugam' *Today* (Singapore, 31 December 2017) at www.todayonline.com/singapore/spore-must-continue-keep-out-islamophobia-shanmugam.

[74] Faris Mokhtar, 'S'pore must continue to keep out of Islamophobia: Shanmugam' (n 73).

[75] 'We have seen how the pursuit of absolute freedom of expression in other countries can give rise to polarising extremism, racism and xenophobia, which have in turn led not only to acrimony between different groups but tragic bloodshed at times. We want to avoid such incidents in Singapore. Our citizens also demand a high level of civility in our public discourse, especially on such sensitive matters. This is because respect, tolerance and courtesy among different races and religions remain fundamental values for Singaporeans.' UNHRC, 'National report submitted in accordance with paragraph 5 of the annex to Human Rights Council resolution 16/21 (Singapore)' (28 October 2015) UN Doc A/HRC/WG.6/24/SGP/1, para 117 (Second National Report (Singapore)).

[76] eg the Minister for Law and Home Affairs has urged the building up of inter-faith relations, to oppose radicalisation and segregationism, and to build a Singaporean identity and interactive common spaces: Shanmugam, 'Inter-Agency Aftercare Group Youth Forum' (n 31).

iv. 2007 Amendments – Encompassing the Virtual

Given the importance of online communication, sections 298 and 298A of the Penal Code were made to apply to online or electronic transmissions, as the impact of such transmissions was 'much wider than face-to-face or hard copy transmissions',[77] magnified in terms both of reach and permanency.[78] The laws on sedition, contempt of court and defamation have also been recognised as applying to virtual speech.[79]

Extending the penal clauses to digital speech sent a strong signal that the Internet is 'not an entirely unregulated space' where calls to violence, including racial slurs, are treated as an acceptable mode of communication.[80] Indeed, the anonymity of digital speech, the lack of a filter in the form of being taken to task by someone in a physical audience, may embolden some in the safety and secluded privacy of their room 'to make more extreme statements and take more extreme views'.[81] To condone such behaviour would be a 'collective failure' in cultivating the Internet as 'an empowering forum for the good of mankind and for the creation of a more robust civic consciousness and civilised society'. It is therefore 'inevitable' that 'public order offences will increasingly take place in the realm of cyberspace', where 'shortened communication synapses often lead to hasty conclusions', such that the Internet 'can curtail tolerance and shorten tempers as well'.[82] Thus public order, which restrains speech and religious freedoms, while usually connoting 'the protection of a public physical space from disorder', now extends to cyberspace. Digital speech can be abused, and given the rapidity with which false digital speech can travel, there is 'no reason why false statements should not be justifiably restricted on the basis of the preservation of public order'.[83] The same argument might not apply with equal force to hurtful or offensive digital speech, where what is at issue is the truth or falsehood of propositions about religion or race, as opposed to digital misinformation that undermines the democratic process.

Courts have declared their readiness to act in the public interest by imposing deterrent sentences 'to rein in irresponsible and extreme online postings' that may imperil 'peace and harmony' within Singapore's multi-racial and multicultural society, as 'mutual respect and tolerance' cannot be taken for granted.[84]

[77] Ho Peng Kee, 'Penal Code (Amendment) Bill' (n 43) col 2175 et seq.

[78] *Public Prosecutor v Tang Koon Huat* [2017] SGDC 221 [27]–[28] ('A moment on Internet, is forever on Facebook.').

[79] *Public Prosecutor v Benjamin Koh* [2005] SGDC 272; *Lee Hsien Loong v Roy Ngerng* [2015] SGHC 320; *AG v Wham Kwok Han Jolovan* [2018] SGHC 222. See Thio Li-ann, 'The Virtual and the Real: Article 14, Political Speech and the Calibrated Management of Deliberative Democracy in Singapore' [2008] *Singapore Journal of Legal Studies* 25.

[80] *Yue Mun Yew Gary* (n 24) [54].

[81] ibid [52].

[82] ibid [54].

[83] Sundaresh Menon CJ (dissenting), *Ting Choon Meng* (n 66) [119].

[84] *Tang Koon Huat* (n 78) [28].

In the context of sections 298/298A, the good of social cohesion of a religiously and racially diverse democratic society is a key factor in justifying restrictions on speech on the basis of its content, mode of communication (whether temperate or abusive) and other contextual features.

v. Porting Over Religion-Related Offences from the Penal Code to the Maintenance of Religious Harmony Act

As part of the project of making the MRHA a 'comprehensive Act' to provide 'a full range of legislative levers' to deal with maintaining religious harmony, offences relating to 'egregious conduct'[85] in relation to religious disharmony were ported over from the Penal Code to the MRHA when it was amended in 2019. Sections 295 (injuring or defiling a place of worship with intent to insult the religion of any class), 296 (disturbing a religious assembly) and 297 (trespassing on burial places) of the Penal Code have been repealed, while the references to 'religion' have been removed from sections 298 and 298A, which now only deal with race-related offences.[86]

Broadly speaking, the matters formerly falling under sections 298 (wounding religious feelings) and section 298A (promoting on religious grounds feelings of enmity, hatred, ill-will) fall within the scope of new section 17F of the MRHA, which borrows the Penal Code terminology and is discussed further below.

The new section 17E creates the offence of urging another person or group of persons, on religious grounds, to use force or violence against any target person or target group in Singapore as identified by religion, ethnicity, descent, nationality, language, political opinion 'or by any other characteristic, whether or not of a similar kind'.[87] This reflects an official acknowledgement of the advent of 'tribal or group politics', insofar as it is envisaged that target groups or their members, defined by immutable traits, ideological or sexual preferences, socio-economic class or any distinguishing marker, may be singled out for physical force or violence. This would in any event be covered by other Penal Code provisions, such as section 267C, which criminalises making documents containing any incitement to violence, which is punishable by five years' imprisonment. Under section 17E, the maximum term of imprisonment has been raised to 10 years, signalling that 'the weaponisation of religion to urge violence or force

[85] Sun Xueling (Senior Parliamentary Secretary to the Minister for Home Affairs), 'Maintenance of Religious Harmony (Amendment) Bill', Singapore Parliamentary Debates: Official Reports, 7 October 2019, vol 94. The speech is also available at www.mha.gov.sg/newsroom/in-parliament/parliamentary-speeches/news/second-reading-speech-for-the-maintenance-of-religious-harmony-amendment-bill-speech-by-sun-xueling-senior-parliamentary-secretary-ministry-of-home-affairs-and-ministry-of-national-development.

[86] As this book goes to print in 2020, there is yet no indication when the amendments to the MRHA will commence.

[87] The explanatory statement accompanying the MRHA Amendment Bill states that 'other characteristics' may include 'atheists, individuals from a specific racial community, who share a similar sexual orientation, or have a certain nationality or descent like foreign workers or new citizens'.

to be used against any person is unacceptable in our society'.[88] Section 17E only applies to instances of physical violence or force, and not to intangible wounded feelings or insult, which some have loosely called 'psychological violence'.[89]

While section 17E(1) and (2) are not religion-specific in terms of the target person or group, sections 17E(3) and (4) identifies the target group on religious grounds, which excludes 'atheists or persons who lack any religious belief or view'; under these subsections, the person urging force or violence against the religiously defined target group does so on non-religious grounds. In short, urging the use of force or violence against any religious groups on any ground is prohibited, as is the urging of force or violence on religious grounds against any religious or non-religious group. While section 298A addresses acts likely to prejudice disharmony between different religious or racial groups, section 17E addresses any type of inter-group conflict, including between religious and irreligious groups, and the possibility that one might urge physical force or violence against the other.[90]

Section 17F(1) is directed at conduct that incites 'feelings of enmity, hatred, ill-will or hostility against, or contempt for or ridicule of' a religious group in Singapore; while section 17F(2) deals with religious insult or the wounding of religious feelings of a religious person. The person engaging in such conduct under sections 17F(1) and (2) refers to a religious leader, with these clauses dealing with inter-religious or intra-religious situations, which would have generally been covered under section 298 and section 298A. Under sections 17(3) and (4), the perpetrator is any person (religious or otherwise) who knowingly engages in conduct designed to incite hatred, insult or wounding, with the additional requirement under section 17(3)(d) and section 17(4)(d) that the said person knows such conduct 'would threaten the public peace or public order' in Singapore. While section 298A imposes punishment of up to three years' imprisonment, the MRHA offence, which delineates a defence of domestic or private communications, provides for imprisonment for up to five years, to denote the gravity of threats to religious harmony. While section 17F(4) covers the same

[88] Sun Xueling, 'Maintenance of Religious Harmony (Amendment) Bill' (n 85).

[89] See, eg, the idiosyncratic equation of 'hate speech and institutionalized discrimination' of groups, including those who define themselves in terms of sexuality, with violence: Anthea Ong (Nominated MP), 'Maintenance of Religious Harmony (Amendment) Bill', Singapore Parliamentary Debates: Official Reports, 7 October 2019, vol 94. 'Hate speech' is an open-textured term, which can cover anything from legitimate criticism to speech that on repetition can increase people's propensity to violence. The difficulty for each political community is to settle on the criteria for 'hate', an impartial arbiter, and to negotiate the extent to which speech that harms and speech that hurts is constitutionally protected. The Law Minister issued a Ministerial Statement on 'Restricting Hate Speech to Maintain Racial and Religious Harmony in Singapore' on 1 April 2019; see Shanmugam (n 48).

[90] The Government has recognised in policy statements the prospect of inter-group conflict on ideological grounds, between religious and 'secular groups', urging both religious groups venturing into the secular domain and 'secular groups which want to strongly push their views and change our social norms' to practise mutual tolerance and restraint: President SR Nathan, 'Building Our Future Singapore in an Uncertain World' (Speech at Opening of Parliament, 18 May 2009) [20].

ground as section 298 in capturing any person who 'knowingly' engages in religious insult or wounding, section 17F(3) is broader than section 298A, which refers to conduct causing disharmony between religious or racial groups that may disturb public tranquillity. Section 17F(3) encompasses situations without an inter-religious dimension, as where an irreligious or secular humanist person, for strategic purpose, incites hostility against a disliked religious group whose views, on questions of public morality for example, he may oppose as obstructions to his preferred ideological agenda.[91]

C. How do we Solve a Problem Like Maria? Sensitivity to the Sentiments Provoked by Fealty to the Sacred

Within a democratic society, a key strategy in not forcing religious citizens to choose between loyalty to deity and polity is through robust protection of religious freedom and other civil liberties; added to this, religious status cannot be invoked to disallow participation in public life, or to disallow the holding of political office.

However, only an imprudent government would discount the gravity of religious conflict within a nation where it has occurred before, which traumatises the national psyche. The standard narrative[92] revolves around past racial riots in 1964, and tensions associated with the *Maria Hertogh* case.[93] Maria was a young Dutch girl separated from her natural parents, who were Dutch Catholics, during the Japanese Occupation; she was adopted and raised as a Muslim by her Malay foster mother, Che Aminah. After the war, her natural parents sought custody of her; Che Aminah arranged for an under-aged Maria

[91] The new MRHA clauses are not general hate-speech legislation but designed to ensure that the use of religion is not abused and weaponised to upset public tranquillity, and against the long-recognised threat to religious harmony caused by religious insult, wounding religious feelings, and inciting hatred and hostility against religious groups in Singapore, the last of which enjoy constitutional freedom of religion guarantees under Art 15, Singapore Constitution. Religious groups may criticise groups that promote a homosexual agenda on a variety of grounds, including public morality, though they may not incite violence against any group on religious grounds. Agendas that seek to enact hate-speech legislation to prohibit criticism of homosexual conduct, for example, would go against existing laws such as the prohibition of sodomy under s 377A of the Penal Code, the purpose of which has been judicially identified to be to maintain public morality, in affirming its constitutionality validity: *Lim Meng Suang v AG* [2015] 1 SLR 26. Hate-speech legislation engages questions of public morality on all sides, and envisages an abandonment of liberal neutrality in favour of a remoralised state. The question is: whose vision of morality prevails? See Gail Mason, 'The symbolic purpose of hate crime law' (n 47).

[92] eg Lim Biow Chuan, 'Penal Code (Amendment Bill)' (n 54) col 2416. The Maria Hertogh incident was also referenced in explaining the Government's circumspect attitude towards outdoor street protests: Deputy Prime Minister Wong Kan Seng, Singapore Parliamentary Debates: Official Reports, 28 February 2008, vol 84, cols 1153–55, cited in *Chee Soon Juan v Public Prosecutor* [2011] 2 SLR 940 [22].

[93] *Maria Huberdina Hertogh v The Consul-General For The Netherlands* [1950] 1 MLR 238. See Syed Muhd Khairudin Aljunied, *Colonialism, Violence and Muslims in Southeast Asia: The Maria Hertogh Controversy and its Aftermath* (Routledge, 2009).

to marry a 22-year-old teacher to gain control of the situation, but the marriage was declared null and void. Maria, who wanted to stay with Che Aminah, was taken into protective custody by the Social Welfare Department. Religious sensitivities were inflamed by the 'irresponsible reporting' of the English press showing photos of Maria in a convent, as some Muslims 'felt that a Muslim girl was being forced to convert to Christianity'.[94] A four-day riot broke out on 11 December 1950, when a British judge decided to award custody of Maria to her natural parents, resulting in the death of 18 persons, with 173 injured and property damage. The aftermath of the case was 'disastrous for race relations between the colonial masters and their Muslim subjects', such that 'Singapore was never to forget the Maria Hertogh riots.'[95]

Courts have invoked the spectre of Maria, as in *Public Prosecutor v Koh Song Huat Benjamin*,[96] where, in speaking of the sentencing approach of general deterrence for sedition involving ill-will and hostility between 'different races or classes', Magnus SDJ noted that '[r]acial and religious hostility feeds on itself'; deterrence was necessary not only because of the 'international security climate', but also because of 'the especial sensitivity of racial and religious issues in our multi-cultural society, particularly given our history of the Maria Hertogh incident in the 1950s and the July and September 1964 race riots'.[97]

The Religious Man is a sensitive man, given to emotional reaction where religious matters are concerned, rather than possessing the detachment one expects the Rational Man, committed to free speech, viewpoint diversity and intellectual enquiry, to exhibit. In discussing the 'real risk' test in relation to contempt of court, the Court of Appeal in *Shadrake v AG* rejected contrary views that the appropriate reference point from which to ascertain whether speech critical of the judiciary would undermine the public confidence in the administration of justice 'may not always be average reasonable persons'. Some persons might be 'less rational' or 'more discriminating'.[98] The Hong Kong Court of First Instance, in *Secretary for Justice v Oriental Press Group*,[99] considered it important not to discount the perspective of 'the person who does not address issues rationally', whereas the Singapore Court of Appeal confirmed that the 'public' must 'comprise the average reasonable person'; while people might respond differently to the same impugned statement, the Court was to make an 'objective decision' whether the statement would undermine public confidence in the courts, 'as assessed by the effect of the impugned statement on the average reasonable person'.[100] The test of the 'fair and reasonable man' as the

[94] Chan Sek Keong, 'Multiculturalism in Singapore: The Way to a Harmonious Society' (2013) 25 *Singapore Academy of Law Journal* 84, [22].
[95] ibid [12].
[96] *Benjamin Koh* (n 79).
[97] ibid [6].
[98] *AG v Shadrake* [2011] 2 SLR 445 [52].
[99] *Secretary for Justice v Oriental Press Group* [1998] 2 HKC 627.
[100] *Shadrake Alan v AG* [2011] SGCA 26 [32].

'anthropomorphic conception of justice' was adopted, the spokesman for which is the court itself.[101]

The legislative formulation of the section 298/298A offences in referencing 'feelings' departs from the 'reasonable man' as embodied by the court; it takes religious sensitivities seriously and holds out a view of religion as provoking or inspiring passions and emotions that can erupt into a public order threat. Rather than trying to promote rational detachment, civility and resilience in religious citizens, the Government has focused on protecting sensitive feelings, which can be dangerous for freedoms if this is the sole or primary consideration. For the Government, the maintenance of 'racial and religious harmony' is 'an important tenet for us when approaching the Rule of Law';[102] this transcends law and order issues, and concerns the quality of relational well-being and a sense of civic solidarity. The Government adopts[103] an 'activist' approach towards ethnic relations and managing threats to social harmony such as anti-Islam feelings and rhetoric. In catering to religious sensibilities, burning holy books like the Bible and Quran would be a crime.

II. PROSECUTING RELIGIOUS OFFENCES – SECTIONS 298 AND 298A

There have been relatively few cases brought under sections 298 and 298A, not all of which are fully reported;[104] in certain circumstances, a 'stern warning' is given in lieu of a prosecution under section 298A. Typically, these decisions are not accompanied by reasons. Stern warnings were given in the following cases:[105]

(a) 2012: Amy Cheong, a Singapore permanent resident, received a 'stern warning' for posting an expletive-filled racist rant on Facebook; she disparaged Malays for their low-cost, lengthy void deck weddings and mocked

[101] ibid, citing Lord Radcliffe in *Davis Contractors Ltd v Fareham Urban District Council* [1956] AC 696, 728.

[102] S Jayakumar, 'Applying the Rule of Law' (2009) 43(1) *The International Lawyer* 83, 85.

[103] 'Need to guarantee position of minorities in Singapore, secure common space: Shanmugam' *The Straits Times* (Singapore, 1 February 2017) at www.straitstimes.com/singapore/need-to-guarantee-position-of-minorities-in-singapore-secure-common-space-shanmugam.

[104] eg Andrew Kiong pleaded guilty and was imprisoned for two weeks for wounding the feelings of others by leaving a card on the car of Mohamad Dahar Dollah that insulted Islam; he had 16 similar cards and had placed eight of them on cars he believed Muslims owned: Shaffiq Alkhatib, 'Man gets 2 weeks' jail for insulting Islam' *Channel News Asia* (Singapore, 7 August 2010); Lee Dji Lin wounded religious feelings by placing raw pork outside her Malay-Muslim neighbour's house; found to have a psychiatric condition, she was subject to a two-year Mandatory Treatment Order: Vanessa Paige Chelvan, 'Women who threw pork at Muslim neighbour's flat sentenced to psychiatric treatment' *Channel News Asia* (Singapore, 30 June 2017). The prosecution brought a s 298 charge for wounding religious feelings when a tourist allegedly said to his taxi driver, a Malay-Muslim, that Muslims were terrorists and that he would burn the driver's Koran. The accused was acquitted as it was not proven beyond a reasonable doubt that these words had been uttered, or that the accused had uttered them: [2018] SGDC 288.

[105] Ministry of Home Affairs, Annex to 'Statement on Offensive Speech and Expression Involving Race or Religion' (7 May 2017) at www.mha.gov.sg/docs/default-source/others/annex---offensive-speech-and-expression-involving-race-or-religion.pdf.

their divorce rate. The insulting post was circulated by one of her friends in cyberspace; a grassroots leader and secretary of the Hougang Inter-Racial and Religious Confidence Circle made a police report against her. She lost her job as an assistant director of membership at the National Trade Union Congress, and returned to Australia.[106]

(b) 2012: A received a conditional warning for posting comments on an online forum labelling the Indian community as 'smelly f***';

(c) 2012: A and B commented online, 'Malays only know how to rob, rape and steal from Chinese'; they were given conditional warnings;

(d) 2014: A posted a comment on a shop's Facebook page saying that Malays were 'ridiculous fools' causing trouble by their dietary requirements, in response to a Malay individual's enquiry about how the shop got a halal certificate. He was given a conditional warning.

A. Prosecution under Section 298: The *Amos Yee Cases* (2015–16)

In one of the most infamous cases involving a section 298 offence, Amos Yee, a teenager who was also a former child actor, was charged, convicted and jailed twice for online postings made in 2015 and 2016 for wounding wounded religious feelings. The first offence occurred on 27 March 2015, some four days after the death of Singapore's first Prime Minister, during a time of national mourning. Yee, then 16, posted an eight-minute video on his Youtube Channel, entitled 'Lee Kuan Yew is finally dead'. In it, he criticised Lee's authoritarian government and policies, comparing Lee to Jesus Christ, describing both as

> power hungry and malicious, but [they] deceive others into thinking that they are compassionate and kind. Their impact and legacy will ultimately not last as more and more people find out that they are full of bull. And Lee Kuan Yew's followers are completely delusional and ignorant and have absolutely no sound logic or knowledge about him that is grounded in reality, which Lee Kuan Yew very easily manipulates, similar to the Christian knowledge of the Bible and the work of a multitude of priests.

In the same video, Yee also superimposed an image of Lee and former British Prime Minister Margaret Thatcher on stick figures depicted as engaging in 'unnatural intercourse'.[107] Two days later, numerous police reports were filed against Yee by members of the public. He was eventually charged under section 292 for the offence of distributing obscene material and under section 298 for uttering words with deliberate intent to wound religious feelings. He was found guilty of both charges in *Public Prosecutor v Amos Yee Pang Sang*[108] and refused the prosecution's recommendation that he undergo probation. He was

[106] Joyce Lim, 'Racist rant: Amy Cheong gets stern warning from police' *The Straits Times* (Singapore, 25 March 2013).

[107] *Public Prosecutor v Amos Yee Pang Sang* [2015] SGDC 215 (*Amos Yee* (DC)) [22].

[108] ibid.

then sentenced to four weeks' imprisonment in September 2015, backdated for time spent in remand.

Yee later ignored police notices to aid in investigations concerning offensive remarks he made against Islam on his blog in November 2015, and left Singapore. Before he returned in April 2016, Yee published vulgar Facebook posts[109] for which he was again charged under section 298 for insulting the religious feelings of Muslims ('Islam reinforces sexism') and Christians ('Responding to the Common Bullshit of Christians').[110]

In convicting him of these subsequence offences, the District Court stated that Yee did not 'lack in his mental capacity to make rational choices', noting his 'contemptuous and irreverent remarks' had the tendency 'to generate social unrest and undermine the religious harmony in our society'. To serve the public interest, the court would not condone or tolerate Yee's conduct.[111] Yee, who expressed remorse,[112] pleaded guilty in September 2016 and was sentenced to six weeks' imprisonment and fined $2,000. Yee's appeal against the District Court decision failed. Yee eventually made his way to the USA, where he was awarded asylum in March 2017. The US immigration judge found the criminal charges against Yee were a 'pretext' to silence his political opinions.[113] A Singapore Ministry of Home Affairs (MHA) statement pointed out that the US decision 'conflated a legitimate difference on tolerance for offensive material with political persecution';[114] other officials clarified Yee was prosecuted not for

[109] Yee posted 'the Islamics seem to have lots of sand in their vaginas too … But don't mind them, they do after all follow a sky wizard and a pedophile prophet. What in the world is a 'moderate muslim'? A f*****g hypocrite that's what! … With all due respect, Christians, you can shove that faith up your ass. Faith! Faith! I'd be damned at this retardation of humanity. F**k you, Christian shits.' Ministry of Law, 'Statement by the Ministry of Law on the Decision granting Asylum in the United States to Amos Yee' (Singapore, 19 April 2017) [11] at www.mlaw.gov.sg/content/minlaw/en/news/videos/statement-on-amos-yee.html.

[110] J Weston Phippen, 'The Teenager who wounded Singapore's religious feelings' *The Atlantic* (30 September 2016) at www.theatlantic.com/news/archive/2016/09/singapore-blogger-religious/502262/.

[111] This decision was not published. Amir Hussain, 'Blogger Amos Yee starts serving 6-week jail term' *The Straits Times* (Singapore, 13 October 2016) at www.straitstimes.com/singapore/courts-crime/blogger-amos-yee-starts-serving-6-week-jail-term; 'Amos Yee gets 6 weeks jail for wounding religious feelings' *Channel News Asia* (Singapore, 29 September 2016) at www.channelnewsasia.com/news/singapore/amos-yee-gets-6-weeks-jail-s-2-000-fine-for-insulting-muslims/3165386.html accessed 5 November 2016.

[112] Amir Hussain, 'Teen blogger Amos Yet gets 6 weeks jail and $2000 fine for wounding religious feelings' *The Straits Times* (Singapore, 29 September 2016) at www.straitstimes.com/singapore/courts-crime/teen-blogger-amos-yee-gets-six-weeks-jail-and-2000-fine-for-wounding. According to his Defence lawyer, Yee admitted not possessing 'any religious, scholastic and/or intellectual ability to discuss religion'. In this instance, no Christian or Muslim religious leaders came forward to say their religious feelings had been affected.

[113] Nirmal Ghosh, 'US appeals board gives asylum nod to Amos Yee' *The Straits Times* (28 September 2017) at www.straitstimes.com/singapore/us-appeals-board-gives-asylum-nod-to-amos-yee; Bill Chappell, 'US grants Asylum to Amos Yee, Young Blogger from Singapore' *npr* (27 September 2017) at www.npr.org/sections/thetwo-way/2017/09/27/553976738/u-s-grants-asylum-to-amos-yee-young-blogger-from-singapore.

[114] Ministry of Law, 'Statement by the Ministry of Law on the Decision granting Asylum in the United States to Amos Yee' (n 107). The UN Human Rights Office for Southeast Asia considered criminal sanctions 'disproportionate' and 'inappropriate', citing 'international protections for

his political opinions but for hate speech against Christians and Muslims, which Singapore 'does not countenance', as 'we have learnt from bitter experience how fragile our racial and religious harmony is'.[115]

The following section will examine how the District Court and High Court interpreted the statutory requirements of section 298, and the constitutional arguments raised by defence counsel in relation to free expression.

i. The Actus Reus and Mens Rea of Section 298

In its judgment on the first set of offences, the District Court found that the reference to 'any person' under section 298 was not confined to a single person but could relate to an entire religious community, consistent with section 2 of the Interpretation Act.[116] Aside from the actus reus of uploading the videos, which Yee clearly did,[117] the question of whether the section 298 offence was satisfied rested on the answer to two main questions:

(a) whether the communication was offensive and wounding; and
(b) whether there was deliberate intent to wound religious feelings.

a. Wounding Religious or Racial Feelings

Imposing legal sanctions on words that wound religious or racial feelings poses a substantive limit to expressive freedoms, but it is not evident what 'wounding religious feelings' entails. Does a bare complaint suffice to establish woundedness, or is there a way to measure feelings to verify the existence of wounds in the form of pain and damage? Are there degrees of harm, and should this factor impact liability and sentencing? Is 'religious feeling' a monolithic category, or does it relate to a range of emotions, such as distress, anger, joy, submission and sorrow?[118] To these complex questions, the District Court cursorily stated that to wound religious feelings 'simply means to give offence to any person'.[119]

freedom of expression and opinion': Johan Nylander, 'UN urges Singapore to release 16 year old blogger Amos Yee' *Forbes* (23 June 2015) at www.forbes.com/sites/jnylander/2015/06/23/un-urges-singapore-to-release-16-year-old-blogger-accused-of-posting-critical-lee-kuan-yew-photos/.

[115] Tham Yuen-C, 'Amos Yee prosecuted for hate speech, not political dissent: Singapore to The Economist' *The Straits Times* (13 April 2017) at www.straitstimes.com/singapore/amos-yee-prosecuted-for-hate-speech-not-political-dissent-singapore-high-commissioner-for.

[116] Cap 1, Rev Ed 2002. The amendments to s 298 in 2007 were meant to allow cases such as *Benjamin Koh* (n 79) to be prosecuted under it, rather than under the Sedition Act. This case involved online remarks directed not at one individual but at the Muslim Malay community at large. Thus, one can infer that Parliament intended for the revised s 298 to apply to communities as well as individuals.

[117] The prosecution pointed out that Yee had also taken 'active steps' to disseminate the video as widely as possible, such as asking 'The Real Singapore' website to publicise the video: 'Prosecution's Closing Submissions' (MAC Nos 902694 to 902696, 8 May 2015) [33]–[34], at www.dodwell-law.com/wp-content/uploads/2015/05/Amos-Yee-8-May-15-Prosecution-Closing-Submissions.pdf, accessed 19 February 2019.

[118] Daniel Statman, 'Hurting Religious Feelings' (2000) 3 *Democratic Culture* 199.

[119] *Amos Yee* (DC) (n 107) [32].

If so, does it matter how sensitive religious groups or particular religious persons might be, and whether the offence given is trivial or serious? Or is 'religious feeling' to be treated as an abstraction? It appears that section 298 might be conceptualised as a statutory right not to be religiously offended, but this begs the question whether such protection is absolute or whether some degree of resilience is expected of the offended believer, who must in a democratic society tolerate and accept the denial of his or her religion by others, as well as the propagation of competing religious or humanist doctrines.

In attempting to drill down into the specifics of religious feelings, it was argued that Yee's words could not wound the religious feelings of Christians, given the Christian teaching on tolerance and forgiveness; minimally, it could not be said with 'absolute certainty' whether their religious feelings were wounded.[120] The High Court, on appeal, found that even if the Christian religion taught forgiveness and letting go of hate, it did not mean that followers of that religion were incapable of having their religious feelings wounded. Forgiveness does not mean being 'impervious' to hurt feelings 'from attacks and insults'; what it entails is not seeking retaliation or holding grudges. It was precisely because 'human followers of religion can get offended when their religions are attacked'[121] that section 298 was necessary. There was no need to show that the feelings of specific individuals were in fact wounded, provided the words, 'using an objective standard', had the capacity to wound.[122]

The Distinct Court, in considering the language and effect of the comments Yee made in the video about Jesus, the 'central figure of Christianity', found these to be 'clearly derogatory and offensive to Christians'. The comments that Christians had 'no real knowledge of the bible' as their understanding was manipulated by a 'multitude of priests' were 'insulting and offensive to the Christian community'.[123] This provided an 'ample basis' on which to infer a deliberate intent to wound Christian religious feelings,[124] as the chief fault element of section 298.

b. Deliberate Intention

The section 298 offence is intent-based and mere utterance alone suffices to constitute the actus reus as no proof of actual wounding or consequences is required, as distinct from the section 298A requirement that the court consider

[120] 'Appellant's Written Submissions' (Magistrate's Appeal No 9108 of 2015/01, 29 September 2015) [63] at http://perma.cc/7PN5-RP7S.

[121] 'Respondent's Submissions' (Magistrate's Appeal No 9108 of 2015/01, 29 September 2015) [102].

[122] 'Justice Tay Yong Kwang's Oral Judgment for Magistrate's Appeal No 9108 of 2015 Amos Yee v Public Prosecutor' (Attorney-General's Chambers, 24 February 2017) [7] at www.agc.gov.sg/home/justice-tay-yong-kwang%27s-oral-judgement-for-magistrate-s-appeal-no.-9108-of-2015-amos-yee-v-public-prosecutor.

[123] *Amos Yee* (DC) (n 107) [33].

[124] 'Respondent's Submissions' (n 121) [82].

whether an act disturbs or is likely to disturb public tranquillity. The mens rea of 'deliberate intention' must be proved beyond reasonable doubt.

The District Court held that the evidence that some Christians were offended by Yee's comments went not to liability but influenced sentencing.[125] This proof was found in Yee's own statement that some '20 negative comments' made 'mostly from people practising Christianity' were left on his Youtube video channel.[126] Since the impact of the expression was not an element of the offence, it was irrelevant that religious leaders made no public statements confirming that their religious feelings as Christians were wounded by Yee's video, or that many Christians, including Yee's former bailor, Vincent Law, stated that their religious feelings were not hurt.[127] That the 'negative reaction' was confined to social media comments was also not deemed surprising, as the video was made 'not by someone who is learned or of special influence' but by a teenager, 'who plainly has a lot of growing up to do'.[128]

As subjective states of mind cannot be proved as a fact, intention must be proved through the 'irresistible inference' drawn from 'all relevant facts', which are to be located in the video and the accused's knowledge 'as to its effect'.[129] Mere knowledge 'of the likelihood of feelings being hurt'[130] was insufficient, consistent with the Orissa High Court's approach in *Narayan Das*.[131] Instead, a conscious deliberate intent to wound religious feelings was required.

This deliberate intent could be inferred from various factors. First, evidence indicating that the making and uploading of the video were premeditated, not carried out impulsively 'on the spur of the moment'.[132] Yee spent two to three days 'preparing the script and shooting the video',[133] indicating this was an endeavour that had been thought through. Second, the accused's state of mind with respect to the nature of what he was trying to communicate and the knowledge of the accused as to the effect of his communication. Deliberate intent was further located in Yee's admission, prior to uploading the video, that 'the video was offensive and would promote feelings of disharmony or feelings

[125] *Amos Yee* (DC) (n 107) [37].

[126] ibid [36].

[127] 'Defence's Closing Submissions' (MAC Nos 902694 to 902696, 8 May 2015) [73] at www.dodwell-law.com/wp-content/uploads/2015/05/Amos-Yee-Closing-Submissions-08.05.15for-webpage-uploading-3.pdf.

[128] *Amos Yee* (DC) (n 107) [39].

[129] ibid [45].

[130] ibid [41].

[131] *Narayan Das v State* AIR 1952 Ori 149 [6].

[132] *Amos Yee (DC)* (n 107) [42]. CK Thakker, Ratanlal Ranchhoddas and Dhirajlal Keshavlal Thakore, *Ratanlal & Dhirajlal's Law of Crimes: A Commentary on the Indian Penal Code* (2005 Reprint) 1187: 'Although the party uttering offensive words might be conscious at the moment of uttering them that they were likely to wound the feelings of his auditors, yet if it were apparent that he uttered them on the spur of the occasion, in good faith, simply to further his argument … he would not … be liable to conviction.' (as cited in the Defence's Closing Submissions (n 127) [83]).

[133] *Amos Yee* (DC) (n 107) [50].

of ill-will within the Christian community'.[134] The High Court likened stirring 'ill-will' to 'wounding somebody's feelings'.[135] Third, the language employed could also go to proving an intent to wound, even if it does not eventuate in actual harm, perhaps because the publication is confined to a small circle of tolerant people.[136] The High Court found from the video's contents that there was 'no doubt' Yee intended to 'deliberately arouse' Singaporeans, whether Christian or not, to enter into 'verbal combat with him' through the method of provocatively using 'vulgarities and insults' to 'arouse emotions'.[137] Fourth, the High Court considered Yee's history and 'apparently unhappy experience' as a former Catholic and altar boy; Yee had left Catholicism and embraced atheism, which he thought favoured 'logic and reasoning'. This provided the background to the words Yee used, which were 'not innocent words uttered without real thought'.[138]

The deliberate intention to wound through online expression did not have to be targeted at a specific group of religious people given the 'vast reach of the Internet'. Even if the intended audience were all Singaporeans who could choose whether or not to view the video, so long as it reached the specific religious community, the words had the capacity to wound. The District Court found the comparison between publishing online and speaking words 'in the privacy of a secluded location' to be 'strange'.[139] Again the focus was on the potential effect of the uploaded post, as the accused was assumed to appreciate that the platform through which he chose to communicate his message had a potentially global audience.

c. Deliberate or Dominant Intent

One argument made by the defence was that the test adopted in *Narayan Das v The State*[140] should be used to construe section 298. This required a 'real or dominant intent' to wound religious feelings. This was absent, as Yee's alleged intent was to 'generate controversy and encourage critical discussion'[141] through his video about whether Lee Kuan Yew as a government leader was as good a person as public sentiment indicated. Yee argued the video was 'essentially secular' and may have wounded the 'secular feelings'[142] of Singaporean Lee

[134] ibid [34].
[135] 'Justice Tay Yong Kwang's Oral Judgment' (n 122) [3]–[4].
[136] *Amos Yee* (DC) (n 102) [38], citing Roberts CJ in *The King v Nga Shwe Hpi* AIR 1939 Ran 199.
[137] 'Justice Tay Yong Kwang's Oral Judgment' (n 122) [3].
[138] ibid [5].
[139] *Amos Yee* (DC) (n 107) [51].
[140] *Narayan Das* (n 131). The real and dominant intent test was applied to ascertain whether the accused's intent was to persuade people he was a living God or whether he sought to deliberately wound the religious feelings of others who were going to worship the inanimate object representing Lord Jagannath, which he described as 'a piece of wood'. The Orissa High Court found his dominant intent was to emphasise his own divinity, not insult Lord Jagannath.
[141] 'Appellant's Written Submissions' (n 120) [78].
[142] ibid [46].

admirers, but there was no evidence of an intent to insult Christians, to whose feelings Yee was 'indifferent'.[143] Yee thus lacked a 'real and dominant' intent to wound religious feelings, as he had in good faith included the words complained of to support his political and 'essentially secular' critique of Lee, as evident in his video title, and that 'drawing the analogy with Jesus and Christians' was to advance another critique against Lee and his policies rather than to wound religious feelings.[144]

The District Court rejected the argument that Amos was 'indifferent' to the video's effect on Christians, showing a lack of deliberate intent or, at worst, that wounding Christian religious feelings was 'an ancillary purpose, and not his primary or dominant intent'.[145] The determinative factor was the 'character of the contents'[146] of the video, not its title or the fact it contained only '10 sentences' referencing Jesus and Christians.

The contents related to two distinct subjects, Jesus and Lee Kuan Yew: in drawing an analogy between them, Yee was pointing to 'the same alleged denigrating similarities' between Lee, Jesus and their followers.[147] The District Court indicated that Yee was 'fully aware' the comparison 'was offensive to the Christian population' and that he had looked up the Sedition Act. District Judge Jasvender Kaur found that Yee's immediate intent 'was to denigrate both subjects'; as there was no ambiguity in intent, the *Narayan* test had no application here.[148] The High Court affirmed that all section 298 required was to prove a deliberate intention to wound religious or racial feelings, 'irrespective of whether there is also another intention, dominant or otherwise'.[149] In describing the inclusion of 'knowingly promotes' in section 298A as mirroring the requirement of 'deliberate intention of wounding' found in section 298, Parliament understood that deliberate intention meant 'nothing more than knowingly';[150] this included things a person 'should have known' would follow from an act, even in the absence of desire to wound religious feelings, as when a Muslim slaughtered a cow for a wedding feast in full view of Hindus.[151]

ii. Fair Latitude to Religious Discussion: Free Speech Values

Presenting Yee's video as a political critique that sought to urge people to feel less afraid of criticising the Government was a strategy to foreground 'the primacy of Article 14';[152] were the court not to protect free speech values, its

[143] ibid [71].
[144] ibid [47], [57].
[145] 'Defence's Closing Submissions' (n 127) [78], [80].
[146] *Amos Yee* (DC) (n 107) [49].
[147] ibid [49].
[148] ibid.
[149] 'Justice Tay Yong Kwang's Oral Judgment' (n 122) [6].
[150] 'Respondent's Submissions' (n 121) [74].
[151] *Mir Chittan v Emperor* AIR 1937 All 13.
[152] 'Appellant's Opening Submission' (Magistrate's Appeal No 9108 of 2015/01, 8 October 2015) [13].

decision would have a chilling effect in 'an age of renewed interests in politics and an emerging sense of ownership in Singapore and what direction our country should take'.[153] The court was urged to 'send the message that truth and reason should be allowed to prevail in the marketplace of ideas'.[154]

The issue was framed as one of how 'to calibrate the tension between the higher order right for Amos to express his views on matters of public interest, and the public interests of protecting morals and public order'.[155] To give effect to the constitutional free speech guarantee as a 'higher order' right, it was argued that the section 298 offence should be subject to a high threshold of requiring proof of wounded religious feelings. Rather than assessing whether the words in the abstract had the capacity to wound or offend, the appellant argued that a distinction should be drawn between 'lawful criticism' of a religion, even if this was robust, harsh or misguided, and merely insulting or wounding religious feelings, such as associating non-halal food with a Muslim religious figure.[156] As section 298 'is not a blasphemy law',[157] free speech could not be subject to the 'overly sensitive feelings' of a religious person or group, as a constitutional right was at stake.[158] It was argued that what Yee said about Christ was just a 'strongly expressed critique'.[159]

The District Court found that Yee's remarks against Christians and Christ[160] were 'invective in nature', flowing from which the District Court was content to state that 'no issue of "fair latitude" for religious discussion or free speech arises'.[161] This test, based on 'good faith', had been derived from *Narayan*, where the purpose of the Indian Penal Code (from which section 298 was derived) was identified as allowing 'all fair latitude to religious discussion', while preventing 'the professors of any religion from offering, under the pretext of such discussion, intentional insults to what is held sacred by others'.[162] Thus a 'warm expression dropped in the heat of controversy' or an argument offered in good faith to vindicate one's own creed rather than to annoy professors of another creed, 'will not fall under the definition contained in this clause'.[163]

Presumably, the judge agreed with the prosecution's argument that Yee's comments fell without the 'fair latitude' to be given religious discussion, given Yee's 'mocking tone' in guising intentional insults as critical discussion; Yee

[153] ibid [6].
[154] ibid.
[155] ibid [12].
[156] 'Appellant's Written Submissions' (n 120) [42].
[157] ibid [40].
[158] ibid [73], [75].
[159] ibid [42].
[160] *Amos Yee* (DC) (n 107) [83].
[161] ibid [51].
[162] Thomas B Macaulay, *The Complete Works of Thomas Babington Macaulay (Illustrated)*, 1st edn (Delphi Classics, 2016) note J, quoted in *Narayan Das* (n 131) [6]–[7].
[163] *Narayan Das* (n 131) [6]–[7].

declared he was not remorseful, despite knowing his videos were 'offensive and promoted ill-will and hostility amongst Singaporeans', as he considered this 'an aspect for freedom of speech and positive change to occur'.[164]

In contrast, the respondents argued that the case was not about free speech or viewpoint diversity but 'the abuse of these freedoms'.[165] The High Court rejected this characterisation as a 'noble disguise of freedom of speech' and desire to generate genuine discussion, as the use of 'vulgarities, and crude language and obscene depiction' did not 'sound like freedom of speech at all'; rather, it was a 'license to hate, to humiliate others and to totally disregard their feelings or beliefs by using words to inflict unseen wounds'.[166] Justice Tay Yong Kwang pointed out that 'real debate and rational discussion' on public issues could 'flourish in an environment of goodwill, reasoning and civil language', rather than be poisoned 'with vulgarities and crude language'.[167] The Singapore model of free speech and political participation thus incorporates a duty of civil discourse, which is required if democracy is to be sustainable, with engaged and engaging citizens. In another context, it was observed that 'temperate, balanced criticism allows for rational debate … and thus may even contribute to the improvement and strengthening of the administration of justice', whereas 'scurrilous and preposterous attacks … are likely to have the opposite effect'.[168] Law thus serves as a gentle civiliser of citizens in the exercise of their liberties.

B. Prosecution under Section 298A: *Imam Nalla Case* (2017)

Unlike section 298, section 298A is framed in relation to causing 'feelings of enmity, hatred or ill-will', or committing acts prejudicial to the maintenance of harmony 'between different religious or racial groups'. It implies a deterioration of relations between at least two different religious or racial groups, as opposed to an actor's (religious or otherwise) wounding the religious or racial feelings of one group.

Nalla Mohamed, an Indian national who was chief Imam at Jamae Chulia Mosque, had lived in Singapore for about a decade. During Friday prayers on 6 January 2017, he uttered an Arabic phrase, 'Grant us help against the Jews and the Christians.' This was recorded on video and uploaded on Facebook on

[164] 'Prosecution's Closing Submission' (n 117) [39]–[40] (8 May 2015) at www.dodwell-law.com/wp-content/uploads/2015/05/Amos-Yee-8-May-15-Prosecution-Closing-Submissions.pdf accessed 19 February 2019.

[165] Prosecution's Skeletal Submissions on Sentencing (6 July 2015) at www.agc.gov.sg/docs/default-source/newsroom-doucments/media-releases/2015/15-7-6_amos-yee-written-skeletal-subs-(with-annexes).pdf.

[166] 'Justice Tay Yong Kwang's Oral Judgment' (n 122) [7].

[167] ibid [11].

[168] *AG v Tan Liang Joo John* [2009] 2 SLR 1132 [19]; see also *Wham Kwok Han Jolovan* (n 79) [73]–[76].

24 February 2017 by a recent Muslim convert, Terence Nunis. This caused a stir within the Muslim community, who felt the video cast them in a negative light. Nunis wrote, 'Islam is not at war with people of other faiths … This is an unbecoming relic of a different age. We should not encourage this sort of thinking or condone this sort of supplication.'[169]

A police report was lodged on 28 February, and, after investigations, Nalla was prosecuted and convicted under section 298A(b) for committing an act he knew was 'prejudicial to the maintenance of harmony between different religious or racial groups and which disturbs or is likely to disturb the public tranquility'. He pleaded guilty, was fined $4,000 and later deported from Singapore.[170] This reflects Singapore's zero tolerance policy for religious leaders who make divisive speeches that would be firmly repudiated. In her sentencing remarks in *Public Prosecutor v Nalla Mohamed Abdul Jameel Abdul Malik*,[171] District Judge Jasvender Kaur noted that Nalla knew that his words could be interpreted as 'asking God to grant Muslims victory against the Jews and Christians'.[172] This was an aggravating factor, compounded by the fact that an Imam leading Friday prayers, who should be aware of the Singapore context, ought to have exercised greater care not to say anything in a sermon 'that may undermine the harmony that exists amongst the different races and religions'; the Imam's comments could 'create friction and conflicts' between different religious groups that Singapore could ill-afford.[173]

Muslim leaders also distanced themselves from the Imam's prayer: the Islamic Religious Council (MUIS) declared there was no room in Singapore for discourse that promoted intolerance, enmity or violence against other communities; Muslim Affairs Minister Yaacob Ibrahim called for calm and unity in a Facebook post, declaring the rejection of 'any speech or actions that foster ill will between communities. That is the Singapore way.' The Mufti Fatris Bakaram made a Facebook post stating that the Muslim community had to ensure its religious texts were read appropriately, otherwise the good name of Islam and Muslims in Singapore would be smeared.[174] The Law Minister commented that

[169] 'Police report lodged over remarks made by imam on Christians and Jews' *Channel News Asia* (Singapore, 28 February 2017) at www.channelnewsasia.com/news/singapore/police-report-lodged-over-remarks-made-by-imam-on-christians-and/3557112.html?cid=FBCNA accessed 7 March 2017.

[170] Jeanette Tan, 'Muslim imam convicted of promoting enmity between religious groups, fined $4000 for comments on Jews, Christians' (*Mothership.sg*, 3 April 2017) at mothership.sg/2017/04/muslim-imam-convicted-of-promoting-enmity-between-religious-groups-fined-4000-for-comments-on-jews-christians/.

[171] MCN-900387-2017 (3 April 2017) at www.statecourts.gov.sg/Resources/Documents/03042017%20Oral%20GD%20-%20PP%20v%20Nalla%20Mohamed%20Abdul%20Jameel%20Abdul%20Malik%20%28website%29.pdf.

[172] ibid [1](i).

[173] ibid at 1(iv) and 2.

[174] The Mufti issued a Statement on Nalla's case dated 3 April 2017, in which he stated the Imam's words had no place in Singapore where communities co-existed peacefully and harmoniously, as they 'made our Jewish and Christian friends wonder why they were being targeted',

these statements demonstrated how strongly the Muslim community valued religious harmony.[175]

Notably, despite the legal action taken, the Imam made reconciliatory gestures towards various religious leaders, who were receptive of them. The District Court took note of these mitigating factors. On 31 March, Nalla requested a meeting with inter-faith representatives, which took place at the Harmony in Diversity Gallery, where he delivered an apology to them (including Christian, Sikh, Taoist, Buddhist and Hindu representatives) and to all Singaporeans. He also visited Rabbi Mordecai Abergel at his synagogue to give him a copy of his Statement of Apology, and was photographed with him and other religious leaders, including Anglican Bishop Terry Kee. He commented that the rabbi and bishop had received him with kindness, pointing out that 'all mortal men make mistakes', and that 'we must move forward consciously for the sake of social trust and religious cohesion'.[176] Members of the Inter-Religious Organisation dressed in religious garb accompanied him to these meetings and to court, demonstrating solidarity. Finally, the Imam had a conciliatory breakfast with Law Minister Shanmugam organised by the Imam of Ba'alwie Mosque, where the press took photographs of both conversing and embracing.[177] Cumulatively, these publicly visible acts demonstrated rapprochement. This was capped by the Muslim Affairs Minister's Facebook page thanking non-Muslims for accepting the Imam's apology and noting that gracious forgiveness reflected 'the Singapore way' of upholding 'mutual respect and harmony for our common good'.[178] This reflects the practice of relational constitutionalism, which seeks to promote durable relationships and social solidarity by cultivating goodwill between religious groups through dialogue, quiet diplomacy and conciliation to diffuse disharmony crises.[179]

The police issued a 'stern warning' to two other parties involved, as the Public Prosecutor assessed their actions to be violations of section 298A(b).

caused suspicion among non-Muslims and damaged the image of Islam and Muslims. This Statement is available at www.muis.gov.sg/-/media/Files/Corporate-Site/Press-Releases/03-Apr-2017--Media-Statement--Mufti-Statement-on-the-Case-of-Mr-Nalla-Mohamed-Abdul-Jameel-Eng.pdf.

[175] Toh Yong Chuan, 'No room for religious extremism in Singapore, says Muslim leaders' *The Straits Times* (Singapore, 5 March 2017) at www.straitstimes.com/singapore/no-room-for-religious-extremism-in-singapore-say-muslim-leaders.

[176] Toh Yong Chuan, 'Shanmugam appreciates imam's sincere apology' *The Straits Times* (Singapore, 6 April 2017) at www.straitstimes.com/singapore/shanmugam-appreciates-imams-sincere-apology; 'Imam has shown sincere remorse, regret, Shanmugam' *Today* (Singapore, 5 April 2017) at www.todayonline.com/singapore/shanmugam-meets-imam-who-made-offensive-remarks-against-jews-christians.

[177] Toh Yong Chuan, 'Minister meets imam who was fined for making offensive remarks and will be headed home' *The Straits Times* (Singapore, 5 April 2017) at www.straitstimes.com/singapore/minister-meets-imam-who-was-fined-for-making-offensive-remarks-and-will-be-heading-home.

[178] 'Imam who made offensive remarks to be repatriated; stern warnings for two others: MHA' *Today* (Singapore, 3 April 2017) at www.todayonline.com/singapore/imam-who-made-offensive-remarks-be-repatriated-stern-warnings-two-others-mha.

[179] Li-ann Thio, 'Relational Constitutionalism and the Management of Inter-Religious Disputes: The Singapore "Secularism with a Soul" Model' (2012) 2 *Oxford Journal of Law and Religion* 446.

They were not prosecuted, being secondary offenders.[180] The first, Nunis, had uploaded the video and disseminated offensive material online, rather than reporting the Imam's actions to the police. The second, NUS academic Syed Muhammad Khairudin Aljunied, made two Facebook posts ('The Imam and the Silly Convert' and 'The Imam and the Wised Up Convert Reloaded') that appeared to support Nalla's offensive remarks; these similarly attracted liability for prejudicing harmony between religious groups. Both parties made public apologies through the MHA and undertook not to repeat their conduct. This plays an educative and socialising function in denoting that it was 'irresponsible and reckless' to sensationalise such issues on social media, which could sow discord within and between communities. MUIS urged the Malay-Muslim community to refer such matters to the authorities in the future, as the two stern warnings issued were 'a strong reminder on what MUIS has always stressed: that the use of social media must be tempered with wisdom and *adab* (ethics and civility)'.[181] In an interview, the Roman Catholic Archdiocese said that religious teachers should be 'aware that they are not just addressing their believers, but also the world as well', which necessitated being 'more cautious not to be seen as slighting other religions'.[182] A Muslim minister noted that though the Nalla case was not about 'slighting religions', it 'also stirs emotions within our community'.[183]

An MHA statement underscored that the phrase Nalla used was 'unacceptable in a multi-racial and multi-religious society'.[184] Nalla clarified the phrase was not in the Quran but from an old Arabic text originating from his village in India.[185] The MHA, in seeking to demonstrate even-handedness, declared that '[a]ny religious leader from any religion' making similar statements would be 'held accountable for their actions'. While Nalla's supplication was not in the Quran, 'the same principles apply, even if such verses are to be found in a religious text'. It asserted that under Singapore law, no one would be allowed 'to preach or act divisively and justify that by reference to a religious text'. This is

[180] 'NUS don and blogger warned by Police in case of imam who made offensive comments against Jews and Christians' *The Independent.sg* (3 April 2017) at theindependent.sg/nus-don-and-blogger-warned-by-police-in-case-of-imam-who-made-offensive-comments-against-jews-and-christians/.

[181] 'Singapore to repatriate imam who made offensive remarks, two others warned' *Malay Mail* (Singapore, 3 April 2017) at www.malaymail.com/news/world/2017/04/03/singapore-to-repatriate-imam-who-made-offensive-remarks-two-others-warned/1348695.

[182] Siau Ming En, 'Social media should not be used to sow discord: Religious leaders' *Today* (Singapore, 4 April 2017) at www.todayonline.com/singapore/social-media-should-not-be-used-sow-discord-religious-leaders.

[183] Masagos Zulkifli, 'Aspirations of Singapore Women (Motion)' Singapore Parliamentary Debates: Official Reports, 4 April 2017, vol 94.

[184] Ministry of Home Affairs, 'MHA Statement on Sentencing of Imam for Offensive Remarks' (9 April 2017) para 5, at www.mha.gov.sg/newsroom/press-release/news/mha-statement-on-sentencing-of-imam-for-offensive-remarks.

[185] Toh Yong Chuan, 'Imam apologises for insensitive remarks, clarifies that remarks were not from Quran' *The Straits Times* (Singapore, 31 March 2017) at www.straitstimes.com/singapore/imam-apologises-for-insensitive-remarks-clarifies-that-remarks-were-not-from-quran.

potentially a limit on religious freedom, insofar as there are 'exhortations in religious texts, from more than one religion, which, inter alia, encourage violence towards people of other religions'.[186] Effectively, such religious doctrine would be outlawed, but this may be justified as part of the price of living in a plural society which generally guarantees religious liberties, short of religiously justified (rightly or wrongly) violence.

i. Rights, Interests, Values – What's at Stake?

Sections 298 and 298A of the Penal Code legally sanction various forms of communication that wound religious/racial feelings and cause disharmony between religious/racial groups. They legally sanction violations of basic standards of civility. By requiring only a 'deliberate intention' to harm, section 298 does not make a connection between hurtful speech and the empirically contingent fact of violence, giving rise to a 'subjective sense of disorder'[187] whenever social norms of civility or propriety are violated. Communications under section 298A are repressed because they possess the tendency to produce violence and disorder, both physical and psychological, through undermining essential social norms.

Where religious sensitivities are recognised as legitimate limits on free speech guarantees, this views the prevention of a certain type of offensive conduct as the state's business. Free speech does not have pre-eminent status in Singapore, unlike other jurisdictions like the US, where it is considered constitutive of national identity, key to democratic participation and the symbol of individual liberty that defines civic membership. However, where the state has no interest in presenting or preserving a set of religious truths, the question of how to measure the legitimacy of religious sensibilities as a free speech limit arises. Does criminal prosecution lie for any criticism of religion? Is it unreasonable for religionists to expect exemption from all criticism and insults, in a secular state where government seeks to preserve religious harmony and reciprocal tolerance to maintain the good of public order?[188] While the state should restrain conduct

[186] Ministry of Home Affairs, 'MHA Statement on Sentencing of Imam for Offensive Remarks' (n 175) para 9. The Law Minister had apparently referred to some biblical passages in Deuteronomy as an example of religious scriptures that invited Christians 'to go out and kill non-believers', according to a news report. The National Council of Churches of Singapore (NCCS) expressed concern that this misrepresented the Bible and Christianity. In a meeting with NCCS, the Minister clarified that scriptural passages had to be contextualised within the Singapore setting, accompanied by explanation to avoid harmful misconstruction. He acknowledged that Christians understood the 'destroy' passages as being confined to a specific historical context and did not entail divine commands to justify violence by Christians against non-believers. NCCS, 'Dialogue with Minister K Shanmugam on "Terrorism and Radicalisation in Southeast Asia and our Challenges"' (13 February 2018) at www.mha.gov.sg/docs/default-source/others/dialogue-with-minister-k-shanmugam-on-terrorism-and-radicalisation-(9-feb-2018).pdf.

[187] Robert Post, 'Hate Speech' in Ivan Hare and James Weinstein (eds), *Extreme Speech and Democracy* (Oxford University Press, 2009) 123, 136.

[188] *Refah Partisi (The Welfare Party) v Turkey* [2003] ECHR 87, para 91.

that incites hatred against religions or races, this does not require insulating all religious discourse from scrutiny and critique: there is a difference between conduct that 'incites' and that 'insults', between harmful and hurtful speech. Some may see a virtue in exercising free speech to engage in religious satire or even ridicule, to challenge religious fundamentalism, or to protest a dominant religion or religious school, as freedom of thought. The case law provides little insight into whether and how these distinctions should be drawn.

Where religious sensitivities are valorised, a blanket prohibition against offensive speech might be adopted in the extreme: this would sound the death knell for freedom of thought and inquiry, under which states are empowered to assess the legitimacy of religious beliefs, as where the Singapore Government requires that sacred scriptures be contextualised and not used to provoke inter-group animosities. A more balanced approach may be to regulate offensive speech not exclusively on the basis of content, but as to the manner in which it is delivered. This could be related to public order and social solidarity, and even to an ethos of tolerance, which gratuitously offensive speech violates. Article 152 may be read as obliging the Government to protect the interests of 'racial and religious minorities' and Malays as indigenous peoples, which includes guarding against wounded religious feelings that thwart the peaceful enjoyment of religious freedom of minorities.[189]

Sections 298/298A may be characterised as expressing a right not to be religiously offended, setting up a clash between free speech rights as expressions of autonomy and a right to be free from offence.[190] In *Public Prosecutor v Koh Song Huat Benjamin*, Magnus SDJ, in addressing seditious speech stirring ill-will between races or classes, stated that 'the right of one person's freedom of expression must always be balanced by the right of another's freedom from offence, and tampered by wider public interest considerations'.[191] The idea that a right like free speech may be limited by the 'rights of others' or competing interests was also evident in *Chee Siok Chin v Minister for Home Affairs*, where the High Court was dealing with public nuisance and the right to assembly. Rajah JC stated that 'Freedom of action invariably ends when conflicting rights and/or interests collide. Contempt for the rights of others constitutes the foundation for public nuisance. All persons have a general right to be protected from insults, abuse or harassment.'[192]

In the context of balancing rights, duties and goods, an essential task is to identify the nature and status of these items. How, then, is the 'freedom from offence' to be characterised?

[189] Arguably, where a minority religion like Islam is connected to an ethnic identity like Malay, this minority religion deserves more protection, as it serves as a proxy for ethnic identity. Niraj Nathwani, 'Freedom of Expression and Religious Feelings' (2009) 1 *Yearbook of Muslims in Europe* 507, 531.

[190] Where this promotes discrimination against a group, it may hinder that group from effectively participating in the democratic processes, justifying restrictions in the name of democratic processes.

[191] *Benjamin Koh* (n 79) [8].

[192] *Chee Siok Chin* (n 40) [136].

Although this is not reflected yet in Singapore jurisprudence, the right not to be religiously offended or have one's religious beliefs insulted has been held to be part of religious freedom in the jurisprudence of the European Court of Human Rights.[193] In decisions like *ES v Austria*,[194] Article 188 of the Austrian Criminal Code, which makes disparagement of religious doctrine an offence, was held not to violate freedom of expression. The Court took at face value the government claim that protecting religious freedom was a 'legitimate aim'. A commentator said that the European Court's treatment of religious and expressive freedoms could lead to the embrace of

> what is effectively a Singapore style model of religious tolerance, a tolerance enforced by a nanny state, rather than a public debate over controversial ideas where the best remedy against stupid and disgusting speech … is more speech exposing that stupidity.[195]

This idea gels with the Singapore prioritisation of maintaining racial and religious harmony as part of the 'social compact', which 'guarantees the safety, security and freedom of religion for all, and creates a common space'[196] where *le vivre ensemble* can exist.

If the right not to be religiously offended were part of religious freedom, the issue of balancing co-equal rights to free speech and religious freedom would arise. The question is whether this conception of a right to religious freedom is able to establish duties on others to avoid religiously offensive expression, which may possibly lead to violence. If this extends to a duty not to mock but to show religious personages respect, this could arguably constitute a duty to participate in a religious practice, which is an oppressive imposition.[197]

If the right not to be religiously offended is independent of religious freedom, it cannot stand as an unenumerated constitutional right, as the prevailing orthodoxy is that such rights must be essential to the political system, such as the right to vote.[198] It might conceivably be a statutory right, drawn from laws on sedition and statutory torts of harassment, which places it formally on a lower legal order than free speech, which has constitutional status. It may fall into the category of a 'constitutional interest', a category recognised in

[193] Ilias Trispiotis, 'The Duty to Respect Religious Feelings: Insights from European Human Rights Law' (2013) 19 *Columbia Journal of European Law* 499.

[194] *ES v Austria* [2018] ECHR 891. Mrs S held two seminars in Vienna entitled 'Basic Information on Islam', in which she criticised the Prophet Muhammad for committing paedophilia in marrying Aisha, a 6-year-old girl, and allegedly consummating this marriage when she was 9 years old while Muhammad was 56.

[195] Marko Milanovic, 'Legitimizing Blasphemy Laws Through the Backdoor: The European Court's Judgment in ES v Austria' *EJILTalk!* (29 October 2018) at www.ejiltalk.org/legitimizing-blasphemy-laws-through-the-backdoor-the-european-courts-judgment-in-e-s-v-austria/.

[196] Ministry of Home Affairs, 'Statement on Offensive Speech and Expression involving Race or Religion' (7 May 2017) at www.mha.gov.sg/docs/default-source/others/statement_on_offensive_speech_and_expression_involving_race_or_religion.pdf.

[197] Nathwani, 'Freedom of Expression and Religious Feelings'(n 189) 520.

[198] *Yong Vui Kong v PP* [2015] 2 SLR 1129.

Shadrake v AG[199] in relation to contempt laws, a permissible ground of derogation under Article 14(2) and the constitutional interest in ensuring public confidence in the administration of justice. While constitutional interests may be located in specified grounds of derogation from constitutional rights, it is unclear how to weigh them.

In the final analysis, one may have the legal right to offend, but it may not be right to offend. Certainly sections 298/298A punish the wounding of religious feelings and err on the side of public order rather than liberty. To promote the responsible exercise of expression, appeal is made to soft constitutional law norms not to denigrate other religions or moral or prudential rules, 'independent of any legal duty' for citizens to display 'appropriate social behaviour' through respecting 'the other races in view of our multi-racial society' and ensuring that 'nothing is said or done which might incite the people and plunge the country into racial strife and violence', unravelling the social fabric.[200]

III. CONCLUDING REFLECTIONS: RELIGIOUS OFFENCES IN A SECULAR STATE AND RELIGIOUS SOCIETY

In a secular state with distinct sources of political and religious authority, it does not make sense to speak of the special protection of sacredness. That stance seems to belong to a pre-modern era in which there was no separation of state and religion, no robust protection of religious freedoms, where blasphemy norms privileged one faith and were discriminatory. In England, a blasphemous libel was composed of 'any contemptuous, reviling, scurrilous or ludicrous matter relating to God, Jesus Christ or the Bible or the formularies of the Church of England as by law established'.[201] This was qualified, in that it was 'not blasphemous to speak or publish opinions hostile to the Christian religion, or to deny the existence of God, if the publication was couched in decent and temperate language'.[202] The test, as approved by the House of Lords in *Lemon*,[203] did not relate to the substance but to the manner in which such doctrines were advocated; nor was a tendency to cause a breach of the peace required. This shift in the definition of blasphemy 'from an offence of heresy to one of incivility',[204] was partially influenced by the rise of secularism; Lord Scarman in *Whitehouse* considered there was a case for retaining the offence of blasphemy, provided it was extended to protect the religious belief and feelings of non-Christians.

[199] *AG v Shadrake* (n 98) [77].

[200] *Benjamin Koh* (n 79) [8].

[201] Lord Scarman, *Whitehouse v Gay News Ltd* [1979] AC 617, 665, referring to the formulation of blasphemy in Art 214, *Stephen's Digest of the Criminal Law*, 9th edn (1950).

[202] *R v Lemon* [1979] AC 617, 665.

[203] ibid (approving of a definition of actus reus in *Stephen's Digest of the Criminal Law*).

[204] Clive Unsworth, 'Blasphemy, Cultural Divergence and Legal Relativism' (1995) 58 *Modern Law Review* 658, 662.

This offence was designed to safeguard public tranquillity, and Lord Scarman opined that in 'an increasingly plural society' it was necessary 'not only to respect the differing religious beliefs, feelings and practices of all' but also 'to protect them from scurrility, vilification, ridicule and contempt'.[205]

In a secular state with a plural religious society, sections 298/298A function as the modern secular form of blasphemy laws, which address an incivility that can precipitate (and historically has done so) violence. There is some sense in legally protecting some sensitivity towards religious sensibilities and loyalties towards the sacred, provided the intent of such religious offences is to secure an effective pluralism, ensure the peaceful coexistence of multiple religious groups and inhibit religious extremism by preserving religious harmony. This caters to the concerns of minorities; and, in taking religion seriously, this view appreciates the central role religion plays in the corporate life and personal identity of believers, and the self-respect that comes from a person's sense that his or her core religious or moral beliefs are worthy. In a sense, just as defamation laws protect our right to a good name, laws that constrain offensive speech and protect wounded religious feelings, whose roots lie in blasphemy laws, 'protect the sense of self-worth and self-esteem of believers'.[206] While freedom to disagree on religious issues must be preserved, such disagreement should be expressed in a manner 'respectful of the centrality of religious beliefs to the very being of believers',[207] as a matter of social discipline and tolerance. This taking religion seriously is reflected in the District Court's observation in *Amos Yee*[208] that religion 'is a very sensitive and passionate subject', noting that Singaporeans pride themselves 'on our multi-ethnic and multi-religious society where everyone is free to practice his religion'. Law thus enforces shared community norms of civility, such as Singapore multiculturalism, which sustains community identity; an acceptance of such laws requires viewing the Government, who decides what constitutes 'disharmony', less like an adversary and more like a cooperative partner.

Nonetheless, some academics and civil society activists have issued calls to repeal section 298.[209] Professor Cherian George argued that laws against racial and religious insult could backfire and undermine social harmony where the law is used in a deleterious manner.[210] Laws like section 298 have invited people to demand state intervention when their subjective religious and racial feelings are wounded,

[205] *Whitehouse* (n 201) 658.

[206] 'Blasphemy strips away self-respect' *The Irish Times* (15 February 2006) at www.irishtimes.com/opinion/blasphemy-strips-away-self-respect-1.1015767.

[207] ibid.

[208] *Amos Yee* (DC) (n 107) [81].

[209] Roy Ngerng, 'Call on AGC to Abolish the Section 298 and Sedition Act Laws and #FreeAmos Yee' *The Heart Truths* (2 May 2015) at thehearttruths.com/2015/05/02/call-on-agc-to-abolish-the-section-298-and-sedition-act-laws-and-freeamosyee/comment-page-1/ (arguing that s 298 duplicates the Sedition Act).

[210] Lianne Chia, 'Laws against racial and religious insult tend to backfire: Cherian George' *Channel News Asia* (27 March 2018) at www.channelnewsasia.com/news/singapore/laws-against-racial-and-religious-insult-tend-to-backfire-10079972.

whether this offence is genuine or manufactured for political gain. Singapore has been unusual in avoiding the ill effects of similar laws in India and Malaysia, which had been 'weaponized by merchants of intolerance and hate' to 'exploit any state-sanctioned right not to be offended in order to gain the upper hand'.[211] Perhaps this is because race and religion 'are not as politicized here as elsewhere'.[212] Thus an 'offended' majority religious or racial group could give full rein to tribalist impulses in invoking the law to oppress a minority religious or racial group.

The Singapore Muslims for Secular Democracy (SM4SD)[213] has also argued that section 298 undermines secularism and 'trades freedom for peace', inhibiting freedom of thought and expression, including the right to criticise ideas, in exchange for social harmony. Further, curbing expressive freedoms for hurting religious sensitivities would preclude the kind of constructive criticism that might helpfully address the 'negative religious feelings' that 'create greater terror, oppression and ruthlessness'; this could flow from extremist readings of theology based on the interpretation of ancient sacred texts, which can radicalise believers, particularly impressionable youths. Chilling speech by penal sanctions, aside from speech inciting violence, misrepresentations or inflammatory profanity that cannot contribute to reasonable discussion, may inhibit the honest, intelligent discussion of important issues, including matters of theology, which can disabuse listeners of false or extremist teachings. They also argued that from a 'purely secular perspective', a secular state would not be concerned with religion or religious affairs.

In a secular state with a constitution based on pluralism rather than absolute truth, the goal of legislation like sections 298/298A is not to preserve religious orthodoxy but to preserve inter-religious and civil peace by safeguarding the feelings of the faithful, and to contain 'emotional' reactions to perceived or actual attacks on one's faith. Emotions are an inevitability, 'which no legal order could pretend to abolish'; thus, disorderly emotions must be managed, while acting in accordance with orderly 'rationality' must be praised.[214] Public order can be threatened by religious disharmony in the context of societies that are not

[211] ibid.

[212] ibid.

[213] 'Section 298 contradicts Singapore's secularism, says Muslim group' *The Online Citizen* (15 December 2015) at www.onlinecitizenasia.com/2015/12/15/section-298-contradicts-singapores-secularism-says-muslim-group/.

[214] For example, in *Ong Kian Cheong* (n 14), Neighbour DJ (at [13]) noted that when a Muslim woman, Farhati bte Ahmad, read a tract she felt 'denigrated her religion Islam and the Prophet Muhammad', she thought a Christian sent her the tract as it 'promoted Christianity', and she 'was angry'. She thought if the publication 'had fallen into the wrong hands', it could foster ill-will 'by Muslims against Christians'. The district judge praised her response thus: 'Acting rationally, she reported the matter to the police for an investigation to be conducted.' In other words, she channelled her emotional feelings into rational, responsive conduct. Another rational, peace-orientated response could have been to ignore the tract and throw it away. In contrast, the Christian couple who distributed the tracts were chastised for 'their intolerance, insensitivity and ignorance of delicate issues concerning race and religion in our multi-racial and multi-religious society': ibid [82]. Had they lived in an environment that adopted a laissez-faire approach towards free speech, the price of which is hearing speech we dislike, their actions would have been unexceptional. Context is key

post-religion but where religious beliefs and commitments are taken seriously, such that the idea of a free marketplace of religious and ideological ideas fades into the elusive realm of utopia. Insults against erroneous religious opinions or criticism about a religion 'seldom have any other effect than to fix those opinions deeper, and to give a character of peculiar ferocity to theological dissension. Instead of eliciting truth, they only inflame fanaticism.'[215]

Laws have a regulatory cost: here, it includes the chilling effect on expressive freedoms, the truncation of religious freedom, particularly religious propagation, whose goal is to seek and promote religious truth. Too much emphasis on 'harmony' can spawn conformism, timidity, and an inability to engage in deep and honest conversations about race and religion in deference to the excessively sensitive;[216] this makes for a thin, superficial veneer of harmony, rather than deep bonds of solidarity based on mutual respect and an ability to disagree with civility on things that matter. Furthermore, these laws encourage individuals to develop a culture of complaints in the face of perceived or actual slights, rather than the temperate resilience that facilitates robust political and religious debates. If citizens do not learn how to deal with dissenting or disturbing views, they may fail to cultivate the civic virtues of tolerance, self-restraint and social resilience, which are the sinews that hold together the harmonious coexistence of distinct ethnic and religious groups within a plural society.

BIBLIOGRAPHY

'Transcript of the Prime Minister's statement to Religious Representatives and Members of the Inter-Religious Council' (Singapore, 30 September 1965) www.nas.gov.sg/archivesonline/data/pdfdoc/lky19650930a.pdf

Aljunied, SMK, *Colonialism, Violence and Muslims in Southeast Asia: The Maria Hertogh Controversy and its Aftermath* (Routledge, 2009)

Alkhatib, S, 'Man gets 2 weeks' jail for insulting Islam' *Channel News Asia* (Singapore, 7 August 2010)

Bakaram, MF, 'Mufti of Singapore, Dr Mohamed Fatris Bakaram's statement on the case of Mr Nalla Mohamed Abdul Jameel' (Media Statement, *Majlis Ugama Islam Singapura*, 3 April 2017) at www.muis.gov.sg/-/media/Files/Corporate-Site/Press-Releases/03-Apr-2017--Media-Statement--Mufti-Statement-on-the-Case-of-Mr-Nalla-Mohamed-Abdul-Jameel-Eng.pdf

in Singapore, and rationality lies not in self-help but in making police complaints, precipitating a centralised response.

[215] Walter Morgan and AG Macpherson, *The Indian Penal Code (Act XLV, of 1860) with Notes* (1861) 217–18.

[216] See Jaclyn L Neo, 'Dimensions of Religious Harmony as Constitutional Practice: Beyond State Control' (2019) 20(7) *German law Journal* 966; Li-ann Thio, 'Irreducible plurality, indivisible unity: Singapore Relational Constitutionalism and cultivating harmony through constructing a constitutional civil religion' (2019) 20(7) *German Law Journa*l 1007.

Balakrishnan, V, 'Speech by Minister for Foreign Affairs Dr Vivian Balakrishnan During The Committee of Supply Debate' (Singapore, Ministry for Foreign Affairs, 1 March 2018) at www.mfa.gov.sg/Newsroom/Press-Statements-Transcripts-and-Photos/2018/03/Min-COS-2018-Speech

Chan Sek Keong, 'Multiculturalism in Singapore: The way to a Harmonious Society' (2013) 25 *Singapore Academy of Law Journal* 84

Channel News Asia, 'Police report lodged over remarks made by imam on Christians and Jews' (Singapore, 28 February 2017) at www.channelnewsasia.com/news/singapore/police-report-lodged-over-remarks-made-by-imam-on-christians-and/3557112.html?cid=FBCNA accessed 7 March 2017

——, 'Amos Yee gets 6 weeks jail for wounding religious feelings' (Singapore, 29 September 2016) at www.channelnewsasia.com/news/singapore/amos-yee-gets-6-weeks-jail-s-2-000-fine-for-insulting-muslims/3165386.html accessed 5 November 2016

Chappell, B, 'US grants Asylum to Amos Yee, Young Blogger from Singapore' *npr* (27 September 2017) at www.npr.org/sections/thetwo-way/2017/09/27/553976738/u-s-grants-asylum-to-amos-yee-young-blogger-from-singapore

Chelvan, VP, 'Women who threw pork at Muslim neighbour's flat sentenced to psychiatric treatment' *Channel News Asia* (Singapore, 30 June 2017)

Cheong, D, 'Boundaries must be drawn to prevent hate speech: K Shanmugam' *The Straits Times* (Singapore, 25 August 2017) at www.straitstimes.com/politics/hate-speech-boundaries-must-be-drawn-says-shanmugam

Chia, L, 'Laws against racial and religious insult tend to backfire: Cherian George' *Channel News Asia* (27 March 2018) at www.channelnewsasia.com/news/singapore/laws-against-racial-and-religious-insult-tend-to-backfire-10079972

conversion.buddhists.sg, Agree to Disagree: Conversations on Conversions (Singapore, 2010) at conversion.buddhist.sg/wp-content/uploads/2016/02/Agree-to-Disagree-Conversations-on-Conversion.pdf

Cram, I, 'The Danish Cartoons, Offensive Expression and Democratic Legitimacy' in Ivan Hare and James Weinstein (eds), *Extreme Speech and Democracy* (Oxford University Press, 2009) 311

Ghosh, N, 'US appeals board gives asylum nod to Amos Yee' *The Straits Times* (28 September 2017) at www.straitstimes.com/singapore/us-appeals-board-gives-asylum-nod-to-amos-yee

Hussain, A, 'Blogger Amos Yee starts serving 6-week jail term' *The Straits Times* (Singapore, 13 October 2016) at www.straitstimes.com/singapore/courts-crime/blogger-amos-yee-starts-serving-6-week-jail-term

——, 'Teen blogger Amos Yet gets 6 weeks jail and $2000 fine for wounding religious feelings' *The Straits Times* (Singapore, 29 September 2016) www.straitstimes.com/singapore/courts-crime/teen-blogger-amos-yee-gets-six-weeks-jail-and-2000-fine-for-wounding

Lee, HL, 'Race, multiracialism and Singapore's place in the world' *The Straits Times* (Singapore, 30 September 2017) at www.straitstimes.com/opinion/race-multiracialism-and-singapores-place-in-the-world

Lee, KY, 'Transcript Of A Press Conference Given By The Prime Minister' (Singapore, Television Singapura Studio, 22 May 1965) at www.nas.gov.sg/archivesonline/data/pdfdoc/lky19650522.pdf

Lim, J, 'Racist rant: Amy Cheong gets stern warning from police' *The Straits Times* (Singapore, 25 March 2013)

Macaulay, TB, *The Complete Works of Thomas Babington Macaulay (Illustrated)*, 1st edn (Delphi Classics, 2016)

Malay Mail, 'Singapore to repatriate imam who made offensive remarks, two others warned' (Singapore, 3 April 2017) at www.malaymail.com/news/world/2017/04/03/singapore-to-repatriate-imam-who-made-offensive-remarks-two-others-warned/1348695

Mason, G, 'The symbolic purpose of hate crime law: Ideal victims and emotion' (2014) 18(1) *Theoretical Criminology* 75

Milanovic, M, 'Legitimizing Blasphemy Laws Through the Backdoor: The European Court's Judgment in ES v Austria' *EJILTalk!* (29 October 2018) at www.ejiltalk.org/legitimizing-blasphemy-laws-through-the-backdoor-the-european-courts-judgment-in-e-s-v-austria/

Millennials of SG, 'I converted to Christianity and My Muslim friends and family condemned me' (5 January 2017) at millennialsofsg.com/2017/01/05/christian-muslim-family/

Ministry of Home Affairs, Annex to 'Statement on Offensive Speech and Expression Involving Race or Religion' (7 May 2017) at www.mha.gov.sg/docs/default-source/others/annex---offensive-speech-and-expression-involving-race-or-religion.pdf

——, 'Statement on Offensive Speech and Expression involving Race or Religion' (7 May 2017) at www.mha.gov.sg/docs/default-source/others/statement_on_offensive_speech_and_expression_involving_race_or_religion.pdf

——, 'Statement by the Ministry of Law on the Decision granting Asylum in the United States to Amos Yee' (Singapore, 19 April 2017) at www.mlaw.gov.sg/content/minlaw/en/news/videos/statement-on-amos-yee.html

——, 'MHA Statement on Sentencing of Imam for Offensive Remarks' (9 April 2017) at www.mha.gov.sg/newsroom/press-release/news/mha-statement-on-sentencing-of-imam-for-offensive-remarks

——, *Maintenance of Religious Harmony White Paper* (Cmd 21 of 1989)

Mokhtar, F, 'S'pore must continue to keep out of Islamophobia: Shanmugam' *Today* (Singapore, 31 December 2017) at www.todayonline.com/singapore/spore-must-continue-keep-out-islamophobia-shanmugam

Morgan, W, and Macpherson, AG, *The Indian Penal Code* (Act XLV, of 1860) with Notes (1861)

Nathan, SR, 'Building Our Future Singapore in an Uncertain World' (Speech at Opening of Parliament, 18 May 2009).

Nathwani, N, 'Freedom of Expression and Religious Feelings' (2009) 1 *Yearbook of Muslims in Europe* 507

National Council of Churches Singapore, 'Dialogue with Minister K Shanmugam on "Terrorism and Radicalisation in Southeast Asia and our Challenges"' (13 February 2018) at www.mha.gov.sg/docs/default-source/others/dialogue-with-minister-k-shanmugam-on-terrorism-and-radicalisation-(9-feb-2018).pdf

National Integration Council, 'Singapore at a Glance' (Singapore, 28 November 2019) at www.nationalintegrationcouncil.gov.sg/living-in-singapore/singapore-at-a-glance

Neo, J, 'Dimensions of Religious Harmony as Constitutional Practice: Beyond State Control' (2019) 20(7) *German law Journal* 966

——, 'Seditious in Singapore! Free Speech and the Offence of Promoting Ill-Will and Hostility between Different Racial Groups' [2011] *Singapore Journal of Legal Studies* 351

New Straits Times, 'Why Malaysia backpedaled on ICERD Ratification' (Malaysia, 24 November 2018) at www.nst.com.my/news/nation/2018/11/434078/why-malaysia-backpedalled-icerd-ratification

Ngerng, R, 'Call on AGC to Abolish the Section 298 and Sedition Act Laws and #FreeAmosYee' *The Heart Truths* (2 May 2015) at thehearttruths.com/2015/05/02/call-on-agc-to-abolish-the-section-298-and-sedition-act-laws-and-freeamosyee/comment-page-1/

Nylander, J, 'UN urges Singapore to release 16 year old blogger Amos Yee' *Forbes* (23 June 2015) at www.forbes.com/sites/jnylander/2015/06/23/un-urges-singapore-to-release-16-year-old-blogger-accused-of-posting-critical-lee-kuan-yew-photos/

Pew Research Center, 'Global Religious Diversity' (4 April 2014) at www.pewforum.org/2014/04/04/global-religious-diversity/

Phippen, JW, 'The Teenager who wounded Singapore's religious feelings', *The Atlantic* (30 September 2016) at www.theatlantic.com/news/archive/2016/09/singapore-blogger-religious/502262/

Post, R, 'Hate Speech' in Ivan Hare and James Weinstein (eds), *Extreme Speech and Democracy* (Oxford University Press, 2009) 123

Prime Minister's Office, *Shared Values White Paper* (Cmd 1 of 1991)

Jayakumar, S, 'Applying the Rule of Law' (2009) 43(1) *The International Lawyer* 83

Shanmugam, K, 'Ministerial Statement on Restricting Hate Speech to Maintain Racial and Religious Harmony in Singapore' (Singapore, Ministry of Home Affairs, 1 April 2019) at www.mha.gov.sg/newsroom/in-parliament/parliamentary-speeches/news/ministerial-statement-on-restricting-hate-speech-to-maintain-racial-and-religious-harmony-in-singapore-speech-by-mr-k-shanmugam-minister-for-home-affairs-and-minister-for-law

——, 'Inter-Agency Aftercare Group Youth Forum on "Dangers of Extremism in the Cyber World: Building Resilience in Youth"' (Ministry of Home Affairs, speech delivered on 11 August 2018) at www.mha.gov.sg/newsroom/speeches/news/inter-agency-aftercare-group-youth-forum-on-dangers-of-extremism-in-the-cyber-world-building-resilience-in-youth

Siau, ME, and Ng, K, 'Community committee 'able to deal with evolving concept of race' *Today* (Singapore, 9 September 2017) at www.todayonline.com/singapore/community-committee-able-deal-evolving-concept-race

Siau, ME, 'Social media should not be used to sow discord: Religious leaders' *Today* (Singapore, 4 April 2017) at www.todayonline.com/singapore/social-media-should-not-be-used-sow-discord-religious-leaders

Statman, D, 'Hurting Religious Feelings' (2000) 3 *Democratic Culture* 199

Tan, J, 'Church in S'pore make police report against Rice Media for "scurrilous attack" in article' (Singapore, *Mothership.sg*, 27 March 2018) at mothership.sg/2018/03/preacher-lou-engle-cornerstone-church-anti-islam/

——, 'Muslim imam convicted of promoting enmity between religious groups, fined $4000 for comments on Jews, Christians' *Mothership.sg* (3 April 2017) at mothership.sg/2017/04/muslim-imam-convicted-of-promoting-enmity-between-religious-groups-fined-4000-for-comments-on-jews-christians/

Tan, YL, 'Sedition and its New Clothes in Singapore' [2011] *Singapore Journal of Legal Studies* 212

Thakker, CK, Ranchhoddas, R, and Thakore, DK, *Ratanlal & Dhirajlal's Law of Crimes: A Commentary on the Indian Penal Code* (2005 Reprint)

Tham, YC, 'Amos Yee prosecuted for hate speech, not political dissent: Singapore to The Economist' *The Straits Times* (13 April 2017) at www.straitstimes.com/singapore/amos-yee-prosecuted-for-hate-speech-not-political-dissent-singapore-high-commissioner-for

The Independent.sg, 'NUS don and blogger warned by Police in case of imam who made offensive comments against Jews and Christians' (3 April 2017) at theindependent.sg/nus-don-and-blogger-warned-by-police-in-case-of-imam-who-made-offensive-comments-against-jews-and-christians/

The Irish Times, 'Blasphemy strips away self-respect' (15 February 2006) at www.irishtimes.com/opinion/blasphemy-strips-away-self-respect-1.1015767

The Online Citizen, 'Section 298 contradicts Singapore's secularism, says Muslim group' (15 December 2015) at www.onlinecitizenasia.com/2015/12/15/section-298-contradicts-singapores-secularism-says-muslim-group/

The Straits Times, 'Islamophobia as bad and unacceptable as terrorism, says PM Lee' (Singapore, 21 June 2017) at www.straitstimes.com/singapore/islamophobia-as-bad-and-unacceptable-as-terrorism-says-pm-lee

——, 'Need to guarantee position of minorities in Singapore, secure common space: Shanmugam' (Singapore, 1 February 2017) at www.straitstimes.com/singapore/need-to-guarantee-position-of-minorities-in-singapore-secure-common-space-shanmugam

——, 'The right to choose one's religion – by a padre' (Singapore, 9 March 1966) 6

Thio, LA, 'Irreducible plurality, indivisible unity: Singapore Relational Constitutionalism and cultivating harmony through constructing a constitutional civil religion' (2019) 20(7) *German Law Journal* 1007

——, 'Relational Constitutionalism and the Management of Religious Disputes: The Singapore "Secularism with a Soul" Model' (2012) 1(2) *Oxford Journal of Law and Religion* 446

——, *A Treatise on Singapore Constitutional Law* (Academy Publishing, 2012)

——, 'Contentious Liberty: Regulating Religious Propagation in a Religiously Diverse Secular Democracy' [2010] *Singapore Journal of Legal Studies* 484

——, 'The Virtual and the Real: Article 14, Political Speech and the Calibrated Management of Deliberative Democracy in Singapore' [2008] *Singapore Journal of Legal Studies* 25.

Today, 'Imam has shown sincere remorse, regret, Shanmugam' (Singapore, 5 April 2017) at www.todayonline.com/singapore/shanmugam-meets-imam-who-made-offensive-remarks-against-jews-christians

——, 'Imam who made offensive remarks to be repatriated; stern warnings for two others: MHA' (Singapore, 3 April 2017) at www.todayonline.com/singapore/imam-who-made-offensive-remarks-be-repatriated-stern-warnings-two-others-mha

Toh, YC, 'Shanmugam appreciates imam's sincere apology' *The Straits Times* (Singapore, 6 April 2017) at www.straitstimes.com/singapore/shanmugam-appreciates-imams-sincere-apology

——, 'Minister meets imam who was fined for making offensive remarks and will be headed home' *The Straits Times* (Singapore, 5 April 2017) at www.straitstimes.com/singapore/minister-meets-imam-who-was-fined-for-making-offensive-remarks-and-will-be-heading-home

——, 'No room for religious extremism in Singapore, says Muslim leaders' *The Straits Times* (Singapore, 5 March 2017) at www.straitstimes.com/singapore/no-room-for-religious-extremism-in-singapore-say-muslim-leaders

——, 'Imam apologises for insensitive remarks, clarifies that remarks were not from Quran' *The Straits Times* (Singapore, 31 March 2017) at www.straitstimes.com/singapore/imam-apologises-for-insensitive-remarks-clarifies-that-remarks-were-not-from-quran

Trispiotis, I, 'The Duty to Respect Religious Feelings: Insights from European Human Rights Law' (2013) 19 *Columbia Journal of European Law* 499

Unsworth, C, 'Blasphemy, Cultural Divergence and Legal Relativism' (1995) 58 *Modern Law Review* 658

Wong, RJJ, 'Practising and professing your faith: Know your rights' *Salt & Light* (15 September 2018) at https://saltandlight.sg/faith/practising-and-professing-your-faith-know-your-rights/

11

Recalibrating the Scales of Criminal Justice in Brunei Darussalam: Religious Penal Clauses 1905–2018

ANN BLACK

I. INTRODUCTION

AFTER ALMOST 100 years of British colonial influence, Negara Brunei Darussalam[1] (Brunei) became fully independent in 1984. The colonial legacy is significant, as the British administration transformed a bankrupt, vulnerable kingdom to one of the most stable, affluent and modern nations in Southeast Asia. Britain saved Brunei from extinction in the 1900s, and again in 1962, when it sent in British troops to save the ruling royal family from an internal anti-royal and pro-democratic uprising. Both events changed the legal system in distinctive ways. The first intervention introduced English laws and legal institutions, whilst the second allowed law-making by emergency order and facilitated an absolute monarchy. The legacy of both British interventions resonates today for law and religion in the Sultanate.

Brunei, on the island of Borneo, has had six centuries of hereditary rule by male Sultans, each a descendant from its first Sultan, Muhammad Shah. It is said that he converted to Islam in order to marry the daughter of another Malay Sultan.[2] In assuming the mantle of Sultan, he relinquished the title of raja but retained the Hindu co-title of Yang Di-Pertuan. Today's Sultan and Yang Di-Pertuan Haji Hassanal Bolkiah Mu'izzaddin Waddaulah (Sultan) is his twenty-ninth successor. As a Sultanate, Brunei's Malay subjects aligned with an

[1] This is the country's official title. *Negara* originates from Sanskrit and means nation; *Brunei* comes from the Sanskrit word Varuna/*Baruna* referring to a nation of seafarers and traders. It changed to Brunei in the reign of Sultan Ahmad (1408–25). *Darussalam* is an Arabic term for 'Abode of Peace'.

[2] Because there is historical debate whether the Sultanate of Johore existed before 1405, many historical accounts simply say 'from a neighbouring kingdom'.

Islamic way of life and law, but there was also harmonisation with its Majapahit Hindu foundations of state and society, and coexistence with the animistic beliefs[3] and ways of the Bornean tribes that did not convert to Islam. From the seventeenth century onwards, the Chinese, with their own religions, also settled in Brunei.[4]

Therefore, prior to European colonisation, Brunei was already ethnically and religiously plural. Europeans brought Christianity into the religious mix, but their missionaries bypassed Muslims as fellow travellers in the Abrahamic tradition, to focus their efforts on converting the 'pagans' – the animistic indigenous 'natives' of Borneo. Today, animism, Hinduism, Buddhism and Christianity have communities in Brunei that make one-third of its population non-Muslim.

In earlier times, Brunei's plural polity allowed criminal sanctions for breaches of religious law and tenets of faith, but these were specific and applicable to the followers of that religion. Muslims received punitive consequences for breaches of Islamic law, whereas the animistic natives meted out their own ritualistic sanctions to violators of their spiritual *adat* (custom). This changed when the British colonisers imposed a common law penal code under which laws on religion were not specific to one religion but applied equally to all, regardless of creed or rank. This, Mansurnoor notes, was a previously 'wholly unknown conception'.[5] Unlike Islamic penal laws that differentiated between genders, between Muslims and non-Muslims, and customary laws that applied differently according to one's social rank, the new colonial laws were neutral and general in both application and enforcement. British penal religious laws, for example, referred to 'places of worship', not to mosques, nor to churches, shrines, temples, synagogues or spiritual places; and to 'objects held sacred by any class of persons', without specifying Bibles, Qurans, statues of Buddha or Shiva, crucifixes, etc. Because of this neutral rather than secular position on religion, the term 'civil' law applies to common law enactments and courts, as distinct from the religious system with Islamic/Syariah law and Syariah courts.

For most of the twentieth century the colonial penal laws had supremacy, but in 1996 the Sultan's birthday *titah*[6] (a royal policy speech) announced that new

[3] Animism is a belief system where the natural and supernatural merge, and in which the spirits of people, animals and deities constantly interact. The link between spiritual and ritual redress is evident in dispute resolution. See Ann Black, 'Survival or Extinction? Animistic Dispute Resolution in the Sultanate of Brunei' (2005) 13 *Willamette Journal of International Law & Dispute Resolution* 1.

[4] After the discovery of oil, the Chinese population increased by more than 200% between 1931 and 1947. Today, half of the Chinese remain temporary residents and less than one-quarter are citizens. Some are stateless. Citizenship, access to land ownership and professional restrictions have led to some Chinese emigrating. See Rozan Yunos, 'The Chinese in Brunei' *Brunei Times* (Bandar Seri Begawan, 30 April 2012).

[5] Moshe Yegar, *Islam and Islamic Institutions in British Malaya* (Magnes Press, 1979) 40; Iik Arifin Mansurnoor, 'Formulating and Implementing a Shari'a-Guided Legal System in Brunei Darussalam: Opportunity and Challenge' (2008) 1(2) *Sosiohumanika* 219, 230.

[6] Most *titah* can be accessed in Malay, with some translated into English, from the Government of Brunei's website at www.rtb.gov.bn/PMO%20Pages/ Titah-View.aspx.

Syariah courts were not just for the implementation of family laws but were to apply '*Qunan Jina'l Islam*' (an Islamic criminal law enactment) in its entirety as required by Allah, the Almighty.[7] Since that time, a policy of recalibrating the nation's laws to reverse colonial legal dominance, including in criminal law, occurred. It also reversed neutrality in religious penal clauses to prioritise the defence of Islam. This policy culminated with the Syariah Penal Code Order 2013 ('2013 Order') and the Syariah Penal Procedure Order 2018 ('2018 Procedure Order').

In reviewing the colonial legacy of contemporary practice, this chapter will argue that while transplanted colonial edicts in the form of religious penal offences remain in the civil system, an equally important colonial legacy is paradoxically Islamic criminal law. Islamic penal offences were recognised, codified and applied by Brunei's colonial courts; and from this colonial foundation, their jurisdiction and significance expanded to be equal to civil offences, particularly concerning religion, and they now surpass those civil offences. In addition, Britain's failure to embed an accountable and democratic process for law-making gave rise to today's absolute monarchy. Imposing Syariah criminal law on Brunei's Muslims and non-Muslims was therefore possible without consultation or a vote.

To explore this paradoxical legal legacy in contemporary Brunei, section II provides the legal background in which religious penal offences developed in both the civil and Islamic streams of law during the British Residency. Section III follows the evolving legal landscape through independence to the present day in which the dominance of civil law subsides and Islamic law shapes Brunei's legal trajectory. Guided by ideology, Brunei adopted an Islamisation agenda, in which law was an important vehicle for a *zikir* (fully Islamic compliant) nation. The pinnacle was the enactment of Syariah criminal law through the 2013 and 2018 Orders. As religious penal clauses are a significant component of these Orders, this legislation and several cases are considered. Section IV deals with the implications and social impact of religious penal clauses for Muslims and non-Muslims in Brunei, and section V tries to gauge contemporary public opinion. In section VI, the chapter concludes that although the dual system of penal laws, each with their own distinctive religious offences, remains in Brunei, the pendulum has swung too far in favour of religious laws. The promotion and protection of one religion, Islam, and one conservative Shafi'i interpretation at the expense of all others, puts in jeopardy the universality of religious freedom in the colonial model.

II. LEGAL BACKGROUND

As noted, Britain intervened twice to shape the legal trajectory in Brunei, and at both times consolidated the position of the Sultan over religious law.

[7] *Titah* delivered 16 July 1996. Reported also in 'Titah' *Borneo Bulletin* (Bandar Seri Begawan, 17 July 1996).

A. Britain Rescues the Sultanate in 1905–06

> The United Kingdom had the awesome responsibility of possessing the power of life or death over the moribund sultanate and in electing to regenerate the dying State, HM government surely chose correctly. As a result, an ancient culture was preserved … to blossom anew.[8]

Brunei received a lifeline when Britain accepted McArthur's recommendation to 'regenerate the dying Sultanate' and agreed to provide direct British administration and financial support. But for McArthur's Report, this British protectorate[9] was destined to be subsumed into the larger neighbouring protectorate of British North Borneo, or joined with Sarawak under the rule of the Brooke family – the white 'rajas' of Borneo. In 1890, Charles Brooke as 'raja' (1868–1917) annexed a part of Brunei – Limbang – with the result that Brunei was divided into two small non-contiguous enclaves.[10] Further incursions by Sarawak were imminent for the impoverished Sultanate, which was beset with internal problems[11] and facing other external threats.[12] At its zenith in the sixteenth and seventeenth centuries, Brunei had been a great thalassocracy,[13] whose control had extended throughout Borneo to the southern Philippines, but at the turn of the twentieth century it had contracted and was 'about to disappear from the kingdoms of the earth'.[14] To save his kingdom, Sultan Hashim acceded to British conditions and signed the Residency Agreement in 1905.[15] From this time, the British imported English law and institutions into Brunei, but the Sultan retained authority for Islam.

As there was no Crown governor, Brunei was technically not a colony, but the difference was purely semantic. The Sultan retained *de jure* authority, but the

[8] Malcolm Stewart Hannibal McArthur, *Report on Brunei in 1904: Introduced and Annotated by HMV Horton* (Ohio University Press, 1987) 69, 128.

[9] In the 1888 Protectorate Treaty, Bruneians formally became protected persons of 'Her Majesty' for defence and protection against attacks of third parties. To ensure Europeans were not subject to the vagaries of local laws, the principle of extra-territoriality applied. A Consul-General, or other officer duly 'appointed by Her Britannic Majesty', would determine any matter, civil or criminal, involving a British subject: Treaty of Protection [1888] *UKTS* 5582 (17 September 1888).

[10] This was despite strong protests from the Sultan and his nobles that Britain was not adhering to the central terms of the Protectorate Treaty that guaranteed protection of Brunei territory.

[11] These included a weak economy, imminent bankruptcy, succession disputes following the death of Sultan Omar Ali Saifuddien, an inability to maintain control and allegiance of its nobles, and dissatisfaction among the people of the Sultanate erupting at times in revolt. See DS Ranjit Singh, *Brunei: 1839–1983: The Problems of Political Survival* (Oxford University Press, 1991) 41.

[12] There were ongoing hostilities with the Sulus of the Southern Philippines and rampant piracy in the waters of northern Borneo, as well as threats from the Brookes in Sarawak. See Lionel Astor Sheridan, *Malaya and Singapore: The Borneo Territories: Development of their Laws and Constitutions* (Stevens & Sons, 1963) 118, 119.

[13] There were no precise borders and control was based on sea domination, not land domination. See Roger Kershaw, 'Marginality Then and Now: Shifting Patterns of Minority Status in Brunei Darussalam' (1998) 29 *Internationales Asienforum* 83.

[14] British Consul-General Peter Leys' letter to Lord Salisbury dated 24 December 1885.

[15] The Agreement was signed by Sultan Hashim and his *wazirs* (noble advisors) on 3 December 1905, and by Sir John Anderson, representing the British Crown, on 2 January 1906.

British Resident, as representative of the Crown, advised the Sultan, who had to take his advice on all matters, excluding issues on the 'Mohammedan' religion. Unlike the Malay Peninsula states, the Sultan's remit did not include Malay customs. This was because McArthur, also the first Resident, wanted to overhaul land ownership and reduce the entitlements of the nobility, all of which were Malay customary practices.[16] Yusof argues this was important in bolstering the Sultan's position over and above the nobles, and was in fact the first step in 'solidifying Brunei as the absolute monarchy of today'.[17] Under the Agreement, the Sultan retained his dignity, royal position and authority over Islam. For all other matters, the Resident's word was law.[18] Tarling writes that 'it does not follow, because the Resident is only the adviser, that the ruler may reject his advice … the fiction … that the Residents are merely advisers must be kept up'.[19] There were several reasons to keep up 'the fiction'. It meant the Sultan maintained the support and confidence of his subjects, which kept the prestige of the institution of monarchy. It also minimised resistance to British rule. Tarling writes that making allies with local elites, in particular indigenous rulers, was a recurring feature of colonialist collaborations.[20] Although the Resident had no superior in Brunei, he was subordinate to other colonial officials, namely the High Commissioner and his Secretary in Singapore, and the Colonial Office in London.

In a short period, Britain established a new system of land ownership, a western-style civil service for managing revenue, taxation, customs and excise, postal services, police, prisons, currency, agriculture, and oversaw public works including roads, wharves and a new capital city. Living standards improved for health, education and sanitation. However, like all colonial regimes, the primary responsibility was to secure law and order. Establishing English-style common law courts applying English laws was foremost in the Resident's administrative reforms. McArthur and others had been unimpressed by Brunei's judicial administration. Hewett, Acting Consul-General, advised the Foreign Office in 1904 that the Sultan's record was one of 'broken promises, lawless acts and outrages against British subjects, denial of justice, and the protection of wrongdoers',[21]

[16] Reform of land ownership on English lines commenced immediately. Despite objections from the Sultan, traditional Bruneian land holdings of *kerajaan* (of the Sultan), *kuripan* (appanages to nobles and officials) and *tulin* (private hereditary domains) were abolished under the 1907 Land Enactment and compensation was paid to the holders, including the Sultan. The 1909 Land Code established a system of land titles and transfer of land. This allowed for ownership of land by British, Chinese and indigenous groups such as the Kedayans.

[17] Rabiqah NHBM Yusof, 'Brunei: Building and Enshrining an Absolute Monarchy' (MPhil thesis, Oxford Brooks University 2017).

[18] Early in the Residency, the young Sultan, through his regents, in 1909 objected to sections of the 1908 Land Code. The voicing of these objections resulted in a reduction of the Sultan's stipend and he was threatened with deposition. See Graham Saunders, *A History of Brunei* (Routledge, 1994) 114.

[19] Nicholas Tarling, *Fall of Imperial Britain in South East Asia* (Oxford University Press, 1993) 73.

[20] Nicholas Tarling, *Nations and States in Southeast Asia* (Cambridge University Press, 1998) 57. Examples of collaborative arrangements with indigenous rulers include the Sultans in Malaya, the emirs in Northern Nigeria and the Kabaka of Uganda.

[21] McArthur, *Report on Brunei* (n 8) 12.

and McArthur wrote 'there is a semblance of a judicature, but little justice. Cases are sometimes tried before the Sultan or *Pengiran Bandahara* … as a rule cases are settled by a system of arbitration among the recognised, if unauthorised headman of kampongs'.[22] The system was a blend of *adat* and Islamic law that enabled Bruneians to settle disputes in personalised and private ways, based on rank, class and religion, through forms of arbitration and mediation. There were no established Syariah courts, judges, police or prisons. Mansurnoor noted an overriding defect was the dominance of the executive in administering justice, which resulted in corruption and injustice.[23] British intervention laid the groundwork for what became a respected judicial system in the decades that followed.

From the British perspective, Brunei needed 'the clearer and stronger rule of the more enlightened European in whose justice and integrity they have perfect confidence'.[24] For the British, 'enlightened' justice resided in the common law. However, the Agreement was honoured, and a place for Islamic law was integral to the new system.

B. Colonial Courts

The British established five courts to administer civil and criminal laws.[25] The rationale for five courts in a population of less than 22,000 was to recognise the principle that the governing law be applicable to the local circumstances. Brunei's plurality was acknowledged through the *Kathi* (later *Kadi*) Courts for Muslims and the Natives' Court for Asiatics and indigenous people presided over by indigenous headmen.[26] This mirrored sentiments expressed by Sir Benson Maxwell, Justice of the Supreme Court of the Straits Settlements, that 'native communities with their own religious and customary principles should not be judged by an inapplicable English law'.[27] Second, the common law system required an appeal and review mechanism. The four magistrates-level courts, which included the *Kathi/Kadi* Courts, could appeal to the Resident's Court,[28] and from there to the Supreme Court of the Colony of the Straits Settlements and ultimately the Privy Council. The appeal avenue from a decision of the *Kathi* Court directly to

[22] ibid 6.

[23] Iik Arifin Mansurnoor, 'Re-establishing Order in Brunei: The Introduction of the British Legal System During the Early Residential Period' (2013) 52(2) *Islamic Studies* 155, 158. He cites the research undertaken by Siti Zaliha in her thesis 'Comparing Brunei's Judicial System With That of Islam'.

[24] British Consul-General Peter Leys' letter to Lord Salisbury dated 24 December 1885.

[25] Section 3 of the Courts Enactment 1908 sets out five courts with civil and criminal jurisdiction: The Court of the Resident with four subordinate courts – Courts of the Magistrate of the First Class, Courts of the Magistrate of the Second Class, Courts of the Native Magistrates and Courts of *Kathis* (later *Kadi*).

[26] Criminal jurisdiction was imprisonment not exceeding three months and fines not exceeding B$10.

[27] Yegar, *Islam and Islamic Institutions* (n 5) 128.

[28] Courts Enactment 1908, s 7. The Resident's Court was presided over by the British Resident or by the District Judge of the Colony of the Straits Settlement (with the Sultan's concurrence).

the Resident (in his position as *Hakim Mahkamah Rayuan*),[29] including retrials, indicates the authority of the Resident vis-à-vis the *kathi* (Islamic judge) even on matters of Islam. When the young Sultan Alam II wrote requesting that all existing Islamic laws and customs of Brunei remain 'inviolate and unchanged',[30] the Resident counselled him that the treaty's rationale was to replace Brunei's obsolete laws to ensure the Sultanate's survival, and warned that if he persisted with this, his stipend would be decreased.[31] All offences punishable by death, of which there were many, had to be heard and determined by the Supreme Court of the Straits Settlements.[32]

i. Religious Clauses in the Colonial Penal Codes

McArthur introduced English criminal law through the Courts Enactment of 1908. There was no need for locally drafted penal laws for Brunei, as the Penal Code of the Straits Settlements was detailed and readily applicable to Brunei's circumstances.[33] It was originally derived from the Indian Penal Code of 1860. Also transplanted were the Straits Settlements' Criminal Procedure Code and the Evidence Act. It was a seamless, reliable, quick way to incorporate common law principles into Britain's latest colonial acquisition.[34]

ii. Specific Religious Penal Offences

There were four specific religious penal clauses in the 1908 Penal Code in a separate Chapter XV entitled 'Offences Relating to Religion'. These were:

> Section 295: … destroys, damages, or defiles any place of worship, or any object held sacred by any class of persons, with the intention of thereby insulting the religion of any class of persons, or with the knowledge that any class of persons is likely to consider such destruction, damage, or defilement as an insult to their religion.
>
> Section 296: … voluntarily causing disturbance to any assembly lawfully engaged in the performance of religious worship or religious ceremonies.
>
> Section 297: … with the intention of wounding the feelings of any person, or of insulting the religion of any person, trespasses on any place of worship or on any place of sepulchre or any place set apart for the performance of funeral rites.
>
> Section 298: … uttering words, making a gesture, or placing an object with deliberate intent to wound the religious feelings of any person.

[29] Nani Suryani Haji Abu Bakar, 'The Impact of British Administration over Brunei's Society: 1906–1984' Second Joint Seminar of FASS UBD and IOC UT: Asian Societies and Cultures in the Eyes of Bruneian and Japanese Researchers (16–18 September 2008) 7 at www.academia.edu/8446348/The_impact_of_British _administration_over_Brunei_s_society_1906_-_1984.

[30] Singh, *Brunei* (n 11) 113.

[31] Abu Bakar, 'Impact of British Administration' (n 29) 8.

[32] The first trial from Brunei before this court was in 1916. It was a trial for the murder of the acting British Resident for Brunei, Ernest Maundrell. The court convicted and executed the accused.

[33] Penal Code of the Straits Settlements, rev edn 1835–1900, Ordinance IV of 1871. Section 25 of the Courts Enactment 1908 adopts the Penal Code of the Colony of the Straits Settlements as Brunei law.

[34] See also the Civil Procedure Code, Laws of the Straits Settlements.

Conviction of an offence under section 295 was punishable by up to two years' imprisonment and/or a fine, with a maximum sentence of one-year's imprisonment for the other three offences. These four original colonial penal offences relating to religion, with almost identical wording, are in all subsequent revisions of the Brunei Penal Code. These include Chapter 22 in the Laws of Brunei 1951 and Chapter 22 in the 1984 Revised Laws. The only difference is an increase in penalties for section 295 to a maximum of five years' imprisonment and/or a fine, and three years for section 296 and section 297. The punishment for a section 298 offence remains one year's imprisonment. Added in 1997 was the new section 297A, on opening graves to interfere with human remains or to remove items of value.[35]

a. Morality Offences

The Penal Code of 1908 contained morality offences, which reflected Christian doctrine, including punishment for acts contrary 'to the order of nature'.[36] Section 377 is identical to provisions in other British colonial laws and remains in the current Penal Code. In 2010, the maximum penalty was reduced from life imprisonment to 10 years and/or a fine; but in July 2017, section 377 was amended to increase the maximum penalty from 10 to 30 years, with whippings.

b. Sedition

The offence of sedition was set out in section 124A of the 1908 Penal Code.[37] Its focus was on words, representations and signs bringing hatred, or exciting dissatisfaction, against the British monarch or the Government in Brunei. The section remains in the current Code, but today it applies to the Sultan and his Government. From 1948, sedition warranted a separate enactment, the Sedition Act (Chapter 24). Its current role in limiting religious and other forms of self-expression in the Sultanate will be discussed in section III.

C. Colonial Penal 'Mohammedan' Laws

The colonial choice of the term 'Mohammedan' for the religion and laws of Islam meant Islamic law was not broad and encompassing but limited and restricted. This contraction of Syariah was nevertheless symbolically beneficial

[35] Punishment is a term of up to seven years' imprisonment and/or a fine.

[36] See also the *hudud* offence of *liwat* in Syariah Penal Code Order 2013, s 82.

[37] The section states 'Whoever by words, either spoken or written, or by signs, or by visible representation, or otherwise, brings or attempts to bring into hatred or contempt, or excites attempts to excite feelings of dissatisfaction towards His Majesty or the Government established by law in the Colony, shall be punished with Penal servitude for life, to which fine may be added, or with imprisonment for a term which may extend to three years, to which fine may be added, or with both.'

for Brunei's Malays and for the Sultan. The Agreement gave him 'authority over Islam', but all enactments went through the State Council. In name, they were made by the Sultan-in-Council, but in fact the Resident fixed legislation, including Islamic laws, in line with British requirements.[38] Family and succession law had the widest scope, but there were penalties for breach of Islamic religious duties. The Mohammedan Laws Enactment of 1912 had 18 sections, of which 12 were penal religious offences. This Enactment was colonial law passed by the State Council and is described as 'colonised' Syariah.[39] The colonial imprint is evident in many of its features.

First, the penalties provided do not accord with outcomes in the Syariah, and adopt the same language and form as all colonial laws. Second, appeals were to the Resident's Court or to the Sultan. There is of course jurisprudential debate about whether appeals from a decision of any Islamic judge is permissible in Islam, but a secular appeal avenue is not. Sultan Alam II requested that a *kathi* sit with the Resident for cases including appeals conducted in his court. This was rejected, but the option for a *kathi* to sit as an assessor in the court was a compromise, with the proviso that the advice of any assessor need not be taken.[40] Third, a form of precedent, a distinguishing feature of the common law, not Islamic jurisprudence, developed. Brunei's *kathis* looked to their earlier decisions, rather than using the Islamic method of *usul-al-fiqh* based on jurisprudential deduction and reasoning from the primary sources of Islamic law.[41] Fourth, as there was no Islamic procedure or evidential rules in the Enactment, English laws filled the lacunae. This continued for decades. In addition, power to enforce a *kathi*'s decision lay with the Magistrate Courts.[42] Fifth, six of the Islamic religious offences came within the jurisdiction of the secular Magistrate Courts.[43] These penal offences included religious teaching without the written permission of the Sultan or teaching false doctrine,[44] the enticement of an unmarried Muslim girl,[45] the absconding of an unmarried girl to live an immoral life,[46] unlawful intercourse with a married Muslim woman (adultery)[47] and

[38] BA Hussainmiya, 'Manufacturing Consensus: the Role of the State Council in Brunei Darussalam' (2000) 31(2) *Journal of Southeast Asian Studies* 321, 325.

[39] Tim Lindsey and Kerstin Steiner, *Islam, Law and the State in Southeast Asia* (IB Taurus, 2012) 337.

[40] McArthur, *Report on Brunei* (n 8) 38.

[41] Lindsey and Steiner, *Islam* (n 39) 337.

[42] Courts Enactment 1908, s 10.

[43] Mohammedan Laws Enactment 1912, s 15(2).

[44] Mohammedan Laws Enactment 1912, s 10. The penalty was a fine of B$25.

[45] Mohammedan Laws Enactment 1912, s 4. The penalty was a fine of up to twice the *mas kahwin* (*mahr* – payment made by the husband to his wife at marriage).

[46] Mohammedan Laws Enactment 1912, s 5. The penalty was imprisonment for no more than one month, or bail if she promised to behave properly. If she failed to improve, the penalty was imprisonment of no more than three months.

[47] Mohammedan Laws Enactment 1912, s 6. Adultery was an offence punishable by imprisonment for a maximum of one year for the man and a fine of up to B$250. For the woman, imprisonment was for no more than six months. Parties who had been in an adulterous relationship could not lawfully marry pursuant to s 6(3).

relationships with kin prohibited by Syariah.[48] The punishment for each of these offences was heavier than for the six offences within the *Kathi* Court's jurisdiction.

The *Kathi* Court had sole jurisdiction over the other six religious offences. In this Court, the *kathi* could summon two or more Muslims of good standing from a list compiled by the Sultan to sit with him as assessors.[49] Fines went into the Mohammedan Religious Fund,[50] whereas previously fines were 'pocketed' by adjudicators.[51] The offences included breach of the religious duty to attend a mosque for Friday prayers (for men),[52] unilaterally breaking an engagement,[53] instigating a broken engagement,[54] a Muslim wife's leaving the marital home,[55] failure of a husband to provide financial support for the family[56] and immoral cohabitation. As regards the last of these, the *kathi* would first order the parties to marry, and failure to comply created the offence.[57]

An interesting offence is the offence of prostitution, because it highlights the interplay between the two streams of law. The *kathi* had power to summon a Muslim woman to warn her to desist from prostitution. If she failed to comply, the case went before the Magistrate Courts, at which stage the woman could be imprisoned for three months and, if convicted on a second offence, banished from Brunei.[58] The relationship between penal offences in the two systems was an ongoing issue, and today is a vexed one, which will be discussed later in section III.D.

D. The Colonial Legacy from the Residency

The colonial legacy from the Residency period was legally transformative. Mansurnoor describes it as revolutionary,[59] as it 'opened Courts of Justice which know no distinction between races and creeds, between rich and poor, between master and slave'.[60] Enforcing 'Mohammedan' laws required the construction of supportive institutions and funding.[61]

[48] Mohammedan Laws Enactment 1912, s 7. Incest was defined as 'any relationship with persons whom one might not marry according to the Mohammedan law'. A conviction carried a term of imprisonment of up to five years for a man, and for a woman, no more than one year.

[49] Mohammedan Laws Enactment 1912, s 15(1).

[50] Mohammedan Laws Enactment 1912, s 18.

[51] Mansurnoor, 'Re-establishing Order' (n 23) 169, citing British official William Hood Treacher.

[52] Mohammedan Laws Enactment 1912, s 3. The penalty was a fine of 50 cents for each absence.

[53] Mohammedan Laws Enactment 1912, s 8. The penalty was to pay the *mas kahwin*, but the gifts would be returned.

[54] Mohammedan Laws Enactment 1912, s 9. The penalty was a fine of B$10 or imprisonment for 14 days.

[55] Mohammedan Laws Enactment 1912, s 11. The penalty was a fine of $10.

[56] Mohammedan Laws Enactment 1912, s 12. The penalty was imprisonment for no more than 10 days or a fine of no more than B$10.

[57] Mohammedan Laws Enactment 1912, s 14. The penalty was a fine of B$10.

[58] Mohammedan Laws Enactment 1912, s 13.

[59] Mansurnoor, 'Re-establishing Order' (n 23) 179.

[60] ibid 180, citing Treacher.

[61] Britain built courthouses, offices and a prison. The Government appointed *Kathis* (public servants supported by the bureaucracy) and recruited religious enforcement police.

By the end of the Residency,[62] Brunei had a respected independent judicial system for civil and religious law, the country was stable, financially sound and well-administered, with little corruption and a comparatively peaceful plural population of many ethnicities and religions.

III. CONTEMPORARY DEVELOPMENTS

The Residency formalised two streams of law, and within each were religious penal offences. This bifurcation continues to the present day. Except for a commensurate increase in penalties in line with inflation, the substance of the first Penal Code of 1908 remains essentially the same in the current Penal Code (Chapter 22). By contrast, in the Islamic law stream, offences, procedures, penalties and jurisdiction for Islamic criminal law have greatly expanded from its 1912 predecessor. The scales for offences against religion have tipped in favour of greater weight for Islamic penal law.

After the end of World War II and Japan's occupation of Brunei, nationalism inspired the desire for greater autonomy and an increased role for Islam. The first step was in 1948, when a board of 18 religious Islamic advisors was established with authority over appeals on Islamic law.[63] This severed the Resident's appellate role in Islamic law cases. In 1955, under the guidance of Sultan Omar, known as the 'father of modern Brunei' and the father of the current Sultan, the Religious Council, State Council and Qadi Courts' Law Act of 1955 replaced the Mohammedan Enactment 1912. Its 12 'infractions of religious precepts' were consolidated in the new Act but, importantly, administration of Islamic law was now under the direct control of Islamic scholars and the religious courts were self-administered separately from the civil courts.[64] From then to today, the Religious Council, with two Committees of Laws and of Courts, is one of the most powerful institutions in the Sultanate.[65] Since independence, a similar but more expansive Religious Council and Kadi's Court Act have replaced the 1955 Act.

A. Britain Rescues the Sultan in 1962

The Constitution of Brunei Darussalam 1959 (Constitution) provided for a partially elected legislature, with 17 members appointed by the Sultan and 16 elected by the people.[66] The elected representatives would always be in the

[62] The Resident's Court was abolished in 1951.

[63] Mansurnoor, 'Shari'a-Guided Legal System' (n 5) 232.

[64] Mansurnoor, 'Re-establishing Order' (n 23) 179.

[65] The Religious Council collects religious taxes (*zakat* and *fitrah*), supervises mosques and imams, registers converts, ensures Sunni Shafi'i school doctrine, administers inheritance matters, implements Islamic law and practices, and advises the Sultan.

[66] From 1951, Brunei was again a protectorate. The Constitution provided for self-governance in all matters other than defence and foreign affairs.

minority but, via the ballot box, it was possible for Bruneians to have input into the direction of law and policy for Brunei. The pro-democracy, anti-aristocratic Brunei People's Party/*Parti Rakyat Brunei* (PRB), which ran on a platform to form a Greater Borneo and to limit the Sultan's powers, won all 16 seats. The message from the people was overwhelming, but the Sultan refused to accept it and prevented the elected representatives from forming a government. Thwarted, the PRB staged a coup against the Sultan. He proclaimed a state of emergency.

Within days, British forces quashed the uprising. The coup leaders fled or were imprisoned, and the PRB was banned.[67] The state of emergency instituted in 1962 to quell the PRB-led uprising continued, and has since been renewed every two years,[68] most recently in 2017.[69] It is ironic that although all the constitutional triggers for a state of emergency proclamation – threat of public danger, external aggression, war or international disturbance – do not exist in the 'Abode of Peace', the Sultan continues to appropriate emergency powers to make any 'orders whatsoever which he considers desirable in the public interest'.[70] The (Emergency) Arbitration Order 2009, (Emergency) Syariah Penal Code Order 2013, (Emergency) Beauty and Health Establishment Order 2016 and (Emergency) Syariah Courts Criminal Procedure Code Order 2018 are amongst the hundreds of emergency orders enacted that bear no link to security threats or dangers.

B. Independence and Commencement of MIB Ideology

At independence in 1984, the Sultan's address to the nation introduced his subjects to the nation's ideology of 'MIB': *Melayu Islam Beraja* (Malay, Islam, Monarchy).[71] The Islam pillar of MIB drove a policy of Islamisation that recalibrated the Sultanate's laws in line with traditional Syariah (*Hukum Shara*) rather than the Bruneian mix of Islamic principles and customs operating prior to the Residency. A Committee on the Modification of Brunei Laws was established to review all laws of Brunei to ensure conformity with Syariah, including criminal laws. A decade later, when Islamisation of laws was well underway,[72] the Sultan

[67] In 2009, the Minister released the last coup member from prison.

[68] Constitution of Brunei Darussalam, Art 83(2); Emergency (Continuation and Validation of Emergency Provisions) Order 2004.

[69] See Proclamation of Emergency (No S12), 12 February 2017 at www.agc.gov.bn/AGC%20 Images/LAWS/ Gazette_PDF/2017/EN/S012.pdf.

[70] Constitution of Brunei Darussalam, Art 83(3).

[71] Scholars such as Muhammad Hadi bin Md Melayong from the MIB Council claim the ideology of MIB commenced in 1360 on the conversion of the first Sultan. It was not until 1984, however, that it was first articulated. See Muhammad Hadi bin Md Melayong, 'Brunei's Golden Period of Expansion' *Borneo Bulletin* (Bandar Seri Begawan, 24 October 2016).

[72] First was the prohibition on the sale and consumption of alcohol (1991) and pork products (1992). Next were laws on banking and finance, including the Islamic Banking Act, with a fully Islamic-compliant bank opening in 1993. The Syariah Courts Act 1998 upgraded the *Kadi* Courts to a three-tier Syariah courts system, followed by the Islamic Family Law Order 1999, Islamic Evidence

publically called for the establishment of Syariah criminal law and procedure. He tasked the Ministry of Religious Affairs (MoRA) with making this a reality. It took 15 years, but in 2013, the Sultan announced by *titah* at his sixty-sixth birthday that he had given his royal consent for the 2013 Order.[73]

The first phase of the 2013 Order commenced in 2014 with *taz'ir* (general offences). The controversial *hudud* offences, with classic penalties of amputation, stoning, executions and whippings, and *qisas* (eye-for-eye retaliation) and *diyat* (blood money) for homicide and bodily injury would follow, 12 months after enactment of a complementary Procedural Order. Although the Procedural Order came into force in March 2018, uncertainty remained as to whether the Sultan's pledge to implement the later phases for *hudud* and *qisas* offences would eventuate. Nine months later, with the Notification of Commencement gazetted, the Sultan fulfilled his commitment to fully implement Syariah criminal law in Brunei. From 3 April 2019, all parts (except for section 94 on pregnancy outside wedlock) commenced.

Amongst the new *hudud* offences, is the religious offence of *irtidad*, apostasy. If proven, an unrepentant apostate can be sentenced to death by execution. The 2018 Procedure Order details the methods for execution as it does for death by stoning. However, it was the two stoning offences of *zina* (adultery in marriage) and especially *liwat* (consensual homosexual acts) that garnered the most international reaction from human rights bodies, governments, non-governmental organisations (NGOs), corporations and the international (but not the Bruneian) media. The words 'Sultan', 'Brunei', 'stoning' and 'gay-sex' dominated headlines across the world. The religious penal offences, also punishable with the death penalty, drew little criticism. Having underestimated a worldwide vigilant, vocal and passionate gay-rights movement, and faced with threats of boycotts and sanctions, the Sultan announced a concession. He would extend the de facto moratorium on capital punishment operating under the civil law to the Syariah system. This placated many international critics whilst pleasing his supporters as the laws were retained. There was no repeal nor amendment of the offending provisions. Execution and death by stoning remain in Bruneian legislation.

C. Religious Penal Offences in the Syariah Penal Code Order 2013

Article 3(1) of the Constitution of Brunei Darussalam provides, 'Save as otherwise expressly provided therein, this order shall apply to Muslims and non-Muslims.' The 2013 Order thus applies to all persons. This marks a significant departure from the first colonial enactment that was for Muslims only. It also

Order 2001, Islamic Adoption of Children Act 2001, Syariah Financial Supervisory Board Order 2006 and Compulsory Religious Education Act 2012.

[73] 'In conjunction with my 66th birthday, with all gratitude, which will save us all, especially the king, from (what will be) demanded by *Allah Subhanahu Wa Ta'ala* on Judgment Day.'

departs from the neutral and general application of religious penal clauses in the civil Penal Code. Clauses specify Muslim[74] or simply any person.[75] Punishments differ in the same way.[76] Non-Muslims, as well as Muslims, can commit offences against tenets of Islam, Islamic morality and Islamic institutions. Some offences and the penalties given also vary according to a perpetrator's gender and marital status.[77]

There are other key differences from earlier Islamic penal laws, including from the amended Religious Council and Kadi's Court Act. First, the 2013 Order expands the nature of conduct that comprises an offence against the religion of Islam. Second, the penalties for offences consolidated from the Religious Council and Kadi's Court Act are increased. Most offences punishable with fines or imprisonment have seen a threefold increase.[78] Third, under *hudud* and *qisas*, a hitherto unknown range of punitive consequences, including stoning, enters the Sultanate.[79] Fourth, offences under the 2013 Order committed by Bruneians outside the territory of Brunei fall under the Syariah Court's penal jurisdiction.[80] Fifth, the death penalty for non-Muslims and Muslims is now possible for several religious offences.[81]

The 2013 Order sets out more than 100 criminal offences. Of these, more than half are 'religious' offences, with the majority for acts contrary to the tenets of Islam, with other offences for acts against Islamic religious authorities and 18 offences for breach of Islamic morality. Given this number, the overview to follow considers examples from each category.

i. *Offences Contrary to the Tenets of Islam*

a. Offence of Apostasy

Apostasy – leaving Islam for another religion, becoming an atheist, or denying a central tenet of the Islamic faith – is a matter of 'grave concern' to Islamic authorities everywhere. Brunei's State Mufti, Haji Awang Abdul Aziz bin Juned,

[74] For example, it is an offence under s 94 for a Muslim woman to be pregnant or give birth out of wedlock.

[75] For example, it is an offence under s 222 for a person to deride the Quran.

[76] For example, offences for drinking liquor or intoxicants differentiate between Muslims and non-Muslims. For a Muslim, it is an offence to drink any alcohol; whereas for non-Muslims, the offence is committed when such drinking occurs in a public place. For a Muslim, the penalty is whipping (40–80 strokes), with a term of imprisonment not exceeding two years for a third or subsequent offence; whilst for a non-Muslim's first offence, the penalty is a fine of up to B$8,000 or imprisonment also for up to two years, or both. However, no whipping is prescribed for non-Muslims.

[77] For example, the penalty for an offence under s 94 is halved when the offender is unmarried.

[78] For example, incitement to neglect religious duties in s 193 of the Religious Council and Kadi's Court Act had a maximum penalty of imprisonment for six months or a fine of B$4,000. In the 2013 Order, imprisonment is for a term of up to three years and/or a fine of B$12,000.

[79] There is no evidence that Bruneians had previously conducted stoning as a punishment for adultery.

[80] Syariah Penal Code Order 2013, s 3(3).

[81] For example, *irtidad*/apostasy, blasphemy and sodomy.

described it as the 'worst crime, the most insolent' and 'a heinous humiliation not only to Islam but to Allah Himself'.[82]

Yet apostasy was not an offence under any of the earlier religious laws, including the Religious Council and Kadi's Court Act. Renunciation of Islam was lawful under section 169 of that Act. It required an apostate to report the fact in writing to the Secretary of the Religious Council. The Act required nothing more. The ease of a 'mere notification' concerned the religious establishment in Brunei, and the Religious Council was reluctant to validate apostasy applications. Lindsey and Steiner report that by 2006 there was a backlog of over 20 apostasy cases before the Council. In 2006, the Council, in consultation with the judges of the Syariah Courts (which replaced Kadi Courts in 1998), decided, without legislative amendment, that the Syariah Court would hear and decide all renunciations of Islam. The Court then could order a lengthy period of counselling to persuade the would-be apostate of his or her error and the gravity of his or her sin, followed by a re-education programme,[83] and finally counselling by a Syariah Court judge, who was required to order the applicant to repent. If there was no repentance and the cumulative persuasive measures failed to deter the applicant, the judge could certify him or her as a *murtad* (apostate). This enabled official changes to be made to name and religion on the apostate's identity card. There were no penalties. The Sarawak High Court noted the availability of a process for renunciation in a Malaysian judicial review case.[84] It involved an Iban Christian who converted from Christianity to Islam to marry in Brunei, and who then, on divorce, sought to convert back to Christianity. Justice Chung held that as her conversion out of Islam was in Brunei Darussalam, she should obtain 'her release from Islam' with the relevant authorities in Brunei Darussalam, as renunciation was not possible in Sarawak. Once obtained in Brunei, she could then apply for a declaration to change her religious identity and registration in Sarawak.

Under the 2013 Order, a Muslim who renounces Islam by declaring he or she is no longer a Muslim is liable for a *hadd* death penalty sentence (subject to the de facto moratorium on execution).[85] There is considerable jurisprudential debate on whether apostasy should be categorised as *hadd* and the validity of the death penalty.[86] Brunei, which previously did not criminalise renunciations, has now adopted the most conservative jurisprudential stance. Imposition of the death penalty is only open when there is proof of apostasy by either two confessions

[82] Haji Awang Abdul Aziz bin Juned, *The Shari'ah Penal Code: An Introduction* (Office of the State Mufti, 2014) 150.

[83] This is run by the Council of Religious Affairs and the Syariah Affairs Department of the Ministry of Religious Affairs.

[84] *Mardina Tiara bt Abdullah Emat @ Margaret ak Emat v Director of Jabatan Agama Islam Sarawak & Ors* [2017] 9 MLJ 293 (High Court, Kuching).

[85] Syariah Penal Code Order 2013, s 112.

[86] See Ann Black, Hossein Esmaeili and Nadirsyah Hosen, *Modern Perspectives on Islamic Law* (Edward Elgar, 2013) 225–26.

of guilt, or *shahadah* (the highest standard – oral eyewitness evidence) given in court by two *syahid* (credible Muslim male witnesses). If the evidence fails to meet these requirements, there is a lesser penalty.[87] A Muslim attempting to renounce Islam receives the same penalty, as does 'any person' convicted of abetting apostasy.[88] In the sections that follow section 112, apostasy/*irtidad* extends to declaring oneself a god[89] or declaring oneself a *rasul* (messenger) or *nabi* (prophet).[90] After any apostasy conviction, the Syariah Court will order that a Muslim offender repent, which – if deemed sincere – will result in an acquittal.[91] This feature of repentance is a recurring and important one in the 2013 Order, and means that many of the Syariah penalties will not be carried out.

The apostasy offences in the 2013 Order import conservative fundamentalist jurisprudence. Although the Quran warns about consequences for 'a believer who turns his back on Islam', these are in the 'hereafter' and do not mandate death.[92] There are *hadiths* that do, and it is an offence to question their veracity.[93] The State Mufti of Brunei justifies the death penalty by *ijma* (consensus of the scholars), which he asserts as *wajib* (obligatory) to enforce.[94] He supports this with a second societal justification. The State Mufti claims there is a trend for apostasy applications, and although he gives no figures from Brunei, he has cited figures from Malaysia, where 5,000 or so Muslims allegedly applied to change their Malay name to non-Malay in order to leave Islam.[95] In his view, laws that allow for renunciation of Islam are wrong, and he endorses the Sultan's 'excellent' vision for *hadd* penalties in Brunei's 2013 Order. Whether *hadd* penalties occur or not, their symbolic importance is paramount.

b. Blasphemy and Heresy

Section 107 of the 2013 Order defines apostasy/*irtidad* more broadly than renunciation, and thereby incorporates acts of blasphemy and heresy under the broad *irtidad* umbrella. In section 107, apostasy extends to an 'act done or word uttered' by a Muslim that is 'contrary to the faith of Islam'. If the required evidence[96] shows that a Muslim brings into contempt a *nabi*, whether the Prophet Mohammad or any prophet, the offender can also face the death penalty.

[87] A maximum of up to 30 years' imprisonment and whipping not exceeding 40 strokes.
[88] Syariah Penal Code Order 2013, s 113.
[89] Syariah Penal Code Order 2013, s 108.
[90] Syariah Penal Code Order 2013, s 109.
[91] Syariah Penal Code Order 2013, s 116.
[92] See, eg, Surahs 47:25 and 2:217 Quran. Sheikh Abdur Rahman, a former Chief Justice of Pakistan, argues there is no reference to death in any of the 20 instances of apostasy in the Quran.
[93] Sahih Bukari 14:395–6: 'Kill the person who abandons his religion.' See later discussion on the *anti-hadith* movement in section IV.B.
[94] Syariah Penal Code Order 2013, s 154. This consensus was reached by early Sunni jurists.
[95] Juned, *The Shari'ah Penal Code* (n 82) 150.
[96] Two confessions or *shahadah* evidence by *syahids*.

The blasphemy net covers several other offences:

- Deriding, ridiculing, insulting, etc, verses of the Quran or *hadith* (narrated traditions of the Prophet Muhammad);
- Denying a *hadith* as a source of authority in the teachings of Islam;
- Denying obligatory matters with *ijma* (consensus of jurists).[97]

Each of these affects Muslim intra-plurality in Brunei, as the weight given to certain *hadiths* and what amounts to *ijma* vary across schools of law and jurisdiction. To criminalise religious debate has a chilling effect on interpretative freedom for Muslims in Brunei.

c. Non-Muslims and Blasphemy

The chilling effects also extend to Brunei's religious minorities, who risk punitive consequences by comparing, discussing or criticising Islam. Although non-Muslims cannot renounce Islam, the definition of apostasy in blasphemy terms to include insulting or denying tenets of Islam extends to all persons. This is akin to the Pakistani provisions for blasphemy, and at least one Pakistani scholar, Dr Anwarallah, was influential in the drafting of the 2013 Order. As a result, there is a range of penal offences in the 2013 Order that apply to 'any person', so the criminal jurisdiction of the Syariah courts, including imposition of the death penalty, now extends to non-Muslims. For example, the offence of 'orally, in writing, by visible representation or in any other manner contempts or brings into contempt' the Prophet Mohammad mandates the death penalty,[98] as does deriding or insulting a verse of the Quran or a *hadith* of the Prophet.[99] Attempting and abetting these offences have similar penalties to those previously outlined for Muslims.

Insulting any aspect of Islam has punitive consequences. Section 220, which applies to any person, sets out seven ways by which a person 'orally, in writing, by visible representation or in any other manner' may insult, make fun of, mock, mimic or ridicule Islam. These seven cover (i) the teachings of Islam, (ii) practices or ceremonies, (iii) words regarded as holy by Muslims, (iv) any law dealing with Islam, (v) any *sahabat* (companion of the Prophet), (vi) tenets of any recognised sect and (vii) any gazetted *fatwa*.[100]

d. Use of 'Islamic' Words by Non-Muslims

Section 217 criminalises non-Muslims using words reserved for Muslims. The Order's Fifth Schedule lists 20 or so words. Penal sanctions apply to their use

[97] See Syariah Penal Code Order 2013, s 111(1).

[98] Syariah Penal Code Order 2013, s 221. If proof does not meet the required standard, the penalty is up to 30 years' imprisonment.

[99] Syariah Penal Code Order 2013, s 111.

[100] Syariah Penal Code Order 2013, s 220. The maximum penalty for an offence under s 220(a)–(g) is three years' imprisonment or a fine not exceeding B$12,000.

in connection with another religion.[101] They include *azan*, *fatwa*, *hadith*, *hajj*, *hukum syaria*, *imam*, *solat*, *wali* and *Allah*. *Allah* is the Arabic and the Malay word for God as the Abrahamic God of Muslims, Christians and Jews. Its inclusion in section 217 means that Bibles or hymn books of the Christian population in Brunei that contain the word *Allah* are now unlawful, and persons in possession of them can face imprisonment for up to three years, a fine up to B$12,000 or both,[102] and the item will be forfeited and destroyed, regardless of the conviction.[103] The Fifth Schedule covers any speech or public statement using a prohibited word,[104] or 'any derivatives or its variation', if it was 'to state or express any fact, belief, idea, concept, act, activity, matter or instances of, or relating to a religion other than the religion of Islam'.[105]

Interestingly, there was debate in the Government's briefings on the new Order as to whether non-Muslims could sing the country's national anthem '*Allah* Bless the Sultan', which begins with the words '*Ya Allah*'. A spokesperson for the Attorney-General responded that non-Muslims should sing the anthem because it is 'a song that is respected by the whole country', in contrast to Christian hymns that only a minority respect.[106] Restrictions on the use of such words are frequently justified because of their potential to confuse Muslims. This paternalistic approach to the need for religious penal clauses is a recurring theme.

ii. Doctrines or Practices Contrary to Islamic Law

Section 207 of the 2013 Order has two parts. The first applies to Muslims who teach or expound any doctrine relating to Islam that is contrary to Islamic law, or who perform or practise any ceremonies contrary to Islamic law. The second part covers non-Muslims who teach, expound or perform ceremonies reserved for Muslims.

a. Black Magic

A new criminal offence under the 2013 Order is practising, advertising for or seeking black magic services, involving 'spirits, evil spirits, ghosts and the like'. The Attorney-General's department called it an 'innovative' offence.[107]

[101] Syariah Penal Code Order 2013, s 217. The penalty is imprisonment for a maximum of three years or a fine not exceeding B$12,000.

[102] Syariah Penal Code Order 2013, s 217(2).

[103] Syariah Penal Code Order 2013, s 217(3).

[104] ibid.

[105] ibid.

[106] Nadzri Zailani, 'Non-Muslims allowed to sing national anthem' *Brunei Times* (Bandar Seri Begawan, 22 April 2014).

[107] 'Practising Black Magic is listed offence in Syariah Law' *Brunei Times* (Bandar Seri Begawan, 4 June 2014).

Accordingly, it conducted workshops on what black magic encompasses and how to secure convictions.[108] There are two targeted groups for these offences. One is the non-Muslim indigenous tribal groups, who follow their traditional animistic practices in which individuals are in constant interaction with the spirit world's many gods. Omens and evil spirits are part of this world, as is augury.[109] These practices originated in pre-Islamic Borneo, and Islamic scholars view them as inferior and primitive.[110] For this reason, when Muslim Malays also have dealings with the spirit world, through spells, magic and omens, visit animist shrines, perform healings and other ceremonies, Brunei's religious officials view it all as heretical and deviant. This is the other target group. Muller's anthropological research showed that although it has been in decline, some Malays still engage in 'superstitious' practices, including visiting *keramat* shrines, which they believe contain spirits who can mediate with God.[111] Visiting and using the services of *bomoh* (shamans and magic healers) are also sinful as forms of black magic. The State Mufti's office distinguishes between traditional healing, which is medicinal, and acts of healing invoking the supernatural.[112] It becomes criminal if the act of healing 'could fall under *syirik* (associating Allah SWT with anything as an equal) … and believes in a separate power or belief besides Allah SWT'.[113] Although already prohibited under the Religious Council and Kadi Court Act, the 2013 Order increases the penalties from three months to two years' imprisonment, and quadruples the maximum fine. It also has fleshed out the sections in more detail and has included two serious offences of 'attempting to cause death by black magic'[114] and where the actual causing of death by black magic is proved mainly by confessional evidence.[115] Again, repentance is encouraged. In order to purify the faith and practices of Bruneian Muslims, the Government's Faith Control Section remains vigilant against shamanism and superstition, and has a 24-hour hotline for 'tip-offs' for the reporting of suspicious activities.[116]

[108] ibid.

[109] Augury is a form of divination to determine the will of the gods revealed through the behaviour of birds, animals, and reptiles. Augurs (witch doctors or shamans) can interpret the signs and omens from the gods, who issue warnings, provide favours, give guidance and foretell the future.

[110] Jay Bernstein, 'The Deculturalisation of the Brunei Dusun' in Robert L Winzeler (ed), *Indigenous Peoples and the State* (Yale University Press, 1997) 167. Animism concerns the current Government just as it did earlier, when those without Holy Scriptures, the non-believers known as *kafirs*, were not entitled to the protections afforded *dhimmis* (people of the book). The conversion campaigns of the Islamic *Da'wah* Centre target *kafirs*, including the Iban, Dusan, Punan, Murut and Belait indigenous peoples. If they convert to Islam, there are incentives in the form of cash payments, houses and other tangible benefits, such as preferential employment opportunities, including in the public service.

[111] Dominik M Muller, 'Sharia Law and the Politics of "Faith Control" in Brunei Darussalam' (2015) 46 *Internationales Asienforum* 313, 329.

[112] Nabilah Haris, 'Local customs, beliefs may not be Syariah compliant' *Brunei Times* (Bandar Seri Begawan, 17 April 2014).

[113] ibid.

[114] Syariah Penal Code Order 2013, s 153.

[115] Syariah Penal Code Order 2013, s 152.

[116] Muller, 'Sharia Law' (n 111) 329.

b. Proselytisation

Numerous penal offences in the 2013 Order protect Islam by prohibiting proselytisation of Muslims. This contrasts with the nation's *da'wah* propagation policy, which actively promotes conversions to Islam. In Brunei, propagating a religion other than Islam is a criminal offence with a penalty of up to five years' imprisonment.[117] Related crimes include persuading a Muslim to change his or her religion, persuading a person having no religion to become a believer of a religion other than Islam,[118] and exposing the beliefs and practices of a religion other than Islam to a minor Muslim child or a child whose parents have no religion.[119] Delivering or giving a publication relating to a religion other than Islam to Muslims or persons with no religion is also an offence.[120] These offences apply to both private and public places.[121]

c. Offences for Breach of Religious Duties

Under the 2013 Order, Muslims must by law fulfil their religious obligations. Although this has always been the case, now, however, the duties have been expanded and detailed, and the penalties multiplied. Breaches include failure to attend Friday prayers;[122] eating, drinking or smoking during Ramadan;[123] selling food, alcohol or cigarettes to persons required to observe Ramadan;[124] non-payment of *zakat* and *fitra*;[125] and drinking alcohol or similar intoxicating drinks; and selling, distributing or possessing alcoholic items.[126]

Non-Muslims found to have encouraged or incited a Muslim not to fulfil any prescribed religious duty can face a year in prison.[127] Non-Muslims cannot consume alcohol in a public place,[128] nor sell, advertise or give alcohol or similar substances to Muslims.[129] Although drinking wine is not contrary to Christianity and is integral to the Christian sacrament of Holy Communion, and rice wine was part of animistic traditional ceremonies, there are significant restrictions on access and consumption. In the same way, the clothing prescriptions of conservative Islam apply in a range of settings, including government

[117] Syariah Penal Code Order 2013, s 209.
[118] Syariah Penal Code Order 2013, s 211. The penalty is imprisonment for a maximum of five years and a fine of up to B$20,000.
[119] Syariah Penal Code Order 2013, s 212. The penalty is imprisonment for a maximum of 5 years and a fine of up to B$20,000.
[120] Syariah Penal Code Order 2013, s 214.
[121] Syariah Penal Code Order 2013, s 215.
[122] Syariah Penal Code Order 2013, s 194.
[123] Syariah Penal Code Order 2013, s 195.
[124] Syariah Penal Code Order 2013, s 195(2).
[125] Syariah Penal Code Order 2013, s 236.
[126] Syariah Penal Code Order 2013, s 104(4).
[127] Syariah Penal Code Order 2013, s 235.
[128] Syariah Penal Code Order 2013, s 104(5).
[129] Syariah Penal Code Order 2013, s 104(6). The penalty is imprisonment of up to two years and/or a fine of B$8,000.

workplaces and schools, under the general catch-all offence of not tarnishing the image of Islam.[130] Cross-dressing is a separate offence, however, and one of the first convictions under the 2013 Order was for this offence in Rosiani's case.

d. Case of Rosiani Hj Metasan, Syariah Subordinate Court

Rosiani was an unmarried male civil servant who allegedly posed as a woman and had female personal items in his bag.[131] He was prosecuted and convicted of the offence of 'posing as a woman' under section 198(1) of the 2013 Order. The Syariah prosecutor advocated that his was an immoral act in Islam that damaged the religion and Malay traditions. The magistrate concluded that Rosiani's actions reflected his moral decadence, and added a general warning that if such activity is not curbed it can 'lead to the spread of social disorder such as homosexuality, free-sexual relations, drug abuse and so on'.[132] In addition to his fine of B$1,000, Rosiani was warned that he must 'return to the right path and to Allah SWT'.

D. Offences against Religious Authority

This category of religious penal offences has political overtones. Designed to protect the state's monopoly over Islam and insulate the Sultan as head of Islam, the Government's Islamic institutions are made immune from criticism. These offences protect the status quo. As head of the religion, the Sultan with the Religious Council can ensure that Islam practised in Brunei supports, not undermines, his absolute monarchy. Islam in Brunei means Sunni Islam 'according to the Shafeite sect'.[133] This diminishes Islam's inherent interpretive plurality. There is only one permissible Islamic path in Brunei, and the 2013 Order ensures that all Islamic teachings and practice conform to it.[134] Religious interpretations that are inconsistent with the Religious Council's conservative Shafeite positions are 'deviationist' and criminalised in the 2013 Order. Muller describes this as a 'passionate demonisation of religious pluralism'.[135]

Only the State Mufti or a person acting on his authority can issue a *fatwa* (a religious scholarly opinion) on an issue of Islamic doctrine or law.[136] A person cannot teach on Islam or Islamic doctrine without the prior approval of the

[130] Syariah Penal Code Order 2013, s 197.
[131] Ak Md Khairuddin Pg Harun, 'Bruneian civil servant fined $1000 for cross-dressing' *Brunei Times* (Bandar Seri Begawan, 11 March 2015).
[132] ibid.
[133] Constitution of Brunei Darussalam, Art 2. See also Religious Council and Kadi's Courts Act, s 43.
[134] The Sultan's *titah* for *Aidil Adha*, dated 7 March 2001, reminds Muslims not to let 'deviants influence them'.
[135] Dominik M Muller, 'Paradoxical Normativities in Brunei Darussalam' (2016) 56(3) *Asian Survey* 415, 415.
[136] Syariah Penal Code Order 2013, s 228(1).

Religious Council.[137] The most encompassing offence for stifling public and open debate is in section 230, which makes it an offence – punishable with up to five years' imprisonment – for any person who 'contempts, neglects, contravenes, *opposes*, or insults any *titah* by the Sultan with respect to religion' (emphasis added). Given that *titah* is the main means for announcing significant new laws or policy in Brunei, it is a significant political as well as religious restraint.

E. Interaction between the Civil and Religious Laws

When the same act or omission is a criminal offence in the two streams of law, it is necessary to decide which court has jurisdiction. Initially there was considerable uncertainty as to whether a person could be tried, charged or even convicted of two offences for the same conduct. Would double jeopardy apply? Would the jurisdiction of one court prevail over the other? By whom and how would jurisdiction be decided? It seems that cases involving crimes covered by both the Islamic and the civil laws are currently referred to the Attorney General's Chambers (AGC), which determine case-by-case if there is a specific crime that should be prosecuted and whether it should be filed in the Syariah courts or civil court. The AGC has not published official guidelines for its determination process.

F. Case of Shahiransheriffuddin bin Shahrani Muhammad 2017 ('*Shahiran*')

The case of *Shahiran* highlights the challenges that arise from of two sets of laws: was his conduct seditious, an offence against religious authority, or both? There is no reported judgment on this case, and the information presented here is from local and international news reports.[138] Shahiran was a government employee. On 16 July 2017, he posted a comment on Facebook (the post was under another name) in which he was critical of a newly released halal regulation and certification policy of MoRA. He expressed the view that the need for many small businesses to hire halal supervisors was too onerous.

The post was deleted very quickly, but there were some screen shots uploaded by Twitter users. The post said:

> From now on all businesses to do with food must hire 'two Halal Muslim supervisors who possess basic knowledge of *Hukum Syarak* and product handling ethics, and at least one Halal supervisor must be present at the business at all times' as part of this new halal licensing thing.

[137] Syariah Penal Code Order 2013, s 229.

[138] 'Brunei Darussalam 2017/2018' (*Amnesty International*, undated) at www.amnesty.org/en/countries/asia-and-the-pacific/brunei-darussalam/report-brunei-darussalam.

> This may also hit people in other industries like cosmetics. My cousin thinking about making soups as a hobby will be impacted.
>
> Get a halal cert or get fined. Halal certs will cost you fucking loads like hiring up to 5/6 new people. Small home-based businesses ARE NOT EXEMPTED.
>
> Fuck you MORA.
>
> Go back to your stupid useless ministry and start investigating why all the sexual offenders are *Ugama* teachers instead of trying to destroy people's livelihoods like this.[139]

The post ended by asking Bruneians 'why we let them (MoRA) destroy our lives and our kids' future?'

In mid-2017, Borneo Bulletin reported that Shahiran was initially charged with one count of sedition under section 4(1)(c) of the Sedition Act, for posting 'inflammatory comments about the Ministry's halal certification policy'. The magistrate held it was a seditious post but adjourned the case until August. Shahiran received bail on his own surety, with the condition that he did not post any adverse comments against the Brunei Government. If found guilty, he faced a maximum fine of B$5,000 and/or a two-year prison sentence. However, in August 2017, an online crowdfunding site was set up to assist Shahiran's defence because, it claimed, MoRA had laid additional charges under Syariah law on 2 August.[140] These charges included insulting (with intention) Islamic law and members of the Islamic Council. Another online site stated that the Religious Enforcement Unit of MoRA questioned him for two days without legal representation, and that Shahiran had asked for, but did not receive, a written copy of the Syariah charges. It was not clear whether the civil and religious charges arising from the one post would proceed and, if so, which would be heard first. On the day Shahiran was due for sentencing for the sedition offence, *Borneo Bulletin* reported that he was not present in court and had 'fled and sought refuge in Canada'.[141] The court issued a warrant for his arrest and entered judgment *in absentia*.

IV. SOCIAL BACKGROUND

A. Negara Zikir

The 2013 Order and 2018 Procedure Order are the culmination of Brunei's national project to establish a *zikir* nation, defined by Brunei's Sultan as one 'that upholds Allah (SWT)'s laws, with noble moral values'.[142] In this Sultanate,

[139] 'The Brunei Project' at www.facebook.com/thebruneiproject.

[140] ibid.

[141] Fadley Faisal, 'Defendant in sedition trial flees before verdict' *Brunei Bulletin* (Bandar Seri Begawan, 15 November 2018).

[142] '*Titah* for the 1433 Hijrah (Islamic New Year)' *Brunei Times* (Bandar Seri Begawan, 30 November 2011).

religion, specifically the religion of Islam, is not only important but drives government policy through the central tenet of state ideology of MIB. In describing the nation, the adjective *zikir* is repeatedly used rather than 'Islamic', possibly because the former is aspirational whilst an Islamic state is a contested term in many Muslim countries, making it, as Harding concludes, ambiguous and 'impossible' to define.[143] However, this clearly enunciated *zikir* direction means that the ethnic, religious and legal pluralism that has been part of life in Brunei for centuries is now incompatible and threatened. The Sultan rejects pluralism in all forms, and has specifically condemned 'religious pluralism' for diverting Muslim thinking and allowing deviant teachings that 'every individual is free to choose their religion' to pollute Brunei.[144] The judges of the Syariah High Court[145] and local religious scholars[146] endorse his viewpoint on religious pluralism. Equally condemned is 'liberal Islam', for tarnishing the image of Islam and misguiding Muslims.[147]

By adhering to MIB, the Sultan's Government strives for a mono-cultural and a Muslim *zikir* nation. However, Brunei today remains a multi-racial and multi-religious. Two-thirds of the 434,000[148] people in Brunei are Malay, the Chinese population is 16 per cent and Indians, indigenous ethnic groups and expatriates, most of whom are non-Muslims, together make up the remaining one-third.[149] A decade earlier, Brunei conducted its last census, in which Muslims made up 66 per cent, Buddhists 13 per cent, Christians 12 per cent, indigenous religions 2 per cent and others 7 per cent of the population. Government data now report that the percentage who are Muslims is currently 75 per cent, which shows the success of the Ministry of Religion's *da'wah* (propagation of Islam) programmes and its restrictions on the practice of other religions. However, the figures remain incomplete, as they do not include residents, including foreign workers, many of whom are from the neighbouring Philippines, nor Brunei's stateless residents, who are mainly the descendants of earlier Chinese immigrants. Regardless, Muslims are the majority, but there is still a significant percentage of the population (approximately 25–37 per cent) who are not.[150]

[143] Andrew J Harding, 'The Keris, The Crescent and the Blind Goddess: The State, Islam and the Constitution in Malaysia' (2002) 6 *Singapore Journal of International & Comparative Law* 154.

[144] Azlan Othman, 'Steer clear of deviant teachings, Muslims told' *Borneo Bulletin* (Bandar Seri Begawan, 2 February 2013).

[145] Khal Baharulalam, 'Don't let external influence rattle Islamic faith, Muslims urged' *Borneo Bulletin* (Bandar Seri Begawan, 15 January 2015).

[146] 'Deepen Islamic knowledge to counter contemporary threats, says Islamic scholar' *Borneo Bulletin* (Bandar Seri Begawan, 3 November 2016).

[147] Baharulalam, 'Don't let external influence rattle Islamic faith' (n 145).

[148] 'Total Population by Country 2019' (*World Population Review*, undated) at www.worldpopulationreview.com/countries.

[149] Brunei Economic Development Board, 'Brunei Economic Development Board: Introducing Brunei, 2013' (undated) at www.bedb.com.bn/why_intro.html.

[150] 'Brunei – Update on Shariah Penal Code and Death Penalty' *Anti-Death Penalty Asia Network* (9 June 2016) at www.adpan.org/2016/06/09/brunei-update-on-shariah-penal-code-and-death-penalty.

Article 3 of the 1959 Constitution embeds the concept of freedom of religion. It states that other religions can be practised 'in peace and harmony' alongside Islam, the 'state' religion.[151] This is significant, as there are no other rights or liberties in the Constitution, neither is the separation of powers, independence of the judiciary or representative government established. Arguably, this is a colonial failing with a lasting impact on human rights in Brunei. Freedom of religion is fragile in a country where religious, executive, legislative power and judicial oversight reside in one person, the Sultan, whose goal is to create a *zikir* nation. Religious freedom also requires the companion freedoms of speech, of the press and of association to be fully realised.

B. Promotion of Islam, But Only Shafi'i School

Under Article 2 of the Constitution of Brunei Darussalam, '"Islamic Religion" means the Islamic Religion according to the Shafeite sect of Ahlis Sunnah Waljamaah (Sunni tradition).'

In Brunei, religion is not a personal matter of faith between a believer and his or her God or gods, but a government matter. Religion is not confined to the private sphere, nor is the Government's role limited to 'this world, but also extends to the next'.[152] The reasoning for recognition of only the Shafi'i school is that one *madhab* will unify, rather than divide, the people.[153] Shafi'i Islam is at the forefront and centre of all activities, and the five target areas for MoRA in 2018 reflect this.[154]

The first target was efficient MoRA administration, including for *hajj* and *zakat*. Within MoRA is the office of the State Mufti, who has sole authority to issue *fatwas* (binding rulings for Muslims in Brunei)[155] and who writes the weekly sermons under the Sultan's supervision,[156] which all imams must give. It is compulsory under the 2013 Order for Muslim men to attend the Friday prayers, so the mosque is a pulpit for delivering the Government's agenda. MoRA conducts seminars, conferences, briefings and workshop on aspects of Islam in workplaces and in the community to strengthen Islamic understanding and prevent aberrant beliefs.[157] The Religious Enforcement Division works to

[151] Constitution of Brunei Darussalam, Art 3(1).

[152] Melayong, 'Brunei's Golden Period' (n 71).

[153] 'Avoid Misguided Teachings' *New Brunei Times* (7 July 2018) at nbd.com.bn/2018/07/07/avoid-misguided-teachings-friday-sermon.

[154] Rokiah Mahmud, '$235.99M allocated to MoRA' *Borneo Bulletin* (Bandar Seri Begawan, 14 March 2017).

[155] Fatwas are generally advisory, but in Brunei it is a criminal offence to disobey a fatwa of the Mufti. See generally on fatwas, Ann Black and Nadirsyah Hosen, 'Fatwas: their Role in Contemporary Secular Australia' (2009) 18(1) *Griffith Law Review* 405.

[156] Marie-Sybille de Vienne, *Brunei: From Age of Commerce to Rentier State* (NUS Press, 2015) 272.

[157] Zee Yusri, 'Call to strengthen Ahli Sunnah Wal Jamai'ah' *Borneo Bulletin* (Bandar Seri Begawan, 10 September 2013).

ensure full compliance by Muslims and non-Muslims with religious laws. The Religious Police report unIslamic behaviour.

The second target was strengthening *da'wah* through more efficient propagation methods and programmes. The *Da'wah* Unit promotes conversions to Islam. Media reports give positive accounts of the financial, as well as spiritual, benefits of conversion. There is also the *Aqidah* (doctrine/faith) Control Section to ensure 'correct' practice of Islam.[158] Eradication of deviance is a MoRA priority, even preoccupation.[159] Shia Islam,[160] Ahmadiyyah, a range of Sufi groups, Al-Arqam, Ba'hai, Silat and Lintau are banned as heretical and deviant forms of Islam. Deviationist teachings are a 'poison to security and could destabilise the country's peace and harmony creating havoc, foes and even spill blood (fighting) among Muslims'.[161]

The third target is 'Syariah law empowerment including the enforcement of procedures and regulations' under the 2013 Order. The Religious Enforcement Division investigates crimes exclusive to the 2013 Order and other Syariah legislation. In 2017, the Syariah Courts heard 148 criminal cases, of which 98 were for *khalwat* (suspicious proximity).

The fourth target is enhancing Islamic education and awareness of MIB principles. Shafi'i Islamic religious education (known as *ugama* instruction) is compulsory at all schools for students aged 7 to 15 years, whether non-Muslim or non-Shafi'i Muslims. This includes non-government schools run by international or faith-based organisations. By law, they cannot teach any religion other than Islam to their students, so the set religious texts only cover Islam.[162] The law prohibits the teaching of other religions or comparative religious studies, even in the handful of schools run and funded by religious denominations. In the three schools run by the Catholic Vicariate, catechism lessons and religious instruction are only possible outside school hours and off school premises.

The fifth target is more efficient processing of halal certification and labelling. A recent amendment extended certification beyond food and consumables to cosmetics, transportation, storage and packaging. It applies to all businesses, whether conducted by Muslims or non-Muslims.

MoRA's approach to inculcating Islam is that from school, to university, to the workplace, Muslims in Brunei are taught one patriarchal conservative form of Islam. Unlike neighbouring Indonesia, where non-state Islamic organisations

[158] Muller, 'Sharia Law' (n 111) 320.

[159] 'His majesty reminds the country to be wary of Akidah Deviation' (*Borneo Post Online*, 23 September 2017) at www.theborneopost.com/2017/09/23/his-majesty-reminds-the-country-to-be-wary-of-akidahdeviation.

[160] See Muller, 'Paradoxical Normativities' (n 135) 424. Shi'ites are the second largest group of Muslims after Sunni adherents.

[161] Azlan Othman, 'Imams Warn against Deviationist Teachings' *Borneo Bulletin* (Bandar Seri Begawan, 4 January 2004).

[162] Compulsory Religious Education Act 2012.

and scholars can operate and compete with state bodies, there is no such avenue in Brunei. As Mansurnoor notes, 'open religious debates … have never taken place'.[163] Accepting, citing or practising in conformity with any other interpretation is a criminal offence under both the 2013 Order and the Sedition Act. Also criminalised as deviationist are liberal or more modern interpretations. Liberal Muslims, the Sultan argues, 'divert Muslim thinking … [they] want Islam to always change in accordance to the time they pass through'.[164] In Brunei, one cannot take a liberal interpretation of a passage in the Quran as Muslims in Turkey and other parts of the world can do, for example to argue that a different interpretation of *liwat* (homosexuality) is available, or that reading a book on world religions is permissible for Muslims and will not corrupt their faith or confuse them. Nor can Muslims, or any person, question the veracity of penalties in Brunei, even ones where the Quran does not specify an earthly punishment.

When an opinion letter published in the *Brunei Times* questioned the appropriateness of stoning to death as the punishment for adultery, arguing instead for 100 lashes based on the Quranic verse, the result was a heresy charge for the author. The accused subsequently confessed and repented in the Syariah Court. He agreed to counselling and a faith purification programme.[165] Debating the veracity of stoning, especially given that for centuries Brunei did not punish adultery that way, is a legitimate debate but it could not be had in Brunei. The State Mufti rejected any questioning of stoning as the appropriate punishment for adultery, because adultery 'is damaging and despicable, dirty, not civilised, and a crime that destroys descendants and violates human dignity. Allowing such a thing is akin to the life of animals because animals do not have a system.'[166]

As noted earlier, the 2013 Order counters interpretative democracy by invoking the criminal offence of apostasy/*irtidad* for denying a *hadith* of the Prophet or *ijma* as a source or authority for a particular teaching of Islam.[167] The Sultan called on the authorities to act to strictly enforce the laws against the infallibility of *hadith* and *ijma*.[168] Imams in their Friday sermons condemned persons:

> Who are anti-*hadith* and prefer their interpretations of Quranic verses without understanding the laws of *hadith*. They should repent and come back to the right path according to correct Islamic teachings. If they are committed to the Al-Quran, they should be the first to defend the *hadith*.[169]

[163] Iik Arifin Mansurnoor, 'Islam in Brunei Darussalam and Global Islam: An Analysis of their Interaction' in Johan Meuleman (ed), *Islam in the Era of Globalisation: Muslim Attitudes towards Modernity and Identity* (Routledge-Curzon, 2002) 88.

[164] Othman, 'Steer clear' (n 144).

[165] 'Confession, Repentance for Questioning Islamic law' *Brunei Times* (Bandar Seri Begawan, 3 June 2013).

[166] 'State Mufti rebuts criticism of Syariah Penal Code Order' *Borneo Bulletin* (Bandar Seri Begawan, 16 May 2014).

[167] Syariah Penal Code Order 2013, s 111(b).

[168] Azlan Othman, 'Imams remind Ummah against anti-Hadith groups' *Borneo Bulletin* (Bandar Seri Begawan, 30 March 2013).

[169] ibid.

C. Legal Restrictions on the Practice of Non-Muslim Religions in Brunei

In his address in 2014, the State Mufti said, 'Everyone sees the reality that Allah the Almighty's Law is beautiful, perfect and fair in nature, be it for Muslims or non-Muslims.'[170] Islam is 'perfect', but the Constitution does allow the practice of other religions in 'peace and harmony'. The interpretation of the 'peace and harmony' qualification is for the protection of Muslims, however, not vice versa. It ensures collective harmony and peace in Brunei by stopping any religious practice of non-Muslims that could offend, confuse or entice Muslims away from Islam. The civil courts' Court of Appeal cannot consider the constitutionality of this interpretation of the qualification, because interpretation of the Constitution is not for the courts but for an Interpretation Tribunal. Its members are appointed by the Sultan at the time he decides whether an interpretation is required.[171] The Constitution does not allow judicial review.[172] Only the Sultan has constitutional authority to amend the Constitution.[173]

A fatwa of the State Mufti set out the MoRA position on non-Muslims:

> Believers of other religions that live under the rule of an Islamic country, according to Islam, may practise their religion or celebrate their religious festivals among their community, with the condition that the celebrations are not disclosed or displayed publicly to Muslims.[174]

A public display of an aspect of any another religion amounts to propagating a religion other than Islam to a Muslim.[175]

Religious worship requires sacred texts, symbols and performance of rituals. Sacred symbols, such as a Hindu *aum*, a statute of Buddha, Roman Catholic rosary beads or the Christian crucifix, cannot be displayed in Brunei, and importation, even for private use, is difficult. In the 2013 Order, a prohibited publication 'relating to religions other than Islam' includes pictures and photographs relating to another religion, such as images of Westminster Abbey, Michelangelo paintings in the Sistine Chapel, the Kamakura Buddha or the Sikh Golden Temple, as well as any 'holy book, fundamental book or text of a religion other than Islam'.[176] The prohibition goes so far as to include any publication with 'quotations, excerpts or citations' from holy books and texts, or those that 'state the history, principles, teachings, characteristics, policies, performances, ceremonies, customs, charitable deeds, dogmas, orders or organisations of that religion' or deal with 'an entity, spiritual power or things worshipped by the

[170] Hakim Hayat, 'State Mufti delivers lecture in Malaysia' *Borneo Bulletin* (Bandar Seri Begawan, 20 August 2014).

[171] Constitution of Brunei Darussalam, Art 86.

[172] Constitution of Brunei Darussalam, Art 84C(1).

[173] Constitution of Brunei Darussalam, Art 85(1).

[174] *Fatwa* (Siri 03/2005), reported in 'Muslims must not follow non-Islamic celebrations' *Borneo Bulletin* (Bandar Seri Begawan, 28 December 2014).

[175] Syariah Penal Code Order 2013, s 209(1).

[176] Syariah Penal Code Order 2013, s 2.

believers of that religion'.[177] Additionally, a further penal offence is committed if these publications are advertised, sent or given to a Muslim or person of no religion.[178] By denying access to materials about the faith of one-third of Brunei's people, their freedom of belief and worship is intentionally limited, and it denies Muslims a wider world-view. There are other, practical restrictions. There is a *fatwa* banning church and temple expansions or renovations, although approval is possible for safety and security repairs.[179]

There is also close monitoring of cultural practices associated with religions other than Islam. Disallowed, on the grounds of confusing Muslims and/or damaging the faith of the Muslim community,[180] are any public displays of Christmas (Santa-related clothing, candles, singing of carols, Christmas trees).[181] Each year, public warnings are given that the display of a Christmas tree or decorations in a store, hotel or other venue, or home window would amount to propagating a religion other than Islam to a Muslim, despite these being cultural, not devotional, activities.[182] There are also limitations on where and for how long Chinese New Year celebrations can take place, and annual permits are required each year except for the main celebration, where the Sultan and members of the royal family join the Chinese community to mark the occasion. The *Borneo Bulletin* reported that 'this has demonstrated the loving monarch's care for the people including the Chinese community'.[183]

Despite these discriminatory practices against minority religions, the prevailing view as expressed by the MIB Supreme Council is that MIB in fact unites the country's people, 'regardless of their ethnicity, race and religion', as Islam brings 'harmony, mutual respect and a better understanding between one another'.[184] The Mufti advocates that in fact the 2013 Order 'has no shortcomings … and is not only created for a specific race, but is for all human beings, and not for a specific time, but for the entire universe up until the hereafter'.[185]

V. PUBLIC OPINION ON BRUNEI'S RELIGIOUS PENAL CLAUSES

> Residents of Brunei-Muara District cheered with joy and happiness … expressed their love and gratitude to the Sultan … [and] will always support His Majesty for the recent implementation of the Syariah Penal Code Order.[186]

[177] ibid.

[178] Syariah Penal Code Order 2013, s 125.

[179] 'Brunei Darussalam 2017/2018' (n 138).

[180] 'Muslims must not follow non-Islamic celebrations' (n 174).

[181] Syariah Penal Code 2013, s 217. The penalty is five years' imprisonment. See also 'Christmas ban to be strictly enforced in Brunei after sharia law introduced' *ABC News* (24 December 2015) at www.abc.net.au/news/2015-12-23/christmas-ban-to-be-strictly-enforced-this-year-inbrunei/7051680.

[182] Syariah Penal Code Order 2013, s 219.

[183] James Kon, 'Their Majesties grace grand CNY celebration' *Borneo Bulletin* (Bandar Seri Begawan, 15 March 2018).

[184] Melayong, 'Brunei's Golden Period' (n 71).

[185] Hayat, 'State Mufti' (n 170).

[186] Rokiah Mahmud, 'Get-together an opportunity to personally greet His Majesty' *Borneo Bulletin* (Bandar Seri Begawan, 25 August 2014).

Unless it is a ringing endorsement of the Sultan's Government, like the one reproduced above, there are few, if any, opportunities for Bruneians to express their opinions on any matter, and particularly about religious penal clauses. Whilst there was gratitude expressed in the mainstream media[187] and online, the initial views were a mix of positive and negative responses. The Sultan reminded his subjects that the Order criminalised negative commentary.[188]

A. Political Avenues for Public Opinion

Brunei does not hold elections and does not have a democratically representative body. This has several consequences for expressing opinions. Without elections and a representative parliament, there is scant need for political parties as their *raison d'être* is to inform the political process. The success of PRB on an anti-royalist agenda in the one election in 1961 and the subsequent rebellion, resulted in a ban on all political parties. Under the Societies Act (Chapter 66), the Minister has thwarted several attempts to start political parties. He can refuse to register and can also deregister any group (five or more persons) that opposes the laws, policy and direction of MIB and the Sultan. When the Brunei National Development Party (BNDP) announced a policy in 1988 calling for parliamentary democracy, elections, the repeal of emergency laws and a constitutional monarchy, it was immediately de-registered and its leader arrested under the Internal Security Act (Chapter 133) (ISA).[189] There is one party currently registered in Brunei, the National Development Party, which fully supports the Sultan, MIB and the status quo. Expressing any views on religion or religious penal clauses is outside their remit.

Without elections, Brunei does not have a representative law-making body in which it is possible to engage in an exchange of views and to scrutinise government policy. Rarely are draft laws published prior to enactment. From 1962 to 2004, the Legislative Council (LegCo) did not operate at all. In 2004, with much fanfare, it was reconstituted, but not as a fully, or even partially, elected body as set out in the Constitution; instead, it is an advisory council to which all members are appointed by the Sultan. It meets once a year, with considerable pomp and ceremony. However, it is a show chamber, as the LegCo has no genuine legislative power and its members remain subservient to the Sultan.[190]

[187] See, eg, Nurhamiza Hj Roslan, 'Syariah law is beautiful and fair: State Mufti' *Brunei Times* (Bandar Seri Begawan, 13 October 2011).

[188] 'Sultan hits back at rare criticism over sharia' *The Star Online* (26 February 2014) at www.thestar.com.my/news/regional/2014/02/26/brunei-sultan-hits-back-at-rare.

[189] Section 3(1) of the Sedition Act and the ISA criminalises 'any act, speech or publication made with the intention of inciting disaffection for the Sultan' and the Government. The ISA allows detention without trial for up to two years, with indeterminate extensions, and specifically ousts judicial review of detention orders.

[190] The 33 members include the Sultan with the Crown Prince, 13 cabinet ministers (*ex officio* members) with 18 other appointed members, two titled persons, seven prominent citizens, and eight

He can appoint and remove members 'at his pleasure', and since 2004, laws enacted by the Sultan no longer require the LegCo's 'advice and consent'.[191] In the 2018 LegCo meeting, the Minister of Religion gave a progress report on Syariah criminal law and announced the gazetting of the 2018 Procedural Order. There were no reports in the media of any questions or discussion. However, the Minister did tell the media, 'If asked by anyone where the democracy of Brunei's MIB is, answer assertively that our democracy is based on the teachings of Islam.'[192]

B. Media Avenues for Public Opinion

Brunei's Constitution does not give any guarantee of freedom of speech or expression. Before the 2013 Order, there was already civil legislation to limit opposition and criticism of the Government, particularly the Sedition Act. The Act criminalises words uttered with a seditious intention;[193] printing, publishing or selling any seditious publication;[194] importing the same;[195] or attempting, preparing or conspiring to do an act with seditious intent.[196] It sets out seven ways to establish a seditious intention. These include raising discontent or disaffection amongst the inhabitants of Brunei Darussalam,[197] promoting feelings of ill-will and hostility between different classes of the population of Brunei Darussalam[198] and, importantly, expressing opinions on religious penal clauses 'to directly or indirectly lower or adversely affect the standing or prominence of the National Philosophy of Melayu Islam Beraja'.[199] *Shahiran* is the only sedition case listed on the website of the Brunei courts, but no report of the decision is given.[200]

In addition to offences in the 2013 Order and the Sedition Act,[201] there is a net of criminal and regulatory laws that further limit free speech in print, broadcast,

representatives from the four districts, who are indirectly elected. A Selection Committee appointed by the Sultan approves their appointment and, after the district elections, makes recommendations to the Sultan. If he rejects a candidate then an alternative candidate must go before the Selection Committee. See Constitution of Brunei Darussalam, sch 2.

[191] Constitution of Brunei Darussalam, Art 39. See Tey Tsun Hang, 'Brunei's Revamped Constitution: The Sultan as the Grundnorm' [2007] 9 *Asian Law* 264.

[192] Aziz Idris and Izah Azahari, 'Minister delivers closing remarks at LegCo' *Borneo Bulletin* (Bandar Seri Begawan, 21 March 2018).

[193] Sedition Act, s 4(1)(b).

[194] Sedition Act, s 4(1)(c).

[195] Sedition Act, s 4(1)(d).

[196] Sedition Act, s 4(1)(a).

[197] Sedition Act, s 3(d).

[198] Sedition Act, s 3(e).

[199] Sedition Act, s 3(g).

[200] See State Judiciary Department Brunei Darussalam, 'Judgments' (undated) at www.judiciary.gov.bn/SJD%20Site%20Pages/Judgments.aspx.

[201] Sedition Act, s 4.

television and social media.[202] As a result, it is difficult to know the opinion of Bruneians on anything, especially on the sensitive issue of Syariah criminal law. The legislation, together with monitoring and blocking by the government agencies,[203] especially now on internet use, serves to guarantee a compliant, obsequious media and a society that self-censors. There are few cases on these issues in the judgments, so it would seem that the Government's policy of 'vigilance'[204] has facilitated an effective self-censoring culture. There are suggestions, however, that administrative penalties, such as travel bans or suspension from government jobs, serve as additional disincentives. Close monitoring of online exchanges, the deputy State Mufti stated, was 'to prevent … deviant ideologies … [as the] internet can contaminate or manipulate people's beliefs'.[205] He called for greater sanctions and more controls on 'virtual books, televisions shows, films, computer games, cyberspace and social networking sites' such as Twitter and YouTube.[206]

The Government justifies censorship as the means to shield Bruneians from negative information. Year after year, Brunei is ranked as 'not free', along with nations such as Cambodia and North Korea.[207] In 2020 Brunei was ranked 152 on the World Press Freedom Index.[208]

C. Opinion of the International Community

Internationally, Brunei's 2013 Order drew both condemnation and applause. The International Commission of Jurists (ICJ) denounced the 2013 Order 'as a blueprint for human rights violations',[209] while Amnesty International claimed it took Brunei back to the 'dark ages', making 'mockery of the country's international human rights commitments', and called for its revocation.[210] The Human Rights Watch Asia Director described the Order as a 'return to medieval

[202] The Undesirable Publications Act, the Censorship of Film and Public Entertainments Act and the Newspaper Act give the Minister of Home Affairs discretion to grant and revoke publishing licences, to shut down newspapers and to bar distribution of foreign publications.

[203] Censorship Board and the Prime Minister's Office. The Internet Code of Conduct requires internet sites to register with the Broadcasting Authority.

[204] 'Instil patriotism to preserve Brunei's dignity, sovereignty' *Borneo Bulletin* (Bandar Seri Begawan, 27 February 2017).

[205] Yusri, 'Call to strengthen' (n 157). He also identified a need to monitor and control NGOs and foreign speakers.

[206] ibid.

[207] See Freedom House, 'Brunei' (undated) at www.freedomhouse.org/country/brunei.

[208] Reporters Without Borders, 'World Press Freedom Index 2020' (undated) at www.rsf.org/en/ranking.

[209] International Commission of Jurists, 'Brunei: New Penal Code a Blueprint forHuman Rights Violations' (27 January 2014) at www.icj.org/brunei-new-penal-code-a-blueprint-for-human-rights-violations.

[210] Amnesty International, 'Brunei Darussalam: Revoke new Penal Code allowing stoning, whipping and amputation' (30 April 2014) at www.amnesty.org/en/latest/news/2014/04/brunei-darussalam-penal-code.

punishment' and 'out of step with the 21st century'.[211] However, the Sultan, the State Mufti and all government spokespersons, including senior members of the judiciary in the civil law system, defended the 2013 Order. Attorney General Hajah Hayati binte Haji Salleh admitted she was not an expert in the field of Syariah law but supported the Sultan's vision to make it a reality.[212] State Mufti Juned responded to the criticism and reassured Bruneians that 'Islamic criminal law is not done out of whim and it is not done simply to be cruel to people; it is done for the good of mankind.'[213] He visited mosques throughout the Sultanate to explain 'the beauty of Syariah criminal law',[214] and outlined how it was 'much more superior' to 'man-made conventional laws'.[215] The Sultan fended off international criticism as 'based on a distorted view of Islam', and received support from Islamic scholars in neighbouring Malaysia.[216] Dato' Seri Sheikh Hj Nooh bin Gadot, the Johor state Islamic advisor, lauded Brunei and the Sultan for showing political will at the very top, as in other countries it is a struggle from the bottom to implement *hudud*. He hoped that 'Allah the Almighty showers the nation with blessings'.[217]

VI. OVERARCHING REFLECTIONS

The colonial legacy for contemporary religious practice and religious penal clauses reverberates in Brunei today in three main ways. The first legacy was that colonial Britain transplanted the common law system into Brunei. This included the standard religious penal clauses found in most British colonies. These offences remain in the current Penal Code but are rarely, if ever, employed, which makes their impact minimal. Frequently, the Sultan and senior figures threaten to use sedition laws, another colonial inheritance, but this use too is sparing. Their potential for use, however, does serve to limit debate and commentary on religious, ethnic, political and other sensitive topics. Britain also brought to Brunei European conceptions of religious freedom regardless of a person's faith, and whilst these concepts lay behind the constitutional protection that all religions be practised in 'peace and harmony', the ascendancy of Islamic law and commencement of the 2013 and 2018 Orders have diminished the protections for religious minorities.

[211] Al Jazeera, 'Brunei enacts new penal code as sultan calls for "stronger" Islam' (4 April 2019) at www.aljazeera.com/news/2019/04/brunei-enacts-sharia-law-sultan-calls-stronger-islam-190403060932396.html.

[212] Hajah Hayati binte Haji Salleh, 'Foreword' in Juned, *The Shari'ah Penal Code* (n 82) xxviii.

[213] Roslan, 'Syariah law' (n 187).

[214] Juned, *The Shari'ah Penal Code* (n 82) xiii.

[215] ibid.

[216] Azlan Othman, 'Experts laud Brunei for introducing Syariah Law' *Borneo Bulletin* (Bandar Seri Begawan, 25 October 2013).

[217] ibid.

The second paradoxical colonial legacy is that colonisation actually strengthened Islamic law and laid the groundwork for today's Syariah criminal laws. From the onset of the Residency, the colonial government oversaw and funded the application and enforcement of Islamic law. It codified Islamic criminal law so that infractions of Islamic duties or breaches of Islamic laws were administered by, and penalties imposed by, the government. The colonial nexus was so close that initially many religious breaches and penalties were under the civil courts' jurisdiction. The colonial model institutionalised religious courts supported by an ever-expanding bureaucracy to administer and enforce Islamic law. Brunei's religious scholars are not independent from government but dependent on it for employment and favour. The bureaucratic legacy is evident in Brunei's powerful religious institutions, none more so than the Religious Council, MoRA, the Office of the State Mufti, the MIB Supreme Council, the Faith/Doctrine Control Section, *Da'wah* Centre, Syariah Affairs Department and the Religious Enforcement Division. The colonial government also professionalised Syariah judicial and prosecutorial services. As a result, the three-tier Syariah courts came to mirror in many ways their common law counterparts rather than a traditional *Kathi* Court. In adjudication, enacted regulations dominated over *fiqh*. The Residency gave the Sultan custody over and authority for Islam, which he retains to the present.

The religious penal clauses contained in the 2013 Order were possible because of the third legacy, namely, that Brunei's contemporary model of governance is a product of colonial concepts and practices. Herein lies another paradox. Prior to the Residency, the Sultan was at the apex of the social hierarchy but his *wazirs* and nobles had areas of control and responsibility over governance, tributes (taxes) and dispute resolution. It was not the absolute and autocratic model of today. In the Residency all power and decision-making, save for Islam, rested exclusively with one man, and this was the blueprint used in the 1959 Constitution, rather than a reversion to the prior power-sharing arrangement. The Constitution transferred the roles and powers of the Resident to the Sultan, who also retained his religious mandate as head of Islam. The merger of both offices created the absolute monarchy of today. When Britain sent troops in support of the Sultan against the pro-democratic anti-monarchy uprising in 1962, an autocratic regime was re-enforced. In overlooking the fledgling democratic yearnings of the people, Britain gave the green light to autocratic rule and legislation by emergency decree of the Sultan.

Use of emergency powers in the 'Abode of Peace' to legislate the most extensive regime of religious penal clauses anywhere in Asia is an abuse of special powers reserved for exceptional and threatening circumstances. To use royal fiat to enact Syariah penal laws without debate by appointees in the LegCo, and without consulting Bruneians, whose lives the Order impacts, is unprecedented in the region.[218] A censored media and a population that lacks freedom of speech

[218] Announced in a *Titah* for the Sultan's 66th birthday on 15 July 2013.

resulted in a veneer of public support for the 2013 Order. It even contained its own penal sanctions against opposition to it ('any law dealing with Islam or MIB')[219] or the *titah*.[220] The Sultan warned:

> [Domestic critics] cannot be allowed to continue committing these insults, but if there are elements which allow them to be brought to court, then the first phase of implementing the Syariah Penal Code Order in April will be very relevant to them.[221]

Under the banner of religion, the state also silences political opposition. At first glance, the rationale that all limitations on religious practice arises from a genuine desire to protect the purity of Islam and ensure Bruneian Muslims enter heaven comes from a protective, if paternalistic place, but the political implications and personal wealth accrued by the Sultan and the royal family make this questionable. The life and rule of Brunei's head of Islam is the antithesis of the simple unostentatious path advocated and lived by the Prophet Mohammad.

The consequence for contemporary practice is an on-going and ever-increasing tension in the relationship between the religious and the civil penal laws in Brunei. During the colonial era, civil law dominated, but the balance has since shifted decisively towards Islamic law. As this chapter has shown, the greatest tipping point in favour of religious penal law was when the Sultan enacted the 2013 Order and the accompanying 2018 Procedure Order. *Hudud* and *qisas* offences tipped the scales even further. This is the nadir of the common law in Brunei. In her response to a question about the future of both streams of criminal law, Attorney General Hajah Hayati said there are 'thoughts of one penal code system', but whether it will 'be a merged code or just based on only Syariah' only time will tell.[222]

BIBLIOGRAPHY

—— Civil Procedure Code, Laws of the Straits Settlements
—— Compulsory Religious Education Act 2012
—— Constitution of Brunei Darussalam
—— Courts Enactment 1908
—— Emergency (Continuation and Validation of Emergency Provisions) Order 2004
—— *Mardina Tiara bt Abdullah Emat @ Margaret ak Emat v Director of Jabatan Agama Islam Sarawak & Ors* [2017] 9 MLJ 293 (High Court, Kuching)
—— Mohammedan Laws Enactment 1912
—— Proclamation of Emergency (No S12), 12 February 2017 at www.agc.gov.bn/AGC%20Images/LAWS/Gazette_PDF/2017/EN/S012.pdf

[219] Syariah Penal Code Order 2013, s 220(d).
[220] Syariah Penal Code Order 2013, s 230.
[221] 'Sultan hits back at rare criticism over sharia' (n 188).
[222] HH Azaraimy, 'Practising a dual criminal justice system' *Borneo Bulletin* (Bandar Seri Begawan, 21 October 2013).

—— Sedition Act
—— Syariah Penal Code Order 2013
—— 'The Brunei Project' at www.facebook.com/thebruneiproject
—— Treaty of Protection [1888] *UKTS* 5582 (17 September 1888)
ABC News, 'Christmas ban to be strictly enforced in Brunei after sharia law introduced' (24 December 2015) at www.abc.net.au/news/2015-12-23/christmas-ban-to-be-strictly-enforced-this-year-inbrunei/7051680
Bakar, NSHA, 'The Impact of British Administration over Brunei's Society: 1906–1984' Second Joint Seminar of FASS UBD and IOC UT: Asian Societies and Cultures in the Eyes of Bruneian and Japanese Researchers (16–18 September 2008) 7, 8 at www.academia.edu/8446348/The_impact_of_British_administration_over_Brunei_s_society_1906_-_1984
Al Jazeera, 'Brunei enacts new penal code as sultan calls for "stronger" Islam' (4 April 2019) at www.aljazeera.com/news/2019/04/brunei-enacts-sharia-law-sultan-calls-stronger-islam-190403060932396.html
Amnesty International, 'Brunei Darussalam 2017/2018' (undated) at www.amnesty.org/en/countries/asia-and-the-pacific/brunei-darussalam/report-brunei-darussalam
——, 'Brunei Darussalam: Revoke new Penal Code allowing stoning, whipping and amputation' (30 April 2014) at www.amnesty.org/en/latest/news/2014/04/brunei-darussalam-penal-code
Anti-Death Penalty Asia Network, 'Brunei – Update on Shariah Penal Code and Death Penalty' (9 June 2016) at www.adpan.org/2016/06/09/brunei-update-on-shariah-penal-code-and-death-penalty
Azaraimy, HH, 'Practising a dual criminal justice system' *Borneo Bulletin* (Bandar Seri Begawan, 21 October 2013)
Bernstein, J, 'The Deculturalisation of the Brunei Dusun' in Robert L Winzeler (ed), *Indigenous Peoples and the State* (Yale University Press, 1997) 159
Baharulalam, K, 'Don't let external influence rattle Islamic faith, Muslims urged' *Borneo Bulletin* (Bandar Seri Begawan, 15 January 2015)
Black, A, 'Survival or Extinction? Animistic Dispute Resolution in the Sultanate of Brunei' (2005) 13 *Willamette Journal of International Law & Dispute Resolution* 1
——, Esmaeili, H, and Hosen, N, *Modern Perspectives on Islamic Law* (Edward Elgar, 2013)
——, and Hosen, N, 'Fatwas: their Role in Contemporary Secular Australia' (2009) 18(1) *Griffith Law Review* 405
Borneo Bulletin, 'Instil patriotism to preserve Brunei's dignity, sovereignty' (Bandar Seri Begawan, 27 February 2017)
——, 'Deepen Islamic knowledge to counter contemporary threats, says Islamic scholar' (Bandar Seri Begawan, 3 November 2016)
——, 'Muslims must not follow non-Islamic celebrations' (Bandar Seri Begawan, 28 December 2014)
——, 'State Mufti rebuts criticism of Syariah Penal Code Order' (Bandar Seri Begawan, 16 May 2014)
——, 'Titah' (Bandar Seri Begawan, 17 July 1996)
Borneo Post Online, 'His majesty reminds the country to be wary of Akidah Deviation' (23 September 2017) at www.theborneopost.com/2017/09/23/his-majesty-reminds-the-country-to-be-wary-of-akidahdeviation
British Consul-General Peter Leys' letter to Lord Salisbury dated 24 December 1885

Brunei Economic Development Board, 'Brunei Economic Development Board: Introducing Brunei, 2013' (undated) at www.bedb.com.bn/why_intro.html

Brunei Times, 'Practising Black Magic is listed offence in Syariah Law' (Bandar Seri Begawan, 4 June 2014)

——, 'Confession, Repentance for Questioning Islamic law' (Bandar Seri Begawan, 3 June 2013)

——, '*Titah* for the 1433 Hijrah (Islamic New Year)' (Bandar Seri Begawan, 30 November 2011)

De Vienne, M-S, *Brunei: From Age of Commerce to Rentier State* (NUS Press, 2015)

Faisal, F, 'Defendant in sedition trial flees before verdict' *Brunei Bulletin* (Bandar Seri Begawan, 15 November 2018)

Freedom House, 'Brunei' (undated) at www.freedomhouse.org/country/brunei

Haris, N, 'Local customs, beliefs may not be Syariah compliant' *Brunei Times* (Bandar Seri Begawan, 17 April 2014)

Harun, AMKP, 'Bruneian civil servant fined $1000 for cross-dressing' *Brunei Times* (Bandar Seri Begawan, 11 March 2015)

Harding, AJ, 'The Keris, The Crescent and the Blind Goddess: The State, Islam and the Constitution in Malaysia' (2002) 6 *Singapore Journal of International & Comparative Law* 154

Hayat, H, 'State Mufti delivers lecture in Malaysia' *Borneo Bulletin* (Bandar Seri Begawan, 20 August 2014)

Hayati, H, HS b, 'Foreword' in Haji Awang Abdul Aziz bin Juned, *The Shari'ah Penal Code: An Introduction* (Office of the State Mufti, 2014) xxviii

Hussainmiya, BA, 'Manufacturing Consensus: the Role of the State Council in Brunei Darussalam' (2000) 31(2) *Journal of Southeast Asian Studies* 321

Idris, A, and Azahari, I, 'Minister delivers closing remarks at LegCo' *Borneo Bulletin* (Bandar Seri Begawan, 21 March 2018)

International Commission of Jurists, 'Brunei: New Penal Code a Blueprint for Human Rights Violations' (27 January 2014) at www.icj.org/brunei-new-penal-code-a-blueprint-for-human-rights-violations

Juned, AAA b, *The Shari'ah Penal Code: An Introduction* (Office of the State Mufti, 2014)

Kershaw, R, 'Marginality Then and Now: Shifting Patterns of Minority Status in Brunei Darussalam' (1998) 29 *Internationales Asienforum* 83

Kon, J, 'Their Majesties grace grand CNY celebration' *Borneo Bulletin* (Bandar Seri Begawan, 15 March 2018)

Lindsey, T, and Steiner, K, *Islam, Law and the State in Southeast Asia* (IB Taurus, 2012)

Mahmud, R, '$235.99M allocated to MoRA' *Borneo Bulletin* (Bandar Seri Begawan, 14 March 2017)

——, 'Get-together an opportunity to personally greet His Majesty' *Borneo Bulletin* (Bandar Seri Begawan, 25 August 2014)

Mansurnoor, IA, 'Re-establishing Order in Brunei: The Introduction of the British Legal System During the Early Residential Period' (2013) 52(2) *Islamic Studies* 155

——, 'Formulating and Implementing a Shari'a-Guided Legal System in Brunei Darussalam: Opportunity and Challenge' (2008) 1(2) *Sosiohumanika* 219

——, 'Islam in Brunei Darussalam and Global Islam: An Analysis of their Interaction' in Johan Meuleman (ed), *Islam in the Era of Globalisation: Muslim Attitudes towards Modernity and Identity* (Routledge-Curzon, 2002) 88

McArthur, MSH, *Report on Brunei in 1904: Introduced and Annotated by HMV Horton* (Ohio University Press, 1987)
Melayong, MHM b, 'Brunei's Golden Period of Expansion' *Borneo Bulletin* (Bandar Seri Begawan, 24 October 2016)
Muller, DM, 'Paradoxical Normativities in Brunei Darussalam and Malaysia' (2016) 56 (3) *Asian Survey* 415.
——, 'Sharia Law and the Politics of "Faith Control" in Brunei Darussalam' (2015) 46 *Internationales Asienforum* 313.
New Brunei Times, 'Avoid Misguided Teachings' (7 July 2018) at nbd.com.bn/2018/07/07/avoid-misguided-teachings-friday-sermon
Othman, A, 'Experts laud Brunei for introducing Syariah Law' *Borneo Bulletin* (Bandar Seri Begawan, 25 October 2013)
——, 'Imams remind Ummah against anti-Hadith groups' *Borneo Bulletin* (Bandar Seri Begawan, 30 March 2013)
——, 'Steer clear of deviant teachings, Muslims told' *Borneo Bulletin* (Bandar Seri Begawan, 2 February 2013)
——, 'Imams Warn against Deviationist Teachings' *Borneo Bulletin* (Bandar Seri Begawan, 4 January 2004)
Reporters Without Borders, 'World Press Freedom Index 2019' (undated) at www.rsf.org/en/ranking
Roslan, NH, 'Syariah law is beautiful and fair: State Mufti' *Brunei Times* (Bandar Seri Begawan, 13 October 2011)
Sheridan, LA, *Malaya and Singapore: The Borneo Territories: Development of their Laws and Constitutions* (Stevens & Sons, 1963)
Singh, DSR, *Brunei: 1839–1983: The Problems of Political Survival* (Oxford University Press, 1991)
State Judiciary Department Brunei Darussalam, 'Judgments' (undated) at www.judiciary.gov.bn/SJD%20Site%20Pages/Judgments.aspx
Tarling, N, *Nations and States in Southeast Asia* (Cambridge University Press, 1998)
——, *Fall of Imperial Britain in South East Asia* (Oxford University Press, 1993)
Tey Tsun Hang, 'Brunei's Revamped Constitution: The Sultan as the Grundnorm' [2007] 9 *Asian Law* 264
The Star Online, 'Sultan hits back at rare criticism over sharia' (26 February 2014) at www.thestar.com.my/news/regional/2014/02/26/brunei-sultan-hits-back-at-rare
World Population Review, 'Total Population by Country 2019' (undated) at www.worldpopulationreview.com/countries
Yegar, M, *Islam and Islamic Institutions in British Malaya* (Magnes Press, 1979)
Yunos, R, 'The Chinese in Brunei' *Brunei Times* (Bandar Seri Begawan, 30 April 2012)
Yusof, RNHBM, 'Brunei: Building an Enshrining an Absolute Monarchy' (MPhil thesis, Oxford Brooks University 2017)
Yusri, Z, 'Call to strengthen Ahli Sunnah Wal Jamai'ah' *Borneo Bulletin* (Bandar Seri Begawan, 10 September 2013)
Zailani, N, 'Non-Muslims allowed to sing national anthem' *Brunei Times* (Bandar Seri Begawan, 22 April 2014)

Index

www.ingramcontent.com/pod-product-compliance
Ingram Content Group UK Ltd.
Pitfield, Milton Keynes, MK11 3LW, UK
UKHW020231290926
15470UKWH00002B/467

9 781509 937295